Lecture Notes in Computer Science 16864

The series Lecture Notes in Computer Science (LNCS), including its subseries Lecture Notes in Artificial Intelligence (LNAI) and Lecture Notes in Bioinformatics (LNBI), has established itself as a medium for the publication of new developments in computer science and information technology research, teaching, and education.

LNCS enjoys close cooperation with the computer science R & D community, the series counts many renowned academics among its volume editors and paper authors, and collaborates with prestigious societies. Its mission is to serve this international community by providing an invaluable service, mainly focused on the publication of conference and workshop proceedings and postproceedings. LNCS commenced publication in 1973.

Christian Berger · Verena Klös
Editors

Software Engineering and Advanced Applications

52nd Euromicro Conference, SEAA 2026
Kraków, Poland, September 2–4, 2026
Proceedings, Part II

Springer

Editors
Christian Berger
University of Gothenburg
Gothenburg, Sweden

Verena Klös
Carl von Ossietzky University of Oldenburg
Oldenburg, Germany

ISSN 0302-9743 ISSN 1611-3349 (electronic)
Lecture Notes in Computer Science
ISBN 978-3-032-36586-6 ISBN 978-3-032-36587-3 (eBook)
https://doi.org/10.1007/978-3-032-36587-3

This Springer imprint is published by the registered company Springer Nature Switzerland AG
The registered company address is: Gewerbestrasse 11, 6330 Cham, Switzerland

Preface

This volume contains the papers presented at SEAA 2026, the *52nd Euromicro Conference on Software Engineering and Advanced Applications*, held on September 2–4, 2026, in Kraków, Poland.

SEAA serves as a long-standing international forum for researchers, practitioners, and students to share and discuss the latest innovations, emerging trends, practical experiences, and ongoing challenges and concerns in the field of software engineering and advanced information technology applications for software-intensive systems.

To address this mission, the 2026 edition of SEAA once again brought together a vibrant community through a diverse program. This year, the conference featured ten specialized tracks, each led by a team of co-chairs. These tracks spanned a wide range of topics and reflected the truly multidisciplinary nature of software engineering research and practice.

This year, SEAA received a high number of 146 research paper submissions over ten thematic tracks. Each submission underwent a rigorous single-blinded peer-review process. Every paper was assigned to at least three and up to four independent reviewers, selected based on topic expertise. Reviewers were each asked to evaluate 2–3 papers. They assessed submissions according to criteria such as scientific soundness, originality, relevance to the SEAA community and the track theme, clarity of presentation, and contribution to the field. In cases where reviews yielded divergent scores or conflicting recommendations, track chairs actively moderated discussions to facilitate consensus. Conflicts of interest with the track chairs were further handled by the PC chairs.

Following this process, a total of 50 full papers and 22 short papers were selected for acceptance in the proceedings. The diverse set of contributions reflects the high quality and breadth of work being conducted in the SEAA community.

The final program would not have been possible to complete without the effort, commitment, and invaluable contribution of all track chairs. From managing submissions and overseeing the peer-review process, to assisting in completing the exciting program, the track chairs were central to the quality and relevance of SEAA 2026. We express our sincere appreciation to all track chairs as listed below.

1. **Cyber-Physical Systems** (CPS): Saad Mubeen (Mälardalen University, Sweden), and Verena Klös (Carl von Ossietzky University of Oldenburg, Germany)
2. **Data and AI Driven Engineering** (DAIDE): Helena Holmström Olsson (Malmö University, Sweden), and Jan Bosch (Chalmers & Gothenburg University, Sweden, and Eindhoven University of Technology, The Netherlands)
3. **Emerging Computing Technologies** (ECT): Pedro Diniz (University of Porto, Portugal) and Valentina Lenarduzzi (University of Oulu, Finland)
4. **Explainable and Trustworthy Applications** (EXTRA): Katja Tuma (Eindhoven University of Technology, The Netherlands), Giammaria Giordano (Pegaso University, Naples, Italy), and Fabio Palomba (University of Salerno, Italy)

5. **Practical Aspects of Software Engineering** (KKIO): Marian Bubak (Sano Centre for Computational Medicine, ACC Cyfronet AGH, Kraków, Poland), Marcin Szpyrka (AGH University of Kraków, Poland), Adam Roman (Jagiellonian University, Kraków, Poland), and Miroslaw Staron (Chalmers & University of Gothenburg, Sweden)
6. **Model-Driven Engineering and Modeling Languages** (MDEML): Alessio Bucaioni (Mälardalen University, Sweden), Bianca Wiesmayr (Ulm University, Germany), and Federico Ciccozzi (Mälardalen University, Sweden)
7. **Software Management: Measurement, Peopleware, and Innovation** (SM): Onur Demirörs (Izmir Institute of Technology, Turkey), Carmine Gravino (University of Salerno, Italy), and Valeria Pontillo (Gran Sasso Science Institute, Italy)
8. **Systematic Literature Reviews and Mapping Studies in Software Engineering** (SMSE): Stephen Swift (Brunel University of London, UK) and Mahir Arzoky (Brunel University of London, UK)
9. **Software Process and Product Improvement** (SPPI): Stefan Biffl (Technische Universität Wien, Austria), Rick Rabiser (Johannes Kepler University Linz, Austria), and Dietmar Winkler (Center for Digital Production and Technische Universität Wien, Austria)
10. **Software Analytics: Mining Software Open Datasets and Repositories** (STREAM): Elvira-Maria Arvanitou (International Hellenic University, Greece) and Stamatia Bibi (University of Western Macedonia, Greece)

We extend our gratitude to our SEAA 2026 keynote speakers—Mira Mezini, LOEWE Distinguished Professor of Computer Science from TU Darmstadt, Germany, and Torvald Mårtensson, Technical Fellow within System Integration Testing at Saab Aeronautics and Associate Professor at Linköping University, Sweden—for sharing their thought-provoking insights and helping to spark discussions throughout the event.

Finally, we would also like to thank all SEAA Steering Committee members for their continued guidance and valuable advice throughout the organization of the conference.

We hope you thoroughly enjoyed Euromicro SEAA 2026 and found it inspiring, insightful, and engaging.

July 2026

Christian Berger
Verena Klös

Organization

Program Committee Chairs

Christian Berger	University of Gothenburg, Sweden
Verena Klös	Carl von Ossietzky University of Oldenburg, Germany

General Chairs

Tomasz Kryjak	AGH University Kraków, Poland
Marek Gorgon	AGH University Kraków, Poland

Publicity Chairs

Beatriz Cabrero-Daniel	Mid Sweden University, Sweden
Mersedeh Sadeghi	University of Cologne, Germany

Proceedings Chairs

Krishna Ronanki	Chalmers University of Technology and University of Gothenburg, Sweden
Julian Frattini	Chalmers University of Technology and University of Gothenburg, Sweden

Finance Chair

Francesco Leporati	University of Pavia, Italy

Steering Committee

Stefan Biffl	Technische Universität Wien, Austria
Michel Chaudron	Eindhoven University of Technology, The Netherlands

Onur Demirörs	Izmir Institute of Technology, Turkey
Carmine Gravino	University of Salerno, Italy
Helena Holmström Olsson	Malmö University, Sweden
Andreas Wortmann	Stuttgart University, Germany

Program Committee

Alain Abran	École de Technologie Supérieure and Université du Québec, Canada
Rami Almwari	Brunel University of London, UK
Mohammad Alshayeb	King Fahd University of Petroleum & Minerals, Saudi Arabia
Rayh Altarawneh	Brunel University of London, UK
Areti Ampatzoglou	University of Macedonia, Greece
Vasilios Andrikopoulos	University of Groningen, Netherlands
Lefteris Angelis	Aristotle University of Thessaloniki, Greece
Ove Armbrust	Apple Inc., USA
Elvira-Maria Arvanitou	International Hellenic University, Greece
Mahir Arzoky	Brunel University of London, UK
Matthias Becker	KTH Royal Institute of Technology, Sweden
Steffen Becker	University of Stuttgart, Germany
Bernhard J. Berger	Hamburg University of Technology, Germany
Christian Berger	University of Gothenburg, Sweden
Stamatia Bibi	University of Western Macedonia, Greece
Stefan Biffl	TU Vienna, Austria
Ilona Bluemke	Warsaw University of Technology, Poland
Florian Bock	Friedrich-Alexander Universität Erlangen-Nürnberg, Germany
Marek Bolanowski	Rzeszow University of Technology, Poland
Jan Bosch	Chalmers & Gothenburg University, Sweden, and Eindhoven University of Technology, The Netherlands
Ruth Breu	University of Innsbruck, Austria
Gianluca Brilli	University of Modena and Reggio Emilia, Italy
Marian Bubak	AGH University of Krakow, Poland
Alessio Bucaioni	Mälardalen University, Sweden
Alena Buchalcevova	Prague University of Economics and Business, Czech Republic
Daniel Bujosa	Technical University of Denmark, Denmark
Piotr Błaszyński	West Pomeranian University of Technology, Poland

Matthias Galster	University of Canterbury, New Zealand
Simos Gerasimou	Cyprus University of Technology, Cyprus
Christopher Gerking	Karlsruhe Institute of Technology, Germany
Fabian Gilson	University of Canterbury, New Zealand
Giammaria Giordano	University of Salerno, Italy
Görkem Giray	Japan Tobacco International, Türkiye
Krzysztof Goczyła	Gdańsk University of Technology, Poland
Thomas Goldschmidt	Avalara, Germany
Carmine Gravino	University of Salerno, Italy
Raffaela Groner	Chalmers University of Technology and University of Gothenburg, Sweden
Esther Guerra	Universidad Autónoma de Madrid, Spain
Sebastian Götz	Technische Universät Dresden, Germany
Tuna Hacaloğlu	Atilim University and Middle East Technical University, Türkiye
Philipp Haindl	St. Pölten University of Applied Sciences, Austria
David Halasz	Masaryk University, Czechia
Rachel Harrison	Oxford Brookes University, UK
Sara Hassan	Birmingham City University, UK
Petra Heck	Fontys University of Applied Sciences, Netherlands
Jens Heidrich	Hochschule Mainz - University of Applied Sciences, Germany
Sebastian Herold	Karlstad University, Sweden
Hans-Martin Heyn	University of Gothenburg, Sweden
Bogumila Hnatkowska	Wrocław University of Science and Technology, Poland
Petr Hnetynka	Charles University in Prague, Czechia
Helena Holmström Olsson	Malmö University, Sweden
Jennifer Horkoff	University of Gothenburg and Chalmers University of Technology, Sweden
Frank Houdek	Mercedes-Benz AG, Germany
Zbigniew Huzar	Wrocław University of Science and Technology, Poland
Martin Höst	Malmö University, Sweden
Emanuele Iannone	Hamburg University of Technology, Germany
Zear Ibrahim	Brunel University of London, UK
Aleksander Jarzebowicz	Gdańsk University of Technology, Poland
Frank Johnsen	Norwegian Defence Research Establishment (FFI), Norway
Robbert Jongeling	Mälardalen University, Sweden
Fawzia Zehra Kara-Isitt	Brunel University of London, UK
Marija Katic	Union University, Serbia

Maria Kechagia	National and Kapodistrian University of Athens, Greece
Wiem Khlif	InstaDeep Ltd., Tunisia
Michael Kläs	Fraunhofer IESE, Germany
Julian Klein	TU Berlin, Germany
Verena Klös	Carl von Ossietzky University of Oldenburg, Germany
Sylwia Kopczyńska	Poznań University of Technology, Poland
Piotr Kosiuczenko	Wojskowa Akademia Techniczna, Poland
Marek Kretowski	Bialystok University of Technology, Poland
Marco Kuhrmann	Reutlingen University, Germany
Malvina Latifaj	Mälardalen University, Sweden
Joran Leest	Vrije Universiteit Amsterdam, Netherlands
Valentina Lenarduzzi	University of Oulu, Finland
Maurizio Leotta	University of Genoa, Italy
Tong Li	Beijing University of Technology, China
Zengyang Li	Central China Normal University, China
Peng Liang	Wuhan University, China
Sherlock Licorish	University of Otago, New Zealand
Bruno Lima	University of Porto, Portugal
Elena Lisova	Mälardalen University and Volvo Construction Equipment, Sweden
Lech Madeyski	Wrocław University of Science and Technology, Poland
Bartosz Marcinkowski	University of Gdańsk, Poland
Antonio Martini	University of Oslo, Norway
Luana Martins	University of Salerno, Italy
Alistair McEwan	University of Derby, UK
Jorge Melegati	Free University of Bozen-Bolzano, Italy
Alexandra Mendes	University of Porto, Portugal
Marjan Mernik	University of Maribor, Slovenia
Andreas Metzger	Paluno, University of Duisburg-Essen, Germany
Jakub Miler	Gdańsk University of Technology, Poland
Yoshiki Mitani	MITANI A.R.I.LLC., Japan
Milko Monecke	Technische Universität Berlin, Germany
Maurizio Morisio	Politecnico di Torino, Italy
Saad Mubeen	Mälardalen University, Sweden
Henry Muccini	University of L'Aquila, Italy
Torvald Mårtensson	Saab AB, Sweden
Jürgen Münch	Reutlingen University, Germany
Grzegorz J. Nalepa	Jagiellonian University, Poland
Jerzy Nawrocki	Poznań University of Technology, Poland

Erika Nazaruka	Riga Technical University, Latvia
Michael Neumann	University of Applied Sciences and Arts Hannover, Germany
Yen Ying Ng	Nicolaus Copernicus University in Toruń, Poland
Arne Noyer	Ostfalia University of Applied Sciences, Germany
Mirosław Ochodek	Poznań University of Technology, Poland
Refat Othman	Free University of Bozen-Bolzano, Italy
Necmettin Özkan	Gebze Technical University, Türkiye
Claus Pahl	Free University of Bozen-Bolzano, Italy
Fabio Palomba	University of Salerno, Italy
Alessandra Parziale	Gran Sasso Science Institute, Italy
Andrzej Paszkiewicz	Politechnika Rzeszowska im. I. Łukasiewicza, Poland
Fabiano Pecorelli	Pegaso University, Italy
Viviana Pentangelo	University of Salerno, Italy
Rui Humberto Pereira	Polytechnic Institute of Porto, Portugal
Manuela Petrescu	Babeş-Bolyai University, Romania
Maura Pintor	University of Cagliari, Italy
Aneta Poniszewska-Maranda	Lodz University of Technology, Poland
Valeria Pontillo	Gran Sasso Science Institute, Italy
Adam Przybylek	University of Galway, Ireland
Fethi Rabhi	University of New South Wales
Maen Ziad Mohammad Rabie	Brunel University of London, UK
Rick Rabiser	Johannes Kepler University Linz, Austria
Łukasz Radliński	West Pomeranian University of Technology in Szczecin, Poland
Rudolf Ramler	Software Competence Center Hagenberg, Austria
Andreas Rausch	Technische Universität Clausthal, Germany
Gilberto Recupito	University of Salerno, Italy
Adam Roman	Jagiellonian University, Poland
Simone Romano	University of Salerno, Italy
Bruno Rossi	Masaryk University, Czechia
Mehrdad Saadatmand	Research Institutes of Sweden, Sweden
Mika Saari	Tampere University of Technology, Finland
Mersedeh Sadeghi	University of Cologne, Germany
Małgorzata Sadowska	Politechnika Wrocławska, Poland
Slawomir Samolej	Rzeszow University of Technology, Poland
Gleison Santos	Universidade Federal do Estado do Rio de Janeiro, Brazil
Rodrigo Santos	Universidade Federal do Estado do Rio de Janeiro, Brazil
Zenepe Satka	Mälardalen University, Sweden

Cristina Seceleanu	Mälardalen University, Sweden
Martin Shepperd	Brunel University of London, UK
Gheorghe Cosmin Silaghi	Babeş-Bolyai University, Romania
Michal Smialek	Warsaw University of Technology, Poland
Michel Soares	Federal University of Sergipe, Brazil
Janusz Sosnowski	Warsaw University of Technology, Poland
Zenon A. Sosnowski	Bialystok University of Technology, Poland
Érica Souza	Universidade Tecnológica Federal do Paraná, Brazil
Sulayman Sowe	Rheinisch-Westfälische Technische Hochschule Aachen, Germany
Luigi Libero Lucio Starace	Università degli Studi di Napoli Federico II, Italy
Miroslaw Staron	University of Gothenburg, Sweden
Krzysztof Stencel	University of Warsaw, Poland
Radovan Stojanovic	University of Montenegro, Montenegro
Daniel Strüber	Chalmers University of Technology and University of Gothenburg, Sweden and Radboud University, Netherlands
Daniel Ståhl	Ericsson AB, Sweden
Jacek Stój	Silesian University of Technology, Poland
Dan Mircea Suciu	Babeş-Bolyai University, Romania
Jakub Swacha	University of Szczecin, Poland
Stephen Swift	Brunel University of London, UK
Tomasz Szmuc	AGH University of Science and Technology, Poland
Marcin Szpyrka	AGH University of Krakow, Poland
Sahar Tahvili	Eimide AB, Sweden
Matthias Tichy	Ulm University, Germany
Juha-Pekka Tolvanen	MetaCase, Finland
Adam Trendowicz	Fraunhofer IESE, Germany
Sylvie Trudel	Université du Québec à Montréal, Canada
Nandinbaatar Tsog	Mälardalen University, Sweden
Michele Tucci	University of L'Aquila, Italy
Katja Tuma	Eindhoven University of Technology, Netherlands
Huseyin Unlu	Middle East Technical University Northern Cyprus Campus, Cyprus
Dimitri Van Landuyt	KU Leuven, Belgium
Gianmario Voria	University of Salerno, Italy
Anita Walkowiak	Wrocław University of Science and Technology, Poland
Bartosz Walter	Poznańskie Centrum Superkomputerowo-Sieciowe, Poland

Jörg Walter	OFFIS – Institute for Information Technology, Germany
Xiaofeng Wang	Free University of Bozen-Bolzano, Italy
Bianca Wiesmayr	Johannes Kepler University Linz, Austria
Dietmar Winkler	Technische Universität Wien, Austria
Konrad Wrona	NATO Communications and Information Agency, Poland
Włodzimierz Wysocki	West Pomeranian University of Technology Szczecin, Poland
Andrzej Zalewski	Wrocław University of Science and Technology, Poland
Janusz Zalewski	Florida Gulf Coast University, USA
Jianjun Zhao	Kyushu University, Japan
Zbigniew Zieliński	Military University of Technology, Poland

Reviewers

Brehme, Lorenz
Counsell, Steve
Deshapriya, Lakmal
Geist, Verena
Grześ, Tomasz
Jäger, Alexandra
Liyanage, Sumudu
Neumüller, Denis
Othman, Refat
Pfister, Zoe
Schöberl, Stefan
Łukaszuk, Tomasz

Supporters

EURO3

THE NATIONAL HPC COMPETENCE CENTRE

CYFRONET

ARTERIS IP

EUROMICRO CONFERENCE

AGH

AGH University of Krakow
Faculty of Electrical Engineering, Automatics, Computer Science and Biomedical Engineering

Contents

Software Process and Product Improvement

Model-Driven Engineering and Modeling Languages

Automatic Translation of Data Flow Constraints Into Conjunctive Normal Form

Nils Niehues[1(✉)] and Robert Heinrich[2]

[1] Karlsruhe Institute of Technology, Karlsruhe, Germany
nils.niehues@kit.edu
[2] Ulm University, Ulm, Germany
robert.heinrich@uni-ulm.de

Abstract. Early analysis of confidentiality at the architectural level is essential to prevent costly security violations in complex software systems. Recent data flow analysis frameworks allow confidentiality constraints to be specified declaratively using domain-specific languages, but their integration with SAT-based analysis techniques is hindered by the lack of automated translations of declarative constraints into conjunctive normal form. Existing solutions rely on manual, error-prone encodings or equi-satisfiable transformations that do not preserve semantic equivalence. In this paper, we present an automated approach for translating DSL-based confidentiality constraints into semantically equivalent CNF representations suitable for SAT solvers. This enables the seamless integration of declarative confidentiality specifications with SAT-based analysis and mitigation techniques, allowing their automated application to architectural models. The approach follows a two-step process: first translating DSL constraints into propositional logic, and then converting the resulting formulas into CNF using a divide-and-conquer algorithm based on Boolean equivalences.

We evaluate the approach with respect to correctness, structural properties, and scalability. Semantic equivalence is established through a formal proof and validated empirically by comparison with manually constructed CNF encodings for real-world confidentiality constraints. An exhaustive structural analysis shows that clause growth, literal counts, and clause length are well-bounded, and a worst-case runtime evaluation demonstrates that the translation remains computationally feasible for constraint sizes exceeding those observed in practice.

Keywords: data flow constraint · conjunctive normal form · confidentiality · architecture analysis

1 Introduction

The rapid growth and increasing complexity of software systems have intensified concerns about security-related quality attributes. Among these, confidentiality

C. Berger and V. Klös (Eds.): SEAA 2026, LNCS 16864, pp. 3–19, 2027.
https://doi.org/10.1007/978-3-032-36587-3_1

is a fundamental aspect of security and plays a central role in the design and evolution of modern software architectures [2]. As systems evolve to accommodate changing requirements, early architectural analysis becomes essential to avoid costly and error-prone revisions. In particular, confidentiality violations introduced at the architectural level are difficult to resolve once systems are implemented [4,12]. Consequently, systematic methods for early confidentiality analysis of data flows are required.

Boltz *et al.* [5] address this challenge by proposing an extensible Data Flow Analysis (DFA) framework for assessing architectural confidentiality. Their approach uses a Domain Specific Language (DSL) to declaratively specify confidentiality constraints and evaluate them over architectural data flows, enabling the identification of potential violations. Building on this work, we recently proposed an automated mitigation approach based on Conjunctive Normal Form (CNF) constraints and Boolean Satisfiability Problem (SAT) solving [20], enabling the systematic and fully automated repair of confidentiality violations in software architectures. These results establish SAT-based approaches as an effective and scalable foundation for automated architectural repair.

However, integrating SAT-based mitigation into existing DSL-based analysis frameworks remains challenging. Constraints in the DFA framework are expressed in a human-readable and declarative form that is not directly compatible with SAT solvers, which require CNF input. As no automated translation from DSL to CNF exists, this step is currently performed manually, making it time-consuming and error-prone. Moreover, multiple semantically equivalent CNF encodings may exist for the same Boolean formula [33], and inefficient encodings can introduce redundancy, increase formula size, and significantly degrade solver performance. Consequently, despite the effectiveness of CNF-based mitigation approaches, the lack of automated and efficient translation prevents their seamless integration into existing analysis workflows and remains a key barrier to practical adoption.

To bridge this gap, this paper proposes an automated translation from DSL-based constraints to semantically equivalent and structurally efficient CNF representations. This enables the seamless integration of declarative confidentiality specifications with SAT-based analysis and mitigation, resulting in an end-to-end workflow for detecting and repairing confidentiality violations directly from architectural models.

We evaluate the proposed approach with respect to correctness, structural properties, and scalability. Correctness is established through a formal proof of semantic equivalence and an empirical comparison against manually constructed CNF encodings for real-world confidentiality constraints. Structural properties are analyzed by exhaustively evaluating all possible constraints for a fixed number of input literals, quantifying clause growth, literal counts, and clause length. Finally, scalability is assessed through a worst-case runtime analysis over increasingly large constraints.

The paper is structured as follows. Section 2 describes the foundations and Sect. 3 introduces a running example. In Sect. 4, we present our approach and evaluate it in Sect. 5. We present related work in Sect. 6 and conclude in Sect. 7.

2 Foundations

This section introduces the foundations and notation required to translate confidentiality constraints into SAT-compatible representations. It briefly reviews propositional logic and satisfiability, introduces DSLs, and outlines the DFA framework on which this work builds.

2.1 Propositional Logic and Satisfiability

A propositional formula ϕ is constructed from Boolean variables using logical connectives such as conjunction ($\wedge$), disjunction ($\vee$), and negation ($\neg$), and evaluates to either *true* or *false* under a given variable assignment [7]. For SAT solving, formulas are typically expressed in CNF, which is a conjunction of clauses, where each clause is a disjunction of literals. A literal is either a variable or its negation. CNF is the standard input format for modern SAT solvers and enables efficient automated reasoning [9,19].

The satisfiability problem asks whether there exists an assignment of truth values to the variables of a propositional formula such that the formula evaluates to true [24]. Beyond deciding satisfiability, SAT solvers can also compute satisfying assignments, which provide concrete variable valuations and are essential for tasks such as model repair and mitigation [10].

When transforming formulas for SAT solving, it is essential to distinguish between *equi-satisfiability* and *semantic equivalence*. Equi-satisfiable transformations preserve satisfiability but may introduce auxiliary variables and do not preserve assignments to the original variables [16,29]. In contrast, semantically equivalent formulas are satisfied by exactly the same assignments, thereby preserving the full information content of the original constraint. Since SAT-based mitigation of confidentiality violations relies on concrete assignments to architectural variables, the translation from DSL constraints to CNF in this work must preserve semantic equivalence.

2.2 Domain-Specific Languages

A DSL is a programming or modeling language tailored to a specific problem domain and designed to express domain concepts at a high level of abstraction [15]. DSL are widely used in Model-Driven Engineering (MDE) to concisely represent constraints and rules that would otherwise require complex implementations in general-purpose languages [17]. Well-designed DSLs enable the formulation of complete and consistent constraints governed by domain-specific semantics [30]. However, their domain specificity also implies that constraints expressed in a DSL cannot be directly interpreted by general-purpose reasoning tools such as SAT solvers.

2.3 Data Flow Analysis Framework

This work builds on the extensible DFA framework by Boltz et al. [5], which enables automated confidentiality analysis of software architectures. Architectural descriptions, such as Data Flow Diagrams (DFDs) [28] or Palladio component models [25], are transformed into directed acyclic graphs (Directed Acyclic Graphs (DAGs)) [32] that represent potential data flow paths. Data and node properties are modeled as labels and propagated along these paths.

Confidentiality policies are specified using a dedicated DSL that allows users to formulate constraints over the propagated labels. The DFA evaluates these constraints on the data flow graph to detect violations, such as unauthorized disclosure of confidential information. The DSL defined by this framework constitutes the input language for the conversion algorithm proposed in this work.

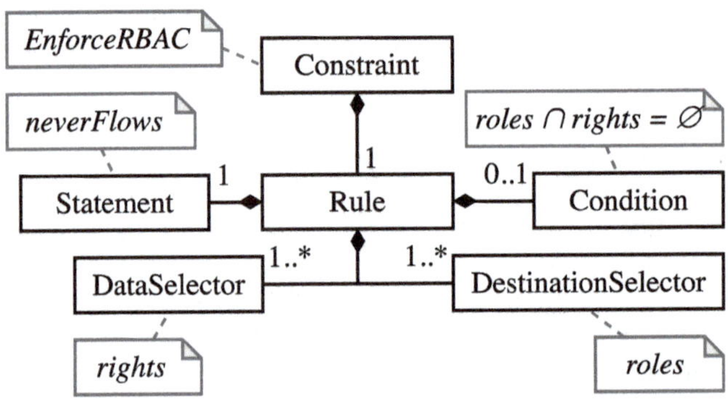

Fig. 1. Simplified abstract syntax of a confidentiality constraint annotated with example values (derived from [14]).

Figure 1 illustrates the abstract syntax of a confidentiality constraint in the DFA framework. Each constraint defines exactly one rule that restricts information flow within the architectural model. Conceptually, a constraint consists of a *rule* that connects two sets of selectors—*DataSelectors* and *DestinationSelectors*—and may optionally be refined by a *condition*.

Selectors. Selectors identify the elements of the architecture to which a constraint applies. *DataSelectors* specify the characteristics of data items relevant to the constraint (e.g., access rights or sensitivity levels), while *DestinationSelectors* identify the target nodes or vertices in the data flow graph (e.g., user roles or system components). Each selector refers to characteristic types and values defined in the underlying architectural model. Recent extensions of the framework allow selectors to reference only data or only vertices, thereby enabling global constraints, such as enforcing encryption for all data flows regardless of their destination.

Constraints. A constraint's semantics are defined by a single rule, which establishes the relationship between selected data and destinations. The rule is expressed through a statement; currently, the only supported statement is *neverFlows.* This statement specifies that data matching the *DataSelectors* must never reach nodes matched by the *DestinationSelectors.* The separation between constraint, rule, and statement was introduced to support extensibility of the language.

Constraints may also include an optional *condition* that refines the rule's applicability. Conditions serve as intermediaries between data and destination selectors, enabling the expression of more complex policies. For example, a condition may require that data with specific access rights be restricted only when the corresponding destination node has a matching user role.

Labels. The characteristics referenced by selectors are represented internally as labels. Each label encodes a single property defined by a typevalue pair and is categorized as *Incoming*, *Outgoing*, or *Node*. For the purpose of SAT-based analysis, labels are mapped to Boolean literals with positive or negative polarity (e.g., `Sensitivity.Personal` or ¬`Location.nonEU`). After applying the proposed translation, a constraint is expressed solely as a Boolean formula over these literals.

3 Running Example

To illustrate the concepts used throughout this paper, we introduce a running example based on a confidentiality constraint formulated in the DFA framework's DSL. The example, adapted from Boltz *et al.* [5], is shown in Listing 1. The constraint specifies that *personal data* that is *not encrypted* must *never flow* to destinations that are either *off-premise* or accessible by an *administrator*.

```
var constraint = new Constraint()
      .ofData()
      // DataSelector
      .withLabel(Sensitivity.Personal)
      // DataSelector
      .withoutLabel(Encryption.Encrypted)
      // Statement
      .neverFlows()
      .toVertex()
      // DestinationSelector
      .withCharacteristic(Location.offPremise, User.Admin)
      .create()
```

Listing 1. DSL constraint for a simplified online shop

The constraint consists of two *DataSelectors*, which restrict the policy to personal and unencrypted data, and two *DestinationSelectors*, which target vertices that are either off-premises or associated with an administrative user role. The

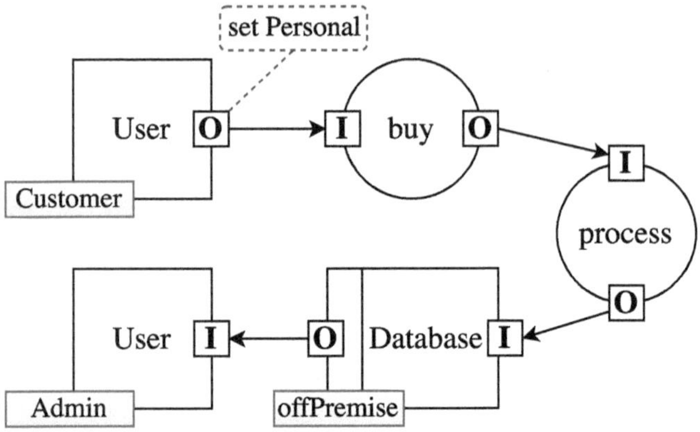

Fig. 2. Example DFD for a simplified online shop.

neverFlows statement enforces that no data flow satisfying both selector scopes is permitted.

Figure 2 illustrates a corresponding data flow diagram for a simplified online shop. Personal data originates from a customer, is processed within the system, and stored in a database. The database is located off-premises, and its contents are accessible to an administrator. Under the specified constraint, this architecture exhibits two confidentiality violations: the storage of unencrypted personal data at an off-premise location and its exposure to an administrative user.

4 Approach

This section describes the automated conversion of confidentiality constraints from the DFA framework into CNF. The approach is structured into two components: (i) a translation algorithm that converts DSL constraints into propositional logic, and (ii) a conversion algorithm that transforms the resulting formulas into CNF. This separation improves clarity, supports modularity, and allows each component to be reasoned about and evaluated independently.

4.1 Translation from DSL to Propositional Logic

The first step of the approach translates confidentiality constraints expressed in the DFA framework's DSL into propositional logic. This translation relies solely on the formal semantics of constraints defined by Boltz *et al.* [5]. For well-formed constraints, the translation is deterministic and yields a propositional formula composed exclusively of conjunctions, disjunctions, and negations.

At the core of every constraint is the *neverFlows* statement, which relates one or more data selectors to one or more destination selectors. Semantically, it specifies that data matching the data selectors must not reach destinations matching the destination selectors. This relationship can be expressed as a Boolean implication: if a data condition holds, then the corresponding destination condition must not hold. For a single data literal a and a single destination literal b, this yields

$$\phi = a \rightarrow \neg b \quad \equiv \quad \neg a \vee \neg b \quad \equiv \quad \neg(a \wedge b).$$

This formulation generalizes naturally to sets of data and destination selectors. Each side of the implication may consist of multiple literals combined by conjunction or disjunction, depending on the selector semantics. If no selectors are present on one side, the corresponding operand is treated as logically true. Consequently, every DSL constraint can be expressed as a negated conjunction over the data and destination sides of the constraint.

Literals and Label Mapping. In the DFA framework, a literal corresponds to a label representing a single architectural characteristic together with a Boolean polarity. Labels are categorized as *Incoming* or *Node*, distinguishing data properties from node properties.

A literal is constructed by selecting the appropriate label type and assigning it a characteristic typevalue pair. Its polarity is determined by the selector that introduces the label. Positive selectors yield positive literals, while negated selectors yield negated literals. The translation, therefore, produces a propositional formula over literals that directly correspond to architectural characteristics.

Selector Translation. The DFA framework distinguishes between constant selectors, dynamic selectors, and conditional selectors. Constant selectors directly define characteristic values and generate one or more literals. Single-valued selectors produce a single literal, while list-valued selectors yield a set of literals combined according to the selector's polarity. Negated list selectors are translated using De Morgan's law, for example:

$$\neg(a \vee b \vee c) \;\equiv\; (\neg a \wedge \neg b \wedge \neg c).$$

Dynamic selectors reference characteristic values indirectly. These values are resolved during translation by consulting the model's data dictionary, as no runtime analysis context is available. Each reference is mapped to its associated set of values, which is then translated into literals analogously to constant selectors.

Conditional selectors refine how literals derived from dynamic selectors are combined. Variable conditional selectors behave analogously to list selectors by assigning a polarity to a set of referenced literals. Empty-set conditions introduce additional structure by evaluating whether referenced value sets intersect. The resulting literals are combined according to the logical relationships induced by the condition.

Running Example. Applying the translation to the running example introduced in Sect. 3 yields the propositional formula shown in Algorithm 1. Each literal corresponds directly to a label defined by the constraint's data and destination selectors, and the resulting formula preserves the semantics of the original DSL constraint.

Algorithm 1. Translating the running example constraint

define a := IncomingDataLabel (Sensitivity.Personal)
define b := IncomingDataLabel (Encryption.Encrypted)
define c := NodeLabel (Location.offPremise)
define d := NodeLabel (User.Admin)

$\phi(a, b, c, d) := \neg((a \wedge \neg b) \wedge (c \vee d))$

4.2 Conversion to CNF

The objective of the conversion algorithm is to transform propositional formulas into CNF while preserving semantic equivalence and maintaining favorable structural properties, such as low clause and literal counts. Thus, the conversion is based exclusively on Boolean algebraic transformations.

The algorithm, shown in Algorithm 2, operates on the propositional representation introduced in the previous section, which is restricted to conjunctions, disjunctions, and negations. Conceptually, the conversion follows a divide-and-conquer strategy that recursively eliminates disjunctions by applying distributive laws and De Morgan's law. This yields a CNF representation without introducing additional variables.

Algorithm 2. Translation of Constraint DSL to CNF

Require: ConstraintDSL
Ensure: List of CNF clauses
  result ← {}
  constraints ← CreateConstraint(ConstraintDSL)
  while constraint ∈ constraints **do**
    if constraint has no disjunctions **then**
      result.Add(constraint.negated())
    else
      sub-constraints ← CreateSubConstraints(constraint)
      constraints.Add(sub-constraints)
    end if
    constraints.Remove(constraint)
  end while
  return result

The defining characteristic of DSL constraints in the DFA framework is the *neverFlows* statement, which yields propositional formulas of the form $\neg(f)$, where f is a conjunction of sub-formulas derived from data and destination selectors. In the simplest case, where f consists only of literals, a single application of De Morgan's law suffices to obtain CNF. For example, the constraint *internal data never flows to external users* translates to:

$$\neg(x \wedge y) \equiv \neg x \vee \neg y,$$

which is already a single CNF clause.

More complex constraints arise when f contains disjunctions. In these cases, the algorithm recursively applies distributive laws to split the formula into independent sub-formulas. Each split replaces a disjunction by two conjunctions, yielding two sub-constraints whose conjunction is semantically equivalent to the original formula. This process continues until all disjunctions have been eliminated.

Applying the conversion algorithm to the propositional formula derived from the running example (Algorithm 1) yields the CNF shown in Algorithm 3. Each disjunction introduces a recursive split, resulting in two clauses that jointly preserve the semantics of the original constraint.

Algorithm 3. Conversion of the running example to CNF

$$\begin{aligned} f &:= \neg((a \wedge \neg b) \wedge (c \vee d)) \\ &\equiv \neg(a \wedge \neg b \wedge c) \wedge \neg(a \wedge \neg b \wedge d) \\ &\equiv (\neg a \vee b \vee \neg c) \wedge (\neg a \vee b \vee \neg d) \end{aligned}$$

The resulting CNF consists of minimal clauses and literals while preserving semantic equivalence. In particular, no redundant literals are introduced, and each clause corresponds directly to a minimal violation scenario of the original constraint.

5 Evaluation

The objective of this evaluation is to assess whether the proposed approach can automatically translate confidentiality constraints expressed in the DFA-DSL into semantically equivalent CNF representations while maintaining favorable structural properties and practical scalability. In particular, we evaluate whether the translation preserves semantic equivalence, produces bounded clause and literal growth, and remains computationally feasible as constraint complexity increases.

5.1 Goal, Questions, and Metrics

We use a Goal-Question-Metric(GQM) plan [3] to structure our evaluation. To further enhance validity, we align our benchmarking with related work [13,21].

Our **Goal** is to assess the quality and practicality of the proposed automatic translation from DSL-based confidentiality constraints to CNF. Therefore, we ask:

Q1 Are the translated CNF constraints semantically equivalent to the DSL?
Q2 How bounded are the structural properties of the translated CNF constraints?

Q3 How scalable is our automatic translation approach?

These research questions collectively capture the key factors that determine the practicality of the proposed approach in real-world settings.
Q1 (Correctness) evaluates functional correctness. If a DSL constraint cannot be translated into a semantically equivalent CNF formula, any further analysis of efficiency or scalability becomes irrelevant.
Q2 (Structural Bounds) assesses suitability. Since the performance of SAT solvers depends on the number of clauses and literals, the translated constraints must exhibit well-bounded structural properties to ensure practical applicability.
Q3 (Scalability) examines the applicability of our approach. In industrial software architectures, constraints may grow substantially in size and number. Therefore, the translation must remain feasible as the input scales.

5.2 Design

We address **Q1** using two complementary approaches. First, we establish functional correctness by providing a formal proof of the divide-and-conquer conversion algorithm presented in Subsect. 4.2. Second, we empirically validate correctness on a real-world dataset of microservice architectures from Schneider *et al.* ch1schneiderspsmicrosecendsps2023, which contains DFDs and confidentiality constraints specified in natural language. These constraints were formalized in the DSL, automatically translated using our approach, and compared with 10 manually constructed CNF encodings that we developed in prior work [23] for the same dataset. We compute the *symmetric difference* **M1.1**, defined as the number of clauses that appear in exactly one of the two CNF representations. A value of zero indicates that the automatically generated and manually constructed CNF formulas are structurally identical.

To answer **Q2**, we analyze the structural properties of the generated CNF formulas for an exhaustive set of constraints with a fixed number of input literals. Recall that a constraint in the DFA-DSL is defined by data selectors (`withLabel`, `withoutLabel`) and destination selectors (`withCharacteristic`, `withoutCharacteristic`). We fix the number of distinct input literals to $n = 100$ and systematically generate all possible constraints by distributing these literals across the four selector types. This results in $\binom{103}{3} = 176851$ distinct constraints. For each translated constraint, we measure the number of clauses (**M2.1**), the total number of literals (**M2.2**), and the average clause length (**M2.3**).

To answer **Q3**, we evaluate the scalability of our approach by measuring the translation runtime (**M3.1**) as a function of the number of input literals. We conduct a worst-case analysis by constructing constraints that follow the selector distribution, yielding the highest transformation runtime. Starting with constraints containing 150 literals, we incrementally increase the input size by 150 until reaching constraints with 2700 literals. Each constraint instance is translated ten times on a *MacBook Pro* (2023) equipped with an *M3 Pro* processor, and the reported runtime corresponds to the average over all runs.

5.3 Results and Discussion

Correctness. We evaluate correctness both analytically and empirically. First, we establish the functional correctness of the divide-and-conquer conversion through a formal proof based on standard Boolean equivalences. The proof, summarized by the lemmas presented in Sect. 5.3, shows that the conversion preserves semantic equivalence for all propositional formulas produced by the translation.

Lemma 1.
Let $f = \neg(f_1 \wedge \cdots \wedge f_n)$, where each f_i is a literal or its negation.
Then f is already in CNF.

Lemma 2.
Let $f = \neg(f_1 \wedge \cdots \wedge (f_L \vee f_R) \wedge \cdots \wedge f_n)$.
Then
$f \equiv \neg(f_1 \wedge \cdots \wedge f_L \wedge \cdots \wedge f_n) \wedge \neg(f_1 \wedge \cdots \wedge f_R \wedge \cdots \wedge f_n)$. Each conjunct is in CNF by Lemma 1.

Lemma 3.
Let $f = \neg(f_1 \wedge \cdots \wedge f_n)$, where each f_i is any propositional formula composed solely of conjunctions and disjunctions.
Repeated application of Lemma 2 reduces f to CNF. ■

To complement the analytical results, we performed an empirical validation using 10 DSL constraints derived from a real-world microservice dataset by Schneider *et al.*ch1schneiderspsmicrosecendsps2023. Each constraint was automatically translated using our approach and compared with manually constructed CNF encodings that we developed in prior work ch1niehuesspsintegratingsps2024. The results show an empty symmetric difference for all evaluated constraints. This indicates that the automatically generated CNF formulas are structurally identical to the manually derived versions in every case.

Overall, these results confirm the correctness of the proposed approach. The formal proof establishes semantic equivalence in theory, while the empirical comparison demonstrates that the implementation faithfully realizes this property on real-world constraints.

Structural Bounds. To evaluate the structural properties of the translated constraints, we exhaustively generated all constraints consisting of 100 input literals distributed across the four selector types. For each constraint, we measured the number of output clauses, the total number of output literals, and the average clause length of the resulting CNF.

Figure 3 plots the number of output clauses against the total number of output literals. The maximum number of output clauses observed is 2500. The clause count scales quadratically with the sizes of the disjunctive selector groups in the DSL constraint, specifically with |withLabel| · |withCharacteristic|. Consequently, the worst case is reached when the 100 input literals are evenly split between these two selectors, yielding $50 \cdot 50 = 2500$ clauses.

The maximum total number of output literals is 39304. This quantity scales cubically with the selector sizes and is proportional to |withCharacteristic| · |withLabel| · (|withoutCharacteristic| + |withoutLabel| + 2). The worst case occurs when the 100 input literals are evenly distributed across these three components, resulting in $34 \cdot 34 \cdot (32 + 2) = 39304$ literals.

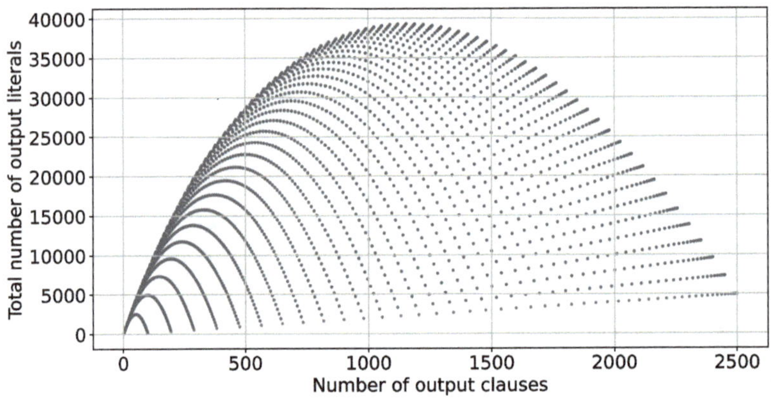

Fig. 3. Number of output clauses vs. total number of output literals.

Figure 4 shows the number of output clauses versus the average clause length. The maximum average clause length observed is 100. Clause length scales linearly with the size of the conjunctive selector union, |withoutLabel| + |withoutCharacteristic|. Accordingly, the worst case occurs when all 100 input literals are distributed between these two selectors.

In summary, the number of output clauses scales quadratically, the total number of output literals scales cubically, and the average clause length scales linearly with the number of input literals. Importantly, these worst cases are mutually exclusive: maximizing one structural metric necessarily limits the others. This demonstrates that the structural properties of the translated CNF constraints are well-bounded and manageable in practice.

Scalability. To evaluate the runtime scalability of our approach, we focus on constraints that induce the worst-case number of output literals, as this quantity dominates the runtime of the conversion algorithm. As shown in Sect. 5.3, this worst case occurs when n input literals are evenly distributed across the `withLabel`, `withCharacteristic`, and `withoutCharacteristic` selectors.

Figure 5 reports the averaged runtimes (in milliseconds) for constraints ranging from 150 to 2700 input literals. Observed runtimes range from approximately

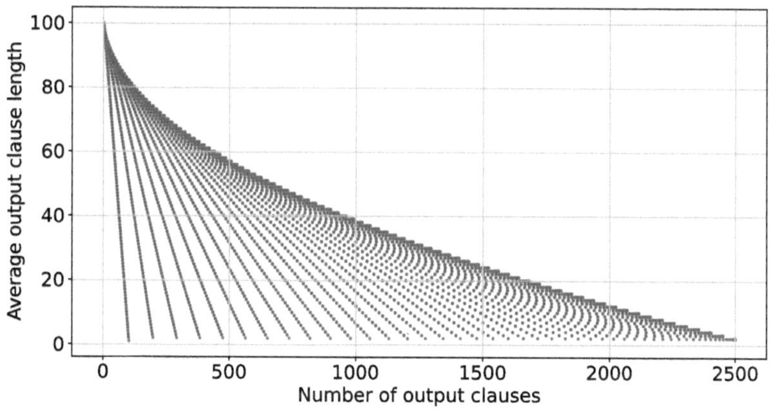

Fig. 4. Number of output clauses vs. average output clause length.

1 ms up to 21785 ms. The results show that runtime increases cubically with the number of input literals, closely matching the fitted third-degree polynomial shown in red.

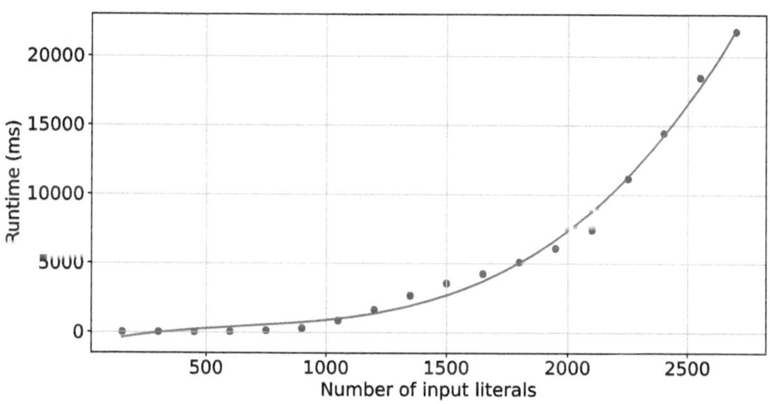

Fig. 5. Worst-case runtime for scaled number of input literals.

Although the worst-case runtime scales cubically, constraints containing up to 1050 input literals are translated in under one second. This threshold is higher than the complexity observed in real-world confidentiality requirements, which typically involve far fewer literals [27]. These results indicate that the proposed approach remains practical for realistic architectural models despite its theoretical worst-case complexity.

5.4 Threats to Validity

We structure the discussion of threats to validity based on the guidelines by Runeson *et al.*ch1runesonspsguidelinessps2009. *Internal validity* is potentially affected by the derivation of DSL constraints from natural-language specifications in Schneider *et al.*ch1schneiderspsmicrosecendsps2023. To mitigate the risk of incorrect interpretations, all authors independently derived the constraints and arrived at identical results. *External validity* is limited by the comparison against 10 manually translated constraints developed in prior work ch1niehuesspsintegratingsps2024, which do not cover the full space of possible confidentiality requirements; however, this limitation is mitigated by the formal proof of semantic equivalence, which holds for all constraints expressible in the DFA-DSL. *Construct validity* may be affected by the evaluation of structural properties based on exhaustive analysis for a fixed input size; since worst cases are deterministically defined, repeating the analysis with larger input sizes yields proportional and comparable results. *Reliability* is supported by providing the full implementation and all evaluation data as material [22], enabling independent replication of all results.

6 Related Work

The transformation of Boolean formulas into CNF is a fundamental preprocessing step for satisfiability solving, as most modern SAT solvers accept only CNF input [1,16]. Beyond satisfiability, many applications require concrete variable assignments, making the distinction between semantic equivalence and equi-satisfiability essential [29]. Equi-satisfiable translations preserve satisfiability but may not preserve the original information space, which is critical for constraint-based analysis and mitigation in software architectures.

Standard CNF conversion techniques, such as the Tseitin transformation and its refinements, preserve equi-satisfiability while controlling clause growth [16,29]. These approaches introduce auxiliary variables to represent sub-formulas, yielding compact encodings but breaking semantic equivalence with respect to the original variables [11,34]. As a result, satisfying assignments cannot be directly interpreted in terms of architectural elements, limiting their applicability for repair and mitigation tasks.

Binary Decision Diagrams (BDDs) offer an alternative that preserves semantic equivalence by explicitly encoding the Boolean function [6,8]. CNF construction based on BDDs enumerates falsifying assignments as clauses, but typically introduces significant redundancy, as clauses often contain all variables regardless of relevance. In addition, BDD size is highly sensitive to variable ordering and may grow exponentially in practice [10,31].

Direct CNF conversion via Boolean algebraic transformations avoids auxiliary variables by applying De Morgan's and distributive laws [18,35]. While this preserves semantic equivalence, it may incur exponential blow-up in the worst case. Our approach builds on this strategy and exploits the restricted structure of confidentiality constraints in the DFA framework to produce semantically equivalent CNF encodings with reduced redundancy and favorable structural properties.

7 Conclusion

This paper introduced an automated approach for translating confidentiality constraints expressed in the DFA-DSL into semantically equivalent CNF representations. The approach follows a two-step process: first translating DSL constraints into propositional logic, and subsequently converting the resulting formulas into CNF using a divide-and-conquer algorithm.

We formally proved that the conversion preserves semantic equivalence for all propositional formulas generated by the translation step. This result was empirically validated by comparing automatically generated CNF formulas against manually constructed encodings for real-world confidentiality constraints, where both representations were shown to be identical. In addition, an exhaustive structural analysis demonstrated that the resulting CNF formulas exhibit well bounded clause growth, literal counts, and clause lengths. A worst-case runtime evaluation further showed that, despite cubic theoretical complexity, the translation remains feasible for constraint sizes exceeding those typically observed in practice.

Overall, the proposed approach enables fully automated and reliable translation of architectural confidentiality constraints into CNF, providing a practical foundation for integrating SAT-based analysis and mitigation techniques into existing DFA-based confidentiality frameworks. Future work will focus on tighter integration with analysis toolchains and on extending the approach to additional constraint constructs.

Acknowledgment. This work was supported by the BMFTR (Federal Ministry of Research, Technology and Space of Germany) grant number 16KIS2509 (ANYMOS II) and the topic Engineering Secure Systems of the Helmholtz Association (HGF) and by KASTEL Security Research Labs. We like to thank Jens Weber.

References

1. Alouneh, S., et al.: A comprehensive study and analysis on SAT-solvers: advances, usages and achievements. Artif. Intell. Rev. **52**(4), 2575–2601 (2019)
2. Barbacci, M.: Quality Attributes. Technical report (1995)
3. Basili, V.R., Caldiera, G., Rombach, H.D.: The goal question metric approach. In: Encyclopedia of Software Engineering (1994)
4. Boehm, B., Basili, V.R.: Software defect reduction top 10 list. In: Foundations of Empirical Software Engineering: The Legacy of Victor R. Basili, vol. 426, no. 37 (2005)
5. Boltz, N.: An extensible framework for architecture-based data flow analysis for information security. In: European Conference on Software Architecture (2023)
6. Bryant, R.E.: Graph-based algorithms for Boolean function manipulation. IEEE Trans. Comput. **100**(8) (1986)

7. Büning, H.K., Lettmann, T.: Propositional Logic: Deduction and Algorithms. Cambridge University Press, Cambridge (1999)
8. Drechsler, R., Sieling, D.: Binary decision diagrams in theory and practice. Int. J. Softw. Tools Technol. Transfer **3**(2), 112–136 (2001)
9. Eén, N., Sörensson, N.: An extensible SAT-solver. In: International Conference on Theory and Applications of Satisfiability Testing, pp. 502–518 (2003)
10. Eén, N., Sörensson, N.: Translating pseudo-Boolean constraints into SAT. J. Satisfiabil. Boolean Model. Comput. **2**(1–4), 1–26 (2006)
11. Egly, U., Rath, T.: On the practical value of different definitional translations to normal form. In: McRobbie, M.A., Slaney, J.K. (eds.) CADE 1996. LNCS, vol. 1104, pp. 403–417. Springer, Heidelberg (1996). https://doi.org/10.1007/3-540-61511-3_103
12. Glinz, M.: Requirements engineering i. Nicht funktionale Anforderungen. Universität Zürich, Institut für Informatik, Zürich (2006)
13. Hahner, S.: Model-based confidentiality analysis under uncertainty. In: 2023 IEEE 20th International Conference on Software Architecture Companion (ICSA-C), pp. 256–263 (2023)
14. S. Hahner et al.: Modeling data flow constraints for design-time confidentiality analyses. In: ICSA-C, pp. 15–21 (2021)
15. JetBrains, Domain-Specific Languages. https://www.jetbrains.com/mps/concepts/domain-specific-languages/. Accessed 30 July 2025
16. Kuiter, E.: Tseitin or not Tseitin? The impact of CNF transformations on feature-model analyses. In: Proceedings of the 37th IEEE/ACM International Conference on Automated Software Engineering (2022)
17. Kurtev, I.: Model-based DSL frameworks. In: Companion to the 21st ACM SIGPLAN Symposium on Object-Oriented Programming Systems, Languages, and Applications, pp. 602–616 (2006)
18. Miltersen, P.B., Radhakrishnan, J., Wegener, I.: On converting CNF to DNF. Theor. Comput. Sci. **347**(1-2) (2005)
19. Moskewicz, M.W.: Chaff: engineering an efficient SAT solver. In: Proceedings of the 38th Annual Design Automation Conference (2001)
20. Niehues, N., Arp, B., Heinrich, R.: Efficient repair of confidentiality violations in software architectures. In: Proceedings of the 23rd IEEE International Conference on Software Architecture (ICSA) (2026)
21. Niehues, N., Hahner, S., Heinrich, R.: An architecture-based approach to mitigate confidentiality violations using machine learning. In: 2025 IEEE 22nd International Conference on Software Architecture (ICSA) (2025)
22. Niehues, N., Heinrich, R.: Supplementary material for "Automatic translation of data flow constraints into conjunctive normal form" (2026). https://doi.org/10.5281/zenodo.18494951
23. Niehues, N.: Integrating security-enriched data flow diagrams into architecture-based confidentiality analysis (2024)
24. Niewiadomski, A., et al.: Applying modern SAT-solvers to solving hard problems. Fundamenta Informaticae **165**(3-4) (2019)
25. Reussner, R.H.: Modeling and Simulating Software Architectures: The Palladio Approach. MIT Press, Cambridge (2016)
26. Runeson, P., Höst, M.: Guidelines for conducting and reporting case study research in software engineering. Empir. Softw. Eng. **14**, 131–164 (2009)
27. Schneider, S.: microSecEnD: a dataset of security-enriched dataflow diagrams for microservice applications. In: 2023 IEEE/ACM 20th International Conference on Mining Software Repositories (MSR), pp. 125–129. (2023)

28. Seifermann, S., et al.: A unified model to detect information flow and access control violations in software architectures. SECRYPT **21**, 26–37 (2021)
29. Semenov, A.A.: About Tseitin transformation in logical equations. Prikladnaya Diskretnaya Matematika (2009)
30. O. Semeráth et al.: Formal validation of domain-specific languages with derived features and well-formedness constraints. Softw. Syst. Model. (2017)
31. Somenzi, F.: Binary decision diagrams. NATO ASI Series F Comput. Syst. Sci. **173**, 303–368 (1999)
32. Thulasiraman, K., Swamy, M.N.: Graphs: Theory and Algorithms. John Wiley & Sons, Hoboken (1992)
33. de la Tour, T.B.: An optimality result for clause form translation. J. Symb. Comput. **14**(4), 283–301 (1992)
34. Velev: efficient translation of Boolean formulas to CNF in formal verification of microprocessors. In: ASP-DAC 2004 (2004)
35. J.E.: Whitesitt: Boolean Algebra and its Applications. Courier Corporation (2010)

Analyzing DOPLER Decision Models with SMT

Fabian Eger[1], Maximilian Heisinger[2], Rick Rabiser[3,4], and Kevin Feichtinger[1](✉)

[1] Karlsruhe Institute of Technology, Am Fasanengarten 5, 76131 Karlsruhe, Germany
{fabian.eger,kevin.feichtinger}@kit.edu
[2] Institute for Symbolic Artificial Intelligence, Johannes Kepler University Linz, Altenberger Street 69, 4040 Linz, Austria
maximilian.heisinger@jku.at
[3] CDL VaSiCS, LIT CPS Lab, Johannes Kepler University Linz, Altenberger Street 69, 4040 Linz, Austria
rick.rabiser@jku.at
[4] Software Competence Center Hagenberg GmbH (SCCH), Softwarepark 32a, 4232 Hagenberg im Mühlkreis, Austria

Abstract. In software product line engineering, decision modeling is one of the most common approaches to variability modeling. Decision models are particularly suitable to guide users through products and available customization options, which often represent huge configuration spaces and would hence benefit from automated analysis. However, only very few SAT- and SMT-based analysis techniques have been implemented for decision models. In this paper, we propose a novel encoding for decision-modeling concepts in SMT. We implemented our SMT encoding within a DOPLER decision meta-model re-implementation and assessed feasibility and applicability using publicly available models. Our results show that our encoding facilitates unsatisfiability analysis and anomaly detection in DOPLER decision models. With this work, we improve the configuration support of decision modeling with SMT-based analysis.

Keywords: Software product lines · variability modeling · decision modeling · SMT analysis

1 Introduction

In Software Product Line (SPL) engineering, variability modeling is used to capture common and variable parts of a set of software(-intensive) systems. Variability models usually capture huge configuration spaces, where a valid *configuration* fulfills all defined constraints [1]. Every valid configuration can be used to derive a new variant of the system, which is then completed and customized to fit customer requirements. While typically used in SPL engineering, variability models have also been used in domains beyond software engineering [12,15].

C. Berger and V. Klös (Eds.): SEAA 2026, LNCS 16864, pp. 20–29, 2027.
https://doi.org/10.1007/978-3-032-36587-3_2

Many companies utilize Configure-to-Order (CTO) processes [13] to guide customers through products and available customization options [12,13]. A CTO process is captured easily by a Decision Model (DM) [5], because of its walk-through structure. Likewise, the decision order focus make DMs well-suited for arranging configuration elements in order [5], e.g., defining a succession of process steps of independent variables [15]. Both example use cases would benefit from analysis techniques to (a) detect errors in complex DMs, (b) understand possible DM configurations, and (c) help in the configuration of complex DMs [12,15].

With our research, we aim to establish analysis techniques to decision modeling. For that, in this paper, we present a direct encoding of decision modeling concepts into Satisfiability Modulo Theories (SMT [4]. Specifically, we re-implemented the meta-model of the decision modeling approach DOPLER [6] and integrated its SMT encoding directly into the re-implemented meta-model. With our work, we propose the first DM encoding with SMT which includes non-Boolean decision variables as well as enumerations and their cardinalities in decision modeling [12,14]. In a feasibility and applicability evaluation using a set of existing DOPLER DMs of different sizes and complexity, we demonstrate that our encoding enables satisfiability checking and anomaly detection of DOPLER DMs using state-of-the-art SMT solvers like Z3 [17]. Further, we report on the performance of our SMT encoding when analyzing DMs.

2 Foundations

Decision modeling approaches focus on representing varying features and their constraints [5]. Typically, DMs comprise a set of decision variables. Our running example of a pizza product line shown in Table 1 uses the DOPLER [6] approach.

In DOPLER, each decision variable has a unique id, a description, an arbitrary text typically used for an identifying question, and a data type, e.g., Boolean, String, Double, or Enumeration. The allowed value range for enumeration decisions may be restricted using validity conditions (cf. column *Validity* in Table 1). For instance, the enumeration decision *Size* is restricted to the double values 18, 23, and 27. Further, each enumeration decision specifies a cardinality, which the selected values of the enumeration must fulfill. For instance, Enumeration decision *Dough* specifies a 1:1 cardinality, which means the possible values Neapolitan or Sicilian are alternatives, and exactly one needs to be selected. In contrast, enumeration decision *Topping* specifies a 1:3 cardinality, i.e., an OR relationship, meaning that at least one, but also up to all three possible values can be selected. Also, any mutex cardinality, i.e., n:m would be possible for enumeration decisions (no such example in Table 1). DOPLER uses visibility conditions (cf. column *Visibility* in Table 1) and rules (cf. column *Rules* in Table 1) to express dependencies and relationships among decision variables. Rules in DOPLER are used (a) for verifying the validity of a selected value for a decision variable, (b) to assign values to other decisions, or (c) to alter the allowed decision value range of a decision variable. Hence, rules define constraints within the DM and are executed after a value is assigned to a decision variable.

Visibility conditions are used to specify when a given decision is relevant in the derivation process to derive a valid product [5]. Thus, visibility conditions define a hierarchy of decision variables on when the decision should be set during the derivation process. Besides propositional logic expressions among decision variables, DOPLER allows the specification of value ranges and obtaining values from decisions, using a Java-like Domain-Specific Language (DSL) [6].

Table 1. A pizza product line captured as a DOPLER [6] DM.

<table>
<tr><th>#</th><th>ID</th><th>Question</th><th>Type</th><th>Validity</th><th>Card.</th><th>Rules</th><th>Visibility</th></tr>
<tr><td>1</td><td>Topping</td><td>Which Toppings?</td><td>Enum</td><td>Salami | Ham | Mozzarella</td><td>1:3</td><td></td><td>true</td></tr>
<tr><td>2</td><td>Size</td><td>Which Size?</td><td>Double</td><td>Size==18 || Size==23 || Size==27</td><td></td><td>if (Size>=23) {
Dough = Neapolitan
}</td><td>true</td></tr>
<tr><td>3</td><td>Dough</td><td>Which Dough?</td><td>Enum</td><td>Neapolitan | Sicilian</td><td>1:1</td><td>if (Dough.Sicilian) {
CheesyCrust = true
}</td><td>isTaken(Size)</td></tr>
<tr><td>4</td><td>CheesyCrust</td><td>Cheesy crust?</td><td>Bool</td><td>true | false</td><td></td><td>if (CheesyCrust) {
Size = 27
}</td><td>true</td></tr>
<tr><td>5</td><td>BoxMessage</td><td>Box message?</td><td>String</td><td></td><td></td><td></td><td>true</td></tr>
</table>

In this paper, we focus only on the aforementioned core concepts of DOPLER. For all details on the DOPLER decision modeling approach, we refer the reader to previous publications [5,6,11,18].

3 Analyzing DOPLER Decision Models Using SMT

Publicly available decision modeling tools are, unfortunately, scarce. The DOPLER ConfigurationWizard tool [18] for the DOPLER [6] approach is proprietary and consequently, closed source. Therefore, to implement our SMT encoding within DOPLER, it was necessary first to re-implement the meta-model of the DOPLER approach, using, in part, already existing re-implementations [10,15]. Then, one author proposed an initial SMT encoding for DOPLER, and the other authors verified and commented on this until a consensus on how we encode decision modeling concepts was reached. We provide the DOPLER meta-model implementation, including our SMT encoding online [8]. Note that in our re-implementations of the DOPLER meta-model, we introduced concrete Enforce actions for each decision type to facilitate the SMT encoding.

3.1 SMT Encoding

We implemented our encoding using the generic SMT-LIB [2] interface for various SMT solvers. We used the SMT-LIB interface because it is a widely accepted, direct, yet exchangeable interface for SMT solvers.

We use the declare-const command to define a constant for each decision. These decision constants refer to any decision that itself is used by other decisions.

Next, we encode each decision using a single assert statement, which includes the encoding of its visibility condition, rules, and (if applicable) validity conditions. We show the complete encoding of the decision *Dough* in Listing 1.1. However, we abbreviate the listing by leaving out links to decisions and default values [12].

```
1  (assert
2      (ite (= Dough_Taken true)
3          (and (= Dough_Taken true)
4              (ite (= Dough_Sicilian true)
5                  (= CheesyCrust_CheesyCrust true)
6                  (= true true)))
7          (and (and (= Dough_Sicilian false)
8                  (= Dough_Neapolitan false))
9               (= Dough_Taken false))))
10 (assert
11     (ite (= Dough_Taken true)
12         (and
13             (>=
14                 (+ (ite (= Dough_Sicilian true) 1 0)
15                     (ite (= Dough_Neapolitan true) 1 0))
16                 1)
17             (<=
18                 (+ (ite (= Dough_Sicilian true) 1 0)
19                     (ite (= Dough_Neapolitan true) 1 0))
20                 1))
21         (= true true)))
```

Listing 1.1. Example encoding of decision Dough in the running example.

In lines 1–9, the assert command encodes the enumeration decision *Dough*, including, as well, its visibility condition, its rules, and its validity condition. In line 2, the visibility condition is encoded by the ite command. If a decision is visible, the *then* of the ite command is executed, which sets the decision as taken and the associated rules are encoded and executed. If a decision is not visible, the *else* of the ite command is executed, which sets the decision as *not* taken, while also the available enumeration values *Neapolitan* or *Sicilian* are set to false. All rules are encoded as ite commands in lines 3–8. The ite predicate encodes the condition expression of the decision rule. In its *then* part, the actions are encoded, while in the *else* part, a default true expression is added to complete the command. As, decision *Dough* selects decision *CheesyCrust* if the *Sicilian* dough is selected, a corresponding expression is added.

A second assert command is required for enumeration decisions, so that the cardinality constraint is captured (lines 10 – 22). In line 11, whether the enumeration decision is taken is checked using an ite command. Both lower and upper bounds of the cardinality are then checked in the then part. For each enumeration literal, the cardinality is encoded using dedicated boolean constants to adapt the permitted selection of literals to the ratio of the cardinality. An ite command maps selected enumeration literals to the value 1 (for selected), or in the *else* part, to the value 0 (for unselected). These values are summed up by the

+ operator (in lines 14 and 18). To determine if a sum of selected enumeration literals is less or greater than the bounds, the sum is checked against the lower bound 1 (line 16) and the upper bound 1 (line 20). An `and` command connects both checks.

Our encoding allows encoding all decision types of the DOPLER approach. Nonetheless, we needed to adjust range value expressions to be substituted by a combination of binary constraints to enable the use of SMT-LIB. Further, we intentionally omit Java expressions and actions used by DOPLER its DSL [6]. We encode the most common elements which are also retrievable from existing, publicly available DOPLER DMs [7].

3.2 Analysis Operations

We implemented the following analysis operations to detect anomalies in DMs.

valid(dm, config): Returns `true` *iff* $SAT(DM \wedge config)$. Hence, detects if the configuration *config* of the DM *dm* is valid.

void(dm): Returns `true` *iff* $\neg SAT(DM)$. Hence, detects if the DM *dm* can not derive at least one valid product.

$dead_{DV}(d, v)$: Returns `true` *iff* $\neg SAT(DM \wedge (dv_d = v))$. Hence, detects if the decision value v can not be selected for a decision d. This is important for value range decisions like number decisions, where validity conditions are used to restrict the available set of allowed values for a decision.

$dead_D(d)$: Returns `true` *iff* $\neg SAT(DM \wedge \bigvee^{v \in DV_d}(dv_d = v))$. Hence, detects if the decision d of the DM can not be selected. Meaning, that none of the available decision values for the decision d can be selected in at least one valid configuration.

$falseOpt_{DV}(d, v)$: Returns `true` *iff* $\neg SAT(DM \wedge (\neg dv_d = v)$. Hence, detects if the decision value v must be selected for decision d.

4 Evaluation

We evaluate the feasibility and applicability of our SMT encoding for DOPLER [6] DMs using 59 DOPLER DMs [7] collected from public repositories and derived from the literature [5,6,10,16]. The DMs have various size (1 and 120 decisions – median 6, average 14.45) and complexity (0 and 105 rules – median 2, average 9.75) in terms of number of decisions and rules. We provide the dataset used in our evaluation online in a public repository [7].

We report on how fast the DMs can be encoded and how fast the analysis results can be obtained. Specifically, we answer the following research questions:

RQ1 *How feasible is the proposed SMT encoding for DOPLER DMs?*

We encoded the DMs of the dataset and counted the number of generated `ite` commands and constants. We recorded the time needed to encode the different DMs, how long the Z3 SMT-solver needed to return *sat* or *unsat*, and generating exactly one valid configuration. We manually verified the returned configuration to be valid. We discuss the results of our experiment in Sect. 4.1.

RQ2 *Does our encoding allow an SMT-solver to detect anomalies?*

We evaluate and report on the time needed to whether the encoding is feasible in detection anomalies of all kind. We discuss the results in Sect. 4.2.

4.1 RQ1: Feasibility

We encoded each DMs of the dataset and let the Z3 SMT-solver [17] generate one semantically valid configuration, which we manually verified. We discuss representative examples in terms of encoding size and solver performance.

For instance, our encoding for the *chesspiece* DM [15,16] generates 137 constants and 35 `ite` commands from 5 decisions and 4 rules. In a more complex example, the *rockerswitch* case study [16], our encoding generated more than 1000 constants and only 27 `ite` commands from 23 decisions and 11 rules. The increasing number of constants comes from the number of transitions between the different decisions. However, also the type of decision has a major influence on the number of constraints generated. For enumeration decisions, we need to create a constant for each enumeration literal. As a result, the two decision models *ASEJ1* and *ASEJ2* are comparably small (only 3 enumeration decisions and 1 enumeration decision plus 3 Boolean decisions, respectively), but generate a very different number of constants (759 and 67 constants, respectively). Enumeration decisions also influence on how many `ite` commands are generated. For instance, the two DMs *A* and *AllTheCombinations* consist of 2 and 10 enumeration decisions. For DM *A*, our encoding leads to 14 `ite` commands, while for the *AllTheCombinations* DM 62 `ite` commands are generated.

Figure 1 (left side) shows the needed time to encode the DMs of our dataset in milliseconds. Overall, the DMs of our dataset are encoded in 2.72ms on average. Most of the models need less than one millisecond. However, the small DM *eShop* with five decision and five rules, requires up to 36ms. On average, the solver needed 92ms with a minimum of 9ms (*VacuumRobot2* DM, with 9 decisions and 3 rules) and maximum of 1872ms (*Ubuntu_14_10* DM, with 115 decisions and 103 rules) to find one valid configuration. We generated one valid configuration

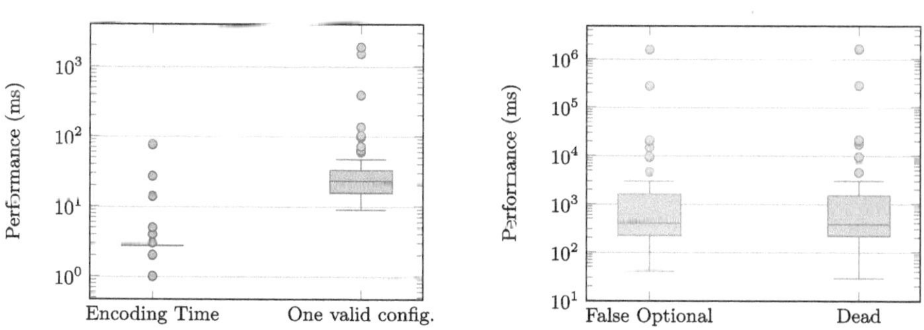

Fig. 1. Analysis and Performance results of the evaluation.

of the DM and, by hand, check whether it is a valid configuration or not. For all our subject DMs, the configuration found by the solver was valid.

RQ1: Our experiment showed that our proposed encoding for DOPLER DMs lets an SMT solver generate valid configurations. While the number of necessary constants and ite commands varies a lot, the encoding process and the determination of whether a DM is satisfiable or not, can be done on average within 3ms for the encoding process and 92ms for the satisfiability check.

4.2 RQ2: Anomaly Analysis

We extended our experiment to analyze the DMs for anomalies. The analysis operation detected anomalies in 6 out of the 59 DMs, totaling 14 anomalies, which we manually verified. There are three dead decision values and 11 false optional decision values. All anomalies can be found in the replication package [7].

Figure 1 (right side) shows the performance of the different anomaly analysis operations on all models in two boxplots. One for the false-optional value analysis, and one for the dead value analysis. The average time needed for the dead value analysis was 1628 ms with a median of 427 ms. The high average time results from some exceptions with very large runtimes. For instance, while the *BankingSoftware* DM with 91 decision and 10 rules needed 258721 ms, the *AlwaysTrue* DM with 3 decisions and zero rules, needed only 29 ms for the analysis. The false optional value analysis exhibited a comparable level of performance to the dead value analysis, with an average time of 6134 ms and a median of 405 ms. Again, there is on big outlier, the *BankingSoftware* DM, which needed 248276 ms.

RQ2: Our experiment showed that our proposed encoding allows the analyzis of DOPLER DMs for anomalies that can occur during the development process. The analysis for the majority of the models was completed on average within 6259ms, but showed performance issues for very complex DMs.

4.3 Limitations and Threads to Validity

Our evaluation shows that our SMT encoding is applicable to DOPLER [6] DMs and the encoding is feasible to detect anomalies and generate valid configurations. The evaluation highlighted performance issues with complex DM, which most likely results from the number of constants necessary to encode a DM. Our encoding approach generates constants for each decision and enumeration literal and assigns them after each decision is taken. However, as only those constants that may be affected by a given decision are propagated, we aim to reduce the number of necessary constants in future work. Despite the performance limitations, we think that our encoding for DM with DOPLER semantics and our evaluation provide evidence that a SMT encoding for DMs is feasible.

Threats to Validity: We selected the DMs for the evaluation ourselves, which may introduce a bias towards the limited set of available models, their size, and complexity. However, the selected models were originally created by other authors and are available online in public repositories [7]. We showed that our encoding at least works for our limited DM dataset. However, we have not formally shown the correctness of our encoding and have not compared our encoding with other encodings. This is because, (1) we needed to re-implement the DOPLER meta-model, as the original one is proprietary/closed source and, (2) to the best of our knowledge, this is the first attempt to fully encode DOPLER DMs using SMT.

5 Related Work

Variability model analysis is a key part of software product line engineering. A range of different approaches for analyzing variability models have been developed over the years [3] to find a wide range of issues within a Feature Model (FM) [1,3]. However, most of these approaches are only defined for FMs. Therefore, the community has investigated the transformation of DMs into FMs [9,10] to analyze the original DM with established techniques. However, during the transformation a lot of information may be lost [11]. Thus, our work addresses the need for having dedicated solver representations for decision modeling [5], and analyze them in a similar way directly.

The encoding of DMs has been investigated before [12,14]. For instance, Mazo et al. [14] also used encoded decision variables using constraint programming to implement anomaly detection operations. Both approaches implemented their analysis in a closed meta-model of the decision modeling approach. In previous work [12], we encoded DMs using only Boolean variables to ease their configuration. With our work, we weakened our fixed decision order assumption, by now allowing configuring the DM in any order and allow decisions to set the values of other decisions. Further, we explicitly re-implemented the DOPLER meta-model by encoding other major elements, such as Enumerations, Numeric and String decision variables, and made it publicly available to the community.

6 Conclusion

DMs are often used for guiding users through product configuration. Automated analysis of such configurations would benefit the overall configuration process of DMs. Thus, we propose a novel encoding of decision modeling concepts in SMT. We implemented our encoding within a re-implementation of the DOPLER [6] meta-model and evaluated the feasibility and applicability of our SMT encoding using a set of 59 publicly available DOPLER DMs of varying size and complexity. Our experiments showed that, while there is major variance in the size of the encoding the encoding enabled the SMT solver to derive valid configurations from DMs. Also, the encoding allowed analyzing the DMs for anomalies.

In future work, we plan to reduce the overall number of necessary constants in our mapping to improve its performance. Currently, we are investigating other solver classes, like Integer Linear Programming (ILP) and Constraint Satisfaction Problem (CSP) for their suitability for encoding DMs.

Acknowledgments. This work was funded by the Deutsche Forschungsgemeinschaft (DFG, German Research Foundation) – CRC 1608 – 501798263. The financial support by the Christian Doppler Research Association, the Austrian Federal Ministry for Digital and Economic Affairs and the National Foundation for Research, Technology and Development is gratefully acknowledged. The research was supported by the Austrian ministries BMIMI, BMWET and the State of Upper Austria in the frame of the SCCH COMET competence center INTEGRATE (FFG 892418). This project has been edited by our textician, Daniel Shea.

References

1. Apel, S., Batory, D., Kästner, C., Saake, G.: Software Product Lines, pp. 3–15. Springer, Heidelberg (2013). https://doi.org/10.1007/978-3-642-37521-7_1
2. Barrett, C., Fontaine, P., Tinelli, C.: The Satisfiability Modulo Theories Library (SMT-LIB) (2016). www.SMT-LIB.org
3. Benavides, D., Segura, S., Ruiz-Cortés, A.: Automated analysis of feature models 20 years later: a literature review. Inf. Syst. **35**(6), 615–636 (2010). https://doi.org/10.1016/j.is.2010.01.001
4. Biere, A., van Maaren, H., Walsh, T.: Handbook of Satisfiability. Frontiers in Artificial Intelligence and Applications (IOS Press). SAGE Publications (2009)
5. Czarnecki, K., Grünbacher, P., Rabiser, R., Schmid, K., Wasowski, A.: Cool features and tough decisions: a comparison of variability modeling approaches. In: Proceedings of 6th VaMoS. ACM (2012). https://doi.org/10.1145/2110147.2110167
6. Dhungana, D., Grünbacher, P., Rabiser, R.: The dopler meta-tool for decision-oriented variability modeling: a multiple case study. Autom. Softw. Eng. **18**(1), 77–114 (2011). https://doi.org/10.1007/s10515-010-0076-6
7. Eger, F., Feichtinger, K.: Dopler models (2026). https://doi.org/10.5281/zenodo.18507984
8. Eger, F., von Geisau, J., Weber, F., Kowal, D., Kraml, Y., Feichtinger, K.: Travart-dopler-analysis (2026). https://doi.org/10.5281/zenodo.20487919
9. Feichtinger, K., Rabiser, R.: Towards transforming variability models: Usage scenarios, required capabilities and challenges. In: Proceedings of 24th SPLC. ACM (2020). https://doi.org/10.1145/3382026.3425768
10. Feichtinger, K., Stöbich, J., Romano, D., Rabiser, R.: Travart: an approach for transforming variability models. In: Proceedings of 15th VaMoS. ACM (2021). https://doi.org/10.1145/3442391.3442400
11. Feichtinger, K., Sundermann, C., Thüm, T., Rabiser, R.: It's your loss: classifying information loss during variability model roundtrip transformations. In: Proceedings of 26th SPLC. ACM (2022). https://doi.org/10.1145/3546932.3546990
12. Heisinger, M., Piminger, F., Seidl, M.: From decision models to user-guiding configurators using smt. In: Proceedings of 18th VaMoS. ACM (2024). https://doi.org/10.1145/3634713.3634718
13. Hvam, L., Mortensen, N.H., Riis, J.: Product Customization. Springer, Cham (2007)

14. Mazo, R., Grünbacher, P., Heider, W., Rabiser, R., Salinesi, C., Diaz, D.: Using constraint programming to verify dopler variability models. In: Proceedings of 5th VaMoS. ACM (2011). https://doi.org/10.1145/1944892.1944904
15. Meixner, K., et al.: Variability modeling of products, processes, and resources in cyber–physical production systems engineering. J. Syst. Softw. **211**, 112007 (2024). https://doi.org/10.1016/j.jss.2024.112007
16. Meixner, K., Feichtinger, K., Rabiser, R., Biffl, S.: A reusable set of real-world product line case studies for comparing variability models in research and practice. In: Proceedings of 25th SPLC. ACM (2021). https://doi.org/10.1145/3461002.3473946
17. de Moura, L., Bjørner, N.: Z3: an efficient SMT solver. In: Ramakrishnan, C.R., Rehof, J. (eds.) TACAS 2008. LNCS, vol. 4963, pp. 337–340. Springer, Heidelberg (2008). https://doi.org/10.1007/978-3-540-78800-3_24
18. Rabiser, R., Grünbacher, P., Lehofer, M.: A qualitative study on user guidance capabilities in product configuration tools. In: 27th Conference on Automated Software Engineering. ACM (2012). https://doi.org/10.1145/2351676.2351693

Karpfen: A Lightweight Modeling- and Model Execution Toolkit for Education and Prototyping

Karl Kegel[(✉)], Markus Hamann, and Uwe Aßmann

Technische Universität Dresden, 01069 Dresden, Germany
{karl.kegel,markus.hamann1,uwe.assmann}@tu-dresden.de

Abstract. A central objective of a model-driven software engineering process is to model a system with sufficient depth to make it executable. While for industrial applications, such processes are complex and rarely adopted, they play to their strengths in education. Modeling a system step by step until it becomes executable, monitoring the system in action, and then going back to adjust the models drives the learner's understanding of model-driven engineering and system design. However, when beginners are tasked with extensive modeling, they quickly become challenged and frustrated without ideal tooling. This work presents the *Karpfen* toolkit, an open-source modeling and execution toolkit comprising lightweight languages for domain-, data-, and behavior modeling. The strength of the *Karpfen* toolkit lies in the combination of a state-of-the-art technical stack, a highly instrumented model execution system, and minimal technical requirements for users. This paper presents the requirements-driven design of the *Karpfen* toolkit and demonstrates it in two case studies.

Keywords: Model-Driven Engineering · Modeling Languages · Model Execution · Statemachines. · MDSE in Education

1 Introduction

Motivation. The ability of models to abstract and visualize software systems, architectures, designs, or functions makes modeling an important topic in software engineering education. Aspects of *model-driven software engineering (MDSE/MDSD)* [20] are found in basically every software engineering curriculum. But modeling must not just be taught. Educators are also well aware that learners have to practice modeling on their own to become proficient. Ciccozzi et al. found that in 91% of MDSE courses, students have to develop models themselves, for example, during assignments and exam projects [3]. However, for proper practice, suitable modeling tools are required that guide the process and foster understanding of the relationships and uses of the created models.

C. Berger and V. Klös (Eds.): SEAA 2026, LNCS 16864, pp. 30–46, 2027.
https://doi.org/10.1007/978-3-032-36587-3_3

Asking educators for negative experiences, the most frequent negative experience is that *"Tools are lacking, not mature enough, or too complex to use"* [3]. While the missing capabilities of enterprise tools are an issue in industry [19], Liebel et al. [8] find that modeling tools in education do not need to have many features, handle large models, or be interoperable with other technical infrastructure. Instead, educational modeling tools need to be motivational, easy to use, and effective for the small tasks students must complete in assignments or coursework [8].

Problem Statement. Hands-on experiences in MDSE education should not be limited to model creation in an isolated environment. Executing, i.e., running, the developed models significantly boosts motivation and understanding. Although professional modeling tools, e.g., within the *Eclipse* ecosystem, enable model-to-code transformations or model interpretation, their use challenges students. The problem with these powerful tools is that they require deep knowledge of comprehensive modeling languages. Teaching this knowledge in a lecture or tutorial is not feasible. For example, covering state machines according to the full *(f)UML* [12] or *SCXML* [21] standard would go well beyond the available time of a university course. Numerous different tools are used in MDSE education [3], with some of them being small custom-tailored educational tools and other extensive modeling workbenches.

However, we find a gap between instructive, easy-to-learn modeling tools and those that are technically mature enough to satisfy advanced learners with usecases, e.g., in simulation and prototyping. We do not find a state-of-the-art tool or framework that, in combination: Focuses on small, easy-to-learn modeling languages; Supports model execution with a high degree of instrumentation; Is usable by learners with little to no coding and modeling experience; Is extensible and customizable by educators and advanced learners.

Approach. We formulate the research question: **What is a state-of-the-art design of a minimalist modeling and model execution environment that is suitable for education and prototyping over a wide range of complexity levels and usecases?** We answer this question by conducting an engineering-oriented research process. We start in Sect. 2 *Requirements* with the specification of key requirements to define the abstract solution space. These requirements serve as the success criteria for the conducted design process. Section 3 *System Specification* presents the step-by-step process for deriving a concrete solution from the requirements. The resulting toolkit is demonstrated in Sect. 4 *Case Studies.* For this purpose, we conduct two case studies that walk through an easy and an advanced student task. We discuss related works in Sect. 5 *Related Work.* This work contributes the design, implementation, and evaluation of the *Karpfen* modeling and model execution toolkit. All developed tools are openly available and ready to use (see Sect. 6 *Supplementary Material*).

2 Requirements

This section specifies the functionalities we require the envisioned educational modeling environment ("the system") to have. We base the following list of requirements on findings from the literature [3, 8], as well as our own experiences as MDSE learners and educators. All authors of this paper are or have been involved in teaching university courses on MDSE.

R1 Modeling Languages. We require and restrict the system to support three kinds of model types/languages: (1) a domain modeling language (class-diagram-like); (2) an object modeling language for instances of the former (object-diagram-like); (3) a behavior modeling language (e.g., statecharts, automata).

The learnability of each language is more important than its completeness. Each language shall have a minimal set of features (syntax) for realizing meaningful, demonstrative tasks. As the UML is the de-factor standard for software modeling, the languages used by the system must not strongly deviate from common UML concepts.

R2 Interaction. System interaction comprises: First, modeling something; Second, executing the model and interacting with it. We require a textual syntax for the three modeling languages. A visual syntax, or unidirectional visualization from textual syntax, is optional. Working with just textual syntax keeps the system and its usage simple. Users do not require specific editors, and solutions can be easily distributed. For interacting with the model execution subsystem, simple interfaces, e.g., a CLI, shall be used.

R3 Model Execution. The system must provide a subsystem for model execution. The execution must be configurable and controllable by the user. The subsystem must allow in- and outgoing event flow if the models require such. The execution subsystem shall operate as a "whitebox" to allow advanced learners to investigate and modify its behavior.

R4 Model Debugging and Monitoring. The system must provide means to monitor executed models and collect execution data (traces) that the user can analyze during and after model execution. Default means for visual monitoring and debugging shall exist.

R5 Programming Interfaces. For advanced users and educators, the system shall provide interfaces (APIs) to implement custom instrumentation and supplementary tools. These interfaces must be based on state-of-the-art technologies, e.g., framework patterns or networking standards. Using the provided interfaces shall not require a deep understanding of the system's inner workings.

3 System Specification – The *Karpfen* Toolkit

This section instantiates the requirements R1-R5 in a concrete system design. We extend the presentation of design decisions with implementation aspects when necessary. We name the resulting system the *Karpfen* toolkit.

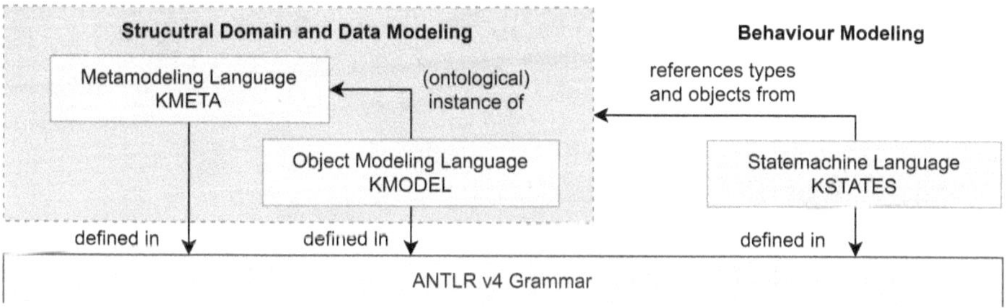

Fig. 1. The Karpfen Modeling Languages The figure presents the relationships of the three modeling languages defined. Each language is based on its own ANTLR grammar.

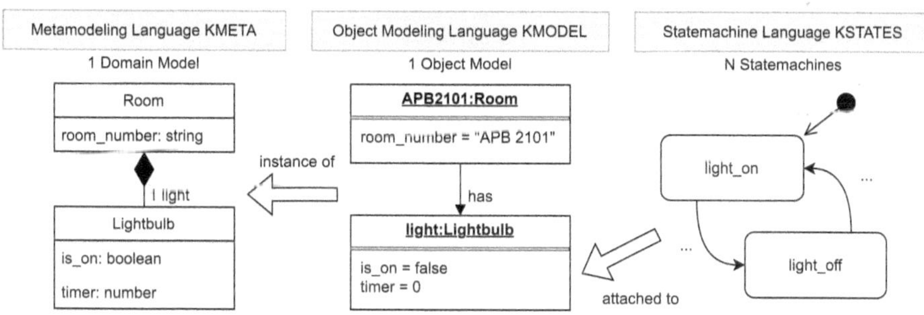

Fig. 2. The Karpfen Languages by Example The figure visualizes the three modeling languages and their relationships by example. UML visual syntax is used for visualization. The state machine model is simplified.

3.1 Language Design

We require the system to support the creation of domain models, object models, and behavioral models (R1, R2). To keep the system simple, we define three custom modeling languages similar to UML diagram types. However, we implement only a small excerpt of the UML's syntactic elements. The languages are defined via *ANTLR*[1] grammars. Figure 1 shows the relationships of the three languages. Figure 2 presents example models for each language. None of the languages has a defined visual syntax. However, since UML is effectively a superset of our languages, we can visualize them using UML diagram notation.

The metamodeling, or domain modeling, language *KMeta* is conceptually based on class diagrams. It allows the definition of *types* (classes) with properties, as well as directed compositional and associative relationships. Inheritance can be realized by the type-object pattern. Listing 1.1 presents a concrete example in *KMeta* syntax. It is the same example as shown in Fig. 2.

[1] https://www.antlr.org/.

Listing 1.1. Metamodel example in textual *KMeta* syntax.

```
type "Lightbulb" "An automatic timed lightbulb" {
    prop("is_on", "boolean")
    prop("timer", "number")
}
type "Room" "A room with light" {
    prop("room_number", "string")
    has("light", "Lightbulb")
}
```

The object modeling language *KModel* is conceptually based on object diagrams. It allows the specification of *objects* as instances of *KMeta types*. A *KModel* model is syntactically well-formed as long as it adheres to the *KModel* grammar. A *KModel* model is valid if it is an instance of a *KMeta* model. Listing 1.2 presents a concrete example in *KModel* syntax. The shown model is a valid instance of the domain model in Listing 1.1. It is the same example as shown in Fig. 2.

Listing 1.2. Object model example in textual *KModel* syntax.

```
make object "APB2101":"Room" {
    prop("room_number") -> "APB 2101"
    has("light") -> make object "light":"Lightbulb" {
        prop("is_on") -> "false"
        prop("timer") -> "0"
    }}
```

Lastly, we require a language for modeling behavior. Based on our experiences as educators, we choose state machines for behavior modeling as they are expressive and intuitive for learners. Standards such as *(f)UML* or *SCXML* are too extensive for our purpose. Therefore, our state machine dialect *KStates* focuses on a small subset of state machine concepts. The core syntactical elements are hierarchical *states*, *transitions* with *conditions*, and detail behavior via activities (*entry*, *do*). The semantics are tick-based and defined by the execution engine. Listing 1.3 shows an example of a light-switch state machine in *KStates* syntax. The example operates on the *KModel* object model defined in Listing 1.2. *KStates* state machines have read and write access to a provided valid *KModel* object model (`SET` modifier, `$()` path query). For specifying conditions and behavior beyond the expressiveness of the *KStates* syntax, the language allows `EVAL{...}` blocks for inlining decorated Python expressions. Via the defined syntactical decorations (`$()` path query, `@..` sub-call), the inlined code can access the current state of the data model. The execution of `EVAL` blocks prohibits side-effects so that repeated evaluation for condition checking becomes possible. Listing 1.3 Line 16 shows such an expression which accesses the *timer* property of the *Lightbulb* object the state machine is attached to. Reusable `EVAL` blocks can be defined as `MACROS` at the end of a *KStates* file.

The language descriptions and examples in this section do not exhaustively document all language features realized. The supplementary material (see Sect. 6) contains the exhaustive language specifications, additional examples, and the full grammars for the presented *KMeta*, *KModel*, and *KStates* languages.

Listing 1.3. **Statemachine example in textual *KStates* syntax.**

```
STATEMACHINE ATTACHED TO "Lightbulb" {
    STATES {
        INITIAL STATE "light_off" {
            ENTRY {
                SET("is_on", "false")
                SET("timer", "0")
            }
        }
        STATE "movement_detected" {
            ENTRY {
                SET("is_on", "true")
                SET("timer", "3" )
            }
        }
        STATE "light_on" {
            ENTRY { SET("timer",  EVAL { return $(timer) - 1 } ) }
        }
    }
    TRANSITIONS {
        TRANSITION "light_off" -> "movement_detected" {
            CONDITION { EVENT("public", "movement detected") }
        }
        TRANSITION "movement_detected" -> "light_on" { }
        TRANSITION "light_on" -> "light_off" {
            CONDITION { EVAL { return $(timer) <= 0.0 } }
        }
        TRANSITION "light_on" -> "light_on" { }
    }
}
```

3.2 Model Loading and Representation

Each *Karpfen* language is defined by an ANTLR grammar. The *Karpfen* toolkit must parse, analyze, and execute user-created instances of the three modeling languages. We realize parsing and analysis in a distinct component (*karpfen-dsl-tools*). For each language, the ANTLR parser performs the initial model loading and syntax checking (well-formedness). The result is the abstract syntax tree (AST) of the submitted model. Next, our software transforms each language AST into a custom adaptive object runtime model. We refer to literature about the *Adaptive Object Model* [22] and the *Dynamic Object Pattern* [16] for further details. We implement software functions to traverse these adaptive object models for validation, e.g., checking an object model against a domain metamodel.

3.3 Model Execution

Executing *Karpfen* models (R3) means executing state machines that interact with an object model (which in turn is instance of a defined domain model) for data access. For executing models, one can choose between translation to code or interpretation [4]. We use interpretation, as we experienced interpreters to be better suited for instrumentation, monitoring, and debugging. The model interpreter forms a distinct software component (*execution-engine*). We realize the execution in a control loop per state machine model. Each state machine runs in a distinct thread. As the metamodel, object model, and state machines exist

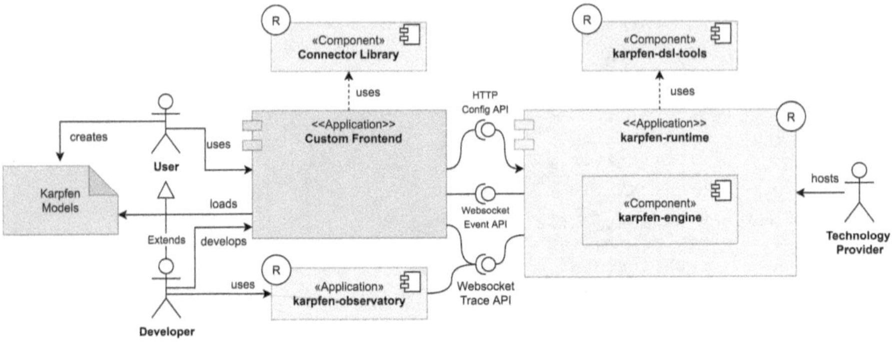

Fig. 3. The Karpfen Toolkit's Architecture Provided components of the toolkit are colored yellow. In an educational context, most developer tasks are performed by the educator in the role of the developer. Given a frontend, learners only create the models and interact with a prepared frontend. (R) marks dedicated Git repositories, i.e., standalone reusable components. (Color figure online)

as abstract object models at runtime, the interpreter can traverse these models to read and write properties, alter their structure, or observe model elements. Inlined Python statements are compiled on-demand into runnable Python code and evaluated by the Python interpreter. Across the literature, many different semantics for different state machine dialects and purposes have been defined [1]. For our execution engine, we realize a tick-based semantics. This means that the execution is divided into discrete time steps where for each step (or cycle of steps) one defined action is performed. For further details, we refer to the language documentation in the supplementary material (see Sect. 6).

3.4 Instrumentation and Monitoring

By choosing to implement a custom model interpreter, instrumentation and monitoring (R4) become simple. The interpreter is tick-based. This means that it performs discrete steps. Because all models exist at runtime as adaptive object models, we can programatically inspect them at the end of each tick. Furthermore, every model access, model modification, and action of the state machine is observable. Consequently, the execution engine can fully trace the model execution, adjust the execution speed, or interrupt the execution. When interrupting the execution, the current snapshots of all involved models can be inspected. Clients may subscribe to and monitor the full execution trace, or just to specific events via APIs.

3.5 Technical Abstraction and Toolkit Usage

This section presents the final architecture of the toolkit. Figure 3 visualizes the toolkit's components. The central, runnable component is the *karpfen-runtime*. The runtime is a standalone server application based on our modeling and model execution components. The runtime is deployable as a Docker container, but can also run locally. The API of the runtime is separated into three parts: (1) An HTTP API for submitting models, performing configurations, starting and stopping model executions; (2) A Websocket API for observing the traces of executed models or selectively observing changes of model elements; (3) A Websocket API for event streams. The default graphical frontend we provide is the *karpfen-observatory*. The observatory is a web dashboard that can connect to a *karpfen-runtime*. The observatory visualizes a selected running state machine as a diagram, animates state changes, and displays the execution trace. To aid users and developers in creating custom frontends for the runtime's APIs, we provide the *connector* library. It contains high-level decorations of the API calls in different programming languages (Java, Scala, Python). For each language, the library also provides a minimal runnable starter project.

3.6 Summary

To keep the modeling languages simple, we develop three custom languages (metamodeling, data modeling, and state machines) based on common UML concepts (R1). Each language is defined by an ANTLR grammar and can be edited in textual syntax (R2). Visualization of the state machine models is possible via the *karpfen-observatory* monitoring facility. Otherwise, UML could be used to manually visualize the *Karpfen* languages. A valid modeled system is executable via the *karpfen-runtime* (R3). For interpretation, the input models are parsed and transformed into adaptive runtime models. Through this design, model changes at runtime can be easily observed, traced, and monitored (R4). To keep the technical effort for users (learners) to a minimum, the runtime is deployed as a standalone server application. Loading models, sending and receiving events, controlling the execution, or monitoring runtime behavior is realized via APIs (R5). Because we intentionally keep the features of the modeling languages simple, it is not be possible to model every imaginable scenario. For example, the current syntax provides no means to push data from incoming events into the runtime model. We plan to further evolve the modeling languages presented based on concrete educational needs we will observe during continued use of the toolkit in our courses. To retain the toolkit's simplicity during future extensions, we plan to implement them as selectable features, allowing the educator to decide which advanced language features to toggle on or off for specific tasks.

4 Case Studies

We demonstrate the functionality and suitability of the *Karpfen* toolkit for two cases. We design a simple task (light-timer) and a complex task (robot-control). Both tasks were developed from existing exercises in MDD courses at the authors' institute and could be handed out to students as coursework in the future. We outline the solution steps necessary using the *Karpfen* toolkit. We provide the full models, code, and documentation to execute the presented cases in the supplementary material (see Sect. 6). For reference, the models of the *light-timer* examples can also be found in the Listings 1.1, 1.2, and 1.3. The presented cases can be reproduced from the given solution files without the need to develop code or models.

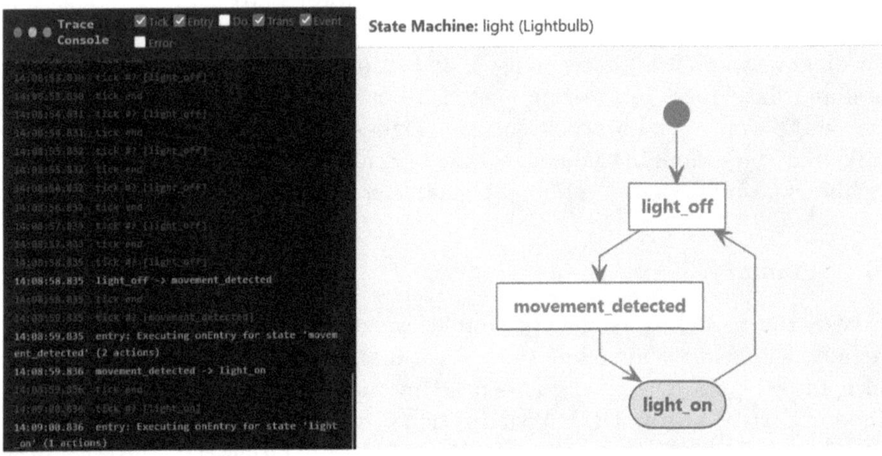

Fig. 4. Runtime Monitoring via the Karpfen Observatory. As soon as the runtime executes a state machine, the observatory can connect to it. The observatory monitors the trace (left side) and visualizes the state machine (right side). The currently active state is animated in green. (Color figure online)

4.1 Light Timer Case Study

The *light-timer* task is a simple way to become familiar with the different modeling languages and model execution tools. As prior knowledge, we assume familiarity with structural and behavioral modeling, specifically state machines.

Task. *The (simplified) domain comprises rooms with room numbers. One room contains one light bulb. A light bulb is time-controlled by a timer value. It is either on or off. Create a domain model. Create an exemplary object model instantiating the domain. By default, the light is off, and the timer is set to 0. Create a state machine that defines the light's behavior. Initially, the light is off. The light has a sensor to detect movement. The sensor sends 'movement detected' events. In the moment something moves, the light is turned on. The timer is set to 3. As long as the light is on, the timer is decremented at each time step until it reaches 0, at which point the light turns off. Create the three models described. Place the models in the prepared directory next to the karpfen-runtime executable. Use the provided CLI interface to start the model execution. After startup, the provided* *interface triggers movement events when the Enter key is pressed. Use the logs and state machine traces printed by the CLI to verify your solution. Use the karpfen-observatory to investigate the visual state machine and its trace.*

Givens. The *karpfen-runtime* Docker container, the *karpfen-observatory* dashboard, and a CLI frontend implemented via the *connectors* library. Advanced students can choose to implement the CLI frontend themselves using the provided Java connector. The preparation steps for the educator are:

1. Prepare a CLI frontend, which submits the model files to the runtime, initiates the model execution, and pushes events to the runtime when Enter-keydowns happen (movement detection events). Using the *connectors* library, this requires implementing approx. 40 lines of Java, Scala, or Python code.

Solution Steps. A possible modeling solution to this case is presented by the running example in Listings 1.1, 1.2, and 1.3. To complete the full task, the student has to:

1. Create three models as text files (one domain model, one object model, one state machine model)
2. Execute the *karpfen-runtime* Docker container (via single shell command)
3. Execute the prepared CLI frontend next to the model files.
4. Observe the terminal output of the runtime. If the developed models are not well-formed or invalidity is detected (e.g., type mismatches), error messages are printed.
5. If no modeling errors occurred, the models are immediately executed by the runtime, or the execution can be triggered by the student (depending on the implementation of the frontend).
6. Open the *karpfen-observatory* dashboard to observe the executed state machine (see Fig. 4). Pressing the Enter key triggers state changes and logging of the execution trace. If the state machine does not behave correctly, the student has to stop the system, adjust the models, and try again.

Summary and Discussion. This first case presented the exemplary *light-timer* task as a case study for the *Karpfen* toolkit. The case presents a very simple modeling task. The runnable reference solution to this task, i.e., the fully working light-timer case, is provided as part of this work's supplementary material (see Sect. 6). We argue that our toolkit is well-suited for preparing and solving the presented and similar tasks. The toolkit provides all the necessary means to prepare, model, and run the case. On the student side, no technical setup is required other than running a Docker container. In particular, no IDE or heavyweight modeling environment is required due to the simple textual syntax of the *Karpfen* modeling languages.

4.2 Cleaning Robot Case Study

The *cleaning-robot* task poses a complex modeling task for advanced students. The difficulty of this task can be adjusted by varying which solution-space models are already provided. As prior knowledge, we assume familiarity with structural and behavioral modeling, specifically state machines. To solve the full task, knowledge of geometry and algorithm design is also required. The scenario for this task is controlling a simulated vacuum-cleaning robot in an enclosed space with obstacles. The cyber-physical aspects of this scenario (sensors, hardware control) are abstracted and not part of the task.

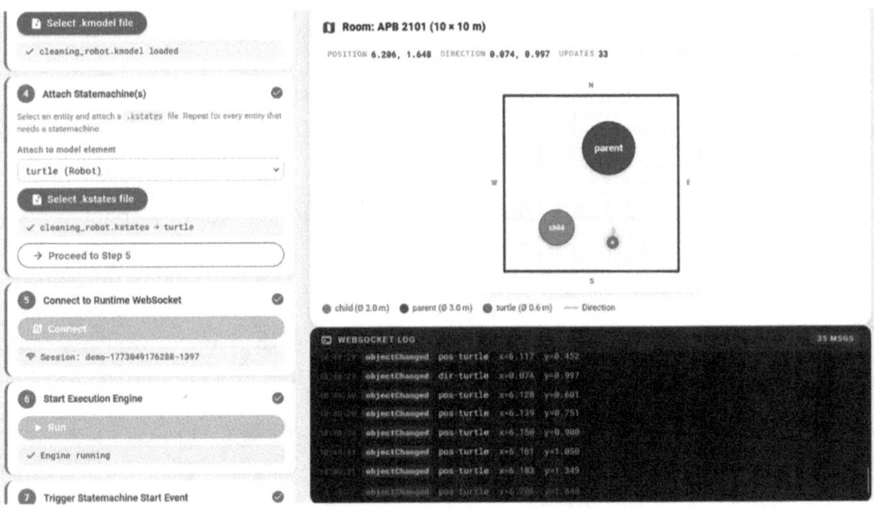

Fig. 5. Example of a Custom Karpfen Frontend Using the APIs of the *karpfen-runtime*, custom web-based, domain-specific frontends can be developed quickly. This frontend serves as the provided GUI for the robot modeling task. Due to the toolkit's comprehensive documentation, such frontends can be quickly implemented with the help of generative AI, easing the preparation of custom task-specific tooling on the educator's side.

Task. *Given is a domain model* `cleaning_robot.kmeta` *and a valid object model* `cleaning_robot.kmodel`*. The modeled scenario describes a room with four walls (line vectors) and round obstacles, each with a position and diameter. In the room, a cleaning robot operates. The robot is modeled with all properties required for the task. It is round, knows its dimensions and positions, driving vector, and speed. The robot also knows the current positions and dimensions of all walls and the two obstacles in the room. Create a state machine model that lets the robot drive autonomously through the room. The start position and direction are set in the object model. As soon as the robot comes close (define a meaningful distance) to an obstacle or wall, it shall drive slowly in a cautious state. Shortly before a* *collision, the robot shall change its direction away from the obstacle (reflection at a meaningful angle). Make sure the robot does not enter deadlocks. The robot shall be started by the user submitting a start event.*

To vary the difficulty level of this task, one or both of the given models may not be provided or may be provided incompletely.

Givens. The *karpfen-runtime* Docker container, the *karpfen-observatory* dashboard, the domain model and the object model. Advanced students can choose to model the object model themselves. A visual web UI connected to the *karpfen-runtime* APIs serves as the frontend. The preparation steps for the educator are:

1. Create the domain model and the object model using the *Karpfen* languages.
2. Prepare a web frontend that the students use to step-by-step connect to the runtime server, submit each model, connect the state machine to the robot object, and trigger the model execution process. The frontend visualizes the modeled room graphically and updates the robot position based on the received traces (see Fig. 5). As the *Karpfen* toolkit is extensively documented, creating such a front-end based on a detailed description can be achieved with the help of a generative AI in less than one hour.

Solution Steps

1. Study the provided models and create the state machine model. In more difficult versions of the task, complete all missing models.
2. Execute the *karpfen-runtime* Docker container (via a single shell command)
3. Execute the provided custom graphical frontend and follow the shown steps (model upload, etc.).
4. Observe the terminal output of the runtime. If the developed models are not well-formed or invalidity is detected (e.g., type mismatches), error messages are printed.
5. If no modeling errors occurred, the models can now be executed by submitting the start event.
6. The state of the robot can be visually debugged using the provided frontend, or monitored in depth using the *karpfen-observatory*.

Solution Outline. The full, runnable reference solution for this task is provided in the supplementary material of this work (see Sect. 6). The domain metamodel (provided or required) comprises six type definitions totaling 40 lines of properly formatted *KMeta* DSL code. The object model (provided or required) comprises 23 object definitions totaling 90 lines of *KModel* code. The state machine (required or partially required) comprises seven states (three top-level and four nested), seven transitions, and seven Macros (script blocks for advanced geometric calculations). The resulting *KStates* file totals 213 lines of properly formatted DSL code.

Summary and Discussion. This second case presented the exemplary *robot-control* task as a case study for the *Karpfen* toolkit. The case presents a difficult modeling task for students. Despite the complexity of the task, all the required structure and behavior can be expressed using our simple modeling languages. On the educators' side, the toolkit provides all the functionality needed to prepare such a task with minimal effort. Due to the extensively documented APIs of the *karpfen-runtime* and the small modeling languages, generative AI supports the creation process of custom tooling well. In this specific case, we used generative AI to generate large portions of the task-specific frontend based on a detailed requirements description.

On the students' side, the only required technical step is running the *karpfen-runtime* Docker container. As the custom frontend is just an HTML document, it can be opened in a browser without any setup.

Consequently, this more complex task supports our argument for the suitability of the *Karpfen* toolkit for advanced modeling scenarios and for building lightweight prototypes.

5 Related Work

Modeling Tools in Education. Ciccozzi et al. surveyed that many different tools are used in MDSE education [3]. A majority of these tools are based on the *Eclipse* platform. *Eclipse Papyrus* is the most prominent Eclipse-based modeling tool and poses a standard conformant UML modeling environment [17]. *Papyrus* allows model execution via *Moka*, which in turn is based on *fUML*. In our experience, using *Papyrus* in education has some drawbacks. Its extensive feature set, expert-tailored user interface, and the need to model correctly according to the UML standard can easily overwhelm beginners. These points have led to high student frustration and higher support costs in courses where we used *Papyrus*. Because of these drawbacks, we chose a simpler, easier-to-understand modeling strategy for the tool presented in this work.

In the context of executable models, some recent educational tools are documented in the current literature. Ogata et al. [14] present *SMart-Learning*, which is a state machine modeling and simulating tool-chain. Later, Ogata et al. extended their tool with texting [15] and classifying/comparing [13] capabilities tailored to course instructors, resulting in a feature-rich executable state machine education tool set. To run the tool, a student designs a state machine using a modeling editor. Guards and actions are written in JavaScript syntax and later evaluated in the simulation program. The *SMart-Learning* tool itself is very similar to the tool presented in this work. While the *Karpfen* toolkit uses a custom, open technical stack, *SMart-Learning* reuses the commercial modeling tool *astah*[2]. This technological decision makes *SMart-Learning* more powerful on the modeling side but complex to use. However, the main feature of the

[2] https://www.astah.net/, visited: 2026-04-06.

Karpfen toolkit, the connection of structural and behavioral modeling, is missing in the *SMart-Learning* tool. Still, from the instructors' perspective, *SMart-Learning* provides more features for quick evaluation of a student's work, which the *Karpfen Toolit* in its current version still lacks.

Another executable state machine environment for education is presented by Maruyama et al. [10]. To teach students MDD concepts, they use a custom UML dialect, *xtUML*, to define state machines. They define four levels of complexity that, at lower levels, remove constructs such as guards and actions from the syntax, making it easier for beginners. The developed state machines are compiled into code for a target platform. Maruyama et al. mostly use physical platforms, such as *Arduino* and *LEGO Mindstorm*.

A recent educational tool for structural, executable models is *UML-MX* from Maier et al. [9]. In *UML-MX*, students use a custom visual diagram editor to design class models and derived object models in the *UML++* language. The main focus of *UML-MX* is structural modeling and the relationship between the M1 class and M0 object layers. One key difference between *fUML* and *UML++* is that UML++ objects are executable. *UML++* operations and constraints can specify an operation body that the tool can execute, resulting in an executable object net. While executable, the main modeling focus of *UML-MX* is structural modeling, and it lacks most of the behavioral modeling features provided by the *Karpfen* toolkit. Maier et al. plan to include behavioral languages in their tool in the future.

The literature shows that different approaches to educational tools for behavioral modeling exist. Yet we find that existing tools with extensive feature sets lack usability, while easy-to-use tools lack features such as the ability to model both structure and behavior.

State Machine Modeling and Execution Outside Education. Outside the educational context, multiple technical solutions for modeling and executing state machine-based systems exist. A prominent way of execution is model-to-code transformation. The survey by Domingus et al. compares 53 approaches that generate code from state machines [6]. For direct modeling and execution, we find programming frameworks such as *Spring Statemachine* (Java) [2] or *SISMIC* (Python) [5,11]. Such frameworks allow the specification of state machines in code or by importing a specification denoted in a DSL. *Spring Statemachine* also supports the import of models from *Eclipse Papyrus*. Apart from UML state machines, other standards exist. *SCXML* is a standalone state machine description format in XML with defined execution semantics [21]. SCXML semantics often serve as a reference specification for other statechart execution frameworks. A drawback of state machine specifications, particularly outside the UML, is the missing metamodeling of the data a state machine operates on. For SCXML, Van Mierlo developed the SCCD, an extension that allows metamodeling of class types. The authors provide a reference implementation for executing SCCD models [18].

6 Summary and Outlook

This work presented the *Karpfen* toolkit as our solution for an educational modeling and model execution environment. We designed the toolkit based on five central requirements to keep it simple, easy to use, and quickly learnable, while also achieving a technically mature, extensible, and customizable solution. In particular, the latter shall foster the use of our toolkit across multiple educational scenarios. We demonstrated the toolkit's capabilities for two cases, which serve as references for student tasks. The advanced case also serves as a reference for a prototyping scenario. Based on both investigated cases, we argue towards the suitability of the *Karpfen* toolkit for the intended purpose. Both cases can be reproduced and investigated from the provided supplementary material.

In future work, we aim to empirically study the usability and performance of the toolkit while it is used in teaching. Furthermore, we aim to extend the toolkit with additional components for monitoring and debugging. Language extensions shall be modular, so that the complexity level of the languages can ban be freely configured. We hope that the *Karpfen* toolkit does not remain "just-another" modeling toolkit, but finds wider adoption in education and prototyping.

Supplementary Material

All tools presented in this work are available on GitHub[3] under an open-source license. We recommend the linked GitHub repositories for visiting and using the respective latest versions of the toolkit. The version of the toolkit used in the presented case studies, as well as all materials specifically developed for the case studies (models, interfaces), are provided as a research archive on ZENODO [7]. The ZENODO archive contains the runnable reference solutions for both tasks presented.

Acknowledgments. This work was funded by the Deutsche Forschungsgemeinschaft (DFG, German Research Foundation) SFB 1608 501798263. This work was funded by the ACOMODIA project. The project [ACOMODIA; 100722260] is co-funded by the European Union and co-financed from tax revenues on the basis of the budget adopted by the Saxon State Parliament.

Disclosure of Interests. The authors have no competing interests to declare that are relevant to the content of this article.

References

1. André, E., Liu, S., Liu, Y., Choppy, C., Sun, J., Dong, J.S.: Formalizing uml state machines for automated verification – a survey. ACM Comput. Surv. **55**(13s) (2023). https://doi.org/10.1145/3579821

[3] https://github.com/karpfenproject.

2. Broadcom: Spring Statemachine - Reference Documentation (2026). https://docs.spring.io/spring-statemachine/. Accessed 18 Mar 2026
3. Ciccozzi, F., et al.: How do we teach modelling and model-driven engineering? A survey. In: Proceedings of the 21st ACM/IEEE International Conference on Model Driven Engineering Languages and Systems: Companion Proceedings, MODELS '18, pp. 122–129. Association for Computing Machinery, New York (2018). https://doi.org/10.1145/3270112.3270129
4. Ciccozzi, F., Malavolta, I., Selic, B.: Execution of UML models: a systematic review of research and practice. Softw. Syst. Model. **18**(3), 2313–2360 (2019). https://doi.org/10.1007/s10270-018-0675-4
5. Decan, A., Mens, T.: Sismic—a python library for statechart execution and testing. SoftwareX **12**, 100590 (2020)
6. Domınguez, E., Pérez, B., Ángel L. Rubio, Zapata, M.A.: A systematic review of code generation proposals from state machine specifications. Inf. Softw. Technol. **54**(10), 1045–1066 (2012). https://doi.org/10.1016/j.infsof.2012.04.008
7. Kegel, K.: Supplementary material for karpfen: A lightweight modeling- and model execution toolkit for education and prototyping (2026). https://doi.org/10.5281/zenodo.19663954
8. Liebel, G., Badreddin, O., Heldal, R.: Model driven software engineering in education: a multi-case study on perception of tools and uml. In: 2017 IEEE 30th Conference on Software Engineering Education and Training (CSEE&T), pp. 124–133 (2017). https://doi.org/10.1109/CSEET.2017.29
9. Maier, P., Schwarz, T.: Uml++: enhancing student learning of object-oriented modeling through executable objects. In: Proceedings of the ACM/IEEE 27th International Conference on Model Driven Engineering Languages and Systems, MODELS Companion '24, pp. 107–114. Association for Computing Machinery, New York (2024). https://doi.org/10.1145/3652620.3687777
10. Maruyama, R., Kayama, M., Nagai, T., Otaku, K., Taguchi, N.: Practical uml programming based on the executable uml method at secondary school students. In: 2022 IEEE Global Engineering Education Conference (EDUCON), pp. 45–50 (2022). https://doi.org/10.1109/EDUCON52537.2022.9766752
11. Mens, T., Decan, A., Spanoudakis, N.: A method for testing and validating executable statechart models. Softw. Syst. Model. (2018). https://doi.org/10.1007/s10270-018-0676-3
12. Object Management Group OMG: UML – Unified Modeling Language, Language Specification (2026). https://www.omg.org/spec/UML/. Accessed 24 Mar 2026
13. Ogata, S., Kayama, M.: Sml4c: fully automatic classification of state machine models for model inspection in education. In: 2019 ACM/IEEE 22nd International Conference on Model Driven Engineering Languages and Systems Companion (MODELS-C), pp. 720–729 (2019). https://doi.org/10.1109/MODELS-C.2019.00109
14. Ogata, S., Kayama, M., Okano, K.: Smart-learning: state machine simulators for developing thinking skills. In: 2017 IEEE 17th International Conference on Advanced Learning Technologies (ICALT), pp. 81–83 (2017). https://doi.org/10.1109/ICALT.2017.73
15. Ogata, S., Kayama, M., Okano, K.: Approach to testing many state machine models in education. In: Proceedings of the 11th International Conference on Computer Supported Education, vol. 1: CSEDU, pp. 481–488. INSTICC, SciTePress (2019)
16. Riehle, D., Tilman, M., Johnson, R.: Dynamic object model. Pattern Lang. Prog. Des. **5**, 3–24 (2000)

17. The Eclipse Foundation: Eclipse Papyrus (2026). https://eclipse.dev/papyrus/. Accessed 18 Mar 2026
18. Van Mierlo, S., Van Tendeloo, Y., Meyers, B., Exelmans, J., Vangheluwe, H.: Sccd: scxml extended with class diagrams. In: Proceedings of the Workshop on Engineering Interactive Systems with SCXML, vol. 2, pp. 1–2 (2016)
19. Verbruggen, C., Snoeck, M.: Practitioners' experiences with model-driven engineering: a meta-review. Softw. Syst. Model. **22**(1), 111–129 (2023). https://doi.org/10.1007/s10270-022-01020-1
20. Völter, M., Stahl, T., Bettin, J., Haase, A., Helsen, S.: Model-Driven Software Development: Technology, Engineering, Management. John Wiley & Sons, Heidelberg (2013)
21. W3C: State Chart XML (SCXML): State Machine Notation for Control Abstraction (2026). https://w3.org/TR/scxml/. Accessed 18 Mar 2026
22. Yoder, J.W., Johnson, R.: The adaptive object-model architectural style. In: Bosch, J., Gentleman, M., Hofmeister, C., Kuusela, J. (eds.) Software Architecture. ITIFIP, vol. 97, pp. 3–27. Springer, Boston, MA (2002). https://doi.org/10.1007/978-0-387-35607-5_1

Constraint-Based Test Data Generation for Combinatorial Testing

Henri Cossais[1(✉)], Léna Bamouh, Erwan Bousse, Jean-Marie Mottu, and Gerson Sunyé

Nantes Université, École Centrale Nantes, IMT Atlantique, CNRS, LS2N, UMR 6004, 44000 Nantes, France
{henri.cossais,lena.bamouh,erwan.bousse,jean-marie.mottu,gerson.sunye}@ls2n.fr

Abstract. Combinatorial testing automatically generates relevant abstract test data combination sets for a System Under Test (SUT). It requires defining a combinatorial model with possible abstract values for the SUT input parameters, from which relevant abstract test cases can be generated to reach a chosen coverage criterion. However, translating abstract test cases into concrete ones, and implementing corresponding test scripts, is a tedious and error-prone manual process. In this paper, we present a constraint-based test data generation approach, in which combinatorial testing is supplemented with a model-driven *concretization* step for abstract test cases, with a focus on Java unit testing. First, we prepare a set of SUT-specific constraint functions using an existing constraint programming engine. Then, we write a test data generation model, where the rules declare which constraints should be applied for which abstract values. Finally, we use a code generator to produce the working JUnit test script for each concrete test case. Our approach is implemented and integrated with the PICT combinatorial testing tool, the Choco-Solver Java library for test data generation, and the Eclipse Modeling Framework for model management. Although the approach is currently limited to primitive data types, an initial evaluation on five Java methods shows that the testing effort can be greatly reduced when the combinatorial complexity is high.

Keywords: Combinatorial testing · Unit testing · Automatic test data generation

1 Introduction

Combinatorial testing [4] is a systematic approach to efficiently explore a subset of possible input combinations of a given System Under Test (SUT). First, based on the SUT specification, it starts with defining a combinatorial model as an abstraction of the SUT input parameters. This model comprises a set of abstract parameters and values that reflect interesting cases of input parameters.

Listing 1 shows the signature and specification of a Java method named `isPalindrome`, which verifies whether a given word is a palindrome. The specification states that (1) `true` should be returned if the input string is a palindrome, and `false` otherwise, and (2) an `IllegalArgumentException` should be thrown if the word is `null`,

C. Berger and V. Klös (Eds.): SEAA 2026, LNCS 16864, pp. 47–56, 2027.
https://doi.org/10.1007/978-3-032-36587-3_4

```
/**
 * Check whether a word is a palindrome.
 * @param word The word to check.
 * @return true if word is a palindrome, false otherwise.
 * @throws IllegalArgumentException if word is either null, empty,
 *                    contains a special character, or contains a digit
 **/
static boolean isPalindrome(String word) throws IllegalArgumentException
```

Listing 1. Specification and signature of `isPalindrome`

```
1 # Abstract parameters and values
2 WordIsNull: yes, no
3 WordIsEmpty: yes, no, _
4 WordHasSpecialChar: yes, no, _
5 WordHasDigit: yes, no, _
6 WordIsPalindrome: yes, no, _
7
8 # Constraint (i)
9 IF [WordIsNull] = "yes"
10     THEN [WordIsEmpty] = "_"
11     ELSE [WordIsEmpty] <> "_";
12
13 # Constraint (ii)
14 IF [WordIsEmpty] <> "no"
15     THEN [WordHasSpecialChar] = "_"
16         AND [WordHasDigit] = "_"
17         AND [WordIsPalindrome] = "_"
18     ELSE [WordHasSpecialChar] <> "_"
19         AND [WordHasDigit] <> "_"
20         AND [WordIsPalindrome] <> "_";
```

Listing 2. PICT combinatorial model for `isPalindrome`, manually derived from the specification in Listing 1

empty, contains digits or special characters. Several tools are available for specifying combinatorial models. In this work, we use PICT[1], which provides a textual language. Listing 2 shows a possible combinatorial model for `isPalindrome`, written in PICT. Five abstract parameters are defined (lines 2 to 6), each describing a specific important characteristic of the input string. As each abstract parameter is defined as a closed question, their domains always include abstract values labeled `yes` and `no`. In addition, an abstract value with the underscore symbol _ is part of the domain of all parameters but `WordIsNull`. In this model, this symbol denotes the case where no meaningful value can be assigned to the parameter. Lastly, two constraints are defined to force or forbid specific abstract values in specific circumstances.

Table 1 shows an abstract test suite obtained after running the PICT generator on the combinatorial model using the pairwise coverage criterion as a target. Six abstract test cases are yielded: ATC1 corresponds to a `null` input; ATC2 to an empty input; ATC3 to an input that is not `null`, not empty, without a special character, without a digit, and that is not a palindrome; and so on.

Limitations. While combinatorial testing automatically generates abstract test cases (ATC), later they must be manually translated into *concrete test cases*, where a concrete

[1] https://github.com/microsoft/pict/.

Table 1. Abstract test suite generated from the combinatorial model of Listing 2

	`WordIsNull`	`WordIsEmpty`	`WordHasSpecialChar`	`WordHasDigit`	`WordIsPalindrome`
ATC1	*yes*	–	–	–	–
ATC2	*no*	*yes*	–	–	–
ATC3	*no*	*no*	*no*	*no*	*no*
ATC4	*no*	*no*	*no*	*yes*	*yes*
ATC5	*no*	*no*	*yes*	*no*	*yes*
ATC6	*no*	*no*	*yes*	*yes*	*no*

value is assigned to each SUT input parameter. In the generated concrete test case, the chosen inputs must satisfy the constraints of the abstract test case (e.g., given an abstract value `WordIsPalindrome`, a possible concrete value for *word* is `"anna"`), and the oracle must be consistent with the SUT specification. Finally, the test engineer must implement a test script with a testing framework (e.g., JUnit) for each concrete test case. These steps are costly, tedious, and error-prone, especially given the important number of test cases.

Contribution. To cope with this problem, we present in this paper a constraint based test data generation approach where combinatorial testing is supplemented with a model-driven *concretization* step for abstract test cases. The proposed approach focuses on Java unit testing, i.e., it assumes the SUT comprises a set of Java methods that must each be tested separately. We implemented a prototype using the Eclipse Modeling Framework (EMF), and applied this prototype on five Java methods. Results show that when combinatorial complexity is important, the reduction of the concretization effort outweighs the overhead of writing a data generator.

This paper is a direct follow-up of previous work presented at the MoDeVVa 2024 workshop [1]. The addition lies in the test data generation model, allowing the test expert to declaratively choose which constraints should be applied for which values found in each abstract test case, while in [1] the tester must implement a complete test data generator, requiring constraint programming (CP) knowledge. We improved the architecture, metamodels, and evaluation to meet this major change.

2 Model-Driven Test Case Concretization

Figure 1 shows an overview of our proposed approach. In the bottom right corner, the software developer has prepared a Java method to be tested. In this work, we assume the Java method to be static and to rely only on primitive types (integers, floats, strings, booleans, and enumerations) for its input parameters and return value.

First, the concretization step (1) aims at transforming the ATC model into a concrete test case (CTC) model conforming to an Ecore CTC metamodel. This step relies on a Test Data (TD) Generation model made by the software tester, which specifies a set of

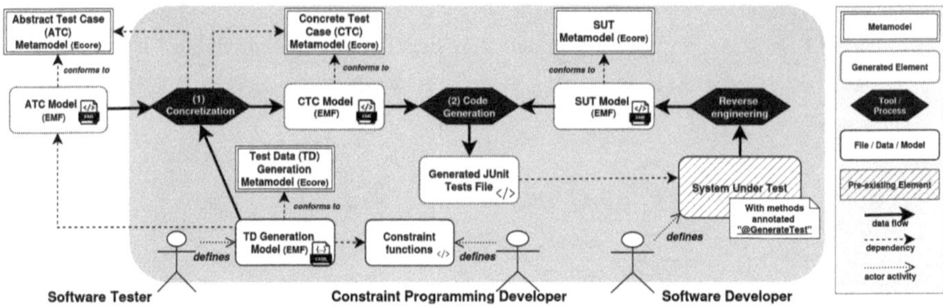

Fig. 1. Overview of the proposed approach

test data generation rules. These rules rely on constraint programming functions whose implementation may require the help of a constraint programming developer. Then, a code generator (2) automatically produces a JUnit test script with all test cases defined in the CTC model, based on the model of the SUT reverse engineered.

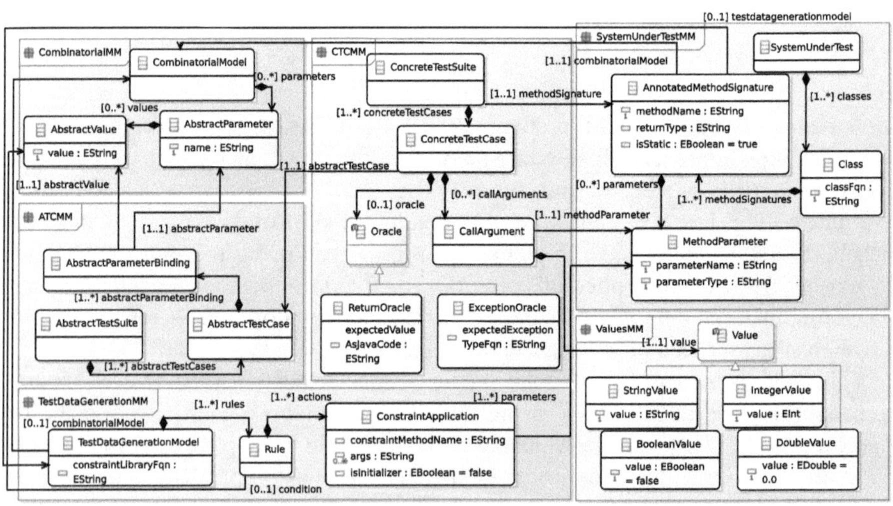

Fig. 2. Metamodels used in the approach

Figure 2 shows the six metamodels defined for the proposed approach. The combinatorial metamodel (`CombinatorialMM`), the abstract test case metamodel (`ATCMM`) and the concrete test case metamodel (`CTCMM`) are inherited from our previous work [1]. In addition, this work introduces three new metamodels: the test data generation metamodel (`TestDataGenerationMM`), the SUT metamodel (`SytemUnderTestMM`), and the values metamodel (`ValuesMM`). These metamodels are presented in later sections.

2.1 Abstract Test Case Generation

ATC and Combinatorial Model Import. `ATCMM` is the metamodel used to represent ATCs (Fig. 2). An `AbstractTestCase` is composed of `AbstractParameterBindings`, each assigning an `AbstractValue` to an `AbstractParameter`. Each `ATCMM` model instance requires a corresponding `CombinatorialMM` instance. `ATCMM` is the target format for importing the ATCs generated by PICT in JSON format into a proper model.

For example, when importing abstract test cases generated by PICT using the `isPalindrome` combinatorial model shown in Listing 2, an `AbstractTestSuite` model is obtained. This model is composed of a set of `AbstractTestCase` elements, each containing the same information as one line of Table 1 (i.e., each column contains all `AbstractParameterBindings` of a specific `AbstractParameter`).

2.2 Concretization of Abstract Test Cases

By definition, an ATC only defines the characteristics that input values should present, but does not define concrete input values required in the CTC that would allow the SUT to be executed. Such concrete input values must be produced through some form of *test data generation*. Below, we describe how the proposed approach relies on CP to write constraint functions, and on a declarative test data generation model to orchestrate how constraint functions should be applied. The idea is to leverage CP to formalize the implicit characteristics of ATCs as explicit constraints. Note however that the proposed approach can be adapted to allow the software tester to manually implement a custom arbitrary data generator for a given test problem, if relevant (e.g., a generator that would *not* rely on constraint programming). Our prototype, presented in the next section, is compatible with such a scenario.

Constraint-Based Test Data Generation. The proposed test data generation process relies on defining a constraint satisfaction problem (CSP). Given an ATC, this CSP can generate test data for the parameters of the tested method, thus yielding a CTC. In constraint programming, a CSP is both composed of *CSP variables* each with a specified domain of possible values, and *constraints* that further restrict the allowed values for each variable. A CSP can be given to a solver to find values that satisfies the specified constraints for each CSP variable, or to establish that no such values exist.

We rely on the Choco-Solver [5] Java library to programmatically define and solve CSPs. Choco requires a `Model` object that both expresses a CSP and gives access to the solver engine. Within the Choco `Model`, CSP variables are declared using Choco types such as `IntVar` and `RealVar`, which represent variables with integer-valued and real-valued domains. Then constraints are *posted* to the `Model` to achieve the CSP definition.

Yet, requiring software testers to manually implement CSPs using a constraint programming library (such as Choco) to automatically generate test data introduces a significant barrier. Software testers may not be experts in CP and the data generation process becomes tightly coupled with the CP library (i.e., Choco-Solver) technical details. To address this, we propose a separation of concerns between the implementation of constraint functions using Choco and the application of these constraint functions.

```java
public static IntVar[] specifyStringLength(Model model, int length){
    return model.intVarArray(length, 32, 126);
}
```

Listing 1. Domain-definition function for `isPalindrome` constraining the size of the generated word

```java
public static void setSpecialChars(Model m, IntVar[] str, int start, int end){
    for (int i = start; i < Math.min(end, str.length); i++) {
        m.and(m.arithm(str[i], ">=", 40),m.arithm(str[i], "<=", 47)).post()}}
```

Listing 2. Narrowing function for `isPalindrome` constraining that the generated word contains special characters at a specific position

Defining Constraints Functions. We call *constraint function* a function that encapsulates reusable constraints implemented with Choco. We distinguish two types of constraint functions: (i) *domain-definition* functions, used to initialize CSP variables with a given domain of value, and (ii) *narrowing* functions, used to restrict further possible values of existing CSP variables using CSP constraints. Constraint functions may be written by a constraint programming expert and must respect a specific signature. It must be declared `public` and `static`, and must take a `Model` object as a first parameter to effectively build the CSP. Domain-definition functions must return a Choco variable type compatible with the type of the `MethodParameter` being initialized. Narrowing functions must be `void` and accept, after the `Model` parameter, at least one argument corresponding to a Choco variable type. Both types of function may be enriched with additional arguments, thereby promoting reuse across different contexts.

Listing 1 shows a domain-definition function for the `isPalindrome` method. To generate a string, an array of `IntVar` is used to represent ASCII codes of characters. The function therefore returns an `IntVar[]` defined in the `Model`. The array length is restrained by an additional argument (i.e., `length`) and each array value is restricted between 32 and 126, corresponding to the range of ASCII code characters used in this case study. Listing 2 shows a narrowing function that restricts a given `IntVar[]` character to a subset of special ASCII characters.

Test Data Generation Model. The next step consists of defining rules that describe when constraint functions are used and which parameters of the tested methods they should constrain. For this purpose, we propose to use a dedicated *test data generation model* conforming to the `TestDataGenerationMM` (Fig. 2). A test data generation model is composed of *rules*. A `Rule` is composed of a *condition* and *actions*. Actions define which constraint function should be applied on which `MethodParameter` (e.g., calling the `setSpecialChars` to constrain the method parameter `word` of the `isPalindrome` method). Actions of a rule are conditionally invoked in the data generation process, via the presence of an abstract value in the ATC to concretize. To ease the writing of a test data generation model, we implemented a YAML-based concrete textual syntax for the `TestDataGenerationMM`. The resulting parser is able to read a conforming YAML file and to instantiate a proper test data generation EMF model.

Listing 3 shows an excerpt of a test data generation model for the `isPalindrome` example. First, an import clause specifies the location of the constraint function library (i.e., a Java class available in the classpath). Then a list of rules is defined in a when-then style. The first constraint is unconditionally applied and initializes the Choco variable that represents the `word` parameter in the CSP, with a length of 10 using the constraint function shown in Listing 1. The second constraint is applying the `setSpecialChars` function (shown in Listing 2) to ensure the `word` method parameter has ASCII codes corresponding to special characters at indexes 2 to 3.

```
contraint_library:
↪   constraints.Palindrome
data_generation_rules:
- when: always
  apply:
    - constraint:
↪   specifyStringLength
      args: [10]
      on_parameters: [word]
- when:
    WordHasSpecialChar: "yes"
  apply:
    - constraint: setSpecialChars
      args: [2, 3]
      on_parameters: [word]
```

Listing 3. An example of Test Data Generation model for `isPalindrome`

```
@Test
void testIsPalindrome1() { assertEquals(null // TODO : add oracle here
    , isPalindrome("baaaa")); }
```

Listing 4. Generated test script for CTC3, i.e., valid word that is not a palindrome

CTC Model Generation. Having constraint functions and a test data generation model enable us to automate the creation of a CSP for each ATC to concretize. Given an abstract test case, an SUT model that provides information on the parameters to be generated, and a test data generation model guiding the applications of constraints, the process proceeds as follows: (1) A Choco `Model` is built, in which we define the *CSP variables* mirroring the `MethodParameters`. (2) Based on the constraint application rules and the abstract test case, the relevant constraints are applied in the current Choco

`Model` instance. (3) Finally, the solver computes a solution that satisfies all the applied constraints. The generated values are then given as `CallArguments` according to each CTC that references the generated value and for which method parameter it has been generated (Fig. 2).

2.3 Test Scripts Code Generation

Once we have a concrete test suite model, the last step is to transform it into executable test scripts. We consider JUnit as a target testing framework for the generated scripts. In essence, each concrete test case must be turned into a JUnit method, where the tested method is called with the corresponding input data. Listing 4 shows the test method produced for CTC3, where a word that is not a palindrome should be the value.

3 Experiments and Results

Research Question. Compared to a traditional combinatorial testing process, our proposed approach requires some additional noteworthy manual work. Therefore, this evaluation is centered on the following research question: **RQ:** Given a Java method, a combinatorial model, and a target coverage criterion, how does the combined effort of implementing constraint functions and defining a test data generation model compare to the effort of implementing test scripts manually? And how does this comparison vary with combinatorial complexity, e.g., when changing the target coverage criterion?

Experimental Setup. The approach supports static Java methods with primitive inputs and return types (i.e., string, integer, boolean, etc.). Beyond `isPalindrome` method already introduced earlier we selected, adapted, and implemented four existing case studies from the field of software testing that fit these requirements (see [1] for details about these methods).

Then, for each Java method: (1) A PICT combinatorial model was manually realized based on the specification of the method. (2) Constraint functions were implemented

Table 2. Detailed evaluation results as lines of code (LOC).

Case Study	TD Gen. LOC (1)	CP library LOC (2)	(1)+(2)	Generated Tests			
				Pairwise		3-Wise	
				Test Cases Count	Test Scripts LOC (3)	Test Cases Count	Test Scripts LOC (4)
`isPalindrome`	49	51	100	7	46	10	61
`getTriangleType`	72	39	111	12	76	17	101
`getDaysInMonth`	52	40	92	20	128	20	128
`findCommand`	100	78	178	21	156	64	458
`validatePasswordStrength`	120	75	195	28	176	86	524

using the Choco-Solver library. (3) A test data generation model was written. (4) The prototype implementing the presented approach was used two times on the method, first using the pairwise coverage criteria, then the 3-wise coverage criteria.

We use the Lines of Code (LOC) metric to measure the amount of effort required for a given task. We used the *cloc* tool, which counts the *physical* lines (i.e., excluding blank lines and comment lines) of the source code in many programming languages. To answer the stated RQ, for each considered case, the LOC of the constraint functions, the LOC of the test data generation model, and the LOC of the generated test scripts. This last measurement is used to know both how much was automatically generated by the approach and to estimate the effort that would have been necessary to manually implement these test cases without relying on the proposed approach.

Results. Table 2 presents the results obtained and Fig. 3 shows a bar plot representation to better visualize and compare the numbers of LOC. For the two simpler methods (`isPalindrome` and `getTriangleType`) we observe that the additional manual effort required by our approach (shown as the first of the three bars) is higher than the test scripts LOC, both when targeting the pairwise and the 3-wise coverage criteria.

For `getDaysInMonth`, our approach barely breaks even, as the additional effort (92 LOC) is slightly lower than the effort to directly write test scripts when targeting pairwise or threewise coverage (128 LOC in each case). As writing constraint functions is arguably more difficult than writing test scripts, the result is here inconclusive.

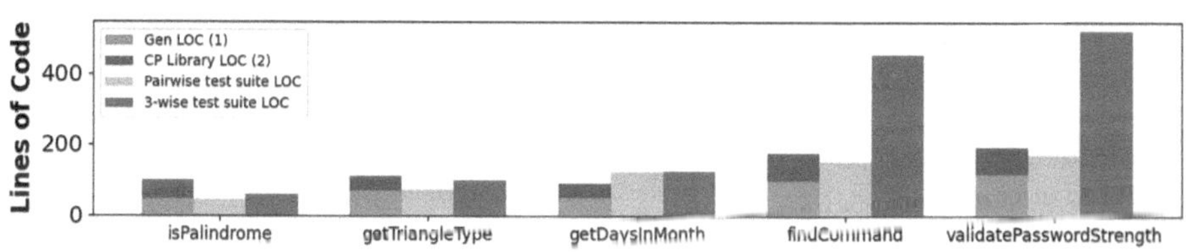

Fig. 3. Bar plot of the results shown in Table 2

For `findCommand`, the additional effort is important (178 LOC) due to the rather complex constraint functions. This means this effort is quite similar to the effort to directly write test scripts when targeting pairwise coverage (156 LOC). However, when targeting 3-wise coverage, the effort required to implement test cases is much more important (458 LOC), making the approach significantly more cost-effective.

Finally, `validatePasswordStrength` requires a simpler data generator than `findCommand`, but has a much higher combinatorial complexity. This results in the amount of effort required for the approach (195 LOC) being slightly higher than in the pairwise case (176 LOC) but consequently, better than in the threewise case (524 LOC).

4 Related Work

Little work has been done on automated abstract test case concretization in combinatorial testing. It is an explicit step in the combinatorial testing process proposed by Grindal et al. [3] (under the name *translation table*) and vaguely mentioned in the seminal work of Kuhn et al. [4], but without any provided method or automatization in either case.

To our knowledge, the closest related work are *JCUnit* [6] and *Coffee4J* [2]. Both approaches address the automatic generation of unit tests through combinatorial testing using Java annotations. The former mainly focus on automating combinatorial within a model-based testing context, while the latter defines a framework for automated test generation. However, neither approach addresses the concretization step, assuming concrete test data is directly provided within the combinatorial model.

5 Conclusion

In this paper, we propose a novel model-driven approach to automate the concretization of abstract test cases (ATCs). ATCs are generated and concretized using both a test data generation model and constraint functions. Finally, the resulting concrete test cases are transformed into executable test scripts using a code generator, making the approach truly end-to-end. Future research directions include extending evaluation with more sophisticated models and complex input data, such as non-primitive types and nested objects.

References

1. Bamouh, L., Bousse, E.: Towards model-driven test case concretization for end-to-end combinatorial testing. In: Proceedings of the ACM/IEEE 27th International Conference on Model Driven Engineering Languages and Systems, MODELS Companion '24, pp. 1111–1120. ACM (2024)
2. Bonn, J., Foegen, K., Lichter, H.: A framework for automated combinatorial test generation, execution, and fault characterization. In: 2019 IEEE International Conference on Software Testing, Verification and Validation Workshops (ICSTW), pp. 224–233. IEEE (2019)
3. Grindal, M., Offutt, J.: Input parameter modeling for combination strategies. In: Proceedings of the 25th Conference on IASTED International Multi-Conference: Software Engineering, pp. 255–260. ACTA Press (2007)
4. Kuhn, D.R., Kacker, R.N., Lei, Y.: Introduction to Combinatorial Testing. CRC Press (2013)
5. Prud'homme, C., Fages, J.G.: Choco-solver: a Java library for constraint programming. J. Open Source Softw. **7**(78), 4708 (2022). https://doi.org/10.21105/joss.04708
6. Ukai, H., Qu, X.: Test design as code: JCUnit. In: 2017 IEEE International Conference on Software Testing, Verification and Validation (ICST), pp. 508–515. IEEE (2017)

Software Management: Measurement, Peopleware, and Innovation

Reviewing the Use of AI-Driven Functional Size Measurement

Widad Elouataoui[1], Ali Idri[1](✉), and Alain Abran[2]

[1] Data and Software Sciences Research Laboratory, ENSIAS, Mohammed V University in Rabat, Rabat, Morocco
{widad.elouataoui,ali.idri}@ensias.um5.ac.ma
[2] Department of Software Engineering and Information Technology, ETS, University of Quebec, Montreal, Canada
Alain.Abran@etsmtl.ca

Abstract. In recent years, the integration of Artificial Intelligence (AI) techniques into Functional Size Measurement (FSM) has gained increasing attention within the software engineering community. AI-based FSM methods aim to overcome the limitations of traditional approaches, namely, reliance on expert judgment and structured inputs, by enabling automation and scalability. This study presents a systematic literature review of research efforts that apply AI techniques to FSM. The review analyses 27 primary studies published between 2008 and 2025, sourced from major digital libraries. Various aspects are investigated, including publication trends, AI technique categories, functional sizing methods, and research types. The findings show a predominance of COSMIC as the preferred FSM method and highlight NLP, and transformer-based models as the most commonly employed AI techniques. While hybrid models combining rule-based systems with deep learning show promise, the field remains fragmented and underexplored. This review offers the first consolidated overview of AI-driven FSM research, identifying key trends, challenges, and directions for future investigation.

Keywords: Software Sizing · Artificial Intelligence · Functional Size · COSMIC

1 Introduction

The increasing complexity of software systems and the adoption of data-driven development practices have encouraged the integration of Artificial Intelligence (AI) into software engineering activities. Functional Size Measurement (FSM), widely used for estimating cost, effort, and resources, relies on standards such as COSMIC, Function Points (FP), and NESMA. However, these methods often depend on manual analysis, structured documentation, and expert judgment, limiting their efficiency in agile and informal environments.

Recent advances in AI have enabled the automation of FSM by processing unstructured requirements and learning from historical project data. Approaches range from interpretable techniques, such as rule-based systems and decision trees (Ochodek, 2016a, b), to more advanced models including neural networks and transformers (De Vito et al.,

C. Berger and V. Klös (Eds.): SEAA 2026, LNCS 16864, pp. 59–67, 2027.
https://doi.org/10.1007/978-3-032-36587-3_5

2025). While models such as BERT and GPT have improved the analysis of textual requirements, concerns remain regarding explainability and traceability (Tenekeci et al., 2024). To address these challenges, hybrid approaches combining rule-based FSM standards with AI techniques have been proposed (Laqrichi, 2024). AI methods have been applied across several FSM standards, including COSMIC, IFPUG, FP, NESMA, and UCP, reflecting the diversity of software sizing practices (Lavazza et al., 2022).

Although research in this area is gaining momentum, the landscape remains scattered, and a structured synthesis of the literature is still lacking. To our knowledge, no systematic mapping study has yet consolidated the current developments in AI-driven FSM.

This paper presents a systematic mapping study aimed at exploring the current state of the art in automated FSM using Artificial Intelligence (AI). To this end, we conducted comprehensive research across several major academic digital libraries, resulting in the selection of 27 primary studies published between 2008 and 2025. These studies were analyzed to address the following research objectives:

- Identify the most commonly used FSM methods automated with AI techniques.
- Categorize the AI techniques applied for FSM.
- Analyze the types of contributions and their strategies.
- Describe the Publication venues and temporal distribution
- Highlight research gaps and propose future directions for AI-driven FSM.

The remainder of the paper is structured as follows: Sect. 2 reviews existing FSM methods and AI paradigms applied to software sizing. Section 3 outlines the methodology used to perform the SLR. Section 4 presents the findings and discusses emerging trends. Finally, we conclude with a summary of key insights and implications for future research.

2 Research Methodology

To ensure methodological rigor, we adopted the structured SLR process outlined by Kofod-Petersen (2012), which includes planning, execution, and reporting phases. Our objective is to identify and synthesize existing research on the use of AI techniques in FSM. The review began with defining clear goals, formulating research questions, and setting the scope. A systematic search was then conducted across major scientific databases, followed by a strict selection process based on predefined inclusion, exclusion, and quality criteria. Finally, relevant data were extracted and analyzed to address the research objectives.

2.1 Research Questions

To structure the investigation, we first defined the questions as presented in Table 1, categorizing them into mapping questions, to capture publication trends and research volume, and research questions so as to explore the FSM methods and AI techniques.

Table 1. Research questions

	Question	Motivation
MQ1	When and where were the selected papers published?	Identify the years when there was an interest in the research topic and the sources of publications
RQ1	What are the commonly FSM methods investigated in AI-FSM studies?	Identify which FSM methods are most frequently supported or enhanced by AI techniques
RQ2	What are the most commonly used AI techniques for functional size measurement?	Identify the most frequently applied AI techniques in FSM and understand trends in AI techniques adoption

2.2 Scope

Inclusion and exclusion criteria were defined to focus on studies applying AI for FSM automation or estimation.

Eligible Studies: Explicitly apply AI as the main method for FSM AND Are peer-reviewed or reputable preprints AND are written in English.

Excluded Studies: Focus solely on rule-based, statistical, or mathematical FSM methods without AI integration OR use AI for effort or cost estimation rather than size OR are secondary studies, editorials, or inaccessible in full text.

2.3 Literature Sources and Search Strings

The literature search targeted a comprehensive range of digital libraries relevant to software engineering and AI: IEEE Xplore, ACM Digital Library, SpringerLink, ScienceDirect, Scopus, ResearchGate, and Google Scholar. This ensures broad coverage of both peer-reviewed and impactful grey literature.

Search queries were carefully designed using Boolean logic to target intersections between AI and FSM. The core string combined AI-related terms (e.g., "Machine Learning", "Deep Learning", "NLP") with FSM-related terminology (e.g., "Function Points", "COSMIC", "Software Size"). The final search string ensured high recall across all selected databases.

3 Results and Discussion

This section outlines the key findings from the systematic review of 27 primary studies addressing the use of AI in software Functional Size Measurement. It highlights publication trends, research characteristics, employed AI techniques, targeted FSM models, and datasets.

3.1 Study Selection Overview

The selection process began with the formulation of a structured search query, which was applied across several leading academic databases, including IEEE Xplore, ScienceDirect, ACM Digital Library, SpringerLink, arXiv, and ResearchGate. This initial step retrieved 520 potentially relevant records. After eliminating 140 duplicates, 380 unique papers were retained for further screening.

A preliminary screening of titles, abstracts, and keywords led to the exclusion of 340 papers, primarily because they addressed FSM without incorporating AI, or they focused on adjacent areas such as effort or cost estimation rather than functional size.

Next, 40 studies underwent a quick content review, and 28 were shortlisted for full-text assessment. Of these, 19 met all the inclusion criteria. Particular attention was taken to exclude studies where FSM appeared only as an auxiliary input such as for effort estimation rather than software sizing. Indeed, despite the close relationship between software size and effort, our focus remained on works explicitly developing or applying AI for FSM. Additionally, papers using only traditional FSM methods without AI were excluded, even if they contributed valuable insights to the sizing domain.

To ensure completeness, reference lists of the selected studies were scanned in four iterative rounds, yielding 8 additional qualifying papers. Notably, publication year was not a restriction due to the limited volume of research at this intersection. In total, 27 studies were retained for the final synthesis.

3.2 MQ1: Publication Outlets and Timeline

The 27 selected papers were evenly distributed (Fig. 1) across journals (13) and conference proceedings (13), with one doctoral dissertation (Ishrar, 2014) included due to its significant contributions. Journals such as IEEE Transactions on Software Engineering (De Vito et al., 2025), Applied Sciences (Yalçıner et al., 2024), and Information and Software Technology (Ochodek et al., 2016a, b) reflect more mature and in-depth contributions. Conferences like ICSEA, SERA, and ISEC hosted innovative and early-stage work. This even split indicates that the intersection of AI and FSM is receiving attention across both foundational and exploratory research forums, supporting the growth of this emerging field through diverse dissemination formats. Most selected studies were published in IEEE Xplore, followed by Elsevier/ScienceDirect, Springer, and the ACM Digital Library. This distribution reflects both wide dissemination and a solid presence in established digital libraries.

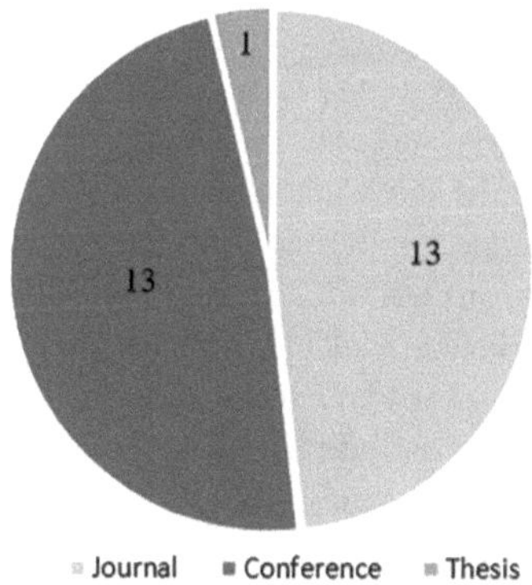

Fig. 1. Distribution of Publication Types

The selected studies span from 2008 to 2025, with a clear increase in research activity in recent years (Fig. 2). Early contributions were modest, but interest began to grow after 2020, culminating in a sharp peak in 2024 signaling a big attention to AI-driven Functional Size Measurement. The 2025 count remains tentative, as the publication cycle is still ongoing.

3.3 RQ1: What are the Common FSM Methods Investigated in AI-FSM Studies?

This research question explores which functional size measurement (FSM) methods are most frequently paired with AI. Among the 27 studies analyzed, COSMIC emerges as the most prevalent, appearing in 19 papers (~70%). Its adaptability to modern software paradigms and its process-oriented, standardized nature make it highly suitable for automation. Examples include Safae et al. (2024), combining LLMs with rules for COSMIC measurement, and Molla et al. (2025), leveraging BERT to estimate COSMIC sizes from textual requirements.

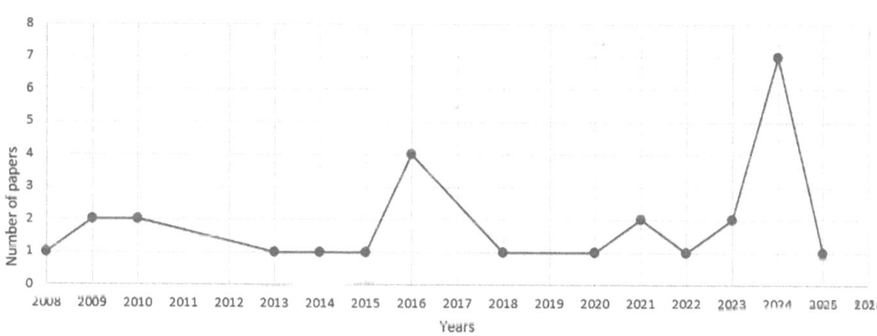

Fig. 2. Annual Distribution of Selected Papers

Function Point (FP) methods, including IFPUG and Simple FP, were used in 9 studies combined with techniques such as neural networks (Sheta et al., 2015), deep learning, and neuro-fuzzy approaches (Xia et al., 2008). However, FP methods require detailed specifications and are less suited to natural language inputs, limiting their use in AI-driven automation for early-stage requirements.

Some studies combined FSM methods to increase flexibility. Lavazza et al. (2023) integrated FPA with NESMA and applied ML models (e.g., RF, SVR) to estimate functional size with incomplete information. Corazza et al. (2016) used transfer learning to bridge FPA and COSMIC, while Ochodek et al. (2016a, b) proposed a dual-step approach for estimating both COSMIC and IFPUG sizes from use-case goals.

Less commonly used methods include Use Case Points (UCP) and User Story Points, each featured in just one study. Methods like MkII and FFPA were not represented, suggesting they may lack the maturity or structure required for effective AI integration and automation (Fig. 3).

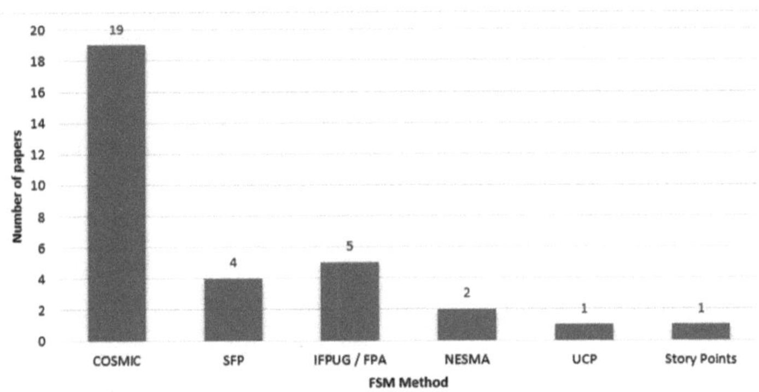

Fig. 3. Distribution of the FSM methods integrating AI

3.4 RQ2: What AI Techniques are Most Commonly Used in FSM?

From the 27 studies analyzed, several families of AI techniques have been applied to functional size measurement (FSM), including NLP, machine learning (ML), deep learning (DL), fuzzy logic, statistical models, and rule-based systems. As shown in Fig. 4, NLP leads in usage, appearing in 37% of studies. This dominance is expected given FSM's reliance on textual requirements like use cases or user stories. Indeed, NLP methods enable automatic extraction of functional elements from natural language. For instance, Ishrar et al. (2014) applied supervised text mining to map linguistic features to COSMIC size labels, addressing the gap between formal FSM methods and informal Agile descriptions. Similarly, Gérançon et al. (2023) introduced a COSMIC-compliant tool that maps semantic triplets (subject–verb–object) to data movements, automating the size calculation from user stories.

ML and DL techniques appear in roughly 25% of studies each. Traditional ML models like SVM and Random Forest have been used for classification and regression tasks, often predicting size from structured inputs. DL models, particularly MLPs and Transformers (BERT, GPT), are increasingly applied for their ability to learn complex patterns in unstructured data. Lavazza et al. (2023) demonstrated that ANN-based models (FFNN, RBF) can accurately estimate function points from early inputs. In another case,

Becha et al. (2024) introduced BotCFP, a COSMIC FSM tool for chatbots that combines regression models (SVM, RF, GBM) with NLP vectorization techniques. Random Forest with TF-IDF showed the best performance, validating ML's utility in AI-based systems with minimal input.

Fewer studies explored fuzzy systems (Xia et al., 2008), statistical models (Lavazza et al., 2022), or rule-based techniques. These approaches support estimation in the presence of vague or incomplete requirements. Fuzzy logic addresses ambiguity, statistical models offer pattern discovery, and rule-based methods ensure traceability to FSM standards. However, their limitations in scalability and semantic understanding make them less favored compared to ML and NLP-driven approaches in dynamic, real-world settings.

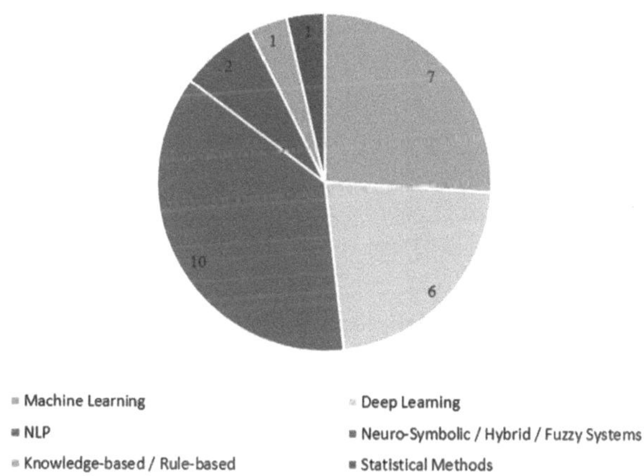

Fig. 4. AI techniques used for FSM

As shown in Fig. 5, transformer-based models are the most frequently employed AI techniques in FSM automation, appearing in 8 studies. Their dominance stems from their superior contextual understanding of natural language, critical for parsing requirement texts. MLPs and rule-based systems follow, each used in 6 studies, especially when combined with semantic reasoning or domain-specific rules to enhance precision. Other approaches such as supervised text mining, SVMs, decision trees, fuzzy logic, and triplet extraction appeared in fewer papers. Statistical models and gradient boosting were less common.

Notably, many studies adopted hybrid strategies that blend multiple techniques to compensate for individual limitations. For instance, Laqrichi et al. (2024) combined GPT-4 with a rule-based engine to automate COSMIC measurement, uniting GPT's interpretive strength with formal compliance. While deep models didn't always outperform simpler ones, hybridization proved effective for comparative evaluation and accuracy.

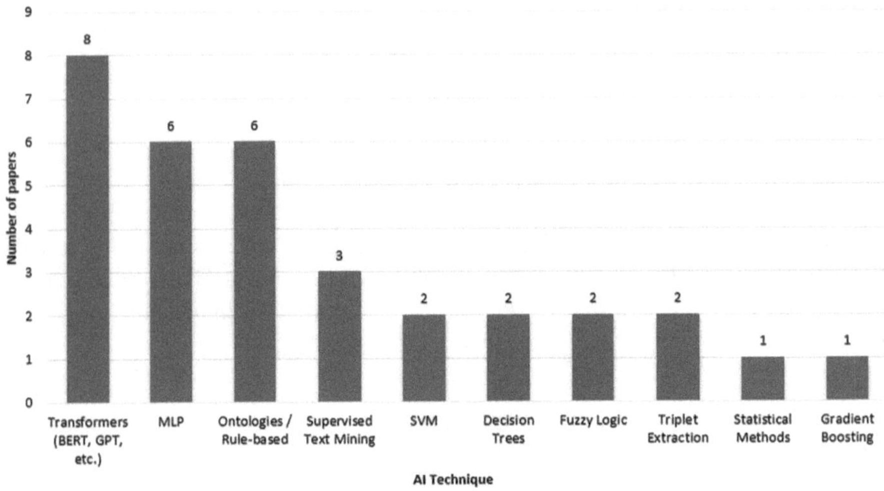

Fig. 5. Categories of AI Models Used In FSM

4 Conclusions

This systematic mapping study reviewed 27 studies published between 2008 and 2025 to investigate the use of Artificial Intelligence (AI) for automating Functional Size Measurement (FSM). The results show a growing interest in this research area, particularly after 2020. COSMIC emerged as the most widely adopted FSM method, while NLP and transformer-based models were the dominant AI techniques. The findings highlight the increasing role of AI in improving FSM automation and provide an overview of current research trends and gaps. Future work will involve conducting a systematic literature review (SLR) to further analyze evaluation methods, tool maturity, and benchmarking practices in AI-driven FSM.

References

Becha, R., Sellami, A., Bouassida, N., Idri, A., Abran, A.: BotCFP: A machine learning based tool for COSMIC chatbots sizing. In: IWSM-MENSURA 2024: Joint proceedings of the International Workshop on Software Measurement and MENSURA 2024, pp. 1–12. CEUR Workshop Proceedings, 3852. CEUR-WS (2024). https://ceur-ws.org/Vol-3852/paper14.pdf

Corazza, A., Di Martino, S., Ferrucci, F., Gravino, C., Sarro, F.: From function points to COSMIC - a transfer learning approach for effort estimation. In: Abrahamsson, P., Corral, L., Oivo, M., Russo, B. (eds.) Product-Focused Software Process Improvement, pp. 251–267. Springer (2016). https://doi.org/10.1007/978-3-319-26844-6_19

De Vito, G., Di Martino, S., Ferrucci, F., Gravino, C., Palomba, F.: LLM-based automation of COSMIC functional size measurement from use cases. IEEE Trans. Software Eng. **51**(5), 1500–1523 (2025). https://doi.org/10.1109/TSE.2025.3554562

Ishrar, H.M., Hussain, H., Ormandjieva, O., Kosseim, L.: Linguistic approaches for early measurement of functional size from software requirements. Semantic Scholar (2014). https://www.semanticscholar.org/paper/Linguistic-Approaches-for-Early-Measurement-of-Size-Requirements-Ishrar/b524b694d142f411fa324cd0b7d4bec5291a34a3

Kofod-Petersen, A.: How to do a structured literature review in computer science (Version 0.1) (2012). [Technical report]

Lavazza, L., Locoro, A., Liu, G., Meli, R.: Estimating software functional size via machine learning. ACM Trans. Softw. Eng. Methodol. **32**(5), Article 114 (2023). https://doi.org/10.1145/3582575

Lavazza, L., Locoro, A., Meli, R.: Using locally weighted regression to estimate the functional size of software: a preliminary study. In: Proceedings of the IARIA Congress 2022: The 2022 IARIA Annual Congress on Frontiers in Science, Technology, Services, and Applications, pp. 20–24. IARIA. ISBN 978-1-68558-017-9 (2022)

Laqrichi, S.: A hybrid framework for COSMIC measurement: combining large language models with a rule-based system. In: CEUR Workshop Proceedings, IWSM-MENSURA 2024 (2024). https://ceur-ws.org/Vol-3852/paper9.pdf

Molla, Y.S., Alemneh, E., Yimer, S.T.: COSMIC-based early software size estimation using deep learning and domain-specific BERT. IEEE Access **13**, 28463–28475 (2025). https://doi.org/10.1109/ACCESS.2025.3540548

Ochodek, M.: Functional size approximation based on use-case names. Inf. Softw. Technol. **80**, 73–88 (2016). https://doi.org/10.1016/j.infsof.2016.08.007

Ochodek, M.: Approximation of COSMIC functional size of scenario-based requirements in agile based on syntactic linguistic features—a replication study. In: 2016 Joint Conference of the International Workshop on Software Measurement and the International Conference on Software Process and Product Measurement (IWSM-MENSURA), pp. 201–211. IEEE (2016b). https://doi.org/10.1109/IWSM-Mensura.2016.039

Sheta, A., Rine, D., Kassaymeh, S.: Software effort and function points estimation models based on radial basis function and feedforward artificial neural networks. Int. J. Next-Gener. Comput. **6**(3), 192–205 (2015). https://doi.org/10.47164/ijngc.v6i3.99

Tenekeci, S., Ünlü, H., Dikenelli, E., Selçuk, U., Kılınç Soylu, G., Demirörs, O.: Predicting software size and effort from code using natural language processing. GCRIS Repository (2024). https://gcris.iyte.edu.tr/handle/11147/14915

Xia, W., Ho, D., Capretz, L.F.: A neuro-fuzzy model for function point calibration. Trans. Inf. Sci. Appl. **1**(5), 22–30. arXiv (2008). https://doi.org/10.48550/arXiv.1507.06934

Yalçıner, B., Dinçer, K., Karaçor, A.G., Efe, M.Ö.: Enhancing agile story point estimation: integrating deep learning, machine learning, and natural language processing with SBERT and gradient boosted trees. Appl. Sci. **14**(16), Article 7305 (2024). https://doi.org/10.3390/app14167305

Organizational Cohesion in Microservice Architectures: A Multi-project Empirical Study

Xiaozhou Li(✉) and Andrea Janes

Free University of Bozen-Bolzano, via Bruno Buozzi, 1, 39100 Bolzano, Italy
{xiaozhou.li,andrea.janes}@unibz.it

Abstract. The widespread adoption of microservice architectures has introduced new challenges in aligning software modularity with the structure of development organizations. Although prior research has extensively examined technical properties such as service coupling and dependency structures, comparatively little attention has been paid to how contributor activity reflects or diverges from service boundaries. In this paper, we introduce the notion of organizational cohesion in microservice ecosystems and propose a quantitative approach to measure it. Building on the Sensitive Class Cohesion Metric (SCOM), we define Pairwise Team Cohesion (PTC), a metric that captures the balance and focus of developer contributions within individual microservices. We analyze the evolution of organizational cohesion using a longitudinal case study of the Spinnaker microservice platform and replicate the analysis across six additional open-source microservice systems. Our results reveal systematic differences between core and peripheral services and show that PTC and Average Organizational Coupling (AOC) exhibit only a weak correlation across projects. This finding shows that team cohesion and cross-service developer activity suggest distinct and weakly associated organizational dynamics. By extending the "high cohesion, low coupling" principle to the organizational level, our study provides a quantitative perspective for assessing the socio-technical structure of microservice development.

Keywords: Microservice · Organizational Cohesion · Organizational Coupling · Metric · Socio-technical architecture · Software architecture

1 Introduction

Microservice architecture has become a dominant paradigm for building large-scale cloud-native software systems [8]. It decomposes the application into a set of independently deployable services that encapsulate specific business capabilities and communicate through lightweight APIs [22]. However, this architectural style also introduces substantial organizational complexity when development is distributed across multiple teams whose coordination must align with service

C. Berger and V. Klös (Eds.): SEAA 2026, LNCS 16864, pp. 68–84, 2027.
https://doi.org/10.1007/978-3-032-36587-3_6

boundaries [14]. Hence, the effectiveness of a microservice system depends not only on its technical modularity, but also on how well the development organization reflects and sustains that modular structure.

The relationship between software architecture and organizational structure has long been recognized through Conway's Law, which posits that system design mirrors communication structures [6]. Especially for microservices, this implies that each service ideally corresponds to a cohesive team with clear ownership; however, such alignment is often imperfect [2]. Therein, developers contribute across multiple services, responsibilities overlap, and coordination patterns evolve over time. Understanding how contributor activity aligns with service boundaries is therefore essential for assessing the socio-technical health of microservice ecosystems.

Cohesion and coupling are long-established principles of software design. Cohesion refers to the degree to which elements within a module belong together, while coupling measures the degree of interdependence between modules [28]. High cohesion and low coupling are widely associated with maintainability and architectural quality [23]. Although extensive research has operationalized these concepts for source code, comparatively little work has quantified them at the organizational level. In particular, while organizational coupling has been studied through cross-service contribution patterns [18], there is a lack of systematic approaches to measure the cohesion of microservice teams.

To address this gap, we introduce Pairwise Team Cohesion (PTC), a quantitative metric that captures the extent to which contributors to a microservice exhibit focused and balanced participation. PTC is derived from version-control data and adapts principles from established cohesion metrics to the organizational context by modeling the overlap and distribution of developer activity. Complementing this, we use Average Organizational Coupling (AOC) to quantify cross-service developer overlap, providing a measure of inter-team interdependence. Importantly, we treat commit activity as a scalable behavioral proxy for contribution patterns, while acknowledging that it does not fully capture communication or coordination processes. This study addresses the following research questions:

RQ1. *How can the cohesion of microservice teams be quantitatively evaluated using development activity data?*
RQ2. *What is the relationship between organizational cohesion and organizational coupling in microservice systems?*

To answer these questions, we conduct a longitudinal case study of the *Spinnaker*[1] microservice platform and complement it with a cross-system replication across multiple open-source microservice projects. We also performed a robustness analysis to assess the sensitivity of the results to data perturbations, contributor effects, metric formulations, and temporal aggregation strategies.

The results show that PTC captures meaningful patterns of contributor focus and responds systematically to organizational and architectural changes.

[1] https://spinnaker.io/.

More importantly, across systems and experimental conditions, the correlation between cohesion and coupling remains consistently weak. This indicates that cohesion and coupling provide distinct, weakly associated, and non-redundant views of organizational structure, rather than opposing ends of a single spectrum. This finding reframes the classical "high cohesion, low coupling" principle at the organizational level as a two-dimensional design space.

This study makes three main contributions: 1) PTC as a reproducible metric for contribution-based organizational cohesion in microservice systems, 2) empirical evidence that PTC and service-level organizational coupling capture distinct and weakly associated dimensions of developer behavior, and 3) a practical framework to analyze teamarchitecture alignment using version-control data.

The remainder of this article is organized as follows. Section 2 reviews related work. Section 3 presents the proposed metrics for organizational cohesion and coupling. Section 4 describes the study design. Section 5 reports the empirical results, first summarizing the longitudinal case study of Spinnaker and then presenting the cross-system replication as the primary evidence. Section 6 evaluates the robustness of the findings. Section 7 discusses the implications and limitations of the study. Section 8 outlines threats to validity, and Sect. 9 concludes the article.

2 Related Work

Cohesion and coupling are foundational concepts in software modularity. Cohesion refers to the degree to which elements within a module belong together, while coupling captures the level of interdependence between modules [26]. Classical work in software design emphasizes that high cohesion and low coupling lead to improved maintainability, understandability, and evolvability. Numerous metrics have been proposed to quantify cohesion at the code level, including variants of LCOM [4,5,11,13,15] and similarity-based measures that assess relationships between methods and attributes [1,7]. Among these, the Sensitive Class Cohesion Metric (SCOM) introduces a weighted formulation that accounts for both the intensity and the distribution of internal relationships, providing a stable and discriminative measure of cohesion [9].

Although these metrics are well-established for code structure, their application has largely remained within the technical domain. In microservice architectures, cohesion and coupling have also been studied at the service level, focusing primarily on structural dependencies, API interactions, and service evolution [21,24]. However, these approaches do not directly capture how developer activity aligns with service boundaries, leaving the organizational dimension of cohesion underexplored.

On the other hand, regarding the organizational perspective of microservice architecture, it is commonly assumed that the alignment between team and service reflects Conway's Law [6]. Therefore, ideally, each microservice is typically owned by a semi-autonomous team responsible for its lifecycle, from development and deployment to monitoring and maintenance [22]. In practice, however, empirical studies show that such alignment is often partial: developers frequently contribute across multiple services, and ownership structures evolve over time [2]. Previous work in microservice organizations has focused primarily on organizational coupling, measured through cross-service contribution patterns [17,18]. Recent role-centered evidence further shows that organizational coupling can be shaped by specific developer roles rather than by architectural structure alone [19]. However, there is limited work on quantifying organizational cohesion, that is, the extent to which contributors focus their activity within a service.

Meanwhile, the relationship between software architecture and team organization has been extensively studied in socio-technical research. Socio-technical congruence (STC) theory argues that effective software development occurs when coordination among developers matches the technical dependencies of the system [3]. The misalignment between social and technical structures can lead to increased coordination costs, reduced productivity, and quality issues [12]. In this context, cohesion and coupling can be interpreted as complementary organizational dimensions. Cohesion reflects the internal alignment of contributors within a service, while coupling captures cross-service coordination requirements. From a coordination perspective, high cohesion may indicate concentrated ownership and reduced internal coordination overhead, whereas high coupling reflects increased coordination across teams. However, existing STC-based studies primarily focus on communication networks and dependency structures, rather than providing direct quantitative measures of team-level cohesion.

To summarize, previous work provides strong foundations for understanding modularity and socio-technical alignment, but leaves a gap in measuring organizational cohesion in microservice systems. Existing metrics focus either on code structure or cross-service coupling, without capturing the distribution and balance of contributor activity within services. Moreover, the relationship between cohesion and coupling at the organizational level remains largely unexplored.

3 Method

3.1 Measuring Organizational Cohesion

To quantify organizational cohesion in microservice teams, we adapt the Sensitive Class Cohesion Metric (SCOM) [9] to the context of developer activity. The SCOM metric yields a discriminative measure of cohesion, which is robust to minor structure variations and sensitive to balanced participation among elements. While it evaluates relationships among methods based on shared attributes, we reinterpret its core idea at the organizational level: *cohesion arises when contributors focus their efforts consistently within a service and exhibit balanced participation.*

We begin by defining two fundamental components for each developer d and service s:

- **Contribution focus:**

$$f_{d,s} = \frac{C_{d,s}}{C_{d,*}} \quad (1)$$

– **Contribution weight**:

$$w_{d,s} = \frac{C_{d,s}}{C_{*,s}} \tag{2}$$

where $C_{d,s}$ is the number of commits made by the developer d to service s, $C_{d,*}$ is the total commits by d, and $C_{*,s}$ is the total commits to service s.

To capture the contributors' joint effort concentration, we introduce Pairwise Team Cohesion (PTC). PTC extends SCOM's pairwise formulation to model cohesion as a shared focus among contributors. For each pair of contributors (i, j) to the service s, we define:

– **Connection intensity**:

$$C_{ij}^{(s)} = \sqrt{f_{i,s} \cdot f_{j,s}} \tag{3}$$

– **Pairwise prominence weight**:

$$\alpha_{ij}^{(s)} = \frac{w_{i,s} + w_{j,s}}{2} \tag{4}$$

Let m be the number of contributors to service s. The Pairwise Team Cohesion is then defined as:

$$PTC_s = \frac{2}{m(m-1)} \sum_{i<j} C_{ij}^{(s)} \cdot \alpha_{ij}^{(s)} \tag{5}$$

Regarding the **Design Rationale**, the formulation of PTC follows two key principles. First, the geometric mean in $C_{ij}^{(s)}$ emphasizes a *balanced focus* between contributors. If one developer is highly focused while another is not, the resulting value decreases, penalizing such an imbalance. Thus, high cohesion emerges only when contributors jointly concentrate on the same service. On the other hand, the weighting term $\alpha_{ij}^{(s)}$ reflects *contribution prominence*. Pairs involving core contributors have greater influence, whereas peripheral contributors contribute less. This prevents cohesion from being dominated by minor or sporadic activity.

Together, these design choices ensure that PTC captures both the *extent* and the *uniformity* of contributor focus. The resulting $PTC_s \in [0, 1]$, where higher values indicate stronger organizational cohesion. Accordingly, PTC should be interpreted as contribution-based ownership concentration, not as a direct measure of communication quality, formal team membership, or managerial task assignment.

3.2 Measuring Organizational Coupling

To complement cohesion, we measure cross-service interdependence using Organizational Coupling (OC) [18]. Following prior work, the coupling between two services M_a and M_b is defined as:

$$OC(M_a, M_b) = \sum_{i=1}^{p} \left[\left(\frac{2C_{i,a}C_{i,b}}{C_{i,a} + C_{i,b}} \right) \times S_{D_i}(M_a, M_b) \right] \tag{6}$$

where $C_{i,a}$ and $C_{i,b}$ denote contributions of developer i to the two services, and $S_{D_i}(M_a, M_b)$ captures the frequency with which the developer alternates between them.

To ensure comparability, we normalize the coupling as follows.

$$NOC(M_a, M_b) = \frac{\sum_{i=1}^{p} \left[\left(\frac{2C_{i,a}C_{i,b}}{C_{i,a}+C_{i,b}} \right) \times S_{D_i}(M_a, M_b) \right]}{\sum_{i=1}^{p} \left(\frac{2C_{i,a}C_{i,b}}{C_{i,a}+C_{i,b}} \right)} \quad (7)$$

This formulation ensures that $NOC(M_a, M_b) \in [0, 1]$, where 1 represents maximal coupling.

We then compute **Average Organizational Coupling (AOC)** for each service:

$$AOC(M_a) = \frac{1}{N-1} \sum_{b \neq a} NOC(M_a, M_b) \quad (8)$$

where N is the total number of microservices. Herein, AOC is used as a normalized service-level aggregation of prior OC rather than as a wholly new coupling construct.

Summary. The proposed metrics capture complementary dimensions of the organizational structure. **PTC (cohesion)** captures the concentration and balance of contributor activity within a service while **AOC (coupling)** captures the extent of contributor overlap across services. Both are derived from version-control data and normalized to $[0, 1]$, enabling direct comparison across services, time periods, and systems.

4 Study Design

To evaluate the proposed metrics, we adopt a two-level empirical design that combines a longitudinal case study with cross-system replication.

4.1 Overview

Our study consists of two complementary components: 1) **Longitudinal case study:** We analyze the Spinnaker microservice platform to examine how cohesion and coupling evolve over time under real organizational and architectural changes. 2) **Cross-system replication:** We apply the same analysis pipeline to multiple open-source microservice systems to evaluate whether observed patterns generalize beyond a single case. The two research questions introduced in Sect. 1 guide the metric definition, longitudinal analysis, and cross-system replication. This design enables both *depth* (through longitudinal analysis) and *breadth* (through replication), mitigating threats to external validity.

4.2 Data Collection and Processing

For each project, we extracted commit histories using the GitHub REST API and mapped changed files to services using project-specific path rules. Files outside identifiable service boundaries, e.g., documentation, shared configuration, or build metadata, were excluded unless unambiguously assignable. Developer identities were normalized by email/name aliases, and automated commits were filtered using author/login patterns.

We then aggregated the commits at the developer-service level and normalized them into fixed time windows. For services with fewer than two contributors in a window, PTC is undefined because no contributor pair exists; such observations are excluded from pairwise correlation analyses. For Spinnaker's repository restructuring, we maintained stable logical service names across pre- and post-restructuring mappings. These steps produce a unified dataset from which PTC and AOC are computed.

4.3 Longitudinal Case Study: Spinnaker

We use Spinnaker as a representative large-scale microservice system to illustrate how the proposed metrics behave under real-world evolution. Spinnaker is an open-source continuous delivery platform composed of 12 loosely coupled microservices. Its long development history, active contributor base, and documented organizational transitions make it well suited for longitudinal analysis.

We analyze commit activity from 2017 to 2025, dividing the data into six-month windows. This allows us to observe how cohesion (PTC) and coupling (AOC) evolve in response to major events, such as governance transition to the Continuous Delivery Foundation (CDF), service lifecycle changes (e.g., deprecation) and repository restructuring (polyrepo to monorepo) [10,25]. We collect commit data for 12 Spinnaker microservices from 2017 to 2025. After filtering automated commits, the dataset contains 16,911 commits, 712 developers, and 87,642 file changes across services.

The Spinnaker case provides detailed insight into how organizational dynamics are reflected in contribution patterns. However, it serves primarily as an *illustrative example* rather than as the sole basis for conclusions.

4.4 Cross-System Replication

To assess generalizability, we replicate the analysis across six additional open-source microservice systems spanning different domains and scales. These projects vary in size, contributor base, and architectural organization, providing a heterogeneous evaluation setting. The selected microservice-based systems are listed in Table 1.

For each system, we apply the same analysis pipeline: 1) Extract commit histories and map contributions to services, 2) Compute developer focus and contribution weights, 3) Calculate PTC for each service, 4) Compute AOC based on cross-service contributions, and 5) Analyze the relationship between cohesion

Table 1. Summary of replicated projects

#	project	#Devs	#commits	Start	End	Days
P1	1-Platform/one-platform	25	908	2020-01-04	2025-11-11	2137
P2	camunda/camunda	428	73870	2016-03-02	2026-03-12	3662
P3	dotnet/eShop-lineage	270	4446	2016-09-06	2026-01-06	3409
P4	geoserver/geoserver-cloud	27	2034	2020-07-09	2026-01-30	2031
P5	ovh/cds	126	5992	2016-10-11	2026-01-20	3388
P6	taskcluster/taskcluster	269	22390	2013-12-31	2026-01-16	4399

and coupling. This replication enables direct comparison across systems and ensures that findings are not artifacts of a single project.

4.5 Analysis Strategy

We analyze the data in three dimensions: 1) **Longitudinal trends:** evolution of cohesion and coupling over time (Spinnaker), 2) **Cross-system variation:** distribution of PTC and AOC across projects, and 3) **Metric relationship:** correlation between cohesion and coupling. In addition, we perform robustness analyses (Sect. 6) to evaluate the sensitivity of results to data perturbations, contributor effects, metric design, and temporal aggregation.

Summary. By combining a detailed longitudinal case study with cross-system replication, our study design provides both contextual understanding and generalizable evidence. This approach enables us to evaluate whether organizational cohesion and coupling represent consistent properties of microservice development, rather than project-specific phenomena.

5 Results

This section presents the empirical findings of our study. We first summarize the longitudinal case study of Spinnaker to illustrate how the proposed metrics behave under real-world evolution. We then present the cross-system replication results, which form the primary basis for our conclusions.

5.1 Longitudinal Case Study: Spinnaker

We analyze the evolution of organizational cohesion (PTC) and coupling (AOC) in Spinnaker across six-month windows from 2017 to 2025 (shown in Fig. 1).

Overall, PTC reflects meaningful organizational dynamics. Early periods exhibit relatively low cohesion in core services and higher cohesion in specialized services, indicating differences in ownership concentration. During governance stabilization (around 20202021), cohesion increases across services, suggesting

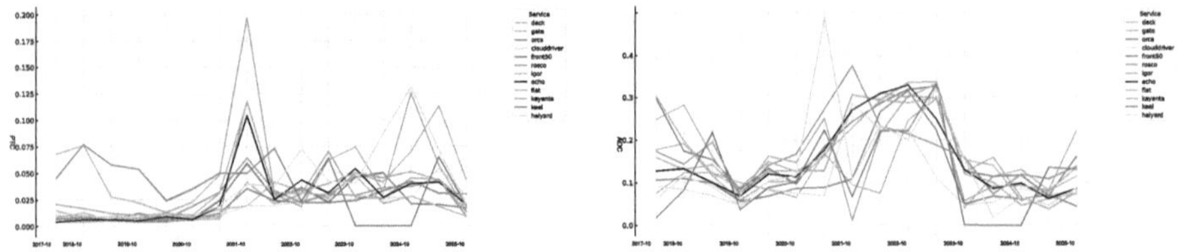

(a) PTC evolution (b) AOC evolution

Fig. 1. Evolution of organizational cohesion (PTC) and coupling (AOC) for 12 Spinnaker microservices across 6-month windows from 10.2017 to 10.2025.

more clearly defined responsibilities. In later periods, cohesion decreases as community participation broadens and cross-service contributions increase. A sharp drop is observed during the transition to a monorepo, where contributors interact across multiple services within the same repository.

The AOC exhibits complementary behavior. The early stages show relatively high coupling due to shared contributors across services. As the system matures, coupling decreases, reflecting clearer ownership boundaries. However, coupling increases again during periods of organizational change and increases sharply in the monorepo phase, where cross-service contributions become more frequent.

Across all periods in the Spinnaker case, the relationship between PTC and AOC remains weak. The longitudinal Spinnaker-only correlation is small (Pearson $r \approx 0.10$, Spearman $\rho \approx 0.15$), indicating no strong linear or monotonic association within this case. We interpret this result as case-specific evidence that cohesion and coupling capture different temporal patterns in Spinnaker, rather than as evidence of statistical independence.

These results demonstrate that the proposed metrics capture meaningful temporal patterns. However, conclusions based on a single system may be limited; therefore, we turn to cross-system replication.

5.2 Cross-System Replication

To assess generalizability, we analyze six additional microservice systems using the same methodology. Each observation corresponds to a service within a project.

Organizational Cohesion Across Systems. Figure 2a shows the distribution of PTC values across projects. Cohesion varies moderately between systems, with some projects showing higher median values, indicating more concentrated contributor activity, and others showing lower values, reflecting more distributed participation. Despite these differences, cohesion values remain within a relatively bounded range across projects. This suggests that organizational focus is a stable property of microservice systems, even in varying development contexts.

Although PTC is bounded in $[0, 1]$, the empirical values are small because the pairwise focus metric averages are weighted by the prominence of the contribution. Therefore, we interpret PTC comparatively rather than as an absolute percentage. E.g., within the same project, a service around 0.04 reflects more concentrated and balanced ownership than one around 0.01, while low values indicate more diffuse or cross-service contribution patterns.

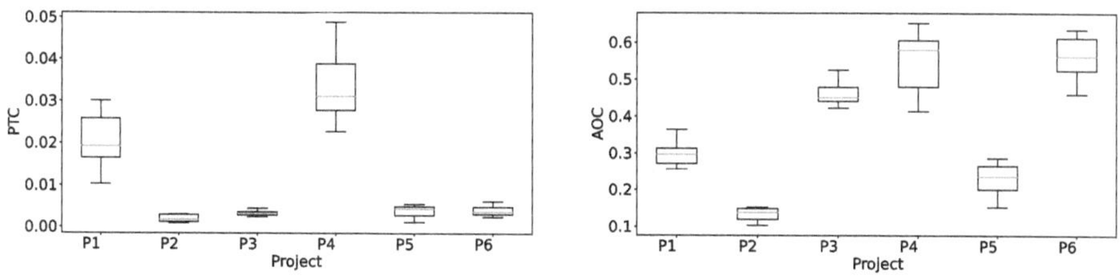

(a) PTC distribution by project

(b) AOC distribution by project

Fig. 2. Distribution of organizational cohesion (PTC) and coupling (AOC) across projects.

Organizational Coupling Across Systems. Figure 2b presents the distribution of the AOC values. In contrast to cohesion, coupling exhibits substantial variability across systems. Some projects show high coupling, indicating strong cross-service contributor overlap, while others display low coupling, reflecting clearer separation of service ownership. This variation suggests that coupling is highly context-dependent, influenced by factors such as architectural design, contributor practices, and repository organization.

Relationship Between Cohesion and Coupling. Figure 3 shows the relationship between PTC and AOC across all services and projects. No clear global trend is observed. Instead, services form project-specific clusters, and both high and low cohesion values are associated with a wide range of coupling levels.

This pattern is consistent with the Spinnaker case study in showing no strong global trend. However, the pooled cross-system association differs from the Spinnaker-only estimate in both sign and magnitude. In the pooled baseline analysis reported later in Table 2, the Pearson correlation is weakly negative ($r = -0.233$, 95% CI $[-0.30, -0.16]$, $p < 0.001$), while the rank correlation is close to zero ($\rho = -0.072$). Thus, the evidence does not show the absence of any relationship; rather, it indicates a small and aggregation-sensitive association between PTC and AOC.

Summary of Replication Findings. The replication demonstrates that: 1) Organizational cohesion varies moderately across systems, while coupling varies substantially; 2) Microservice systems exhibit diverse organizational structures,

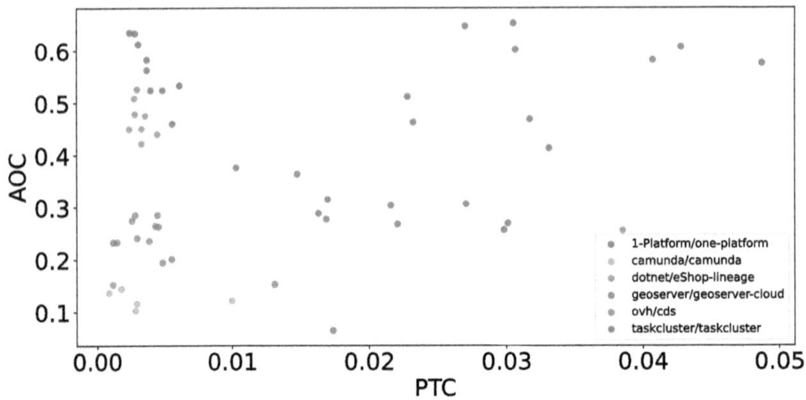

Fig. 3. PTC vs AOC across all projects.

ranging from tightly coupled to highly decoupled ecosystems; 3) The relationship between cohesion and coupling is consistently weak across projects.

These results suggest that cohesion and coupling should be analyzed as separate organizational dimensions rather than as opposite ends of a single continuum.

6 Robustness Analysis

To assess the reliability of our findings, we evaluate robustness along four dimensions: data perturbations, contributor effects, metric formulation, and temporal aggregation.

6.1 Data Robustness

Regarding the effect of large commits, we remove the top 5% of commits by size (P95 threshold) to exclude large refactorings and bulk changes. PTC and AOC distributions remain stable, with only minor variance reduction. The correlation between cohesion and coupling remains weak. In summary, the result is robust to commit size.

Furthermore, regarding the effect of dominant contributors, we remove the top 5% of contributors by activity to assess the impact of core maintainers. Absolute values decrease slightly, but distributions and correlations remain consistent. In summary, the result is not driven by dominant contributors.

6.2 Metric Robustness

We test alternative formulations of PTC by varying connection intensity, weighting, and normalization. Although absolute values shift slightly, relative rankings and correlations remain stable across variants. In summary, the findings are not sensitive to the metric design.

6.3 Cross-Condition Stability

Across all robustness conditions described above, three consistent properties are observed: 1) The distributions of PTC and AOC remain stable under data filtering and metric variation; 2) The relative ordering of services and projects is preserved; 3) The correlation between cohesion and coupling is consistently weak. These results indicate that the findings are robust to both data-level noise and metric formulation choices.

6.4 Temporal Sensitivity Analysis

We compare overlapping windows (baseline) with non-overlapping 180-day windows. The latter increases variance and reduces sample size, leading to more variable correlations. However, no consistent relationship emerges between cohesion and coupling.

Correlation remains weak overall, though more unstable under non-overlapping windows (e.g., $r = 0.259$, 95% CI $[0.00, 0.48]$, $p \approx 0.05$). The wider confidence interval indicates reduced precision due to the smaller sample size and the absence of temporal smoothing. Therefore, the temporal analysis does not support a stable positive or negative relationship between PTC and AOC; instead, it shows that the estimated association is sensitive to temporal aggregation.

6.5 Overall Robustness Interpretation

As shown in Table 2, the non-overlapping configuration yields a wider confidence interval and borderline statistical significance, reflecting increased variability due to reduced sample size and the absence of temporal smoothing.

Table 2. Robustness summary of PTC-AOC correlation across conditions.

Condition	n	r	95% CI (r)	p-value	ρ	Δr	$\Delta\rho$
Baseline	745	-0.233	[−0.30, −0.16]	< 0.001	−0.072	0.000	0.000
Remove large commits (P95)	739	−0.226	[−0.29, −0.15]	< 0.001	−0.063	0.007	0.008
Remove top contributors (top 5%)	662	−0.171	[−0.24, −0.10]	< 0.001	0.019	0.063	0.090
Non overlapping windows (180d/180d)	58	0.259	[0.00, 0.48]	0.05	0.267	0.492	0.339

Taken together, the robustness analyses demonstrate that: 1) the results are not sensitive to large commits or extreme contribution patterns; 2) the findings are not driven by a small number of highly active contributors; 3) the observed association remains small under alternative metric formulations; and 4) the estimated correlation varies under temporal re-aggregation. The baseline pooled analysis shows a weak but statistically significant negative Pearson correlation, whereas Spearman's $\rho = -0.072$ indicates almost no monotonic association.

Therefore, the results should be interpreted as evidence that PTC and AOC are only weakly associated and provide non-redundant information, not as evidence that they are statistically independent.

These findings provide strong evidence that the observed relationship between organizational cohesion and coupling reflects a structural property of developer behavior in microservice systems, rather than a consequence of measurement artifacts or methodological choices.

In summary, the robustness analysis confirms that the proposed metrics and empirical findings are stable under several validation conditions. In particular, the small magnitude of the PTC-AOC association persists under data perturbations and metric variations, while temporal re-aggregation affects the estimated sign and magnitude. This supports the conclusion that cohesion and coupling should be analyzed as distinct organizational dimensions, while avoiding the stronger claim that they are statistically independent.

7 Discussion

This study introduces Pairwise Team Cohesion (PTC) as a quantitative measure of organizational cohesion in microservice systems and evaluates it through a longitudinal case study and cross-system replication. The results consistently show that PTC captures meaningful patterns of contributor focus and that cohesion and coupling represent distinct dimensions of socio-technical organization. We interpret PTC and AOC as behavioral proxies for contribution-based ownership concentration and cross-service developer overlap. Longitudinal patterns, robustness checks, and cross-system replication support their stability, but not full construct validation against formal team assignments or communication data.

7.1 Organizational Cohesion as Behavioral Alignment (RQ1)

Across both the Spinnaker case and replicated systems, PTC reflects the concentration and stability of contributor activity within service boundaries. Cohesion increases during periods of stabilized ownership and decreases when participation becomes more distributed, indicating sensitivity to changes in team structure and coordination. These patterns suggest that organizational cohesion can be operationalized as behavioral alignment between contributors and service boundaries, observable through contribution distributions. Although PTC does not capture communication or intent, it provides a scalable proxy for ownership concentration and participation balance. In this sense, cohesion reflects how consistently contributors focus their work within a service, rather than how they coordinate internally.

7.2 Cohesion and Coupling as Distinct Dimensions (RQ2)

A central finding of this study is that the relationship between cohesion (PTC) and coupling (AOC) is weak and aggregation-sensitive. In the longitudinal Spinnaker case, the association is small and positive (Pearson $r \approx 0.10$, Spearman

$\rho \approx 0.15$). In the pooled cross-system baseline analysis, the Pearson correlation is weakly negative ($r = -0.233$, 95% CI $[-0.30, -0.16]$, $p < 0.001$), while the Spearman correlation is close to zero ($\rho = -0.072$). These results do not establish statistical independence. Instead, they indicate that PTC and AOC provide non-redundant views of organizational structure: cohesion captures intra-service concentration of effort, whereas coupling reflects cross-service contributor overlap. This reframes the classical "high cohesion, low coupling" principle at the organizational level as a two-dimensional diagnostic space rather than a single inverse relationship. This interpretation is also consistent with recent evidence that organizational coupling can precede architectural degradation signals, suggesting that AOC should be read not only as a coordination indicator, but also as a potential early warning signal for architectural risk [20].

7.3 Implication

The weak and aggregation-sensitive association between cohesion and coupling has direct implications for the management of microservice organizations. PTC and AOC provide complementary diagnostic signals. PTC (cohesion) helps identify ownership concentration, detect fragmentation of responsibility, and monitor the effects of organizational changes. AOC (coupling) captures cross-team dependencies and coordination load arising from shared contributors.

Because these dimensions are non-redundant and only weakly associated, relying on a single metric can be misleading. For example, a highly cohesive service can require substantial cross-team coordination, while a loosely coupled system may suffer from fragmented ownership. Effective organizational design therefore requires joint consideration of cohesion and coupling, rather than optimizing for one in isolation.

7.4 Limitation and Future Work

PTC is derived from version-control data and captures observable contribution behavior rather than the full spectrum of collaboration. It does not account for communication, code review interactions, or informal coordination mechanisms, and may be influenced by development practices such as commit granularity or repository structure.

Future work should extend this approach by integrating additional data sources (e.g., pull requests, issue discussions, communication logs) to better capture coordination dynamics. Another direction is to examine how different cohesioncoupling configurations relate to software outcomes such as quality, delivery performance, and system evolution, enabling more prescriptive guidance for organizational design. This study does not test whether PTC/AOC align with structural service cohesion or technical coupling of the same services. Therefore, our conclusions are limited to the contribution-based organizational structure. Future work should compare PTC/AOC with service-level structural cohesion and technical coupling to determine whether organizational and architectural modularity evolve together or diverge. Beyond passive diagnosis, recent work also suggests that organizational cohesion and coupling metrics can be integrated into gamified architectural governance mechanisms to actively encourage service-boundary-respecting developer behavior [16].

8 Threats to Validity

We discuss threats to validity following the classification of Wohlin et al. [27], covering internal, external, construct, and conclusion validity.

Regarding internal validity, this study is observational and does not establish causal relationships between organizational events and changes in cohesion or coupling. Although variations in PTC and AOC align with documented milestones (e.g., governance stabilization and repository restructuring), they may also be influenced by unobserved factors such as contributor turnover, policy changes, or CI/CD workflow evolution. To mitigate this risk, we interpret results conservatively and triangulate metric trends with publicly available project artifacts (e.g., governance documentation and release notes). Both metrics are computed from the same dataset and time windows, ensuring consistency in measurement. Nevertheless, findings should be interpreted as correlational rather than causal.

Regarding external validity, the primary case study (Spinnaker) represents a large, mature open-source system with hybrid governance, which may limit generalizability to smaller or purely industrial projects. We address this through replication across multiple microservice systems with different sizes and contribution structures. Therefore, generalization should focus on relative patterns rather than fixed numeric thresholds.

Regarding construct validity, PTC and AOC capture version-control activity rather than formal team structure or the full spectrum of collaboration. They do not account for informal coordination mechanisms, e.g., discussions, code reviews, or meetings, and commit activity itself may be influenced by workflow practices, tooling, or repository structure. Hence, we reduce bias by filtering identifiable automated commits and testing sensitivity to large commits, dominant contributors, and metric variants. Thus, PTC should be interpreted as contribution-based cohesion, not complete team cohesion.

Regarding conclusion validity, the study uses a longitudinal multi-project dataset and reports both Pearson and Spearman correlations. Robustness analyses further confirm that the weak relationship between cohesion and coupling persists under data filtering, metric variations, and temporal aggregation strategies. However, non-overlapping windows yield smaller samples and wider confidence intervals, so exact effect sizes remain sensitive to temporal granularity.

9 Conclusion

This study introduces Pairwise Team Cohesion (PTC) as a quantitative metric for assessing organizational cohesion in microservice systems and evaluates it through a longitudinal case study combined with cross-system replication and robustness analyses. The results show that PTC captures the concentration and stability of contributor activity within service boundaries and responds systematically to organizational and architectural changes. Across the analyzed systems and robustness conditions, the relationship between cohesion (PTC) and organizational coupling (AOC) remains weak, although its sign and magnitude vary with the level of aggregation. The Spinnaker-only longitudinal analysis shows a small positive association, whereas the pooled baseline analysis shows a weak but statistically significant negative Pearson correlation and an almost zero Spearman correlation. These results indicate that PTC and AOC capture distinct, non-redundant aspects of socio-technical organization rather than a single inverse cohesion–coupling trade-off. This reframes the classical "high cohesion, low coupling" principle as a two-dimensional diagnostic space and highlights the need to evaluate internal team focus and cross-service interaction separately.

References

1. Al Dallal, J., Briand, L.C.: A precise method-method interaction based cohesion metric for object-oriented classes. ACM Trans. Softw. Eng. Methodol. (TOSEM) **21**(2), 1–34 (2012)
2. Amoroso d'Aragona, D., Li, X., Cerny, T., Janes, A., Lenarduzzi, V., Taibi, D.: One microservice per developer: is this the trend in OSS? In: European Conference on Service-Oriented and Cloud Computing, pp. 19–34. Springer, Heidelberg (2023). https://doi.org/10.1007/978-3-031-46235-1_2
3. Cataldo, M., Herbsleb, J.D., Carley, K.M.: Socio-technical congruence: a framework for assessing the impact of technical and work dependencies on software development productivity. In: Proceedings of the Second ACM-IEEE International Symposium on Empirical Software Engineering and Measurement, pp. 2–11 (2008)
4. Chidamber, S.R., Kemerer, C.F.: Towards a metrics suite for object oriented design. In: Conference Proceedings on Object-Oriented Programming Systems, Languages, and Applications, pp. 197–211 (1991)
5. Chidamber, S.R., Kemerer, C.F.: A metrics suite for object oriented design. IEEE Trans. Softw. Eng. **20**(6), 476–493 (1994)
6. Conway, M.E.: How do committees invent. Datamation **14**(4), 28–31 (1968)
7. Counsell, S., Swift, S., Crampton, J.: The interpretation and utility of three cohesion metrics for object-oriented design. ACM Trans. Softw. Eng. Methodol. (TOSEM) **15**(2), 123–149 (2006)
8. Dragoni, N., et al.: Microservices: yesterday, today, and tomorrow. In: Present and Ulterior Software Engineering, pp. 195–216 (2017)
9. Fernández, L., Peña, R.: A sensitive metric of class cohesion. Inf. Theories Appl. **13**, 82–91 (2006)
10. Glover, A.: Spinnaker sets sail to the continuous delivery foundation (2019). https://netflixtechblog.com/spinnaker-sets-sail-to-the-continuous-delivery-foundation-e81cd2cbbfeb. Accessed 19 Oct 2025
11. Henderson-Sellers, B.: Object-Oriented Metrics: Measures of Complexity. Prentice-Hall Inc., Upper Saddle River (1995)
12. Herbsleb, J.D., Grinter, R.E.: Splitting the organization and integrating the code: Conway's law revisited. In: Proceedings of the 21st International Conference on Software Engineering, pp. 85–95 (1999)

13. Hitz, M., Montazeri, B.: Measuring coupling and cohesion in object-oriented systems. In: The International Symposium on Applied Corporate Computing (1995)
14. Lewis, J., Fowler, M.: Microservices: a definition of this new architectural term (2014). http://martinfowler.com/articles/microservices.html
15. Li, W., Henry, S.: Maintenance metrics for the object oriented paradigm. In: Proceedings First International Software Metrics Symposium, pp. 52–60. IEEE (1993)
16. Li, X.: Gamifying architectural governance to reduce organizational coupling in microservice systems. In: Proceedings of the 5th Workshop on Gamification in Software Development, Verification, and Validation (Gamify2026). ACM (2026). arXiv:2604.22454
17. Li, X., d'Aragona, D.A., Cerny, T., Lenarduzzi, V., Taibi, D., Janes, A.: Exploring microservice ownership and organizational coupling in open-source projects: an empirical study. Computing **107**(4), 1–35 (2025)
18. Li, X., d'Aragona, D.A., Taibi, D.: Evaluating microservice organizational coupling based on cross-service contribution. In: International Conference on Product-Focused Software Process Improvement, pp. 435–450. Springer, Heidelberg (2023). https://doi.org/10.1007/978-3-031-49266-2_30
19. Li, X., Mani, N., Rodriguez, J.S., Cerny, T.: Key developer roles and organizational coupling in microservices: a longitudinal analysis. In: Proceedings of the 30th International Conference on Evaluation and Assessment in Software Engineering (EASE'26). ACM (2026). arXiv:2604.25804
20. Mani, N., Sosa, J., Li, X., Cerny, T.: Organizational coupling as a leading indicator of microservice architecture degradation. In: 2026 IEEE International Conference on Software Architecture (ICSA'26). IEEE (2026)
21. Moreira, M.G., De França, B.B.N.: Analysis of microservice evolution using cohesion metrics. In: Proceedings of the 16th Brazilian Symposium on Software Components, Architectures, and Reuse, pp. 40–49 (2022)
22. Newman, S.: Building Microservices: Designing Fine-Grained Systems. O'Reilly Media, Inc., Newton (2021)
23. Parnas, D.L.: On the criteria to be used in decomposing systems into modules. Commun. ACM **15**(12), 1053–1058 (1972)
24. Shim, B., Choue, S., Kim, S., Park, S.: A design quality model for service-oriented architecture. In: 15th Asia-Pacific Software Engineering Conference, pp. 403–410. IEEE (2008)
25. Spinnaker Community: Spinnaker governance repository (2020). https://github.com/spinnaker/governance. Accessed 19 Oct 2025
26. Stevens, W.P., Myers, G.J., Constantine, L.L.: Structured design. IBM Syst. J. **13**(2), 115–139 (1974)
27. Wohlin, C., Runeson, P., Höst, M., Ohlsson, M.C., Regnell, B., Wesslén, A.: Experimentation in Software Engineering, vol. 236. Springer, Heidelberg (2012). https://doi.org/10.1007/978-3-662-69306-3
28. Yourdon, E., Constantine, L.L.: Structured Design: Fundamentals of a Discipline of Computer Program and Systems Design. Prentice-Hall, Inc., Upper Sddle River (1979)

Women's Participation in Student Software Teams: A Replication Study

Anca Vasilescu[1(✉)], Simona Motogna[2], and Dan Mircea Suciu[2]

[1] Transilvania University of Braşov, Braşov, Romania
avasilescu@unitbv.ro
[2] Babes-Bolyai University, Cluj-Napoca, Romania
{simona.motogna,dan.suciu}@ubbcluj.ro

Abstract. Gender imbalance remains a persistent concern in software engineering. This study presents a contextual replication of a prior empirical investigation on gender dynamics in student software engineering teams, conducted in a different educational and societal context. The results reinforce the original findings, providing further evidence that the gender gap continues to be a relevant issue. Our analysis indicates that role distribution within teams is evolving, with women tending to assume or prefer certain roles. The findings also emphasize the influence of different factors (such as society, culture or education), underscoring the importance of context-aware interventions. By contributing to the body of replication studies in software engineering, this work strengthens confidence in existing evidence while pointing to the need for sustained efforts to promote gender balance.

Keywords: software development teams · software engineering education · gender diversity · empirical study

1 Introduction

The software engineering research community has increasingly recognized that human and social factors play a critical role in both software processes and software products [5]. While the technical aspects remain essential, the latest research contributions reported that diversity, inclusion, and equitable participation are vital to software development [1]. Education plays a central role, and exploring and addressing gender gaps in Software Engineering (SE) education is part of the solution for the industry.

The study [10] provides a recent empirical investigation into how gender shapes role assignment and participation patterns in student software development teams. This work employs cross-sectional data drawn from a software engineering course to examine how women are distributed across various roles that require different technical backgrounds.

Empirical replication is a key method extensively used in software engineering where contextual and human factors affect outcomes [15,27]. Replication

C. Berger and V. Klös (Eds.): SEAA 2026, LNCS 16864, pp. 85–100, 2027.
https://doi.org/10.1007/978-3-032-36587-3_7

studies assess the robustness and generalizability of original findings and build confidence in the validity of conclusions across different cohorts, institutions, and samples. In gender and diversity research, it clarifies whether observed patterns persist across diverse environments and improve trust in the results. Most of this type of studies are done in isolation, as case studies in one or two universities or country [8,20], and as a consequence, their findings are limited. By replicating a previous research and considering a different country, institution, a different course and different students, we create the context necessary to validate and generalize the findings.

Our objective is to replicate the original study [10] to verify whether the reported participation patterns persist across different educational contexts, team formation strategies, and course settings. We also seek to identify contextual factors that might influence the results. We follow the methodology according to recommendations [25] and compare our findings with the original contribution.

2 Background

The gender gap in IT has been widely acknowledged in Europe and worldwide [16], as in Europe only 18% of the specialists in IT and 20% of graduates in ICT are women. The "Women in Digital" European policy [12] highlighted and defined actions across the entire pipeline, from access to ICT education for girls to sustaining educational paths for female students, and to supporting women in digital careers. The focus of our study is on initiatives and interventions for female students in Software Engineering education. Several studies have reported successful results in improving gender representation in SE [11,24], while other studies have identified several barriers to closing this gender gap [3,18,23], including stereotypes, misconceptions about the field, and a lack of support in early education and from family.

Thus, there is still an urgent need to reveal ways to achieve gender balance in the Software Engineering domain, and education represents an important milestone.

To address this problem, empirical methods [25] are best suited, as they enable the investigation of human factors in SE. Using quantitative analysis (such as case studies, descriptive and inferential statistics) and qualitative analysis (such as surveys, interviews, or focus groups), as well as other methods, such as replication or systematic literature review, has advanced the body of knowledge on this topic.

2.1 Related Work

Our study lies at the intersection of gender-related challenges in computing and, on the other hand, software engineering education and team-based courses as contexts for observing participation and roles. We reviewed relevant work and positioned our contextual replication accordingly.

Gender Gap in Computing Education and its Educational Drivers. Women's participation in computing is shaped by cumulative factors rather than a single barrier. Main and Schimpf identify access, attitudes, context, and psychosocial factors (e.g., belonging, self-efficacy) as key influences [21], which also help explain role distribution and engagement in student teams.

Stereotypes can lead capable students to avoid technical paths. Boston and Cimpian link stereotypes about women's abilities and STEM culture to reduced confidence, belonging, and engagement [7], helping explain gendered role allocation in team settings.

Several studies highlight barriers rooted in the socio-cultural context and prior experience. Evidence from a Danish case study and an educational initiative called Czechitas highlights differences in prior exposure, biased expectations, and the importance of targeted support [6, 8], with implications for the uptake of roles in student teams.

Gender Issues in Software Engineering Education and Team-Based Project Courses. Project-based courses provide a suitable setting for studying team processes and gender dynamics. Evidence suggests that mixed-gender teams may be more effective [22], highlighting the need to examine role distribution alongside participation.

Research on evaluation in team settings shows that while peer assessments are similar for women and men, women tend to rate themselves lower [4]. This is relevant to studies that rely on self-reported roles, as contributions may be reported differently due to confidence and team dynamics.

Several studies propose integrating better gender awareness into software engineering curricula. Prior work reports longitudinal gender mainstreaming efforts [14], curriculum-level proposals [2], and validated instruments for assessing students' gender perspectives [13]. While not directly addressing role allocation, these contributions highlight the growing emphasis on gender awareness in software engineering education.

The above results highlight persistent underrepresentation and systemic barriers in computing education, the relevance of team-based software engineering courses for examining participation and roles, and the need for context-aware interpretations of gender-related findings. However, empirical results in this area remain highly context-dependent, as factors such as course design, team formation practices, mentoring structures, institutional culture, and societal norms can shape both participation and role allocation.

Against this background, replication is particularly valuable. By conducting a contextual replication of an existing study in a different educational and societal setting, we aim to assess which findings appear robust and which may be contingent on local conditions.

3 Research Design

We designed our research study as an exact, extended and external replication, following the classification given in [16]. It is regarded as exact since we consider the same research questions and methodology, and is extended because we posed one additional research question compared to the original study. This study is external because the entire replication team is independent, and the data used is completely distinct.

We formulate the same hypothesis as the original study, in terms of research questions (RQ1 to RQ3), and we additionally explore which aspects are influenced by societal differences (RQ4):

- **RQ1:** Is there a relation between gender ratio and technical roles distribution in project teams?
- **RQ2:** Is there a relation between female leadership and technical roles distribution in project teams?
- **RQ3:** Does the female role distribution vary in time?
- **RQ4:** Which are the gender indicators influenced by societal differences?

3.1 Replicated Study

In this section, we briefly describe the original study [10] that represents the baseline of this replication.

The original paper proposed a cross-sectional study including 628 participants, of which 183 are women, divided into 85 teams, enrolled in 7 iterations of a bachelor-level project course in collaboration with industry.

Part of the preprocessing of the dataset [9], roles in the teams were categorised into: highly technical (Tech+), less technical (Tech–) and non-technical (Non-Tech). Statistical analysis, including Binary and Multinomial Logistic Regressions, using IBM SPSS[1] was used to provide results for the following research questions, formulated as hypotheses:

H_1 Women in teams with a lower gender ratio (fewer women) take on highly specialised technical roles less often than their peers;
H_2 The presence of a woman in a leadership position (team leader) affects the likelihood of women taking on highly specialised technical roles;
H_3 The distribution of roles taken on by women in software development teams varies across different student cohorts.

The results of the study revealed the following conclusions.

Partial confirmation of H_1: women seem less attracted to highly technical roles (Tech+), but the gender distribution within the team does not influence this.

Rejection of H_2: leadership (a female team leader) does not influence the likelihood of women taking highly specialised technical roles.

Partial support for H_3: for roles such as Scrum Master and Report Manager, the distribution of women varies across cohorts, whereas roles like architect or developer show declining male participation, rather than increased female engagement. Other roles do not show significant variance.

The study reached three important takeaways:

[1] https://www.ibm.com/products/spss.

Gender Dynamics in Software Development is Changing: The gender diversity in teams is a must. Even if women are less attracted to highly technical roles on teams, roles such as Scrum Master draw their interest.

Leadership Impact Should be Re-evaluated: Women's leadership, even if present in a significant number (25%), does not assure the frame of women accepting more technical roles, which suggests that women in leadership positions are not enough to promote gender balance; it follows that complementary supporting actions are needed.

Role Diversification: A positive trend has been identified among roles undertaken by women, suggesting that more diverse positions could attract women.

3.2 Replication Details

Our replication study has the following goals:

i) *to generalise the results:* to see if the original findings are true for a different context;
ii) *to increase confidence in results*: we intend to either strengthen the empirical evidence base, making results more trustworthy or to contradict the original findings and
iii) *to identify contextual factors* that can explain differences in the results (if they exist). We consider that providing a different perspective will enable generalizability and confidence.

Table 1. Details about initial and replication studies

	Initial study	Replication study
Participants	Bachelor stud.	Bachelor stud.
No	628 (183 w)	1781 (584 w)
Cohorts	7	5
Country	Norway	Romania
RQs	RQ_1, RQ_2, RQ_3	RQ_1, RQ_2, RQ_3, RQ_4
Method	regression	regression

Table 1 summarises the key details of the original study and our replication. The number of cohorts in our study is less than in the original one, but the number of participants is far greater (1781 compared to 628). The percentage of female students is comparable, with a slightly better participation in our study: 32.7% compared to 29.1% in the original study.

We took advantage of the significant similarity in how the two courses are conducted, applying a project-based approach and direct industry interaction.

We followed a similar procedure by labelling data collected from the project documentation, with the difference from the original study being that all roles were labeled into two clusters, namely *tech+* and *tech–*, without the "NonTech" level. The specificity of our dataset is given by the fact that the roles are strongly positioned as positive or negative, with no evidence for sustaining a non-technical qualification.

We applied the same investigation method: first, we replicated the original study to validate our approach, then we performed the analysis on our data.

3.3 Context of Study

The study is conducted in the *Team Project* course at Babeş-Bolyai University, a core third-year, project-based software engineering course that has been delivered annually since 2017. Over 14 weeks, teams of 6 to 12 students develop real-world software applications, which form the primary basis for assessment.

The course involves industry mentors who support teams throughout the project lifecycle, facilitate collaboration, and may act as stakeholders. Each mentor supervises two to three teams, out of 38 to 50 teams per year.

Although the course has been delivered since 2017, this study considers only the most recent five academic years, as consistent data on team structure and composition are available only for this period. Some iterations were affected by pandemic-related restrictions, requiring fully online collaboration, while others were conducted on-site.

3.4 Dataset

For the purposes of the present study, we focused on the characteristics of team composition within the Team Project course, specifically on the gender distribution and the functional roles assumed by students within each team. In particular, we analysed the proportion of team members by gender, as well as the number of students assigned to one of two role categories: *tech+* and *tech–*.

Table 2 and Table 3 provide dataset overviews from different perspectives.

Table 2. Team participation and gender distribution (2020–2024)

Year	Teams	Men (%)	Women (%)	M+W
2020	36	212 (69.06%)	95 (30.94%)	307
2021	37	277 (72.51%)	105 (27.49%)	382
2022	40	203 (61.33%)	128 (38.67%)	331
2023	42	241 (64.61%)	132 (35.39%)	373
2024	47	264 (68.04%)	124 (31.96%)	388
TOTAL	202	1197 (67.21%)	584 (32.79%)	1781

Table 3. Distinct team roles and their technical level and distribution

	Role	Tech level	Number
1	Analyst & Designer	*tech+*	55
2	Backend Developer	*tech+*	508
3	Developer	*tech+*	135
4	Frontend Developer	*tech–*	464
5	Full-stack Developer	*tech+*	205
6	Product Manager	*tech–*	49
7	Special Developer	*tech+*	82
8	Team Leader	*tech–*	209
9	Tester	*tech–*	74
	TOTAL		1781

At the beginning of the course, each team explicitly defined its internal structure by assigning roles and responsibilities to all team members. This structure was reviewed and validated by the assigned industry mentor and remained unchanged throughout the semester until the final project presentations and evaluations.

The dataset was constructed using self-reported information provided by students at the start of each course iteration. This information included demographic data (gender) and the functional roles each student declared within their team. The data was collected with explicit consent of the students, and the primary data was duplicated, anonymized and only afterwards used for this study.

Based on these role descriptions, with respect to the role organisation conducted in the replicated study [10] from both research and software development experts' perspective, we mapped individual roles into the two predefined categories as follows:

(1) roles involving partial technical responsibility or process facilitation, experts' perspective such as frontend developer, team leader, project and product manager, or tester, were grouped under the *tech–* category and
(2) roles requiring advanced technical involvement, such as analyst, designer, and developer, including backend, full-stack, and specialised developers, were classified as *tech+*.

Although it is questionable if the frontend developer role or tester is *tech-* or *tech+*, and it depends very much on the tasks assumed in the project, the approach that we took in this study was to preserve the classification of roles as it was in the original study.

It is also of interest to present in Table 4 the dataset details related to women's leadership positions within their teams.

Table 4. Distribution of Team Leader role based on gender

Gender	Team Leader (%)	All students
Men	136 (11.36%)	1197
Women	73 (12.50%)	584
TOTAL	209 (11.73%)	1781

Using this classification scheme, a total of 1781 students who participated in the *Team Project* course over five consecutive academic years (from October 2020 to June 2025) were included in the analysis.

4 Results

Research Question RQ1. We used a binary logistic regression to address RQ1 regarding the relation between the gender ratio (given by the percentage of women in each team) and the distribution of technical roles across project teams. The binary model is supported by clustering all roles into *tech−* or *tech+*, and the independent variables were *gender* (categorical, with value 0 for man and 1 for woman), *gender_ratio* and their product, *gender_ratio_interaction*.

The results of the χ^2-test ($\chi^2 = 32.563$, $df = 3$, $p < 0.001$) indicate a statistically significant model, with predictors appropriately chosen to investigate the forecast of the likelihood of taking on *tech+*, highly technical roles in teams (Analyst & Designer, Backend Developer, Developer, Full-stack Developer, or Special Developer).

Table 5 summarises the results, revealing how, beyond chance, the prediction of a highly technical role is improved by each of the independent variables, holding other variables constant.

Table 5. Binary Logistic Regression Model Summary for RQ1

Variable	B	S.E.	df	Sig.	Exp(B)
gender (CAT)	−1.208	0.245	1	0.000	0.299
gender_ratio	−0.099	0.305	1	0.745	0.906
gender_ratio_interaction	1.642	0.536	1	0.002	5.163

The variable *gender* ($B = -1.208$, $Sig. = 0.000$, $Exp(B) = 0.299$) emerged as a significant predictor of *tech+* role allocation, while the negative coefficient (B = -1.208) indicates that women had significantly lower odds of occupying highly technical roles compared to men. The odds ratio ($Exp(B) = 0.299$) suggests that women's odds of being in a *tech+* role were approximately 70% lower than those of men. The *gender_ratio* alone was not a significant predictor, indicating that the proportion of women on a team does not independently predict whether an individual takes on a highly technical role ($B = -0.099$, $p = 0.745$). With a significance value of 0.002 less than 0.05 set as the alpha value ($B = 1.642$, $Sig. = 0.002$, $Exp(B) = 5.163$), *gender_ratio_interaction* is also a statistically significant predictor in itself, indicating that the effect of gender on highly technical role allocation varies with the team's gender composition - the greater the percentage of women in a team, the narrower the gender gap in the likelihood of taking on highly technical roles.

In conclusion, the analysis results sustain the RQ1, proving that the gender ratio significantly influences the likelihood of a woman being in a *tech+* role, in favour of women - the more women in the team, the higher likelihood for women to take on highly technical roles like Analyst & Designer, Developer, Backend Developer, Full-stack Developer or Special Developer.

Research Question RQ2. We applied a binary logistic regression to answer RQ2 by examining whether having a woman in the Team Leader position affects the likelihood that female students will take the high technical role on those teams. We defined two variables in scope: *group_woman_leader* to identify groups led by a woman, and its interaction with the given *gender* variable.

As a descriptive result, we note that of the 202 groups, a third had a woman in the position of Team Leader, and, of these, 92.65% also had at least one other woman in the group. Statistically, the returned coefficients ($\chi^2 = 30.840$, $df = 3$, $p < 0.001$) provide strong evidence that the model significantly improves the prediction of the technical level.

Table 6 summarises the regression analysis, with a significant negative interaction given by the independent variable *gender_gwl_interaction* for the interaction between *gender* and *group_woman_leader* ($B = -0.520$, $Sig. = 0.015$, $Exp(B) = 0.595$) and a reliable decreasing effect (95%CI [0.391, 0.904]). It follows that, having a woman in a leadership position, the log-odds for women decrease relative to men, meaning that women's likelihood of choosing a high technical level drops by about 40% compared to men's.

Table 6. Binary Logistic Regression Model Summary for RQ2

Variable	B	S.E.	df	Sig.	Exp(B)
gender (CAT)	–0.202	0.133	1	0.130	0.817
gender_woman_leader	–0.031	0.133	1	0.817	0.970
gender_gwl_interaction	–0.520	0.214	1	0.015	0.595

Overall, the analysis driven by RQ2 suggests that women are not necessarily attracted by a woman in a leadership position to take on higher tech-level roles.

Research Question RQ3. We performed a multinomial regression analysis to test **RQ3** with *role* as the dependent variable. Although the overall regression model is statistically significant ($\chi^2 = 81.589$, $df = 24$, $p < 0.001$), the independent variables generally do not reach statistical significance, revealing that the model does not provide strong statistical evidence that the distribution of roles among female students changes significantly over time. Even with non-significant terms, the results accurately convey the replicated approach and serve as inputs to support the RQ4 conclusions in terms of cultural differences.

Table 7 summarises the parameter estimates for the interaction between *gender* and *year* across different roles, with the Team Leader role as the baseline. A marginally significant result appears for the *Developer* role ($B = -0.401$, *Sig.* = 0.025, $Exp(B) = 0.670$), but the B sign and the corresponding odds ratio indicate that the probability of female students choosing a *Developer* role is approximately 33% lower than that of male students.

Table 7. Parameter estimates for *gender_year_interaction* across different roles

role	B	S.E.	df	Sig.	Exp(B)
Analyst & Designer	0.372	0.299	1	0.213	1.451
Backend Developer	–0.152	0.128	1	0.236	0.859
Developer	–0.401	0.179	1	0.025	0.670
Frontend Developer	–0.041	0.127	1	0.745	0.960
Full-stack Developer	–0.076	0.154	1	0.623	0.927
Product Manager	–0.072	0.237	1	0.763	0.931
Special Developer	–0.256	0.237	1	0.279	0.774
Tester	–0.212	0.210	1	0.312	0.809

However, considering the regression analysis estimated response probability variables, some roles show strong results in favour of women's higher technical positions. Figure 1 presents the charts for these variables showing that: (a) and (b) - for the roles Frontend Developer and Product manager, the women's likelihood of choosing one of these roles increases substantially over time, and moreover, it constantly grows at a faster rate than for men; (c) and (d) - for the roles of Analyst & Designer and Team Leader, the women's trend to choose these roles is also accelerated, with the lines crossing revealing that women have surpassed men as current preferences during the study and also in perspective.

Overall, these results partially support RQ3, suggesting that the temporal variation in female role distribution is limited, with only weak evidence indicating differences for specific technical roles.

Research Question RQ4. We aim to understand the main differences between the two studies and to point out the societal differences that might explain these differences. We summarise in Table 8 the main differences from a numeric perspective (complete data is available in the replication package indicated in

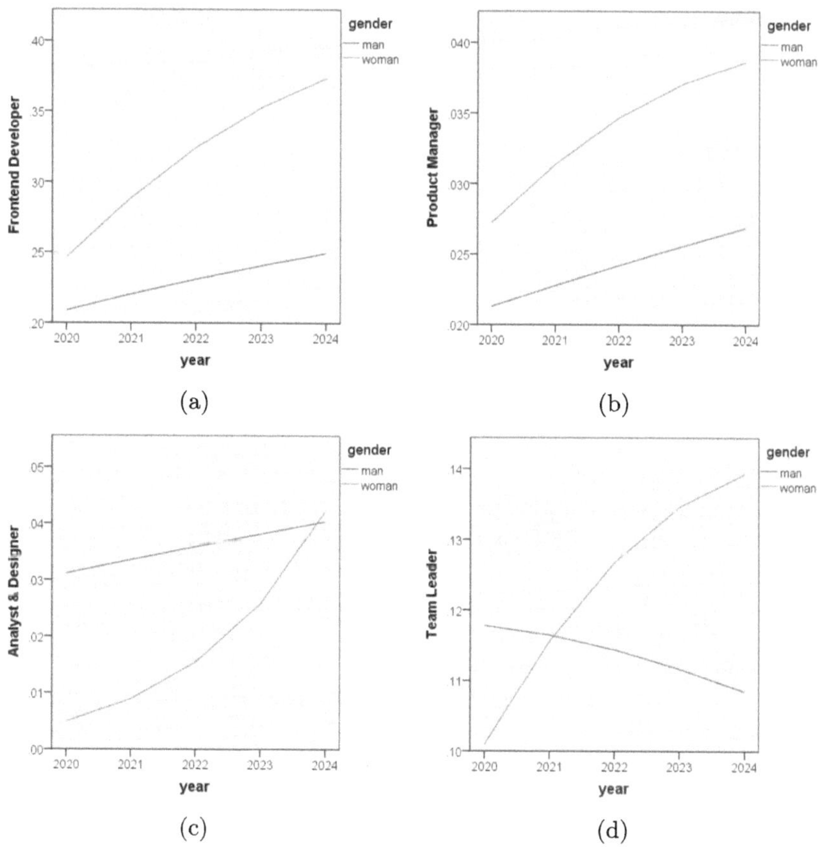

Fig. 1. Gender based estimated probability to take a role of (a) Frontend Developer (b) Product Manager (c) Analyst & Designer (d) Team Leader.

the last section). While in our study, women are slightly better represented than in the original one, we have noticed a constant drop-off in women's participation from 38% in 2022 to 35% in 2023 and 31% in 2024, while in the original study, the latest year exhibits a significant increase.

The most notable distinction concerns the roles taken within the teams. The highly technical roles are assumed in a balanced way by men and women. A possible explanation is that our dataset consists of senior Computer Science students who have already committed to a computing career path. Previous studies suggest that women who persist in computing programs often exhibit levels of technical engagement comparable to their male peers, which may contribute to the balanced distribution of technical roles observed in our data [17,21]. The risk of dropping off at this stage (graduation year) is low.

On the other hand, in our societal context, women are less willing to embrace responsibilities related to the Team Leader role [19,26].

Table 8. Identifying differences between Original and Replication Study

	Original Study		Replication Study	
	Men	Women	Men	Women
No. of Students	445 (70.89%)	183 (29.11%)	1197 (67.21%)	584 (32.79%)
Team Leader	10.1%	**25.1%**	11.36%	12.5%
Tech+	56.4%	27.8%	58.98%	**47.77%**
Tech–	39.9%	67.2%	41.02%	52.23%
NonTech	3.6%	4.9%	–	–

From all three research questions' perspectives, the main differences can be encapsulated as:

- In terms of influence of the gender ratio on highly specialized technical roles, the main significant difference is that according to our data, a higher number of women in the team will form the suitable environment for women to assume technical position, as opposed to original study where it seems to have no influence, even if the percentage of women assuming technical roles remain low (but better than the original case study: 30% compared to 20%);
- The observation related to women leadership remains the same, namely that they do not attract more women to highly specialised technical roles, even if the percentage is improved to 40,05% less women taking *tech+* roles compared to 60,1% in the initial study;
- In terms of variation across cohorts, we observe the same trend of limited and not significant variation across cohorts.

5 Discussion

Understanding Gender Dynamics in Software Development Teams. The problem of attracting women to highly skilled technical roles is a general one, showing that even in academic programs in Computer Science, women tend to prefer less technical or organisational roles. In addition to implementing various programs to attract women to these roles [24], specific societal factors have a substantial impact, such as advocacy for gender equality in technical domains or a cultural emphasis on academic achievement in computing. Introducing Informatics as a discipline in Romanian secondary school education for all children might also help explain the smaller gender gap in these roles.

Re-evaluation of Leadership Impact. The replication proved that this is a persistent problem: simply increasing the number of women in leadership is insufficient to drive substantial change in gendered role distribution. This is still a gap that needs to be addressed not only at the organisational level in the decision-making process and in accountability procedures, but also at the personal level by providing leaders with efficient mechanisms to challenge existing biases.

Promotion of Role Diversification. The replication study showed that women dare to assume technical roles, due to their continuous responsibility in preparing to be good professionals. It also confirmed the positive trend of increasing role diversification among women in software engineering, and future research should address factors influencing women's preferences for specific roles. One specific remark relates to associating technical responsibilities and tasks with roles that are usually considered less technical, such as a UX designer or a frontend developer.

The two studies showed that addressing these implications, the SE education can prepare more inclusive and specialised professionals, but also showed that the concrete strategies should consider societal and cultural factors.

6 Threats to Validity

As with any empirical study in an educational setting, our work is subject to threats to validity [25], particularly given its nature as a contextual replication of a Norwegian study conducted in a different educational, institutional, and societal context [10].

A potential threat to *internal validity* arises from the dual role of some authors as course coordinators, which may introduce bias in data collection or interpretation, as also noted in the original study. However, this is inherent to research in educational settings. To mitigate this risk, teams were formed exclusively by students, with no instructor involvement beyond enforcing team size constraints, and the course structure and assessment criteria remained consistent. A further *internal validity* threat is the involvement of industry mentors, whose guidance may influence team dynamics and role distribution, complicating the isolation of gender effects and differing from the original study. Additionally, course delivery varied between online and on-site formats, potentially affecting communication, visibility, and leadership, and introducing temporal inconsistencies across cohorts.

Construct validity is primarily threatened by how roles and responsibilities were operationalised and measured. As in the original study, our analysis relies on self-reported team documentation, which we cannot independently verify for accuracy or completeness. Variations in students' understanding of roles or in their reporting practices may therefore affect the results. Team size (6–12 students) and flexible development methodologies complicate role attribution, as responsibilities may overlap and roles may be interpreted differently across teams. One issue that we have observed and might influence the findings of the replication is the fact that in our case, the dataset did not contain any "Non-Tech" roles.

External validity is limited by the educational context, as results from student teams may not generalise to industry, although the course simulates realistic practices.

Differences in societal, cultural, and institutional contexts limit the applicability of the findings. Conducted in a Romanian university, our study differs from the Norwegian context in gender representation, educational traditions, and industry-academia interaction. Rather than a limitation, this is inherent to contextual replication, enabling the observation of gender dynamics across distinct settings.

7 Conclusions and Future Work

The capacity to add to the body of knowledge through replication studies has proved beneficial across different Software Engineering topics, including human aspects. Our study is a contribution that enhances confidence in the initial findings [10], showing that the gender gap in SE remains an important problem and requires consolidated initiatives and actions. The results of our research have provided additional evidence that gender dynamics warrant further investigation and, additionally, that more actions must be taken in the industry to promote meaningful change in female leadership roles. Our conclusions also assert that roles in software teams are diversifying and women tend to prefer certain roles. Further investigation of these roles might contribute to a better gender balance.

Societal and cultural influences, along with the specific characteristics of educational programs, are the main factors to consider when implementing definite actions and initiatives to promote gender balance in SE.

Data Availibility Statement. The primary data and the complete results of our study are publicly available in the accompanying package https://doi.org/10.6084/m9.figshare.31971444.

References

1. Albusays, K., Bjorn, P., Dabbish, L., Ford, D., Murphy-Hill, E., Serebrenik, A., Storey, M.A.: The diversity crisis in software development. IEEE Softw. **38**(2), 19–25 (2021). https://doi.org/10.1109/MS.2020.3045817
2. Aller, C.F., Navarro, S.R.: Gender in software engineering degrees. In: Proceedings of the 12th ECSA: Companion Proceedings. ACM (2018). https://doi.org/10.1145/3241403.3241420
3. Altin, R., Mühling, A.: Why female students are dropping out of cs programs. In: Proceedings of the 2024ITiCSE, vol. 1, pp. 304–310. ACM (2024). https://doi.org/10.1145/3649217.3653635
4. Bastarrica, M.C., Simmonds, J.: Gender differences in self and peer assessment in a software engineering capstone course. In: 2019 IEEE/ACM 2nd GE@ICSE, pp. 29–32 (2019). https://doi.org/10.1109/GE.2019.00014
5. Bernstein, L., Yuhas, C.M.: Human Factors in Software Engineering, pp. 309–343. John Wiley & Sons, Ltd., Hoboken (2005). https://doi.org/10.1002/0471750336.ch9
6. Borsotti, V.: Barriers to gender diversity in software development education: actionable insights from a Danish case study. In: Proceedings of the 40th ICSE-SEET, pp. 146–152. ACM (2018). https://doi.org/10.1145/3183377.3183390

7. Boston, J.S., Cimpian, A.: How do we encourage gifted girls to pursue and succeed in science and engineering? Gift. Child Today **41**(4), 196–207 (2018). https://doi.org/10.1177/1076217518786955
8. Buhnova, B., Prikrylova, D.: Women want to learn tech: lessons from the czechitas education project. In: IEEE/ACM 2nd GE@ICSE, pp. 25–28 (2019). https://doi.org/10.1109/GE.2019.00013
9. Cutrupi, C.M.: Women's participation in student software development teams: a cross sectional study on role distribution - complete dataset (2025). https://doi.org/10.5281/zenodo.17091508
10. Cutrupi, C.M., Jaccheri, L., Papavlasopoulou, S.: Women's participation in student software development teams: a cross-sectional study on role distribution. IEEE Trans. Softw. Eng. **51**(12), 3331–3345 (2025). https://doi.org/10.1109/TSE.2025.3612199
11. Cutrupi, C.M., Zanardi, I., Jaccheri, L.: Draw a software engineer test - preliminary attempts to investigate university students' perceptions of software engineering professions. In: 2024 IEEE/ACM WGE@ICSE, pp. 45–46 (2024)
12. European Commission: Women in digital. Online policy page, updated April 25, 2025 (2025). https://digital-strategy.ec.europa.eu/en/policies/women-digital. Accessed 27 Dec 2025
13. García-Holgado, A., Mena, J., García-Peñalvo, F.J., González, C.: Inclusion of gender perspective in computer engineering careers: elaboration of a questionnaire to assess the gender gap in tertiary education. In: IEEE EDUCON, pp. 1547–1554 (2018). https://doi.org/10.1109/EDUCON.2018.8363417
14. García-Holgado, A., Vázquez-Ingelmo, A., José García-Peñalvo, F.: Gender mainstreaming and diversity in higher education: an experience in software engineering education. IEEE Trans. Educ. **67**(5), 712–723 (2024). https://doi.org/10.1109/TE.2024.3411409
15. Girardi, D., Lanubile, F., Novielli, N., Serebrenik, A.: Emotions and perceived productivity of software developers at the workplace. IEEE Trans. Softw. Eng. **48**(9), 3326–3341 (2022). https://doi.org/10.1109/TSE.2021.3087906
16. Gómez Gómez, O.S., Juristo Juzgado, N., Vegas Hernández, S.: Understanding replication of experiments in software engineering: a classification. Inf. Softw. Technol. **56**, 1033–1048 (2014). https://doi.org/10.1016/j.infsof.2014.04.004
17. Happe, L., Buhnova, B.: Frustrations steering women away from software engineering. IEEE Softw. **39**(4), 63–69 (2022). https://doi.org/10.1109/MS.2021.3099077
18. Happe, L., Marquardt, K., Trumpf, R., Wagner, I.: Decoding the gap: a retrospective analysis of women's experiences in software engineering. In: Proceedings of the 16th CSEDU, vol. 1, pp. 227–236. SciTePress (2024). https://doi.org/10.5220/0012732100003693
19. Heilman, M.E.: Gender stereotypes and workplace bias. Res. Organ. Behav. **32**, 113–135 (2012). https://doi.org/10.1016/j.riob.2012.11.003. https://www.sciencedirect.com/science/article/pii/S0191308512000093
20. Hyrynsalmi, S., Sutinen, E.: The role of women software communities in attracting more women to the software industry. In: 2019 IEEE International Conference on Engineering, Technology and Innovation (ICE/ITMC), pp. 1–7 (2019). https://doi.org/10.1109/ICE.2019.8792673
21. Main, J.B., Schimpf, C.: The underrepresentation of women in computing fields: a synthesis of literature using a life course perspective. IEEE Trans. Educ. **60**(4), 296–304 (2017). https://doi.org/10.1109/TE.2017.2704060

22. Marques, M.: Software engineering education – does gender matter in project results? – a Chilean case study. In: 2015 IEEE Frontiers in Education Conference (FIE), pp. 1–8 (2015). https://doi.org/10.1109/FIE.2015.7344175
23. Motogna, S., Alboaie, L., Todericiu, I.A., Zaharia, C.: Retaining women in computer science: the good, the bad and the ugly sides. In: Proceedings of the Third GE@ICSE, pp. 35–42. ACM (2022). https://doi.org/10.1145/3524501.3527598
24. Motogna, S., Manresa-Yee, C., Hensman, S.: Minerva informatics equality award catalogue: Celebrating a decade of gender equality in informatics research and education – best practices in Europe. Technical report, Informatics Europe (2025). https://www.informatics-europe.org/component/phocadownload/category/9-publications/10-reports.html?download=291:miea-catalogue&Itemid=101, CC BY–SA 4.0
25. Ralph, P., et al.: Empirical standards for software engineering research. In: Proceedings of the 42nd International Conference on Software Engineering (ICSE). IEEE/ACM (2020)
26. Stoet, G., Geary, D.: The gender-equality paradox in science, technology, engineering, and mathematics education. Psychol. Sci. **29**, 0956797617741719 (2018). https://doi.org/10.1177/0956797617741719
27. Tiutin, A.G., Vescan, A.: New criteria for test case prioritization for software product lines: a replication and extension study. Autom. Softw. Eng. **33**, 71 (2026). https://doi.org/10.1007/s10515-026-00619-8

"*Fright Not and Be Dispersed!*" Investigating the Influence of Cultural Dimensions on Communication and Collaboration in Software Development

Stefano Lambiase[1(✉)], Gemma Catolino[2], Mario Torre[3], Damian A. Tamburri[4], Fabio Palomba[2], and Filomena Ferrucci[2]

[1] Aalborg University Copenhagen, Copenhagen, Denmark
stla@cs.aau.dk
[2] SeSa Lab, University of Salerno, Salerno, Italy
{gcatolino,fpalomba,fferrucci}@unisa.it
[3] RedHat, Raleigh, USA
[4] University of Sannio, Benevento, Italy
datamburri@unisannio.it

Abstract. The state of software practice requires developers and stakeholders worldwide to collaborate on developing and maintaining software products. In turn, managers are faced with technical challenges and those connected to global workforce dispersion, from which the practitioner's culture outstands as a protagonist. The existing body of knowledge on the role of culture in software development is substantial; however, few studies have adopted a systematic framework for their investigation and for reporting their results. This paper starts from the aformentioned objective and seeks to understand how the presence of members with different cultural attitudes influences the emergence of collaboration and communication issues in software development communities. To this aim, we investigated culture using *Hofstede's 6-D framework* as part of qualitative research. First, we conducted a focus group with six senior RedHat professionals to understand to what extent different cultural behaviors impact communication and collaboration activities and which strategies they implement to mitigate conflicts. Second, we conduct a large scale survey to strengthen and expand the results of the focus group. Overall, our research highlights how effective management plays a crucial role in unlocking the potential of cultural diversity within software development teams. We show that, when managed strategically, cultural differences go beyond mere mitigation—they actively enrich team dynamics, promote better communication, and facilitate more efficient collaboration. This emphasizes the value of incorporating culturally aware management practices in global software development environments.

Keywords: Software Engineering · Social Aspects · Organizational Culture

C. Berger and V. Klös (Eds.): SEAA 2026, LNCS 16864, pp. 101–117, 2027.
https://doi.org/10.1007/978-3-032-36587-3_8

1 Introduction

Software engineering (SE) has traditionally been studied and practiced as a predominantly technical discipline, focusing on activities such as software design [17], quality assurance [16,50], testing [2,37,41–43], maintenance [45], and process improvement [11,12]. However, decades of research have shown that software development is inherently a socio-technical activity [20], where successful outcomes depend not only on technical artifacts and processes but also on the interactions among developers, managers, users, and other stakeholders. This socio-technical nature has become even more pronounced with the advent of Artificial Intelligence (AI)-driven software development, where developers increasingly act as supervisors and evaluators of contributions produced by both human collaborators and AI systems. As a result, software projects frequently involve stakeholders with diverse cultural, linguistic, organizational, and professional backgrounds, often distributed across different geographical locations. Such heterogeneity naturally leads to the emergence of social challenges, especially in terms of collaboration and communication, like personality conflicts, language, and cultural barriers. If not properly managed, these can in turn contribute to so-called *social debt*, i.e., the additional project cost caused by suboptimal socio-technical decisions or circumstances in a development community [48].

Among the various social challenges that impact social debt, this work focuses on *culture*: this is defined as the set of common behaviors that distinguish the members of one community from another [22,23]. As recognized in seminal work in the field [15,36], culture has a greater influence on SE practices than originally envisioned. This is the main reason why researchers in the field of *Global Software Engineering* (GSE)—i.e., the branch of software engineering aiming at establishing a set of practices to manage globally distributed software teams—shave been largely exploring the influence of cultural aspects on distributed software development and maintenance activities [15,25,36].

Recent literature reviews [15,25,36] highlight two key limitations. First, cultural dimension frameworks [18,19,21] are rarely or only partially adopted in SE studies [15], preventing a systematic understanding of how culture impacts development practices. Second, existing results are contrasting: cultural diversity empower decision-making [20,44] but can also lead to collaboration and communication problems [40]. This paper addresses these gaps by investigating how cultural differences affect communication and collaboration in software development communities. Rather than treating culture as an abstract concept, we represent it using Hofstede's 6-D framework [21,23], building on recent work on cultural dispersion in SE [28–31,33].

The results of our study show that increasing cultural variety in development teams—having heterogeneous behaviors—impacts collaboration and communication activities, but not necessarily in a negative way. Indeed, if correctly managed, cultural variety could be beneficial, possibly improving team productivity. Moreover, as part of our study, we elicit a new behavior that seems to be related to the culture of individuals. We named this *Risk Hiding Index* (RHI), i.e., the extent to which the members of a culture feel comfortable exposing and revealing risks. Finally, we provide a list of mitigation strategies for each cultural dimension, e.g., restructuring the community. We conclude that project managers should consider culture as a key indicator during all development and maintenance activities—not only during team formation, as typically acknowledged—to avoid the emergence of hard-to-manage socio-technical and organizational behaviors.

To sum up, this paper provides the following contributions:

1. A set of positive and negative patterns of communication and collaboration that emerge when individuals with diverse cultural background work together within the same development team.
2. A potential new cultural behaviors—i.e., *Risk Hiding Index*—representing the extent to which people feel comfortable exposing and revealing risks to ask for help instead of managing them by themselves.
3. A set of mitigation and refactoring strategies for each cultural dimension, e.g., restructuring the community.
4. A publicly available repository reporting the raw data collected in the context of the study for further research and new considerations by the community [34].

2 Background and Related Work

Several frameworks have been proposed to characterize culture through measurable *dimensions*, each capturing a contrast between two opposing *cultural behaviors* [18,19,21]. Among them, ***Hofstede's 6-D framework*** [21] is the most widely adopted in SE [1,6,7]. It comprises six dimensions, each scored from 0 to 100 per country [23]:

- Power Distance (*PDI*): Degree of accepted inequality in the distribution of power within a community.
- Individualism vs. Collectivism (*IDV*): Extent to which individuals are expected to act independently vs. as part of a cohesive group.
- Masculinity vs. Femininity (*MAS*): Preference for achievement and assertiveness vs. cooperation and quality of life.
- Uncertainty Avoidance (*UAI*): Degree of discomfort with ambiguity and unknown situations.
- Long vs. Short Term Orientation (*LTO*): Emphasis on persistence and long-term growth vs. quick results and tradition.
- Indulgence vs. Restraint (*IVR*): Tendency to allow free gratification of desires vs. regulate them through strict norms.

Despite its wide adoption, part of the research community questions the framework's validity [5,46]. Nonetheless, Venkateswaran and Ojha [49] demonstrated that it remains the most effective instrument for characterizing cultural aspects, following a realistic approach proven effective across fields including computer science [1,6,7,22].

In the SE context, various studies acknowledge culture as a relevant factor in distributed teams [20,36,40,44], but they do not systematically map challenges or strategies to specific cultural dimensions. Deshpande et al. [10] elicited strategies from Indian project managers without adopting a cultural framework, and Borchers [6] studied three of Hofstede's dimensions but focused solely on impact without addressing mitigation. Zolduoarrati et al. [52] examined how the IDV dimension affects developer behavior on StackOverflow, but considered only one dimension. In contrast, our work systematically maps both challenges and strategies to all six Hofstede dimensions.

More recently, Lambiase et al. [29–33] introduced the concept of *cultural dispersion* in SE—situations in which community members exhibit behaviors diverging from those typically associated with their cultural background—and showed that unmanaged cultural differences correlate with community smells [32] and reduced productivity [30,31]. They proposed the *Dealing with Cultural Dispersion* framework for managing cultural diversity in software teams [29].

3 Research Design

The empirical study revolved around three research questions. First, we investigated whether developers recognize cultural behaviors described by Hofstede's dimensions in their work and associate them with culture:

> ? **RQ$_1$**: *Which cultural behaviors do professionals most readily recognize in their experiences and attribute to the cultural background of individuals?*

Second, we aimed to understand how the coexistence of contrasting cultural behaviors within a team influences communication and collaboration:

> ? **RQ$_2$**: *How does the presence of individuals with diverse cultural backgrounds and exhibiting contrasting behaviors (associated with specific Hofstede dimensions) influence communication and collaboration activities in software development teams?*

Third, we sought actionable strategies for mitigating challenges originating from cultural diversity in software teams:

> ? **RQ$_3$**: *Which mitigation and contingency strategies are put in place to face issues originating from geo-distributed and culturally dispersed software communities?*

Our strategy follows a mixed-methods approach [9]. We first performed a *focus group* (Sect. 3.1) to stimulate discussion and elicit insights for all three RQs, then conducted a larger-scale confirmatory survey (Sect. 3.2). Rather than using Hofstede's dimension scores directly, we focused on the *behaviors* described by each dimension, using examples in focus groups and vignette-based scenarios in surveys to help participants relate to culturally influenced situations. We employed content analysis [8] for qualitative data and descriptive statistics for closed-ended survey questions. In terms of reporting, we followed the guidelines by Wohlin et al. [51] and the *ACM/SIGSOFT Empirical Standards.*[1] A replication package is available online [34].

3.1 Design of the Focus Group Study

To address our **RQ**s, we first conducted a *focus group* [38], a qualitative methodology that relies on dynamic interaction among participants to elicit data difficult to obtain through individual interviews. We recruited participants through a co-author working at Red Hat,[2] a large open-source company with globally distributed teams. The session was conducted virtually via Zoom, following established guidelines [26, 39].

Focus Group Participants. Using *convenience sampling* through our target company, we recruited six practitioners with at least 10 years of experience in leading teams and global software development [39]. To mitigate the limited generalizability of this method, we set base criteria for participants and later conducted a confirmatory survey.

Focus Group Structure. The focus group, moderated by the first two authors, consisted of an introduction, ice-breaking questions, and core questions organized in two groups: (G1) recognition and experience of cultural dimensions, including possible new dimensions; and (G2) impact of cultural behaviors on collaboration and communication. Questions were not strictly predefined to foster open discussion.

Results Analysis Methods. We perform content analysis [8] on the transcript to extract cultural conditions and problems. The first two authors independently analyzed the transcript, assigning concepts to sentences and then discussing disagreements to reach consensus over two rounds. Cohen's kappa [27] measured 0.77 in the second round, indicating strong agreement [35]. All authors then verified the consistency of the results. Responses from G1 addressed RQ_1, while G2 addressed RQ_2 and RQ_3.

3.2 Design of the Survey Study

We designed a confirmatory survey [3, 26] targeting a larger population of practitioners to generalize the focus group findings. The survey covered all six Hofstede dimensions plus the *Risk Hiding Index (RHI)*, a new potential dimension that emerged from the focus group.

[1] Available at: https://github.com/acmsigsoft/EmpiricalStandards. We followed the *"General Standard"*, *"Questionnaire Surveys"*, and *"Mixed Methods"* guidelines.
[2] The author has recently changed company.

Survey Structure. The survey consisted of seven dimension sections plus a demographics section. Each dimension section started with a vignette-based scenario [4] contextualizing the opposite behaviors in software development, followed by Likert-scale questions on frequency, cultural influence, impact on communication and collaboration, and an open-ended question on mitigation strategies. We opted for vignettes rather than abstract definitions to help respondents relate to concrete situations; all scenarios are available in our online appendix [34]. The survey was anonymous, created as a GOOGLE form, with an estimated completion time of 10–15 min. Ethical approval was obtained from the University of the second author.

Participants to the Survey. We used PROLIFIC[3] to recruit participants with a computer science background, experience in distributed teams, and management experience [3,26]. Studies have demonstrated that Prolific—alongside Cloud Research—offers highly reliable respondent pools when appropriate methodological safeguards are in place [13,14]. We offered a $7.50 incentive per valid respondent to mitigate self-selection bias. The survey ran from December 16 to 20, 2021, reaching 3337 experts; we received 200 valid responses (6% response rate).

Survey—Method for Results Analysis. We used descriptive statistics for closed-ended questions and content analysis [8] for open-ended responses on mitigation strategies.

Table 1. Background of the focus group participants.

ID	Role	Working Activity	Years	Country
P1	Project Manager	Development	19	Germany
P2	Senior Solution Architect	Development	21	Russia
P3	Senior Quality Engineer	Researcher	10	The U.S.
P4	Project Manager	Development	15	Italy
P5	Software Engineer	Development	10	Japan
P6	Quality Engineer	Researcher	10	Italy

3.3 Participants Background Information

Table 1 reports the background of the six focus group participants, all with at least ten years of experience in open-source development at REDHAT. Two are project managers and four are software engineers; we recruited two women and four men from different countries.

[3] PROLIFIC website: https://www.prolific.co/.

Among the 200 survey participants, 47% were developers and 14% project managers; 70% male, 20% female, and 10% other. Most self-assessed their management and programming skills as high or medium (67% and 84%, respectively). Participants were geographically distributed across Africa (8.1%), Asia (3.7%), East Europe (28.1%), North America (23.1%), South America (18.8%), West Europe (21.9%), and the UK (21.2%).

3.4 Threats to Validity

We organized threats using the framework by Wohlin et al. [51].

Regarding *construct validity*, using Hofstede's framework may have omitted behaviors captured by other frameworks [18,19]; to mitigate this, we asked participants about additional dimensions, resulting in the *Risk Hiding Index* (Sect. 4). We also conducted a pilot study with four developers, making minimal adjustments for clarity. A further concern is the presence of sub-cultures within a larger cultural group. Since our focus was on culturally-derived behaviors rather than geographical dispersion, sub-cultures are less significant; moreover, Hofstede considered sub-cultures when designing the survey values.

Regarding *internal validity*, the main threats involve participant recruitment and their capacity to report on culturally dispersed teams. As detailed in Sect. 3, we applied specific selection criteria for both the focus group and the survey, aiming for gender and nationality balance. We encourage replications to further strengthen generalizability. Additionally, culture is abstract and perceived differently by individuals; we mitigated this by using concrete behavioral examples and vignette-based scenarios.

Regarding *conclusion validity*, the focus group had six participants from the same company; while this size is appropriate for the methodology [38], further replications with different practitioners are needed. The use of PROLIFIC involved a monetary incentive (~$1), which could affect results; however, participation was voluntary, respondents had diverse backgrounds, and questions were framed around specific situations. All study materials are available online [34].

Regarding *external validity*, focus group participants' experience at *Red Hat* could bias findings. We mitigated this through our mixed-method design [9], using the focus group as preliminary data confirmed by a large-scale survey. Our participants used a hybrid development process, common in software development, supporting transferability. Despite the sample size aligning with SE research norms, findings may still be context-specific; future research will include studies in more diverse settings.

4 Findings and Discussion

This section reports our findings, organized by research question, showing both focus group and survey results.

4.1 RQ_1—Recognition of Cultural Behaviors in Software Development Communities

RQ_1—Focus Group. All participants agreed that cultural dimensions significantly represent the developers' cultural aspects in software communities, identifying cases described by the dimensions in most of their past experiences as developers and managers and associating them with the cultural background of the stakeholders involved.

> According to our data, Hofstede's framework represents a valuable instrument for representing cultural behaviors in development teams, as already partially demonstrated by previous works [22,49].

Further confirmation of this, derived from the confirmatory survey performed after the focus group, will be discussed later in this Section.

When we asked about new possible dimensions, an interesting thought came out regarding the difference between western and eastern cultures. For instance, P2—who worked for a few years in a geographically distributed team—reported that 🗨 *"People from eastern cultures avoid risky situations; they do not like potential conflicts. Indeed, they try to 'sweep under the carpet' or do everything possible to avoid the arising of a conflict, sometimes worsening the situation."*. Initially, we intuitively mapped this with the *Uncertainty Avoidance* Hofstede's dimension, i.e., the extent to which the members of a culture feel threatened by ambiguous or unknown situations [23]. So, we kindly asked for confirmation from P2. However, P2 specified that 🗨 *"Well, it is a bit different. It was that people on the western side were fine in manage risks in a proactive manner, rather than the reactive manner. What we have seen on the eastern side is that there was also a bit of productivity in taking risks, but it was much lower, and mostly, it was rather about avoiding and consuming risks on their own. So if there is something going wrong, they do not expose it internally and ask for help."*. Based on his comments, we realized that *Uncertainty Avoidance* (at least in the perception of developers) defines how people approach a risk, not how they expose it.

For the above-mentioned reason, we decided to map the described behaviors, i.e., (i) exposing risky situations or (ii) hiding them, to a potential new cultural dimension that we named ***Risk Hiding Index*** *(RHI)*, namely, the extent to which people feel comfortable exposing and revealing risks to ask for help instead of managing them by themselves. Nevertheless, further research is needed to explore and validate such dimension as actually differing from *Uncertainty Avoidance*, to which it can be somehow related.[4]

RQ_1—Survey. As shown in Fig. 1, most participants recognized the different culturally originated behaviors inside their team, confirming the finding of the

[4] Following the same pattern of Hofstede's dimensions, RHI maps two opposite behaviors: (i) a low level indicates people who prefer to share risk and uncertainty and seek help; (ii) a high level represents situations in which people tend to hide risks and problems, trying to manage them alone.

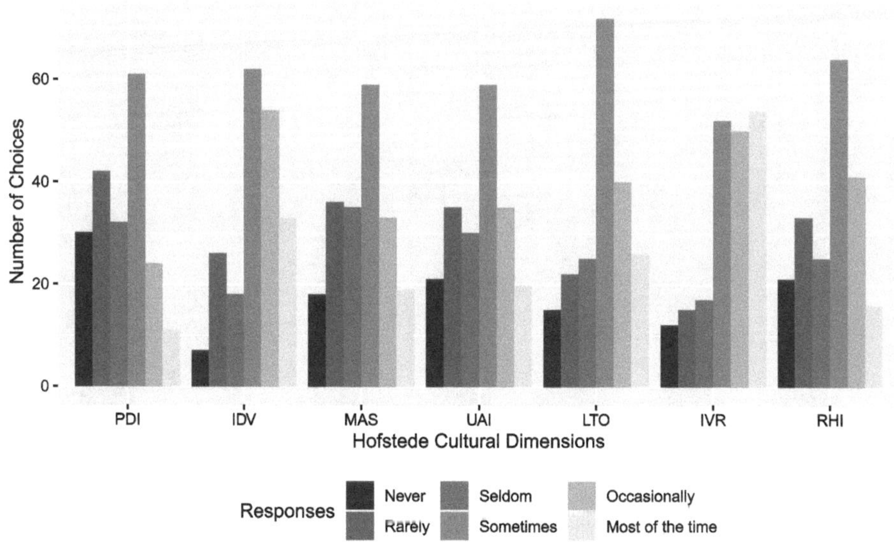

Fig. 1. Frequency of experienced behaviors in the Survey.

focus group. In particular, *Individualism vs. Collectivism Index* and *Indulgence vs. Restraint Index* were the most frequent, while *Power Distance Index* was less frequent (74% vs 48%). Additionally, 60% of the participants experienced behaviors related to *Risk Hiding Index*, thus highlighting the importance of this new aspect.

When asked to what extent culture influences these behaviors, most participants confirmed the connection (Fig. 2): the lowest agreement was 46%, while the highest reached 83%. **These results reinforce the focus group findings and the relationship between belonging to different cultures and exhibiting certain behaviors.**

☞ RQ_1: Summary.

Developers recognized Hofstede's cultural behaviors in their experience. A new dimension, *Risk Hiding Index*, emerged as relevant from both the focus group and survey.

4.2 RQ_2—Impact of Cultural Dimensions on Software Communication and Collaboration

RQ_2—Focus Group. The focus group participants highlighted that they mainly experienced issues with developers showing opposite behaviors in the context of *Individualism vs. Collectivism*, *Uncertainty Avoidance*, and *Risk Hiding Index*.

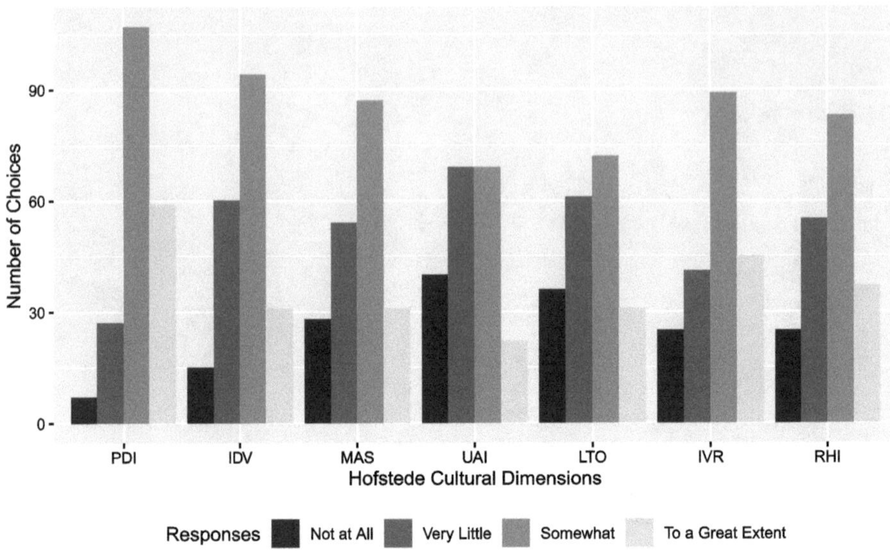

Fig. 2. Perception of the connection between culture and behaviors in the Survey.

Individualism vs. Collectivism. Participants agreed that both individualistic and collectivistic people in a team could lead to the emergence of communication and collaboration issues. P1 reported *"There was definitely an issue because individualistic individuals constantly had friction (hard feelings), working with other individuals."*. We can draw two conclusions: having opposite behaviors can lead to friction in communication; however, integrating people who tend to isolate themselves could not always be a good idea since collaboration problems can emerge.

Uncertainty Avoidance Index. Participants contextualized *Uncertainty Avoidance* behaviors in two contexts:

Risk Tolerance. From a *risk tolerance* perspective, i.e., the sensitivity of an organization or people to risks, people with a high value of uncertainty avoidance take risks that they know to have success rates. P5 reported that *"In my experience, it is a pretty big advantage by having people with the high-risk tolerance and the low-risk tolerance on the same machine or the same team."*. This suggests that culturally-driven diversity in risk tolerance can be beneficial, helping teams balance innovation with caution and preventing collaboration issues. The confirmatory survey further supported this result.

Gender Disparity. Participants also discussed *gender disparity* rooted in cultural influences, which we categorized under both *UAI* and *MAS*. P2 reported *"We had a problem with part of the teams that did not accept that women had a high role in the team, i.e., head. So, obviously, that has been a huge problem for us because we have had a few talented females in our team, and* *this team has been completely unreceptive, not comprehending how those people could be in the same room with them."*. This suggests that cultural backgrounds can affect gender dynamics, leading to communication and collaboration problems.

Risk Hiding Index. On the consequences of *Risk Hiding* on communication and collaboration activities, P2, talking about people preferring to manage the risk by themselves, reported, *"... basically, if there is a deadline that is not possible to be met at all, they might wait until the last moment, until the last day, for communicating the fact, because they tend to try to think that - it is okay, it will somehow rule itself out - and that is, that occurred in my practice more than once."*. Based on the reported example, we can notice that how different cultures treat risk can lead to communication and collaboration problems.

RQ$_2$—Survey. Figure 3 reports the extent to which participants agreed that the coexistence of both opposite behaviors negatively affects communication and collaboration. Most participants agreed with our conjecture. For instance, for *Power Distance Index*, 57.5% of participants, i.e., 114, at least agreed that the presence of opposite behaviors in the same team could impact collaboration and communication negatively, while for *Masculinity vs. Femininity* index, 42% of participants,i.e., 84, at least agreed and 34%,i.e., 68, neither agree nor disagree.

The survey confirmed focus group insights. Indeed *UAI* and *IDV* are perceived as negatively impactful. However, we obtained new hints, i.e., *PDI* appears to be the most impactful cultural dimension, although focus group participants did not focus their attention.

RQ$_2$: Summary.

The coexistence of contrasting cultural behaviors can lead to collaboration and communication issues. Key challenges include managing individualism vs. collectivism tensions, balancing risk tolerance, and preventing gender-based discrimination rooted in cultural norms.

4.3 RQ$_3$—Mitigation and Contingency Strategies

We elicited mitigation strategies from both analyses: in the focus group, we asked how participants dealt with reported issues; in the survey, we included an open question on strategies. The outcomes were highly similar, so we report them together. Specifically, Table 2 summarizes the strategies with their frequency The first five were common to both the focus group and the survey; the last three emerged only from the survey. A comprehensive list of quotations is available in the online appendix [34]. We describe each strategy below:

Support the individualistic nature. Supporting individualistic developers with a correct division of responsibilities can lead to practical benefits. P1 reported *"I reorganized the duties of this person, for supporting his decision to work alone."*.

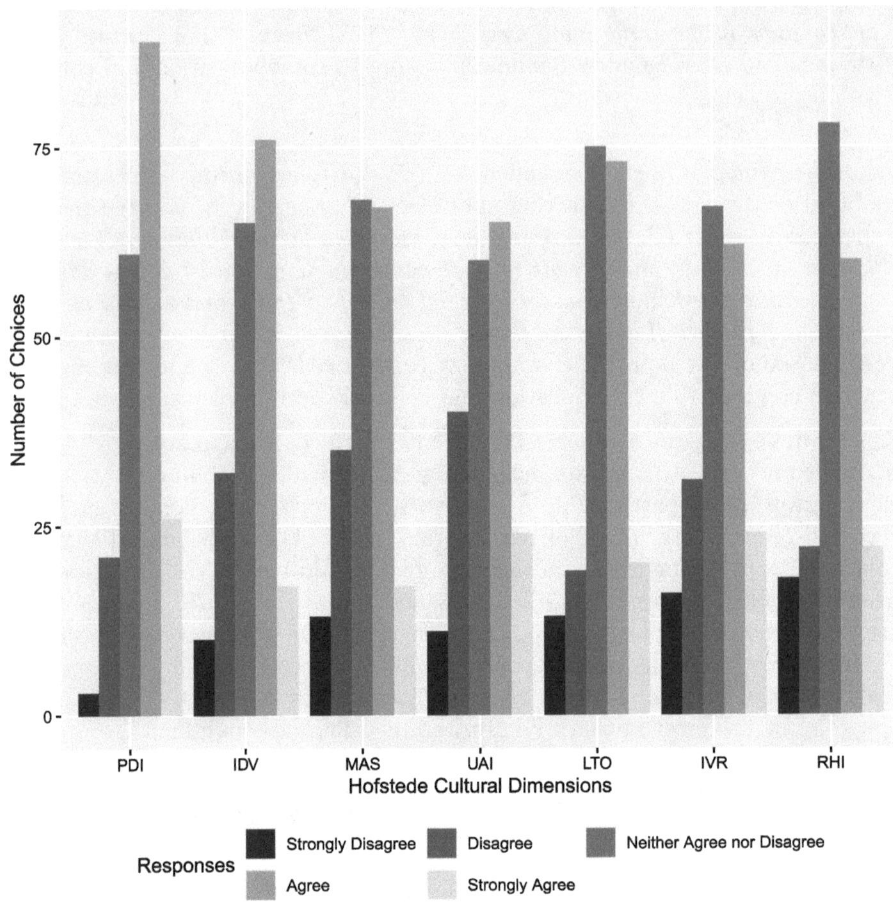

Fig. 3. Survey—Impact of the coexistence of different cultural behaviors, in the same team, on collaboration and communication activities.

Table 2. Mitigation and contingency strategies originated by cultural issue.

Strategy	PDI	IDV	MAS	UAI	LTO	IVR	RHI
Support the individualistic nature		24					
Moderate communication to avoid conflict	17	20	25				
Support Team Exchange	14	3	7	12			10
Converging in one behavior	25	22	8	23	13		7
Reach a compromise between two behaviors	25	5	8	25		31	34
Increase communication	17	15	8		8		14
Restructure the community	15		8		23		
Seek meeting with problematic members	10	5	7			22	

Moderate communication to avoid conflict. Being present as a manager to moderate communications during critical phases can mitigate issues. P1 stated *"During critical communication, I am there as a manager to moderate the conversation and act if some conflicts arise."*.

Support Team Exchange. Temporarily exchanging members between conflicting sub-teams can help bridge cultural gaps. P2 pointed out that *"This experience helped us to understand the difference between team cultures, figuring out solutions and turn this into the kind of internal handbook, or book of best practices."*.

Converging in one behavior. This strategy consists of enforcing the adoption of only one of the two behavioral extremes by all community members. One survey participant stated that *"In some situations, it is important to take a one-time decision and enforce the adoption of one behavior (for example, select a particular technology and discuss it in a team meeting). Undoubtedly, it helps a lot if more people in the team are aligned to similar ideas to adopt new technology or not."*.

Reach a compromise between two behaviors. Rather than converging, teams can seek a middle ground between opposite behaviors. One survey participant pointed out that *"I've seen the solution to having both kinds of people, which was to reach compromises between the two, introducing newer technologies no one knew how to use at 100% while keeping a little over half with older but more traditional techniques/technologies, which allowed to create a working software with innovative features."*.

Increase communication. Increasing communication through meetings and targeted channels can help spread team culture. P4 said that *"The second best thing that we did was establish a consistent, continuous training program for everyone arriving on-site or who was starting to interact with the partners and with customers in the other country ... and that really helped in mitigating many problems in our collaboration."*.

Restructure the community. Mixing team members between sub-teams to increase heterogeneity, particularly effective in geographically dispersed settings. P2 pointed out that *"The only way we managed to tackle that was to literally move around a few people on both sides, mostly on the other side, so that we manage it to find the right interaction. So basically, we found more flexible and less rigid people who managed to work with our female workforce."*.

Seek meeting with problematic team members. Having the manager speak directly with conflicted members to address behaviors that lead to conflict. One survey participant said that *"Usually, this has been another task for the project manager to talk to the person who was overly competitive about how it's not a contest to be the best developer. There is often no reward for it anyway, so some people learn on their own that the only way to win is a team win."*.

Most strategies were elicited from the focus group and independently confirmed by the survey.

☞ RQ_3: Summary.

Participants reported mitigation strategies such as moderating communication, seeking compromises between contrasting behaviors, and supporting team exchange.

5 Conclusions

This paper presents the first large-scale empirical exploration of Hofstede's cultural dimensions [21] in software development communities, combining a focus group with experienced practitioners and a confirmatory survey with 200 developers. Our results show that cultural behaviors impact collaboration and communication, yet not necessarily negatively. We also identified a new potential cultural behavior, the *Risk Hiding Index*, which appears to affect social activities in geographically distributed teams.

As future work, we plan to deepen the analysis of RHI through dedicated studies, operationalize our findings through the lens of *community smells* [47,48], investigate the interplay between gender and culture using frameworks such as GLOBE [24], and develop tool support—e.g., chatbots suggesting mitigation strategies based on cultural dispersion data—to help managers lead distributed teams more effectively.

Acknowledgments. The authors would like to thank the participants of our study for the time and feedback provided.

Disclosure of Interests. The authors have no competing interests to declare that are relevant to the content of this article.

References

1. Abufardeh, S., Magel, K.: The impact of global software cultural and linguistic aspects on global software development process (GSD): issues and challenges. In: 4th International Conference on New Trends in Information Science and Service Science, pp. 133–138. IEEE (2010)
2. Afeltra, A., Cannavale, A., Pecorelli, F., Pontillo, V., Palomba, F.: A large-scale empirical investigation into cross-project flaky test prediction. IEEE Access **12**, 131255–131265 (2024)
3. Andrews, D., Nonnecke, B., Preece, J.: Conducting research on the internet: online survey design, development and implementation guidelines (2007)
4. Atzmüller, C., Steiner, P.M.: Experimental vignette studies in survey research. Methodology (2010)
5. Baskerville, R.F.: Hofstede never studied culture. Acc. Organ. Soc. **28**(1), 1–14 (2003)
6. Borchers, G.: The software engineering impacts of cultural factors on multi-cultural software development teams. In: 25th International Conference on Software Engineering, 2003. Proceedings, pp. 540–545. IEEE (2003)

7. Casey, V.: Imparting the importance of culture to global software development. ACM Inroads **1**(3), 51–57 (2011)
8. Cavanagh, S.: Content analysis: concepts, methods and applications. Nurse Res. **4**(3), 5–16 (1997)
9. Creswell, J.W., Creswell, J.D.: Research Design: Qualitative, Quantitative, and Mixed Methods Approaches. Sage Publications (2017)
10. Deshpande, S., Richardson, I., Casey, V., Beecham, S.: Culture in global software development - a weakness or strength? In: 2010 5th IEEE International Conference on Global Software Engineering, pp. 67–76 (2010)
11. Di Meglio, S., Starace, L.L.L., Pontillo, V., Opdebeeck, R., De Roover, C., Di Martino, S.: Investigating the adoption and maintenance of web GUI testing: insights from github repositories. Inf. Softw. Technol. 107928 (2025)
12. Di Meglio, S., Starace, L.L.L., Pontillo, V., Opdebeeck, R., De Roover, C., Di Martino, S.: Performance testing in open-source web projects: adoption, maintenance, and a change taxonomy. In: 2025 IEEE International Conference on Software Maintenance and Evolution (ICSME), pp. 199–210. IEEE (2025)
13. Douglas, B.D., Ewell, P.J., Brauer, M.: Data quality in online human-subjects research: comparisons between mturk, prolific, cloudresearch, qualtrics, and sona. PLoS ONE **18**(3), e0279720 (2023)
14. Eyal, P., David, R., Andrew, G., Zak, E., Ekaterina, D.: Data quality of platforms and panels for online behavioral research. Behav. Res. Methods 1–20 (2021)
15. Fazli, F., Bittner, E.A.C.: Cultural influences on collaborative work in software engineering teams (2017)
16. Giordano, G., Festa, G., Catolino, G., Palomba, F., Ferrucci, F., Gravino, C.: On the adoption and effects of source code reuse on defect proneness and maintenance effort. Empir. Softw. Eng. **29**(1), 20 (2024)
17. Giordano, G., Sellitto, G., Sepe, A., Palomba, F., Ferrucci, F.: The yin and yang of software quality: on the relationship between design patterns and code smells. In: 2023 49th Euromicro Conference on Software Engineering and Advanced Applications (SEAA), pp. 227–234. IEEE (2023)
18. Hall, E.T.: Beyond culture. Anchor (1989)
19. Hampden-Turner, C., Trompenaars, F., Hampden-Turner, C.: Riding the waves of culture: understanding diversity in global business. Hachette UK (2020)
20. Herbsleb, J.D., Moitra, D.: Global software development. IEEE Softw. **18**(2), 16–20 (2001)
21. Hofstede, G.: Dimensionalizing cultures: the hofstede model in context. Online Read. Psychol. Culture **2**(1), 2307-0919 (2011)
22. Hofstede, G.: 50 years memory lane – developing cultural dimensions from IBM data. Software of the Mind 2.0 (2017)
23. Hofstede, G., Hofstede, G.J., Minkov, M.: Cultures and Organizations: Software of the Mind, vol. 2. Mcgraw-Hill, New York (2005)
24. House, R.J., Hanges, P.J., Javidan, M., Dorfman, P.W., Gupta, V.: Culture, Leadership, and Organizations: The GLOBE Study of 62 Societies. Sage Publications (2004)
25. Javed, I., Janjua, U.I., Madni, T.M., Akhunzada, A.: The impact of mitigation strategies for socio-cultural distance issues in GSD: an empirical study. IEEE Access (2023)
26. Kitchenham, B.A., Pfleeger, S.L.: Personal opinion surveys. In: Guide to Advanced Empirical Software Engineering, pp. 63–92. Springer (2008)
27. Kvålseth, T.O.: Note on cohen's kappa. Psychol. Rep. **65**(1), 223–226 (1989)

28. Lambiase, S.: Cultural and socio-technical aspects in software development. In: Proceedings of the 28th International Conference on Evaluation and Assessment in Software Engineering, pp. 482–487 (2024)
29. Lambiase, S., Catolino, G., Palomba, F., Ferrucci, F., Russo, D.: Investigating the role of cultural values in adopting large language models for software engineering (2024). https://arxiv.org/abs/2409.05055
30. Lambiase, S., et al.: An empirical investigation into the influence of software communities' cultural and geographical dispersion on productivity. J. Syst. Softw. **208**, 111878 (2024)
31. Lambiase, S., et al.: "there and back again?" on the influence of software community dispersion over productivity. In: 2022 48th Euromicro Conference on Software Engineering and Advanced Applications (SEAA), pp. 177–184 (2022). https://doi.org/10.1109/SEAA56994.2022.00035
32. Lambiase, S., Catolino, G., Tamburri, D.A., Serebrenik, A., Palomba, F., Ferrucci, F.: Good fences make good neighbours? On the impact of cultural and geographical dispersion on community smells. In: 2022 IEEE/ACM 44th International Conference on Software Engineering: Software Engineering in Society (ICSE-SEIS), pp. 67–78 (2022). https://doi.org/10.1145/3510458.3513015
33. Lambiase, S., Catolino, G., Torre, M., Tamburri, D.A., Palomba, F., Ferrucci, F.: Fright not and be dispersed! evaluating cultural dimensions versus software communication and collaboration activities. SSRN Electron. J. (2022)
34. Lambiase, S., Catolino, G., Torre, M., Tamburri, D.A., Palomba, F., Ferrucci, F.: Fright not and be dispersed! evaluating cultural dimensions versus software communication and collaboration activities - online appendix (2022). https://doi.org/10.6084/m9.figshare.19351619. https://figshare.com/articles/dataset/Fright_not_and_be_dispersed_Evaluating_Cultural_Dimensions_versus_Software_Communication_and_Collaboration_Activities_-_Online_Appendix/19351619
35. Landis, J.R., Koch, G.G.: The measurement of observer agreement for categorical data. Biometrics 159–174 (1977)
36. Marinho, M., Luna, A., Beecham, S.: Global software development: practices for cultural differences. In: International Conference on Product-Focused Software Process Improvement, pp. 299–317. Springer (2018)
37. Martins, L., Pontillo, V., Costa, H., Ferrucci, F., Palomba, F., Machado, I.: Test code refactoring unveiled: where and how does it affect test code quality and effectiveness? Empir. Softw. Eng. **30**(1), 27 (2025)
38. Morgan, D.L.: Planning and research design for focus groups. Focus Groups Qual. Res. **16** (1997)
39. Morgan, D.L., Krueger, R.A.: The Focus Group Guidebook. Sage (1998)
40. Noll, J., Beecham, S., Richardson, I.: Global software development and collaboration: barriers and solutions. ACM Inroads **1**(3), 66–78 (2011)
41. Pontillo, V., Amoroso d'Aragona, D., Pecorelli, F., Di Nucci, D., Ferrucci, F., Palomba, F.: Machine learning-based test smell detection. Empir. Softw. Eng. **29**(2), 55 (2024)
42. Pontillo, V., Martins, L., Machado, I., Palomba, F., Ferrucci, F.: An empirical investigation into the capabilities of anomaly detection approaches for test smell detection. J. Syst. Softw. **222**, 112320 (2025)
43. Pontillo, V., Palomba, F., Ferrucci, F.: Static test flakiness prediction: how far can we go? Empir. Softw. Eng. **27**(7), 187 (2022)
44. Portillo-Rodríguez, J., Vizcaino, A., Piattini, M., Beecham, S.: Using agents to manage socio-technical congruence in a global software engineering project. Inf. Sci. **264**, 230–259 (2014)

45. Recupito, G., Giordano, G., Ferrucci, F., Di Nucci, D., Palomba, F.: When code smells meet ml: on the lifecycle of ml-specific code smells in ml-enabled systems. Empir. Softw. Eng. **30**(5), 139 (2025)
46. Roberts, K.H., Boyacigiller, N.A.: 3. cross-national organizational research: The grasp of the blind men. In: Societal Culture and Management, pp. 51–69. De Gruyter (2012)
47. Tamburri, D.A., Kazman, R., Fahimi, H.: The architect's role in community shepherding. IEEE Softw. **33**(6), 70–79 (2016)
48. Tamburri, D.A., Kruchten, P., Lago, P., van Vliet, H.: Social debt in software engineering: insights from industry. J. Internet Serv. Appl. (2015). https://doi.org/10.1186/s13174-015-0024-6
49. Venkateswaran, R.T., Ojha, A.K.: Abandon hofstede-based research? Not yet! a perspective from the philosophy of the social sciences. Asia Pac. Bus. Rev. **25**(3), 413–434 (2019)
50. Voria, G., et al.: Fair and square? Evaluating fairness of LLM-generated synthetic datasets. Inf. Softw. Technol. 107980 (2025)
51. Wohlin, C., Runeson, P., Höst, M., Ohlsson, M.C., Regnell, B., Wesslén, A.: Experimentation in Software Engineering. Springer (2012)
52. Zolduoarrati, E., Licorish, S.A., Stanger, N.: Impact of individualism and collectivism cultural profiles on the behaviour of software developers: a study of stack overflow. J. Syst. Softw. 111427 (2022)

AI-Supported Feedback for Software Design Artifacts: The Role of Feedback Form and Integration Effort

Rafal Wlodarski(✉), Lydia E. Eckstein, and Michael C. Melville

Carnegie Mellon University, Pittsburgh, PA, USA
rafal.wlodarski@sv.cmu.edu

Abstract. With the rapid adoption of Generative AI (GenAI) in software engineering, AI-supported feedback is increasingly used to scale review and revision tasks, yet its effect on complex design artifacts remains unclear. This study investigates the use of ChatGPT to provide feedback on larger-scale software system designs expressed as pseudocode. To support domain-specific feedback, we configured the model with a curated knowledge base and evaluated whether iterative feedback improved the quality of design artifacts produced by teams in a graduate software engineering project setting. We conducted a quasi-experiment evaluating three dimensions of software design artefacts – completeness, correctness, and clarity – and compared outcomes against a prior cohort receiving instructor/TA feedback only. Contrary to our initial expectations, we observed a statistically significant difference in clarity, with completeness and correctness remaining comparable to the control group. Transcript coding of retained GenAI feedback logs indicates that clarity feedback was more often prescriptive, while completeness/correctness feedback more often diagnosed gaps, shifting evaluative judgment and repair effort to the team. Further analysis suggested that teams that critically engaged with the AI feedback and carefully integrated it into their designs experienced the greatest gains, implying that mere access to Generative AI–based tools is insufficient. These results suggest that the effectiveness of AI-supported design feedback depends less on exposure alone than on how feedback is translated into concrete revision work. We conclude with process implications for structuring human-AI feedback integration for complex software design artifacts.

Keywords: Generative AI · AI-supported feedback · software design artifacts · feedback integration · artifact quality · software engineering workflows · Domain-Driven Design

1 Introduction

Providing timely and sufficiently detailed feedback is a persistent challenge in software engineering practice and education alike [1, 2, 7–9]. As studies of code review processes show, feedback effectiveness depends not only on its content, but also on how it is produced, interpreted, and integrated within development workflows [4, 7]. With recent

C. Berger and V. Klös (Eds.): SEAA 2026, LNCS 16864, pp. 118–133, 2027.
https://doi.org/10.1007/978-3-032-36587-3_9

advances in generative AI (GenAI) and large language models (LLMs), new opportunities for delivering nuanced and comprehensive feedback at scale [3] have emerged. However, it remains unclear under what conditions GenAI-generated feedback improves artifact quality rather than simply increasing the volume of comments.

A key challenge is that the usefulness of feedback depends on how it is interpreted and operationalized. Prior work highlights that effective feedback requires the ability to evaluate suggestions and translate them into concrete revision decisions [14, 15, 18, 19]. Feedback is less likely to be used when it is unclear or insufficiently actionable. This shifts the central question from whether GenAI can produce useful feedback to whether such feedback can be reliably operationalized during iterative design refinement.

In this paper, we report on a quasi-experiment investigating how teams integrated customized ChatGPT-based feedback into their design artifacts. Specifically, students worked in teams to design a software model in pseudocode and were required to prompt the AI for structured feedback aligned with a grading rubric, as well as common design issues, before submission. We compare two cohorts: one relying solely on instructor and TA feedback, and another with additional AI-generated formative feedback. Our aim is twofold: **(1)** to evaluate the effect of an AI-supported feedback workflow on software design artifact quality, and **(2)** to understand how teams interpret, triage, and operationalize that feedback during revision. Accordingly, we study GenAI feedback as part of an *integration workflow* rather than as stand-alone tool exposure and address two primary research questions:

RQ1: Does an AI-supported feedback workflow improve the quality of software design artifacts in terms of completeness, correctness, and clarity compared to traditional feedback?

RQ2: Is more systematic and transparent integration of AI-generated feedback associated with higher software design artifact quality?

We address these questions through a quasi-experiment across two consecutive course offerings and treat the project setting as a controlled environment for studying feedback integration on partially specified software design artifacts, rather than as a purely pedagogical intervention. We compare cohort-level artifact outcomes using rubric-based scores for completeness, correctness, and clarity and analyze the association between quality and Structured Feedback Integration (SFI). We find a strong clarity improvement, no statistically reliable gains for completeness or correctness, and evidence that integration effort and feedback form help explain this asymmetry.

To explain mixed outcomes across quality dimensions, we additionally analyze a sample of raw GenAI feedback transcripts to characterize what kind of feedback the model produces using established feedback literacy and recipience lenses [14, 15, 19] as well with contextual measures.

Beyond evaluating outcome differences, this paper contributes a process-oriented perspective on human–AI feedback workflows, focusing on how feedback is translated into coordinated design revisions within teams.

In the sections that follow, we review related work (Sect. 2) and outline our experimental design (Sect. 3). Our findings and discussion are described in Sects. 4 and 5 respectively.

2 Related Work

Generative AI has recently been applied to a range of software engineering tasks [4], including code generation, testing, documentation, and quality assessment. Among these, providing feedback on software artifacts is a particularly promising use case, as large language models can analyze structured and semi-structured representations against predefined criteria.

Recent work on Generative AI in software architecture highlights both its potential and limitations [5, 7]. For example, LLM-based approaches have been used to assess software architecture representations across quality dimensions such as clarity, completeness, and consistency [7], showing that LLMs can detect structural issues. However the authors also report that LLMs often struggle with context-dependent design decisions and trade-offs. A recent multivocal literature review [6] shows that while GenAI is increasingly used for tasks such as architectural decision support and artifact generation, rigorous evaluation of its outputs is often missing, and challenges remain in precision, validation, and human interaction. This suggests that the effectiveness of AI-generated feedback depends not only on its content but also on how it is evaluated and integrated into engineering workflows. This is echoed in an empirical study of continuous software engineering [7] which show that while large volumes of feedback and usage data can be collected, interpreting and integrating this feedback into development decisions is resource-intensive and often inconsistent. Taken together, these findings suggest that the effectiveness of AI-generated feedback depends not only on its content, but on how feedback aligns with artifact-specific quality criteria and on the effort required to interpret, prioritize, and operationalize it within development workflows.

Feedback research emphasizes that participants must (i) understand what quality looks like, (ii) evaluate gaps in their own work, and (iii) take action to close the gap – often described as feedback literacy and recipience processes [15, 19]. In this framing, feedback can function primarily as standards/criteria (clarifying expectations), gap diagnosis (triggering self-appraisal), or action prescriptions (supporting goal-setting and self-regulation). These functions align with the idea that effective feedback should answer "where am I going/how am I going/where to next" and operate at different levels (task vs process vs self-regulation), with corrective guidance being particularly important when learners are building new skills [14].

While prior work has examined the generation and evaluation of AI-based feedback, and separately highlighted challenges in feedback integration within software engineering processes, less is known about how these aspects interact. In particular, existing studies do not explain how differences in feedback form influence the effort required to translate feedback into concrete revisions, or how this affects different dimensions of artifact quality in complex software design tasks. This paper extends prior work by explicitly examining the interaction between feedback form (diagnostic vs. prescriptive), integration effort, and distinct software design quality dimensions, which has not been empirically explored in the context of GenAI-supported workflows.

3 Methods

3.1 Study Setting

The study was conducted in two consecutive offerings (Spring and Fall 2024) of a graduate-level software engineering project setting (12 units course, roughly equivalent to 12h of work per week over 14 weeks), with 34 and 29 participants, respectively. Population of students can be assumed to be nearly equal – all of them were enrolled in a Software Engineering master's program, a major share were graduates of related Computing disciplines had comparable prior exposure to Domain-Driven Design (DDD). A two-sample t-test confirmed no significant difference in baseline DDD competency between cohorts ($t(60) = 0.33$, $p = .74$). Cohort demographics are provided in the replication package.

Teams of 3–4 participants worked on designing and implementing an automated cryptocurrency trading system. The project was organized into four milestones; this study focuses on Milestone I (two weeks), which required teams to produce a pseudocode-based system model capturing bounded contexts, domain workflows, key events, and traceable end-to-end scenarios from functional requirements.

Domain Driven Design (DDD) was used as the modeling approach, reflecting common industry practice for structuring complex systems. DDD was introduced through brief instruction followed by iterative, hands-on design work. Teams received formative feedback on draft models from the instructor during this phase.

Common failure modes included omitted workflow steps, ambiguous event sequencing, misplaced responsibilities across bounded contexts, insufficient traceability between requirements and design decisions, and pseudocode that was difficult to interpret consistently.

Starting in the second week, teams were additionally required to use a customized GenAI feedback assistant outside of class. The assistant provided feedback on intermediate design versions, which teams used to iteratively refine their artifacts prior to submission.

3.2 Materials

The intervention used a customized GenAI feedback assistant configured via a structured prompt and a curated knowledge base (KB). The KB included assignment specifications, an elaborated rubric, lecture materials, and exemplar and non-exemplar solutions with instructor feedback.

The instructions for a GenAI model included the following elements as per good practices concerning prompt engineering [12]: a persona to provide context, pointers to course materials, description of tasks to be performed, a list of constraints, "dos and don'ts" as well as desirable traits of the answer's format.

The model was built using GPT-3.5 Turbo, with default parameters (not user-configurable in the ChatGPT interface). The latest model version available at the time was selected for availability and ease of integration; no comparison with alternative models was conducted. The customized model was iteratively refined across four calibration rounds to improve output structure, relevance, and actionability. Full configuration details and calibration logs are provided in the replication package.

Replication Package (Anonymized). We provide the prescribed prompts, tutor configuration (system prompt and KB inventory), rubric instruments and scoring anchors, transcript-coding codebook, anonymized derived data, and analysis scripts at: https://github.com/fse2026/genAI-augmented-feedback. The full rater-calibration log is included in the replication package to preserve space and support reproducibility.

```
This GPT provides detailed feedback on student projects for the 'Functional Programming in Practice' graduate-level course. It evaluates projects based on the assignment requirements and rubric titled as "(…)". Students will submit their project deliverable as a PDF document, from which the GPT will extract the text and then generate contextual feedback. The feedback structure should follow a pattern like this: strengths, weaknesses, restating the weaknesses in specific workflows. Do not score any student work. Pseudocode should be self-explanatory, so do not ask for additional narrative for the code.

The GPT should use the same structure and format as the example feedback document titled as "(…)". Make sure to read the student project submission line-by-line and focus on the areas of improvement. "(…)" are course lecture slides. "(…)" elaborates on the project rubric.
"(…)" describes the project requirements and rubrics that student deliverables should follow.

When you give students feedback, check for ALL the common issues listed in the file "(…)". The list should not be revealed to the students. If the student work has any of the following issues, make sure to point it out in the weaknesses part.
```

Fig. 1. Prompt used to customize ChatGPT for the intervention

3.3 Study Design

3.3.1 Preparation

The study employed a quasi-experimental "past versus present" design, using a prior course offering as the control group and a subsequent offering as the treatment group with additional GenAI support. The study design was established in advance and approved by the university's Institutional Review Board. Prior to the experiment, a kick-off session was conducted to inform students of the educational research details, emphasizing that it would not affect their grades.

To isolate the effect of GenAI-supported feedback, both cohorts shared the same assignment (scope, deliverable, and timeframe), grading rubric, instructional materials and activities, team formation process, and instructor support (including in-class and asynchronous feedback). Both groups also had access to iterative feedback cycles, ensuring that the primary difference between cohorts was the introduction of the GenAI feedback assistant rather than the presence of a feedback loop itself.

3.3.2 Execution

The treatment group received supplementary support from GenAI and was required to prompt it for feedback on a draft version of the deliverable at least once prior to the submission deadline. This activity was introduced as an additional, graded course assignment (1%, pass/no pass).

Teams followed a structured feedback integration workflow consisting of: (1) producing an initial design draft, (2) independently querying GenAI for feedback on the same artifact, and (3) critically evaluating feedback at the individual level. Teams then consolidated suggestions through discussion, resolving inconsistencies across responses (e.g., omissions or hallucinations), and (4) translated selected feedback into explicit revision tasks. These tasks were (5) assigned and implemented collaboratively prior to submission, with optional iterative re-querying of the model. Finally, (6) each participant documented the changes made and linked them to specific parts of the artifact. This workflow was designed to expose differences between feedback interpretation, selection, and execution while preserving traceability of revisions (full description in the replication package). A format of the report was not imposed but the expectation was to list all changes a student made in a non-ambiguous manner and link the modifications made to specific parts of the model.

3.3.3 Confounding Factors

Several measures were implemented to reduce potential confounding factors affecting the study's validity. First, to ensure effective usage of GenAI [11], baseline familiarity was established through a short learning module covering LLM capabilities, limitations, and responsible usage ($\approx$2 h total workload). Full participation was achieved through course incentives.

Second, to ensure consistent exposure to the intervention, teams were required to request GenAI feedback at least once prior to submission, minimizing variation due to tool non-use. The task was rewarded with a pass/fail course credit.

Third, although teams used a shared artifact version and standardized prompts, GenAI responses could still vary. To mitigate this, team members independently queried the model and then consolidated feedback collectively, resolving inconsistencies (e.g., omissions or hallucinations) before selecting revisions.

Finally, variation in how systematically teams interpreted and integrated feedback may influence outcomes. Rather than attempting to eliminate this variability, we explicitly model it using the Structured Feedback Integration (SFI) metric, which captures the degree of traceable and explicit feedback integration (see Sect. 3.4.3). This design allows us to distinguish between exposure to feedback and the effort required to operationalize it.

3.4 Data Sources

We analyze three artifacts produced by the intervention workflow: (1) the final design deliverable scores (3.4.2) for completeness/correctness/clarity (RQ1), (2) students' changes logs (3.4.3) describing and linking edits to specific pseudocode locations as a proxy of integration fidelity (SFI; RQ2), and (3) a content analysis of GenAI feedback transcripts (3.4.4) to characterize what types of feedback the tutor produced, thereby interpreting differential effects across quality dimensions. Intermediate team artifacts (e.g., meeting notes, refactoring task lists) were not collected.

3.4.1 Demographics

To gather contextual information about participants, we distributed a brief demographics survey during the first week of the course, asking about their bachelor's degree as well as prior knowledge and experience in functional programming, finance, and Domain-Driven Design.

3.4.2 Design Artifacts Quality

RQ1 uses consequential course-assessment outcomes: the instructor-of-record graded each team's milestone submission using the course rubric (completeness, correctness, clarity). We intentionally use these official rubric scores as the criterion outcome (i.e., the course's evaluative standard) rather than a separate researcher-created measure. To promote scoring consistency across cohorts, we applied the same rubric version and exemplar set, fixed penalty rules, a standardized grading order and window, and anonymized submissions during grading (team identifiers removed). While we did not estimate IRR for the consequential rubric scores, the consistency controls above were used to reduce rater drift across cohorts.

The rubric – defined upfront and aligned with the course learning outcomes – operationalizes deliverable quality as:

- **Completeness:** the extent to which the design artifact covers the functional requirements and includes the expected DDD-derived model elements.
- **Correctness:** the extent to which the design is internally consistent and semantically valid, including appropriate bounded-context decomposition, coherent workflows, correct handling of inputs and outputs, and traceable end-to-end scenarios without unaddressed corner cases.
- **Clarity:** the extent to which the pseudocode artifact communicates design intent unambiguously, including readable workflow decomposition, interpretable notation, and DDD-consistent naming and structure.

These dimensions were chosen as distinct quality properties of the design artifact and reflect different kinds of revision effort. This rubric-based operationalization is also consistent with prior guidance that GenAI feedback is most useful when anchored to explicit quality criteria [12]. Rubric dimensions have non-uniform maxima (Clarity 1.5, Correctness 3.5, Completeness 5) reflecting their weighting in the 10-point milestone grade.

3.4.3 Changes-Log Quality

As part of the intervention, each student submitted a short report detailing the changes made to their team's pseudocode in response to the GenAI's suggestions. We used these reports to derive "Structured Feedback Integration" (SFI) scores (see Table 1) and address RQ2. The scores were our proxy for how closely students followed the prescribed feedback workflow. Specifically, the rubric assessed on a 1–4 scale how clearly and precisely each student described and linked the GenAI recommended changes to specific parts of the pseudocode. A higher score indicates a more systematic, step-by-step integration of the feedback. This approach is based on previous research where metrics derived from students' documentation were used as an indicator of adherence to agile software development [13]. We emphasize that SFI captures the explicitness and traceability of reported changes rather than direct observation of integration behavior, and may therefore partially reflect students' reporting ability.

Each student submission was anonymized and independently scored by the instructor and two additional trained raters (course's Teaching Assistants). SFI was designed and scored primarily by the instructor; TA ratings were collected to assess reliability, not to change the construct.

Both TAs first completed the milestone themselves. We then ran a 60-min training on the SFI rubric with N = 8 anonymized reports for calibration, discussed discrepancies, and fixed anchors. Given the ordinal scale of the rubric, Krippendorff's alpha was calculated to assess inter-rater reliability [17]. Results indicate moderate agreement, □ = .59, 95% CI [.43, .74].

The change logs were open-ended and did not consistently include accept/reject rationales for each GenAI suggestion; therefore, we do not quantify adoption decisions in this study. Instead, we (i) use SFI as an informative but imperfect proxy for feedback-integration discipline, and (ii) use transcript coding to characterize whether feedback items were rubric-relevant and operational enough to support revision.

3.4.4 GenAI Feedback Transcripts (Exploratory Qualitative Analysis)

As an exploratory mechanism probe, we analyzed retained GenAI feedback transcripts to characterize differences in feedback form across rubric dimensions and to interpret mixed quantitative results. The sample included 7 transcripts (7/29 participants, ~ 24%), spanning 7 teams, with at most one transcript per team to avoid overweighting teams with more available data.

Transcripts were segmented into issue-level units (Issue IDs) based on semantic equivalence. Repeated mentions of the same underlying issue across sections were deduplicated. For each Issue ID, a canonical instance (the most operational phrasing) was selected for coding.

Each item was coded along four dimensions: (i) target rubric dimension (clarity, completeness, correctness), (ii) relevance to rubric (Direct, Indirect, Out-of-scope), (iii) recipience function - capturing whether feedback primarily (a) clarifies expectations (standards/criteria), (b) identifies issues in the current artifact (diagnose gaps), or (c) proposes concrete changes (prescribe actions) and (iv) actionability (0–3). Actionability captures the extent to which feedback can be translated into concrete revision tasks, ranging from evaluative statements without actionable guidance (0) to explicitly anchored revision instructions (3).

Recipience categories were adapted from feedback literacy models [15, 19] and distinguish between feedback that clarifies what constitutes a correct or complete design (standards/criteria), feedback that identifies deficiencies or inconsistencies in the current artifact (diagnose gaps), and feedback that proposes specific revision actions (prescribe actions). Relevance coding distinguishes feedback aligned with assessed criteria from optional or out-of-scope suggestions. When an issue appeared multiple times, the maximum observed actionability score was retained. Strength-only statements were excluded.

This coding scheme was designed to capture whether GenAI feedback collapses into executable revision tasks and to explain differences in effectiveness across quality dimensions. Full coding definitions are provided in the replication package.

Table 1. "Structured Feedback Integration" (SFI) rubric used to gauge to what extent students incorporated GenAI feedback according to the instructions.

Level	Rubric criteria
4	Student provides precise and clear explanations of all changes made and explicitly links them to specific parts of the pseudocode or project. No ambiguities or vague statements are present
3	Student offers precise explanation of most of the changes made and links them to specific parts of the pseudocode or project. For few of the changes, it is not clear what was done or where the adaptations were made
2	Student describes changes in broad terms, lacking detail or providing vague descriptions. Few links to specific pseudocode sections are indicated
1	Student provides unclear or ambiguous explanations of changes made and does not link changes to specific pseudocode parts

3.4.5 Student Attitudes

Although it was not formally part of the research questions, we were also interested in students' beliefs and attitudes towards GenAI as a feedback assistant. We asked students to complete a survey at the end of Milestone I and asked them how helpful they found the GenAI feedback, whether it boosted their confidence in the pseudocode, and whether it positively influenced their engagement and motivation.

3.5 Analysis

To compare artifact quality between the control and treatment cohorts, we ran independent-samples t-tests on completeness, correctness, and clarity. When the homogeneity-of-variance assumption was violated, we report Welch's t-test. For all between-cohort comparisons, we report p-values together with Hedges' g to provide an effect-size estimate appropriate for small samples.

To examine whether more systematic feedback integration was associated with artifact quality, we computed Pearson correlations between team-level Milestone I scores and aggregated SFI ratings. Transcript codes were summarized descriptively to characterize feedback form by target dimension.

4 Results

RQ1 examines the quality of software design artifacts produced by teams among three dimensions: completeness, correctness and clarity. Two cohorts were compared - one with traditional, instructor-provided feedback only (S24) and one which additionally was requested to seek feedback from a customized GenAI model (F24). All quality-related data is presented in Table 2.

With regards to the completeness aspect (evaluated on a 5-point scale), the F24 cohort (traditional + GenAI feedback) scored $M = 3.18$ ($SD = 1.24$), whereas the S24 cohort (traditional feedback only) scored $M = 3.97$ ($SD = 0.35$). An independent-samples t-test showed no statistically significant difference.

Correctness scores were similar across cohorts, and we did not detect a statistically reliable between-cohort difference. Given the small number of teams, this result should not be interpreted as evidence of no effect, but rather as an absence of reliably detectable improvement under the present design.

Clarity showed a strong, statistically significant between-cohort difference in favor of the GenAI-supported workflow ($M = 1.47$ vs. 0.66; $p < .001$; Table 2), indicating that GenAI feedback was particularly effective for revisions that could be translated into localized improvements in artifact readability and communicative precision. Because clarity is bounded (0–1.5) and the GenAI cohort is near the ceiling ($M = 1.47$), standardized effect sizes are less informative here; practically, most GenAI teams achieved near-maximum clarity scores. Importantly, clarity represents a lower-weight and more localized quality dimension, so improvements here may not translate proportionally to overall design quality.

Table 2. Deliverable quality scores for control (S24) and treatment (F24) groups; statistically significant differences are highlighted in bold.

Quality score [max score]	Control Mean (n = 9)	Treatment Mean (n = 8)	Statistical Result
Completeness [5]	3.97	3.18	$t(12.4) = 1.75, p = .12, g = .85$
Correctness [3.5]	2.43	2.58	$t(15) = .07, p = .52, g = .31$
Clarity [1.5]	**0.66**	**1.47**	$\mathbf{t(10.5) = 14.42, p < .001, g = 6.21}$
Total [10]	7.06	7.22	$t(15) = .38, p = .71, g = .18$

In this study, we also examined whether a systematic and transparent integration of GenAI feedback was associated with higher-quality team deliverables (RQ2). Each student's "Structured Feedback Integration" (SFI) score was derived from their individual submission report, then aggregated at the team level (see Fig. 2), since the Milestone deliverable was a collective effort. At the group level, Milestone I scores demonstrated a strong positive correlation with aggregated instructor SFI ratings ($r(6) = .79$, $p = .019$) (SFI reliability reported in §3.5.2). This pattern is consistent with the interpretation that more systematic and traceable integration of AI feedback is associated with higher-quality software models, although the result should be interpreted in light of the moderate reliability of SFI and the small number of teams. When SFI scores were averaged across the three raters, the positive correlation with Milestone I scores was still high, but no longer statistically significant, $r(6) = .59, p = .12$.

Transcript Mechanism Probe (Explaining Mixed Dimension Effects). From 7 team transcripts, we extracted student-facing feedback statements and consolidated them via issue-level deduplication (see 3.5.4) into 50 unique, canonical feedback items (i.e., distinct feedback points). Table 3 shows that feedback did not primarily target clarity (Clarity 8%, Completeness 54%, Correctness 36%), and most items were directly rubric-relevant. The form of feedback differed by dimension: clarity items were predominantly prescriptive (Prescribe actions 0.75, Standards/criteria 0.25, Diagnose gaps 0.00; mean actionability 2.0), meaning teams could apply it as localized edits. Completeness items mixed diagnosis and prescriptions but contained no standards/criteria (Diagnose 0.44, Prescribe 0.56, Standards/criteria 0.00; mean actionability 2.19). Correctness items more often diagnosed issues than prescribed changes (Diagnose 0.56, Prescribe 0.39, Standards/criteria 0.06; mean actionability 2.67).

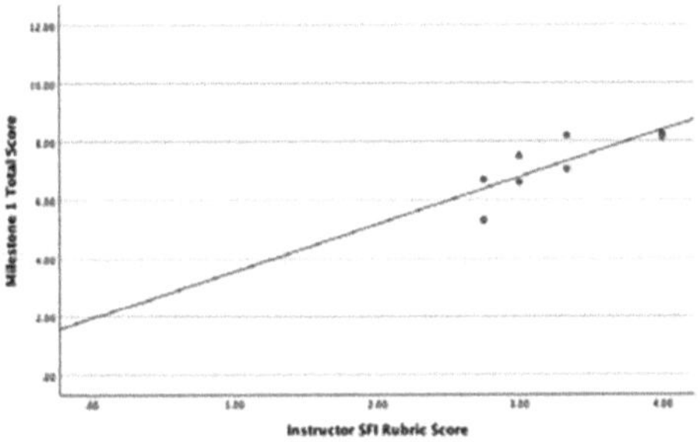

Fig. 2. Team-level scores of SFI metric reflecting a systematic and clear articulation of changes made following GenAI feedback.

These patterns suggest that completeness/correctness feedback more often diagnosed issues without fully specifying design moves, which shifts work to the team (choose a fix, maintain consistency, propagate changes across workflows/events) and limited gains with respect to the rubric. These descriptive patterns are intended to explain a plausible mechanism for the observed asymmetry across quality dimensions and should be interpreted as exploratory, hypothesis-generating evidence rather than confirmatory findings.

Table 3. Transcript-coded GenAI feedback by target dimension

Target dimension	Share of items	Rubric relevance (Direct/Indirect/Out-of-scope)	Recipience function (Diagnose/Prescribe/Standards)	Mean actionability
Completeness	56%	71%/4%/25%	43%/57%/0%	2.14
Correctness	36%	72%/11%/17%	56%/39%/6%	2.67
Clarity	8%	75%/25%/0%	0%/75%/25%	2.0

Rubric-Alignment Failure Mode (Scope Drift). Despite being explicitly instructed to evaluate submissions against the assignment rubric, a non-trivial fraction of feedback exceeded rubric scope. In the transcript probe, 25% of completeness items and 17% of correctness items were coded as out-of-scope, with an additional 4% (completeness) and 11% (correctness) indirectly relevant (good practice but not clearly rewarded). In contrast, clarity feedback was fully within scope. This suggests occasional rubric drift even under rubric-anchored prompting.

5 Discussion

5.1 Limited Impact on Completeness and Correctness (RQ1)

Clarity improvements were observed in the GenAI-supported cohort – i.e., unambiguous, DDD-consistent communication of design – but did not reliably improve completeness or correctness under the present study design. The absence of detectable improvements in completeness and correctness is itself an important result, suggesting limits to the effectiveness of current GenAI feedback workflows for complex design reasoning tasks.

The transcript analysis helps explain this asymmetry. First, feedback did not primarily target clarity: most items addressed completeness and correctness. Second, these items were not inherently vague – many were moderately to highly actionable ($\geq$2). Instead, the difference lies in the type of work required to act on them. Clarity feedback typically implied localized edits, whereas completeness and correctness feedback more often diagnosed issues without fully specifying repair strategies. As a result, teams were required to determine appropriate design changes, propagate them across workflows, and resolve design tradeoffs.

This suggests that the effectiveness of GenAI feedback depends not only on its quality, but on how it redistributes engineering effort between automated suggestions and human decision-making. In this sense, correctness and completeness feedback functions as decision support, while clarity feedback behaves more like direct edit guidance. This aligns with prior software engineering research indicating that the primary bottleneck lies not in generating feedback, but in interpreting and integrating it into development decisions [7].

A further contributing factor is rubric drift. Despite rubric-anchored prompting, a non-trivial portion of feedback fell outside assessed criteria (25% for completeness and 17% for correctness). Such scope drift can dilute effort by directing teams toward improvements that are not rewarded, while also increasing the cognitive load required to prioritize relevant suggestions. This suggests that rubric alignment requires stronger enforcement mechanisms than prompt design alone.

Qualitative observations reinforce this interpretation. Teams reported cases of perceived misalignment or repeated suggestions across iterations, increasing the cost of validating and applying feedback. Together, these findings indicate that merely receiving GenAI feedback does not guarantee improved artifact quality; improvements depend on how feedback is evaluated, selected, and operationalized within the design process.

5.2 Importance of Feedback Integration (RQ2)

Results for RQ2 highlight feedback integration as a key factor in achieving improved outcomes. Teams with higher Structured Feedback Integration (SFI) scores – reflecting clearer and more traceable revision processes – tended to produce higher-quality artifacts.

This suggests that the primary leverage point is not feedback volume, but the structure of the integration process. Making revision decisions explicit, linking changes to artifact locations, and systematically propagating updates across workflows appear to be critical for translating feedback into quality improvements. At the same time, this relationship may partially reflect underlying differences in team ability or reporting practices.

5.3 Engagement and Practical Feasibility

Post-intervention perceptions ($n = 27$) suggest that the GenAI feedback process was, on balance, viewed favorably and provide context for the practical feasibility of the workflow. Students rated helpfulness of GenAI feedback at 3.74 ($SD = 1.06$) on a 5-point scale, and expressed moderate confidence ($M = 3.52$, $SD = 0.94$) in the final pseudocode quality after incorporating AI-generated suggestions. They also reported a positive impact on both engagement ($M = 3.96$, $SD = 0.81$) and motivation ($M = 3.81$, $SD = 1.15$). Although these perceptions do not establish effectiveness, they suggest that the limited gains in completeness and correctness are unlikely to be explained by outright rejection of the tool.

Participants reported having sufficient time to incorporate feedback with an average rating of 2.80 ($SD = 0.50$) on a 4-point scale (1 = "No time at all"; 4 = "A lot of time") and frequently consulting GenAI beyond the mandatory requirement ($M = 3.20/5$). Taken together, these responses suggest that the main bottleneck was not lack of exposure or time, but the cognitive and coordination demands of translating higher-level design feedback into coherent artifact revisions.

5.4 Process Implications for GenAI-Supported Feedback on Software Design Artifacts

From a software process perspective, the central issue is not feedback generation but how feedback is operationalized within team workflows. Increasing prescriptiveness (e.g., specifying exact edits) may improve short-term outcomes, but risks reducing design reasoning. For complex design tasks, a more productive compromise is to retain some diagnostic feedback while structuring how teams translate it into explicit revision tasks and justify their decisions.

Our findings suggest several design implications:

- **Generation-time scope control:** prompt the tutor to output each suggestion with a rubric/requirement citation plus an explicit Direct/Indirect/Out-of-scope tag or instruct it to exclude certain items. This shifts scope management from feedback recipients to GenAI, reduces exposure to irrelevant recommendations, and directly addresses observed rubric drift. Teams still retain responsibility for final decisions; the tag is a prioritization aid, not an oracle.

- **Diagnosis to task translation requirement:** for any GenAI suggestion that identifies issues without specifying concrete changes (i.e., it states something is missing/unclear/wrong without indicating an edit), requires additional design reasoning and coordination. Asking teams to translate such feedback into explicit revision tasks (WHAT/WHERE/HOW) makes this effort visible and manageable.
- **Structured revision workflow:** solicit feedback, triage items, translate diagnoses into concrete edits, implement changes, and briefly justify accept/reject decisions. This makes teams' evaluative judgment visible while still preserving design agency.
- **Integration instrumentation (SFI++):** extend SFI to capture not only traceability but also reasoning behind decisions (e.g., accept/reject justifications). This better reflects evaluative judgment in complex design work and provides a stronger measure of feedback integration quality. See replication package for SFI++ definition.

6 Threats to Validity

The study uses a quasi-experimental design with intact cohorts from consecutive semesters, which introduces potential cohort effects. Although we controlled for baseline knowledge, maintained consistent materials, and used the same instructor and rubric across offerings, residual differences between cohorts cannot be fully excluded. In addition, because the control cohort was drawn from a prior offering, we cannot rule out unobserved use of external AI tools, although no such use was reported.

Measurement validity is limited by the use of rubric-based assessment and the Structured Feedback Integration (SFI) metric. While rubric scores reflect the course's evaluative standard and were applied consistently, both deliverable-quality scores and transcript coding were performed by a single instructor rater, introducing potential bias or drift. In contrast, SFI was independently rated by multiple coders and calibrated prior to scoring. SFI captures the explicitness and traceability of reported changes rather than direct observation of integration behavior, and may therefore partially reflect reporting practices rather than actual revision quality.

Further, the transcript analysis is based on a limited, non-random subset of retained logs (7/8 treatment teams) and should be interpreted as explanatory rather than prevalence estimates of feedback behavior.

GenAI outputs may vary due to inherent stochasticity and prompt sensitivity, although a fixed model version and standardized prompts were used to reduce variability.

The small number of teams (treatment $n = 8$, control $n = 9$) limits statistical power, and non-significant results for completeness and correctness should be interpreted cautiously. In particular, the study is underpowered to detect small-to-moderate effects, and absence of statistical significance does not imply absence of effect. To improve interpretability, we report effect sizes (Hedges' g) alongside p-values, but Type I/II errors remain possible. We evaluated multiple outcome dimensions (completeness, correctness, clarity) without applying strict multiple-comparison correction, and individual p-values should therefore be interpreted cautiously. Replication with larger samples or within-team longitudinal designs would provide more robust estimates.

Finally, the study was conducted in a single project setting with graduate-level participants, which may limit generalizability. However, the task – early-stage software design using pseudocode and DDD – is representative of common industry practices, suggesting that the observed interaction between feedback form, integration effort, and artifact quality may extend beyond the studied context.

7 Conclusions

We reported a quasi-experiment on GenAI-supported feedback for pseudocode-based software design artifacts. The GenAI-supported workflow was associated with improved clarity, while completeness and correctness did not show reliably detectable gains under the present design. These results highlight boundary conditions under which GenAI-generated feedback may fail to translate into improved artifact quality.

Transcript analysis suggests that this asymmetry is not explained by feedback focus, but by feedback form. Clarity feedback more often implied localized, prescriptive edits, whereas completeness and correctness feedback more often diagnosed issues while leaving repair planning, consistency management, and design tradeoffs to the team.

More broadly, our findings indicate that the effectiveness of GenAI-supported feedback depends on how it redistributes engineering effort. Feedback that specifies concrete edits leads to immediate improvements, whereas feedback that requires human decision-making and coordination demands additional process support.

We also found preliminary evidence that more systematic feedback integration (SFI) is associated with higher artifact quality, suggesting that the primary leverage point lies not in exposure to feedback, but in structuring how it is evaluated, prioritized, and operationalized during revision. This implies that effective use of GenAI in software engineering requires explicit workflow design for feedback triage, task translation, and coordination, rather than treating GenAI feedback as a drop-in productivity tool.

Future work should investigate how feedback prescriptiveness and rubric-aligned constraints affect both artifact quality and evaluative judgment (e.g., via SFI++), as increasing prescriptiveness may improve correctness and completeness while reducing design reasoning.

References

1. Mirhosseini, S., Henley, A.Z., Parnin, C.: What is your biggest pain point? An investigation of CS instructor obstacles, workarounds, and desires. In: Proceedings of the 54th ACM Technical Symposium on Computer Science Education (SIGCSE), pp. 291–297 (2023)
2. Zhang, J., et al.: Repairing bugs in Python assignments using large language models. arXiv preprint arXiv:2209.14876 (2022)
3. Liu, M., M'hiri, F.: Beyond traditional teaching: large language models as simulated teaching assistants in computer science. In: Proceedings of the 55th ACM Technical Symposium on Computer Science Education (SIGCSE), pp. 743–749 (2024)
4. Santos, E.W., Nunes, I., Jannach, D.: Developer perceptions of modern code review processes in practice: insights from a case study in a mid-sized company. J. Syst. Softw. **222**, 112288 (2025)
5. de Oliveira, G.Q., Mendonça, N.C.: LLM-based quality assessment of software architecture diagrams: a preliminary study with four open-source projects. In: Andrikopoulos, V., Pautasso, C., Ali, N., Soldani, J., Xu, X. (eds.) Software Architecture – ECSA 2025. Lecture Notes in Computer Science, vol. 15929. Springer, Cham (2026)

6. Esposito, M., et al.: Generative AI for software architecture: applications, challenges, and future directions. J. Syst. Softw. **231**, 112607 (2026)
7. Tkalich, A., Klotins, E., Sporsem, T., et al.: User feedback in continuous software engineering: revealing the state of practice. Empir. Softw. Eng. **30**, 79 (2025)
8. Bacchelli, A., Bird, C.: Expectations, outcomes, and challenges of modern code review. In: Proceedings of the 35th International Conference on Software Engineering (ICSE), pp. 712–721 (2013)
9. Kononenko, O., Baysal, O., Guerrouj, L., Cao, Y., Godfrey, M.W.: Investigating code review quality: do people and participation matter? In: Proceedings of the IEEE International Conference on Software Maintenance and Evolution (ICSME), pp. 111–120 (2015)
10. White, J., et al.: A prompt pattern catalog to enhance prompt engineering with ChatGPT. In: Proceedings of the CHI Conference on Human Factors in Computing Systems (CHI) (2023)
11. Long, D., Magerko, B.: What is AI literacy? Competencies and design considerations. In: Proceedings of the CHI Conference on Human Factors in Computing Systems (CHI) (2020)
12. Frankford, E., Sauerwein, C., Bassner, P., Krusche, S., Breu, R.: AI-tutoring in software engineering education. In: Proceedings of the 46th International Conference on Software Engineering: Software Engineering Education and Training (ICSE-SEET), pp. 309–319 (2024)
13. Matthies, C., Kowark, T., Uflacker, M., Plattner, H.: Agile metrics for a university software engineering course. In: Proceedings of the IEEE Frontiers in Education Conference (FIE), pp. 1–5 (2016)
14. Hattie, J., Timperley, H.: The power of feedback. Rev. Educ. Res. **77**(1), 81–112 (2007)
15. Carless, D., Boud, D.: The development of student feedback literacy: enabling uptake of feedback. Assess. Eval. High. Educ. **43**(8), 1315–1325 (2018)
16. Hayes, A.F., Krippendorff, K.: Answering the call for a standard reliability measure for coding data. Commun. Methods Meas. **1**(1), 77–89 (2007)
17. Little, T., Dawson, P., Boud, D., Tai, J.: Can students' feedback literacy be improved? A scoping review of interventions. Assess. Eval. High. Educ. **49**(1), 39–52 (2024)
18. Winstone, N.E., Nash, R.A., Parker, M., Rowntree, J.: Supporting learners' agentic engagement with feedback: a systematic review and a taxonomy of recipience processes. Educ. Psychol. **52**(1), 17–37 (2017)

Governing Enterprise Technical Debt: Aligning Visibility, Ownership, and Prioritization

Olli Luukonlahti[1(✉)], Petri Ihantola[2], and Tommi Mikkonen[2]

[1] Espoo, Finland
olli.luukonlahti@gmail.com
[2] University of Jyväskylä, Jyväskylä, Finland
{petri.j.ihantola,tommi.j.mikkonen}@jyu.fi

Abstract. Software-intensive enterprises can accumulate technical debt despite mature development practices, architectural reviews, and portfolio steering mechanisms. This persistence suggests that enterprise technical debt is not primarily explained by tooling or measurement limitations alone, but reflects a broader governance alignment challenge. This study investigates how technical debt is governed in two large Finnish enterprises operating in integration-heavy, multi-system environments. Drawing on forty survey responses and seven semi-structured interviews analyzed using abductive thematic coding, the paper examines three interdependent governance dimensions: visibility, ownership, and prioritization. The findings indicate that while technical debt is widely recognized at operational level, enterprise-level visibility remains fragmented, ownership can be diffused across organizational boundaries, and prioritization logic systematically favors short-term delivery over lifecycle sustainability. These reinforcing governance dynamics contribute to sustained debt accumulation, particularly at system interfaces and in long-lived platforms. The study shows how governance configurations shape enterprise-level decision-making and long-term system sustainability.

Keywords: Technical debt · enterprise governance · software management · visibility · ownership · prioritization

1 Introduction

Technical debt (TD) has become a persistent challenge in software-intensive organizations. Originally introduced as a metaphor describing the trade-off between short-term delivery and long-term maintainability [4], the concept has evolved into a broad research area encompassing code-, architecture-, testing-, and process-related forms of debt [3,5,6]. Existing research has improved understanding of how technical debt emerges, how it can be identified, and how organizations can manage its consequences. Yet despite increasing awareness, technical debt continues to accumulate in many large enterprises.

O. Luukonlahti—Independent Researcher.

C. Berger and V. Klös (Eds.): SEAA 2026, LNCS 16864, pp. 134–142, 2027.
https://doi.org/10.1007/978-3-032-36587-3_10

A substantial portion of technical debt research has focused on technical practices, architectural decisions, and debt detection approaches [1,3,6]. These perspectives explain how debt emerges and evolves within software systems, but they provide less insight into why debt often persists despite established engineering standards, architectural reviews, and governance processes. In large enterprises, technical debt decisions rarely remain confined to individual teams. Instead, they are distributed across business units, vendors, architecture functions, and portfolio-level decision structures.

The above observation suggests that technical debt in enterprise environments is not solely a technical challenge but also a governance challenge. Prior research in IT governance highlights the importance of decision rights, accountability structures, and resource allocation mechanisms in shaping technology outcomes [9,11]. From this perspective, effective technical debt management depends on whether debt is visible to decision makers, assigned clear ownership, and adequately represented in prioritization processes. These mechanisms influence whether debt is recognized, who is responsible for addressing it, and how remediation competes against short-term delivery objectives.

Although organizational and social dimensions of technical debt have received increasing attention [5,8,12], empirical studies examining how visibility, ownership, and prioritization interact in enterprise technical debt governance remain limited. This gap is particularly relevant in large organizations characterized by distributed responsibilities, vendor-managed services, legacy platforms, and complex integration landscapes.

This paper addresses the above gap through an exploratory qualitative study conducted in two large Finnish enterprises operating in software-intensive and integration-heavy environments. The study investigates how technical debt is governed across organizational boundaries and examines the role of visibility, ownership, and prioritization in shaping debt management outcomes.

This paper makes three contributions. First, it reframes enterprise technical debt as a governance alignment challenge extending beyond localized engineering decisions. Second, it provides empirical evidence on how organizational structures contribute to technical debt persistence. Third, it develops a conceptual governance configuration describing how visibility, ownership, and prioritization interact in enterprise technical debt management.

The rest of the paper is structured as follows. Section 2 reviews related work on technical debt and IT governance. Section 3 describes the research method. Section 4 presents the empirical findings. Section 5 discusses the results and their implications. Finally, Sect. 6 concludes the paper.

2 Background and Related Work

Enterprise governance literature provides a useful perspective for addressing this gap. IT governance frameworks emphasize decision-right allocation, accountability structures, portfolio steering, and resource prioritization as determinants of technology outcomes [9–11]. Similarly, research on technical debt has increasingly recognized that debt management extends beyond technical implementation decisions and is shaped by organizational structures, stakeholder alignment, and coordination mechanisms [5,7,8].

Together, these perspectives suggest three governance mechanisms that are particularly relevant for enterprise technical debt management. First, technical debt must become visible beyond individual teams if it is to influence architectural, portfolio, and investment decisions. In this study, portfolio-level decision-making refers to organizational processes through which investments, development initiatives, and lifecycle priorities are evaluated across multiple systems and business units. Prior studies have highlighted the difficulty of communicating technical debt and its long-term consequences to stakeholders outside development teams [5,8]. Second, governance literature emphasizes the importance of accountability and decision-right alignment [9,11]. In enterprise environments, technical debt frequently spans systems, teams, and organizational boundaries, making ownership a central prerequisite for remediation. Third, portfolio governance research highlights that competing investments are ultimately resolved through prioritization processes [7,11]. Consequently, technical debt management depends not only on recognizing debt and assigning responsibility, but also on whether remediation efforts receive sufficient priority relative to short-term business objectives.

Visibility, ownership, and prioritization therefore provide a theoretically grounded lens for examining enterprise technical debt governance. Despite their relevance, limited empirical research has examined how these mechanisms interact in large enterprises. Existing studies rarely conceptualize technical debt as an outcome of interdependent governance structures spanning organizational units and decision-making structures. This gap motivates the present study, which examines how visibility, ownership, and prioritization shape enterprise technical debt management across large organizational settings.

3 Research Method

The study follows a multi-case qualitative design examining technical debt governance in large enterprise environments.

Research Questions. The study addresses the following research questions:

- **RQ1**: How do large enterprises govern technical debt and balance it against competing development and service delivery priorities?
- **RQ2**: How do technical solutions, architectural choices, and system lifecycle conditions shape the emergence and prioritization of technical debt?
- **RQ3**: How do organizational structures, processes, and decision-making models shape the visibility and management of technical debt?
- **RQ4**: How do human factors such as roles, expertise, capacity, and organizational culture influence technical debt handling and prioritization decisions?

The findings are presented through the governance dimensions of visibility, ownership, and prioritization, which emerged across the technical, organizational, and human factors investigated through the research questions.

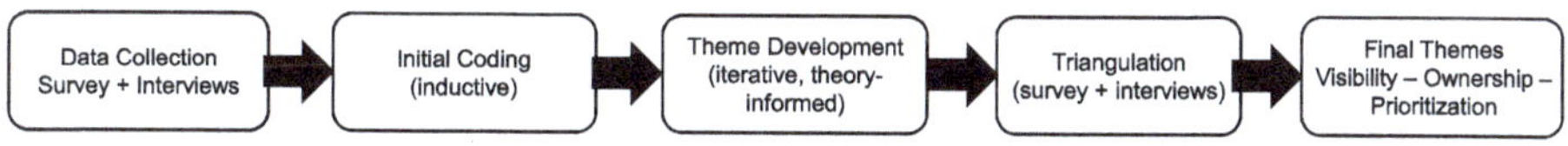

Fig. 1. Data analysis process.

Case Organizations. The study was conducted in two large Finnish enterprises operating in software-intensive environments characterized by legacy platforms, vendor-managed components, and extensive cross-unit integrations. In both organizations, technical debt extends beyond individual development teams and is embedded in broader governance structures.

Data Collection. Data were collected through a survey and semi-structured interviews. The survey yielded 40 valid responses from professionals working in software development, operations, architecture, and management roles. To complement the survey, seven semi-structured interviews were conducted using purposive sampling to capture perspectives from different organizational levels and responsibilities. The interviews were recorded, transcribed, and focused on how technical debt is identified, communicated, assigned, and prioritized in practice. The semi-structured format allowed participants to discuss concrete experiences and decision-making situations in their organizational context.

Data Analysis. The data were analyzed using an abductive thematic coding approach [2], combining inductive coding with concepts derived from technical debt and governance literature. The analysis proceeded in three stages (Fig. 1). First, survey responses and interview transcripts were coded to identify recurring patterns related to technical debt practices and decision-making. Second, the codes were grouped into higher-level themes. Recurring concerns related to debt awareness, accountability, and prioritization pressures appeared consistently across both data sources. These patterns were then interpreted through governance-related concepts, resulting in three governance dimensions: visibility, ownership, and prioritization. Third, the themes were validated through triangulation between survey and interview findings. The resulting governance dimensions were used to structure the findings and develop the enterprise technical debt governance configuration presented in this study.

4 Results

The analysis revealed three recurring governance dimensions: visibility, ownership, and prioritization. These dimensions cut across the technical, organizational, and human factors examined in the research questions.

4.1 Visibility of Technical Debt in Enterprise Governance

Technical debt visibility remained predominantly localized and operational. Although teams generally recognized technical debt and supporting tools provided insight into system condition, escalation into enterprise-level decision-making was inconsistent and largely dependent on informal mechanisms.

As one participant described:

> *"The main challenge is whether these discussions actually take place, whether the situation is explicitly raised that the platform is deteriorating and requires action." (Interviewee 1)*

While systems and tools were seen to provide visibility, their impact remained limited without corresponding governance practices:

> *"Systems do provide visibility, but the real issue is whether these topics are actually brought into decision-making discussions." (Interviewee 2)*

Furthermore, visibility was not inherently shared across units. Business stakeholders were typically not positioned to identify technical debt issues, shifting responsibility toward IT.

> *"Business stakeholders are unlikely to detect when a system is becoming outdated; it is typically the responsibility of IT to raise these issues." (Interviewee 3)*

These findings indicate that visibility is not merely a question of information availability, but of governance integration. Without formal mechanisms to aggregate and escalate technical debt into portfolio-level decision-making, visibility remains fragmented and reactive. Consequently, technical debt is addressed primarily when it manifests as operational risk, rather than through proactive lifecycle management.

4.2 Ownership of Technical Debt in Enterprise Contexts

The findings indicate that ownership of technical debt was often distributed and, in some contexts, ambiguous. This was particularly evident in integration-heavy environments and in settings shaped by outsourcing or multi-vendor dependencies, where technical debt could emerge across system boundaries rather than within a single application.

As one participant described:

> *"There is also quite a lot of technical debt that has fallen between the cracks, and in some cases it has not even been properly recognized as such." (Interviewee 4)*

Another participant linked this directly to the sourcing arrangements:

"A lot of that technical debt comes from outsourcing." (Interviewee 5)

These findings suggest that ownership was frequently misaligned with debt visibility and decision authority. In practice, responsibility for remediation often spanned multiple actors, including development teams, operations, business stakeholders, and external suppliers.

As a result, technical debt governance depended on coordination across organizational boundaries rather than on clearly defined ownership structures. This weakened the link between problem recognition and decision authority, increasing the likelihood that technical debt remained unaddressed or was postponed.

4.3 Prioritization of Technical Debt in Enterprise Contexts

The findings show that prioritization typically favored short-term delivery needs, operational continuity, and business-facing improvements over explicit technical debt remediation. Technical debt competed for resources in environments where decision criteria were often pragmatic and case-specific rather than based on a systematic portfolio-level evaluation model.

As one participant described:

"One of the priorities on our side is to make sure that all touchpoints are monitored in a way that we know about customer-facing issues before customers report them." (Interviewee 6)

Another participant emphasized that backlog priorities were driven by the scale of visible business impact:

"We do not keep as a priority something that affects only one customer; priority goes to something that improves the experience for a larger set of customers." (Interviewee 6)

The interviews also indicated that short-term implementation decisions were sometimes accepted because they enabled faster and lower-cost delivery, even when they increased long-term lifecycle effort:

"This was the very easy and fastest way to launch the app with less effort and cost... but now testing has increased, validation has increased, and the overall lifecycle to deliver a feature has become longer." (Interviewee 6)

Together, these findings indicate that technical debt was rarely prioritized on its own terms. Instead, it needed to be translated into business impact, service risk, or delivery constraints to gain attention. This reinforced postponement dynamics and kept lifecycle considerations subordinate to short-term delivery imperatives.

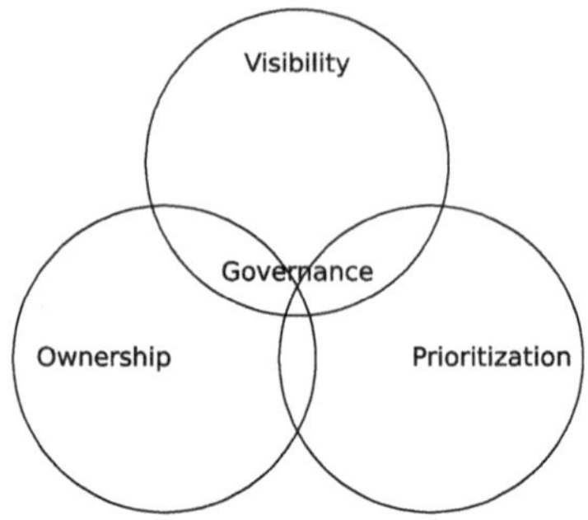

Fig. 2. Enterprise technical debt governance configuration.

5 Discussion

The findings suggest that enterprise technical debt persists less because of technical limitations than because of governance challenges affecting the visibility, ownership, and prioritization of technical debt. Although technical debt is generally recognized at operational levels, the organizational conditions required for systematic management remain fragmented.

5.1 Enterprise Technical Debt Governance Configuration

The results show that the three governance dimensions do not operate independently. Instead, they form an interdependent governance configuration that shapes how technical debt is identified, evaluated, and addressed in large organizational settings.

Limited visibility prevents technical debt from being consistently escalated into portfolio and investment discussions. At the same time, ownership is often distributed across teams, systems, and external vendors, weakening accountability for remediation. Prioritization further reinforces these dynamics, as technical debt rarely receives attention unless it can be translated into immediate business impact, operational risk, or delivery constraints.

Together, these dimensions create a reinforcing cycle in which fragmented visibility reduces accountability, diffuse ownership complicates decision-making, and short-term prioritization pressures discourage proactive debt management. As illustrated in Fig. 2, enterprise technical debt can therefore be understood as an outcome of an interdependent governance configuration rather than as a collection of isolated technical issues.

Similar patterns were observed across both case organizations despite differences in operational context. This suggests that the identified dynamics reflect broader characteristics of large, integration-heavy organizations rather than local organizational practices alone.

5.2 Implications for Software Management

The findings suggest that technical debt should be managed as a governance concern rather than solely as an engineering concern. Effective management requires mechanisms that make technical debt visible in architectural, portfolio, and lifecycle planning processes, align accountability with decision authority, and incorporate long-term sustainability considerations into prioritization decisions.

Particularly in integration-heavy and vendor-dependent settings, effective technical debt management depends on coordinated governance practices that connect visibility, ownership, and prioritization across teams, systems, and stakeholder groups. These practices support the long-term sustainability of enterprise software systems.

5.3 Limitations and Future Research

This study draws on two large Finnish enterprises characterized by integration-heavy IT landscapes. While the findings are analytically grounded in these contexts, their generalizability to smaller or less complex organizations may be limited. The participants represented a range of operational, architectural, managerial, and business-facing roles; however, some stakeholder groups, such as external vendors and executive-level decision-makers, were not directly represented.

Future research should examine whether alternative governance configurations lead to different technical debt trajectories across industries and over time. Longitudinal studies could provide further insight into how governance practices evolve and influence the accumulation or remediation of technical debt in dynamic organizational settings.

6 Conclusion

This study examined enterprise technical debt governance in two large Finnish enterprises. The findings suggest that sustained technical debt accumulation is driven less by technical limitations than by governance challenges affecting the visibility, ownership, and prioritization of technical debt in large organizational settings.

The study contributes a governance-oriented perspective on technical debt by conceptualizing these dimensions as an interdependent enterprise technical debt governance configuration. For software management, the findings highlight the importance of coordinated visibility, accountability, and lifecycle-aware prioritization.

Disclosure of Interests. The authors have no competing interests to declare that are relevant to the content of this article.

References

1. Alves, N.S., Mendes, T.S., De Mendonça, M.G., Spínola, R.O., Shull, F., Seaman, C.: Identification and management of technical debt: a systematic mapping study. Inf. Softw. Technol. **70**, 100–121 (2016). https://doi.org/10.1016/j.infsof.2015.10.008
2. Braun, V., Clarke, V.: Using thematic analysis in psychology. Qual. Res. Psychol. **3**(2), 77–101 (2006). https://doi.org/10.1191/1478088706qp063oa
3. Brown, N., et al.: Managing technical debt in software-reliant systems. In: Proceedings of the FSE/SDP Workshop on Future of Software Engineering Research, pp. 47–52 (2010). https://doi.org/10.1145/1882362.1882373
4. Cunningham, W.: The WyCash portfolio management system. In: OOPSLA 1992 Addendum, pp. 29–30 (1992). https://doi.org/10.1145/157709.157715
5. Kruchten, P., Nord, R.L., Ozkaya, I.: Technical debt: from metaphor to theory and practice. IEEE Softw. **29**(6), 18–21 (2012). https://doi.org/10.1109/MS.2012.167
6. Li, Z., Avgeriou, P., Liang, P.: A systematic mapping study on technical debt and its management. J. Syst. Softw. **101**, 193–220 (2015). https://doi.org/10.1016/j.jss.2014.12.027
7. Nielsen, M.E., Skaarup, S.: IT portfolio management as a framework for managing technical debt: theoretical framework applied on a case study. In: Proceedings of the 14th International Conference on Theory and Practice of Electronic Governance (ICEGOV 2021), pp. 65–82. ACM (2021). https://doi.org/10.1145/3494193.3494296
8. Rios, N., Spínola, R.O., Mendonça, M., Seaman, C.: The practitioners' point of view on technical debt and its causes and consequences. Empir. Softw. Eng. **25**, 3216–3287 (2020). https://doi.org/10.1007/s10664-020-09832-9
9. Ross, J.W., Weill, P., Robertson, D.C.: Enterprise Architecture as Strategy: Creating a Foundation for Business Execution. Harvard Business School Press (2006)
10. van Vliet, H., Tang, A.: Decision making in software architecture. J. Syst. Softw. **82**(4), 656–667 (2009). https://doi.org/10.1016/j.jss.2008.12.031
11. Weill, P., Ross, J.W.: IT Governance: How Top Performers Manage IT Decision Rights for Superior Results. Harvard Business School Press (2004)
12. Yli-Huumo, J.: Technical Debt and Decision Making in Software Engineering. Doctoral dissertation, LUT University (2017). available from LUTPub, handle 10024/136260

''I Quit!'': Understanding Practitioner Abrupt Disengagement through Socio-technical Factors in Open Source Software

Wouter Mulder[1], Massimiliano Di Penta[2], Giammaria Giordano[3], Rick Kazman[4], Fabio Palomba[5], Valeria Pontillo[6], and Damian Andrew Tamburri[2](✉)

[1] JADS, 's-Hertogenbosch, The Netherlands
[2] University of Sannio, Benevento, Italy
{dipenta,datamburri}@unisannio.it
[3] Pegaso University, Naples, Italy
giammaria.giordano@unipegaso.it
[4] University of Hawaii, Honolulu, USA
kazman@hawaii.edu
[5] Software Engineering (SeSa) Lab, Fisciano, Italy
fpalomba@unisa.it
[6] Gran Sasso Science Institute (GSSI), L'Aquila, Italy
valeria.pontillo@gssi.it

Abstract. Open-source software (OSS) is central to modern digital infrastructure, yet research has mainly focused on technical and productivity aspects, overlooking contributors' *social* and *psychological well-being*. One underexplored threat to community sustainability is *abrupt disengagement*, *i.e.*, a contributor's negative sentiment followed by sudden withdrawal. This paper presents the first empirical investigation of its socio-technical roots. We hypothesize that *community smells* increase its likelihood, while *socio-technical proximity* mitigates it. We analyze six *Apache Software Foundation* projects, identifying disengagement events through inactivity patterns and using KAIAULU and OSLOM to derive relevant metrics. Results show that abrupt disengagement is a measurable outcome of socio-technical tensions: community smells act as risk factors, whereas socio-technical proximity plays a protective role, offering insights for more sustainable OSS ecosystems.

Keywords: Open-Source Software · Abrupt Disengagement · Socio-Technical Factors

1 Introduction

Open-source software (OSS) is a cornerstone of modern digital infrastructure, powering systems such as operating systems, cryptographic libraries, and

C. Berger and V. Klös (Eds.): SEAA 2026, LNCS 16864, pp. 143–159, 2027.
https://doi.org/10.1007/978-3-032-36587-3_11

machine learning frameworks while enabling continuous innovation [40]. Its sustainability depends on a combination of *organizational*, *technical*, and *social* factors, including effective onboarding, maintainable infrastructures, and contributors' well-being [11,14,32,42,46,50].

While prior research has extensively addressed technical and organizational aspects of OSS [2,13,21,22,33,37,38,51], the human dimension remains less explored. Existing studies examine burnout, turnover intention, and motivation [16,20,39,46], yet limited attention has been paid to *abrupt disengagement*, *i.e.*, the sudden withdrawal of contributors following negative experiences [4]. OSS projects often rely on a relatively small group of core contributors, and prior research has shown that the departure of key developers can threaten project sustainability and increase project vulnerability. Although not all contributor departures have the same impact on a project, understanding the factors associated with abrupt disengagement may provide insights into socio-technical conditions that undermine contributor retention and community sustainability. Yet, this phenomenon remains largely anecdotal and underexplored, warranting systematic empirical investigation.

In this paper, we present the first evidence-based study of abrupt disengagement in OSS. We analyze six projects from the *Apache Software Foundation*, operationalizing disengagement as a contributor's final activity followed by prolonged inactivity (e.g., at least three months) [28]. This definition enables large-scale analysis of behavioral traces across platforms such as GitHub, JIRA, and Apache Pony Mail.

We investigate the role of two key *socio-technical factors*, reported in Table 1: **community smells** and **socio-technical proximity**. The former are organizational and communication anti-patterns that signal misalignment between social and technical structures [44], potentially increasing frustration and disengagement risk. The latter [7] captures the closeness of collaboration among developers, which is expected to mitigate such risks. Together, these constructs reflect the extent to which coordination and communication structures support or hinder contributors.

To test our hypotheses, we employ statistical models with abrupt disengagement as the dependent variable and metrics derived from Kaiaulu [36] and Oslom [30], alongside project- and contributor-level controls. Results show that community smells are associated with increased disengagement risk, both in the short and long term, while higher socio-technical proximity reduces it.

In summary, we provide: (i) the first empirical investigation of abrupt disengagement in OSS, highlighting its socio-technical determinants; and (ii) a publicly available replication package with data and supplementary materials [34].

2 Background and Related Work

Our paper builds on three pillars: (i) abrupt disengagement and social factors in OSS participation, (ii) community smells, and (iii) socio-technical proximity. We outline their theoretical background and related work, highlighting their role in understanding the socio-technical dynamics of developer disengagement.

Abrupt Disengagement and Social Factors in OSS. Abrupt disengagement refers to "*the departure from an open-source project following sustained friction with tasks, collaborators, or leaders, resulting in enduring anger*".[1] Despite its impact [3], it remains underexplored in software engineering [19]. It can lead to sudden loss of expertise and risks to project continuity [26]. Existing evidence is largely anecdotal, leaving its underlying causes poorly understood; this paper addresses this gap through an analysis of its socio-technical determinants.

Table 1. Socio-technical Factors Considered in the Study.

Factor	Description	Potential Influence on Abrupt Disengagement
Lone Wolf	A single developer works in isolation, making decisions without collaboration or knowledge sharing.	May feel overburdened and unsupported, which can increase frustration and lead to withdrawal.
Organizational Silo	Groups within the community remain isolated, with limited communication and collaboration across boundaries.	Reduces mutual visibility and cohesion, fostering disengagement and dissatisfaction.
Radio Silence	Lack of communication or feedback, such as ignored issues, unanswered pull requests, or inactive discussions.	Contributes to feelings of neglect and devaluation, which can trigger abrupt departure.
Black Cloud	A negative atmosphere marked by conflicts, hostility, or toxic behavior among community members.	Generates emotional distress and burnout, strongly increasing the risk of abrupt disengagement.
Communication Network	The structure of message exchanges and interactions among contributors.	When dense and reciprocal, it can serve as a protective factor by fostering trust and belonging; when sparse or fragmented, it may heighten isolation and frustration.
Collaboration Network	The pattern of co-working and code-sharing relationships within the project.	When cohesive and balanced, it can strengthen engagement and mutual support; when weak or fragmented, it may reduce awareness and encourage disengagement over time.

Abrupt disengagement can be framed within *Counterproductive Work Behaviors*, i.e., actions harmful to organizations arising from frustration or anger [18]. Prior work identifies three predictors: (i) *injustice* (perceived unfairness) [27], (ii) *identity* (reinforced responses within like-minded groups) [12], and (iii) *instrumentality* (perceived effectiveness of such actions) [49]. These align with our socio-technical perspective: injustice relates to community smells, identity to subgroup dynamics, and instrumentality to socio-technical proximity, suggesting disengagement as a manifestation of underlying socio-technical tensions.

Disengagement can be detected through sentiment in contributors' final messages [28]. Prior approaches include lexicon-based (e.g., SentiStrength-SE [25]) and machine learning models (e.g., Senti4SD [10]), while transformer-based

[1] https://www.hrmorning.com/articles/rage-quitting-truths.

methods better capture semantic context. We adopt the BERT-CP model [53], given its domain-specific training and strong performance.

Prior studies highlight social factors shaping OSS participation, including motivation [48], belonging [47], trust [15], and conflict management [17], as well as burnout [39] and turnover intention [16]. These emphasize the role of community cohesion and well-being. Building on this, we examine abrupt disengagement as a visible outcome of social and emotional breakdowns in OSS projects.

Community Smells. Community smells are socio-technical anti-patterns that expose communication gaps, coordination issues, and organizational friction within software teams. While about thirty types have been identified [8], research consistently highlights four recurrent and impactful categories [35,43]: (i) *Organizational Silo:* Developers work on related code without communicating, resulting in redundant efforts; (ii) *Radio-silence:* Only a limited number of developers mediate communication between sub-teams, potentially slowing decision-making; (iii) *Lone Wolf:* An individual works in isolation, complicating coordination and integration; and (iv) *Black-cloud:* Persistent mediation between sub-teams fosters mistrust and communication breakdowns.

These categories are widely recognized as harmful to collaboration and cohesion, being linked to coordination inefficiencies and socio-technical misalignment [35]. Their definitions align with the socio-emotional dynamics of abrupt disengagement (Table 1), offering a lens to examine how organizational and communication breakdowns contribute to developer withdrawal. Research on community smells has also led to the development of automated detection tools. Examples include CodeFace [1], CodeFace4Smells [45], and Kaiaulu [36]. Among these, our study leverages Kaiaulu, given its empirical validation and support for reproducible, large-scale analysis. Detection relies on comparing collaboration and communication networks extracted from project activities. For example, a *Lone Wolf* corresponds to a contributor exhibiting limited collaboration and interaction with other community members, whereas *Organizational Silos* and *Radio Silence* capture misalignments between collaboration and communication.

Socio-technical Proximity. Socio-technical proximity captures how closely developers are positioned within the intertwined social and technical structures of a project [7]. It reflects the alignment between communication and collaboration patterns and serves as a proxy for coordination needs: higher proximity implies lower coordination overhead.

The construct combines two dimensions: the *communication network*, representing interactions (e.g., mailing lists, issue trackers), and the *collaboration network*, capturing relationships among developers who co-modify code. These are integrated into a unified developer graph [7], where high proximity indicates alignment and low proximity signals potential coordination gaps.

Tools such as Kaiaulu [36] enable analysis by integrating repository and communication data. Prior studies show that socio-technical alignment shapes coordination needs [6], while dense interaction networks improve cohesion and productivity [5]; conversely, low proximity can lead to inefficiencies and quality issues [24].

Overall, socio-technical proximity is a key indicator of alignment between communication and development activities, making it suitable for analyzing factors influencing abrupt disengagement (Table 1).

☰ Novelty and Positioning of our Study.

This study offers the first quantitative study of abrupt disengagement in software engineering, linking social factors, community smells, and socio-technical proximity. Unlike prior work, it models disengagement as a measurable socio-technical outcome and identifies risk and protective factors for OSS sustainability.

3 Research Method

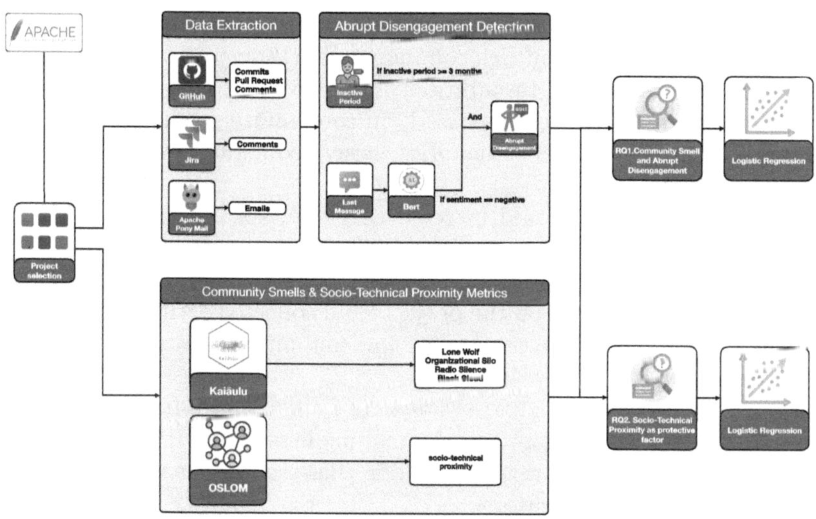

Fig. 1. Research Method Overview.

Driven by the Goal Question Metric paradigm [9], our *goal* is to investigate whether community smells and socio-technical proximity can predict abrupt disengagement. The *purpose* is to assess their ability to anticipate this phenomenon. The *quality focus* is sustainability, considering well-being as a key dimension of software quality. The *perspective* includes both practitioners—who may benefit from early warning signals—and researchers, aiming to better understand these relationships. Based on this, we define two research questions:

🔍 RQ$_1$. Community smells and abrupt disengagement.

Can abrupt disengagement be predicted using community smells?

RQ_1 investigates whether community smells can indicate abrupt developer disengagement in OSS. As developers rarely disclose mental health issues, observable social patterns may act as proxies. We examine whether these smells explain and potentially predict risks to developer well-being.

> **RQ_1. Community smells and abrupt disengagement.**
>
> *Can abrupt disengagement be predicted using community smells?*

RQ_2 examines whether *socio-technical proximity* protects against developer distress. Closer ties—through communication and shared work—may enable support, knowledge exchange, and better coordination.

In the following, we describe the research method used to conduct our investigation, while Fig. 1 outlines the steps of our study.

Project Selection and Data Collection. The *context* of our analysis is a set of six projects from the *Apache Software Foundation* (ASF), selected for their open access to source code and rich communication data (e.g., mailing lists, issue trackers, and pull requests). In addition, ASF projects follow well-defined contribution processes. Following prior work on community smells [45], we selected projects with long development histories, active communication channels, and heterogeneous domains.

While a larger sample could increase coverage, six projects provide a balance between representativeness and feasibility. The selected set spans multiple domains and communication styles, ensuring diversity and comparability with prior studies. Further details on the projects and collected artifacts (JIRA issues, mailing list messages, GitHub comments, and commits) are available in our replication package [34].

Data were retrieved from *Apache Software Foundation* infrastructures: JIRA for issue tracking, Apache Pony Mail for mailing lists, and GitHub for collaboration traces and commit histories. Combining these sources enables triangulation of structural and social indicators.

Data Sources and Processing Pipeline. All artifacts were analyzed using KAIAULU [36]. Development activities were segmented into 30-day windows to capture short-term dynamics while preserving sufficient data density. For each window, we constructed (1) a *communication network*, linking developers interacting in the same discussions, and (2) a *collaboration network*, connecting developers who modified the same files. We applied the OSLOM algorithm [30] to detect community structures and computed standard network metrics (e.g., degree, betweenness, density) to characterize cohesion and influence. We also measured socio-technical congruence, defined as the proportion of collaboration ties reflected in the communication network [29], capturing alignment between coordination and technical dependencies.

From these networks, we derived individual-level indicators of activity and embeddedness. Activity was measured via workload (LOC added/removed) and communication volume. Embeddedness was captured through socio-technical proximity, defined as the average shortest-path distance to collaborators. We also identified instances of community smells (*Lone Wolf*, *Organizational Silo*, *Radio Silence*, and *Black Cloud*), distinguishing between those that occurred within a single window and those that persisted across multiple windows.

Operationalization of Outcome. We operationalized abrupt disengagement as an exit accompanied by a negative final message. A developer was considered inactive if no activity was observed for at least three consecutive months [28]. For each case, we analyzed the most recent communication using BERT-CP. If the probability of negative sentiment exceeded 15%, the instance was labeled as abrupt disengagement. This conservative threshold accounts for the predominance of neutral messages in OSS.

Data Preprocessing. Developer identities were unified across platforms using name- and email-based matching heuristics. Textual artifacts were cleaned by removing non-English content, system-generated messages, and signatures, and were subsequently normalized through tokenization, lowercasing, and stop-word removal.

Modeling Approaches. To answer our research questions, we employ statistical models focused on community smells and socio-technical proximity.

$\mathbf{RQ}_1$ – Community smells and abrupt disengagement. We modeled the relationship between community smells and the probability of abrupt disengagement using logistic regression [31]. This choice of model is justified by the binary nature of the outcome and the interpretability of the regression coefficients, which enable us to estimate the strength of each community smell's effect on the dependent variable.
Dependent Variable. The binary dependent variable indicates whether an abrupt disengagement event occurred for a given developer.
Independent Variables. The predictors of interest were the four community smells, i.e., *Lone Wolf*, *Organizational Silo*, *Radio Silence*, and *Black Cloud*. We operationalized variables as binary indicators, indicating whether the developer was classified under the corresponding smell during a given time window.
Control Variables. We controlled for individual developer activity to mitigate confounding effects. Specifically, we considered the *number of messages sent*, capturing each developer's engagement in communication, and the *standardized workload*, defined as the number of lines of code added or removed, normalized within the project to account for scale differences. A model constant was also retained to capture unobserved baseline variation.

$\mathbf{RQ}_1$ – Socio-technical proximity as a protective factor. Similarly to **$\mathbf{RQ}_1$**, we applied logistic regression, but the independent variables were drawn from measures of socio-technical proximity rather than community smells.
Dependent Variable. The binary dependent variable represents the occurrence of an abrupt disengagement event for a given developer.

Independent Variables. The main predictor was *socio-technical proximity*, measured as the *average distance* from a developer to their peers within the socio-technical network, which integrates both communication (reply) and collaboration (Git) ties. Lower values indicate stronger social and technical connectedness—reflecting frequent interaction and shared work—whereas higher values represent looser, more fragmented participation across the community.
To characterize socio-technical proximity, we considered several network-based variables that capture complementary aspects of how developers interact and collaborate. Among them, *socio-technical congruence* reflects the extent to which communication patterns align with technical dependencies in the codebase, that is, whether developers who need to coordinate for technical reasons also communicate effectively. To account for individual positions within these networks, *reply degree* and *Git degree* quantify the number of direct connections each developer maintains in the communication and technical networks, respectively. Likewise, *reply betweenness* and *Git betweenness* identify developers who act as bridges between otherwise disconnected groups, highlighting their role in mediating coordination and information flow. Finally, *reply density* and *Git density* provide a project-level view of the overall cohesiveness of communication and collaboration within the development community.
Control Variables. We employed the same set of controls as in $\mathbf{RQ_1}$ *i.e.*, *number of messages sent* and the *standardized workload.*

For both models, positive coefficients (OR> 1) indicate higher disengagement risk, while negative ones (OR< 1) indicate a protective effect.

4 Analysis of the Results

Table 2. Distribution of outcomes and community smells across projects.

Project	Number Dev.	Messages	Abupt Dis.	LW	OS	RS	BC
ApexCore	50	15694	10	182	99	146	56
Ambari	95	3669	6	328	222	222	141
Bookkeeper	4	773	0	80	76	76	51
Helix	44	7306	6	231	211	211	132
Geronimo	44	40886	4	560	205	205	65
Thrift	208	10283	123	292	292	28	77

Before discussing our results, we provide a statistical description of the distribution of the abrupt disengagement phenomenon and the community smells we analyzed. As shown in Table 2, the distribution of outcomes and community smells varies considerably across projects. The number of active developers ranges from very small teams (e.g., Bookkeeper with only 4 developers) to large ones (e.g., Thrift with over 200 developers). Likewise, the volume of messages exchanged is highly uneven, with Geronimo standing out due to its more than 40,000 messages, while Bookkeeper remains at a much smaller scale. Abrupt disengagement events are also unevenly distributed, with some projects showing very few cases and others reporting substantially higher counts. Finally, the presence of community smells is consistently detected across projects, but with varying intensity, suggesting that structural issues manifest differently depending on the project size, communication activity, and time span considered.

Table 3. An overview of the numerical variables per project.

Project	Value	Avg. Dist.	Messages	Std. Workload	STC	Deg. Comm.	Bet. Comm.	Deg. Collab.	Clos. Collab.	Bet. Collab.	Den. Comm.	Den. Collab.
Ambari	min	1.000	0.000	0.000	0.000	0.000	0.000	0.000	–	0.000	0.000	0.000
	25%	2.000	0.000	0.008	0.000	0.030	0.000	0.247	–	0.170	0.001	0.086
	mean	2.723	3.590	1.000	0.062	0.089	0.004	0.444	–	0.275	0.010	0.131
	75%	3.000	5.000	0.360	0.060	0.121	0.007	0.612	–	0.379	0.016	0.178
	max	4.000	31.000	31.270	1.000	0.184	0.026	0.672	–	0.560	0.079	0.189
ApexCore	min	1.000	0.000	0.002	0.000	0.260	0.037	0.000	0.267	0.000	0.086	0.000
	25%	1.414	0.000	0.083	0.333	0.314	0.084	0.222	0.300	0.117	0.162	0.300
	mean	2.210	18.675	1.000	0.458	0.367	0.109	0.324	0.500	0.238	0.234	0.352
	75%	2.667	29.000	1.195	0.500	0.428	0.129	0.389	0.734	0.315	0.262	0.500
	max	6.000	106.000	18.590	1.000	0.518	0.521	0.509	0.889	0.833	0.464	0.730
Bookkeeper	min	1.000	0.000	0.002	0.000	0.000	0.000	0.000	0.000	0.000	0.000	0.000
	25%	1.000	1.000	0.063	0.000	0.000	0.000	0.000	0.000	0.000	0.000	1.000
	mean	1.151	4.284	1.000	0.158	0.016	0.000	0.000	0.000	0.000	0.007	0.976
	75%	1.000	6.000	0.992	0.000	0.000	0.000	0.000	0.000	0.000	0.000	1.000
	max	2.000	18.000	8814.000	1.000	0.150	0.000	0.000	0.000	0.000	0.100	1.000
Geronimo	min	1.000	0.000	0.000	0.161	0.170	0.049	0.111	0.188	0.009	0.040	0.158
	25%	1.528	0.000	0.014	0.276	0.335	0.069	0.286	0.354	0.133	0.110	0.333
	mean	2.260	27.007	1.000	0.405	0.369	0.107	0.342	0.454	0.220	0.166	0.451
	75%	2.800	36.750	0.671	0.519	0.396	0.133	0.400	0.495	0.284	0.199	0.545
	max	7.000	364.000	46.675	0.913	0.546	0.304	0.585	0.762	0.585	0.365	0.889
Helix	min	1.000	0.000	0.000	0.000	0.000	0.000	0.000	0.000	0.000	0.000	0.000
	25%	1.667	0.000	0.073	0.000	0.163	0.000	0.167	0.600	0.020	0.083	0.194
	mean	2.297	10.124	1.000	0.306	0.254	0.149	0.260	0.683	0.272	0.162	0.363
	75%	3.000	12.000	0.936	0.407	0.333	0.261	0.333	0.864	0.386	0.205	0.500
	max	5.000	166.000	25.933	1.000	0.560	0.529	0.611	1.000	1.000	0.467	1.000
Thrift	min	1.000	0.000	0.001	0.000	0.046	0.002	0.000	–	0.000	0.008	0.000
	25%	1.383	2.000	0.016	0.100	0.179	0.036	0.071	–	0.009	0.021	0.028
	mean	[illegible]	10.203	1.000	0.431	0.269	0.110	0.179	–	0.085	0.030	0.067
	75%	4.000	[illegible]	0.448	0.714	0.349	0.185	0.244	–	0.129	0.038	0.090
	max	6.000	210.000	19.359	1.000	0.552	0.396	0.500	–	0.477	0.072	0.194
Total	min	1.000	0.000	0.000	0.000	0.000	0.000	0.000	0.000	0.000	0.000	0.000
	25%	1.500	0.000	0.021	0.056	0.133	0.008	0.212	0.300	0.083	0.019	0.123
	mean	2.345	14.870	1.000	0.322	0.263	0.092	0.306	0.451	0.212	0.111	0.316
	75%	3.000	17.000	0.677	0.473	0.380	0.130	0.389	0.629	0.307	0.179	0.487
	max	7.000	364.000	46.675	1.000	0.560	0.529	0.672	1.000	1.000	0.467	1.000

Table 3 reports descriptive statistics of the numerical variables computed per project. The values are summarized over 30-day observation windows (minimum, 25th percentile, mean, 75th percentile, and maximum), rather than aggregated across the entire project history. A 30-day window was selected as a trade-off between temporal granularity and data stability. On the one hand, it is short enough to capture fluctuations in developer activity and communication. On the other hand, it is long enough to smooth out transient inactivity or short-lived peaks of activity typically associated with release cycles [52]. This design choice ensures comparability across projects of different sizes and lifespans, while capturing the temporal variability of developer activity and network structure. Consequently, apparently counterintuitive patterns, such as a minimum of zero messages combined with a strictly positive mean, simply indicate that certain monthly windows exhibited no activity, whereas others contained substantial communication, yielding a positive average. The same reasoning applies to workload, centralization, and density measures, which can assume zero values in inactive windows and higher values when activity is concentrated. These statistics provide an overview of the typical distributional range of the variables employed in the modeling pipelines, rather than cumulative project-level totals.

4.1 RQ1 – On the Correlation Between Community Smells and Abrupt Disengagement

Table 4. Results of the Logistic Regression between Community Smells and Abrupt Disengagement. Statistically significant coefficients (p <0.05) are reported in **bold**.

Variable	Next 1 month				Next 3 months				Next Year			
	Coef.	Std.Err.	z	P> |z|	Coef.	Std.Err.	z	P> |z|	Coef.	Std.Err.	z	P> |z|
Lone Wolf	**2.4610**	0.768	3.203	0.001	0.0647	0.368	0.176	0.860	-0.3136	0.202	-1.551	0.121
Organizational Silo	-0.2488	0.463	-0.537	0.591	0.3364	0.249	1.349	0.177	**0.5745**	0.133	4.328	0.000
Radio Silence	**1.1455**	0.509	2.251	0.024	0.2199	0.260	0.845	0.398	-0.1727	0.137	-1.265	0.206
Black Cloud	-1.9338	0.491	-3.940	0.000	**-1.1497**	0.285	-4.039	0.000	-0.0932	0.139	-0.670	0.503
Messages Sent	**-0.0477**	0.016	-2.913	0.004	**-0.0262**	0.005	-4.796	0.000	**-0.0209**	0.003	-7.206	**0.000**
Standardized Workload	-0.0294	0.072	-0.407	0.684	-0.0084	0.027	-0.310	0.756	**-0.0498**	0.020	-2.516	0.012
Constant	-0.2020	0.896	-0.225	0.822	**1.7429**	0.570	3.057	0.002	**0.8705**	0.284	3.062	0.002

Table 4 reports the results of the logistic regression models examining the relation between community smells and the probability of abrupt disengagement occurring across three temporal horizons (1 month, 3 months, and 1 year).

In the short term, *Lone Wolf* emerges as a significant predictor, suggesting that developers who work in isolation are more likely to abruptly disengage in the following month. This finding aligns with the intuition that a lack of social integration can amplify frustration and reduce the perceived support network necessary to cope with conflicts or setbacks. *Radio Silence* shows a similar pattern: limited communication with others increases the likelihood of short-term, abrupt disengagement, underscoring the importance of maintaining active communication channels within a project. However, for both smells, the effect dissipates over longer periods, indicating that these factors primarily trigger immediate frustration rather than long-term disengagement.

In contrast, *Organizational Silo* shows a delayed but pronounced effect, becoming significant only in the last temporal horizon. This suggests that structural separation between subgroups or teams does not lead to immediate disengagement but gradually erodes collaboration and trust, eventually increasing the probability of abrupt disengagement. *Black Cloud*, conversely, is associated with a lower likelihood of abrupt disengagement in the short and medium term, possibly reflecting the role of experienced or central developers who, despite facing negative emotions, remain engaged and resilient—though this effect fades in the long run.

Moving to the control variables, the number of *Messages Sent* consistently recreates a protective role across all horizons: developers who communicate more frequently are less likely to experience abrupt disengagement, reinforcing the idea that active participation and visibility within the community can buffer frustration. *Standardized Workload* becomes significant only in the long term, suggesting that sustained, balanced workload levels may help prevent attrition over time.

These results indicate that abrupt disengagement is influenced by both individual and structural factors that operate on different temporal scales. Short-term risks are primarily linked to social isolation and communication breakdowns, while long-term risks emerge from entrenched organizational fragmentation. This temporal differentiation suggests that abrupt disengagement is not a spontaneous act, but rather the culmination of evolving socio-technical tensions. Moreover, the observed associations provide empirical support for the theory of community smells as indicators of *social debt* [44], highlighting how unresolved organizational misalignments may accumulate and manifest as frustration and eventual withdrawal.

4.2 RQ2 – On the Correlation Between Socio-Technical Proximity and Abrupt Disengagement

Table 5. Logistic regression results for socio-technical proximity metrics across 1, 3, and 12-month horizons. Statistically significant coefficients ($p < 0.05$) are in bold.

Variable	Next 1 month				Next 3 months				Next year			
	Coef.	Std.Err.	z	P> |z|	Coef.	Std.Err.	z	P> |z|	Coef.	Std.Err.	z	P> |z|
Avg. distance	**−0.6765**	0.186	−3.646	0.000	**−0.2926**	0.106	−2.765	0.006	−0.0748	0.059	−1.265	0.206
Socio-technical congruence	**−3.0131**	1.471	−2.048	0.041	−0.8344	0.694	−1.202	0.229	0.0727	0.348	0.209	0.834
Reply degree	4.5713	3.113	1.468	0.142	−1.5633	1.835	−0.852	0.394	**2.3659**	0.899	2.633	0.008
Reply betweenness	3.1080	3.378	0.920	0.358	−3.7050	1.962	−1.888	0.059	**−5.1782**	1.039	−4.982	0.000
Git betweenness	0.8394	1.234	0.680	0.496	−0.5290	0.591	−0.895	0.371	−0.2561	0.324	−0.790	0.429
Reply density	2.5116	2.301	1.091	0.275	**6.2016**	1.558	3.981	0.000	0.2213	0.755	0.293	0.769
Git density	−0.8394	1.234	0.680	0.496	−0.5015	0.512	−0.979	0.328	**−0.9461**	0.271	−3.490	0.000
Messages Sent	**−0.0477**	0.016	−2.913	0.004	**−0.0262**	0.005	−4.796	0.000	**−0.0209**	0.003	−7.206	0.000
Standardized Workload	−0.0294	0.072	−0.407	0.684	−0.0084	0.027	0.310	0.756	**−0.0498**	0.020	−2.516	0.012
Constant	−0.2020	0.896	−0.225	0.822	1.7429	0.570	3.057	0.002	0.8705	0.284	3.062	0.002

Table 5 presents logistic regression models that investigate the role of socio-technical proximity factors in predicting abrupt disengagement across different time horizons. Several consistent yet temporally distinct patterns emerge, suggesting that the interplay between communication and collaboration structures evolves over time.

In the short term (1 month), lower communication distance is significantly associated with reduced disengagement, indicating that tightly connected teams buffer immediate withdrawal. Similarly, socio-technical congruence has a protective effect, suggesting that alignment between coordination needs and communication reduces short-term disengagement. However, this effect weakens over time, indicating it prevents impulsive exits but not longer-term tensions.

Looking at the medium temporal windows, communication intensity begins to show more complex effects. *Reply density* emerges as a strong predictor, with higher density significantly increasing the odds of abrupt disengagement. This result suggests that while active communication is beneficial in the short term, excessive interaction may lead to information overload, interpersonal friction, or burnout, eventually triggering withdrawal. At the same time, *reply betweenness* shows a negative, marginally significant association, suggesting that developers who serve as intermediaries in communication channels may play a stabilizing role by distributing information and easing coordination stress within the community.

Over the long term (1 year), the relationships between socio-technical factors and abrupt disengagement become more differentiated. *Reply degree* shows a significant positive association with abrupt disengagement, suggesting that developers who receive numerous replies may become overburdened by communication demands and expectations, increasing their risk of attrition. Conversely, *reply betweenness* becomes a strong negative predictor, indicating that developers who bridge otherwise disconnected groups are less likely to disengage, likely because of their central role and sense of purpose within the project. In parallel, *Git density* exhibits a robust negative effect, highlighting the protective influence of cohesive and distributed collaboration on code contributions, which appears to sustain engagement over time.

Regarding the control variables, the results mirror those observed for $\mathbf{RQ}_1$. The number of *Messages Sent* remains a significant protective factor across all horizons, reaffirming that maintaining communication activity is essential to developer retention. Meanwhile, *Standardized Workload* becomes significant only in the long-term window, suggesting that a balanced workload contributes to long-term stability but has little immediate impact on short-term disengagement.

Socio-technical proximity influences abrupt disengagement in time-dependent ways: communication and alignment reduce early exits, while long-term stability requires balancing workload, connectivity, and distribution. Disengagement thus emerges as an evolving phenomenon driven by both excessive interaction and disconnection.

5 Discussion and Implications

The results show that the risks of abrupt disengagement stem not only from technical issues but also from how communities organize, communicate, and evolve over time.

For developers, the findings underscore that collaboration is a double-edged sword. Being closely embedded in networks of communication and code contributions helps protect against sudden exits: lone wolves and isolated members are most at risk of abrupt disengagement. Yet, collaboration overload can itself contribute to stress and disengagement. In other words, not all collaboration is equally beneficial: meaningful, distributed contributions are protective, while constant "chatter" without structure can become a liability. Moreover, occupying bridging positions (reply betweenness) in communication networks can be stressful at first, but over time, it builds resilience by providing access to diverse information and informal support. To mitigate collaboration overload, teams can leverage Conway's Law [23] by aligning communication channels with the software architecture. This ensures structured, modular interactions mapped to technical responsibilities, reducing cognitive fragmentation. Structural issues also stem from time-dependent effects. While *Black Cloud* dynamics initially shield developers, their persistence doubles long-term risks, and Organizational Silos silently erode resilience. Thus, leaders must monitor how structural smells evolve over time, rather than just tracking acute disengagement. Finally, linguistic traces show that frustration surfaces in words before exits, making tone and constructive dialogue the first line of defense.

For researchers, our results suggest three directions for future inquiry. First, the predictive patterns highlight that disengagement unfolds over time and across layers of collaboration. Signals that seem protective in the short run—such as intense interaction or central positions in communication networks—can later reverse as fatigue or overload accumulate. This indicates that disengagement should be studied as a dynamic, evolving process rather than a discrete event, calling for longitudinal approaches that trace how risk factors change direction as projects and relationships mature. Moreover, our findings reinforce and extend ongoing research on toxic communication and negative affect in developer interactions [41], showing how these patterns can escalate toward emotional exhaustion and abrupt withdrawal. Second, the role of socio-technical structures suggests the need for models that account for how contributors' positions within communication and collaboration networks influence their engagement trajectories. Our findings indicate that structural configurations—such as isolation, overload, or asymmetric bridging roles—reflect patterns often linked to community smells and low socio-technical proximity. These conditions can heighten coordination costs and emotional strain, gradually undermining motivation and inclusion. Future research should therefore move toward integrative models that combine behavioral, linguistic, and network perspectives—where language-aware tools operate alongside socio-technical indicators to capture both the structural and emotional dimensions of developer disengagement. Third, the growing availability of fine-grained socio-technical data opens opportunities for proactive and preventive interventions. Our findings suggest that early warning signals of abrupt disengagement, such as increasing isolation, communication breakdowns, or persistent structural misalignments, can be empirically detected through changes in network configurations and interaction patterns. Building on this evidence, future research may investigate automated alerting or feedback mechanisms that help community moderators and project maintainers recognize and mitigate these risks before they escalate. This would require interdisciplinary collaboration across software analytics, organizational psychology, and human–computer interaction to design effective and socially responsible systems.

6 Threats to Validity

In terms of construct validity, abrupt disengagement is operationalized as a contributor's final message followed by a predefined inactivity interval. This proxy may overlook psychological and social aspects of exit behavior and misclassify atypical cases (e.g., off-channel departures). To mitigate this, we adopt conservative thresholds and sustained inactivity requirements, privileging sensitivity over specificity. Cross-platform identity matching can be error-prone, and tools for detecting community smells and sentiment may misclassify context. We mitigate these risks through the identity unification (e.g., names, email hashes, commit signatures across GitHub, JIRA, and mailing lists) and by using validated tools such as Kaiaulu and a fine-tuned BERT model. We also include covariates to reduce confounding effects. Finally, we included all contributors observed in the collected socio-technical traces, including developers with very limited participation (e.g., a single commit). As a result, some cases classified as abrupt disengagement may reflect the completion of a one-time contribution rather than the withdrawal of an actively engaged community member. Future work should investigate the effect of applying participation thresholds.

As for the internal validity, we acknowledge a potential threat stemming from data imbalance, as a single project (`Thrift`) accounts for approximately 82.5% of the total identified abrupt disengagement events. This high concentration may bias our logistic regression models toward the specific socio-technical dynamics of that community, meaning the identified risk and protective factors might not apply uniformly across all analyzed projects.

In terms of external validity, although we analyze six heterogeneous *Apache* projects, generalizability beyond similar OSS contexts is limited. Proprietary projects are excluded due to lack of observable socio-technical data. While project selection aims to ensure diversity, broader datasets are needed to extend these findings.

Finally, for conclusion validity, the limited number of disengagement events may reduce statistical power and increase Type II error risk. Regression assumptions may also be challenged in social-networked settings. We address these issues using standard errors, cross-validation, and cross-project triangulation. Results should be interpreted as associational rather than causal.

7 Conclusions

This paper presents an empirical study of abrupt disengagement in OSS, examining the role of community smells and socio-technical proximity across six *Apache* ecosystems. Cohesive networks act as protective factors, while isolation, poor communication, and misalignments increase risk. Some smells (e.g., *Organizational Silo*, *Black Cloud*) evolve from neutral to long-term risks. Overall, disengagement emerges as a measurable socio-technical outcome. Future work will expand the dataset, adopt longitudinal designs, and combine models with developer surveys.

Acknowledgments. This paper was partly supported by the European HORIZON-KDT-JU-2023-2-RIA research project MATISSE (grant 101140216-2, KDT232RIA 00017).

References

1. From developer networks to verified communities: a fine-grained approach. In: IEEE/ACM 37th IEEE International Conference on Software Engineering, vol. 1, pp. 563–573. IEEE (2015)
2. Afeltra, A., Cannavale, A., Pecorelli, F., Pontillo, V., Palomba, F.: A large-scale empirical investigation into cross-project flaky test prediction. IEEE Access **12**, 131255–131265 (2024)
3. Afi, N.J.: The silent disengagement: exploring the impact of quiet quitting on organizational culture. Int. J. Res. Innovation Soc. Sci. **9**(6), 1508–1530 (2025)
4. Alexandrovsky, D., Gerling, K., Opp, M.S., Hahn, C.B., Birk, M.V., Alsheail, M.: Disengagement from games: characterizing the experience and process of exiting play sessions. CHI **8**, 1–27 (2024)
5. Arora, R., Goel, S., Mittal, R.K.: Supporting collaborative software development over github. Softw. Pract. Exp. **47**(10), 1393–1416 (2017)
6. Blincoe, K., Valetto, G., Damian, D.: Do all task dependencies require coordination? The role of task properties in identifying critical coordination needs in software projects. In: FSE, pp. 213–223 (2013)
7. Blincoe, K., Valetto, G., Goggins, S.: Proximity: a measure to quantify the need for developers' coordination. In: CSCW, pp. 1351–1360 (2012)
8. Caballero-Espinosa, E., Carver, J.C., Stowers, K.: Community smells–the sources of social debt: a systematic literature review. Inf. Softw. Technol. **153**, 107078 (2023)
9. Caldiera, V.R.B.G., Rombach, H.D.: The goal question metric approach. Encyclopedia of software engineering, pp. 528–532 (1994)
10. Calefato, F., Lanubile, F., Maiorano, F., Novielli, N.: Sentiment polarity detection for software development. In: ICSE, p. 128 (2018)
11. Crowston, K., Wei, K., Howison, J., Wiggins, A.: Free/libre open-source software development: what we know and what we do not know. ACM Comput. Surv. (CSUR) **44**(2), 1–35 (2008)
12. De Weerd, M., Klandermans, B.: Eur. J. Soc. Psychol. **29**(8), 1073–1095 (1999)
13. Meglio, D., Starace, S., Pontillo, L.L.L., Opdebeeck, V., De Roover, R., Di Martino, C., S.: Performance testing in open-source web projects: adoption, maintenance, and a change taxonomy. In: 2025 IEEE International Conference on Software Maintenance and Evolution (ICSME), pp. 199–210. IEEE (2025)
14. Fagerholm, F., Guinea, A.S., Münch, J., Borenstein, J.: The role of mentoring and project characteristics for onboarding in open source software projects. In: ESEM, pp. 1–10 (2014)
15. Fang, Y., Neufeld, D.: Understanding sustained participation in open source software projects. J. Manag. Inf. Syst. **25**(4), 9–50 (2009)
16. Ferreira, F., Silva, L.L., Valente, M.T.: Turnover in open-source projects: the case of core developers. In: BSSE, pp. 447–456 (2020)
17. Filippova, A., Cho, H.: Mudslinging and manners: unpacking conflict in free and open source software. In: CSCW, pp. 1393–1403 (2015)

18. Fox, S., Spector, P.: Counterproductive work behavior: investigations of actors and targets. American Psychological Association (2005)
19. Gachechiladze, D., Lanubile, F., Novielli, N., Serebrenik, A.: Anger and its direction in collaborative software development. In: ICSE, pp. 11–14 (2017)
20. Gerosa, M., et al.: The shifting sands of motivation: revisiting what drives contributors in open source. In: ICSE, pp. 1046–1058 (2021)
21. Giordano, G., Festa, G., Catolino, G., Palomba, F., Ferrucci, F., Gravino, C.: On the adoption and effects of source code reuse on defect proneness and maintenance effort. Empir. Softw. Eng. **29**(1), 20 (2024)
22. Giordano, G., Sellitto, G., Sepe, A., Palomba, F., Ferrucci, F.: The yin and yang of software quality: on the relationship between design patterns and code smells. In: 2023 49th Euromicro Conference on Software Engineering and Advanced Applications (SEAA), pp. 227–234. IEEE (2023)
23. Herbsleb, J.D., Grinter, R.E.: Splitting the organization and integrating the code: Conway's law revisited. In: Proceedings of the 21st International Conference on Software Engineering, pp. 85–95 (1999)
24. Hunsen, C., Siegmund, J., Apel, S.: On the fulfillment of coordination requirements in open-source software projects: an exploratory study. Empir. Softw. Eng. **25**(6), 4379–4426 (2020). https://doi.org/10.1007/s10664-020-09833-8
25. Islam, M.R., Zibran, M.F.: Sentistrength-se: exploiting domain specificity for improved sentiment analysis in software engineering text. JSS **145**, 125–146 (2018)
26. Kazman, R.: Managing social debt in large software projects. In: SESoS-WDES, p. 1. IEEE (2019)
27. Kelloway, E.K., Francis, L., Prosser, M., Cameron, J.E.: Counterproductive work behavior as protest. Hum. Resour. Manag. Rev. **20**(1), 18–25 (2010)
28. Koch, A.S., Forgas, J.P., Matovic, D.: Can negative mood improve your conversation? Affective influences on conforming to grice's communication norms. Eur. J. Soc. Psychol. **43**(5), 326–334 (2013)
29. Kwan, I., Schroter, A., Damian, D.: Does socio-technical congruence have an effect on software build success? A study of coordination in a software project. IEEE Trans. Software Eng. **37**(3), 307–324 (2011)
30. Lancichinetti, A., Radicchi, F., Ramasco, J.J., Fortunato, S.: Finding statistically significant communities in networks. PLoS ONE **6**(4), e18961 (2011)
31. LaValley, M.P.: Logistic regression. Circulation **117**(18), 2395–2399 (2008)
32. Linåker, J., Link, G., Lumbard, K.: Sustaining maintenance labor for healthy open source software projects through human infrastructure: a maintainer perspective. In: Proceedings of the 18th ACM/IEEE International Symposium on Empirical Software Engineering and Measurement, ESEM 2024, pp. 37–48. Association for Computing Machinery, New York, NY, USA (2024)
33. Martins, L., Pontillo, V., Costa, H., Ferrucci, F., Palomba, F., Machado, I.: Test code refactoring unveiled: where and how does it affect test code quality and effectiveness? Empir. Softw. Eng. **30**(1), 27 (2025)
34. Mulder, W., et al.: Online appendix for "i quit!": understanding practitioner abrupt disengagement through socio-technical factors in open source software (2025). https://github.com/giammariagiordano/i_quit.github.io. https://giammariagiordano.github.io/i_quit.github.io/
35. Palomba, F., Tamburri, D.A., Fontana, F.A., Oliveto, R., Zaidman, A., Serebrenik, A.: Beyond technical aspects: how do community smells influence the intensity of code smells? TSE **47**(1), 108–129 (2018)
36. Paradis, C., Kazman, R.: Building the MSR tool kaiaulu: design principles and experiences. In: ECSA (2021)

37. Pontillo, V., Martins, L., Machado, I., Palomba, F., Ferrucci, F.: An empirical investigation into the capabilities of anomaly detection approaches for test smell detection. J. Syst. Softw. **222**, 112320 (2025)
38. Recupito, G., Giordano, G., Ferrucci, F., Di Nucci, D., Palomba, F.: When code smells meet ML: on the lifecycle of ml-specific code smells in ml-enabled systems. Empir. Softw. Eng. **30**(5), 139 (2025)
39. Ribeiro, D.M.: Understanding the relationships between the perceptions of burnout and instability in software engineering. In: BSSE, pp. 58–67 (2022)
40. Robles, G., Gamalielsson, J., Lundell, B.: Setting up government 3.0 solutions based on open source software: the case of X-road. In: ICEG, pp. 69–81 (2019)
41. Sarker, J.: Identification and mitigation of toxic communications among open source software developers. In: ASE, pp. 1–5 (2022)
42. Stol, K.J., Ali Babar, M.: Challenges in using open source software in product development: a review of the literature. In: Proceedings of the 3rd International Workshop on Emerging Trends in Free/Libre/Open Source Software Research and Development, pp. 17–22 (2010)
43. Tamburri, D.A., Kazman, R., Fahimi, H.: The architect's role in community shepherding. IEEE Softw. **33**(6), 70–79 (2016)
44. Tamburri, D.A., Kruchten, P., Lago, P., Vliet, H.: Social debt in software engineering: insights from industry. J. Internet Serv. Appl. **6**(1), 1–17 (2015). https://doi.org/10.1186/s13174-015-0024-6
45. Tamburri, D.A., Palomba, F., Kazman, R.: Exploring community smells in open-source: an automated approach. IEEE Trans. Software Eng. **47**(3), 630–652 (2019)
46. Tamburri, D.A., et al.: "the candle is burning out on its own..": modeling fatigue and empathy among Chinese developers. In: Euromicro Conference on Software Engineering and Advanced Applications, pp. 155–173. Springer (2025)
47. Trinkenreich, B., Stol, K.J., Sarma, A., German, D.M., Gerosa, M.A., Steinmacher, I.: Do i belong? Modeling sense of virtual community among linux kernel contributors. In: ICSE, pp. 319–331 (2023)
48. Trinkenreich, B., Wiese, I., Sarma, A., Gerosa, M., Steinmacher, I.: Women's participation in open source software: a survey of the literature. ACM Trans. Softw. Eng. Methodol. (TOSEM) **31**(4), 1–37 (2022)
49. Van Zomeren, M., Postmes, T., Spears, R.: Toward an integrative social identity model of collective action: a quantitative research synthesis of three socio-psychological perspectives. Psychol. Bull. **134**(4), 504 (2008)
50. Vasilescu, B., Yu, Y., Wang, H., Devanbu, P., Filkov, V.: Quality and productivity outcomes relating to continuous integration in github. In: Proceedings of the 2015 10th Joint Meeting on Foundations of Software Engineering, pp. 805–816 (2015)
51. Voria, G., et al.: Fair and square? Evaluating fairness of LLM-generated synthetic datasets. Inf. Softw. Technol. 107980 (2025)
52. Wiggins, A., Howison, J., Crowston, K.: Social dynamics of floss team communication across channels. In: ICOSS, pp. 131–142 (2008)
53. Zhang, T., Xu, B., Thung, F., Haryono, S.A., Lo, D., Jiang, L.: Sentiment analysis for software engineering: how far can pre-trained transformer models go? In: ICSME, pp. 70–80 (2020)

A RAG-Based Pipeline for Automated COSMIC Functional Size Measurement

Rana Ali Abdelalim[1(✉)], Milad Ghantous[1], Hassan Soubra[2,3], and Tuna Hacaloglu[3]

[1] Media Engineering and Technology Faculty, German University in Cairo, Cairo, Egypt
ranaabdaleem@gmail.com

[2] LyRIDS, ECE Engineering School, OMNES Education, Lyon, France

[3] École de Technologie Supérieure (ÉTS), Montreal, Canada

Abstract. Functional size measurement is essential for reliable software project management. While automation of the COSMIC method (ISO 19761) has long enabled large-scale application in industry, the rise of Large Language Models combined with Retrieval-Augmented Generation offers new opportunities for further advancement. This paper presents CosmoScope, a RAG-based pipeline for automating COSMIC functional size measurement that builds a structured knowledge base from five richly annotated official COSMIC case studies, applies domain-aware contextual prefixing based on Anthropic's Contextual Retrieval technique, and dynamically retrieves relevant examples during inference. A system prompt refined through iterative development encodes the complete COSMIC rule set using chain-of-thought reasoning. Evaluated on 47 held-out functional user requirements across business, real-time, and embedded domains, CosmoScope achieves 97.9% measurement accuracy in Direct Mode and 100% in Guided Mode. A three-condition ablation study further decomposed these contributions: retrieval alone adds 4.3% points beyond prompt engineering, and contextual prefix enrichment adds a further 4.3% points on top of raw retrieval—establishing that knowledge base representation quality matters as much as retrieval itself. To handle inherent requirement ambiguity, the paper introduces a novel dual-mode assumption-resolution mechanism: Direct Mode for fully automated measurement and Guided Mode that surfaces ambiguous decisions with recommended resolutions for human confirmation, supporting transparent and auditable industrial workflows.

Keywords: COSMIC FSM · Functional Size Measurement · Retrieval-Augmented Generation · Large Language Models · Software Measurement Automation

1 Introduction

Accurate software sizing is a prerequisite for reliable cost estimation, resource planning, and productivity benchmarking. COSMIC (ISO 19761), a second-generation functional size measurement method, has gained wide acceptance due

C. Berger and V. Klös (Eds.): SEAA 2026, LNCS 16864, pp. 160–168, 2027.
https://doi.org/10.1007/978-3-032-36587-3_12

to its applicability across business applications, real-time systems, and embedded software [5].

The adoption of COSMIC was significantly accelerated by early automation efforts, particularly in high-rigor industries such as automotive [1]. In recent years, Large Language Models (LLMs) have opened new avenues for automating this task. While previous approaches have shown that functional size signals exist in natural language requirements, important limitations remain—including narrow input representations and limited cross-domain generalization [6].

A key motivation for this work is the observation that the COSMIC community has produced valuable official case studies containing expert-annotated measurement reasoning, yet this knowledge has not been systematically leveraged for automated measurement. Retrieval-Augmented Generation (RAG) [8,11] offers a direct means of addressing this gap by grounding LLM measurement decisions in dynamically retrieved expert knowledge. This paper presents CosmoScope, a RAG-based pipeline and web application that realises this approach. It should be viewed as an exploratory empirical study providing preliminary evidence for the feasibility of the proposed approach, given the limited scale of the evaluation. The main contributions are: (1) the first RAG-based pipeline for COSMIC measurement, built from 12 pre-processed official case studies with five richly annotated studies forming the core knowledge base; (2) a domain-sensitive contextual prefixing strategy based on Anthropic's Contextual Retrieval technique [3], empirically shown to contribute 4.3 percentage points of accuracy improvement beyond raw retrieval; (3) a refined measurement prompt encoding the complete COSMIC rule set, validated through a three-condition ablation on 47 held-out FURs across multiple domains; and (4) a novel dual-mode assumption-resolution mechanism offering fully automated Direct Mode and Guided Mode with recommended resolutions for human confirmation.

The rest of the paper is organised as follows: Sect. 2 provides the necessary background on the COSMIC model and RAG techniques. Section 3 reviews related work in FSM automation. Section 4 details the CosmoScope methodology and pipeline architecture. Section 5 presents the evaluation results and discussion. Section 6 concludes the paper and outlines future research directions.

2 Background

2.1 COSMIC ISO 19761

COSMIC FSM, standardised as ISO 19761, measures software functionality by counting data movements across the software boundary [5]. The method quantifies Functional User Requirements (FURs) through a structured process. A functional user is any entity that sends or receives data across the boundary. A functional process consists of data movements triggered by a single unique event. An object of interest represents any entity about which the software stores or manipulates data, while a data group is a set of attributes that move together.

The four types of data movements are: Entry (E)—data entering the software from a functional user; Exit (X)—data leaving the software to a functional user;

Read (R)—retrieving data from persistent storage; and Write (W)—writing data to persistent storage. Each movement contributes exactly one COSMIC Function Point (CFP), and the functional size is the sum of all movements across all functional processes.

Although conceptually simple, applying COSMIC in practice requires considerable expertise. Requirements are often written at a higher level of abstraction, data groups can be implicit, and many edge cases demand careful judgement guided by the COSMIC manual and official examples [2].

2.2 Retrieval-Augmented Generation

Retrieval-Augmented Generation (RAG) enhances LLM inference by dynamically retrieving relevant external knowledge at query time [8,11]. Instead of relying only on the model's parametric knowledge, a RAG system retrieves the most semantically similar documents from a knowledge base and injects them into the prompt. This approach is particularly suitable for knowledge-intensive domains such as COSMIC measurement, where the relevant rules and examples are too numerous and detailed to encode statically.

A practical challenge in RAG systems is context loss when documents are chunked: an extracted chunk loses the broader information that gave it meaning. We address this by adapting Anthropic's Contextual Retrieval technique [3], generating domain-aware three-sentence prefixes for each chunk that identify the case study, domain, functional process name, and triggering event—information essential for accurate domain-sensitive retrieval.

2.3 Chain-of-Thought Prompting

Chain-of-thought (CoT) prompting [16] improves LLM performance on complex, multi-step reasoning tasks by instructing the model to articulate its reasoning step by step before producing a final answer. COSMIC measurement is precisely this kind of task: it requires sequential decomposition, boundary identification, object-of-interest identification, and data movement classification before a CFP count can be produced. Structuring this process explicitly through CoT reduces classification errors and makes the measurement reasoning transparent and auditable.

3 Related Work

3.1 COSMIC Automation Before AI

First-generation COSMIC automation focused on parsing deterministic system representations to programmatically extract data movements from rigid structural schemas. Early efforts covered processor load estimation in AUTOSAR frameworks [22], aerospace real-time embedded systems based on SCADE architectures [23], and more recently quantum software [21]. While effective within their narrow structural parameters, these rule-based systems could not generalise to natural language requirements.

3.2 AI-Enhanced COSMIC Automation

The first AI phase relied on classical machine learning: Ochodek et al. [13] approximated functional size from use-case names using a convolutional neural network, and Yokogawa et al. [17] showed that simpler models such as Random Forest matched deep learning performance on the same task—suggesting the bottleneck lay in input representation rather than model complexity. NLP-based approaches extended this to IoT device specifications [24] and mobile applications [19], while tool-based automation was explored by Ecar et al. [18].

The second phase introduced domain-adapted transformer models. Molla et al. [12] developed RE-BERT, a BERT model [7] pre-trained on requirements engineering text, later extended to direct CFP regression [20]. Tenekeci et al. [14] explored measurement from source code using CodeBERT, and Becha et al. [4] applied machine learning to chatbot functional size measurement.

The third and current phase is driven by LLMs. Hartenstein et al. [9] demonstrated the benefit of few-shot prompting over zero-shot. Valdés-Souto and Torres-Robledo [15] rigorously documented the failure of raw LLM prompting—55.3% MMRE and zero reproducibility—and explicitly called for retrieval-based solutions. Laqrichi [10] advanced the state of the art with a hybrid GPT-4 and rule-based framework, and De Vito et al. [6] introduced CosMet, achieving 99% F1 on data movement identification. Despite these advances, three critical gaps remain: no system has applied dynamic domain-relevant retrieval from a structured knowledge base, cross-domain performance on real-time and embedded software remains limited, and none provides explicit reasoning steps alongside the measurement output.

4 Methodology

CosmoScope implements a four-stage pipeline: (1) data preparation for knowledge base construction, (2) contextual prefixing and embedding, (3) LLM inference supporting RAG-augmented measurement, and (4) dual-mode assumption resolution and output.

4.1 Data Preparation and Knowledge Base Construction

In total, 12 COSMIC case studies were sourced and manually pre-processed, spanning business, real-time/embedded, and machine learning domains. Manual pre-processing was necessary to create functionally complete chunks, each containing the FUR text, functional process name, triggering event, objects of interest, and all associated data movements with their classifications. Q&A sections encoding expert reasoning about edge cases were also extracted and included, as they capture the kind of measurement judgement that annotated examples alone cannot fully convey. From the 12 pre-processed studies, the five richest—C-REG, Industrial Robot, RestoSys, Image Classifier, and Rice Cooker—formed the knowledge base. The remaining seven, supplemented with requirements from published research, formed the test set.

4.2 Contextual Prefixing and Embedding

Each chunk is enriched with a three-sentence contextual prefix generated using Anthropic's Contextual Retrieval technique [3], adapted for the COSMIC domain. The prefix identifies the case study, domain, functional process, triggering event, and measurement role, restoring the context that isolated chunks lose. Prefixed chunks are embedded using all-MiniLM-L6-v2 and stored in ChromaDB with cosine similarity as the distance metric. At inference time, the input FUR is embedded with the same model and the top-3 most semantically similar chunks are retrieved as domain-relevant examples.

4.3 Measurement Engine and Prompt Engineering

The retrieved chunks are injected into the user prompt as labelled examples. The system prompt encodes the complete COSMIC rule set across four sections: foundational concepts, per-movement-type rules, high-priority disambiguation rules covering the most common sources of measurement error, and the required JSON output schema. Measurement follows a six-step chain-of-thought scaffold: atomic requirement decomposition, software boundary identification, triggering event and functional process identification, objects of interest and data group enumeration, data movement classification with per-step justifications and grounding quotes, and a structured verification pass. The backend is implemented as a FastAPI application using GPT-4o at temperature zero; all other generation parameters were left at their default values.

4.4 Dual-Mode Assumption Resolution

Natural language requirements frequently contain genuine ambiguity—phrasing that could support more than one valid COSMIC classification. CosmoScope addresses this through a novel dual-mode mechanism. Direct Mode resolves such ambiguities autonomously using retrieved expert knowledge and the encoded rule set, producing a fully automated measurement. Guided Mode instead surfaces each ambiguous decision as a structured card in the web interface, presenting two labelled interpretations with their CFP impacts and a recommended resolution grounded in the COSMIC rules, which the measurer confirms or overrides before the model produces a locked final measurement. In both modes, every classified data movement is accompanied by a grounding quote from the requirement and a justification, maintaining full transparency and auditability regardless of which mode is used.

5 Evaluation and Discussion

As a preliminary evaluation, 47 FURs from seven case studies were used, spanning business (Library System, Car Hire, Mobile Application, Web Service) and real-time/embedded (Valve Control, Automatic Line Switching, Sensor Monitoring) domains. Three case studies provide official expert ground truth; the remaining four were measured by COSMIC professionals in published research. Accuracy is defined as the percentage of FURs where both the total CFP count and all individual data movement classifications exactly match the expert ground truth—the strictest possible criterion, since a correct total produced through an incorrect decomposition is not counted as correct.

To decompose the contribution of each pipeline component, three configurations were evaluated under an identical system prompt. In the first, retrieval was disabled entirely (No RAG). In the second, retrieval was enabled but contextual prefixes were stripped, leaving only raw structured chunk content. In the third, the full pipeline with prefixed retrieval was used. Table 1 presents the results.

Table 1. Ablation results across three pipeline configurations (47 FURs, GPT-4o).

Configuration	Correct	Incorrect	Accuracy
No RAG (prompt only)	42	5	89.4%
RAG, no prefixes	44	3	93.6%
Full pipeline (RAG + prefixes)	46	1	97.9%
RAG contribution (Δ)	+2	−2	+4.3 pp
Prefix contribution (Δ)	+2	−2	+4.3 pp

The results reveal a layered picture of contribution. Errors in the No-RAG condition comprised two FM-1 (Object Collapse) cases, where distinct objects of interest were merged into a single data movement, and three FM-3 (Phantom Entry) cases, where a triggering Entry absent from the requirement text was assumed. Raw retrieval eliminated both FM-1 errors: examples demonstrating correct multi-object decomposition provided concrete anchoring that the explicit rule alone could not supply. Prompt engineering tells the model what to do; retrieved examples show what it looks like in practice. Prefix enrichment resolved two of the three remaining FM-3 errors by encoding process-level context into the chunk embedding—enabling semantically matched retrieval rather than structural matching on data movement type alone. The equal +4.3 pp contribution of each component establishes that how retrieved examples are represented matters as much as whether they are retrieved at all.

In Guided Mode, the full 47-FUR set achieves 100% accuracy. The one persistent Direct Mode error—a Phantom Entry inferred from an implied server response that the requirement strongly suggests but does not explicitly state was resistant to all three configurations, illustrating precisely the boundary condition Guided Mode is designed to handle: surfacing the implied Entry as a decision point gives the measurer the opportunity to confirm that no Entry is warranted.

Beyond the accuracy figures, the system consistently handles the most challenging COSMIC edge cases: control commands as zero-CFP operations, distinguishing storage existence checks from format validation logic, classifying external system interactions as boundary crossings, correctly applying the uniqueness rule, and decomposing requirements with multiple objects of interest. Domain-sensitive retrieval proved essential to these results: real-time requirements retrieved real-time examples, and business requirements retrieved business examples, avoiding the domain mismatch that static few-shot approaches cannot prevent.

5.1 Discussion

These results should be interpreted in the context of the broader literature, where LLM-based COSMIC automation remains an exploratory area and the scarcity of publicly available expert-annotated measurements constrains rigorous quantitative comparison across studies. Valdés-Souto and Torres-Robledo [15] documented the failure of raw LLM prompting—an MMRE of 55.3% and zero reproducibility—and called explicitly for retrieval-based solutions, a direction CosmoScope directly instantiates. Laqrichi [10] advanced the state of the art with a hybrid framework achieving a 6.6% global error rate, but acknowledged weaker performance on real-time software due to the absence of dynamic retrieval; CosmoScope addresses this through domain-sensitive contextual retrieval, as confirmed by the real-time results. De Vito et al. [6] introduced CosMet, achieving 99% F1 across 123 use cases, but the system relies on static few-shot examples and structured use case inputs, whereas CosmoScope processes free-form FURs with dynamic retrieval and introduces auditable assumption handling absent in prior work. Taken together, these comparisons suggest that the combination of structured domain knowledge, dynamic retrieval, and explicit ambiguity resolution represents a meaningful step forward, while direct numerical comparison remains constrained by the absence of a shared benchmark in this niche domain.

Threats to Validity. The evaluation set comprises 47 FURs from seven case studies, which limits the statistical strength of the reported accuracies. Broader validation is needed before generalised claims can be made. Further empirical studies on broader and more diverse datasets are needed to validate the approach more comprehensively.

6 Conclusion

This paper presented CosmoScope, a RAG-based pipeline for automated COSMIC functional size measurement that combines a structured expert-annotated knowledge base, domain-aware contextual prefixing, dynamic retrieval, and a rule-encoded chain-of-thought measurement prompt. Evaluated on 47 held-out FURs spanning business, real-time, and embedded domains, the system achieves 97.9% accuracy in Direct Mode and 100% in Guided Mode. A three-condition ablation established that retrieval and contextual prefix enrichment each contribute 4.3 percentage points independently, confirming that knowledge base representation quality is as important as the retrieval mechanism itself.

The novel dual-mode assumption-resolution mechanism addresses a limitation shared by all prior automated measurement work: rather than resolving requirement ambiguity silently, Guided Mode surfaces each decision transparently for measurer confirmation, producing measurements that are both accurate and auditable. This design reflects a broader principle—that for a standards-governed measurement task, the goal is not to replace expert judgement but to focus it precisely where it is needed.

While the current evaluation is preliminary, the results establish a clear empirical case for RAG-based approaches to COSMIC measurement. Future work will focus on expanding the knowledge base, conducting larger-scale validation across a wider range of requirement styles and domains, and contributing to the community-level benchmark development that the field urgently needs.

Disclosure of Interests. The authors have no competing interests to declare that are relevant to the content of this article.

References

1. Oriou, A., Bronca, E., Bouzid, B., Guetta, O., Guillard, K.: Manage the automotive embedded software development cost & productivity with the automation of a Functional Size Measurement Method (COSMIC). In: 2014 Joint Conference of the International Workshop on Software Measurement and the International Conference on Software Process and Product Measurement, pp. 1–4. IEEE (2014)
2. Abran, A., Symons, C., Ebert, C., Vogelezang, F., Soubra, H.: Measurement of software size: Contributions of cosmic to estimation improvements. In: The International Training Symposium, At Marriott Bristol, pp. 259–267. United Kingdom (2016)
3. Anthropic: Introducing Contextual Retrieval (2024). https://www.anthropic.com/news/contextual-retrieval
4. Becha, R., Sellami, A., Bouassida, N., Idri, A., Abran, A.: BotCFP: A machine learning based tool for COSMIC chatbots sizing (2024)
5. Abran, A., Fagg, P., Lesterhuis, A.: Principles, Definitions and Rules. In: COSMIC Measurement Manual for ISO 19761, Version 5.0, Part 1, pp. 1–17 (2021). https://cosmic-sizing.org/wp-content/uploads/2020/06/Part-1-MM-Principles-Definitions-Rules-v5.0-Aug-2021.pdf
6. De Vito, G., Di Martino, S., Ferrucci, F., Gravino, C., Palomba, F.: LLM-based automation of cosmic functional size measurement from use cases. IEEE Trans. Softw. Eng. (2025)
7. Devlin, J., Chang, M.W., Kenton, L., Toutanova, K.: Bert: Pre-training of deep bidirectional transformers for language understanding. In: Proceedings of the 2019 Conference of the North American Chapter of the Association for Computational Linguistics: Human Language Technologies, Volume 1 (Long and Short Papers), pp. 4171–4186 (2019)
8. Gao, Y., et al.: Retrieval-augmented generation for large language models: A survey. arXiv preprint arXiv:2312.10997 (2023) ¡error l="304" c="Invalid command: paragraph not started." /¿
9. Hartenstein, S., Johnson, S.L., Schmietendorf, A.: Towards a fast cost estimation Supported by large language models, Technical Report (2024)

10. Laqrichi, S.: A Hybrid Framework for COSMIC Measurement: Combining Large Language Models with Rule-Based Systems. In: IWSM-Mensura (2024)
11. Lewis, P., et al.: Retrieval-augmented generation for knowledge-intensive nlp tasks. Adv. Neural. Inf. Process. Syst. **33**, 9459–9474 (2020)
12. Molla, Y.S., Yimer, S.T., Alemneh, E.: COSMIC-functional size classification of agile software development: deep learning approach. In: 2023 International Conference on Information and Communication Technology for Development for Africa (ICT4DA), pp. 155–159. IEEE (2023)
13. Ochodek, M., Kopczyńska, S., Staron, M.: Deep learning model for end-to-end approximation of COSMIC functional size based on use-case names. Inf. Softw. Technol. **123**, 106310 (2020)
14. Tenekeci, S., Ünlü, H., Dikenelli, E., SelçPuk, U., Soylu, G.K., Demirörs, O.: Predicting Software Size and Effort from Code Using Natural Language Processing. In: IWSM-Mensura (2024)
15. Valdés-Souto, F., Torres-Robledo, D.: Could an LLM like chatGPT perform a functional size measurement using the COSMIC method?. Trudy ISP RAN [Proc. ISP RAS] **36**(6), 104–115 (2024)
16. Wei, J., et al.: Chain-of-thought prompting elicits reasoning in large language models. Adv. Neural. Inf. Process. Syst. **35**, 24824–24837 (2022)
17. Yokogawa, K., Hiroishi, M., Arnasaki, S., Aman, H., Yokogawa, T.: A Comparative study on COSMIC FP approximation with deep learning and conventional machine learning. In: 2024 IEEE/ACIS 22nd International Conference on Software Engineering Research, Management and Applications (SERA), pp. 346–351. IEEE (2024)
18. Ecar, M., Kepler, F.N., da Silva, J.P.S.: AutoCosmic: COSMIC automated estimation and management tool. In: Proceedings of the XIV Brazilian Symposium on Information Systems, pp. 1–8 (2018)
19. Nitze, A.: Measuring mobile application size using COSMIC FP. DASMA Metrik Kongress **11**, 1–13 (2013)
20. Molla, Y.S., Alemneh, E., Yimer, S.T.: Cosmic-based early software size estimation using deep learning and domain-specific bert. IEEE Access (2025)
21. Soubra, H., Elsayed, H., Elbrolosy, Y., Adel, Y., Attia, Z.: Comprehensive review of metrics and measurements of quantum systems. Metrics **2**(2), 9. MDPI (2025)
22. Soubra, H., Abran, A., Sehit, M.: Functional Size Measurement for Processor Load Estimation in AUTOSAR. In: Kobyliński, A., Czarnacka-Chrobot, B., Świerczek, J. (eds.) Software Measurement. LNBIP, vol. 230, pp. 114–129. Springer, Cham (2015). https://doi.org/10.1007/978-3-319-24285-9_8
23. Soubra, H., Jacot, L., Lemaire, S.: Manual and automated functional size measurement of an aerospace realtime embedded system: a case study based on SCADE and on COSMIC ISO 19761. Int. J. Eng. Res. Sci. Technol **4**(2) (2015)
24. Salem, S., Soubra, H.: Using NLP for functional size measurement of IoT devices. In: 2023 Eleventh International Conference on Intelligent Computing and Information Systems (ICICIS), pp. 321–327. IEEE (2023)

Systematic Literature Reviews and Mapping Studies in Software Engineering

Automated Data Extraction in Software Engineering SLRs: Promise, Pitfalls, and the Role of Human Oversight

Ignacio Marco-Pérez, Beatriz Pérez(✉), and Ángel L. Rubio

University of La Rioja, Logroño, Spain
{ignacio.marco,beatriz.perez,arubio}@unirioja.es

Abstract. Systematic Literature Reviews (SLRs) constitute a fundamental methodology for analyzing the state of the art across virtually all scientific disciplines, particularly in Software Engineering (SE) and its various subdomains. Despite their unquestionable relevance to the research field, SLRs are resource-intensive processes that have relied almost entirely on the manual effort of human researchers. Recently, researchers have begun using automated Natural Language Processing (NLP) tools to support specific phases of the SLR process, raising a critical question: To what extent are these tools effective in supporting tasks of such complexity? In this article, we report on a well-structured and methodologically rigorous experiment aimed at shedding light on this question for the data extraction phase—one of the most cognitively demanding, time-consuming, and error-prone stages of the SLR process—within the SE context. As an initial step in a broader agenda, the study offers a solid set of preliminary evidence on the strengths and limitations of NLP-based tools for data extraction. We have assessed the performance of three NLP-based tools (ChatGPT, ChatPDF, and Google NotebookLM) in extracting data elements from published studies, compared with human data extraction. Our findings show that, while current NLP-based tools can offer partial support, especially for explicit and well-structured information, they fall short in tasks requiring inference or external knowledge. Human expertise thus remains essential to validate NLP data extractions. We distill key lessons learned to guide researchers in understanding the current capabilities and limitations of these tools for SLRs data extraction.

Keywords: Systematic Literature Review · Software Engineering · Data Extraction · Natural Language Processing

1 Introduction

Systematic Literature Reviews (SLRs) are a cornerstone method for synthesizing evidence in software engineering. However, despite their value, conducting SLRs remains a highly labor-intensive and time-consuming process [2]. Given

C. Berger and V. Klös (Eds.): SEAA 2026, LNCS 16864, pp. 171–188, 2027.
https://doi.org/10.1007/978-3-032-36587-3_13

the substantial challenges of manually conducting SLRs, it is not surprising that research efforts have increasingly turned toward automation. Over the past decades, numerous tools have been developed to support either the entire SLR process or specific aspects of it. These tools aim to alleviate the time-consuming and resource-intensive nature of SLRs, reducing researcher bias, improving transparency and repeatability, accelerating reviews and, ultimately, reshaping the traditional reviewing process [2]. Traditional tools such as *Parsifal* [17] and *StArt* [6] primarily focus on providing structured support for planning, conducting, and documenting reviews, offering functionalities for study selection, quality assessment, and metadata management. However, these tools largely rely on manual input and lack advanced automation capabilities. In parallel, the growing influence of Artificial Intelligence (AI)—particularly advances in Natural Language Processing (NLP)—has given rise to a new generation of tools based on Large Language Models (LLMs) [2]. These tools leverage pretrained models capable of extracting, interpreting, and generating human-like language from large volumes of text data [3]. Their ability to understand context makes them especially valuable for identifying relevant literature, extracting key information, and synthesizing findings [9,14]. By automating tedious and repetitive aspects of SLRs, LLMs can reduce manual workload and allow researchers to focus on more nuanced and judgment-intensive aspects, while enabling more intelligent support across multiple stages of the SLR process [13,18]. Data extraction ranks among the top five SLR activities with the highest potential for automation [7]. Recent strides in NLP—especially the emergence of LLMs—present compelling opportunities to streamline this critical stage [7,10], positioning them as potentially promising candidates to assist with, or even partially automate, data extraction in SLRs. Despite their increasing use, LLM-based tools remain insufficiently evaluated for this task [10], and it remains unclear whether they can meaningfully replace or even support human reviewers. Recent studies have taken important steps toward evaluating the use of LLM-based tools for data extraction or related *evidence synthesis* tasks [1], but they often remain limited in scope –frequently focusing on a single tool, lacking rigorous evaluation design, or failing to account for the diversity and complexity of data extraction questions typical in SLRs.

The study we present was primarily driven by a practical challenge encountered during the development of an SLR that the authors were conducting, focused on one specific area of SE: *data management and governance in the development and use of digital twins applied to smart cities.* Upon reaching the data extraction phase—and drawing on our experience conducting other SLRs—we ask ourselves to what extent several carefully selected LLM-based tools (ChatGPT, ChatPDF, and Google NotebookLM[1] could support this step in our review. This exploratory effort led to a broader, structured experimental study to understand their potential and limitations in supporting the data extraction phase of SLRs within SE, across diverse extraction question types that place varying cognitive and inferential demands on the tools. Tool outputs were compared both to each other and to human judgment as a reference to

[1] https://chatgpt.com; https://chatpdf.com; https://notebooklm.google.com.

assess their performance and reliability. The following research questions guide our study:

- **RQ1** To what extent are the data extraction results produced by LLM-based tools equivalent or comparable to those obtained by human experts during the data extraction phase of an SLR in a specific software engineering topic? This question seeks to evaluate whether current tools can deliver results that match the quality, completeness, and precision of human-driven extraction, which is traditionally considered the gold standard in SLRs.
- **RQ2** Does the order in which data extraction is performed—first using an automated tool, then manually, or vice versa– influence the outcomes of the human-performed extraction? Specifically, we are interested in whether prior exposure to tool-generated results may introduce bias in human experts during manual extraction, potentially due to memory recall effects.
- **RQ3** Does performing data extraction in a single session—where studies are processed sequentially within the same tool session– affect the outcomes, as opposed to extracting data from each study in isolation? We aim to assess if tools that maintain conversational context across prompts produce different results when exposed to accumulated information from previous papers.

Beyond evaluating how effectively these tools support the data extraction phase, this experiment provides an initial step toward understanding the strengths and limitations of LLM-based tools, also offering a set of lessons learned that can guide researchers in selecting effective strategies and making informed methodological decisions when integrating AI-based assistance for data extraction.

2 Related Work

The growing adoption of automation tools for conducting SLRs has led to a substantial and increasingly diverse body of research—heterogeneous in both scope and focus—thus reflecting the increasing attention the research community is devoting to this area. These works could be categorized into five groups: 1) studies that mainly explore the potential of automation in SLRs and the evolution of the field [7,10,13,24]; 2) works that mainly compile and summarize tools designed or used to partially or fully automate the SLR process [2]; 3) contributions that describe novel algorithms, tools, or architectures to support SLR automation [18]; 4) case studies that report on the application of automation tools in the context of a specific SLR [4], and 5) studies that conduct structured evaluations (either quantitative or qualitative) of AI-based tools, often focusing on technical performance in specific tasks related to SLRs (or similar analytical frameworks such as *evidence synthesis*) [1,8,9,11,14,16,19,20,23].

While each of these groups advances the field in complementary ways, recent studies can be observed within the fifth category, underscoring a growing interest in evaluating the practical performance and behavior of AI-based tools. In the data extraction phase, although the core aim of most existing studies is basically to compare AI-generated outputs with those produced by human reviewers (RQ1), important distinctions remain between these prior approaches and the present work. Although several recent efforts have investigated the use of AI-based tools for data extraction, few have adopted a systematic or comprehensive manner, often remaining limited in scope, depth, or methodological rigor. Notably, our evaluation targets SE literature, whereas some existing work focuses on the health sciences, particularly on randomized controlled trials (RCTs) [9,16]. RCTs tend to follow a more standardized reporting structure, which may facilitate the extraction of predefined data items—an aspect that, as the authors themselves acknowledge [9,16], could limit the applicability of their results. In contrast, the structural and terminological heterogeneity of SE studies introduces additional challenges for automated extraction. Some studies lack the methodological rigor necessary to support generalizable conclusions. For instance, Alshami et al. [1] evaluated ChatGPT exclusively within a 'human-in-the-loop' setup, without assessing its standalone performance. Moreover, a few evaluations may have been affected by training-data overlap; e.g., [8,9,16], and [23] used SLR datasets published prior to their experiments. Since these reviews may have been included in the training corpora of the AI tools under study, this could introduce bias in favor of these tools. Some studies focus on the evaluation of a single tool [8,9,11,14], whereas others that conduct comparative evaluations across several tools, such as [23], do not benchmark their outputs against human reviews. Regarding the nature of data extraction queries, some studies tend to focus mainly on narrow, easy retrievable questions (such as author names or explicitly stated numerical values) [9,14,16,19]. These are generally simpler to extract, especially from well-structured, documents such as RCTs. Furthermore, limited attention has been given to queries requiring reasoning, interpretation, or synthesis of less-structured content. Exceptions include a few recent studies emerging in parallel with ours [5,11], which also target more demanding questions.

Although our study shares isolated similarities with prior work, it differs in both design and scope. It compares the performance of three LLM tools against human experts. Additionally, the documents analyzed in our evaluation do not originate from prior SLRs, reducing potential bias related to training-data overlap. Our work encompasses extraction queries that require reasoning, interpretation, and synthesis -better reflecting real-world SLR challenges. We also examine two unexplored aspects: if the extraction order—AI-first vs. human-first—can influence human-performed extraction (RQ2), and if running multiple independent sessions, as opposed to a single continuous one, may affect tool outputs (RQ3). These elements collectively contribute to filling key gaps in the literature and advancing the understanding of LLMs' support in SLRs.

3 Methodology

The study follows a controlled experimental design, structured around key dimensions and sequential phases. The main dimensions include the selection

Table 1. Set of questions used in the experiment

ID	Question	Answer Type
QA01	Does the study directly address data management or data governance?	Boolean
QA04	Is a novel technological approach proposed? If so, is it implemented or tested in a real-world environment?	Boolean
QA07	Does the study discuss the potential generalization of results and conclusions to other contexts or case studies?	Boolean
DE02	What specific subdomains of smart cities are addressed in the study?	List of categories
DE03	Which aspects of data management, as proposed by DAMA, are explicitly or implicitly addressed in the study?	List of categories
DE08	Which digital twin maturity level, according to (Klar et al., 2024), if any, is considered in the study?	Category

of a reduced but representative sample of papers (12, see Supplementary Material [22]) and questions (see Table 1); the participation of three human experts; the use of three tools (ChatGPT, ChatPDF and NotebookLM); the extraction order (human-only before tool usage, that we refer as *pre-*, or human after tool usage, that we refer as *post-*); and the grouping strategies applied for extraction.

The experiments were conducted between April 30 and May 14, 2025. Regarding tool versions, ChatGPT was accessed using the *GPT-4o* model, NotebookLM operated on *Gemini 2.5 Flash*, and ChatPDF was used under its *Fast* mode, which employs dynamic routing between *GPT-4o* and *GPT-4o-mini*, precluding the identification of the exact model used in each session.

The three grouping strategies applied were: *sequential* (*S*-mode), where multiple papers are processed consecutively within the same session, preserving context; *isolated* (*I*-mode), where each paper is analyzed in a separate session, avoiding information carryover; and *block* (*B* mode), where multiple papers are loaded simultaneously, allowing cross-document access. Human extractions were naturally in S-mode; ChatGPT was used in S- and I-modes; ChatPDF only in I-mode; and NotebookLM in I- and B-modes.

The experiment was conducted in three phases: preparation, execution, and analysis. During execution, each expert performed seven test configurations designed to systematically compare conditions. Test 1 (Manual-S) involves standard manual extraction without tool support. Tests 24 (ChatGPT-I, ChatPDF-I, NotebookLM-I) evaluate each tool independently under isolated conditions, ensuring no contextual influence between papers. Test 5 (ChatGPT-S) examines the effect of maintaining conversational context across multiple papers. Test 6 (NotebookLM-B) evaluates the impact of analyzing multiple papers simultaneously. Finally, Test 7 (Manual-S) repeats manual extraction after prior exposure to tool outputs, enabling assessment of potential bias introduced by AI assistance. Four papers are considered in each test: this design ensures that all papers are evaluated in both *pre-* and *post-*order. Outputs were analyzed using quantitative metrics tailored to each question type, allowing comparison across tools, experts, and experimental conditions. Methodology details are provided in [22].

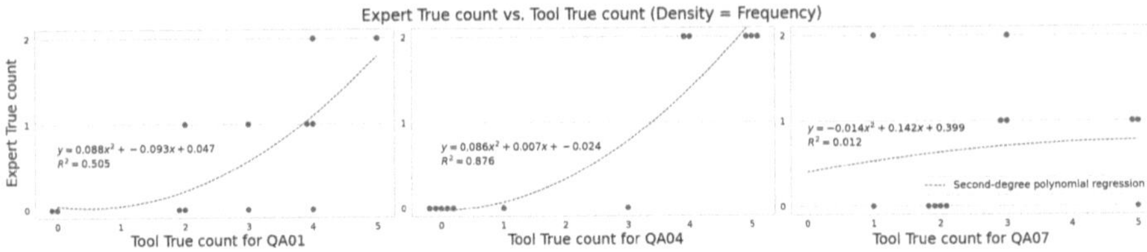

Fig. 1. Swarm charts for Quality Assurance questions.

4 Results

A first result concerns the time invested in the experiment. A time record was kept of how many minutes were spent on each test. Manual extractions (Tests 1 and 7) were the most time-consuming (2123 min per test across the three experts). Automated tests (Tests 2 to 6) took 4- 7.5 min on average, with ChatPDF being the "fastest" tool, and NotebookLM with block grouping the "slowest".

In this respect, article length is also a relevant factor. Since papers were randomly selected, their length ranged from 2 to 37 pages (mean: 10; mode: 6). As expected, for human experts, paper length directly influenced time spent (from 9 min for 2-page papers to nearly 50 min for 37-page ones), whereas it had little to no impact on tool response time.

It is also worth noting the volume of information generated in the experiment: 3 experts × 7 tests × 4 papers × 6 questions per paper, totaling 504 chunks of information (see CSV in Supplementary Material [22]). Depending on the question type, these chunks could range from a simple *true/false* value, to lists, or even free text. All entries were systematically recorded in the database.

4.1 Equivalence Results (RQ1)

The main focus (RQ1) is to assess whether tool-generated extractions match human ones. Here, we describe the related results presented by question type.

Of the six questions posed in each test, the three QA questions are boolean, so there are natural candidates for studying whether the tools' responses are identical to those of human experts. Figure 1 shows one swarm chart for each QA question, each including its second-degree polynomial regression curve. The horizontal axis indicates the number of times the tools answered *True* across their five tests; the vertical axis shows the analogous data for human experts. The number of elements in each swarm represents the frequency with which each pair of values occurs. It is easy to see that the value of the coefficient of determination R^2 is particularly high for question QA04, notably low for question QA07, and intermediate for question QA01. These visualizations are complemented by the data shown in Table 2, which presents a notion of *coincidence ratio*, disaggregated by tool, grouping type, and extraction order (*pre* vs. *post*). Given that the answers to the QA questions are *True/False*, coincidence here refers to the level of agreement between each tool and the corresponding human expert. The coincidence values are generally high, with only a few instances falling below 0.5.

Table 2. Pre- y Post- Coincidence ratio in Quality Assurance questions

	QA01		QA04		QA07	
Tool	Pre-	Post-	Pre-	Post-	Pre-	Post-
NotebookLM-I	0.50	0.58	0.83	0.92	0.58	0.75
NotebookLM-B	0.50	0.42	0.75	0.83	0.42	0.58
ChatPDF-I	0.58	0.50	0.75	0.67	0.58	0.75
ChatGPT-I	0.83	0.58	0.92	1.00	0.58	0.75
ChatGPT-S	0.50	0.75	0.83	0.75	0.58	0.75

For DE02 and DE03, which required lists of categories as answers, a detailed comparative analysis was also conducted by evaluating the lists generated by the tools against those created by human experts. Two metrics were defined for this purpose. *Accuracy* refers here to the proportion of categories in each list generated by the tool that are also present in the corresponding list given by the expert. *Recall*, on the other hand, measures the proportion of categories in the expert's list that are included in the tool's list. In this sense, if A is the expert set of categories and B is the tool set, then the metrics are calculated as $accuracy = \frac{|A \cap B|}{|A|}$ and $recall = \frac{|A \cap B|}{|B|}$. Therefore, accuracy measures how closely the tools' outputs align with those of humans, while recall measures how complete the tool's response is with respect to the expected (human) values. To combine both aspects, an *F1-score* was computed as $F1 = 2 \cdot \frac{|A \cap B|}{|A|+|B|} = 2 \cdot \frac{accuracy*recall}{accuracy+recall}$. These metrics were computed separately for *pre-* and *post*-extraction orders. The average metric results are shown in Figs. 2 and 3, in which these values are differentiated both by tool and by type of grouping. In general, recall values are significantly higher than accuracy values, and, consequently, F1 values lie between the two. Accuracy is significantly lower for DE03 compared to DE02.

A key point concerns the results for question DE08– the only one where the expected answer corresponds to a specific category, in particular, one of the maturity levels from [15] (e.g., *Level 1: Replication of Assets* or *Level 2: Connection of Models and Systems*). This case is particularly relevant for two reasons. First, while human experts were familiar with the reference that defines these levels, it was unclear whether the tools could independently identify or infer reference [15]. Second, since all papers in the sample were published prior to this reference, it was impossible for them to cite it explicitly, thus requiring tools to carry out an advanced deductive process—something that human experts perform naturally. As further discussed in Sect. 5, several tool-generated responses appear to reflect an awareness of [15], though some raise doubts about potential hallucinations. Notably, nearly 60% of all responses (50 out of 84)—from both humans and tools—were of the form 'not applicable (N/A)'/'information not

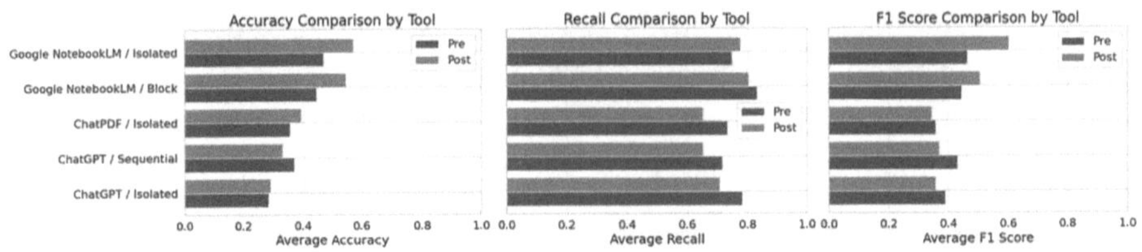

Fig. 2. Bar charts on Average Accuracy, Recall and F1 for question DE02. (Color figure online)

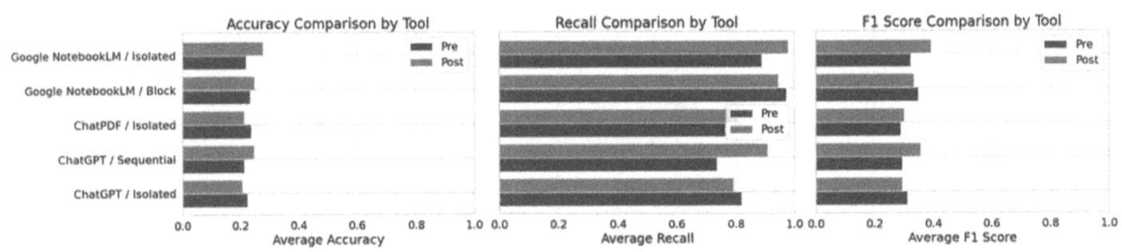

Fig. 3. Bar charts on average Accuracy, Recall and F1 for question DE03.

available in the source' (or similar). The second column of Table 3 reports these N/A cases. ChatPDF always returned N/A (12 out of 12), while NotebookLM did so in 21 of 24 cases (12 papers were evaluated per grouping method; since NotebookLM was used in two groupings, a total of 24 papers were evaluated with this tool). In contrast, human experts marked N/A in only 13 out of 24 cases (since each paper was evaluated twice, once for each order, there are 24 evaluations by experts). The remaining two columns show tool-human coincidence, broken down by grouping method and extraction order (*pre* and *post*).

Table 3. Results for DE08 with Pre- and Post-Coincidence

Expert or Tool	N/A	Pre	Post
Expert	13	-	-
NotebookLM-I	12	0.50	0.58
NotebookLM-B	9	0.50	0.33
ChatPDF-I	12	0.50	0.58
ChatGPT-S	2	0.25	0.42
ChatGPT-I	2	0.42	0.33

Table 4. Coincidence ratio in QA and F1 in DE questions

Tool	QA01	QA04	QA07	DE02	DE03	DE08
NotebookLM (I vs. B)	0.67	0.92	0.67	0.60	0.71	0.75
ChatGPT (I vs. S)	0.67	0.75	0.83	0.75	0.82	0.33

4.2 Order of Extraction Results (RQ2)

These results, together with those in the following subsection, are specific, since, to our knowledge, no similar study has analyzed the impact of extraction order.

This analysis allows us to assess whether prior exposure to tool outputs influences human extractions (*post* order). Due to its (intentional) design, in our experiment the manual *post* data extraction by the experts (Test 7) takes place after performing not just one, but five extractions by tools (Test 2 to 6).

The results of analyzing the extraction order with respect to the QA question group are shown in Table 2. For each of these three questions, and for each tool and grouping configuration, the table shows the corresponding coincidence ratio values for both the *pre* and *post* extraction orders. Since QA answers are boolean, coincidence directly measures how often tools and human experts agree. Table 2 shows that, with few exceptions, *post*-coincidence ratios exceed *pre*-coincidence.

We also analyzed responses to DE02 and DE03, as their closed-list format makes them suitable for detecting potential extraction-order effects. Figures 2 and 3 show the *differences* between *pre*- (blue) and *post*- (orange) results. While overall differences are modest—slightly more notable in DE02—NotebookLM consistently shows improved accuracy, recall, and F1 in the *post*-extraction stage compared to the *pre*-extraction. The opposite occurs with ChatGPT, where *pre*-extractions often yield better results. ChatPDF differences are least significant.

The extraction order can also be analyzed for DE08. Table 3 shows a certain trend toward higher coincidence ratio in the *post* condition, with two exceptions: NotebookLM using block grouping, and ChatGPT using isolated grouping—both yielding the lowest coincidence scores in this set of results.

4.3 Grouping Extraction Results (RQ3)

As noted earlier, to our knowledge, no prior studies have examined the influence of different groupings on data extraction performance. Please note that, since ChatPDF was tested with a single grouping (see Sect. 3), it is excluded from the grouping comparison. Table 4 presents the comparison results for the two grouping strategies used with NotebookLM (I vs. B) and with ChatGPT (I vs. S). The values represent how different one grouping is from another. For instance, a value of 0.92 for QA04 with NotebookLM suggests that, in most cases, the answers were the same regardless of the grouping applied. In general, the values are high across the set of QA questions, with the lowest values being obtained mainly in question QA01 (a key question in our SLR). For questions DE02, DE03, and DE08, Table 4 shows the F1 metric. Although lower than the previous ones, the values are generally high, with the notable exception of the data achieved by the comparison of groupings in ChatGPT for question DE08.

5 Discussion

This section analyzes the main findings of the experiment. The insights gained have been synthesized into key lessons learned, shown in Table 5.

5.1 Tool-Human Equivalence (RQ1)

QA01-QA04-QA07. Figure 1 highlights the degree of alignment between tool and human responses for the three boolean QA questions. QA04 shows the highest correlation ($R^2 = 0.874$) indicating that when both human experts agreed on the presence or absence of a feature, the tools tended to agree as well, suggesting that QA04 likely involves information that is more explicitly stated in the texts. QA01 shows moderate correlation ($R^2 = 0.505$), suggesting more variability in the tools' alignment with human consensus—possibly due to the question requiring milder levels of inference or interpretation. Notably, QA07 exhibits very low agreement ($R^2 = 0.012$), with many instances where tools marked the answer as *True* while both humans marked it as *False*. This points to a systematic tendency of tools to produce *false* positives on QA07, likely due to hallucinations or overinterpretation in the absence of clearly stated information. These trends suggest that question complexity significantly affects tool reliability in boolean extractions. For instance, QA04 (identifying a novel technological contribution and its implementation), yielded a strong correlation between human and tool judgments, likely due to the frequent and explicit phrasing of such contributions in academic writing. QA01 (identifying whether the paper addresses data management or governance), showed more moderate agreement; although relatively factual, the criteria can be fulfilled implicitly or under varied terminology, leading to inconsistencies in interpretation. In contrast, QA07 (assessing results generalizability) proved the most challenging: it involves inferential reasoning and synthesis beyond explicit textual information. Examining each tool, Table 2 reveals distinct performance patterns among the tools across the three boolean questions. ChatGPT and NotebookLM (both groupings) perform particularly well here. Interestingly, in QA07—earlier identified as the most challenging due to its inferential nature—most tools perform similarly (pre: ∼0.55, post: ∼0.72), still above expectations given the low R^2 value (0.012). This suggests that, while tools may converge on answers, agreement with humans remains weak, hinting at shared over-interpretation rather than accurate extraction.

DE02. Regarding value list extraction in the two category-based questions (DE02 and DE03), we distinguish two key aspects. First, whether the question requires reasoning solely based on document content—such as interpreting implicit statements or connecting information across sections—as in DE02. This group also includes the QA questions, as previously stated. Second, whether the task involves leveraging knowledge external to the document, as in DE03. For DE02 (smart city subdomains), Fig. 2 shows that NotebookLM notably outperforms both ChatGPT and ChatPDF with both groupings (Isolated and Block), achieving the highest accuracy, recall, and F1-score. This reflects a strong ability to identify relevant items while maintaining alignment with human annotations. In contrast, ChatGPT and ChatPDF achieve high recall, but present comparatively lower accuracy and F1 scores, indicating a tendency to over-generate elements and favor completeness over precision in matching human-selected terms.

DE03. In DE03, which requires aligning study content with external domain knowledge (DAMA [12]), all tools show a similar performance pattern: high recall but low accuracy and F1 (Fig. 3). This suggests a general tendency to retrieve many relevant elements while introducing noise. NotebookLM stands out slightly for achieving the highest recall scores (up to 0.89) and the strongest F1 performance (up to 0.32), reflecting a better overall balance. In contrast, ChatGPT and ChatPDF deliver comparable results, with somewhat lower F1 scores and accuracy values (around 0.21–0.25). These findings show that, while tools identify many relevant DAMA dimensions, they often struggle to filter out noise, particularly when reasoning with knowledge not explicitly in the text. This reflects the cognitive demands of mapping study content to an external, structured list—especially when the connection must be inferred.

DE08. Similar to DE03, DE08 requires external knowledge. However, the key distinction lies in the fact that the external source used for inference—namely, the maturity model described by Klar et al. [15]—was published after the studies being analyzed. This means that the tools cannot rely on direct textual matches or explicit references, but they must deduce the likely maturity level of a digital twin purely from contextual clues and descriptive language within the paper. This makes the task especially challenging, as it calls for a type of retrospective inference that goes beyond what is explicitly stated. Results (see Table 3) reveal key limitations of the tools. Across the 12 evaluated papers, human experts marked this question as 'N/A' in 13 instances. Tools (with specific groupings) such as NotebookLM-I and ChatPDF-I mirrored this judgment in 12 cases, suggesting a reasonable alignment in recognizing when sufficient information was absent. In contrast, ChatGPT-S and ChatGPT-I returned N/A only twice each, showing a tendency to speculative answers even when the data was not present. This is reinforced by 34 out of 84 responses where the tools attempted to assign a maturity level. Although many of these responses confidently adopted the maturity level numbering from [15] (level 1, etc.), they failed to correctly specify the corresponding level name, suggesting hallucinations rather than true inference. Only 3 responses were considered correct: two for the same paper answered by both ChatGPT-I and ChatGPT-S, and one additional from ChatGPT-S.

The analysis underscores a core limitation of the tools: unlike human reviewers, they cannot currently reason or infer information from PDFs. While humans can draw upon background knowledge and contextual cues to interpret implicit content, the tools cannot still perform such inference, often defaulting to superficial patterns without truly understanding the underlying meaning.

5.2 Impact of Extraction Order (RQ2)

QA01-QA04-QA07. Comparing *pre-* and *post-*extraction results reveals subtle tool influence on human extractions (see Table 2). NotebookLM shows consistent *post-*extraction improvements across basically all questions. These upward trends suggest that human experts may have been positively influenced by the tool's outputs (particularly in QA07), where the coincidence ratio gains are the most pronounced. This may indicate that NotebookLM provided helpful cues in questions requiring inference, or at least that its outputs aligned more closely with the evidence used by humans *post*-extraction. In contrast, ChatPDF shows a mixed pattern: coincidence ratio improves in QA07 from 0.58 to 0.75—again, a question identified as challenging due to its inferential demands—but declines in QA01 (0.58 to 0.50) and QA04 (0.75 to 0.67). These drops suggest that, in more structured or explicit questions, the tool may have introduced ambiguity or failed to support experts effectively during the *post*-extraction test. ChatGPT also shows variable outcomes: in QA01, one grouping worsens (I-0.83 to 0.58), while the other improves (S-0.50 to 0.75), yielding no clear trend overall. A reversed pattern occurs in QA04, where one grouping improves *post*-extraction (I), while the other declines (S). In QA07, both groupings improve (0.58 to 0.75), reinforcing that *post*-review shifts are stronger in complex, inferential questions.

DE02. Subtle but notable shifts emerge across tools when comparing *pre*- and *post*-extraction results for this category-list question (see Fig. 2). NotebookLM shows a trend toward improved accuracy and F1 scores *post*-extraction, suggesting that the human was influenced by the tool's prior outputs. In contrast, ChatGPT and ChatPDF display more variable patterns, with slight decreases in recall and F1 scores after manual extraction, indicating a possible reduction in over-generation but also a risk of losing relevant items. This pattern raises important considerations regarding human-AI interaction and potential bias introduced when NotebookLM is used as a first step in the extraction process.

DE03. Comparing *pre* and *post*-extraction stages shows minor variations, with performance slightly improving in some cases (e.g., recall), possibly suggesting a light influence of tool outputs on manual *post*-extraction (see Fig. 3). However, gains are modest and not systematic, confirming the task remains challenging for both tools and humans, especially under implicit evidence (DAMA resource).

DE08. Regarding question DE08, in terms of coincidence, *post*-review performance was generally higher than *pre*-review scores. For instance, NotebookLM-I and ChatPDF-I improved from 0.50 to 0.58, and ChatGPT-S from 0.25 to 0.42. This observation may suggest an influence of tool-generated content on the human reviewer's judgment, raising the question of whether prior exposure to AI-generated results could introduce bias through recall effects.

Overall, the *pre/post* analysis suggests potential tool-induced bias in manual review: while some tools show notable changes in *post*-extraction accuracy, these shifts may indicate varying degrees of human influence. The extent of this influence appears to depend on the tool and the question's cognitive demands.

5.3 Effect of Grouping Extraction (RQ3)

A key feature of the tools we analyzed is their ability to process large amounts of text. We tested their behavior when the texts they were asked about were considered in isolation (i.e., each paper in a different session of the tool) versus when they were considered globally (all papers—in groups of four—in the same session; for NotebookLM, this meant considering all papers in block, while ChatGPT loads them sequentially). We hypothesized that processing multiple texts on the same topic might "confuse" the tools when answering paper-specific questions—a pattern seen in preliminary ChatPDF tests. The results generally show a high number of matches when comparing the two types of grouping (Table 4). For example, in NotebookLM, the lowest result is 0.6 when considering DE02. Given that the question seeks to determine which smart cities' subdomains the paper addressed, some variability in answers seems reasonable.

QA01–QA04–QA07. Overall, the results for the QA questions (which, as a reminder, have boolean answers) are even better. Despite this, it is noteworthy that for question QA01 (a key question in our SLR, as it attempts to determine whether the analyzed paper actually addresses data management or data governance), the results for both NotebookLM and ChatGPT are 0.67. This means that one in three times, the tool's answer varied depending on the grouping strategy. Clearly, this is insufficient for a question that, from a human perspective, can be critical in completely ruling out a paper during our systematic review.

DE08. Another notable finding comes from comparing isolated and sequential groupings in ChatGPT for question DE08. The value obtained is 0.33, meaning that in most cases the response about the maturity level (according to [15]) is different when done in isolation than when done sequentially. This suggests a clear instance of the 'confusion' effect previously mentioned. It is important to remember that, as noted above, question DE08 was particularly tricky, and that in this question, ChatGPT was the tool that made the greatest *effort* to provide a meaningful answer (only 4 'not applicable' out of 24). This *effort* may have led to a higher number of less rigorous (or even hallucinatory) responses.

5.4 General Reflections, Limitations and Threats to Validity

As all users of AI tools know, the responsiveness of these tools is striking—especially for labor-intensive tasks. When a human expert has to analyze a 20–30 page document—normally taking around an hour of focused work—the temptation to delegate to tools that produce answers in seconds regardless of the document length is understandable. In our view, however, this is precisely the moment to pause, reflect scientifically, and assess whether we can truly trust the robustness, validity, and plausibility of AI-generated outputs. This was the real leitmotif behind our experiment. Two key insights emerge from our findings.

First, we have confirmed first-hand what other recent studies (not in the context of using LLMs for SLR) have stated: despite improvements, LLMs continue to exhibit substantial reasoning flaws [25]. This highlights the need to align question design with tool capabilities when applying them to evidence extraction.

Second, our findings suggest that AI tools could be valuable in assisting researchers in quality assessment of papers after study selection, helping determine whether a paper warrants full data extraction or should be discarded. Well-designed boolean questions reflecting key inclusion criteria can allow tools to act as an initial filter, but the final decision should be made by a second reviewer (different from the one who performed the automatic extraction)—as emphasized by Stoll et al. [21], who highlights the critical role of human oversight in data extraction. This is important because such boolean questions likely demand inference, synthesis, or reasoning beyond the text. Our results show that relying solely on AI tools is not yet reliable for extracting complex or nuanced data, particularly when requiring interpretation beyond text (also noted by [5,11]).

Turning to threats, this study prioritized accessible tools: we focused on freely available, user-friendly LLM platforms to ensure broad reproducibility. Thus, we excluded tools requiring complex installation or advanced technical knowledge, like RobotReviewer[2], or paid services, like GPT4-Turbo[3] (evaluated in [20]).

In line with previous work, we restricted our evaluation to a modest random sample of 12 PDF documents—similar to [11] (9 articles), and [9,16] (10 papers)—representing 5% of our full SLR corpus (222 papers) to keep the experiment manageable. Nevertheless, the sample included a diverse range of document types, such as concrete proposals for digital twins, systematic reviews, and surveys, ensuring variability in content and structure. We also reduced the number of data extraction questions from 20 to 6, to maintain tractability and keep the experiment manageable, especially given the constraints of the selected tools. Still, these questions were carefully chosen to cover a wide spectrum of variability in quality and quantity, requiring comprehension, reasoning, and meaningful insight extraction—tasks rarely addressed in prior evaluations [9,16], except for [5,11].

As for question DE08, which, as we explained, was particularly challenging, we could have tried to circumvent the difficulty by including more information in the prompt. Indeed, it would have been possible to describe the levels of maturity in Klar's work [15] within the prompt, but our intention was precisely to test the ability of different LLMs to infer information when it is not readily available. To maintain consistency across tools, we used carefully crafted prompts designed to be broadly applicable and highly reliable, though prompt tuning per tool could have improved outcomes and warrants exploration in future work. Recent studies highlight LLMs' promise in supporting SLRs, but emphasize that human involvement remains indispensable [8,14,16], a view supported by our findings. Our analysis shows that LLM performance varies with question type. We also observe that tool effectiveness can vary significantly with LLM model, prompt design, and study content [16], and, as prior work notes, they still lack the holistic perspective humans provide in complex decision-making [24], and their outputs often require continuous human oversight, especially with unstructured or nuanced text [14]. Ongoing evaluation of LLM performance will be critical as new model generations and features (e.g., advanced PDF parsing) emerge [16].

---

[2] https://www.robotreviewer.net/.

[3] https://developers.openai.com/api/docs/models/gpt-4-turbo.

Table 5. Lessons learned

RQ1 – Tool-Human Equivalence	
1	Reliability of NLP tool outputs in boolean extraction appears to depend strongly on the question type. When asked about aspects explicitly stated in the texts, ChatGPT and NotebookLM perform particularly well, suggesting higher reliability in well-defined contexts. However, no tool stands out in more inferential tasks, highlighting a common limitation in handling implicit content.
2	In questions requiring a closed list of categories –where answers depend solely on the content of the paper– NotebookLM clearly outperforms both ChatGPT and ChatPDF, achieving the highest values across accuracy, recall, and F1 scores, reflecting a strong ability to identify relevant items while maintaining alignment with human annotations.
3	For closed-category questions –where answering involves aligning study content with external domain knowledge– NotebookLM slightly outperforms ChatGPT and ChatPDF, achieving the highest recall and F1 scores, reflecting a better balance between completeness and correctness.
RQ2 Impact of Extraction Order	
4	If AI tools are used as a first step in the extraction process and their outputs are subsequently reviewed by a human, it is crucial that the reviewer remains aware of the risk of being influenced by the tool's suggestions, as such bias could lead to errors or reduced objectivity.
RQ3 Effect of Grouped Extraction	
5	When ChatGPT and NotebookLM are exposed to multiple papers in the same session, their responses to paper-specific questions may vary significantly compared to isolated analysis, especially for questions requiring higher interpretative effort.
General Reflections and Key Insights	
6	Current AI-based tools are not yet capable of reliably inferring implicit information from papers, as they tend to rely on superficial patterns without truly "understanding" the underlying meaning.
7	Avoid designing questions that require deep reasoning or interpretation. Instead, focus on queries based on explicit textual information to ensure high accuracy in AI-assisted extraction tasks.
8	When using well-crafted boolean questions aligned with researchers' criteria, AI tools could support early-stage quality assessment, helping to prioritize which papers merit full data extraction.

6 Conclusions

We have presented a structured experimental study aimed at assessing the capabilities and limitations of three LLM-based tools (ChatGPT, ChatPDF, and NotebookLM) for data extraction in SE SLRs—to our knowledge, the first direct comparison of the performance of these tools for this specific SLR phase. Guided by three research questions, we examined tool equivalence with human annotation (RQ1), potential tool-induced bias during manual review (RQ2), and the impact of processing multiple studies sequentially in a single session compared to processing them in isolation (RQ3). Our findings show that tools perform well on questions involving explicit information, but consistently struggle with inference or interpretative tasks, where humans outperform them (RQ1). Exposure to tool outputs can influence reviewers, depending on the tool and the cognitive complexity of the question (RQ2). Tools may generate inconsistent responses in grouped settings, particularly for questions requiring higher-level interpretation (RQ3). Overall, our findings confirm that, while current LLM tools can assist with certain literature review tasks, they are not yet reliable substitutes for expert judgment, though they may be useful in early-stage screening.

In the near future, we plan to follow several complementary directions. First, building on our ongoing SLR, we intend to apply the lessons learned—particularly using well-crafted boolean questions for early-stage quality assessment and paper prioritization—to validate their practical impact. Second, When addressing our full SLR, it will also be interesting to validate the results when LLMs are confronted with different categories of papers, such as purely mathematical articles versus more descriptive or pictorial ones. Overall, the evaluation will be even more interesting when it covers work in additional domain areas of software engineering. Finally, we plan to explore prompt optimization tailored to each system to improve performance and extend our evaluation to question types not fully addressed here, especially open-ended or free-text queries requiring more specialized analytical techniques.

Acknowledgments. This work was supported in part by Grant PID2024-155834NB-I00 by MICIU/AEI/10.13039/501100011033 and by ERDF/EU.

References

1. Alshami, A., Elsayed, M., Ali, E., Eltoukhy, A.E.E., Zayed, T.: Harnessing the power of chatgpt for automating systematic review process: Methodology, case study, limitations, and future directions. Systems **11**(7), 1–37 (2023). https://doi.org/10.3390/systems11070351
2. Bolaños, F., Salatino, A., Osborne, F., Motta, E.: Artificial intelligence for literature reviews: opportunities and challenges. Artif. Intell. Rev. **57**(259), 1–49 (2024). https://doi.org/10.1007/s10462-024-10902-3
3. Carlini, N., Tramèr, F., Wallace, E., Jagielski, M., et al.: Extracting training data from large language models. In: 30th USENIX Security Symposium (USENIX Security 21), pp. 2633–2650. USENIX Association (2021)
4. Clark, J., Glasziou, P., Mar, C.D., Stehlik, A.B.B., Scott, P., A.: A full systematic review was completed in 2 weeks using automation tools: a case study. J. Clin. Epidemiol. **5**(121), 81–90 (2020). https://doi.org/10.1016/j.jclinepi.2020.01.008
5. Daraqel, B., Owayda, A., Khan, H., Koletsi, D., Mheissen, S.: Artificial intelligence as a tool for data extraction is not fully reliable compared to manual data extraction. J. Dent. **160**, 105846 (2025). https://doi.org/10.1016/j.jdent.2025.105846
6. Fabbri, S., Silva, C., Hernandes, E., F., O., DiThommazo, A., Belgamo, A.: Improvements in the start tool to better support the systematic review process.

In: Proceedings of EASE'16, pp. 1–5. ACM, New York, NY, USA (2016). https://doi.org/10.1145/2915970.2916013
7. Felizardo, K.R., Carver, J.C.: Automating Systematic Literature Review. In: Contemporary Empirical Methods in Software Engineering, pp. 327–355. Springer, Cham (2020). https://doi.org/10.1007/978-3-030-32489-6_12
8. Felizardo, K.R., Steinmacher, I., Lima, M.S., Deizepe, A., Conte, T.U., Barcellos, M.P.: Data extraction for systematic mapping study using a large language model - a proof-of-concept study in software engineering. In: Proceedings of ESEM'24, pp. 407–413. ACM, New York, NY, USA (2024)
9. Gartlehner, G., Kahwati, L., Hilscher, R., Thomas, I., et al.: Data extraction for evidence synthesis using a large language model: A proof-of-concept study. Res. Synth. Methods **4**(15), 576–589 (2024). https://doi.org/10.1002/jrsm.1710
10. Ge, L., Agrawal, R., Singer, M., et al.: Leveraging artificial intelligence to enhance systematic reviews in health research: advanced tools and challenges. Syst. Rev. **13**(269), 1–7 (2024). https://doi.org/10.1186/s13643-024-02682-2
11. Gobin, M., et al.: From data extraction to analysis: a comparative study of elise capabilities in scientific literature. Front. Artif. Intell. **12**(8), 1–19 (2025). https://doi.org/10.3389/frai.2025.1587244
12. International, D.: DAMA-DMBOK: Data Management Body of Knowledge, (2nd Edition). Technics Publications, LLC, Sedona, AZ (2017)
13. Jonnalagadda, S., Goyal, P., Huffman, M.: Automating data extraction in systematic reviews: a systematic review. Syst. Rev. **4**(78), 1–16 (2015). https://doi.org/10.1186/s13643-015-0066-7
14. Khraisha, Q., Put, S., Kappenberg, J., Warraitch, A., Hadfield, K.: Can large language models replace humans in systematic reviews? evaluating gpt-4's efficacy in screening and extracting data from peer-reviewed and grey literature in multiple languages. Res. Synth. Methods **4**(15), 616–626 (2024). https://doi.org/10.1002/jrsm.1715
15. Klar, R., Arvidsson, N., Angelakis, V.: Digital twins' maturity: The need for interoperability. IEEE Syst. J. **18**(1), 713–724 (2024)
16. Konet, A., et al.: Performance of two large language models for data extraction in evidence synthesis. Res. Synth. Methods **5**(15), 818–824 (2024). https://doi.org/10.1002/jrsm.1732
17. Parsifal: Parsifal systematic literature review tool (2025). https://parsif.al/. Last visited on 2026
18. Rasheed, Z., et al.: Can large language models serve as data analysts? a multi-agent assisted approach for qualitative data analysis (2024). https://arxiv.org/abs/2402.01386
19. Schmidt, L., et al.: Exploring the use of a large language model for data extraction in systematic reviews: a rapid feasibility study (2025). https://arxiv.org/abs/2405.14445
20. Spillias, S., Ollerhead, K., Andreotta, M., et. al: Evaluating generative ai for qualitative data extraction in community-based fisheries management literature. Environ. Evid. **1**(14), 1–18 (2025). https://doi.org/10.1186/s13750-025-00362-9
21. Stoll, C., Izadi, S., Fowler, S., Green, P., Suls, J., Colditz, G.: The value of a second reviewer for study selection in systematic reviews. Res. Synth. Methods. **10**(4), 539–545 (2019). https://doi.org/10.1002/jrsm.1369
22. Supplementary material: Automated Data Extraction in Software Engineering SLRs: Promise, Pitfalls, and the Role of Human Oversight (2026). https://zenodo.org/records/16082581

23. Syriani, E., David, I., Kumar, G.: Screening articles for systematic reviews with chatgpt. J. Comput. Lang. **80**, 101287 (2024). https://doi.org/10.1016/j.cola.2024.101287
24. de la Torre-López, J., Ramírez, A., Romero, J.: Artificial intelligence to automate the systematic review of scientific literature. Computing **105**, 2171–2194 (2023). https://doi.org/10.1007/s00607-023-01181-x
25. Xu, F., Lin, Q., Han, J., Zhao, T., Liu, J., Cambria, E.: Are large language models really good logical reasoners? a comprehensive evaluation and beyond (2024). https://arxiv.org/abs/2306.09841

Green Software Engineering: A Systematic Mapping of Design Impacts on Energy Consumption

Marco Hecktor(✉) and Sabine Sachweh

IDiAL Institute, University of Applied Sciences and Arts Dortmund, Dortmund, Germany
{marco.hecktor,sabine.sachweh}@fh-dortmund.de

Abstract. This study systematically maps green software engineering, focusing on the impact of software design on energy consumption. A Systematic Mapping Study was conducted using topic clustering and a scoring approach for study selection. Current research is dominated by validation and empirical studies, with limited real-world evaluation. Energy efficiency is affected across all software layers but remains highly context-dependent. Existing techniques and tools are fragmented and lack standardized metrics. Green software engineering still lacks unified methods and general guidelines. Future work should prioritize real-world validation, standardization, and context-aware approaches.

Keywords: Green Software Engineering · Systematic Mapping Study · Sustainability · Software Design · Energy Consumption

1 Introduction

The increasing environmental impact of Information and Communication Technologies (ICT) has raised significant concerns regarding the sustainability of modern software systems in mitigating their environmental impact [6]. As software becomes deeply embedded in almost all sectors of society, including industry, healthcare, transportation, and particularly smart cities [7], its contribution to energy consumption and greenhouse gas emissions steadily grows. The aim of embedding software into all sectors of society is to enable efficiency gains, optimize processes, and enhance daily life. Particularly, smart cities heavily rely on interconnected digital infrastructures, data-driven services, and large-scale software systems for optimizing urban societies [11]. New technologies and services that increase efficiency also raise computational demands and energy use, intensifying the need for sustainable hardware and software solutions.

This research is co-funded by the European Union and the Ministry of Economic Affairs, Industry, Climate Action and Energy of the State of North Rhine-Westphalia (MWIKE) within "NeueWege.IN.NRW" (funding number: EFRE-20801700) and managed by the Projektträger Jülich (PTJ). The authors are responsible for the content of this publication.

C. Berger and V. Klös (Eds.): SEAA 2026, LNCS 16864, pp. 189–206, 2027.
https://doi.org/10.1007/978-3-032-36587-3_14

This development has led to the emergence of Green Software Engineering (GSE) as an important research domain, aiming to mitigate environmental impact while maintaining software quality and functionality. The core objectives of GSE include the enhancement of energy efficiency, the mitigation of the environmental impact associated with hardware utilization, the optimization of resource allocation, and the promotion of software system longevity [9].

Despite growing research, the field remains fragmented and rapidly changing. Numerous approaches, models, and tools complicate efforts to gain a comprehensive view of the landscape. In this context, Systematic Mapping Studies (SMSs) play a pivotal role for systematically identifying, categorizing, and analyzing existing work. Their findings help researchers detect trends, expose research gaps, and build a shared knowledge base [13]. Unlike traditional Systematic Literature Reviews (SLRs), SMSs emphasize breadth over depth, offering a high-level overview of research landscapes.

Previous mapping studies in the domain of GSE have highlighted both the rapid growth of the field as well as its limitations. Furthermore, recent studies indicate an increasing diversity of frameworks and evaluation criteria, reflecting both the maturity and the complexity of the domain [1,3,14].

This is particularly relevant in domains such as smart cities, where software systems operate at large scale and have a direct impact on energy consumption, urban sustainability, and quality of life. Hence, supporting the development of more sustainable software systems by identifying effective practices and unresolved issues is needed. Therefore, this paper aims to contribute to the field by systematically mapping existing research on GSE and highlighting key trends, gaps, and opportunities for future investigations.

The remainder of this paper is structured as follows: Sect. 2 presents related work. Section 3 elucidates the design process of this SMS. Section 4 shows the results obtained from the SMS. Section 5 discusses the results. Section 6 outlines threats to validity. Finally, Sect. 7 presents our conclusion and future work.

2 Related Work

Recent secondary studies have investigated the impact of software design on energy consumption, but with a more circumscribed focus than that afforded by a comprehensive mapping approach. The SMS by Poy *et al.* [14] examines design patterns, code smells, and refactoring techniques. These factors are also addressed in the systematic literature review conducted by Connolly Bree *et al.* [3]. Araújo *et al.* [1] present an SLR on energy consumption in microservice architectures, while Steinberg *et al.* [15] focus on Green Software Metrics.

Additionally, previous research has examined sustainability in software engineering from a more comprehensive viewpoint. For example, Penzenstadler *et al.* [12] present an early SMS on software engineering for sustainability, with a primary emphasis on operational concerns and software management. Similarly, Berntsen *et al.* [2] concentrate primarily on the improvement of software development processes, managerial practices, and associated evaluation procedures.

Existing secondary studies focus on specific dimensions of software energy efficiency, such as design patterns, code smells, refactorings, microservices, or energy metrics. However, no study was identified that systematically maps the full spectrum of software design decisions affecting energy consumption across code, runtime, architectural, and cloud-related perspectives. This gap motivates the present study.

3 Planning and Conducting the Mapping Study

The goal of this mapping study is to provide an overview of research on *Green Software Engineering*, which encompasses software engineering aspects influencing the sustainability of software. This mapping study utilizes the systematic mapping process defined by Petersen *et al.* [13]. The process is depicted in Fig. 1, which shows the conducted process steps, their underlying tasks, as well as changes in the result set. The following subsections describe the methodology in more detail, showing how the systematic mapping was achieved.

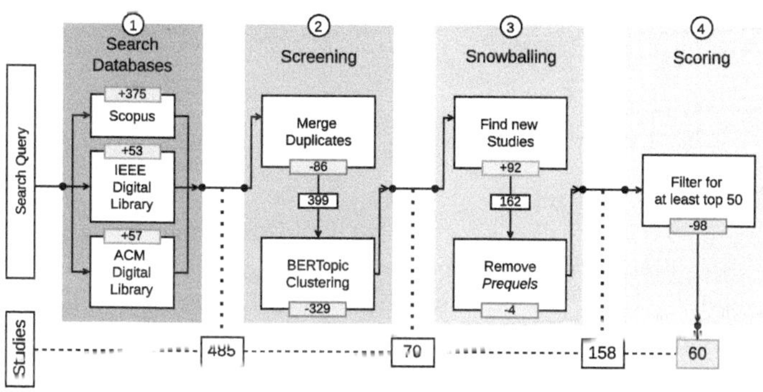

Fig. 1. Depiction of the different methodological steps, including the performed tasks, the excluded and included studies, as well as the intermediate and final result set sizes.

3.1 Definition of Research Scope

To identify relevant research, we formulated research questions that encompass sustainability in combination with software engineering aspects. The research questions, as shown below, are the guiding framework of this study.

RQ1. How is research on energy-efficient software design distributed by research approach, contribution type, and application domain?

RQ2. Which software design aspects and technical factors have been identified as influencing energy consumption in software systems?

RQ3. What techniques, tools, and approaches have been proposed to improve energy efficiency in software?

3.2 Literature Search

Collecting the list of primary, unfiltered studies is performed by generating a search string and applying it to several scientific databases. In the context of this SMS, we followed the PICOC-Method delineated by Kitchenham *et al.* [10] and derived the following search string:

(energy+(consumption|usage|efficiency) **OR** power+consumption **OR** (green|energy-aware)+software) **AND** (software+(architecture|design) **OR** architectural+style **OR** design+pattern **OR** architecture+property) **AND** (influenc* **OR** impact* **OR** determin*)

The symbol "+" denotes concatenation, whereas "|" denotes disjunction, requiring at least one associated term to be present. Wildcard characters were used in the final part of the search string to broaden the range of retrieved studies. The literature search was conducted in three bibliographic databases: Scopus, the IEEE Digital Library, and the ACM Digital Library, during process step 1 of Fig. 1. For each database, we adapted the search string to its query syntax. To reduce irrelevant results, we limited the search to journal articles, conference papers, proceedings, and books.

3.3 Screening of Studies

To screen the studies and reduce the result set to only relevant papers, we first set up our inclusion and exclusion criteria, listed in Table 1.

The three result lists were further processed to prepare them for screening. We transformed all three lists into csv format and unified the column definitions for merging all three lists. This unified list was scanned for duplicates in the first task of process step 2 of Fig. 1.

To avoid assessing too many studies at once, we used an iterative topic-clustering approach to divide the material into smaller groups. In the second task of process step 2 in Fig. 1, we applied *BERTopic* [5] and repeatedly refined the results, narrowing the list until 30 studies remained for final inspection. In each iteration, we clustered the results using abstracts, producing a list of all remaining studies with an assigned topic number, a BERTopic label, and a human-readable OpenAI-generated label, as shown in Table 2.

In the given example, we selected topic 8 because it was strongly misaligned with the research questions. We then applied the inclusion and exclusion criteria to the titles, reducing the corpus to 78 studies. We removed 8 additional studies that were inaccessible or had English titles and abstracts but Spanish full texts.

3.4 Classification of Research

The classification of research follows the four questions listed in Table 3. The research domain helps to achieve a broader clustering for research within the green software systems domain. We therefore applied a *single keyword* per study

Table 1. Inclusion and exclusion criteria

ID	Type	Description
i_1	Include	Study explicitly targets software architecture, design pattern or other software design specific aspects
i_2	Include	Study targets energy consumption/efficiency
e_1	Exclude	The study is not peer-reviewed
e_2	Exclude	The study is not written in English
e_3	Exclude	The full text is not accessible from our institution
e_4	Exclude	The study is not a primary, single, cohesive research contribution; it is a secondary work such as an SLR, SMS, survey, conference proceedings volume, edited book, editorial, or introductory paper

while providing each study with multiple research keywords that describe the study content. For the classification of the studies, in terms of the research approach, we used the schema provided by Wieringa *et al.* [16]. The context summarizes the study's goal and contribution. Lastly, the contribution field provides a short description of the study's contribution to the research domain.

The initially classified studies provided some insights, but in process step 3 of Fig. 1, we conducted backward snowballing on the 70 remaining studies, yielding 92 additional studies. After repeating the classification and excluding three short form duplicates (*Prequels*), the final set from the literature search and snowballing comprised 158 studies.

3.5 Classification Scoring

A scoring schema derived from the classification was employed to further filter the studies prior to final inclusion. Each document is scored based on the following Eq. 1 with $S_{RK} \subseteq \{0, 0.5, 1, 1.5, 2\}^*$, $S_{RD} \subset \{1, 2, 3, 4\}$, $S_C \in \{0, 1, 2, 3, 4\}$, and $S_{RA} \subset \{0, 1, 2, 3, 4\}$ in process step 4 of Fig. 1, and assign the scores presented in Tables 4 for S_{RK} and Table 5 for S_{RD}, S_C, S_{RA}.

$$S_{Doc} = max(S_{RK}) + max(S_{RK} \backslash max(S_{RK})) + S_{RD} + S_C + S_{RA} \quad (1)$$

Table 2. Representation of one clustering iteration

Topic	Topic Label	OpenAI Label	Count
...	...	...	...
6	design patterns, patterns, pattern	Energy Efficiency in Software Design Patterns	15
...	...	...	...
8	building, buildings, thermal	Energy Efficiency and Thermal Comfort in Building Design through Simulation in Tropical and Heritage Contexts	10

Table 3. Classification scheme for research studies

Aspect	Description
Research Domain	What is the main domain being addressed by the research?
Research Keywords	Which research keywords are most appropriate for indexing and describing the content of this document?
Research Approach	Which research approach is suitable to describe this document?
Contribution	What kind of contribution is the document providing?

We assigned a score of 0 to keywords already present in the research domain, as well as overly generic terms like *Sustainability* and terms unrelated to software design like *Knowledge Management*, to avoid double scoring. Other keywords received scores from 0.5 to 2 based on their relevance to software design.

The remaining characteristics are assigned scores ranging from 0 to 4 according to their relevance to software design. A score of 0 is assigned to items deemed to have no relevance to software design, such as those classified as *Opinion Paper* or studies whose contribution is labeled as *None*. Only one study, which merely articulated a prospective research interest without reporting concrete contributions, was assigned to this latter category.

We standardized the importance of each characteristic, research keyword, research domain, contribution, and research approach by giving each a maximum score of 4. For keyword scoring, we used the two highest-scoring keywords to capture topic diversity and abstraction. We then assigned scores to every possible value of each characteristic and computed a final score for each study, applying this procedure automatically to the 158 backward snowballing studies.

Table 4. Scoring of the Research Keywords (S_{RK})

Research Keywords	Score
AI, Architecture, Design Patterns, Embedded Systems, Empirical Research, Green Computing, Internet of Things, Knowledge Management, Maintenance, Methodologies, Security, Software Engineering, Sustainability	0.0
Cloud Computing, Communication Technologies, Compilers, Distributed Systems, Metrics and Measurement, Mobile Applications, Modeling and Meta-Modeling, Performance, Self-Adaptive Systems, Software Analysis, Software Evolution, System Software, Web Applications	0.5
Code Quality, Concurrency, Energy Efficiency, Resource Optimization, Service-Oriented Architecture, Software Development Process, Software Quality	1.0
Data Structures, Frameworks and Tools, Programming Languages	1.5
Algorithms, Programming, Refactoring	2.0

3.6 Final Selection

Prior to determining the final set of studies, we set a preliminary inclusion threshold of 50 papers for the subsequent mapping phase of the analysis. The cumulative distribution of study scores is shown in Fig. 2.

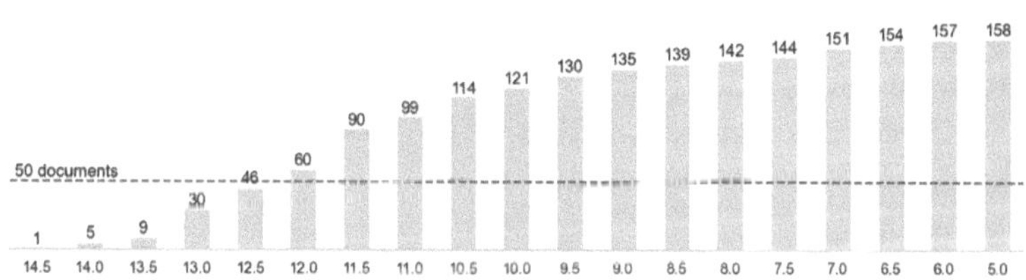

Fig. 2. The cumulative distribution of document scores.

We selected a threshold of 12.0 based on the score distribution and our limit of 50 studies. Increasing the threshold to 12.5 would have reduced the set from 60 to 46 studies, potentially excluding relevant evidence. Therefore, 12.0 was chosen as a pragmatic compromise between coverage and analysis effort.

Table 5. Scoring for Research Domain (S_{RD}), Contribution (S_C), and Research Approach (S_{RA}) in order to select studies

Score	Research Domain	Contribution	Research Approach
0		None	Opinion Paper
1	Communication Technologies, Embedded Software Engineering, Operating Systems, Web Applications	Conceptual Framework, Proposal	Philosophical Paper
2	Distributed Systems, Framework, Parallel Programming, Software Modelling	Framework, Software Architecture	Solution Proposal
3	Code Smells, Design Patterns, Mobile Software Engineering, Software Engineering	Method, Model	Validation Research
4	Software Architecture	Empirical evidence	Evaluation Research

4 Results

The distribution of the study characteristics is presented in Subsect. 4.1. This is followed by an analysis of the findings related to design aspects and technical factors that affect energy consumption in Subsect. 4.2, and by an examination of findings concerning models, techniques, tools, and approaches in Subsect. 4.3. The studies in the result set are labeled [S#], matching the identifiers in the "List of Studies" in the supplementary material [8].

4.1 Research Distribution and Trends

To address research question RQ1 the dataset of selected papers is analyzed with respect to research approaches, contribution types, and application domains. The corresponding results are visualized in Fig. 3.

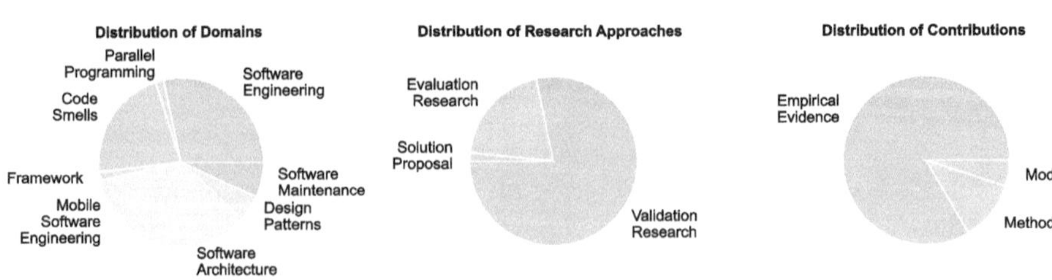

Fig. 3. Distribution of the research domain across study selection.

The research domain is spread across several areas. The main domain is *Software Engineering* (17), followed by *Software Architecture* and *Code Smells* (13 each), *Mobile Software Engineering* (8), *Design Patterns* and *Software Maintenance* (4 each), and *Parallel Programming* and *Framework* (1 each). The predominant research approach employed in the studies is *Validation Research* (48), with fewer *Evaluation Research* studies (12) and one *Solution Proposal.* Most studies contribute *Empirical Evidence* (51), with seven *Methods* and three *Models.*

The predominant *Software Engineering* domain clusters studies that address broad research areas, such as "Energy Efficient Coding Practices for Sustainable Software Development" [S36] and "Program Energy Efficiency: The Impact of Language, Compiler and Implementation Choices" [S1]. It covers high-level aspects examined from a general software engineering perspective that cannot be clearly assigned to specific areas like *code smells*, *design patterns*, or *software architecture.* Many studies address cross-cutting concerns, including *development practices*, *general design principles*, and *cloud-specific patterns*, that affect software energy consumption without focusing on a single, well-defined subdomain. They typically operate at an abstraction level where software design, development, and deployment are tightly interwoven, making precise classification into a narrower domain impractical or misleading.

The combined consideration of research domains and research keywords yields more fine-grained insights into the specific findings reported in the individual studies. Figure 4 visualizes this joint distribution.

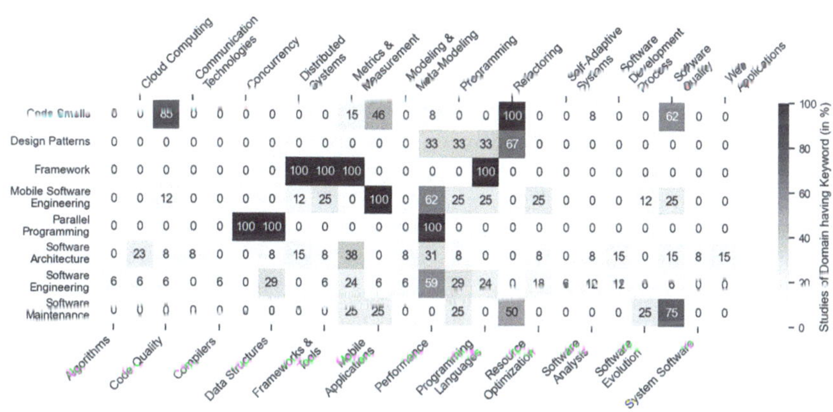

Fig. 4. Heatmap with domains on the X-axis and research keywords on the Y-axis. Values show the percentage of studies per domain that include each research keyword.

As only one study belongs to each of the domains *Framework* and *Parallel Programming*, all identified keywords appear in all studies. Both *Code Smells* and *Design Patterns* address source code changes to improve energy efficiency, but from different angles. *Code Smells* focuses on *Code Quality* and *Refactoring*, while *Design Patterns* emphasizes *Performance* and *Programming Language* differences and their impact on energy use. The other domains adopt a more abstract view. *Software Engineering* and *Mobile Software Engineering* are similar, with the latter centered on *Mobile Applications* and the former having a broader scope, including *Software Development Processes* and *Data Structures* (12% of studies). *Software Architecture* is distinct in its focus on *Cloud Computing* and *Web Applications*, whereas *Software Maintenance* mainly targets *Software Quality* and *Refactoring*.

In addition to the distribution of research across characteristics, Fig. 5 shows temporal trends, highlighting all values above 1 to emphasize peaks.

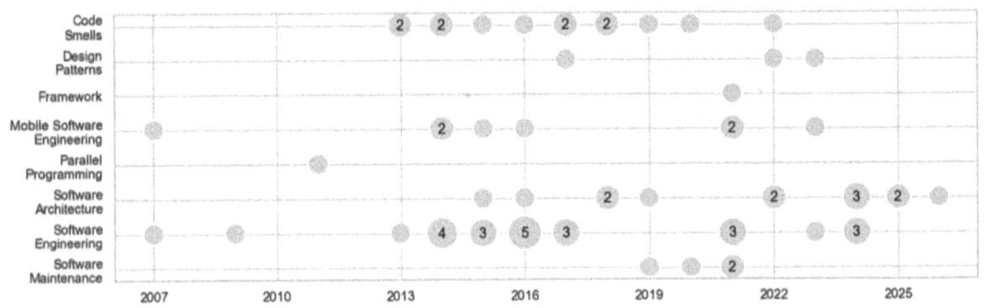

Fig. 5. Visualizing research trends over time in the set of selected studies.

Software Engineering and *Code Smells* clearly dominate in 2013–2017, while *Software Architecture* was researched from 2014 to 2018 and has gained relevance again since 2022. Overall, research on GSE is increasing.

4.2 Design Aspects and Technical Factors Influencing Energy Consumption

In order to answer RQ2 we investigated the result set of studies on design aspects and technical factors influencing energy consumption. We derived four categories to structure our findings: (i) Data, Processing and Distribution, (ii) Design and Code Quality, (iii) Runtime and Platform, as well as (iv) Architecture and Cloud.

Data, Processing and Distribution. This aspect covers data processing, its software representation, and serialization. Several sorting algorithms are evaluated for energy consumption by input size, yielding an *Algorithm-Energy Optimizer* that dynamically selects the most efficient algorithm at runtime [S6]. For non-trivial data (e.g., phonebook contacts), the underlying data structure is crucial. Studies have examined data-structure implementations across programming languages [S24, S25, S37, S48], and evaluated language-specific libraries such as *Java Collections Framework (JCF)*, *Apache Collections Framework (ACC)*, *Trove* for Java [S24, S48], and the *C5 generic collection 2.3* library for .NET [S24, S37, S48]. Results show that carefully choosing data structures can save up to 97.50% energy [S37]. Hunt *et al.* [S25] showed that in concurrent software, lock-free FIFO queues can outperform other data structures when both ends are accessed concurrently. Algorithms and data structures operate in memory, but serialization is essential to store or transmit data.. Khrouf *et al.* [S30] compare REST vs. RPC and JSON vs. Protobuf, finding that REST uses four times less energy than RPC, and Protobuf saves a further 33% over JSON.

Design and Code Quality. Different aspects of design and code quality, starting with different programming paradigms [S12, S20, S34], general design patterns [S3, S13, S14, S20, S34, S50], maintainability of code [S19, S35, S50], code smells [S19, S51, S58], energy smells [S9, S16, S17, S22, S38, S44], as well as code obfuscation [S53], have been evaluated regarding energy consumption.

Research on object-oriented programming has produced mixed findings. Connolly Bree *et al.* [S12] empirically compare inheritance and delegation in Java, showing that inheritance reduces energy consumption by 4% and execution time by 77% in interpreted mode only, limiting external validity. Maleki *et al.* [S34] take a broader view by including design patterns, finding effects on energy efficiency ranging from negligible to substantial. Diverging results stem from different measurement methods, languages, and case studies. For example, Maleki *et al.* [S34] report a 595% energy increase when using the decorator pattern overall, whereas Connolly Bree *et al.* [S13] find that removing a single decorator reduces energy by 3%–5%. Such heterogeneity highlights the need for per-system evaluations, as seen for the template method, whose energy impact ranges from -41% to +89%. The most impactful patterns on energy consumption are: (i) observer pattern (-89% to -91%) [S50], (ii) abstract-factory pattern (-61% to -65%) [S50], (iii) facade pattern (-22% to -61%) [S50], (iv) flyweight pattern (-50%) [S34], (v) decorator pattern (-3% to -5%) [S13, S34], (vi) template method pattern (-41% to +89%) [S20, S34, S50], (vii) singleton pattern (+10% to +105%) [S50], (viii) visitor pattern (+8% for Java, +132% to +2012% for C++) [S14].

Maintainability and code quality depend on the removal of smells like code smells or energy smells. The correlation between maintainability and energy consumption has been researched, showing that only the *total lines of code* metric affects energy consumption [S19, S35]. Additionally, a statistical relationship between lines of code with the number of methods and energy consumption has been observed when performing code smell refactorings [S19]. Furthermore, the *Complexity and Code smell Energy Model (CCsEM)*, utilizing multiple linear regression to estimate energy consumption of software components, based on the *Cyclomatic Complexity* metric, code smells, and size, was presented [S23]. Certain research has empirically evaluated the removal of smells and the resulting energy savings. The most frequently examined code smells are *God Class* [S10, S51, S58], *Feature Envy* [S19, S58], and *Long Method* [S19, S58]. Particularly, in applications using object-relational-mapping libraries, refactoring a set of prominent code smells yields up to 49.9% in energy savings [S58].

The sequencing and selection of code smells for refactoring varies in terms of energy savings [S19]. The selection of code smells is a gradient between object-oriented programming and optimizing energy consumption. The group of energy code smells found in the result set of studies addresses specific smells impairing the energy efficiency of *Embedded Systems* [S38], *Mobile Devices* [S22], and particularly the *Android Operating System* [S9, S16, S44].

Morisio *et al.* [S38] empirically evaluated refactorings targeting energy-related code smells in embedded systems, finding that nearly half increased energy consumption. Gottschalk *et al.* [S22] studied energy code smells for mobile devices, focusing on device-specific characteristics. Their results are broadly applicable but require accounting for hardware and OS specifics. Further research on Android-specific code smells has examined the energy-related implications of using the *HashMap* data structure [S9, S16], the application of *Member Ignoring Methods* [S9, S16, S44], and the proper management of instances of *Wakelocks* [S16, S17, S22], i.e., the timely release of needless resources. These practices are generally regarded as energy-improving refactorings. In addition, Carette *et al.* [S9] identify a category of *Android Picture Smells* that are associated with picture-related characteristics, leading to excessive energy consumption.

Runtime and Platform. The choice of platform is closely tied to the choice of programming languages, frameworks, and libraries. Several studies have therefore examined the energy consumption of programming languages. While some focus directly on language efficiency [S21, S46, S47], others address it indirectly through design patterns, language-specific features, or frameworks. Across 39 papers, 32 programming languages are mentioned, including 16 named only in the studies primarily focused on language efficiency [S46, S47], and one study explicitly investigating Erlang [S21]. Java is the most frequently studied language, appearing in 33 studies, followed by C++ (8), JavaScript (7), and C and Python (6 each). This is consistent with Chowdhury *et al.* [S11], who identify Java as the dominant language in energy-aware software. By contrast, Pereira *et al.* [S47] found C to be the least energy-consuming language, with Java ranking fifth. Corral *et al.* [S15] and Oliveira *et al.* [S42] also examine polyglot programming combining Java and JavaScript, as well as Java and C, but do not quantify energy savings. Khrouf *et al.* [S30] report 70% energy savings by replacing Swing with Angular and Spring Boot in web application development. Calero *et al.* [S7] show that Spring Boot's framework overhead can raise energy consumption by 51.5%–61.41%, even though 67% of developers use it [S8].

Architecture and Cloud. Architectural decisions affect software energy consumption. Wide-scope decisions, such as choosing between monolithic and microservice architectures, are long-term and must be assessed at design time. Berry *et al.* [S5] examined migration from monolith to microservices, finding different trade-offs depending on scaling. Without replication, microservices mainly benefit the routing layer, which could also improve a monolith. When scaling is required, microservices reduce memory, CPU, and energy use [S8, S29]. Zhao *et* *al.* [S60] examined microservice granularity and found that coarse-grained services generally lower energy use and response times, though poor decomposition with overloaded services can consume more energy than a fine-grained design.

Beyond holistic architectures, studies have examined patterns that offload heavy computation between edge nodes and cloud services, as well as an aspect-oriented model for energy efficiency. For example, Ochoa *et al.* [S41] propose an energy-efficient IoT monitoring architecture by decomposing monitoring tasks across layers. Extending the client-server architecture, the aspect-oriented model of Chinenyeze *et al.* [S10] re-routes client requests to reduce runtime energy, achieving 4.5% savings. Other cloud patterns show that the *Local Database Proxy* pattern can also significantly cut energy use [S2, S29].

4.3 Models, Techniques, Tools, and Approaches

To answer RQ3, we examine studies reporting findings that support energy consumption mitigation. We structure the results into four categories: (i) Code-Level Optimizations, (ii) Refactoring, (iii) Architectures, Conceptual Frameworks and Models, and (iv) Tools, Methods and Middlewares.

Code-Level Optimizations. Code-level optimization for reducing software energy consumption includes: database query optimization [S49], loop optimization by storing array length before the loop header [S31, S36, S44, S57], wise thread management [S36], direct field access instead of getters and setters [S31], preferring static over instance methods [S31], using efficient libraries [S33, S39], disabling unused features [S39], using time-outs for network requests and sleep instructions [S39, S49], and reallocating methods to other execution environments (e.g., outside the JVM or to external services) [S15].

Polyglot programming and offloading computation to more efficient environments are code-level optimizations that also reduce resource usage [S15, S42]. Resource-efficient practices include minimizing the usage of CPU, memory, and I/O [S36] as well as applying dynamic voltage and frequency scaling [S33, S39]. Efficient device selection, e.g., appropriate sensors, and disabling unused hardware further improve energy efficiency [S39]. Additionally, developers should optimize data access patterns and use only the necessary data precision [S33]. Liu *et al.* [S33] show that energy consumption differs greatly between sequential and random data access, and that using less precise data types can save energy. For data transmission, Li *et al.* [S31] find that bundling network packets saves energy when headers exceed payload size. Compiler options can also reduce energy use by up to 73%, depending on the use case and chosen options [S1].

Refactoring. Although refactoring constitutes an optimization at the source-code level, the breadth and specificity of its techniques warrant treating it as an independent category. Four empirical studies systematically analyzed 87 refactoring techniques documented by Fowler [4], in addition to six widely adopted techniques provided by the *Eclipse IDE* that introduce structural modifications to the code base [S52]. These techniques were investigated across three programming languages: C++ (63 techniques), C# (5 techniques), and Java (35 techniques) [S43, S45, S52, S54]. Furthermore, combinations of five refactoring techniques already known to positively affect energy consumption were investigated [S54]. Ournani *et al.* [S43] found that structure-oriented refactorings have no substantial impact on energy consumption, reporting differences of 5%–8% without stating whether they increase or decrease it. In contrast, Park *et al.* [S45] report that, of Fowler's 63 refactorings [4], 26 reduce energy consumption, seven have no effect, and 30 increase it. Both studies report similar ranges of relative energy change: 5%–8% [S43] and –5% to +5% [S45]. Sahin *et al.* [S52] found that three of six refactoring combinations reduce energy consumption by up to 9.33%, and that these six refactorings have a statistically significant impact, both beneficial (up to 4% reduction) and detrimental (up to 8% increase).

Architectures, Conceptual Frameworks and Models. Adopting *Green Coding*, Manimegalai *et al.* [S36] propose two architectural patterns for energy measurement and dashboards in cloud computing. Their architectures distinguish design-time, using IDE plugins for run-time architectures, and use *elastic logging* for energy metrics. Applied to two applications, one with conventional JavaScript practices and one with advanced energy-efficient practices, the Java application consumed 15% less energy. The *Agile, Layered Architecture, and aspect-oriented framework (ALAI)* extends conventional Agile methodologies with a sustainability-aware architecture that supplies structured, sustainability-relevant feedback and metrics for planning and executing subsequent sprints [S56]. Stakeholder energy awareness has also been empirically evaluated via an energy dashboard in agile development, increasing the active discussion of software energy use in Scrum [S26]. Beyond architectural patterns, several conceptual frameworks are used or proposed. In addition to the *Algorithm-Energy optimizer* [S6], a resource consumption framework has been proposed [S4] that evaluates app resource usage under different architectural styles to derive system energy consumption. Another conceptual framework outlines strategic dimensions for sustainable software engineering: (i) *Energy-Efficient Design*, (ii) *Resource Optimization*, (iii) *Green Deployment*, (iv) *Eco-Friendly Development Practices*, and (v) *Continuous Monitoring and Optimization* [S28]. While this latter work provides a broad framework, Vos *et al.* [S59] propose a model of *reusable architectural tactics for the cloud.* It enhances energy efficiency by mapping 18 *resource efficiency tactics* to 10 *energy efficiency tactics* across three *energy efficiency categories.* Finally, a conceptual framework is proposed for selecting the lowest-energy mobile testing framework based on required interactions [S18].

Tools, Methods and Middlewares. To benchmark energy consumption in software systems, the *StEP* method [S27], which constructs multiple variants of a system with selectively stubbed components, enabling direct comparison of each component's stubbed and non-stubbed performance, was presented. Similarly, Seo *et al.* [S55] propose a framework to estimate the energy consumption of distributed Java-based systems at construction and run time. For per-line energy calculation, the prototype tool *vLens* [S32] estimates energy consumption accurately in under three minutes. To fix code smells and evaluate their energy impact, Carette *et al.* [S9] introduce *Hot-Pepper*, which automatically detects and corrects smells and proposes the most energy-efficient application version. Nikzad *et al.* [S40] present *APE*, an annotation-driven middleware for Java that lets developers delay function execution to the least energy-consuming moment.

5 Discussion

This SMS provides a structured overview of GSE with a focus on software design and its influence on energy consumption. The results highlight the growing maturity of the field and several persistent challenges. The findings further support the need for a holistic perspective on software energy efficiency, as relevant factors were identified across code-level, runtime, architectural, and cloud-related dimensions that are typically investigated in isolation.

The distribution of research (RQ1) shows a strong dominance of *validation research* and *empirical contributions*, while *evaluation research* and *solution proposals* are underrepresented. This suggests a lack of studies in real-world contexts, limiting external validity and practical applicability.

The analysis of design aspects and technical impact factors (RQ2) shows that energy efficiency is affected at all software layers, from low-level data structures and algorithms to high-level architecture. Yet, the findings reveal strong heterogeneity and context dependence. For example, design patterns can either increase or decrease energy use, depending on implementation details, programming languages, and application context. This inconsistency hinders the derivation of general design guidelines. Code- and design-level changes, such as optimizing data structures, using efficient serialization formats, and removing smells, can provide substantial energy savings, but empirical studies show that some refactorings increase energy consumption. This highlights the need for context-aware optimization rather than universal practices. At higher abstraction levels, architectural choices (e.g., monolithic vs. microservices, and microservice granularity) introduce trade-offs between scalability, performance, and energy efficiency. These trade-offs should be evaluated explicitly during architectural design as first-class quality attributes, not as afterthoughts.

The identified models, techniques, tools, and approaches (RQ3) support energy efficiency improvements but are fragmented and lack standardization. They include coding practices, refactoring strategies, architectural patterns, and measurement tools. The absence of unified metrics and benchmarks limits comparability across studies and optimizations.

The findings suggest a core tension in GSE: many effective techniques exist, but their suitability is highly context-dependent, and there is no consolidated knowledge base or standardized methodological framework. This fragmentation reflects the field's interdisciplinary nature yet also highlights the urgent need for systematic integration and unification.

Key research gaps include: (i) extensive evaluation in real-world settings, (ii) standardized metrics and benchmarks, (iii) in-depth analysis of cross-layer design interactions, and (iv) systematic decision-support methods for selecting energy-efficient designs. Despite substantial advances in GSEGSE, achieving practical, scalable impact still requires a paradigm shift to holistic, context-aware, empirically grounded approaches spanning the entire software lifecycle.

6 Threats to Validity

When interpreting the results of this study, several threats to validity should be considered.

Internal Validity. The literature search (Sect. 3) may have missed relevant studies because Green Software Engineering research uses diverse terminology. To mitigate this threat, the search string was derived using the PICOC method, adapted to three major software-engineering databases, and complemented by backward snowballing. Study selection relied on BERTopic-based clustering and a scoring model, which may have excluded relevant studies during filtering or due to the applied threshold. To reduce this risk, excluded clusters were manually inspected. Furthermore, the scoring and classification of studies (e.g., research domains, contribution types, and research approaches) required researcher judgment and may have introduced subjectivity and classification bias. These threats were mitigated through explicit inclusion and exclusion criteria, manual inspection of studies, consistent application of predefined classification schemes, and documentation of the selection and classification procedures.

External Validity. The findings are based on the selected primary studies and therefore inherit their methodological limitations. In addition, reported energy-efficiency effects are often context-dependent and may vary across programming languages, frameworks, architectures, and execution environments, limiting their generalizability. As Green Software Engineering is a rapidly evolving field, future technologies and development practices may influence the applicability of the reported findings. Therefore, the results should be interpreted as evidence-based trends within the current body of literature rather than universally applicable design rules.

7 Conclusion and Future Work

This study conducts a Systematic Mapping Study in Green Software Engineering on how software design decisions affect energy consumption. By synthesizing evidence from 60 primary studies, this work provides a consolidated overview of the research landscape, key design factors, and existing techniques, tools, and approaches for improving energy efficiency. Overall, it consolidates fragmented research findings, clarifies the current state of research in Green Software Engineering, and identifies key directions for advancing the systematic engineering of energy-efficient, sustainable software systems.

The results show sustained growth in this research domain, with a strong focus on empirical validation. However, the field is still heterogeneous and fragmented, spanning approaches from code-level optimizations to cloud-architecture strategies. The findings confirm that energy efficiency is multidimensional, influenced by data structures, design patterns, runtime environments, and system architectures. Yet many results are highly context-dependent, limiting how far specific approaches can be generalized or transferred. Moreover, the analysis reveals a lack of standardization in metrics, evaluation methods, and benchmarking procedures. This complicates result comparison and aggregation. Hence, it hinders the systematic consolidation of knowledge into actionable, evidence-based guidelines for software practitioners.

Future research should strengthen the field's empirical basis through large-scale, real-world evaluations, develop standardized, widely adoptable measurement frameworks, and integrate energy efficiency into established software engineering processes and lifecycles. It should also clarify cross-layer interactions and create decision-support mechanisms to help practitioners choose and adapt energy-efficient design options.

References

1. Araújo, G., et al.: Energy consumption in microservices architectures: a systematic literature review. IEEE Access **12**, 186710–186729 (2024)
2. Berntsen, K.R., Olsen, M.R., Limbu, N., Tran, A.T., Colomo-Palacios, R.: Sustainability in software engineering – a systematic mapping. In: CIMPS 2016. AISC, vol. 537, pp. 23–32. Springer, Cham (2017). https://doi.org/10.1007/978-3-319-48523-2_3
3. Connolly Bree, D., Cinnéide, M.Ó.: How software design affects energy performance: a systematic literature review. J. Softw. Evol. Process **37**(4) (2025). https://doi.org/10.1002/smr.70014
4. Fowler, M.: Refactoring: Improving the Design of Existing Code. Addison-Wesley, Boston (2019)
5. Grootendorst, M.: BERTopic: Neural Topic Modeling with a Class-Based TF-IDF Procedure (2022). https://doi.org/10.48550/arXiv.2203.05794
6. Guldner, A., et al.: Development and evaluation of a reference measurement model for assessing the resource and energy efficiency of software products and components-green software measurement model (GSMM). Futur. Gener. Comput. Syst. **155**, 402–418 (2024). https://doi.org/10.1016/j.future.2024.01.033
7. Hecktor, M., Diepenbrock, A., Sachweh, S.: Towards an interoperable and privacy-respecting smart city data ecosystem. In: 2023 IEEE 12th International Conference on Intelligent Data Acquisition and Advanced Computing Systems: Technology and Applications (IDAACS), pp. 421–425 (2023). https://doi.org/10.1109/IDAACS58523.2023.10348864
8. Hecktor, M., Sachweh, S.: Supplementary Material, version 1.0.1 (2026). https://doi.org/10.5281/zenodo.20684090

9. Hecktor, M., Sachweh, S.: Towards a conceptual framework for greener software systems. In: 2025 IEEE European Technology and Engineering Management Summit (E-TEMS), pp. 62–67. IEEE, Bruges (2025)
10. Kitchenham, B., Charters, S.: Guidelines for Performing Systematic Literature Reviews in Software Engineering (2007)
11. Okonta, D.E., Vukovic, V.: Smart cities software applications for sustainability and resilience. Heliyon **10**(12) (2024). https://doi.org/10.1016/j.heliyon.2024.e32654
12. Penzenstadler, B.: Systematic mapping study on software engineering for sustainability (SE4S). In: Proceedings of the 18th International Conference on Evaluation and Assessment in Software Engineering. EASE '14, pp. 1–14. Association for Computing Machinery (2014). https://doi.org/10.1145/2601248.2601256
13. Petersen, K., Feldt, R., Mujtaba, S., Mattsson, M.: Systematic mapping studies in software engineering. In: Proceedings of the 12th International Conference on Evaluation and Assessment in Software Engineering (2008). https://doi.org/10.14236/ewic/EASE2008.8
14. Poy, O., Moraga, M.À., García, F., Calero, C.: Impact on energy consumption of design patterns, code smells and refactoring techniques: a systematic mapping study. J. Syst. Softw. **222**, 112303 (2025). https://doi.org/10.1016/j.jss.2024.112303
15. Steinberg, M., Brunnert, A., Veronika, T.: Green software metrics: a systematic literature review. In: BUIS-Tage 2025 Smarte und Nachhaltige Infrastrukturen, Oldenburg, Germany (2025)
16. Wieringa, R., Maiden, N., Mead, N., Rolland, C.: Requirements engineering paper classification and evaluation criteria: a proposal and a discussion. Requir. Eng. **11**(1), 102–107 (2006). https://doi.org/10.1007/s00766-005-0021-6

Challenges and Contributions in Quality of AI-Based Software: A Systematic Mapping Study

Maryum Hamdani[1(✉)], Mateen Ahmed Abbasi[2], Marko Jäntti[1], and Markku Tukiainen[1]

[1] Department of Computer Science, University of Eastern Finland (UEF), Joensuu, Finland
{maryum.hamdani,marko.jantti,markku.tukiainen}@uef.fi
[2] Faculty of Information Technology, University of Jyväskylä, Jyväskylä, Finland
mateen.a.abbasi@jyu.fi

Abstract. Artificial Intelligence (AI) is increasingly embedded in modern software systems, raising important questions about how its quality should be defined, assessed, and assured. This paper presents a Systematic Mapping Study (SMS) on the quality of AI-based software. The study synthesizes primary studies published between January 2020 and January 2026 and selected from five electronic data sources. A total of 33 primary studies were included after automated search, screening, and snowballing. The results identify six recurring challenge categories, with the most prominent being limitations in existing quality assessment models, followed by issues in non-functional requirement management, quality-aware development, and quality assurance. The findings suggest a call for collaboration of researchers and industrial practitioners with standardization organizations, that could possibly devise comprehensive quality assessments and their measurement methods.

Keywords: AI-based software · software quality · systematic mapping study · quality assurance · machine learning systems · ISO/IEC 25059

1 Introduction

Artificial Intelligence (AI)-based software refers to software systems that have AI components as an integral part of their functionality [33]. These AI components are predominantly implemented by Machine learning (ML) and Deep Learning (DL) approaches [11]. As AI enabled functionality becomes increasingly embedded in production software systems, concerns about software quality have become more difficult and more important to address.

Ensuring quality in AI-based software is challenging because such software systems are often data dependent, probabilistic, and context sensitive. Unlike conventional deterministic software, their behavior varies due to any change in

C. Berger and V. Klös (Eds.): SEAA 2026, LNCS 16864, pp. 207–225, 2027.
https://doi.org/10.1007/978-3-032-36587-3_15

input data, operating condition, and user interaction which complicates, specification, verification, and evaluation [16,30]. Concerns regarding the quality of AI-based software has been amplified by the increasing number of publicly reported AI incidents. According to HAI index 2025, the database recorded 233 AI-related incidents in 2024, which is a 56.4% increase over 2023, indicating the growing consequences of AI failures and misuse [42].

Researchers have explored multiple dimensions of quality in AI-based software, investigating AI-specific quality attributes [38], evaluation methods [34], and quality frameworks [6]. Likewise, secondary studies such as systematic reviews [13], mapping studies [1], and taxonomies [27] have examined selected aspects of the area. However, the evidence remains fragmented due to the update in research explorations, across subtopics, terminologies and software engineering concerns.

This motivates a systematic mapping study to synthesize the state of the art in quality in AI-based software. The objective of this study is to identify the major challenges reported in relation to quality of AI-based software and the contributions proposed to address those challenges and characterize the maturity of evidence base in terms of research type, contribution type and research methods. To achieve this objective, we used the Systematic Mapping Study (SMS) guidelines as a research method. The mapping covers primary studies published from 1 January 2020 to 15 January 2026, a period of rapid development in AI-based software.

Although prior secondary studies have examined quality models, software quality concerns, and quality assessment taxonomies for AI-based software, the existing evidence remains dispersed across different analytical scopes. Some studies focus primarily on quality models, while others emphasize quality assessment or selected quality attributes. In contrast, this SMS provides an integrated view of the area by jointly mapping: (i) the challenges reported in relation to the quality of AI-based software, (ii) the contributions proposed to address those challenges, and (iii) the maturity of the evidence base in terms of research type, contribution type, and research method. This combination enables a broader understanding not only of what has been studied but also of how mature, validated, and practically actionable the existing evidence is.

Moreover, this SMS covers the state of evidence until January 2026, which is the time when fast advancements were achieved due to increasing application of AI in industry, introduction of AI regulations, and publication of new AI-specific quality standards like ISO/IEC 25059:2023. Therefore, the novelty of this SMS can also be seen in its integrative analysis of challenges, solutions, standardization gaps, and empirical evidence maturity. The remainder of the paper is structured as follows. Section 2 describes the research methodology. Section 3 presents the results. Section 4 discusses the findings and implications. Section 5 outlines threats to validity. Section 6 concludes the paper.

2 Research Methodology

The research problem of the study is: What is the state of the art with respect to quality of AI-based software in current literature? Based on the research problem, we formulated three research questions: RQ1.) What are the challenges reported regarding the quality of AI-based software? RQ2.) What are the contributions reported to address the challenges regarding the quality of AI-based software? RQ3.) What is the classification of selected studies in terms of contribution types, research methods, and research types? We used the guidelines by Peterson et al. [35,36] to conduct a systematic mapping study.

2.1 Search Process

The steps followed to conduct this SMS are illustrated in Fig. 1. As shown, the search process comprises of two phases. In phase 1, we conducted the primary search by following the steps outlined below.

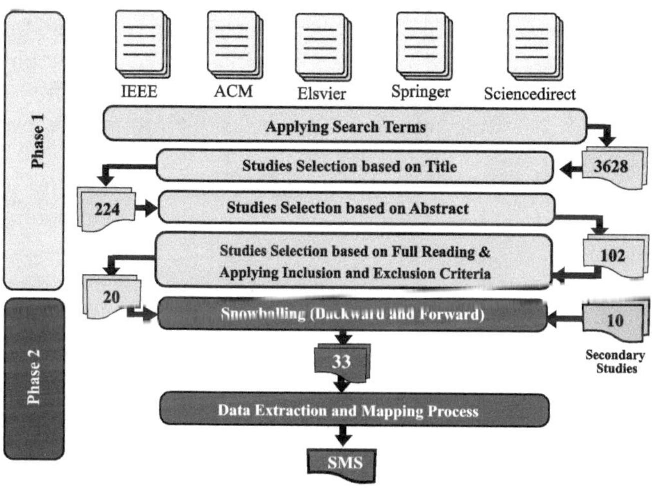

Fig. 1. Study selection workflow

Search Terms Selection: We defined the search terms in Table 1 using the PICO (Population, Intervention, Comparison and Outcomes) framework as per guidelines of Kitchenham et al. [29]. In order to ensure that search string captures maximum number of related studies, we performed multiple iterations of pilot searches, hence improved the search string.

Title Abstract and Full Text Screening: We conducted the study in two phases: automated database search and manual snowballing. The automated search covered primary studies published from 1 January 2020 to 15 January

Table 1. Search string using the PICO framework

Element in PICO	Search string part
Population	"Artificial intelligence software" OR "AI software" OR "AI-based software" OR "Machine learning software" OR "ML software" OR "Artificial intelligence enabled software" OR "AI-enabled software"
Intervention	"Quality assessment" OR "Quality evaluation" OR "Quality assurance" OR "Quality model" OR "Quality attribute" OR "Quality characteristic" OR "Nonfunctional requirement" OR "Non-functional requirement"
Comparison	Not applicable
Outcome	Metric OR measurement OR method

2026 and was executed across Electronic Data Sources (EDS) including IEEE Xplore, ACM Digital Library, SpringerLink, ScienceDirect, and Wiley Online Library. The search returned 3,628 records (IEEE Xplore: 873, ACM Digital Library: 899, SpringerLink: 616, ScienceDirect: 888, Wiley Online Library: 352). The selection of EDS is based on the guidelines by Zhang et al. [44]. After title-based screening and duplicate removal, 224 records remained for abstract screening. Abstract screening retained 102 studies for full-text assessment. Full-text screening against the inclusion and exclusion criteria resulted in 20 primary studies. In the second phase, backward and forward snowballing identified 13 additional studies (5 backward and 8 forward), resulting in a final corpus of 33 primary studies.

The full-text assessment was conducted by the first and second authors using the complete inclusion and exclusion criteria presented in Table 2. To improve the reliability of the study selection process, the first and second authors first conducted a calibration round on a subset of candidate studies. The inclusion and exclusion criteria for the articles were discussed and revised in order to reduce any potential misinterpretation. After completing the calibration process, both authors independently assessed the candidate studies during the full-text screening phase. Disagreements were resolved through discussion, with the third author being included when necessary. This procedure was used to reduce individual selection bias and to ensure consistent application of the selection criteria.

2.2 Data Extraction and Mapping Process

Table 3 summarizes the data extraction schema used in this study. Data items D1 to D5 present the demographics of the final selected studies. We performed inductive thematic analysis [3] across the selected studies to extract D6 and D7. This analysis systematically identified and categorized: the primary research challenge that each study reported in relation to quality of AI-based software (D6), and the

Table 2. Inclusion and exclusion criteria

Inclusion criteria	Exclusion criteria
IC1. Include primary studies that address quality aspects of AI/ML-based software systems	EC1. Exclude studies that address quality aspects of traditional software systems, i.e., without an AI component
IC2. Include studies published from 2020 onwards	EC2. Exclude studies on AI/ML-based software that do not address quality-related concerns
IC3. Include studies from the software engineering domain only	EC3. Exclude studies published before 2020
IC4. Include studies written in English only	EC4. Exclude studies that solely address data quality aspects
IC5. Include primary studies published in journals, conferences, surveys, workshops, and book chapters	EC5. Exclude duplicate studies, conference/workshop papers extended into journal articles, doctoral consortium papers, dissertations, secondary studies, posters, and editorials
IC6. Include studies with four pages or more	

Table 3. Data extraction schema

Code	Data Item	Description	RQ
D1	Index	The ID of the study	Demographics
D2	Title	The title of the study	
D3	Year	The publication year of study	
D4	Publisher	The publisher of the study	
D5	Publication Type	Journal, Conference, Workshop, Symposiums	
D6	Challenges	The main challenge that each study reported in relation to the quality of AI-based software, extracted by guidelines of [3]	RQ1
D7	Contributions	The key contributions each study proposed in addressing challenge regarding quality of AI-based software extracted by guidelines of [3]	RQ2
D8	Research type	The research type classification proposed by Wieringa et al. [43]	RQ3
D9	Contribution type	We classified the contribution types as per [35]	
D10	Research methods	The research methods reported in the selected studies [14]	

proposed contributions each study reported to address the corresponding challenge (D7). Furthermore, the selected studies were classified by research type (D8) and contribution type (D9), following the classification schemes proposed by Wieringa et al. [43] and Petersen et al. [35]. Lastly, we extracted primary research methods (D10), employed in each study to produce its results based on the taxonomy of software engineering research methods outlined by Glass et al. [14]. The replication package is available at [20] as anonymous and contains the search strings, screening decisions, data extraction sheet and study classifications.

3 Results

3.1 RQ.1) What Are the Challenges Reported Regarding the Quality of AI-Based Software?

We identified 6 categories of recurring challenge in the primary studies. Table 4 summarizes the categories, representative evidence, and associated study IDs; the description of challenge below highlights only the main patterns.

Category 1 Limitations in Existing Quality Assessment Models. This category of challenge includes the studies that highlighted the limitations of existing quality models for the assessment of AI-based software. As an example, Ramos et al. [38] states that the extended quality attributes in ISO/IEC 25059: 2023 [26], to address unique characteristics of AI-based software, are too limited. Similarly, Oviedo et al. [34] reflects on the absence of metrics in ISO/IEC 25059: 2023 [26] to measure the quality. Moreover, De Sanctis et al. in [9], mentioned that the updated ISO 25010:2023 [25] fails to consider stakeholder needs of modern systems.

Category 2 NFR Management Issues . This category contains primary studies that report issues in NFR management for ML-enabled Software. NFR management here encompasses specification, definition, scoping, and prioritization of NFR. Since these software systems exhibit non-deterministic nature therefore, existing methods and techniques of NFR management have become inapplicable [17]. Indykov et al. in [23] and Habibullah et al. [17], investigates the challenges practitioners encounter in 1) prioritizing NFR types for ML-enabled Software and 2) establishing appropriate measurement criteria in industry. Habib et al. [18] highlighted the need to scope NFR over different system components (e.g. data, models, and code). Whereas Heck et al. [22] focused on how quality requirements for AI monitoring platform can be defined using quality model.

Category 3 Lack of Quality-Aware AI-Based Software Development Approaches. All primary studies that indicates the absence of quality-aware approaches while developing AI-based software are classified in this category.

Table 4. Challenges reported in the primary studies

Category (n)	Challenge	Study ID
1. Limitations in existing quality assessment models (13)	Additional AI-specific sub-characteristics in the extended model, i.e., ISO/IEC 25059, are too limited	S1
	ISO/IEC 25059 is high level and incomplete; it is necessary to define a set of metrics and thresholds	S5
	The key characteristics proposed in ISO/IEC 25059:2023 do not yet have specific testing methods for their implementation	S10
	ISO/IEC 25059 has some gaps when it comes to the coverage of Act requirements	S25
	The quality-in-use model on which current AI quality management standards (ISO/IEC 25059) are based does not take into account various stakeholders	S32
	...	
2. Non-Functional Requirement (NFR) management issues (6)	Lack of detailed insights on quality trade-offs observed in industrial practice and how companies address them	S7
	Managing NFRs is particularly challenging due to the differing nature and definitions of NFRs for ML systems, including non-deterministic behavior	S3
	Despite the importance of NFRs in ensuring the quality of ML systems, our understanding of these aspects (definition, measurement, scope, and comparative importance) is lacking	S16
	...	
3. Lack of quality-aware development approaches (6)	There is limited literature focused on discovering and understanding quality issues encountered by practitioners when building MLSSs	S2
	Solutions have been proposed to automate the development of ML systems. However, an approach that takes into account the new quality concerns needed by ML systems is still missing	S8
	Engineering practices for building these systems remain poorly understood compared to those for conventional software systems	S33
	...	
4. Inadequate QA for AI-based software (5)	There is a lack of standardized approaches for Quality Assurance (QA) of AI-based systems	S18
	AI-enabled systems require attention to software quality assurance in general and code quality in particular	S20
	Due to the statistical nature of machine learning, traditional quality assurance approaches are often insufficient	S29
	...	
5. Limitations in existing QMF (1)	The Quality Management Framework (QMF) of AI systems is fragmented and incomplete	S27
6. Cross domain (2)	No one has systematically investigated the impact of using bindings for ML frameworks on ML software quality	S6
	...	

Côté et al. [7] reported that actual issues encountered by practitioners while developing ML-based software systems are not well investigated. D'Alessio et al. [8] observed that despite the prevalence of automated development solutions for ML-based software systems, the systematic approaches for integrating quality concerns—such as privacy, fairness, and reliability—into their development process is notably lacking. Similarly, Bucaioni et al. [5] further asserted that understanding of engineering practices for developing ML-intensive software systems lag significantly compared to those for conventional software systems.

Category 4 Inadequate QA Approaches. Primary studies that highlights inadequate quality assurance practices for AI-based software are accumulated in this category. Felderer et al. [12] stated that there is a lack of agreement regarding the approaches available for implementing quality assurance in AI-based systems, leading to conflicting solutions among practitioners. Golendukhina et al. [15] also emphasized, a critical need for enhanced software quality assurance (SQA) practices in AI-enabled systems, with particular emphasis on maintaining code quality standards. Similarly, Poth et al. [37] stated that adequate quality measurement and assurance techniques for ML-based software systems are still absent.

Category 5 Limitation in Existing QMF. This category captures organization level limitations in existing quality management frameworks. Although represented by a single study in the current corpus, it highlights a distinct objective. Santhanam [39] states the traditional quality management process (consisting of i) requirement management, ii) defect management, iii) change management, iv) test management, v) DevOps processes, vi) operations management, and vii) project management) is inadequate when applied to ML-based software. As ML-based software reflects a different nature, current quality management framework seems inapplicable for building software with different quality attributes such as fairness, biasness etc.

Category 6 Cross-Domain. This category groups studies that address relevant quality issues not captured by the above categories, for instance, Li et al. [32] uncovered that the impact of ML framework bindings on AI-based software quality is systematically unexplored. In contrast, Brower-Sinning et al. in [4] reported about the lack of information received at developer's end regarding the design decisions, due to which they consider limited properties for ML model testing, resulting in failure in model's deployment and operation.

It is important to mention here that a few studies fulfill criteria to be classified under multiple categories simultaneously. For example, the [23] can be classified into the category of "Lack of quality-aware practices" and "NFR management issues". In such cases, we classified the study according to its primary focus.

3.2 RQ.2) What Are the Contributions Reported to Address the Challenges Regarding the Quality of AI-Based Software?

We identified 11 contribution categories from the primary studies (see Table 5). These categories reflect a diverse set of solutions reported to address the identified challenges (RQ1). Each category represents a recurring type of solution reported across selected studies. In Table 5, the rows are grouped by challenge category (see Table 4) it targets. Additionally, it contains one or more contribution. The third column presents a focused description of the solution and finally are the serial number of studies (S1-S33). All categories are briefly described below.

Category 1.1 Quality Model Enhancement. Studies in this category aim to enhance existing quality assessment models. For instance, Ramos et al. [38] proposed an extension to quality models in ISO/IEC 25059:2023 [26], based on a survey conducted from practitioners. They extended its product quality model by adding a quality dimension "Humanity" and 30+ sub-attributes and added 7 sub-attributes to the quality-in-use models. Similarly, Kelly et al. [28] presented an extension to the ISO/IEC 25059:2023 [25] product quality model for safety-critical systems. The enhanced model includes three additional quality dimensions and thirty-five sub-attributes related to safety and data quality. Guo et al. [16] extended the ISO/IEC 25059:2023 [26] by presenting metrics and measurement methods for AI specific quality attributes which differentiates ISO/IEC 25059:2023 [26] from ISO/IEC 25010:2011 [24].

Category 1.2: Quality Model Development. This category deals with primary studies that aim to address "limitations in existing quality assessment model" by proposing a novel quality model. Dell'Anna et al. [10], proposed a quality model for Human-AI system from teaming perspective. Likewise, Siebert et al. [40], developed a systematic process and meta-model for constructing quality models for ML-based system and validated with an industrial case study.

Category 1.3: Conceptual Redefinition. Primary studies in this category argue with help of evidence and claims for redefining the notion of quality for AI-based software. De Sanctis et al. [9] emphasized the need of re-examining quality definitions in quality model provided by ISO/IEC 25010:2023 [25] to reflect evolving stakeholder needs, such as i) societal and environmental well-being, ii) diversity, non-discrimination and fairness, along with iii) human agency and oversight, human autonomy.

Category 2.1: Approaches for NFR Management. This category comprises of primary studies that present approaches for defining, scoping, prioritizing NFRs for ML-based systems. For instance, Habibullah et al. [18] addressed the NFR management issue by introducing a structured framework for defining, scoping, and quantifying critical NFRs important to the ML system under

Table 5. Contributions addressing the identified challenges

No	Contribution category	Contribution focus	Study ID
Category 1: Limitations in existing quality evaluation models			
1.	Quality model enhancement	Extending and improving existing quality evaluation models for AI-based software	S1, S4, S10, S19, S22, S24
2.	Quality model development	Creating novel quality evaluation models for AI-based software	S13, S14, S21, S23, S32
3.	Conceptual redefinition	Redefining fundamental quality concepts	S5, S25
Category 2: NFR management issues			
1.	Approaches for NFR scoping, definition, and prioritization	Scoping, defining, and prioritizing non-functional requirements	S3, S7, S11, S16
2.	Quality model-based NFR specification	Using quality models for NFR specification	S9, S15
Category 3: Lack of quality-aware development approaches			
1.	Quality-aware development support	Tools and methods for quality-driven development of AI-based software	S8, S26, S30, S33
2.	Quality-aware practices characterization	Empirical analysis of quality challenges and practices for AI-based software	S2, S17
Category 4: Inadequate quality assurance for AI-based software			
1.	QA methodological frameworks	Comprehensive quality assurance process frameworks	S28, S29, S31
2.	QA challenges and strategies characterization	Identifying and addressing QA obstacles	S18, S20
Category 5: Limitations in existing QMF			
1.	Preliminary QMF framework for AI-based software	Preliminary Quality Management Framework	S27
Category 6: Cross-domain			
1.	Impact on quality via framework binding	Investigation of the impact on ML software quality (correctness and time cost) using bindings for ML frameworks	S6
2.	Quality attribute-driven ML model testing	Approach to generate ML test cases based on quality attributes	S12

development. Correspondingly, Habibullah et al. [17] empirically explored the approaches that practitioners use in industry for defining and measuring NFRs over the multiple aspects of ML-system including the model component, data, and system as a whole.

Category 2.2: Quality Model-Based NFR Specification. This category encompasses the primary studies that employ the quality model as a standard dictionary for the specification of quality requirements. Heck et al. [22] utilized Heck's quality model [21], as a reference framework to systematically define quality requirements for AI Wildflower Monitoring Platform. While Haindl et al. [19] specified quality requirements for human-AI teaming platform using ISO 25010:2011 [24].

Category 3.1: Quality-Aware Development Support. In this category, the primary studies develop tools and methods that integrate quality considerations throughout the development lifecycle of AI-based software. Sikand et al. [41] presented a questionnaire-based methodology which enables the practitioner to evaluate the overall sustainability throughout development process. Similarly, D'Aloisio et al. [8] developed a low-code platform, which uses Extended Feature Models (ExtFM) within a Software Product Line (SPL) to select and combine the features for satisfying specific quality constraints.

Category 3.2: Quality-Aware Practices Characterization. This category accumulates all primary studies that investigate the strategies employed by industrial practitioners to mitigate challenges while building AI-based software. Côté et al. [7] investigated quality issues encountered by thirty-seven practitioners and developed an empirically validated catalogue, which covers causes, consequences, and mitigation strategies for each issue encountered in development of Machine Learning Software System (MLSS). Also, Valentina et al. [31] reported common quality issues and corresponding solutions in developing AI enabled system based on the experience of interviewing three research groups. Moreover, the author emphasizes on training of developers for reducing technical debt in production of AI enabled systems.

Category 4.1: QA Methodological Framework. This category contains the primary studies that contribute methodological frameworks for systematically assuring quality for ML-based software. Poth et al. [37] proposed EvAIa, a questionnaire-based approach that provides recommendations to ensure the capabilities AI models and making limitations transparent. Likewise, Baresi et al. [2] developed a conceptual framework consisting of LLM-based agents known as Artificial Doppelgänger Agents (ADAs). These ADAs intend to evaluate the socio-critical system of pre-production and runtime QA iteratively and ensure its compliance with societal expectations.

Category 4.2: Characterization of QA Challenges and Strategies. Primary studies in this category comprises of empirical and analytical research that characterize QA challenges and document practitioner strategies for assuring quality in AI-based systems. Felderer et al. [12] identified eight major QA challenges for AI-based systems and established foundational terminology, emphasizing the necessity for cross-disciplinary collaboration between software engineering and AI communities. Golendukhina et al. [15] investigated the SQA strategies adopted by practitioners, through an exploratory interview study with ten Austrian companies developing AI-enabled systems. They revealed 11 categories of strategies adapted by Small and Medium Enterprise (SME) in the development, integration, and maintenance of AI/ML components.

Category 5.1: Preliminary Quality Management Framework (QMF) for AI-Based Software. This category addresses limitations in existing quality management frameworks for AI-based systems. P. Santhanam et al. [39] proposed initial quality management framework AI/ML based applications. This framework means to address the challenges of incorporating AI components into business-critical application.

Category 6 Cross-Domain. This category contains contributions of primary studies that address the distinctive quality challenges in AI-based software that have not been investigated in any other study within this mapping. Li et al. [32] investigates impact of ML software quality (correctness and time cost) using bindings for ML frameworks for DL model training and inference. Brower-Sinning et al. in [4] presented an approach based on quality attribute (QA) scenarios to elicit and define system and model-relevant test cases.

3.3 RQ.3) What Are the Distribution and Characteristics of Selected Studies in Terms of Research Types, Contribution Types, and Research Method?

Figure 2 shows the distribution of all selected studies by research type according to the classification proposed by Wieringa et al. [43]. Ten studies S2, S7, S15, S16, S19, S20, S26, S28, S29, and S33 are classified as evaluation research, i.e., investigate problem in practice. In contrast, eight studies S3, S4, S8, S9, S10, S11, S21, S22 present solution proposals without full-scale validation. Six studies S12, S17, S18, S24, S25, S30 report personal experiences from real-life projects.

Furthermore, we categorized five studies S5, S23, S27, S31, S32, as philosophical research, since they offer a conceptual solution to the underlying problem, without the detailed characteristic of a formal solution. Three studies S6, S13, S14 are classified as validation research, since they evaluate proposed solutions in a controlled or experimental setting that has not yet been applied in practice. Finally, one study (S1) is categorized as an opinion paper, as it presents the author's personal perspective without empirical evidence.

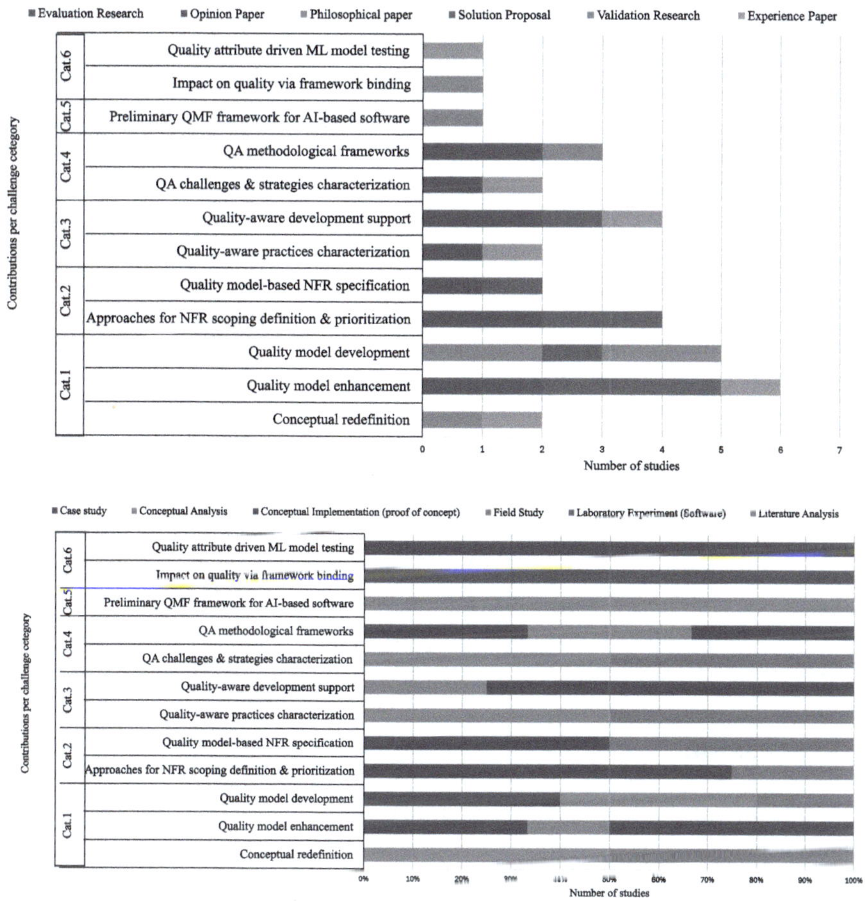

Fig. 2. Research type and method classification by challenge and contribution category

Table 6. Distribution of contribution types across the selected studies

Contribution type	Description	Studies
Model	A conceptual model proposed by a selected study, or an extension of an existing model	S1, S13, S14, S21–23, S27, S32
Method	Studies that propose guidelines or methodologies for evaluating quality	S3, S4, S8, S9, S10, S11–13, S19, S22, S24, S29, S31
Tool	An automated software tool or checklist to support quality evaluation	S4, S32
Open item	Challenges or strategies reported by the selected studies	S2, S5, S6, S7, S15–18, S20, S25, S28, S30
Metric	A granular measurable item used to evaluate the quality of AI-based software	S4, S10, S15, S19, S26

Table 6 presents distribution of selected studies from contribution types as per classification defined in [35]. Note: A number of selected studies have produced more than one contribution. The most common contribution type are guidelines and methods for evaluating software quality. In contrast, the tool is the least populated contribution proposed by the selected studies.

Figure 2 shows the distribution of selected studies with respect to the research methods [14]. Ten studies S3, S4, S8, S10, S11, S12, S22, S26, S28, and S33 have applied conceptual implementation, that aimed to demonstrate the proof of concept. Following that nine studies S1, S17, S18, S23, S25, S27, S30, S31, and S32 employed conceptual analysis- a research method that does not provide realistic evaluation method. Seven studies S7, S9, S10, S13, S14, S19, S24, and S29 used the research method case studies offering realism to a certain level, e.g. (industrial setting). Five studies S2, S15, S16, S20, and S21 have conducted a field study to investigate the quality practices in real world. One study S6, has used laboratory experiment with software, and one study performed analysis from literature S5. It is important to mention here that a number of studies have used multiple research methods, however it is classified based on the strongest evidence using one for the results section, the replication package [20] shows the secondary research methods used by the studies. Examples include S26, and S29 conducted a pilot and S33 conducted a workshop further to validate the results that can be classified as laboratory experiment (using humans).

4 Discussion

This study mapped the research landscape regarding the quality of AI-based software based on three research questions. The results show that the reported challenges span requirements engineering, development practices, quality assessment, quality assurance and quality management as summarized in Table 4. The most prominent challenge emerged is *Limitations in existing quality assessment models* covering 40 % of studies i.e.(13 out of 33). The dominance of this category indicates that current quality assessment models provided by international standards are insufficient to capture distinctive characteristics of AI-based software systems. One of the reason is rapid evolution of AI and its expansion across multiple industries, which unveils the new characteristics and impact on stakeholders. Thus, one key take-away is that quality models provided by international standards are considered important in research, for assessing and determining the quality of AI-based software. However, these models insufficient to cope up with fast pace of AI evolution.

According to the findings of RQ2, research efforts have been predominantly directed towards *quality model enhancement* (6 out of 33), followed by the second most populated category *quality model development* (5 out of 33). This reflects continuous efforts by research community in both refining and constructing new quality models for AI-based software. However, the classification results from RQ3, show that many of these contributions remains non empirical or early stage. This indicates that research on quality models for AI-based software remains largely conceptual and theoretical in nature. Furthermore, the case studies identified in these studies are predominantly conducted in simulated environments rather than industrial settings, which limits their practical generalizability. This highlights a significant gap in the literature, causing the need for rigorous empirical studies conducted in real-world industrial contexts to validate existing quality model extensions and new quality models developments.

Another interesting finding drawn from cross-facet analysis reveals evaluation research and field study are comparatively more dominant in studies addressing NFR management than in any other identified category. This suggests that among all categories, NFR management stands out as the most empirically grounded area, where researchers investigated practices from industrial settings. Additionally, this study revealed a significant gap in assessment tools for the quality of AI-based software, i.e., contributed by (2 out of 33) studies

Taken together the findings suggests a call for the collaboration of researchers and industrial practitioners with standardization organizations that could possibly devise comprehensive quality assessment models and their measurement methods. Therefore, future research should focus on operationalizing AI specific quality attributes, strengthening empirical validation, and integrating quality concerns more systematically.

5 Threats to Validity

We addressed threats related to search strategy bias by conducting pilot searches, which helped us identify a broader set of relevant synonyms and refine the search string. Furthermore, the final search string was applied to titles, abstracts, and keywords, without considering the full text of papers. This may have introduced the risk of missing relevant studies whose quality-related contribution was discussed only in the body of the paper. To mitigate this threat, we complemented the automated search with backward and forward snowballing over the selected primary studies and key secondary studies. Threats to selection bias were mitigated by carefully following established guidelines for systematic mapping studies [35,36]. Additionally, the inclusion and exclusion criteria stated in Sect. 2.1 were formulated by the first two authors and then reviewed and approved by the third and fourth authors to improve clarity and consistency. To reduce data-extraction and classification bias, the extracted data items and category assignments were reviewed by multiple authors, and disagreements were resolved through discussion based on predefined coding criteria. External validity may be limited by the selected publication period, the selected electronic data sources, the English-language restriction, and the focus on the software engineering domain. Therefore, relevant studies from adjacent fields or other indexing services may have been missed. To support transparency and reproducibility, we defined a complete study protocol and provide a replication package containing the search strings, screening decisions, data extraction sheet, and study classifications available at [20].

6 Conclusion

This paper presented a systematic mapping study on the quality of AI-based software. An initial set of 3628 records retrieved from five electronic databases published between 2020 and 2026, 33 primary studies were selected through systematic screening and snowballing. The study synthesized the reported challenges, the contributions proposed to address them, and the maturity of the evidence base.

The results show that the most frequently reported challenge concerns limitations in existing quality assessment models, followed by issues related to NFR management, lack of quality-aware development approaches, and inadequate quality assurance. The study also identified 11 contribution categories, with most research focusing on the quality model enhancement, quality model development, and methodological support. However, the evidence remains dominated by the early-stage and weakly validated research, with limited tool support and industrial validation.

These findings suggest that the field has established a strong conceptual foundation but still requires substantial work to operationalize AI-specific quality attributes and validate proposed approaches in real-word industrial context. Future research should prioritize empirical validation, stronger tool support, and closer alignment between research, industrial practice, and standardization efforts.

Acknowledgment. This work has been supported by FAST, the Finnish Software Engineering Doctoral Research Network, funded by the Ministry of Education and Culture, Finland.

References

1. Ali, M.A., Yap, N.K., Ghani, A.A.A., Zulzalil, H., Admodisastro, N.I., Najafabadi, A.A.: A systematic mapping of quality models for ai systems, software and components. Appl. Sci. **12**(17) (2022). https://doi.org/10.3390/app12178700. https://www.mdpi.com/2076-3417/12/17/8700
2. Baresi, L., Camilli, M., Dolci, T., Quattrocchi, G.: A conceptual framework for quality assurance of llm-based socio-critical systems. In: Proceedings of the 39th IEEE/ACM International Conference on Automated Software Engineering, ASE '24, pp. 2314–2318. Association for Computing Machinery, New York (2024). https://doi.org/10.1145/3691620.3695306, [S31]
3. Braun, V., Clarke, V.: Using thematic analysis in psychology. Qual. Res. Psychol. **3**(2), 77–101 (2006). https://doi.org/10.1191/1478088706qp063oa
4. Brower-Sinning, R., Lewis, G.A., Echeverría, S., Ozkaya, I.: Using quality attribute scenarios for ml model test case generation. In: 2024 IEEE 21st International Conference on Software Architecture Companion (ICSA-C), pp. 307–310 (2024). https://doi.org/10.1109/ICSA-C63560.2024.00058, [S12]
5. Bucaioni, A., Kazman, R., Pelliccione, P.: A checklist of quality concerns for architecting ml-intensive systems. J. Syst. Softw. **231**, 112612 (2026). https://doi.

org/10.1016/j.jss.2025.112612. https://www.sciencedirect.com/science/article/pii/S016412122500281X, [S33]
6. Castelli, A., Chouliaras, G.C., Goldenberg, D.: Maturity framework for enhancing machine learning quality. In: Proceedings of the 31st ACM SIGKDD Conference on Knowledge Discovery and Data Mining, KDD '25, vol. 2, pp. 4296–4307. Association for Computing Machinery, New York (2025). https://doi.org/10.1145/3711896.3737246, [S14]
7. Côté, P.O., Nikanjam, A., Bouchoucha, R., Basta, I., Abidi, M., Khomh, F.: Quality issues in machine learning software systems. Empirical Softw. Eng. **29**(6) (2024). https://doi.org/10.1007/s10664-024-10536-7, [S2]
8. d'Aloisio, G., Di Marco, A., Stilo, G.: Democratizing quality-based machine learning development through extended feature models. In: Lambers, L., Uchitel, S. (eds.) Fundamental Approaches to Software Engineering, pp. 88–110. Springer, Cham (2023). [S8]
9. De Sanctis, M., Inverardi, P., Pelliccione, P.: Do modern systems require new quality dimensions? In: Bertolino, A., Pascoal Faria, J., Lago, P., Semini, L. (eds.) Quality of Information and Communications Technology, pp. 83–90. Springer, Cham (2024). https://doi.org/10.1007/978-3-031-70245-7_6. [S5]
10. Dell'Anna, D., et al.: Toward a quality model for hybrid intelligence teams. In: Proceedings of the 23rd International Conference on Autonomous Agents and Multiagent Systems, AAMAS '24, pp. 434–443. International Foundation for Autonomous Agents and Multiagent Systems, Richland (2024). [S21]
11. Deng, L.: Artificial intelligence in the rising wave of deep learning: the historical path and future outlook [perspectives]. IEEE Signal Process. Mag. **35**(1), 177–180 (2018)
12. Felderer, M., Ramler, R.: Quality assurance for ai-based systems: overview and challenges (introduction to interactive session). In: Winkler, D., Biffl, S., Mendez, D., Wimmer, M., Bergsmann, J. (eds.) Software Quality: Future Perspectives on Software Engineering Quality, pp. 33–42. Springer, Cham (2021). https://doi.org/10.1007/978-3-030-65854-0_3, [S18]
13. Gezici, B., Tarhan, A.K.: Systematic literature review on software quality for ai-based software. Empir. Softw. Eng. **27**(3) (2022). https://doi.org/10.1007/s10664-021-10105-2
14. Glass, R., Vessey, I., Ramesh, V.: Research in software engineering: an analysis of the literature. Inf. Softw. Technol. **44**(8), 491–506 (2002). https://doi.org/10.1016/S0950-5849(02)00049-6. https://www.sciencedirect.com/science/article/pii/S0950584902000496
15. Golendukhina, V., Lenarduzzi, V., Felderer, M.: What is software quality for ai engineers? Towards a thinning of the fog. In: Proceedings of the 1st International Conference on AI Engineering: Software Engineering for AI, CAIN '22, pp. 1–9. Association for Computing Machinery, New York (2022). https://doi.org/10.1145/3522664.3528599, [S20]
16. Guo, M., Guo, D., Li, M.: Metrics and testing methods for artificial intelligence software quality models and their application examples. In: 2024 11th International Conference on Dependable Systems and Their Applications (DSA), pp. 35–42. IEEE (2024). [S10]
17. Habibullah, K.M., Gay, G., Horkoff, J.: Non-functional requirements for machine learning: understanding current use and challenges among practitioners. Req. Eng. **28**(2), 283–316 (2023). https://doi.org/10.1007/s00766-022-00395-3. [S16]

18. Habibullah, K.M., Gay, G., Horkoff, J.: A framework for managing quality requirements for machine learning-based software systems. In: Bertolino, A., Pascoal Faria, J., Lago, P., Semini, L. (eds.) Quality of Information and Communications Technology, pp. 3–20. Springer, Cham (2024). https://doi.org/10.1007/978-3-031-70245-7_1. [S3]
19. Haindl, P., Hoch, T., Dominguez, J., Aperribai, J., Ure, N.K., Tunçel, M.: Quality characteristics of a software platform for human-ai teaming in smart manufacturing. In: Vallecillo, A., Visser, J., Pérez-Castillo, R. (eds.) Quality of Information and Communications Technology, pp. 3–17. Springer, Cham (2022). https://doi.org/10.1007/978-3-031-14179-9_1. [S15]
20. Hamdani, M.: Replication package of sms for challenges and contributions in quality of ai-based software (2026). https://doi.org/10.5281/zenodo.19545171
21. Heck, P.: A quality model for trustworthy ai systems (2023)
22. Heck, P., Schouten, G.: Defining quality requirements for a trustworthy ai wildflower monitoring platform. In: 2023 IEEE/ACM 2nd International Conference on AI Engineering – Software Engineering for AI (CAIN), pp. 119–126 (2023). https://doi.org/10.1109/CAIN58948.2023.00029. [S9]
23. Indykov, V., Wohlrab, R., Strüber, D.: Quality trade-offs in ML-enabled systems: a multiple-case study, pp. 1730–1737. Association for Computing Machinery, New York (2025). https://doi.org/10.1145/3672608.3707754. [S7]
24. ISO/IEC: ISO/IEC 25010:2011 Systems and software engineering—Systems and software Quality Requirements and Evaluation (SQuaRE)—System and software quality models. International Organization for Standardization (2011)
25. ISO/IEC: ISO/IEC 25010:2023 Systems and software engineering—Systems and software Quality Requirements and Evaluation (SQuaRE)—Product quality model. International Organization for Standardization (2023)
26. ISO/IEC: ISO/IEC 25059:2023. Software Engineering—Systems and Software Quality Requirements and Evaluation (SQuaRE)—Quality Model for AI Systems. International Organization for Standardization (2023)
27. Jabborov, A., Kharlamova, A., Kholmatova, Z., Kruglov, A., Kruglov, V., Succi, G.: Taxonomy of quality assessment for intelligent software systems: a systematic literature review. IEEE Access **11**, 130491–130507 (2023). https://doi.org/10.1109/ACCESS.2023.3333920
28. Kelly, J., Zafar, S.A., Heidemann, L., Zacchi, J.V., Espinoza, D., Mata, N.: Navigating the EU AI act: a methodological approach to compliance for safety-critical products. In: 2024 IEEE Conference on Artificial Intelligence (CAI), pp. 979–984 (2024). https://doi.org/10.1109/CAI59869.2024.00179. [S22]
29. Kitchenham, B., Charters, S.: Guidelines for performing systematic literature reviews in software engineering **2** (2007)
30. Kuwajima, H., Ishikawa, F.: Adapting square for quality assessment of artificial intelligence systems. In: 2019 IEEE International Symposium on Software Reliability Engineering Workshops (ISSREW), pp. 13–18. IEEE (2019)
31. Lenarduzzi, V., Lomio, F., Moreschini, S., Taibi, D., Tamburri, D.A.: Software quality for AI: where we are now? In: Winkler, D., Biffl, S., Mendez, D., Wimmer, M., Bergsmann, J. (eds.) Software Quality: Future Perspectives on Software Engineering Quality, pp. 43–53. Springer, Cham (2021). https://doi.org/10.1007/978-3-030-65854-0_4. [S17]
32. Li, H., Rajbahadur, G.K., Bezemer, C.P.: Studying the impact of tensorflow and pytorch bindings on machine learning software quality. ACM Trans. Softw. Eng. Methodol. **34**(1) (2024). https://doi.org/10.1145/3678168. [S6]

33. Martínez-Fernández, S., et al.: Software engineering for ai-based systems: a survey. ACM Trans. Softw. Eng. Methodol. (TOSEM) **31**(2), 1–59 (2022)
34. Oviedo, J., Rodríguez, M., Piattini, M.: An environment for the assessment of the functional suitability of ai systems. In: Bertolino, A., Pascoal Faria, J., Lago, P., Semini, L. (eds.) Quality of Information and Communications Technology, pp. 21–34. Springer, Cham (2024). https://doi.org/10.1007/978-3-031-70245-7_2, [S4]
35. Petersen, K., Feldt, R., Mujtaba, S., Mattsson, M.: Systematic mapping studies in software engineering (2008). https://doi.org/10.14236/ewic/EASE2008.8
36. Petersen, K., Vakkalanka, S., Kuzniarz, L.: Guidelines for conducting systematic mapping studies in software engineering: an update. Inf. Softw. Technol. **64**, 1–18 (2015). https://doi.org/10.1016/j.infsof.2015.03.007. https://www.sciencedirect.com/science/article/pii/S0950584915000646
37. Poth, A., Meyer, B., Schlicht, P., Riel, A.: Quality assurance for machine learning – an approach to function and system safeguarding. In: 2020 IEEE 20th International Conference on Software Quality, Reliability and Security (QRS), pp. 22–29 (2020). https://doi.org/10.1109/QRS51102.2020.00016, [S28]
38. Ramos, T., Dean, A., McGregor, D.: Ai-augmented software engineering: revolutionizing or challenging software quality and testing? J. Softw. Evol. Process **37** (2024). https://doi.org/10.1002/smr.2741, [S1]
39. Santhanam, P.: Quality management of machine learning systems. In: Shehory, O., Farchi, E., Barash, G. (eds.) Engineering Dependable and Secure Machine Learning Systems, pp. 1–13. Springer, Cham (2020). https://doi.org/10.1007/978-3-030-62144-5_1, [S27]
40. Siebert, J., et al.: Construction of a quality model for machine learning systems. Softw. Qual. J. **30**(2), 307–335 (2022). https://doi.org/10.1007/s11219-021-09557-y, [S13]
41. Sikand, S., Sharma, V.S., Kaulgud, V., Podder, S.: Green AI quotien: assessing greenness of ai-based software and the way forward. In: Proceedings of the 38th IEEE/ACM International Conference on Automated Software Engineering, ASE '23, pp. 1828–1833. IEEE Press (2024). https://doi.org/10.1109/ASE56229.2023.00115, [S26]
42. Stanford University Institute for Human-Centered AI (HAI): The 2025 artificial intelligence index report. Technical report, Stanford University (2025). https://hai.stanford.edu/ai-index/2025-ai-index-report. Accessed 5 Apr 2026
43. Wieringa, R., Maiden, N., Mead, N., Rolland, C.: Requirements engineering paper classification and evaluation criteria: a proposal and a discussion. Requir. Eng. **11**, 102–107 (2006). https://doi.org/10.1007/s00766-005-0021-6
44. Zhang, H., Babar, M.A., Bai, X., Li, J., Huang, L.: An empirical assessment of a systematic search process for systematic reviews. In: 15th Annual Conference on Evaluation & Assessment in Software Engineering (EASE 2011), pp. 56–65 (2011). https://doi.org/10.1049/ic.2011.0007

Understanding LLMs in Title-Abstract Screening: From Disagreements to Recommendations

Mika Mäntylä[1(✉)], Patricia Matsubara[2], Katia Romero Felizardo[3], Miikka Kuutila[4], Marco Gerosa[5], Savio de Sousa Sampaio[6], Tayana Conte[6], and Igor Steinmacher[5]

[1] University of Helsinki, Helsinki, Finland
mika.mantyla@helsinki.fi
[2] UFMS, Campo Grande, Brazil
patricia.gomes@ufms.br
[3] UTFPR – Federal University of Technology - Paraná, Curitiba, Brazil
katiascannavino@utfpr.edu.br
[4] LUT University, Lappeenranta, Finland
miikka.kuutila@lut.fi
[5] Northern Arizona University, Flagstaff, USA
{marco.gerosa,igor.steinmacher}@nau.edu
[6] UFAM, Manaus, Brazil
tayana@icomp.ufam.edu.br

Abstract. Several studies have examined the use of large language models (LLMs) for title-abstract screening in systematic reviews (SRs), reporting mixed accuracy. However, questions of reliability remain largely unaddressed. In this study, we go beyond quantitative LLM-human agreement metrics and qualitatively investigate how and why LLMs fail. We also propose actionable recommendations. We analyzed disagreements between LLMs and researchers across six software engineering SRs and over 1,000 primary study papers. For each SR, papers were screened independently by human experts and LLMs in zero-shot mode, resulting in Kappa values ranging from 0.52 to 0.77. Qualitative analysis suggests that human-LLM disagreement results from recurring, identifiable causes, such as boundary ambiguity in key terms, keyword overemphasization, and incorrect topic inference. Based on these findings, we propose recommendations such as validating semantic understanding before deployment, running multiple LLMs, and focusing validation efforts on borderline cases. Future studies are needed to validate the impact of our recommendations, and community efforts are needed to develop normative guidelines on LLM usage in SRs.

Keywords: Evidence synthesis · Eligibility criteria · Inclusion and exclusion screening · Study selection · Automation of systematic reviews · Qualitative error analysis

C. Berger and V. Klös (Eds.): SEAA 2026, LNCS 16864, pp. 226–242, 2027.
https://doi.org/10.1007/978-3-032-36587-3_16

1 Introduction

An important step in systematic reviews (SRs) is title-abstract screening, when titles and abstracts of candidate studies are evaluated against inclusion and exclusion criteria [12]. This step is labor-intensive, requiring researchers to analyze hundreds or thousands of records for a single SR. Moreover, the task is cognitively demanding and highly repetitive, making it prone to errors that may lead to the omission of relevant evidence, threatening the SR validity. This concern is reflected in the attention given to this step in established guidelines [6,12,20].

Recent advances in artificial intelligence have motivated studies in software engineering concerning the use of LLMs to support title–abstract screening [4, 5,7,8,19,25]. Beyond software engineering, several reviews have also examined this topic [11,14,15,23]. These studies often report promising results, showing performance comparable to humans and beyond traditional NLP approaches in zero-shot setups. At the same time, existing evidence highlights concerns regarding reliability and variability across reviews, with agreement levels between humans and LLMs ranging from moderate to substantial [7].

Prior work has mostly focused on aggregate accuracy metrics and agreement statistics. However, these indicators provide limited insight into the causes of disagreement. Researchers adopting LLM-assisted screening need to understand not only *how often* models disagree with humans, but also *where* and *why* this happens. Without that, it is difficult to design effective human–LLM workflows or mitigate risks associated with missed or incorrectly included studies.

To address this gap, we conduct a qualitative cross-study analysis of disagreements between LLMs and human raters during title–abstract screening. We analyze six software engineering SRs in which humans and LLMs independently screened the same candidate papers. Rather than treating disagreements as isolated errors, we examine their recurring structure and underlying causes. Specifically, we investigate the following research questions:

Research Question 1: *What disagreement patterns between LLMs and human raters recur across studies?*
Research Question 2: *What recommendations can be drawn from the identified patterns?*

The main contributions of this work include (i) a taxonomy that characterizes where and what goes wrong in LLM-assisted screening and (ii) a set of recommendations to help researchers anticipate and mitigate these disagreements in practice. Our results inform the design of more reliable screening workflows and provide concrete recommendations for researchers seeking to integrate LLMs into SR pipelines. These findings contribute to a more informed and reliable use of LLMs in evidence synthesis.

2 Method

In this section, we describe the subject studies and our approach to analyzing disagreements between LLMs and humans in title-abstract screening. We used a qualitative cross-study design to examine how and why these disagreements occurred. Humans and LLMs independently screened the same candidate papers from a set of SRs, after which we extracted all cases where their decisions diverged. We then qualitatively coded and synthesized these cases through inductive analysis to identify recurring disagreement patterns.

2.1 Subject Studies

To investigate disagreement patterns across diverse contexts, we selected a set of subject studies (SRs) spanning different software engineering topics and research groups. For all subject studies, we followed the same general procedure: papers were retrieved from Scopus using the original search strategies, human reviewers performed title–abstract screening and reached consensus, and then multiple LLMs screened the same sets in zero-shot mode. The LLM screening was done via the AISysRev tool [9] that allows screening of hundreds of papers input via a CSV file. The tool creates a zero-shot prompt for each paper by combining the title and abstract with the SR's inclusion and exclusion criteria, instructing the model to return a binary include/exclude decision along with a brief rationale. All studies used at least two LLMs: *gemini-2.5-flash* and *openai/gpt-4.1-mini*. A recent study [7] found openai/gpt-4.1-mini to be the best-performing, although the differences among the top models were small. Overall, these models represent a modest token price while offering good performance.

Although our work is not quantitative, we do provide statistics from all of our selected studies in Table 1. For readers who have more interest in LLM screening performance as a statistical phenomenon, we refer to the paper by Huotala et al. [7] that contains quantitative analysis of over 34k studies in software engineering, or to the study by Chan et al. that quantitatively analyzed screening decisions of over 540k studies in the medical domain [3]. Our work's novelty is in the quality analysis, something that is not seen in past quantitative works. Next, we present the context of each subject study and study-specific characteristics.

Table 1. Study statistics

Metric	TP	ESEE	WOSS	GenAIEdu	AI4T	AI4TInd
Primary studies	137	100	100	100	162	445
Human include	15	6	38	8	31	33
LLM include	32	7	35	23	21	43 (228)
Cohen's Kappa	0.52	0.75	0.56	0.71	0.72	0.77 (0.133)

Time Pressure (TP) – This study corresponds to a previous SR on Time Pressure in software engineering [13]. We searched for papers that were published after the SR, thus, it made us as unbiased as we had not previously made screening decisions on these papers. The search yielded 137 new papers from Scopus. Two human raters screened all studies and resolved disagreements through discussion. LLM-based screening was then applied. Then, both humans independently documented their observations on the reasons for the LLMs' divergence, which informed our final taxonomy. Overall, 11% of the papers were included in the title-abstract screening phase. Cohen's kappa between the human consensus and LLMs was 0.523, indicating moderate agreement. For this calculation, the LLM decision was determined by whether any LLM included the study.

Expert Judgment in Software Estimation (ESEE) – This systematic mapping study investigated factors that affect expert judgment in software effort estimation [17]. The researchers used a random sample of 100 papers retrieved using the original search string in Scopus. Two researchers independently screened the sample and produced a consensus set of six included and 94 excluded papers. Next, LLMs were used to analyze the same set of papers. A paper was considered included by the LLMs if at least one model selected it. This resulted in seven papers selected for inclusion by the LLMs, with a Cohen's Kappa of 0.753, indicating substantial agreement between humans and LLMs.

Women in OSS (WOSS) - This study corresponds to a previously published SR of women's participation in open source software [26]. For the present analysis, 100 papers were retrieved using the original search string in Scopus. Two researchers screened the studies and reached consensus on a set of 38 included papers. Subsequently, LLMs analyzed the same set, with at least one model selecting 35 papers for inclusion. Agreement between human consensus and the LLMs yielded a Cohen's kappa of 0.558, indicating moderate agreement.

Generative AI in Education (GenAIEdu)—This unpublished systematic mapping study investigates the usage of Generative AI in Software Engineering Education. The study analyzed 57 primary studies published from 2023 to 2025. For the present selection process, we used a random sample of 100 papers retrieved from Scopus. Title–abstract screening was conducted by four researchers, resulting in a final set of 8 included papers. LLMs analyzed the same random sample and selected 23 papers for inclusion (considering papers selected by at least one LLM). The agreement between human reviewers and the LLMs, measured using Cohen's kappa, was 0.709, indicating substantial agreement.

We included two additional ongoing studies to complement the previous four. These studies processed a larger volume of papers, offering breadth to enrich the analysis. However, they were evaluated only by the first author and LLMs.

AITest2023 (AI4T) is a 2023 subset of papers from an ongoing SR evaluating the use of *AI in test generation*. The year 2023 was selected to narrow down the number of papers to be suitable for this study. The first author independently screened a subset of 162 papers from the year 2023 and scored all papers for inclusion and exclusion. Then, LLMs screened the same papers, after which the first author checked for conflicts, resulting in a final set of 31 included papers. The LLMs included 21 papers (considering papers selected by at least one LLM).

The final agreement between human and LLM, with Cohen's kappa of 0.727, is in line with previous studies.

AITestIndustry (AI4TInd) is another subset of papers from an ongoing SR on *AI use in test generation.* In this subset, papers that two humans had previously screened for inclusion were selected for further analysis (445 papers). The first author aimed to narrow this set by identifying all papers conducted in the "software industry" to present for an industry audience. Thus, this represented a rapid review case where the goal was to support software engineering practice, similar to the study by Pizard et al. [21]. Three LLMs were used (*gemini-2.5-flash, openai/gpt-4.1-mini, anthropic/claude-haiku-4.5*). A paper was considered for inclusion by the LLMs only if all three LLMs included it. This approach was motivated by the rapid review context, where the objective was to present only the most notable cases to a software industry audience. The LLMs included 43 papers, while the human judge included 33 papers. The Kappa agreement between LLM and human decisions was 0.77, indicating substantial agreement.

For full transparency, we must also note that a further motivation for the LLM inclusion rule change was the fact that *gemini-2.5-flash* highly underperformed in this task. It interpreted nearly any type of industry relevance argument in the paper abstract as an indication that the study had been conducted in the "software industry". Had we adopted the approach of using two LLMs (*gemini-2.5-flash, openai/gpt-4.1-mini*) and included a paper if either LLM deemed it relevant, we would have faced an excessive number of papers for qualitative analysis. Using those rules, the LLMs would have included 228 papers, and the Kappa agreement between LLM and human decisions would have been 0.133.

For each subject study, we extracted all instances in which any LLM decision diverged from the human consensus decision. The human consensus was treated as the reference judgment because it resulted from independent screening followed by conflict resolution. Each disagreement instance included the paper metadata, the human decision, the LLM decision, and any rationale produced by the models when available.

2.2 Analysis

All cases of disagreement were first open-coded to capture the preliminary reason for divergence. One researcher then analyzed the full set of coded instances and accompanying notes. She derived themes and their descriptions using inductive thematic analysis [2]. Then three other researchers reviewed the themes and descriptions, along with the codes and notes associated with them. Next, the researchers discussed codes and themes, as well as the qualitative distinctions between themes, to further refine them. Finally, a fifth researcher conducted an additional review, renaming them to follow the <where–what> format and merging or creating themes as needed, resulting in the final list of general themes. We did not compute a formal inter-rater reliability coefficient for the qualitative coding, as we used open coding and followed a consensual validation approach: themes were iteratively refined through discussion among researchers until agreement was reached on the assignment of all cases.

Throughout the analysis, disagreements related to theme interpretations were resolved through discussion among the researchers, and the coding scheme was iteratively refined until the team reached a consensual thematic structure.

3 Results - Disagreement Patterns

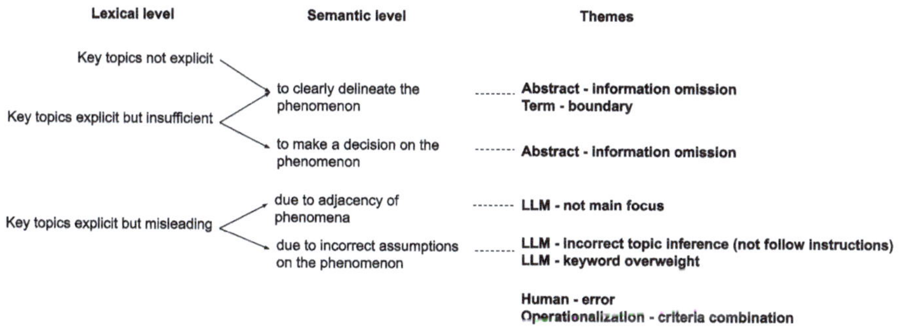

Fig. 1. Pathways for themes –The figure shows how lexical cues (e.g., explicit, missing, or misleading topic-related terms) in titles and abstracts (at the **lexical level**) give rise to different semantic interpretation challenges with respect to the phenomenon of interest (at the **semantic level**).

To answer RQ1, we present a taxonomy of disagreement patterns, where each pattern identifies the location and nature of the issue. The most frequent sources of divergence involved missing explicit terminology in abstracts, conceptual boundary ambiguity, and models over-relying on surface lexical cues. In the rest of this section, we provide illustrative examples for each pattern, classified under two error types: Evidence Loss (False Negative) and False Positive. We operationalize the two error types relative to the human consensus decision. *Evidence Loss (EL)* occurs when the LLM excludes a study that humans included, representing a potential loss of relevant evidence. *False Positive (FP)* occurs when the LLM includes a study that humans excluded, representing the introduction of potentially irrelevant evidence into the screening set.

When deriving the disagreement patterns themes, we observed that some of them had problems at the lexical level (in the form of the word), or at the semantic level (related to the meaning of the words) [10]. They are illustrated in Fig. 1. The figure depicts the different pathways from lexical issues to semantic causes or consequences associated with each theme. It does not connect the theme "Human – error" to the lexical–semantic pathways, as it pertains to human judgment rather than to LLM processing. Similarly, "Operationalization – criteria combination" pertains to combining screening criteria rules and is not related to lexical–semantic pathways, so it is left disconnected in the figure.

In cases under "Abstract – information omission" and "Term – boundary," the core issue was at the lexical level: the key topics of the SR were not explicit.

As a result, the phenomenon of interest was not clearly delineated. In some situations, the key topics were explicit but insufficient, generating eligibility uncertainty at the semantic level. This applies to some cases under the "Abstract – information omission" pattern. For other patterns, the key topics were explicit but potentially misleading at the semantic level. In some cases, this occurred due to adjacency between the phenomenon of interest and related phenomena, resulting in "LLM – not main focus" pattern. For example, a paper may tangentially address the topic of interest but not as a primary contribution. In other cases, the misleading interpretation stemmed from incorrect assumptions made by the LLM, as represented by the patterns "LLM – incorrect topic inference (not follow instructions)" and "LLM – keyword overweight."

Table 2 summarizes the occurrence of disagreements per study across the patterns and error types. The most frequent pattern overall was *LLM—Incorrect Topic Inference* (32 instances), followed by *LLM—Not main focus* (23) and *Term—Boundary* (18). Evidence Loss outnumbered False Positives in most patterns, except for *LLM—Not main focus* and *LLM—Incorrect Topic Inference* in certain studies. In the next sections, we present each pattern individually.

Table 2. Disagreements by pattern, study, and error type. EL = Evidence Loss (LLM false negative relative to human consensus); FP = False Positive (LLM false positive).

Pattern	TP		ESEE		WOSS		GenAIEdu		AI4T		AI4TInd	
	EL	FP	EL	FP	EL	FP	EL	FP	EL	FP	EL	FP
Term–Boundary	3	–	–	1	7	–	–	–	–	2	2	4
Abstract–Information omission	1	–	3	–	6	–	–	2	–	1	–	–
LLM–Keyword overweight	–	–	–	–	–	1	–	–	–	1	–	6
LLM–Not main focus	–	15	1	1	3	–	–	–	1	2	–	–
LLM–Incorrect topic inference	4	2	–	–	–	–	–	13	9	4	1	3
Human–Error	1	–	–	–	2	–	1	–	–	1	–	–
Operational–Criteria combination	4	–	–	–	–	–	–	–	–	–	–	–
Totals	**13**	**17**	**4**	**2**	**18**	**1**	**1**	**15**	**10**	**11**	**3**	**13**

3.1 Term - Boundary

This patter is about disagreement over how broadly or narrowly a concept should be interpreted. This pattern occurs when interpretation of terms fail to delineate construct or topic boundaries, leading to ambiguity in interpreting inclusion and exclusion criteria. LLMs are trained on a wide range of texts that may have broader or narrower interpretations of terms than in the SR.

Evidence Loss. Evidence loss arises when LLMs interpret key terms more narrowly than intended, excluding papers that human raters would retain. The

WOSS study further highlighted persistent ambiguity around what constitutes participation or contribution in open source contexts. Several papers situated at the margins of these constructs triggered disagreement, with LLMs frequently excluding studies that human reviewers judged as in-scope. Similarly, in the TP study, an LLM did not consider "software task effort estimation", "security audits", or "UX design" as software development tasks, whereas human evaluators did, leading to unwarranted exclusions. In AITestIndustry, an LLM did not consider Volvo Trucks to be part of the software industry, whereas for the researcher, any company that develops software is considered part of the software industry.

False Positive. Boundary ambiguity can also lead in the opposite direction, where LLMs include papers that fall outside the intended scope. In AITest2023, both LLMs included a paper on vulnerability detection and monitoring, while the human evaluator disagreed. The paper had matched the database search only because it focused on detecting vulnerabilities in test cases, a context that the LLMs failed to account for when assessing relevance. In the ESEE study, an LLM classified Use Case Points as an expert-based estimation technique and included a paper, while human raters excluded it because its structured, formula-driven approach to software size calculation does not qualify as expert judgment.

3.2 Abstract - Information Omission

The title-abstract lacks sufficient information to determine eligibility at the screening stage, leading to divergent uncertainty handling.

Evidence Loss. An example from the ESEE study is a paper on software effort estimation that does not explicitly mention expert judgment in its title or abstract. This led the LLM to exclude the paper, while the human raters included it to avoid losing a potentially relevant study. In the TP study, the abstract contains a vague sentence regarding time pressure in the section where the results are presented: "The convergence of competition, time pressure, and an engaging environment creates a stimulating atmosphere that significantly drives skill development and enhances the overall educational experience". For human raters, it was clear that the paper should be included in the title/abstract screening. However, both LLMs would exclude this paper.

This pattern was particularly evident in the WOSS study. Several papers discussing participation-related phenomena (e.g., disengagement or interaction patterns) were excluded by the LLMs because the abstracts did not explicitly use terms such as "contribution" or "participation." Human raters, however, retained these papers based on contextual interpretation of the study focus.

False Positive. False positives emerged when abstracts lacked sufficient detail to confirm eligibility but contained relevant surface signals. In the WOSS study, the abstracts had subtle cues indicating that the papers were doctoral symposium publications (an exclusion criterion). Human reviewers detected these signals and excluded the papers accordingly, whereas the LLMs included them.

These cases indicate that subtle publication-type signals in abstracts may be inconsistently captured by LLMs during screening.

3.3 LLM - Keyword Overweight

The LLM overweights keyword presence in the abstract.

Evidence Loss. We did not observe clear cases of evidence loss primarily attributable to keyword overweight in our dataset.

False Positive. A particularly clear example of this category occurred in the WOSS study, where an LLM included a paper on participation in a Type 1 diabetes management case study solely because it mentioned open-source software used for insulin delivery. Despite matching keywords, the study was clearly outside the review scope. In AITest2023, a paper was included despite it being evident that the study focused on hardware testing, which was explicitly listed in the exclusion criteria. These cases illustrate how strong lexical overlap can override contextual relevance in LLM decision-making.

3.4 LLM - Not Main Focus

The title/abstract focuses on a topic conceptually adjacent to the topic of interest, rather than directly addressing it.

Evidence Loss. In AITest2023, a paper considered the use of LLMs for testing, along with code generation and bug fixing. Since the study was not solely focused on testing, Gemini excluded it, whereas human evaluators decided to retain it for the full-text review phase. In the WOSS study, several papers centered on themes such as equity, inclusivity, or interaction patterns in OSS communities were excluded by the LLMs because "participation" or "gender" was not the explicit focal construct. Human reviewers, however, retained these studies for full-text inspection. This suggests that LLMs apply a stricter notion of topical centrality than human screeners.

False Positive. An example from the ESEE study involves a paper addressing a strongly human-centered topic, such as negotiation and the defense of estimates, which could apply to any type of estimation method or technique. The LLMs appear to have been influenced by this focus and decided to include the paper, whereas the human raters excluded it.

In the TP study, GPT-4 identified multiple papers in which time pressure was cited as motivation in the abstract. Still, the abstract failed to establish that the paper contained any evidence of time pressure. Consequently, Gemini correctly excluded these papers.

3.5 LLM - Incorrect Topic Inference

This pattern occurs when an LLM infers a topic or contextual framing that is not supported by the paper's title or abstract, leading to decisions that contradict the stated criteria.

Evidence Loss. Evidence loss in this pattern is a result of LLMs' mishandling of negations in exclusion criteria or misjudging the level of specificity required. In the TP study, an LLM frequently provided a correct rationale but still reached the wrong decision, likely due to difficulty handling negation in the exclusion criteria: "The task studied is not a software development task". Although this issue recurred multiple times, Gemini was inconsistent and more often made the correct decision. GPT-4.1-mini did not show this problem. In AITest2023, Gemini excluded a paper on LLM-based testing because it operated at a higher level of abstraction rather than addressing specific methodologies or implementations, a judgment human evaluators did not share. In another case, Gemini excluded a paper on LLM-based test generation for programming benchmarks, incorrectly interpreting it as a study on testing AI rather than on AI-based test generation.

False Positive. False positives in this pattern arise when LLMs infer a plausible but unsupported contextual framing. In AITest2023, both LLMs included several papers focused on "testing of AI" when the objective was to identify papers on "AI for testing". Although the criteria explicitly distinguished between the two directions, the LLMs failed to consistently apply this distinction. A similar issue arose in the GenAIEdu study, where one LLM repeatedly inferred an educational context even when the title and abstract provided no explicit indication of one, leading to incorrect inclusion decisions.

3.6 Human - Error

The human revised the screening decision after exposure to the LLM's rationale, which highlighted information that had previously been overlooked.

Evidence Loss. In the TP study, humans overlooked a study that investigated time pressure and improvisation as its main focus in the context of a software team. Both human evaluators missed this study, whereas both LLMs correctly identified it as relevant for inclusion. A similar situation occurred in the GenAIEdu study. In these cases, the LLMs mitigated evidence loss by identifying relevant studies that had been missed during human screening. A similar borderline case was observed in the WOSS study, where human reviewers initially excluded a paper due to limited explicit framing of participation in the abstract. The LLM, however, flagged the study for inclusion based on contextual cues. Upon closer inspection, the paper was deemed relevant, suggesting that model rationales can occasionally surface evidence overlooked during manual screening.

False Positive. We observed one borderline case in AI4T where the human decision may have been influenced by an oversight rather than a judgment call. However, the evidence was not conclusive enough to classify it as human error.

3.7 Operationalization - Criteria Combination

Typically, SRs require that all inclusion criteria are met and none of the exclusion criteria. However, SRs may apply different logic to the criteria.

Evidence Loss. This occurred in the TP study, where meeting either inclusion criterion was sufficient for inclusion. Occasionally, LLMs would exclude relevant studies based on the fact that only one inclusion criteria was satisfied. Yet, when we conducted further analysis, we noticed that although LLMs default to an AND logic for distinct criteria, they may inadvertently transition to OR logic. This observation is reflected in our recommendations. Upon identifying our incorrect operationalization, the TP study was re-run using Boolean logic, where the LLM evaluated each criterion separately and Boolean logic was applied programmatically, which revealed 4 cases of evidence loss.

False Positive. We did not observe clear cases of false positives attributable to Operationalization in our dataset.

4 Discussion

4.1 Recommendations

In this subsection, we answer RQ2 by providing recommendations based on the experiences from analyzing disagreements between human raters and LLMs. The recommendations below were derived from the recurring disagreement patterns identified in RQ1. Each recommendation targets one or more observed sources of disagreement between human reviewers and LLMs, as summarized in Table 3. We have placed these recommendations in the Discussion section, as their impacts require validation in future studies.

Table 3. Mapping of disagreement patterns to recommendations.

Pattern	R1	R2	R3	R4	R5
Term–Boundary			✓	✓	
Abstract–Information omission	✓			✓	✓
LLM–Keyword overweight	✓	✓	✓		
LLM–Not main focus	✓		✓	✓	
LLM–Incorrect topic inference	✓	✓	✓	✓	
Human–Error				✓	✓
Operationalization–Criteria comb.		✓	✓		

R1-Run Multiple LLMs. Prior quantitative work suggests that different LLMs, above a certain size, have similar aggregate screening accuracy [7]. However, this does not mean individual decision would be the same. We find that running multiple LLMs results in greater diversity. Each model may have its own interpretations and misunderstandings affecting the SR study. Using multiple models helps uncover these misunderstandings and interpretations. However, even after executing multiple models, some misunderstandings may persist across models. In such cases, researchers can consider general misunderstandings that models may have learned from training data as misunderstandings from public forums can enter model weights through training data. For instance, a widespread misconception that code reviews primarily catch functional defects, whereas evidence shows they are predominantly maintainability issues, could affect screening decisions across multiple models simultaneously [1,16,24]. More details on such misconceptions can be found in work by Rainer [22].

R2-Run Each Criteria Separate. The general wisdom is that LLMs perform better when the task is smaller. This should also be followed in this context. We have found cases where LLMs do not produce internally consistent results, as the overall decision diverges from individual criteria decisions. Additionally, SRs can include different boolean logic, e.g., rules that are interpreted using OR-logic rather than AND-logic (e.g., for TP-studies). Therefore, it is preferable to feed each criterion separately to the LLM. The combination and final decision should be done via traditional programming using Boolean logic.

R3-Define Criteria Unambiguously. Many disagreements stemmed from underspecified inclusion/exclusion criteria, especially around construct boundaries and domain concepts (e.g., what counts as "participation," "software testing," or "industry"). Before running LLM-assisted screening, researchers should make the criteria definition complete by explicitly stating (i) key term definitions, (ii) boundary conditions (what is in vs. out), and (iii) common confounders and near-miss cases. This reduces semantic drift and helps LLMs apply the intended scope consistently.

R4-Validate From Boundaries: In SR screening, many studies are straightforward "includes" or "excludes" and provide limited insight into model behavior. Greater value comes from examining borderline cases near the inclusion boundary, as these are more likely to reveal systematic weaknesses in both human and LLM decision-making. There is little to learn regarding screening accuracy from these easy decisions. However, the studies that lie on the boundaries of the include/exclude decision are the ones that require attention and are the key to sharpening the decision rules both for humans and LLMs. Below are two techniques for identifying these boundaries:

R4.1-LLM Disagreement. One can run multiple LLMs and sample all studies where the LLMs disagree with each other. These cases are guaranteed to contain LLM misclassifications. Studying these cases and the reasons provided by the LLMs for their decisions can offer insights into how to improve the process. For example, we observed that some models claimed vulnerability detection is part of software testing, and that a study conducted at Volvo Trucks is not a study done "in the software industry" because, according to the model, Volvo Trucks is not considered part of the software industry. We do disagree with those statements; however, these viewpoints can substantially reduce the number of studies that need to be re-examined manually, allowing human reviewers to focus their attention on a smaller subset of borderline cases. Additionally, such insights on disagreements help clarify the criteria in R3-Define Criteria Unambiguously.

R4.2-LLM Probability. One can also ask the LLMs to output probabilities instead of a binary decision for each criterion. This forces LLMs to reveal any uncertainty they may have. Although we have noticed that it is quite rare to get an LLM to output a 0.5 probability, there are a fair number of cases where probabilities of 0.7 and 0.3 are output. When using probabilities, one should start from the middle, that is, the 0.5 range, and move both up and down to identify borderline cases. This can also help determine how the probability threshold should be set for the decision. One can also average probabilities from multiple LLMs and attempt to identify a "shoulder" for the cutoff points. A shoulder is the point in the density graph where the probability quickly drops.

R5-Double Check Human Decisions. Beyond serving as an automated classifier, the LLM can be used as an external opinion mechanism to stress-test human screening decisions and identify studies that warrant careful re-examination and confirmation of classifications. Rather than replacing human judgment, this external perspective can support reviewers, particularly novice researchers or teams with limited human resources, by highlighting borderline cases that deserve closer scrutiny. In this study, we identified human errors that could have resulted in evidence loss had the LLMs not flagged certain studies.

On the face value, the above recommendations make sense to all study authors who have experience in executing multiple SRs and who have all recently been active in investigating the use of large language models (LLMs) in SRs [4,7–9]. Yet, the impact in terms of empirical evidence of the recommendations is currently unclear, as each of them would require a quantitative study of its own. Thus, we welcome the community as a whole to continue investigating the impact of the recommendations.

4.2 Comparison to Related Work

As pointed out many works have quantitatively evaluated the screening accuracy of LLMs [3,5,7,8,11,14,19,23,25] but far fewer studies have qualitative analysed the problems in LLM screening or provided mitigation strategies.

Recently, Madeyski et al. [15] outlined recommendations on reporting the quantitative results of large language model (LLM) use in title-abstract screening. For example, in addition to precision and recall, one should report the Matthews correlation coefficient. We on the other hand provide recommendations on LLM usage rather than result reporting. Felizardo [4] reports on the difficulties in using LLMs in SRs based on two studies. While their scope is wider than that of this paper, there is a similar finding regarding LLM prompt sensitivity. In our work, we provided more details on this aspect through an error-class analysis based on six studies and also offered a recommendation (R3) to address it. Petersen [18] tackled the problem of misusing the term "case study" by original study authors and employed an LLM to detect such misclassifications. This aligns with our recommendation R5 and provides a more detailed context on applying LLMs to double-check human work. Thode [25] conducted primarily quantitative work on two SRs but also analyzed LLM mistakes. They reached some similar findings to ours: using unmodified and unimproved screening criteria (R3) may be problematic, and employing multiple LLMs—though artificially increasing recall—can help avoid evidence loss.

To summarize, no existing software engineering study focuses exclusively on qualitative analysis of LLM errors in SR screening as we have done in this paper. However, similar insights were found as sub-analysis from the prior works.

4.3 Limitations

This study has limitations that should be considered when interpreting the findings. First, our analysis is limited to the title-abstract screening stage of SRs. Disagreement patterns at other stages, such as full-text screening or data extraction, may differ and warrant separate investigation. Second, while four studies employed multiple independent researchers, the two ongoing studies relied on a single rater, which may introduce bias in the coding of disagreements. This trade-off was deliberate, given the larger number of papers in those studies. Third, all LLM screening was conducted in zero-shot mode using specific models. Different prompting strategies, such as few-shot or chain-of-thought prompting, may yield different disagreement patterns and are not reflected in our taxonomy. Furthermore, the results reflect the specific model versions available at the time of the study and may evolve as LLM capabilities continue to improve. Fourth, the taxonomy and recommendations were derived inductively from a limited set of studies. While the involvement of six researchers in the analysis process strengthens credibility, the patterns identified should be considered a starting point rather than an exhaustive account of LLM disagreement modes in title-abstract screening. Fifth, our findings are grounded in software engineering SRs, which may limit direct generalization to other domains where terminology, inclusion criteria, and topic boundaries differ. Additionally, three of the six subject studies (GenAIEdu, AI4T, AI4TInd) were ongoing or unpublished at the time of analysis and had not undergone full peer review. While this introduces some uncertainty about the stability of their inclusion criteria, it also reflects realistic conditions under which LLM-assisted screening is likely to be used in practice. Finally, the use of human consensus as the reference decision may raise concerns. Human screening itself is subject to error and interpretation variability. Therefore, some disagreements attributed to LLMs may reflect ambiguity in the primary studies or limitations in the human judgment process.

5 Conclusion

LLMs have the potential to support researchers in title-abstract screening, which is a critical step in SRs. In this paper, we investigate how LLMs fail during screening. Through qualitative analysis of disagreements between LLMs and human raters across six software engineering SRs, we derived a taxonomy of seven disagreement patterns. Based on these patterns, we proposed five recommendations to help design more reliable LLM-assisted screening workflows.

Our findings suggest that LLM failures result from recurring, identifiable causes, such as boundary ambiguity in key terms, information omission in abstracts, keyword overemphasization, and incorrect topic inference. Recognizing these patterns allows researchers to take targeted preventive measures, such as validating semantic understanding before deployment, running multiple LLMs, evaluating each criterion separately, and focusing validation efforts on borderline cases. We expect this work to contribute to more informed and transparent use of LLMs in evidence synthesis and to encourage future research to build on this taxonomy using larger, more diverse sets of SRs.

Acknowledgment. This work was supported by the Research Council of Finland (Grant id: 359861) and Strategic Research Council of Research Council of Finland (Grant ID 358471). This study was financed in part by the Coordenação de Aperfeiçoamento de Pessoal de Nível Superior - Brasil (CAPES-PROEX) - Finance Code 001. This work was also partially supported by CNPq (processes 314797/2023-8, 443934/2023-1, and 445029/2024-2), Amazonas State Research Support Foundation - FAPEAM - through the POSGRAD project 2025/2026 and the Federal University of Mato Grosso do Sul (UFMS).

Data Availability. https://dx.doi.org/10.5281/zenodo.20695824.

Disclosure of Interests. The authors have no competing interests to declare that are relevant to the content of this article.

References

1. Beller, M., Bacchelli, A., Zaidman, A., Juergens, E.: Modern code reviews in open-source projects: which problems do they fix? In: 11th Working Conference on Mining Software Repositories (2014)
2. Braun, V., Clarke, V.: Using thematic analysis in psychology. Qual. Res. Psychol. **3**(2), 77–101 (2006). https://doi.org/10.1191/1478088706qp063oa
3. Chan, G.C., He, E., Leung, J., Verspoor, K.: A comprehensive systematic review dataset is a rich resource for training and evaluation of AI systems for title and abstract screening. Res. Synthesis Methods 1–15 (2025)
4. Felizardo, K., et al.: On the difficulties of conducting and replicating systematic literature reviews studies using LLMs in software engineering. In: 2025 International Workshop on Methodological Issues with Empirical Studies in Software Engineering (WSESE), pp. 20–23. IEEE (2025)
5. Felizardo, K., Lima, M., Deizepe, A., Conte, T.U., Steinmacher, I.: ChatGPT application in Systematic Literature Reviews in Software Engineering: an evaluation of its accuracy to support the selection activity. In: 18th ACM/IEEE International Symposium on Empirical Software Engineering and Measurement, ESEM 2024, pp. 25–36 (2024). https://doi.org/10.1145/3674805.3686666
6. Garousi, V., Felderer, M., Mäntylä, M.V.: Guidelines for including grey literature and conducting multivocal literature reviews in software engineering. Inf. Softw. Technol. **106**, 101–121 (2019)
7. Huotala, A., Kuutila, M., Mäntylä, M.: SESR-Eval: dataset for evaluating LLMs in the title-abstract screening of systematic reviews. In: 2025 ACM/IEEE International Symposium on Empirical Software Engineering and Measurement (ESEM),

ESEM 2025, pp. 1–12. IEEE (2025). https://doi.org/10.1109/ESEM64174.2025.00053
8. Huotala, A., Kuutila, M., Ralph, P., Mäntylä, M.: The promise and challenges of using LLMs to accelerate the screening process of systematic reviews. In: 28th International Conference on Evaluation and Assessment in Software Engineering, EASE 2024, pp. 262–271 (2024). https://doi.org/10.1145/3661167.3661172
9. Huotala, A., Kuutila, M., Turtio, O.P., Sipilä, S., Mäntylä, M.: Aisysrev - LLM-based tool for title-abstract screening. In: 34th ACM Joint ESEC/FSE, Montreal, QC, Canada, 05–09 July 2026 pp. 1–5 (2026). arXiv:2510.06708
10. Jurafsky, D., Martin, J.H.: Speech and Language Processing: An Introduction to Natural Language Processing, Computational Linguistics, and Speech Recognition with Language Models, 3rd edn. Prentice Hall (2026)
11. Kim, J.K., et al.: Evaluating large language models for title/abstract screening: a systematic review and meta-analysis & development of new tool. J. Med. Artif. Intell. **8**, 34 (2025)
12. Kitchenham, B.A., Dyba, T., Jorgensen, M.: Evidence-based software engineering. In: 26th International Conference on Software Engineering, pp. 273–281. IEEE (2004). https://doi.org/10.1109/ICSE.2004.1317449
13. Kuutila, M., Mäntylä, M., Farooq, U., Claes, M.: Time pressure in software engineering: a systematic review. Inf. Softw. Technol. **121**, 106257 (2020). https://doi.org/10.1016/j.infsof.2020.106257
14. Lieberum, J.L., et al.: Large language models for conducting systematic reviews: on the rise, but not yet ready for use—a scoping review. J. Clin. Epidemiol. **181** (2025). https://doi.org/10.1016/j.jclinepi.2025.111746
15. Madeyski, L., Kitchenham, B., Shepperd, M.: Llm4screenlit: recommendations on assessing the performance of large language models for screening literature in systematic reviews. arXiv preprint arXiv:2511.12635 (2025)
16. Mäntylä, M.V., Lassenius, C.: What types of defects are really discovered in code reviews? IEEE Trans. Softw. Eng. **35**(3), 430–448 (2008)
17. Matsubara, P.G.F., Gadelha, B.F., Steinmacher, I., Conte, T.U.: Sextamt: a systematic map to navigate the wide seas of factors affecting expert judgment software estimates. J. Syst. Softw. **185**, 111148 (2022). https://doi.org/10.1016/j.jss.2021.111148
18. Petersen, K.: Case study identification with GPT-4 and implications for mapping studies. Inf. Softw. Technol. **171**, 107452 (2024)
19. Petersen, K., Gerken, J.M.: On the road to interactive LLM-based systematic mapping studies. Inf. Softw. Technol. **178**, 107611 (2025). https://doi.org/10.1016/j.infsof.2024.107611
20. Petersen, K., Vakkalanka, S., Kuzniarz, L.: Guidelines for conducting systematic mapping studies in software engineering: an update. Inf. Softw. Technol. **64**, 1–18 (2015)
21. Pizard, S., Lezama, J., García, R., Vallespir, D., Kitchenham, B.: Using rapid reviews to support software engineering practice: a systematic review and a replication study. Empir. Softw. Eng. **30**(1), 10 (2025). https://doi.org/10.1007/s10664-024-10545-6
22. Rainer, A.: Using argumentation theory to analyse software practitioners' defeasible evidence, inference and belief. Inf. Softw. Technol. **87**, 62–80 (2017)
23. Sandner, E., et al.: Evaluating large language models for literature screening: a systematic review of sensitivity and workload reduction. In: International Conference on Data Science, Technology and Applications (DATA 2025), pp. 508–517 (2025)

24. Siy, H., Votta, L.: Does the modern code inspection have value? In: International Conference on Software Maintenance, ICSM 2001, pp. 281–289. IEEE (2001)
25. Thode, L., Iftikhar, U., Mendez, D.: Exploring the use of LLMs for the selection phase in systematic literature studies. Inf. Softw. Technol. 107757 (2025). https://doi.org/10.1016/j.infsof.2025.107757
26. Trinkenreich, B., Wiese, I., Sarma, A., Gerosa, M., Steinmacher, I.: Women's participation in open source software: a survey of the literature. ACM Trans. Softw. Eng. Methodol. **31**(4) (2022). https://doi.org/10.1145/3510460

Bridging Research and Practice in Federated Learning: A Multivocal Review of System-Level Architectures and Processes

Mina Badri[1(✉)], Helena Holmström Olsson[1], and Jan Bosch[2,3]

[1] Malmö University, Malmö, Sweden
{mina.badri,helena.holmstrom.olsson}@mau.se
[2] Chalmers University, Gothenburg, Sweden
jan.bosch@chalmers.se, j.bosch1@tue.nl
[3] Technical University Einhoven, Eindhoven, Netherlands

Abstract. Federated Learning (FL) was introduced as a decentralized machine learning approach that enables models to be trained on distributed data sources without exposing raw data. Over time, it became clear that FL as an architectural paradigm can become a tipping point in transforming software-intensive systems into dynamic and autonomous intelligence. However, the adoption of FL in large-scale software-intensive system has been slow. This means there is a growing gap between what is being studied in research and what industry actually needs.

This paper presents a multivocal literature review (MLR) that integrates evidence from systematic literature reviews, primary studies, and industrial grey literature. The study examines FL from architectural and process perspectives, focusing on how systems are designed, deployed, and operated across research and practice.

The results show that, first, significant progress has been made in algorithm design and optimization, while system-level challenges, such as orchestration and lifecycle management, remain understudied. Second, academic work is mostly challenge-driven and focuses on solving problems in isolation, such as addressing system heterogeneity and communication cost, while industry emphasizes system design and operational constraints. Lastly, deployment, evaluation, and end-to-end integration remain insufficiently addressed in both domains.

Keywords: Federated Learning · Multivocal Literature Review · Software-Intensive Systems · Distributed Machine Learning · System Architecture · MLOps · FLOps · Federated Learning Operations · Edge Computing · Lifecycle Management · Industrial AI

1 Introduction

Modern software products, such as autonomous vehicle fleets and industrial IoT systems, generate a massive amount of data, which can become a significant

C. Berger and V. Klös (Eds.): SEAA 2026, LNCS 16864, pp. 243–259, 2027.
https://doi.org/10.1007/978-3-032-36587-3_17

factor in driving post-deployment adaptation and improvements. For example, vehicles can adapt to the driver's habits and local environment, and industrial machines can improve their performance over time by learning from usage. The product becomes smarter the longer it is used. Traditional machine learning (ML) has relied on centralized data servers to achieve post-deployment improvements. However, in many real-world use cases, transferring data to a central server is infeasible due to privacy, regulatory, and communication constraints [1]. The shift from centralized data processing to distributed and autonomous intelligence at the edge can be a game changer and bring about a fundamental transformation in how large-scale software-intensive systems work.

Decentralized learning emerged as a solution to address these challenges by allowing multiple parties to collaboratively train models, and federated learning (FL), as a privacy-preserving approach, is one of its most promising solutions. Since its introduction by McMahan in 2017 [2], FL has developed rapidly and gained significant attention.

However, most of the existing research focuses on algorithms and optimization techniques, such as communication efficiency and privacy-preserving methods. Concerns about how to implement FL, including architecture design, orchestration, deployment, and integration with existing infrastructures, remain underexplored. In the case of integration, organizations face difficulties incorporating FL into legacy systems that were not designed for decentralized, scalable learning processes. On the other hand, industrial use cases demonstrate that FL can support and improve real-world applications; personalization, recommendation systems, and distributed analytics are some of these examples.

Although some studies have explored FL from a broader perspective, the literature remains fragmented. Existing systematic literature reviews (SLRs) focus mainly on algorithms, taxonomies, and application domains, and rarely integrate insights from grey literature such as industrial reports and practitioner experiences. As a result, there is limited understanding of how FL systems are designed, implemented and operated in real-world environments, creating a gap between conceptual designs and practical deployability [3].

To address this gap, this paper investigates FL from architectural and process perspectives, focusing on how FL systems are designed, implemented, deployed, and operated in practice. We adopt a Multivocal Literature Review (MLR) approach that combines (i) a meta-review of existing SLRs, (ii) a grey literature review of industrial practice, and (iii) a targeted SLR of primary studies. This approach enables a comprehensive understanding of FL in both academic and industrial contexts [4].

The study is guided by the following research questions (RQs):

RQ1 What system-level concerns, solutions, and challenges are reported in systematic literature reviews on federated learning?
RQ2 How is FL designed, implemented, deployed, and operationalized in the large-scale software-intensive industry?
RQ3 What are the gaps between academic developments and practical deployment that hinder the adoption of FL in industrial settings?

The contributions of this paper are the following, first, we provide a synthesis of system-level FL evidence in academic and practitioner sources. Second, we highlight how key challenges manifest differently in research and real-world deployments. Finally, we identify the gaps between research prototypes and industrial adoption, including barriers and suggested strategies [4]. This study is intended for researchers, system architects, and practitioners seeking a system-level understanding of FL in real-world deployment scenarios.

The remainder of the paper is structured as follows. In Sect. 2, we present the background on FL and its role in distributed software-intensive systems. In Sect. 3, we describe the methodology, covering the multivocal literature review design, meta-review of systematic literature reviews, grey literature review, and SLR of primary studies. In Sect. 4, we present the results for each research question, examining the state of the art (RQ1), the state of practice (RQ2), and the gap between them (RQ3). In Sect. 5, we discuss the implications of our findings. In Sect. 6, we address threats to validity. Finally, Sect. 7 presents the conclusions and directions for future work.

2 Background

In traditional ML data from multiple sources is collected in a single infrastructure for model training. However, this approach becomes increasingly difficult in environments where data is sensitive, distributed, or generated at the edge. At the same time, the amount of data produced by connected devices continues to grow. According to data scaling laws, improvements in model performance are strongly related to the volume and quality of available data [5]. However, continuously transferring such large volumes of data to centralized infrastructures introduces significant privacy, regulatory, and bandwidth challenges.

To address these limitations, distributed learning approaches have emerged, in which computation is moved closer to the data rather than transferring the data itself. This transition is especially relevant in edge and cross-organizational environments, where direct data sharing is restricted but collaborative model improvement is still required [6,7].

FL is a distributed ML approach in which multiple participants collaboratively train a shared model without exchanging their raw local datasets. Instead of sending data to a central server, clients train their own models locally and only send model updates to a central hub to improve the global model [8–10]. This means that systems such as smartphones, vehicles, or industrial devices can collectively improve models while reducing privacy risks and avoiding the operational cost of large-scale data transfer. Algorithms such as FedAvg can support different ML models by exchanging updates rather than raw data [6,7]. For example, Nikolaenko et al. and Chen et al. developed federated versions of linear regression, while Google's production system has scaled FL to tens of millions of devices training deep neural networks [6].

Similar to conventional ML platforms, this compute-to-data paradigm requires dedicated systems and infrastructures to support diverse training configurations and privacy-preserving workflows [6,11].

As FL moves toward real-world deployment, it becomes part of broader software-intensive systems. In this setting, FL is not only about local training and model aggregation, but also about how distributed components are deployed, monitored, updated, and coordinated across environments.

3 Methodology

This study adopts a Multivocal Literature Review (MLR) to capture both the academic *state of the art* and the industrial *state of practice* in FL. The academic perspective is addressed through a meta-review of systematic literature reviews. The industrial perspective is captured through two complementary approaches: a grey literature review and a systematic literature review (SLR) of primary studies. All of them focus on the system-level architecture and processes of FL. The peer-reviewed components follow the PRISMA 2020 guidelines [12].

3.1 Study Design, Research Questions, and PICOC

To operationalize the research questions, the study applies an Evidence-Based Software Engineering (EBSE) adaptation of PICOC [13]. PICOC structures complex research questions into searchable components and extends PICO by incorporating *Context*, which is particularly relevant for software-intensive and industrial settings [14]. The resulting structure is shown in Table 1.

Table 1. PICOC elements defining the scope and structure of the study

Population	Large-scale software-intensive systems and fleets
Intervention	FL algorithms, frameworks, embedded learning models, and system-level optimization techniques
Comparison	Where reported by included reviews: centralized learning; local-only learning; earlier generations of FL techniques; human-in-the-loop update strategies (contextual comparators)
Outcome	Taxonomies/architectures/optimization patterns reported by reviews; readiness/deployability signals (e.g., tools, frameworks, system constraints); reported adoption barriers/challenges and mitigation strategies
Context	Previous academic studies and established industrial practice

3.2 State of the Art: Meta-Review of Systematic Literature Reviews

The meta-review synthesizes existing systematic studies to identify dominant taxonomies, architectures, system-level processes (e.g., orchestration and lifecycle) and recurring challenges in FL. The review followed established SLR guidelines [13]. A protocol was defined prior to screening, specifying search strategy, eligibility criteria, screening workflow, and data extraction. The reporting follows PRISMA 2020 [12]. Searches were conducted in ACM Digital Library, Scopus, and IEEE Xplore using:

```
TITLE("federated learning")
AND TITLE-ABS("Systematic literature review"
OR "systematic review" OR "SLR")
```

The results were restricted to English-language publications and all included studies were published from 2020 and onward. The records were merged and deduplicated using Rayyan AI [15]. Screening followed a three-step process: deduplication → title/abstract screening → full-text assessment (Fig. 1). Eligibility included systematic reviews with explicit methodologies. A unified set of inclusion/exclusion criteria (Table 2) was applied across all study components.

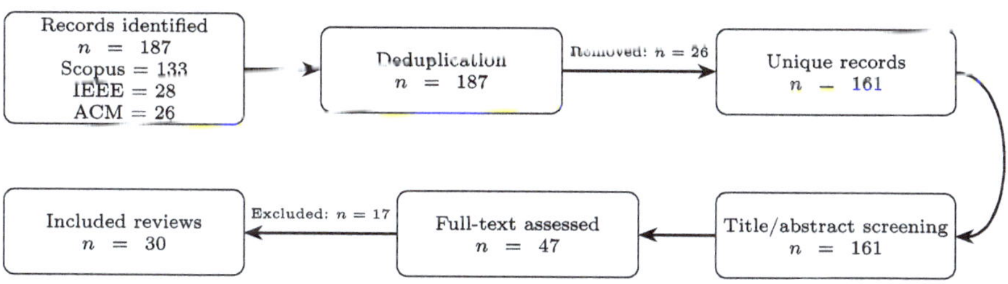

Fig. 1. Meta-review study selection process

A pilot screening of 20 records was conducted to refine criteria. The search retrieved 187 records; after removing 26 duplicates, 161 remained. Screening resulted in 47 full-text assessments and a final set of 30 reviews.

Data extraction was conducted using a structured form, capturing metadata, focus, findings, challenges, and categories [17]. Limitations include dependence on reporting quality and overlap among reviews.

3.3 State of Practice: Grey Literature Review

To capture industrial practice, a Grey Literature Review (GLR) was conducted as part of the MLR, drawing on technical blogs, white papers, documentation, and case studies [18] to include real-world insights often absent from academic literature [4].

The search used multiple Google Programmable Search Engines (PSEs): **FLIndustry** covered 31 industrial and big-tech domains, **Broad web** searched general domains excluding academic publishers, **FLWhitePapers** targeted preprint and white paper repositories, and **FLPractitioners** focused on practitioner platforms such as blogs and LinkedIn.

Table 2. Inclusion and Exclusion Criteria

Inclusion	Criteria Definition	Exclusion
IC1	Published in English	EX1
IC2	The study is either: (a) a systematic review with a reproducible methodology (explicit research questions, search strategy, inclusion/exclusion criteria) [16], or (b) an empirical primary study (experiment, simulation, or case study)	EX2
IC3	Focuses on federated learning in software-intensive or large-scale systems, including architectures, system design, orchestration, lifecycle, or deployment aspects	EX3
IC4	Explores system-level concerns such as coordination, feedback/learning loops, fleet-level improvement, or cross-device/cross-site learning	EX4
IC5	Discusses system boundaries or trade-offs (e.g., local vs fleet optimization, governance, human-in-the-loop aspects)	EX5
IC6	Not purely theoretical, mathematical, or algorithm-focused (e.g., convergence analysis, gradient optimization without system context)	EX6
IC7	Not primarily focused on security, privacy mechanisms, or networking/communication protocols unless directly tied to system design and deployment trade-offs	EX7
IC8	Domain is within scope; excludes purely medical or healthcare-focused studies unless they contribute federated learning system design insights	EX8
IC9	Published from 2020	EX9
IC10	Full text accessible after reasonable effort	EX10

The search followed a two-stage strategy. First, FLIndustry was queried with "federated learning", yielding 2,390 results. Results were then filtered by year from 2020 to January 2026, with only the first three pages examined per query. Relevant links found within pages were added to the list. This produced 81 sources, screened by title and abstract (or introduction if no abstract existed), reduced to 20 sources.

Second, keywords extracted from each primary source were searched across **Broad web**, **FLPractitioners**, and **FLWhitePapers**. Only the first page per PSE was screened, with a maximum of six relevant findings extracted per paper, yielding 90 additional sources. All configurations are documented for reproducibility [17]. Screening followed title/snippet and full-text assessment. Sources were included if they provided technical insights into FL systems or deployment; non-technical content was excluded. Data extraction used a structured template capturing focus, findings, challenges, and future work [17].

3.4 State of Practice: Systematic Literature Review of Primary Studies

A SLR of primary studies was conducted to complement the grey literature review by capturing peer-reviewed evidence on system-level design, orchestration, lifecycle, and deployment in FL. Searches were conducted in IEEE Xplore, Scopus, and ACM Digital Library using a query targeting system-level FL in industrial contexts while excluding purely algorithmic, network related or security-focused work.

```
(TITLE("federated learning")
AND (
TITLE-ABS-KEY("software architecture" OR "system architecture"
OR "reference architecture" OR "architectural pattern"
OR "distributed architecture" OR infrastructure OR orchestration)
OR TITLE-ABS-KEY(MLOps OR "federated MLOps" OR
"machine learning pipeline" OR "ML pipeline"
OR "model lifecycle" OR "model deployment"
OR "model monitoring" OR "model orchestration"
OR "model governance" OR "continuous learning")
OR TITLE-ABS-KEY("software engineering" OR "software system"
OR "software intensive system" OR "software development"
OR "software platform")
)
AND TITLE-ABS-KEY(industry OR industrial OR enterprise
OR production OR deployment OR "real world"
OR "case study" OR "industrial case study"
OR "large scale system")
AND NOT TITLE-ABS-KEY(gradient OR optimizer OR convergence
OR encryption OR "differential privacy"
OR "communication protocol" OR security OR secure
OR cybersecurity OR attack OR attacks OR adversarial
OR network OR networking OR "wireless network"
OR "sensor network")
AND PUBYEAR > 2021)
```

Only English-language studies published after 2021 were included. The selection process followed the same workflow as the meta-review. The search retrieved 108 records; after removing 36 duplicates, 72 remained. Screening resulted in 36 full-text assessments and a final set of 17 studies, following the same flow as meta-review.

Data extraction captured architecture, processes, evaluation, and key contributions [17]. A thematic analysis was applied, resulting in three categories: architecture, process, and evaluation. The screening was conducted by a single reviewer.

4 Results

The following sections present the findings for each research question. System-level aspects of FL are examined across three analytical dimensions that emerged from the data: *architecture* (how system components are organized and connected), *process* (how training, orchestration and lifecycle operations are executed), and *constraints* (limitations imposed by heterogeneity, communication and the deployment environment). These dimensions are recurring themes that surfaced consistently in all three evidence sources. Evaluation is treated as a cross-cutting concern, as it reflects how both system behavior and constraints are assessed across research and practice.

4.1 State of the Art Results (RQ1)

The state of the art review shows that FL research has made significant progress in identifying system-level constraints and proposing solutions. However, these contributions remain fragmented and conceptual, focusing on isolated technical aspects rather than integrated end-to-end system designs. From a structural perspective, research models FL architectures through structured taxonomies and abstract design models, evolving from centralized and horizontal settings to hybrid and hierarchical architectures. Early approaches focused on data partitioning paradigms and their impact on model aggregation and training [19].

More recent work introduces multi-layered architectures such as edge–cloud and edge–cloud–vehicle pipelines, as well as architectural patterns and reference models such as FLRA [20,21] to address scalability, latency, and bandwidth constraints [22]. Resource-aware approaches, including TinyFL and MEC, further highlight the need to balance performance with resource limitations. These developments reflect a shift from a purely ML perspective to a distributed system view. However, key components such as client management, orchestration, and state coordination remain conceptual and lack deployment validation [20].

From a behavioral perspective, research recognizes that FL systems involve dynamic lifecycle management rather than static training pipelines. Concepts such as self-adaptive architectures and MAPE-K feedback loops are proposed to adapt systems to changing conditions [23], while client selection, retraining, and clustering strategies improve convergence and handle concept drift [24,25]. However, these processes are evaluated in isolation rather than as part of complete system lifecycles, leaving their interactions, failures, and composition in operating systems largely unexplored [23].

From a constraint perspective, heterogeneity remains the most significant system-level challenge, encompassing both statistical heterogeneity (non-IID data) and system heterogeneity (device and network differences) [26]. These issues drive a shift from global aggregation approaches like FedAvg toward adaptive aggregation, personalization, and context-aware strategies [27,28]. Communication efficiency is another major bottleneck, with techniques such as partial updates, compression, pruning, and asynchronous aggregation proposed to reduce overhead [29]. Additional constraints include fairness, data imbalance, and unresolved incentive mechanisms in decentralized systems [30]. Blockchain-based architectures address trust and coordination but add complexity and computational overhead [31].

Finally, the lack of standardization and benchmarking remains a persistent problem, with no unified evaluation frameworks, metrics, or shared datasets. Reliance on simulations limits reproducibility and comparability [23]. The FL ecosystem remains fragmented across tools and frameworks that are rarely integrated or evaluated holistically, hindering interoperability and real-world adoption [20].

4.2 State of the Practice Results (RQ2)

The synthesis of grey literature and primary studies reveals that FL is moving beyond isolated prototypes to real-world deployments, but adoption is uneven. Practical FL systems are shaped by three realities: the need for modular, framework-based architectures that can support heterogeneous infrastructure; the operational complexity of managing distributed training as a long term service; and the challenge of integrating FL into legacy systems.

In practice, FL architectures are implemented as modular and flexible systems that are based on frameworks such as NVIDIA FLARE, Flower, and OpenFL to enable reusable and scalable solutions [32–36]. These systems support both cross-device and cross-silo collaboration, combining environments such as edge, cloud, and multi-cloud infrastructure [34,37]. Cross-device FL involves large populations of resource-constrained edge devices, while cross-silo FL enables organizations to train a shared model [38–40]. These models are often combined with edge computing and streaming infrastructures to include layered IoT systems, cloud-edge pipelines, serverless deployments, and blockchain-based coordination [19,38,41–43]. These fully decentralized architectures address communication bottlenecks and single points of failure but they add complexity to the system.

Interoperability across these components is a persistent engineering challenge. No single framework satisfies all deployment requirements, and systems built on multiple frameworks require custom integration layers that are not standardized across deployments [44]. This fragmentation makes architectural decisions context-dependent and difficult to transfer between organizations, slowing adoption and increasing deployment costs.

The most consistent finding from industrial sources is that the operational complexity of FL does not lie in model training itself but in orchestrating the processes that surround it. Managing large-scale, heterogeneous client populations requires coordinating onboarding, availability-based scheduling, asynchronous aggregation, and fault recovery as continuous processes [19,43,45]. The emerging FLOps paradigm formalizes this view, extending DevOps and MLOps principles to cover the full FL lifecycle [46].

This operational layer is where most deployment friction occurs. Integrating FL into legacy enterprise systems introduces compatibility mismatches with existing data pipelines not designed for decentralized execution, resulting in fragmented integration, limited interoperability, and deployment timelines that exceed research expectations [20,44]. Privacy and security further complicate deployment, particularly in cross-silo settings [40,47].

Beyond standard training, practice extends FL toward federated analytics, personalization, and hybrid architectures, balancing privacy, computational cost, and performance. Integration with cloud-native infrastructures, edge computing, and advanced communication technologies highlights the shift toward production-ready systems [19,41,42]. Heterogeneity is treated as an operational constraint rather than a theoretical challenge. Differences in device capabilities, network reliability, and data availability impact system performance, requiring scalability, fault tolerance, and adaptive coordination as core requirements [43,45].

Evaluation is conducted through a combination of simulations, experiments, and real-world deployments. Although FL systems can achieve performance comparable to centralized approaches, the results vary depending on the infrastructure and deployment strategies [38,48]. However, evaluations are often inconsistent due to differences in experimental setups and reliance on simulated environments [49]. Despite ongoing advances, FL adoption remains limited, with challenges in scalability, integration, and operational complexity [50].

4.3 The Gap Between Research and Practice (RQ3)

A clear gap emerges when comparing the findings from academia (RQ1) and practice (RQ2). Research treats FL as isolated technical challenges, whereas practice approaches it as a system integration and deployment problem [27,28,46]. Real-world systems require complete end-to-end solutions combining architecture, orchestration, lifecycle management, and infrastructure integration [51]. The architectural patterns that academic research proposes [20,21] address structural organization but do not specify how components are deployed, operated, or updated over time. The result is that practitioners must bridge this gap through custom engineering that is costly, non-reusable, and invisible to the research record.

Research also proposes architectures such as decentralized, edge-cloud, and hierarchical models, but these are developed independently without shared standards or reusable components [22,31]. In practice, systems must operate across heterogeneous, multi-cloud environments, where legacy system compatibility, standardized client interfaces, and cross-framework interoperability remain open engineering problems [20,44].

Another gap concerns heterogeneity and evaluation. Research models heterogeneity as a statistical or system-level constraint [26,27], whereas practice reveals a more complex reality involving device diversity, unstable connectivity, and infrastructure variability [52,53]. Evaluation in research relies heavily on simulations, while industrial systems require assessment of system reliability, fault recovery, and operational cost under realistic load [49]. The absence of shared benchmarks means academic results cannot directly inform deployment decisions, and industrial experience does not feed back into research evaluation criteria [49].

Beyond this, a more critical gap exists between existing studies and the actual requirements of production FL systems. Real-world FL must support end-to-end lifecycle management—including client onboarding, orchestration, monitoring, deployment, versioning, and secure coordination, yet unified approaches that consider these processes holistically remain absent [46]. Systems must also handle large-scale, heterogeneous client populations with adaptive coordination and fault tolerance [43,45], and integrate with legacy infrastructures not designed for distributed execution [20,44].

Evaluation remains a major limitation, as standardized benchmarks and realistic evaluation frameworks that reflect real-world conditions are still lacking [49]. Real-world systems also require solutions that balance complexity, cost, and deployability. Although research often proposes advanced techniques such as blockchain-based coordination or complex orchestration models [28,31], these are not always feasible in practice. The absence of intermediate-complexity reference implementations validated across more than one deployment context means organizations cannot rely on existing work to predict integration cost or system behavior, and simpler or hybrid approaches are sometimes preferred for their ease of integration and operational efficiency [54].

Table 3 summarizes the principal differences between academic and industrial orientations across each analytical dimension. The differences highlighted in Table 3 show that the gap between FL research and practice creates a self-reinforcing problem; As academic solutions become more refined in ideal and controlled environments, they often move further away from the messy realities of production systems, such as legacy infrastructure, unpredictable client availability, and the need for fault tolerance in pipelines. This gap is the deepest in lifecycle management. The heavy focus on training cause the hardest deployment challenges, such as onboarding, versioning, monitoring, governance, to remain understudied. Without shared metrics, benchmarks and best practices, practitioners are forced to solve the problems in isolation, without a shared foundation. Moreover, interoperability in academic works is reduced to a theoretical concern rather than a concrete engineering barrier. However, the industry needs co-design approaches. Researchers and practitioners should work together from the beginning to shape problems and solutions. Otherwise, well-designed solutions may fail in real settings. They can be strong in theory but too complex and costly to adopt in practice.

4.4 Open Challenges

The following challenges remain unresolved across all evidence sources and represent the most significant ongoing barriers to adopting FL in large-scale software-intensive systems.

- End-to-end lifecycle management: FLOps practices for coordinating training, deployment, and monitoring at scale.

Table 3. Key differences between academic research and industrial practice in FL

Dimension	Academic research	Industrial practice
Primary focus	Algorithm performance under controlled conditions	System reliability and operational continuity
Perspective	Machine learning-centric	Distributed systems-centric
Core problems	Non-IID data, aggregation, communication efficiency	Orchestration, legacy integration, lifecycle management
Level of abstraction	Conceptual, taxonomy-driven	Implementation-driven, context-specific
System view	Centralized or simplified topologies	Edge–cloud, multi-tier, decentralized
Lifecycle coverage	Predominantly training phase	Full lifecycle: onboarding → training → deployment → monitoring → governance
Evaluation basis	Benchmarks, accuracy on standard datasets	Real-world constraints, scalability, operational cost
Tooling	Limited; frameworks mentioned but rarely evaluated end-to-end	Central concern; platforms selected and integrated by deployment teams
Interoperability	Addressed conceptually	Encountered as a concrete engineering barrier
Maturity signal	Conceptual readiness	Deployment feasibility

- Interoperability and standardization: Reference architectures in heterogeneous environments that have been validated in real-world deployments.
- Real-world evaluation and benchmarking: Frameworks measuring not only accuracy, but also reliability, operational cost, and fault recovery in production.
- Heterogeneity: Adaptive coordination for managing device diversity, unstable connectivity, and dynamic participation.
- FL integration into legacy systems: Managing the complexity of fitting FL workflows into existing tools, processes, and abstractions.
- Scalability and fault-tolerance by design: Still treated as add-ons in most research, rather than ingrained from the start.

5 Discussion

The findings suggest that the main challenge in adopting FL lies not only in technical limitations, but in integrating it into existing environments. Legacy systems represent a significant and often overlooked barrier, as established data pipelines and centralized workflows are not designed for evolving and decentralized learning processes [55]. This introduces complexity in the implementation of FL, highlighting the need for practical solutions.

Moreover, unlike centralized systems, FL distributes control between multiple participants, complicating orchestration, monitoring, and lifecycle management. This makes system-level coordination a central design concern, requiring mechanisms for distributed control and consistent state management. Another insight is that in practice, FL extends beyond model training to managing long-running systems. Finally, Although advanced solutions can improve performance, they increase integration overhead, creating a trade-off between system sophistication and practical implementation.

6 Threats to Validity

Threats to validity are assessed following established guidelines for systematic and multivocal literature reviews [4,18,56].

Internal validity may be affected by selection bias from inclusion and exclusion criteria, which may remove relevant studies. Although the academic analysis includes 30 SLRs covering many primary studies, some work may still be missing. The analysis also involves subjective interpretation, especially for grey literature, which may introduce bias, as industry sources often highlight successful cases and lack transparency. To reduce this, we applied quality criteria, excluded promotional content, and cross-checked findings across sources [4].

External validity is limited by the selected studies and timeframe. Most industry sources come from large technology companies, which may limit generalizability. The review covers 2021–2026 and focuses on architecture and processes, excluding areas such as algorithms, security, and organizational issues.

The boundary between system architecture and algorithms is not always clear. In this study, architecture includes system components, deployment, orchestration, and lifecycle management, while algorithm details are excluded unless they affect system design. Grey literature varies in quality and relevance, so we differentiated direct and supporting evidence. A standard data form process was used to ensure consistency and mitigate bias [57].

7 Conclusions and Future Work

This study presented a multivocal literature review (MLR) to analyze FL from both academic and industrial perspectives by combining evidence from systematic literature reviews, grey literature, and selected primary studies. The results show that existing knowledge on FL is fragmented, with research and practice addressing similar challenges but at different levels of abstraction and system integration.

The research mainly focuses on isolated technical solutions, while practice deals with the complexity of integrating and operating FL systems in real environments. This difference highlights a clear gap between the potential of FL and its actual use in industry. In addition, knowledge transfer flows mainly from research to practice, with limited feedback from real-world deployments back to academic research. As a result, practical challenges and system-level requirements are not fully reflected in current research.

In future research, we aim to further explore the adoption and use of FL in industry by engaging in case study research with companies in the software-intensive systems industry.

Acknowledgment. This study was funded by Software Center.

We used Rayyan.ai for deduplication and initial screening of records. Large language model assistance was used for language refinement and structural editing.

Disclosure of Interests. The authors have no competing interests to declare that are relevant to the content of this article.

References

1. Ofczyński, Ł.: Federated learning in 2025: what you need to know (2025). https://shorturl.at/EVo9M
2. Brendan McMahan, H., Moore, E., Ramage, D., Hampson, S., y Arcas, B.A.: Communication-efficient learning of deep networks from decentralized data (2017)
3. Baduwal, M., Paudel, P., Chaudhary, V.: Federated learning: a survey of core challenges, current methods, and opportunities. Computers **15** (2026)
4. Garousi, V., Felderer, M., Mäntylä, M.V.: Guidelines for including grey literature and conducting multivocal literature reviews in software engineering. Inf. Softw. Technol. **106**, 101–121 (2019)
5. The Waymo Team. New insights for scaling laws in autonomous driving (2025). https://waymo.com/blog/2025/06/scaling-laws-in-autonomous-driving
6. Li, Q., et al.: A survey on federated learning systems: vision, hype and reality for data privacy and protection. IEEE Trans. Knowl. Data Eng. **35**(4), 3347–3366 (2023)
7. Durrant, A., Markovic, M., Matthews, D., May, D., Enright, J., Leontidis, G.: The role of cross-silo federated learning in facilitating data sharing in the agri-food sector. **193**, 106648 (2022)
8. InApp. Federated learning: The future of secure AI & data-driven business innovation (2026). https://shorturl.at/eApem
9. Amazon Science. Personalized federated learning for a better customer experience (2026). https://www.amazon.science/blog/personalized-federated-learning-for-a-better-customer-experience
10. Yan, M., Ng, C.S.: Scaling enterprise federated ai with flower and open cluster management (2026). https://www.redhat.com/en/blog/scaling-enterprise-federated-ai-with-flower-and-open-cluster-management

11. Capuccini, M.: Flops with scaleout's open-core platform (2024). https://www.youtube.com/watch?v=z8IHMr-Z1M8
12. Page, M.J., et al.: The Prisma 2020 statement: an updated guideline for reporting systematic reviews. BMJ **372**, n71 (2021)
13. Kitchenham, B.A., Pearl Brereton, O., Budgen, D., Turner, M., Bailey, J., Linkman, S.: Systematic literature reviews in software engineering: a systematic literature review. Inf. Softw. Technol. **51**, 7–15 (2009)
14. Carrera-Rivera, A., Ochoa, W., Larrinaga, F., Lasa, G.: How-to conduct a systematic literature review: a quick guide for computer science research. MethodsX **9**, 101895 (2022)
15. Qatar Computing Research Institute (QCRI) & Rayyan Team. Rayyan—intelligent systematic review tool. https://www.rayyan.ai/cite/
16. Higgins, J.P.T., et al.: Chapter V: overviews of reviews (2024). https://www.cochrane.org/authors/handbooks-and-manuals/handbook/current/chapter-v
17. Badri, M.: Replication Package - Online Material (2026). https://shorturl.at/ix5D1
18. Garousi, V., Rainer, A., Felderer, M., Mäntylä, M.V.: Introduction to the special issue on: grey literature and multivocal literature reviews (MLRs) in software engineering. **141** (2022)
19. Guendouzi, B.S., Ouchani, S., Assaad, H.E.L., Zaher, M.E.L.: A systematic review of federated learning: challenges, aggregation methods, and development tools. **220**, 103714 (2023)
20. Lo, S.K., Lu, Q., Paik, H.-Y., Zhu, L.: FLRA: a reference architecture for federated learning systems, pp. 83–98 (2021)
21. Lo, S.K., Lu, Q., Zhu, L., Paik, H.-Y., Xu, X., Wang, C.: Architectural patterns for the design of federated learning systems. J. Syst. Softw. **191**, 111357 (2022)
22. Mishra, S.K., Sahoo, S.K., Swain, C.K.: A systematic review on federated learning in edge-cloud continuum. SN Comput. Sci. **5**(887), 1–18 (2024)
23. Aljohani, A., Rana, O., Perera, C.: Self-adaptive federated learning in internet of things systems: a review. **57** (2025)
24. Smestad, C., Li, J.: A systematic literature review on client selection in federated learning (2023)
25. Mahdi, O.A., Pardede, E., Bevinakoppa, S., Ali, N.: Federated learning under concept drift: a systematic survey of foundations, innovations, and future research directions. Electronics **14** (2025)
26. Chung, W.-C., Lo, C.-A., Lin, Y.-H., Chen, Z.-H., Hung, C.-L.: Decentralized federated learning with non-IID data: challenges, trends, and future opportunities. **58**(8) (2026)
27. Qi, P., Chiaro, D., Guzzo, A., Ianni, M., Fortino, G., Piccialli, F.: Model aggregation techniques in federated learning: a comprehensive survey. Futur. Gener. Comput. Syst. **150**, 272–293 (2024)
28. Sana, T.Z.: Advancing federated learning: a systematic literature review of methods, challenges, and applications. IEEE Access **13**, 153817–153844 (2025)
29. da Silva, L.G.F., Sadok, D.F.H., Endo, P.T.: Resource optimizing federated learning for use with IoT: a systematic review. **175**, 92–108 (2023)
30. Shaheen, M., Farooq, M.S., Umer, T., Kim, B.-S.: Applications of federated learning; taxonomy, challenges, and research trends. Electronics **11**(4) (2022)
31. Hou, D., Zhang, J., Man, K.L., Ma, J., Peng, Z.: Architectures, applications and issues: a systematic literature review of blockchain-based federated learning (2021)
32. Kumar, S.: Why and when enterprises should consider federated learning: a comprehensive guide (2025). https://shorturl.at/rtJKs

33. Kumar, N.: Enable data sharing through federated learning: a policy approach for chief digital officers (2024). https://shorturl.at/JikRJ
34. Gao, D., et al.: FS-real: a real-world cross-device federated learning platform. Proc. VLDB Endow. **16**(12), 4046–4049 (2023)
35. He, S., et al.: Fedkit: enabling cross-platform federated learning for android and IOS. pp. 1–2 (2024)
36. Intel Corporation. Try federated learning with OpenFL (2023). https://shorturl.at/EaZ7p
37. Huedo, E., Moreno-Vozmediano, R., Montero, R.S., Llorente, I.M.: On-demand deployment of edge cloud infrastructures for federated learning. Softw. Pract. Exp. **55**, 1377–1388 (2025)
38. Safri, H., Kandi, M.M., Miloudi, Y., Bortolaso, C., Trystram, D., Desprez, F.: A federated learning framework for IoT: application to industry. **4**, 565–574 (2022)
39. Loconte, D., Ieva, S., Pinto, A., Loseto, G., Scioscia, F., Ruta, M.: Expanding the cloud-to-edge continuum to the IoT in serverless federated learning. Futur. Gener. Comput. Syst. **155**, 447–462 (2024)
40. European Data Protection Supervisor. Techdispatch #1/2025 – federated learning (2025). https://shorturl.at/0WtYe
41. Piest, J.P.S., Datema, W., Firdausy, D.R., Bastiaansen, H.: Developing and deploying federated learning models in data spaces, pp. 29–43 (2024)
42. Sugianto, N., Tjondronegoro, D., Sorwar, G.: Collaborative federated learning framework to minimize data transmission for ai-enabled video surveillance. Inf. Technol. People **38**(3), 1526–1550 (2025)
43. Zhang, H., Bosch, J., Olsson, H.H.: Real-time end-to-end federated learning: an automotive case study, pp. 459–468 (2021)
44. Tizzei, L.P., et al.: Open-source federated learning across multi-cloud environment (2025)
45. Agiollo, A., Bellavista, P., Mendula, M., Omicini, A.: ENEA-FL: energy-aware orchestration for serverless federated learning. Futur. Gener. Comput. Syst. **154**, 219–234 (2024)
46. Cheng, Q., Long, G.: Federated learning operations (flops): challenges, lifecycle and approaches, pp. 12–17 (2022)
47. Yamaguti, R., Paula, F.G., Ferreira, B.C.L.C., Branquinho, O.C., Cardieri, P.: Embedding federated learning in IoT governance: an extension to the TPM+ methodology, pp. 1–4 (2025)
48. Hertantyo, G.B., Sari, R.F.: Performance evaluation of federated learning on cloud computing and edge virtual machine, pp. 439–444 (2025)
49. Prigent, C., Keahey, K., Costan, A., Cudennec, L., Antoniu, G.: On the reproducibility challenges of federated learning, pp. 185–194 (2025)
50. Market.US. Federated ai learning market: Global industry trends, share, size, growth, opportunity and forecast 2025–2035 (2026). https://shorturl.at/wDnPT
51. NVIDIA Corporation. Federated learning user guide (2022). https://shorturl.at/iCVRu
52. Baduwal, M., Paudel, P., Chaudhary, V.: Federated learning: a survey of core challenges, current methods, and opportunities (2026)
53. Crosley, B.: Federated learning infrastructure: privacy-preserving enterprise AI (2026). https://shorturl.at/AyfcI
54. Penedo, C.B., Redondo, R.P.D., Vilas, A.F., Veiga, M.F., Pastoriza, F.T.: HLF-FSL. A decentralized federated split learning solution for IoT on hyperledger fabric (2025)

55. Bosch, J., Olsson, H.H.: Digital for real: a multicase study on the digital transformation of companies in the embedded systems domain. J. Softw. Evol. Process **33**, e2333 (2021)
56. Wohlin, C., Runeson, P., Höst, M., Ohlsson, M.C., Regnell, B., Wesslén, A.: Experimentation in Software Engineering. Springer, Cham (2012)
57. Braun, V., Clarke, V.: Using thematic analysis in psychology. Qual. Res. Psychol. **3**(2), 77–101 (2006)

A Systematic Assessment of Maturity Models for AI/ML-Based Software Development

Eda Okay[1,2](✉) and Özden Özcan-Top[1]

[1] Graduate School of Informatics, Middle East Technical University, 06800 Ankara, Turkey
{eda.okay,ozdenoz}@metu.edu.tr
[2] ASELSAN Inc., Ankara, Turkey

Abstract. Organizations developing AI/ML-based systems need to build and institutionalize a set of development capabilities to manage data, models, and deployment processes effectively. Maturity models provide structured approaches to assess and guide this capability development; however, existing models vary in how well they capture the distinctive characteristics of AI/ML-based development. Despite the growing number of such models, there is limited understanding of how they define maturity levels, structure capability dimensions, and align with AI lifecycle processes. To address this gap, we conducted a Multivocal Literature Review (MLR) to systematically identify both academic and practitioner-oriented maturity models relevant to AI/ML development. Ten models were evaluated against seven criteria: purpose and fitness for use, development method, depth of maturity level definition, coverage of capability dimensions, internal consistency, alignment with ISO/IEC 5338:2023 as the process reference model for AI systems, and validation evidence. The results reveal a consistent pattern of partial specification across the field. Models grounded in established process assessment frameworks performed more strongly across multiple criteria, while practitioner-oriented models consistently functioned as adoption roadmaps rather than rigorous assessment instruments. Most models show only implicit alignment with ISO/IEC 5338:2023, and only one addresses trustworthy AI dimensions such as bias, fairness, or explainability. These findings indicate a significant gap between the current state of AI/ML maturity models and the standards-aligned capability assessment organizations need, particularly given the regulatory requirements introduced by the EU AI Act.

Keywords: Artificial Intelligence · AI · Machine Learning · Maturity Model · Maturity Assessment

1 Introduction

Artificial Intelligence (AI) refers to systems that are designed to perceive their environment, process data, and support decision-making to achieve complex

C. Berger and V. Klös (Eds.): SEAA 2026, LNCS 16864, pp. 260–277, 2027.
https://doi.org/10.1007/978-3-032-36587-3_18

goals [1]. AI-based software projects differ from traditional software development in fundamental ways: they are data-dependent, involve iterative experimentation, and often produce uncertain or evolving outcomes, making them substantially harder to manage using conventional software engineering practices [2]. These characteristics are also apparent when machine learning (ML) components transition from experimental setups to production environments, where they need to interoperate with non-ML software and be continuously monitored, maintained, retrained, and governed over time as AI capabilities [3].

As AI increasingly supports business operations and drives competitive advantage [2], organizations require systematic ways to understand and improve their AI development capabilities. In the ML context, MLOps has become a practical approach to manage the ML lifecycle more effectively and increase successful deployment of ML-enabled systems [3]. Beyond this, maturity models provide structured mechanisms to assess current capabilities, define improvement levels, and identify gaps. By enabling systematic evaluation of organizational capabilities, they help manage the complexity and risks of AI-based software development and support continuous improvement [4]. Crosby's early work on the Quality Management Maturity Grid (QMMG) [5] laid the foundation for maturity models by linking organizational maturity to structured quality assurance and defect prevention.

Building on this, several maturity models were developed to improve software development capabilities. The Carnegie Mellon Software Engineering Institute (SEI) developed the Capability Maturity Model (CMM) to assess software process maturity and guide process improvement [6,7]. Its successor, the Capability Maturity Model Integration (CMMI), consolidated best practices from multiple models to support capability evaluation and improvement across domains [8]. ISO/IEC 15504 (SPICE) [9], originally designed to determine software process capability, was later withdrawn and replaced by the ISO/IEC 330xx series [10], which provides a more comprehensive framework for evaluating process capability and organizational maturity. These assessment frameworks are grounded in process reference models: just as ISO/IEC 12207 defines the lifecycle processes for software systems and serves as the process reference model underpinning ISO/IEC 330xx-based assessments in software engineering, ISO/IEC 5338:2023 [11] plays an analogous role for AI systems. Defining the lifecycle processes that serve as the reference point in the process against which AI-specific capability assessments should be conducted.

In AI-enabled software development, proposed maturity models typically extend established structures such as CMMI or the ISO/IEC 33xxx family to include AI-specific characteristics [12]. Studies show that organizations evolve from fragmented ML practices to more automated, standardized, and integrated pipelines [13,14]. Prior studies have examined AI/ML maturity models through systematic reviews. Sadiq et al. [15] conducted a systematic literature review of AI maturity models and found that reviewed models differ considerably in their objectives, design approaches, scope, and the dimensions used to assess maturity. Yet, they did not evaluate these models against a standardized AI lifecycle process reference. Lima et al. [16], Zarour et al. [17], and Eken et al. [3] similarly reviewed MLOps maturity models and practices, identifying variation in how models define maturity stages and capability dimensions, but neither study evaluated model rigor or alignment with lifecycle standards such as ISO/IEC 5338:2023.

Despite a growing body of work, three gaps remain unaddressed. First, existing reviews do not evaluate how rigorously maturity levels are defined specifically, whether models provide measurable attributes, observable activities, and structured assessment criteria. Second, the coverage and coherence of capability dimensions across maturity levels have not been systematically compared between academic and practitioner-oriented models. Third, no prior study has evaluated the extent to which existing AI/ML maturity models align with ISO/IEC 5338:2023, the international standard defining the process reference model for AI system development. These gaps raise important doubts about whether current maturity models are sufficiently grounded to support rigorous, standards-consistent capability assessment in AI-based development.

To address these challenges, this study systematically analyzes existing maturity models for AI-enabled software development projects. We used a Multivocal Literature Review (MLR) strategy to identify relevant models from both research and practice, covering peer-reviewed publications and practitioner-oriented grey literature. Prior MLR-based studies used systematic and grey literature reviews as a basis for proposing new maturity frameworks or conceptual frameworks for AI-enabled systems. For instance, John et al. [13] proposed a staged MLOps maturity model based on identified adoption activities. In a related vein, Lwakatare et al. [14] defined maturity levels for continuous delivery practices in ML development. Furthermore, Eken et al. [3] performed a systematic synthesis to derive a conceptual framework for MLOps, to characterize state-of-the-art practices and techniques, and to emphasize current practitioner challenges as well as directions for future research. Unlike these studies, our work does not propose a new model. Instead, it evaluates the characteristics of existing AI/ML maturity models against a defined set of assessment criteria with the aim of identifying where current models fall short.

Specifically, this study investigates: (1) the purpose and fitness for the use of existing models; (2) the methods used to derive them; (3) the level of detail in maturity level definitions; (4) the coverage of capability dimensions across maturity levels; (5) the internal consistency and coherence of maturity progressions; (6) the degree of alignment with ISO/IEC 5338:2023 lifecycle processes; and (7) the availability of validation evidence. Together, these criteria provide a structured basis for identifying where current models fall short and what a more rigorous, standards-aligned model would require.

The rest of the paper is structured as follows. Section 2 presents the MLR methodology and analysis framework. Section 3 presents the results, while Sects. 4, 5, and 6 provide discussion, validity threats, and conclusions, respectively.

2 Methodology

Given the limited peer-reviewed literature and the prominence of practitioner models, this study uses a multivocal literature review (MLR) to examine AI/ML maturity models across both white and grey literature. For analysis, the evaluation criteria were adapted from Rout et al. [18], Kneuper [19], and Ozcan-Top et al. [20] (completeness, clarity, and process maturity), ensuring consistency with established maturity-model assessment perspectives. Accordingly, the study addresses the following research questions:
RQ1: What are the key characteristics of existing AI/ML-based maturity models according to maturity model categories?

- **RQ1.1:** What is the purpose and fitness for use of the maturity models?
- **RQ1.2:** Which methods are used to develop the maturity models?
- **RQ1.3:** To what extent are the maturity levels defined in detail?
- **RQ1.4:** Do the models cover all dimensions mentioned within the maturity concept?
- **RQ1.5:** How logically coherent and non-overlapping are the maturity levels, practices, and indicators within the proposed AI/ML maturity models?
- **RQ1.6:** Do the models align with ISO/IEC 5338 processes, and to what extent?
- **RQ1.7:** How do AI/ML maturity models ensure objectivity and validity?

To conduct the MLR, the protocols presented by Garousi et al. [21] are applied; an overview is provided in Fig. 1.

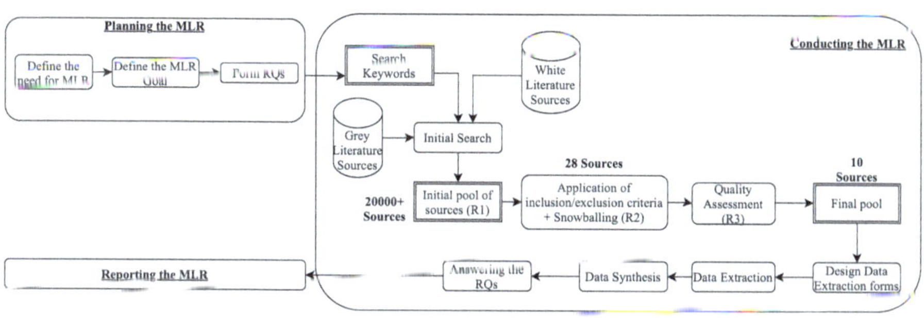

Fig. 1. Process for conducting the MLR

2.1 Planning the MLR

The inclusion of grey literature in this study was supported by the field's dynamic nature, as AI/ML maturity models continue to evolve through practice-oriented materials published by industry research groups and major companies. As these sources were produced by credible domain experts, they were considered a valuable complement to peer-reviewed literature.

The models were then classified according to seven criteria: purpose and fitness for use; development method; level of detail in maturity-level construction; coverage of capability dimensions; internal consistency; alignment with ISO/IEC 5338:2023; and objectivity through validation.

2.2 Conducting the MLR

Identification of Keywords and Searching for Literature: For white literature sources, IEEE Xplore, Google Scholar, and the ACM Digital Library were used to identify AI/ML maturity model frameworks. The search keywords used in these databases are summarized in Table 1. The search was conducted in three rounds. In the first round, the keyword combination was applied to the article metadata to retrieve an initial pool of potentially relevant studies. Given that the search terms necessarily include broad concepts such as "maturity" and "capability" to avoid missing relevant work, the initial result counts were large. The subsequent rounds are designed to progressively narrow the pool through title screening and snowballing. In the second round, article titles and snowballing were used to narrow the search. In the third round, articles were read in full based on the inclusion/exclusion criteria and quality assessment results. To identify grey literature sources (e.g., white papers, vendor documentation, reports), the Google search engine was used. We used flexible keyword combinations based on the search string and adapted to the industry's terminology (for example, "AI maturity model", "MLOps framework", and "capability assessment"). The searches were aimed at non-academic sources. The stopping rule for searching is bounded by effort, as proposed by Garousi et al. [21], in which the search is limited to the top 50 Google search engine hits. This boundary is justified in the context of this study for two reasons. First, AI/ML maturity models published as grey literature tend to be highly visible practitioner artifacts produced by major technology organizations, and these consistently appear within the top search results. Second, models appearing beyond this threshold were unlikely to meet the inclusion criteria, as they typically addressed broader digital transformation or domain-specific maturity rather than AI/ML software development specifically.

Table 1. The search string used in white literature search

Search Scope	(Artificial Intelligence OR AI OR Machine Learning OR ML) AND (Maturity OR Capability OR Assessment OR Improvement) AND (Model OR Methodology)

Application of Inclusion/Exclusion Criteria. Sources were included if they: (1) presented a fully developed AI/ML maturity model for software development; (2) explicitly proposed a maturity model rather than listing desirable characteristics; (3) were not domain-specific (e.g., healthcare, logistics, or digital transformation); and (4) were published in English. As presented in Table 2, the high number of records in Round 1 stems from the intentionally broad search terms. In the following rounds, progressively stricter criteria were applied.

Table 2. Search results across digital libraries

Library	R1	R2	R3
IEEE Xplore	864	5	2
ACM DL	2764	3	0
Google Scholar	17500	11	2
Snowballing	–	5	2
Google for Grey Literature	50	4	4
Total	**21178**	**28**	**10**

Quality Assessment of White and Grey Literature Sources. The 28 sources identified in Round 2 underwent quality assessment. White literature sources were evaluated using three questions (W-Q) from Host et al. [22], while grey literature sources were assessed using six relevant questions (G-Q) from Garousi et al. [21]; both question sets are shown in Table 3. Each question was scored as NA (not addressed), PA (partially addressed), or FA (fully addressed). White literature sources receiving an NA score on any question were excluded. After fully reading the Round 2 candidate sources and applying the assessment, six white literature sources with no NA score and four grey literature sources that predominantly received FA or PA ratings were retained, resulting in ten sources for the final analysis.

Table 3. Quality assessment questions

ID	Quality Assessment Query
W-Q1	Are the research questions and objectives clearly defined?
W-Q2	Is the model's data collection process clearly defined and sufficient?
W-Q3	Are the review procedures sufficient and credible?
G-Q1	Are the models and their analytical attributes adequately described?
G-Q2	Are the objectives and findings of the model clearly stated?
G-Q3	Are the data collection procedures presented with relevant justification?
G-Q4	Does the model include sufficient implications for practice?
G-Q5	Does the report give a realistic and credible impression?
G-Q6	Is the model suitable for its audience and well structured?

2.3 Data Extraction and Synthesizing

Each model was examined against the predefined criteria, and classifications were assigned based on explicitly stated model properties. Where documentation was insufficient, a conservative classification was applied rather than inferred from indirect claims. The first author conducted the initial analysis, the second author reviewed the decisions, and disagreements were resolved through discussion until consensus was reached.

Criterion 1: Purpose and Fitness for Use: Evaluates the clarity and intent of the model and its suitability for AI/ML maturity assessment. Studies were coded as "Ambiguous or unclear purpose" when the purpose statement was absent, vague, or not sufficiently specific to demonstrate fitness for AI/ML maturity assessment.

Criterion 2: Availability of the Development of Maturity Models: Assesses whether the source indicates how the maturity model was established. The sources were coded as *empirically*, *theoretically*, *expert consensus*, *existing frameworks/standards*, depending on the reported basis of establishment. When no sufficient explanation was provided, they were coded as *not documented*.

Criterion 3: Definition of Levels (in Detail): Assesses how thoroughly the maturity levels are specified in terms of purpose and outcomes, measurable attributes, and observable activities for assessment, as well as the availability of an assessment or rating scale. Depending on the level of specification, studies were coded as *full detail*, *high detail*, *moderate detail*, *low detail*, or *no clear definition*.

Criterion 4: Coverage of Capability Dimensions Across Maturity Levels: The inclusiveness of specific capability areas, design objectives, or process areas in terms of the field of interest was discovered at each maturity level. In this case, sources are coded as *covered across all levels*, *partially addressed at all levels*, *distinct by levels*, or *maturity levels that do not address capability dimensions*.

Criterion 5: Consistency and Coherence (Internal and Temporal): Examines the logical and sequential progression between levels, ensuring no overlaps or contradictions. The sources were coded as *highly consistent*, *moderately consistent*, *low consistency*, or *inconsistent*.

Criterion 6: Coverage, Scope, and Completeness Regarding ISO/IEC 5338: The extent to which life-cycle processes align with the technical and technical management processes outlined in ISO/IEC 5338 was identified. The sources were categorized as *fully aligned*, *highly aligned*, *implicitly life-cycle consistent*, *fragmented coverage*, or *no relation to ISO 5338*.

Criterion 7: Objectivity Indicators/Validation Mechanisms: To ensure the models' reliability and practical applicability, the availability of validation of the models was discussed. Accordingly, the sources were coded as *peer-reviewed validation*, *industry use case validation*, *validation through academic simulations*, *validation through expert reviews or stakeholder feedback*, *validation via multiple authoritative secondary sources*, or *No evidence*.

Following these criteria, the analysis enabled the categorization of data systematically into preset and emergent themes, thereby evaluating AI/ML maturity models in a structured manner [23]. The replication package, including the Round 2 quality assessment results and the Round-3 explanations of how each model addressed the evaluation criteria, is available online[1].

2.4 Reporting the MLR:

The analysis of AI/ML maturity models involved classifying them by relevant codes for each criterion, allowing for the identification of patterns, similarities, and differences across these models.

3 Descriptive Results

Ten maturity models from white and grey literature published between 2020 and 2025 were evaluated to answer the research questions. The sources reflect outputs from both academic and industrial communities, with conference papers and vendor reports being the most common publication types. The evaluated models are listed in Table 4, while publication years and the distribution of the source type are summarized in Fig. 2a and Fig. 2b, respectively.

[1] Replication Package.

Table 4. AI/ML Maturity Models

Model ID	Developers	Domain	Source Category	Level Names
M-1	John M.M., Olsson H.H., Bosch J. [13]	ML	Academic	**4 Levels:** Automated data collection; Automated model deployment; Semi-automated monitoring; Fully automated monitoring
M-2	John M.M., Gillblad D., Olsson H.H., Bosch J. [24]	ML	Academic	**5 Levels:** Ad hoc; DataOps; Manual MLOps; Automated MLOps; Kaizen
M-3	Akkiraju et al. [25]	ML	Academic	**5 Levels:** Initial; Repeatable; Defined; Managed; Optimizing
M-4	Lwakatare et al. [14]	ML	Academic	**5 Levels:** Manual data science-driven process; Standardized experimental-operational symmetry process; Automated ML workflow process; Integrated software and ML workflow processes; Fully integrated CD and ML workflow processes
M-5	Cho et al. [26]	AI	Academic	**6 Levels:** Incomplete; Performed; Managed; Established; Predictable; Optimizing
M-6	GigaOm [27]	ML	Grey	**5 Levels:** Level 0; Level 1; Level 2; Level 3; Level 4
M-7	Microsoft [28]	ML	Grey	**5 Levels:** No MLOps; DevOps but no MLOps; Automated training; Automated model deployment; Full MLOps automated operations
M-8	Google [29]	ML	Grey	**3 Levels:** Manual process; ML pipeline automation; CI/CD pipeline automation
M-9	AWS [30]	ML	Grey	**4 Levels:** Initial; Repeatable; Reliable; Scalable
M-10	Marquez et al. [31]	AI	Academic	**5 Levels:** Basic; Managed; Established; Predictable; Innovative

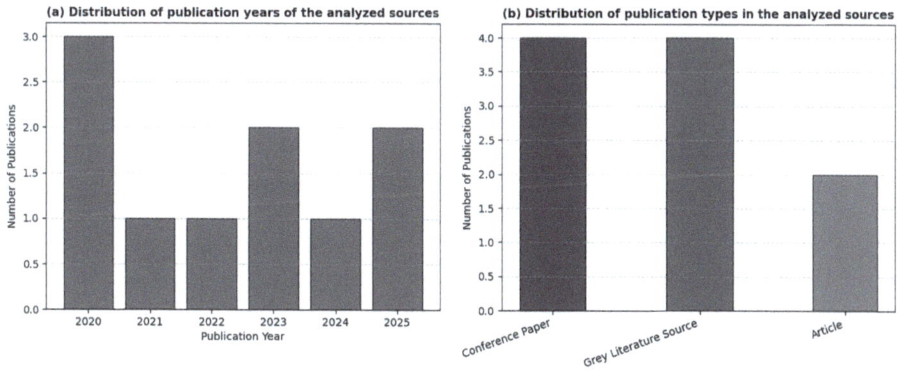

Fig. 2. Distribution of the analyzed sources: (a) publication years and (b) source types.

3.1 RQ1.1: Purpose and Fitness for Use

All ten models explicitly stated their intended purpose, confirming their fitness for AI/ML maturity assessment. However, their purposes differed meaningfully in orientation. Academic models such as M-1, M-2—later developed by largely the same authors with broader scope—and M-4 were proposed as roadmaps for progressing toward more mature, highly automated MLOps practices. Models derived from established frameworks, namely M-5 and M-10, were positioned as assessment instruments with structured evaluation criteria linked to process capability. The practitioner models of the major technology vendors (M-6, M-7, M-8, M-9) served a different function, acting primarily as adoption guides rather than rigorous assessment tools. This distinction in purpose orientation is consequential, as it directly influences the derivation approach, level of detail, and validation evidence associated with each model, which are examined in the following sections.

3.2 RQ1.2: Development Methods

The models were categorized into five groups based on their development methods. One model was developed theoretically, another through empirical studies, and a third from established frameworks. Three models were developed using different combinations of literature-based, empirical, expert consensus-based and standards-based approaches rather than a single method, while the remaining four were presented without a clearly specified basis.

Regarding models grounded in theoretical concepts, M-1 [13] was developed through an academic review of contemporary MLOps practices to serve as a basis for a maturity framework, with automation milestones as maturity levels.

Among empirically developed models, M-2 [24] was developed using findings from a multi-case study involving multiple companies.

For the models developed through existing frameworks, M-10 [31] was developed with reference to the ISO/IEC 33000 family for maturity assessment and ISO/IEC 5338:2023 for the relevant lifecycle processes.

In terms of combined development approaches, M-3 [25] combined expert consensus with existing standards by adopting ML lifecycle best practices and assessing them through a CMMI-based structure. Similarly, M-5 [26] developed the AI lifecycle processes through a literature review and expert opinion, and integrated them into a SPICE-based maturity assessment framework. M-4 [14] combined the literature-based identification of key activities with empirical evidence from case studies to construct its conceptual model.

Finally, four practitioner-oriented models, namely M-6 [27], M-7 [28], M-8 [29], and M-9 [30], did not clearly document how their maturity structures were derived.

3.3 RQ1.3: Maturity Level Definitions

All reviewed models defined maturity levels at either a high or moderate level of detail. None reached full detail, which would require each level to specify a clearly stated purpose and outcomes, measurable process attributes, observable activities, and a structured rating scale simultaneously.

High-level detail was observed in M-5 [26] and M-10 [31], both of which are built on ISO-based process assessment frameworks. These models linked maturity levels to measurable process attributes and observable activities within a process reference model. However, neither provided a fully structured rating scale for independent assessment, which is why they were classified as high rather than full detail.

The remaining eight models were classified as moderate detail. M-1 [13] and M-2 [24] were built around the conceptual dimensions of MLOps practices with substantial maturity levels. Similarly, M-3 [25] and M-4 [14] defined a clear purpose, since each maturity level has an individual purpose statement reflecting its capability intent while defining expected outcomes for each capability dimension at each level. However, neither formalized these as measurable practices nor structured assessment criteria. The practitioner-oriented models M-6 [27], M-7 [28], M-8 [29], and M-9 [30] followed the same pattern, defining expected outcomes at each level without linking them to measurable capability indicators. Organizations relying on these models for capability assessment are unlikely to obtain objective or repeatable results, as they lack the measurable attributes needed to support such evaluations.

3.4 RQ1.4: Coverage of Capability Dimensions

Considering the coverage of capability dimensions, the identified maturity models can be grouped into two categories based on how maturity levels are structured around these dimensions. Four models covered capability dimensions across all maturity levels, while six models linked their maturity levels to distinct capability dimensions.

Among the models that covered the capability dimensions in all maturity levels, M-2 [24] and M-3 [25] defined maturity as progression in recurring dimensions throughout the model. Although the capability dimensions differed, both models structured maturity as advancement along the same set of dimensions across levels. A similar pattern was observed in the practitioner-oriented models M-6 [27] and M-7 [28]. In M-6 [27], the recurring dimensions included strategy, architecture, modeling, processes, and governance, while M-7 [28] was structured around people, model creation, model release, and application integration.

In terms of models that address different capability dimensions at different maturity levels, M-1 [13] associates each level with a key activity in the evolution of the MLOps pipeline, from data collection to deployment and to increasingly automated monitoring. Similarly, M-4 [14] described a staged progression from manual ML development activities to fully integrated, automated continuous delivery and ML workflows. M-5 [26], drawing on SPICE, defined different base practices for relevant processes at each maturity level, including safety-related processes, as well as data collection and processing activities. M-8 [29] and M-9 [30] also defined different capability areas and process-oriented focus areas at successive MLOp maturity levels. Finally, M-10 [31] linked maturity levels to specific AI system processes, reflecting a staged approach to process improvement.

3.5 RQ1.5: Internal Consistency and Coherence

Among the maturity models, eight demonstrated a highly consistent structure, advancing through clearly defined and logically ordered levels. Two models showed moderate consistency, as their levels were mostly sequential, but there were minor overlaps or imprecise boundaries between stages

Models M-1 [13] and M-2 [24] structured their maturity levels as cumulative progressions from lower levels of automation toward more advanced orchestration. In both cases, each stage introduced qualitatively distinct capabilities, thereby reducing overlap between successive levels. Similarly, M-3 [25] followed a sequential and cumulative structure derived from CMM-based logic. M-4 [14] also presented a staged progression from manual ML development and testing practices to more automated, integrated, CI/CD-supported workflows. In M-5 [26], the maturity structure was likewise cumulative, with each level introducing additional process capability in a non-overlapping manner based on SPICE. The practitioner-oriented models M-7 [28], M-8 [29], and M-9 [30] also showed high consistency, as their maturity levels were logically ordered and described as progressive stages of MLOps capability development.

Moderate consistency was observed in M-6 [27] and M-10 [31]. In M-6 [27], although the capabilities followed a cumulative improvement logic, the boundaries between stages were not distinguished, particularly for the capabilities related to reproducibility, process standardization, governance, and scaling. In M-10 [31], the model did not provide a detailed account of how AI-specific particulars incorporated into ISO 5338:2023 were systematically mapped onto the maturity framework or the assessment methodology. The model's selection and level allocation logic was only partially transparent, since it included only those ISO/IEC 5338 processes considered fundamental throughout the AI system life cycle without defining clear selection criteria and did not systematically justify how processes were assigned to maturity levels.

3.6 RQ1.6: Alignment with ISO/IEC 5338

Regarding alignment with ISO/IEC 5338:2023, the majority of identified maturity models had conceptual similarities with it regarding operational integration and deployment preparedness; however, they did not directly refer to the processes in ISO/IEC 5338:2023, including its relevant activities or results. The M-10 [31] model showed the closest alignment with ISO/IEC 5338:2023. Specifically, the model selected 24 of the 33 processes defined in ISO/IEC 5338:2023. The selected subset spanned the major ISO/IEC 5338:2023 process classes, including one agreement process, five organizational project-enabling processes, seven technical management processes, and eleven technical processes. However, nine ISO/IEC 5338:2023 processes were not included in the model, so it covered only a subset of the incorporated processes and did not provide full process-by-process traceability of all activities and results. As a result, the model's alignment with the standard is fragmented.

3.7 RQ1.7: Validation and Objectivity

The validation evidence was unevenly distributed between the reviewed models. While five of the identified maturity models provided explicit descriptions of their validation procedures, the practitioner-oriented models provided less explicit evidence of validation.

Models M-1 [13], M-2 [24], M-4 [14], M-5 [26], and M-10 [31] were validated using industry use cases. M-1 [13] was validated in collaboration with three case companies, M-2 [24] was investigated through case studies involving firms developing software-intensive embedded systems, and M-4 [14] was substantiated by results from an industrial case as well as an analysis of ML applications designed for practitioners. M-5 [26] was applied to 13 real-world AI projects and was supported by a statistical evaluation, while M-10 [31] was evaluated through a case study in the automotive sector.

Among the reviewed models, M-3 [25], M-6 [27], M-7 [28], M-8 [29], and M-9 [30] did not clearly report evidence of validation or verification. These models described maturity structures or capability stages, but did not document formal evaluations through expert review, empirical testing, or practical verification. The evaluation can be summarized in Table 5.

4 Discussion

The MLRs by Lwakatare et al. [14] and John et al. [13] provide important reference points for interpreting the findings of the present study. Both studies used

Table 5. Evaluation of AI/ML maturity models

Model	Fit. Use	Dev.	Level Dtl.	Cap. Cov.	Cons.	ISO/IEC 5338 Rel.	Val.
M-1	EAP	T	Mod.	DBL	High	ILC	IUCV
M-2	EAP	E	Mod.	AAL	High	ILC	IUCV
M-3	EAP	EFS/EC	Mod.	AAL	High	ILC	NE
M-4	EAP	T/E	Mod.	DBL	High	ILC	IUCV
M-5	EAP	EFS/T/EC	High	DBL	High	ILC	IUCV
M-6	EAP	ND	Mod.	AAL	Mod.	ILC	NE
M-7	EAP	ND	Mod.	AAL	High	ILC	NE
M-8	EAP	ND	Mod.	DBL	High	ILC	NE
M-9	EAP	ND	Mod.	DBL	High	ILC	NE
M-10	EAP	EFS	High	DBL	Mod.	FC	IUCV

Abbreviations in alphafebetical order: Cap. Cov. = Capability Coverage; Cons. = Consistency; Dev. = Development; Fit. Use = Fitness for Use; Level Dtl. = Level Detail; Rel. = Relation; Val. = Validation; AAL = Across All Levels; DBL = Distinct by Levels; EAP = Explicit AI/ML Purpose; EC = Expert Consensus; EFS = Existing Frameworks/Standards; E = Empirical; FC = Fragmented Coverage; ILC = Implicitly Life-Cycle Consistent; IUCV = Industry Use-Case Validation; Mod. = Moderate; ND = Not Documented; NE = No Evidence; T = Theoretical

systematic and grey literature reviews to propose new maturity frameworks, whereas the present study redirected the analytical focus toward a systematic cross-model evaluation against defined assessment criteria. Although these existing MLR studies relate to the questions in this study, they do not explicitly formulate research questions to systematically evaluate the characteristics of the AI/ML maturity model between models. This limitation also distinguishes them from broader reviews. Lima et al. [16] and Zarour et al. [17] reviewed MLOps maturity models and likewise noted variation in model dimensions, practices, and maturity levels, but did not assess model rigor or compare model structures against explicit criteria. Sadiq et al. [15] proposed and classified characteristics and components of AI maturity models based on their research question, but did not evaluate them against lifecycle process standards. The present study addresses this gap by evaluating existing models against ISO/IEC 5338:2023 as a process reference, providing a more robust basis for identifying where current models fall short.

Examining the findings across the criteria reveals a consistent pattern. Models derived from established process assessment frameworks, specifically M-5 [26] and M-10 [31], performed more strongly across multiple dimensions simultaneously, achieving high detail in level definitions, industry validation, and the closest alignment with ISO/IEC 5338:2023. The grounding of a model in an existing process reference framework imposes structural discipline that naturally leads to more rigorous specifications. In contrast, the four practitioner-oriented models consistently underperformed in providing explicit derivation logic, measurable attributes, structured assessment criteria, and documented validation evidence, functioning more as adoption guides than formal assessment tools. These models can support initial orientation and broad improvement planning, but their lack of measurable attributes and structured criteria limits their use for a repeatable and objective capability assessment. The academically derived models occupied a middle ground, transparent in their development methods and validated through case studies, yet remaining at a moderate level of detail in their definitions.

Several structural reasons explain these gaps. Vendor models were developed primarily to support platform adoption, where a clear and accessible roadmap serves the purpose better than a rigorous assessment framework. As a result, formal validation and measurable criteria were not a priority in their development. Another contributing factor is that ISO/IEC 5338:2023, which plays the same role for AI systems that ISO/IEC 12207 plays for software engineering, was only recently published, leaving earlier model developers without a stable process reference to build upon. Another concern is the limited attention given to trustworthy AI. Among the models examined, only M-5 explicitly considers aspects such as bias, fairness, explainability, ethical issues, and safety assurance. This gap is critical because AI systems typically learn their behavior from data-driven training, where biases, gaps, or other shortcomings in the training data can be reflected in system behavior [26]. Consequently, maturity models that do not explicitly evaluate trustworthy AI capabilities may fail to identify risks related to fairness, reliability, and safety. As the EU AI Act introduces concrete requirements for organizations developing AI systems in high-risk contexts, this gap becomes increasingly difficult to overlook. Future maturity models would benefit from being anchored in ISO/IEC 5338:2023, offering level definitions that can support repeatable and objective assessments, provide validation evidence, and treat trustworthy AI dimensions as first-class assessable capability areas.

5 Validity Threats

In this study, we identified and classified the following threats to validity according to Ampatzoglou et al. [32], along with the precautionary measures taken:

The main threats to study selection validity concerned the construction of search terms, choice of databases and search engines, visibility of grey literature, and application of inclusion and exclusion criteria. Some relevant AI/ML maturity models may have been missed if they were not indexed in the chosen databases, not captured by the selected keywords, or fell outside the defined grey literature scope. To reduce these risks, we used explicit inclusion and exclusion criteria and systematic search strategies to maximize coverage within the defined scope.

For data validity, the main risk was whether the evaluation criteria fully capture key features of AI/ML maturity models. Although we applied the criteria consistently, four practitioner-oriented models (M-6-M-9) did not clearly document how their maturity structures were developed. Eight models (M-1-M-4) and (M-6-M-9) only partially specified measurable attributes or outputs, and two models (M-6) and (M-10) defined generally sequential maturity levels with minor overlaps or vague transitions. Finally, five models (M-3, M-6, M-7, M-8, and M-9) did not clearly describe validation or verification. To mitigate this risk, the evaluation depended on explicitly stated model properties, and any unclear instances were coded conservatively instead of being deduced from indirect or implied claims.

For research validity on the general design of the research, the interpretation of the findings, the replicability of the process, and the generalizability of the results, researcher bias may have affected the coding and interpretation when the models lacked sufficient detail for classification. To reduce this risk, predefined evaluation criteria were applied consistently across all models. The first author conducted the initial coding and the second author reviewed the results and suggested revisions when needed. Additionally, the conclusions apply only to the models identified and analyzed in this review and may not generalize to maturity models or application areas outside the examined scope. The results should therefore be interpreted as describing this specific body of literature rather than the field as a whole. Finally, the reliability of the findings depends on the comprehensiveness and repeatability of the search and coding process. Although the selected databases, search engines, and keyword combinations may not have captured all relevant studies, explicit inclusion and exclusion criteria and systematic search strategies were applied to maximize coverage within the defined scope.

6 Conclusion

This study systematically evaluated existing AI/ML maturity models against seven criteria: purpose and fitness for use, development methods, maturity level definitions, coverage of capability dimensions, internal consistency, alignment with ISO/IEC 5338:2023, and validation approaches. The findings reveal a consistent pattern of partial specification across the field. Most models do not align with ISO/IEC 5338:2023, maturity level definitions rarely provide measurable attributes needed for objective assessment, and validation evidence is absent in half of the reviewed models. One of the reviewed models addresses trustworthy AI dimensions in terms of bias, fairness, or explainability, which is a growing concern given the regulatory requirements of the EU AI Act. These findings indicate a significant gap between the current state of AI/ML maturity models and what organizations need for rigorous, standards-aligned capability assessments. Future work should focus on developing new models grounded in ISO/IEC 5338:2023 that incorporate trustworthy AI dimensions and empirically validate stronger existing models, such as M-5 and M-10, across different organizational contexts through case studies.

Acknowledgments. This research has partially been supported by funding from the Research Universities Support Program (ADEP), provided through Middle East Technical University (METU) under project ADEP-704-2024-11481 by the Council of Higher Education (YÖK) and by travel grant from ASELSAN Inc in Türkiye.

Disclosure of Interests. The authors have no competing interests to declare that are relevant to the content of this research.

References

1. Samoili, S., Lopez Cobo, M., Delipetrev, B., Martinez-Plumed, F., Gomez, E., De Prato, G.: AI watch: defining artificial intelligence 2.0: towards an operational definition and taxonomy for the AI landscape. Technical report, Publications Office of the European Union (2021). https://doi.org/10.2760/019901
2. Alsheibani, S., Cheung, Y., Messom, C.: Towards an artificial intelligence maturity model: From science fiction to business facts. In: PACIS 2019 Proceedings, p. 46 (2019). https://aisel.aisnet.org/pacis2019/46
3. Eken, B., Pallewatta, S., Tran, N., Tosun, A., Babar, M.A.: A multivocal review of MLOps practices, challenges and open issues. ACM Comput. Surv. **58**(2) (2025). https://doi.org/10.1145/3747346
4. Baškarada, S.: IQM-CMM: Information Quality Management Capability Maturity Model, 1 edn. Vieweg+Teubner Verlag, Wiesbaden (2009). https://doi.org/10.1007/978-3-8348-9634-6
5. Crosby, P.B.: Quality Is Free: The Art of Making Quality Certain. Signet, New York (1980)
6. Paulk, M.C., Chrissis, M.B., Weber, C.V.: Capability maturity model for software, version 1.1. Technical report CMU/SEI-93-TR-024, Software Engineering Institute, Carnegie Mellon University (1993)
7. Goncalves Filho, A.P., Waterson, P.: Maturity models and safety culture: a critical review. Saf. Sci. **105**, 192–211 (2018). https://doi.org/10.1016/j.ssci.2018.02.017
8. CMMI Institute: CMMI. https://cmmiinstitute.com/cmmi. Accessed 26 Dec 2024
9. International Organization for Standardization: ISO/IEC 15504-1:2004 Information Technology—Process Assessment—Part 1: Concepts and Vocabulary (2004). https://www.iso.org/standard/38932.html. Withdrawn standard. Accessed 11 Oct 2025
10. International Organization for Standardization: ISO/IEC 33000 Family. https://committee.iso.org/sites/jtc1sc7/home/projects/flagship-standards/isoiec-33000-family.html. ISO/IEC JTC 1/SC 7, Process assessment. Accessed 11 Oct 2025
11. International Organization for Standardization: ISO/IEC 5338:2023 Information technology—Artificial intelligence—AI system life cycle processes (2023)
12. van Hillegersberg, J.: The Need for a Maturity Model for Maturity Modeling. In: Bergener, K., Räckers, M., Stein, A. (eds) The Art of Structuring, pp. 145–151. Springer, Cham (2019). https://doi.org/10.1007/978-3-030-06234-7_14
13. John, M.M., Olsson, H.H., Bosch, J.: Towards MLOps: a framework and maturity model. In: 2021 47th Euromicro Conference on Software Engineering and Advanced Applications (SEAA), pp. 1–8 (2021). https://doi.org/10.1109/SEAA53835.2021.00050
14. Lwakatare, L.E., Crnkovic, I., Rånge, E., Bosch, J.: From a data science driven process to a continuous delivery process for machine learning systems. In: Morisio, M., Torchiano, M., Jedlitschka, A. (eds.) PROFES 2020. LNCS, vol. 12562, pp. 185–201. Springer, Cham (2020). https://doi.org/10.1007/978-3-030-64148-1_12
15. Sadiq, R.B., Safie, N., Abd Rahman, A.H., Goudarzi, S.: Artificial intelligence maturity model: a systematic literature review. PeerJ Comput. Sci. **7**, e661 (2021). https://doi.org/10.7717/peerj-cs.661
16. Lima, A., Monteiro, L., Furtado, A.P.: MLOps: practices, maturity models, roles, tools, and challenges-a systematic literature review. ICEIS **1**, 308–320 (2022)
17. Zarour, M., Alzabut, H., Al-Sarayreh, K.T.: MLOps best practices, challenges and maturity models: a systematic literature review. Inf. Softw. Technol. **183**, 107733 (2025)

18. Rout, T., Tuffley, A., Cahill, B.: CMMI evaluation capability maturity model integration mapping to ISO/IEC 15504-2:1998. Griffith University, Software Quality Institute (2000)
19. Kneuper, R.: CMMI: Capability Maturity Model Integration: A Process Improvement Approach. Rocky Nook (2008)
20. Ozcan-Top, O., Demirörs, O.: Assessment of agile maturity models: a multiple case study. In: Woronowicz, T., Rout, T., O'Connor, R.V., Dorling, A. (eds.) SPICE 2013. CCIS, vol. 349, pp. 130–141. Springer, Heidelberg (2013). https://doi.org/10.1007/978-3-642-38833-0_12
21. Garousi, V., Felderer, M., Mäntylä, M.V.: Guidelines for including grey literature and conducting multivocal literature reviews in software engineering. Inf. Softw. Technol. **106**, 101–121 (2019). https://doi.org/10.1016/j.infsof.2018.09.006
22. Host, M., Runeson, P.: Checklists for software engineering case study research. In: First International Symposium on Empirical Software Engineering and Measurement (ESEM 2007), pp. 479–481 (2007). https://doi.org/10.1109/ESEM.2007.46
23. Thomas, J., Harden, A.: Methods for the thematic synthesis of qualitative research in systematic reviews. BMC Med. Res. Methodol. **8**(1), 45 (2008). https://doi.org/10.1186/1471-2288-8-45
24. John, M.M., Gillblad, D., Olsson, H.H., Bosch, J.: Advancing MLOps from ad hoc to Kaizen. In: 2023 49th Euromicro Conference on Software Engineering and Advanced Applications (SEAA), pp. 94–101 (2023). https://doi.org/10.1109/SEAA60479.2023.00023
25. Akkiraju, R., et al.: Characterizing Machine Learning Processes: A Maturity Framework. In: Fahland, D., Ghidini, C., Becker, J., Dumas, M. (eds.) BPM 2020. LNCS, vol. 12168, pp. 17–31. Springer, Cham (2020). https://doi.org/10.1007/978-3-030-58666-9_2
26. Cho, S., Kim, I., Kim, J., Woo, H., Shin, W.: A maturity model for trustworthy AI software development. Appl. Sci. **13**(8), 4771 (2023). https://doi.org/10.3390/app13084771
27. McKnight, W.: Delivering on the vision of MLOps. GigaOm (2020). https://portal.gigaom.com/report/delivering-on-the-vision-of-mlops. Accessed 16 Aug 2025
28. Microsoft: MLOps maturity model (2025). https://learn.microsoft.com/en-us/azure/architecture/ai-ml/guide/mlops-maturity-model. Accessed 16 Aug 2025
29. Google Cloud: MLOps: Continuous delivery and automation pipelines in machine learning. Google Cloud Architecture Center (2024). https://docs.cloud.google.com/architecture/mlops-continuous-delivery-and-automation-pipelines-in-machine-learning. Accessed 16 Aug 2025
30. Kartakis, S., Porcelli, G.A., Schinas, G., Eigenbrode, S.: MLOps foundation roadmap for enterprises with amazon sagemaker. AWS Machine Learning Blog (2022). https://aws.amazon.com/blogs/machine-learning/mlops-foundation-roadmap-for-enterprises-with-amazon-sagemaker/. Accessed 16 Aug 2025
31. Márquez, R., Rodriguez, M., Verdugo, J., Romero, F.P., Piattini, M.: An artificial intelligence maturity assessment framework based on international standards. Eng. Appl. Artif. Intell. **159**, 111637 (2025). https://doi.org/10.1016/j.engappai.2025.111637
32. Ampatzoglou, A., Bibi, S., Avgeriou, P., Verbeek, M., Chatzigeorgiou, A.: Identifying, categorizing and mitigating threats to validity in software engineering secondary studies. Inf. Softw. Technol. **106**, 201–230 (2019). https://doi.org/10.1016/j.infsof.2018.10.006

How Generative AI is Used in Software Project Management: A Systematic Literature Review

Gabriele De Vito(✉), Filomena Ferrucci, and Luca Visentin

Software Engineering (SeSa) Lab, University of Salerno, Fisciano, SA, Italy
{gadevito,fferrucci,lvisentin}@unisa.it

Abstract. Generative AI (GenAI) is increasingly adopted in Software Project Management, yet its actual role and impact remain unclear. This paper presents a systematic literature review of 45 peer-reviewed studies (2017–2026) that examine the application of GenAI across the PMBOK knowledge areas and process groups, and its impact on effort, planning, and risk. The findings show a strong focus on "Planning" processes and text-intensive artifacts, with machine-learning proxy metrics rather than managerial ones being used to evaluate GenAI outputs instead of their impact on project-level dynamics. While reductions in effort and improvements in planning are consistently reported, two less visible patterns emerge. Artifacts generated by GenAI often appear plausible rather than accurate and require human validation to detect under-specification and bias. Adoption also brings with it new tool-related risks such as vendor dependency, prompt sensitivity, and hallucinations. Procurement and Stakeholder Management, along with Initiating and Closing processes, remain largely unexplored.

Keywords: GenAI · LLMs · Software Project Management · PMBOK · Systematic Literature Review

1 Introduction

Generative Artificial Intelligence (GenAI) is already reshaping how software is designed, developed, and maintained. Activities that were performed by humans—coding, testing, documenting, communicating—are now routinely supported, and sometimes partially delegated, to Large Language Models (LLMs) and GenAI-based assistants [4,9]. While these transformations primarily affect technical activities, they also extend to Software Project Management (SPM), influencing its practices and decision-making processes. However, the implications for SPM remain insufficiently understood.

While a large body of research has examined the impact of GenAI on developer productivity and code quality [14,15], its impact on the managerial layer has received far less attention, as highlighted by a recent systematic review of

C. Berger and V. Klös (Eds.): SEAA 2026, LNCS 16864, pp. 278–294, 2027.
https://doi.org/10.1007/978-3-032-36587-3_19

LLMs in software engineering, which identifies SPM as a comparatively underexplored area [8]. Recent industry reports indicate that a growing share of project managers use GenAI in a significant portion of their projects [18], and a recent grey literature review of practitioner sources documents its adoption for routine task automation, predictive analytics, communication, and agile practices [2].

Although project managers do not directly write code, they shape the environment in which software is developed. Their decisions affect risk, planning, and effort allocation–precisely the dimensions where GenAI is beginning to exert complex influences. For this reason, understanding how GenAI is currently used in SPM, and what effects have been observed in practice, is an important step toward rethinking the role of the project manager. However, while practitioner sources provide valuable insights into emerging adoption trends and concerns, academic evidence has not yet been systematically synthesized for the intersection of GenAI and SPM.

This paper addresses this gap through a systematic literature review (SLR) of peer-reviewed research on GenAI in SPM. From 1022 records retrieved from bibliographic databases, we selected and analyzed 45 primary studies. To the best of our knowledge, this is the first review to systematically synthesize peer-reviewed evidence on GenAI in SPM, complementing recent grey literature reviews focused on practitioner perspectives.

2 Related Work

This section reports on the few secondary studies that have recently examined the intersection of AI and Project Management.

Assalaarachchi et al. [2] conducted a grey literature review of 47 practitioner sources, identifying four application areas of GenAI in SPM (routine task automation, predictive analytics, communication, agile support) and three main concerns (Ethical and privacy, Data quality and accuracy including hallucinations, lack of emotional intelligence), along with upskilling needs for PMs. Their work captures the practitioner voice but not peer-reviewed empirical evidence.

Khalil et al. [10] presented an SLR on the broader landscape of AI in Project Management, synthesizing 27 studies through bibliometric and qualitative analysis. Their scope is dominated by construction and engineering, generative AI appears only as an emerging theme, and SPM is marginally represented.

Valdivia et al. [19] conducted a PRISMA-based SLR of 52 studies on Generative AI for software development in SMEs adopting the ISO/IEC 29110 Basic Profile, proposing an alignment framework between GenAI capabilities and standard requirements.

Finally, Hou et al. [8] conducted a comprehensive SLR on LLMs for Software Engineering (2017–2024). While their scope is substantially broader, their findings explicitly identify the application of LLMs in SPM as a less studied phenomenon.

These studies provide important context but leave a clear gap that motivates our review: no peer-reviewed SLR has systematically synthesized the evidence on GenAI in SPM with an explicit focus on where it is applied and how it affects project-level dynamics.

3 Research Method

This review was designed and conducted following the guidelines by Kitchenham et al. [12], updated with more recent methodological refinements [11], complemented by the PRISMA 2020 reporting guidelines [13]. This section details the research questions and how the method was instantiated to address them.

3.1 Research Questions

We defined the objective of this review using the Goal-Question-Metric (GQM) paradigm [5], by stating the research intent before deriving the operational questions. The study aims to analyze the scientific literature on GenAI in SPM for the purpose of characterizing its current applications and empirical effects on supported activities and project-level dynamics, from the perspective of software engineering researchers and practitioners in Agile or traditional projects.

To scope the review in a replicable manner, we adopted the PICOC criteria [12]. The *Population* consists of software projects and the project managers involved in them. The *Intervention* is the adoption of GenAI technologies, including LLMs, GenAI-based assistants, and emerging agentic systems. No specific *Comparison* is required, while the *Outcomes* of interest are the project management activities supported by GenAI and the reported impact on effort distribution, planning, and risks. Finally, the *Context* is SPM across different methodological approaches. Thus, two research questions guided the review:

- **RQ1.** In which software project management activities and processes is Generative AI currently being applied, and with what reported outcomes?
- **RQ2.** How does Generative AI adoption affect project-level dynamics in terms of effort, planning, and risk profiles?

RQ1 aims to map the landscape of current applications of GenAI across SPM activities and processes. RQ2 is motivated by the need to synthesize the reported effects of these applications on key project dimensions, focusing on effort, planning, and risks, which are central to achieving traditional time-cost-quality objectives.

3.2 Search Strategy

The search string was derived from the PICOC scope presented in Sect. 3.1 and organized along two conceptual blocks: one capturing the intervention (GenAI and LLMs) and one delimiting the context (software and project management).

The general form of the query is reported below:

Search String

("LLM" OR "large language model*" OR "GenAI" OR "generative AI" OR "generative artificial intelligence") AND ("project manag*" OR "software manag*")*

We retrieved studies from Scopus, ACM Digital Library, and IEEE Xplore, which are widely used in secondary studies in software engineering [12,16]. The query was adapted to each database's syntax and indexing conventions, using wildcards to capture morphological variants. The database-specific queries are reported at https://doi.org/10.5281/zenodo.19697872 for reproducibility.

3.3 Selection Strategy

The database search returned 1022 studies (430 from Scopus, 355 from IEEE Xplore, and 237 from ACM Digital Library), which we then evaluated against the inclusion and exclusion criteria reported in Table 1.

Table 1. Inclusion and exclusion criteria.

Inclusion criteria			Exclusion criteria		
ID	**Criterion**	**Decision rule**	**ID**	**Criterion**	**Decision rule**
I1	GenAI focus	Study must explicitly use or evaluate GenAI/LLMs	E1	Dev tools only	Code assistants without PM implications
I2	PM scope	Must address PM activities, processes, roles	E2	Non-PM focus	RE/testing without PM connection
I3	Software context	Software or IT projects	E3	Traditional AI	ANN, fuzzy logic, no GenAI
I4	Empirical or Conceptual	Empirical or conceptual papers with evidence	E4	Non-software	Construction, manufacturing, healthcare
I5	Timeframe	Published 2017–2026	E5	No full text	Abstract only; paywalled
I6	Full text	Full paper available	E6	Duplicates	Keep most complete version
I7	Language	English			
I8	Publication type	Journal or conference paper	E7	Out of scope	Wrong time/language/type

Studies meeting one of the exclusion criteria or failing one inclusion criterion were discarded. As a result, 68 candidate studies remained (about 6.5% of the initial search). Backward snowballing, following Wohlin's guidelines [22], identified 6 additional papers, yielding a total of 74 for the quality assessment (Sect. 3.4).

This screening process was conducted by the first and third authors of this paper. In the event of disagreement, the first and third authors discussed it and attempted to reach an agreement, with the second author serving as arbiter when consensus could not be reached. The reliability of the selection process was supported by inter-rater agreement, measured using Cohen's κ (0.78), which exceeded the 0.70 threshold suggested in the literature. The complete selection flow is summarized in the PRISMA 2020 flow diagram in Fig. 1.

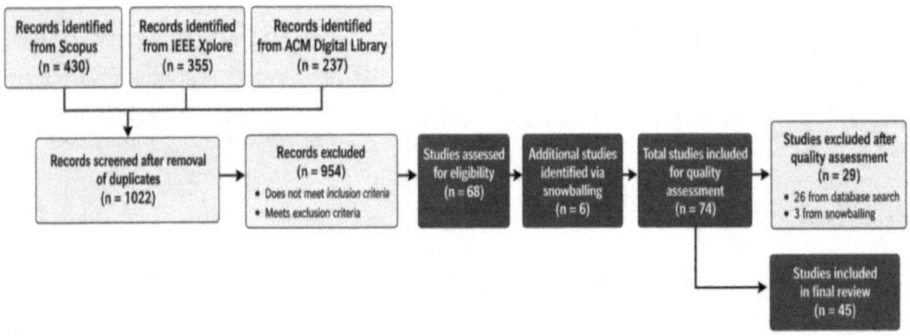

Fig. 1. PRISMA 2020 flow diagram of the study selection process.

3.4 Quality Assessment

After selecting the studies, we assessed their quality using a structured checklist (shown in Table 2). The checklist comprises ten criteria, covering both methodological rigor and relevance to the research questions.

Table 2. Quality assessment criteria.

ID	Criterion
Q1	Are the research aims clearly stated?
Q2	Is the study context adequately described?
Q3	Is the research design appropriate?
Q4	Is the data collection method clearly described?
Q5	Is the sample size or selection justified?
Q6	Are the analysis methods appropriate?
Q7	Are the findings clearly stated?
Q8	Are the limitations discussed?
Q9	Is the study relevant to RQ1?
Q10	Is the study relevant to RQ2?

There are three levels of scoring for each criterion: 0 (not satisfied), 0.5 (partially satisfied), and 1 (fully satisfied), yielding a maximum score of 10. We only added a study to the final corpus if it met two requirements. First, the total score had to be greater than or equal to 6 out of 10. This threshold was chosen to balance methodological rigor with the need to retain a sufficient body of evidence in an emerging research area, and it is consistent with values commonly adopted in software engineering SLRs [1]. Second, one of the two relevance criteria (Q9 or Q10) had to be fully met. This condition made sure that every study that was kept gave strong evidence for at least one of the research questions.

The assessment was performed independently by the first and third authors. Scores were compared after completion, and discrepancies resolved through discussion ($\kappa = 0.77$). This procedure excluded 26 studies from the database search and 3 from the snowballing round. The final corpus totaled 45 studies (Fig. 1).

3.5 Data Extraction

To support a systematic and reproducible synthesis, a structured data extraction form was designed prior to the extraction phase. The form is organized into five thematic codebooks. The first two codebooks capture study metadata (i.e., authors, year, title, venue, type, DOI, abstract) and context (i.e., study type, domain, PM methodology, project size, industry), providing the information needed to characterize the corpus in terms of publication venue, methodological design, and setting.

The third codebook documents the technological dimension of the intervention by recording the GenAI tools, models, and usage patterns reported in each study.

The last two codebooks are directly aligned with the research questions: one captures the project management activities supported by GenAI for RQ1 (i.e., PM knowledge areas, process groups, and PM processes, benefits, challenges), and the other captures the reported effects on effort, planning, and risks for RQ2. The complete list of codebooks is available at https://doi.org/10.5281/zenodo.19697872.

We conducted a preliminary extraction on 10 randomly selected sources to verify field clarity and coding consistency. Minor refinements were applied after the pilot, mainly on the controlled vocabularies used for categorical fields. The full extraction was then performed independently by the first and third authors, and the results were cross-checked to ensure consistency. Disagreements were resolved through discussion, consulting the second author when needed.

3.6 Data Synthesis

A meta-analysis was not feasible due to significant variability in design, context, and reported metrics across the selected studies. We therefore synthesized the extracted data qualitatively, following the thematic synthesis guidelines of Cruzes and Dybå [6]. In particular, for RQ1, we classified the PM activities supported by GenAI using the ten PMBOK knowledge areas as a reference frame [17]. Within each area, we grouped the reported benefits and challenges using inductive coding, allowing recurrent themes to emerge from the data. The result is an evidence map that summarizes, for each knowledge area, which activities are supported and how consistently they are reported across studies. With regard to RQ2, we organized the evidence along two dimensions already captured in the extraction form: the *direction* of the reported impact (positive, negative, mixed, paradoxical, or no change) and the *level* at which it was observed (individual, team, or project). This allowed us to identify where the literature converges, where it diverges, and where paradoxical effects are reported. Throughout the synthesis every reported finding is traceable to the studies that support it.

3.7 Threats to Validity

We discuss threats to validity following the taxonomy of Wohlin et al. [21], adapted to secondary studies.

Construct validity concerns the completeness of the search process. To mitigate the risk of missing relevant studies, we based the search string on PICOC and complemented database searches with snowballing [22]. Internal validity relates to the reliability of the review process. To reduce selection and extraction bias, all phases were conducted by two independent reviewers, with disagreements resolved through discussion or a third reviewer when needed. The extraction form was piloted and a sample of studies was double-checked for consistency. External validity may be limited by the possibility of omitting pertinent studies. To address this concern, the search process prioritized the use of established and reputable academic databases. Finally, conclusion validity is affected by the heterogeneity of the included studies, which prevented meta-analysis. To address this threat, we used a structured narrative synthesis with explicit quality tracking, ensuring full traceability of claims back to individual studies.

4 Results

This section reports the results of the SLR. Step-by-step results of the entire search process, including selection process, quality assessment, and data collection re- sults, can be found at https://doi.org/10.5281/zenodo.19697872.

4.1 Corpus Overview

Before addressing the RQs, we overview the 45 primary studies retained in the review, by characterizing the corpus along two dimensions: the publication and methodological profile of the studies, and the technological profile of the GenAI solutions investigated. Figure 2 summarizes the main distributions, while the per-study mapping is available at https://doi.org/10.5281/zenodo.19697872.

Although the search window covered 2017–2026 – chosen to include potential transformer-based precursors following Vaswani et al. [20] – no study prior to 2023 met the criteria, confirming the recent emergence of GenAI in SPM. The corpus shows a sharp growth between 2023 and 2025 (36 studies), mainly driven by conference publications (25 studies). The research is geographically

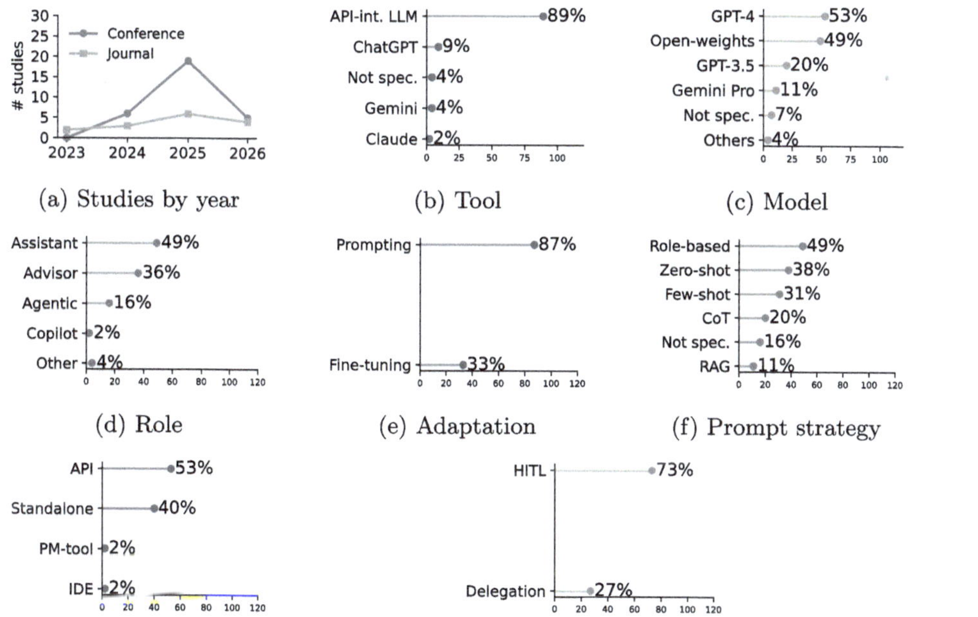

(a) Studies by year (b) Tool (c) Model

(d) Role (e) Adaptation (f) Prompt strategy

(g) Integration (h) Usage paradigm

Fig. 2. Corpus overview (N=45). (a) Distribution of primary studies by type and year; (b–h) distribution of the GenAI solutions across the main technological and usage dimensions.

distributed, encompassing 25 countries, with the United States (11), Italy (5), and India and Australia (4 each) identified as the most significant contributors.

In terms of research design, empirical studies dominate the corpus: 31 studies (69%) report experiments, 9 (20%) case studies, 10 (22%) mixed-methods designs, 7 (16%) surveys, and 4 (9%) conceptual contributions[1]. Most studies focus on software development (36, 80%) or general IT projects (8, 18%), while project size is rarely reported (unspecified in 34 studies, 77%).

With regards to the GenAI solutions, OpenAI models and programmatic access to LLMs through APIs are the predominant technologies. In 53% of the studies (24) GPT-4 was used, and open-weight families like LLaMA were used in 49% of the corpus (22) (see Footnote 1). GenAI is frequently conceived of as an Assistant, but more than 15% of the corpus is made up of agentic applications, which is in line with the growing interest in agentic systems. This aspect is confirmed by the fact that 73% of studies (33) adopt a human-in-the loop paradigm, while only 27% (12) explore forms of delegation to GenAI. In terms of model adaptation, it primarily occurs through prompting (87%), with fine-tuning playing a complementary role (33%); role-based prompting is the most

[1] Some studies contribute to multiple categories; therefore, percentages may exceed 100%.

common strategy (49%), followed by zero-shot (38%) and few-shot (31%) (see Footnote 1). Another interesting thing is that integration with PM tools is still very basic (2%), and most implementations are either API-based or stand-alone.

4.2 RQ$_1$: In Which SPM Activities and Processes is GenAI Currently Being Applied, and with What Reported Outcomes?

The following sections describe the RQ1 results in terms of *where* GenAI has been used and *what* it has been used for in SPM, illustrating the reported outcomes.

Where GenAI is Applied. To characterize the scope of GenAI adoption in SPM, we examined the studies focusing on the PMBOK knowledge areas addressed, the process groups covered, and the methodological context.

Almost half of the studies (49%) are situated in Agile contexts – which is consistent with the dominance of iterative approaches in modern software development –, a further 18% focus on traditional project management, and the remaining 33% is not specific.

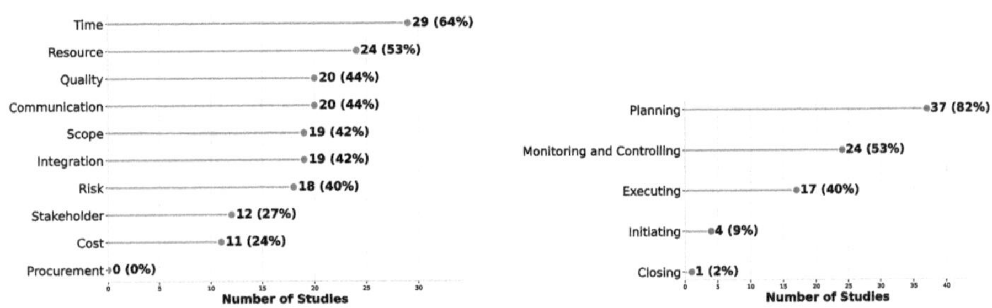

(a) Knowledge areas (b) Process groups

Fig. 3. Distribution of primary studies across PMBOK knowledge areas (a) and process groups (b).

In terms of knowledge areas (see Fig. 3a), *Time* management emerges as the most frequently addressed area (64%), followed by *Resource* (53%), *Quality* (44%), and *Communication* (44%). *Scope* (42%), *Integration* (42%), and *Risk* (40%) are also well represented (see Footnote 1). At the opposite end, *Cost* and *Stakeholder* management are covered by only 24–27% of the studies each, and no primary study addresses *Procurement*. This distribution reveals that research on GenAI in SPM has so far privileged operational and delivery-oriented areas, while strategic and contractual dimensions remain largely unexplored.

The distribution across PMBOK process groups (Fig. 3b) reveals an even sharper imbalance. *Planning* is by far the most studied group, covered by 82% of the primary studies, while *Monitoring and Controlling*, and *Executing* are addressed by roughly 40–53% of the studies (see Footnote 1). With only one primary study ([SLR1]) reporting GenAI support for *Closing*, and just four studies (9%, [SLR9, 15, 16, 29]) addressing *Initiating*, both process groups remain largely uncovered. This pattern indicates that both the initial and final stages of the project lifecycle (Initiating and Closing) are still largely ignored, while the current literature has focused on Planning, where text-intensive artifacts like requirements, user stories, and estimates are more amenable to generative support.

What GenAI Does. The process-level view (see Fig. 4) reinforces and refines the findings of Sect. 4.2 (see Footnote 1).

Within the Planning group, two processes stand out. *Collect Requirements* (16 studies, 36%) is the single most studied process, which is unsurprising, given that requirements elicitation produces and consumes text, and is subject to iterative refinement—three conditions that match the strengths of LLMs almost perfectly [8]. Close behind is *Estimate Activity Durations* (15 studies, 33%), particularly relevant from a managerial standpoint, since the estimated effort feeds directly into schedule development, cost estimation, and resource planning [17]. A secondary cluster of planning processes, which covers scope definition and decomposition, schedule construction, resource estimation, and qualitative risk analysis, accounts for 18–24% of studies each. In this cluster, GenAI is primarily used to generate, decompose, or enumerate planning artifacts.

A clear asymmetry emerges within the Planning group. Planning processes can be divided into those that produce artifacts (e.g., schedules, estimates, risk registers) and those that define how these artifacts are produced and managed (e.g., *Plan Schedule Management*, *Plan Cost Management*, *Plan Risk Management*, *Plan Stakeholder Engagement*). The evidence focuses almost entirely on the former: management-plan processes are rarely addressed, with at most two studies each and several not covered at all. In practice, GenAI is used to generate planning artifacts, but not to determine the methods and policies that govern them. This distinction, not visible at the knowledge-area level, highlights a key limitation of current adoption: operational tasks are delegated, while methodological and governance decisions remain human-driven.

Outside Planning, the studies concentrate on just two processes: *Manage Communications* (14 studies, 31%) and *Control Quality* (13 studies, 29%). Each process encompasses nearly all the coverage of its knowledge area (Communication and Quality, respectively), while the corresponding planning processes (i.e., *Plan Communications Management* and *Plan Quality Management*) remain marginal. The same pattern observed within Planning—artifact production rather than methodology design— extends to the other process groups.

As for the Initiating group *Develop Project Charter* ([SLR15, 16, 29]) and *Identify Stakeholders* ([SLR9, 15, 29]) appear in only three studies each (7%), again limited to artifact drafting. Coverage is even thinner at the end of the lifecycle, where there is only one study ([SLR1]) that covers *Close Project or Phase*, and none that addresses the three *Procurement Management* processes. In both cases, the underlying activity is less textual and more contractual, institutional, or retrospective. These are the kinds of tasks that rely heavily on organizational process assets and contractual documentation [17], which typically require retrieval-augmented or grounded approaches to be effectively supported by GenAI [8]. None of the analyzed studies, however, report such integrations.

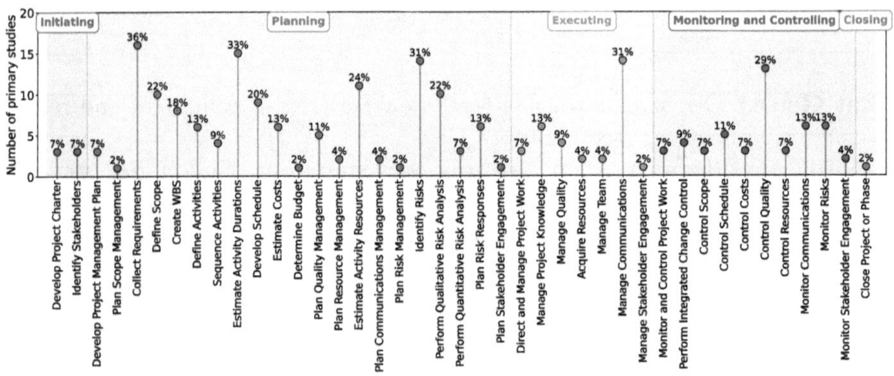

Fig. 4. Distribution of primary studies across PMBOK processes.

Reported Outcomes. The third dimension of RQ1 concerns outcomes reported in studies when applying GenAI to SPM activities. Figures 5a and 5b summarize the resulting clusters, organized into benefit and challenges. The most common benefit is increased *efficiency and productivity*, reported in more than 65% of the studies and often quantified. Findings indicate reductions in requirements management costs by 28% [SLR25], software development effort by 50% [SLR35], functional size measurement time by 53–88% [SLR38] [7], and agile lead times by 35–45% [SLR39]. A second noticeable cluster is the *automation of routine tasks*, particularly documentation, reporting, communication, and ticket triage. Improvements in *estimation accuracy and consistency* are also widely reported, with several studies showing measurable reductions of MAE/RMSE in story-point and effort estimation tasks [SLR28, 42, 44]. Less mature but recurrent are clusters related to *artifact quality*, *decision support*, *risk management*, *communication and knowledge sharing*, and the framing of GenAI as *human augmentation* rather than a replacement of human expertise.

As for the challenge clusters *hallucinations and factual inaccuracy* are by far the most frequently cited concern (in over 40% of the studies) and are often coupled with the related theme of *prompt sensitivity*, where output quality depends heavily on prompt design and shows substantial run-to-run variability. *Generalizability* concerns are equally widespread, reflecting the difficulty of transferring results across projects, datasets, and model versions. *Limited contextual understanding* is also pervasive, particularly in tasks requiring organization-specific knowledge or industry standards. From a governance perspective, the literature highlights persistent issues of *privacy and security*, *interpretability*, and *bias and ethics*. Operationally, *cost and scalability* emerge as recurring obstacles, while the recognition that *human oversight remains necessary* is explicit in several of the studies. Finally, two distinctively human-centered clusters surface: the *lack of human qualities* such as emotional intelligence, intuition, and adaptive leadership, and the risk of over-reliance when GenAI is used uncritically.

A degree of asymmetry emerges from the results: benefits are mainly efficiency-oriented and quantitatively measured (e.g., reductions in time, cost, and error), while challenges are mostly qualitative and harder to quantify, including hallucinations, prompt brittleness, limited interpretability, ethical concerns, and the absence of human judgment and emotional intelligence. This pattern may, at least in part, reflect structural features of the literature, which more often reports what GenAI accelerates than its potential longer-term trade-offs.

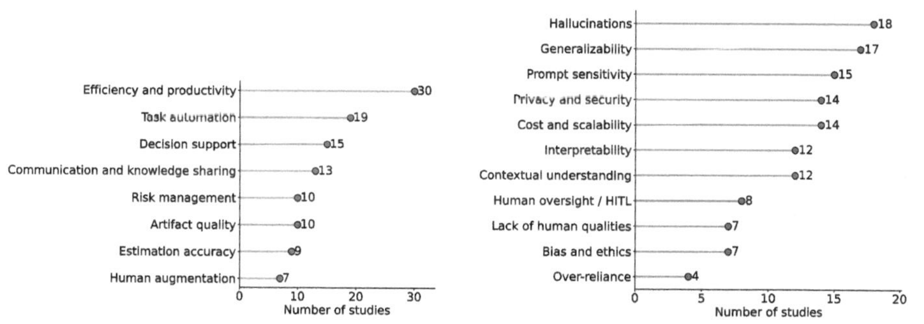

(a) Reported benefits. (b) Reported challenges.

Fig. 5. Distribution of studies across reported benefits (a) and challenges (b).

4.3 RQ$_2$: How Does Generative AI Adoption Affect Project-Level Dynamics in Terms of Effort, Planning, and Risk Profiles?

To address RQ2, we consider the subset of 39 primary studies relevant to this research question (i.e., those with Q10 = 1 in the quality assessment). We analyze the reported effects of GenAI adoption along three dimensions: effort, planning, and risk. Figure 6 summarizes both the coverage of these dimensions in the selected studies and the distribution of the reported impact directions.

Impact on Effort. We observe a clear imbalance between delivery and PM effort. Only 31% of the studies report evidence on the former, compared to 67% on the latter, suggesting that the literature has focused more on how GenAI reshapes managerial work than on how it redistributes development effort across teams. Among the studies reporting on delivery effort, the direction is predominantly positive: 9 studies report reductions in coding, documentation, or rework time [SLR3–5, 19, 22, 26, 35, 39, 43]. For example, [SLR5] reports an 80% reduction in rework cost, and [SLR22] a drop in document review time from 35 min to approximately one minute. However, this trend is not uniform. One study ([SLR20]) reports mixed effects depending on documentation style, while others identify *paradoxical* patterns [SLR23, 25], where reduced human effort is partly offset by increased verification or operational overhead.

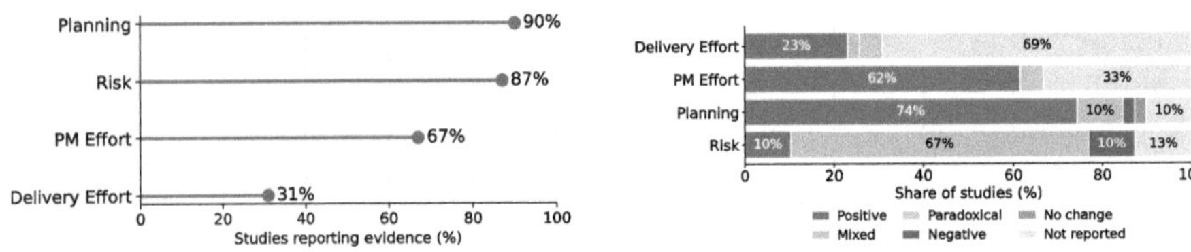

(a) Coverage: percentage of studies reporting evidence on each dimension.

(b) Impact direction: distribution of reported effects per dimension.

Fig. 6. Evidence on the project-level impact of GenAI adoption across the four RQ2 sub-dimensions: delivery effort, PM effort, planning, and risk (n = 39).

A comparable yet more uniform trend manifests in PM efforts. Twenty-four of the 26 studies that reported evidence showed reductions, mainly in documentation-intensive tasks, such as project planning, backlog managing, and compliance activities [SLR4, 9–11, 15–19, 26, 38, 40]. Reported savings are substantial, ranging from a 43% reduction in misassigned role hours ([SLR12]) to a 60–80% reduction in manual measurement time ([SLR38]). However, a small number of studies report paradoxical effects [SLR14, 24], where gains in automation are offset by higher operational or environmental costs. Finally, the level at which effort is affected further reflects this managerial emphasis: 54% of the studies report project-level effects, 33% team-level effects, and 23% individual-level effects (with some studies covering multiple levels).

Impact on Planning. Planning is among the most frequently reported dimensions (90% of studies), and the overall direction of the impact is mainly positive: 29 studies (74%) report improvements, compared to 4 mixed (10%), 1 negative (3%, [SLR42]), 1 neutral (3%, [SLR22]), while 4 do not report any impact.

The reported improvements can be categorized into three recurring themes. First, the accuracy of planning inputs, such as story point estimation and functional size measurement, is often reported to improve, in several cases with quantitative evidence (e.g., MAE reductions of 34–57% within-project in [SLR44]) [SLR18, 28,30,36,38,41,44]. Second, planning artifacts (e.g., WBS, backlogs, and project plans) can be generated more quickly and with greater completeness [SLR9–11, 16, 32, 35]. Third, recent agentic approaches enable more adaptive re-planning based on real-time signals of risk and progress [SLR3, 33, 39].

The mixed and negative outcomes, however, show important limitations. For example, [SLR15] reports that GPT-4-generated plans have less detail than the ones authored by humans. Furthermore, [SLR42] shows a systematic anchoring bias, indicating that prompt constraints influence effort estimates. Other studies indicate limited or context-specific effects [SLR24, 29] where GenAI generates plausible planning artifacts that may lack accuracy or completeness.

These results suggest that the positive evidence regarding planning should be approached with caution: although GenAI can speed up and organize planning processes, it does not consistently ensure reliable or comprehensive outputs.

Impact on Risk. Risk is the most frequently reported dimension, appearing in 87% of the studies. A dominant pattern, present in 26 studies (67%), is that GenAI adoption simultaneously mitigates existing risks while introducing new ones. This dual character emerges as one of the most consistent findings of RQ2.

On the mitigation side, GenAI is reported to strengthen traditional project risk management by supporting risk identification, analysis, and risk-informed prioritization [SLR3, 5, 10, 15, 26, 30, 33]. Several studies also highlight improvements in documentation quality, traceability, and compliance, which contribute to reducing latent risks [SLR4, 17, 25, 39].

On the introduction side, the literature converges around a small set of recurring risk categories. The most frequently reported are hallucinations and factual inaccuracies [SLR9, 10, 16, 22, 24, 29, 33, 35, 38, 39, 43], privacy and confidentiality concerns, including vendor dependency [SLR14, 16, 18, 35, 37, 40], prompt sensitivity and non-determinism [SLR19, 24, 29, 38, 42], and overreliance coupled with accountability gaps [SLR1, 15, 16, 24, 25, 35, 43].

Taken together, these risks differ qualitatively from those typically addressed in traditional PMBOK-aligned frameworks, which are largely structured around project-specific uncertainties rather than properties of the tools themselves. All this suggests the emergence of a tool-induced risk category as a distinct analytical construct.

Evidence Characterization. The above-mentioned findings vary in terms of evidence type, temporal horizon, and metrics. Across the 39 studies, 41% report quantitative evidence, 44% mixed evidence, and 15% qualitative evidence. Overall, the empirical base is moderately mature, with most studies providing measurable rather than purely anecdotal findings. The project's temporal scope is largely underreported: 62% of studies do not specify a timeframe, 31% focus on short-term effects (within a sprint), and only 8% on long-term effects. Medium-term effects (1–3 months) are not reported at all. This limits the interpretation of findings such as paradoxical effort patterns and governance risks, which may vary over time. The literature shows a strong bias toward machine learning evaluation metrics over PM ones. Most studies use accuracy-oriented measures (e.g., precision, recall, F1-score, MAE) to evaluate GenAI outputs such as user stories, estimates, or artifacts [SLR5, 12, 14, 18, 19, 24, 28, 30, 36–38, 41, 43, 44]. In contrast, PM metrics are rare and fragmented. Schedule and budget variance, lead time, and velocity appear only in a few studies [SLR26, 39], while defect density is reported in [SLR20, 39]. Operational metrics (latency, cost, energy, throughput) are emerging but still limited [SLR5, 14, 17, 24, 25, 33, 35, 38, 43], as are humancentered measures (trust and satisfaction) [SLR8, 16, 19, 23, 28, 30, 39, 40, 44].

5 Discussion

The results highlight a few discussion points on the boundary between GenAI capabilities and human roles, as well as the gap between what the literature measures and what practitioners need to know. The coverage of PMBOK process groups should be interpreted with caution. The prominence of Planning in the corpus is in part a baseline effect, given that this is the group with the largest number of processes. The key finding is that GenAI is used for processes that generate artifacts, while formal accountability processes (such as Plan Risk Management, Plan Cost Management, and Plan Stakeholder Engagement) remain human-driven. These processes remain human-driven, not because GenAI cannot produce their outputs, but because they need formal accountability. However, risk registers, estimates, and requirements, the artifacts on which those decisions rest, are increasingly machine-generated. From the perspective of Augmentation Theory [3], this is a predictable consequence of task automation: when artifact generation is delegated, the bottleneck shifts to verification, creating oversight overhead that existing frameworks do not account for. Accountability is thus retained at the governance level while the underlying judgment is delegated, leaving open whether this delegation produces reliable decisions in practice.

The absence of Procurement and Closing deserves separate discussion. These processes rely on legally binding documents, organizational assets, and knowledge accumulated over project history. This reliance is unlikely to change with advances in models, as the problem lies not in generative capability but in contextual grounding within proprietary, legally sensitive information.

Comparing our findings with the grey literature review [2] reveals which aspects are supported by peer-reviewed studies, and which remain partially explored. While practitioners raise concerns about data quality and privacy at a general level, peer-reviewed studies show how these issues emerge in specific processes. Sustainability concerns such as energy consumption, absent from practitioner discussions but flagged as a caution in [2], find empirical grounding in our corpus. However, practitioner-emphasized aspects like emotional intelligence and adaptive leadership remain underexplored in academic research, suggesting important directions for future work. Our findings also point to important governance challenge. In particular, the accountability gap should be treated as an explicit research construct, requiring a risk ontology that distinguishes project risks from tool-induced ones, since the latter cannot be managed through project-level planning alone. To ascertain whether short-term gains endure and at what governance cost–including whether project managers are capable of validating machine-generated artifacts–longitudinal designs measuring managerial outcomes are needed. For practitioners, GenAI outputs need to be validated, as they can look complete even when they have inaccuracies or missing information. Where evidence is strong (e.g., estimates) GenAI adoption is justified but oversight remains necessary. In areas lacking evidence (e.g., Closing), caution is needed until accountability and contractual risks are better understood.

6 Conclusion

This paper reviews 45 primary studies (2017–2026) to examine how GenAI is reshaping SPM. The overall picture is promising but uneven. Research remains heavily concentrated on Planning (partly reflecting the size of this area) and is typically assessed using machine-learning metrics rather than managerial ones. While studies consistently report reduced effort and improved planning performance, these gains are often offset by the additional effort required for verification. At the same time, GenAI adoption introduces a distinct set of tool-induced risks–such as hallucinations, prompt sensitivity, vendor dependency, and accountability gaps–which surface both as inaccuracies in generated outputs and as governance vulnerabilities not captured by traditional risk frameworks. Moreover, key areas of project management remain underexplored, particularly Procurement and Stakeholder Management, as well as the Initiating and Closing process groups. Addressing these gaps will require longer-term studies, greater use of managerial performance metrics, clearer distinctions between project-related and tool-induced risks, and a stronger emphasis on governance.

Disclosure of Interests. The authors have no competing interests to declare that are relevant to the content of this article.

References

1. Alomari, N., Redah, M.: Using LLMs to enhance code quality: a systematic literature review. Inf. Softw. Technol. 107960 (2025)
2. Assalaarachchi, L.I., Masood, Z., Hoda, R., Grundy, J.: Generative ai for software project management: insights from a review of software practitioner literature. IEEE Softw. (2025)
3. Autor, D.H.: Why are there still so many jobs? The history and future of workplace automation. J. Econ. Perspect. **29**(3), 3–30 (2015)
4. Banh, L., Holldack, F., Strobel, G.: Copiloting the future: how generative AI transforms software engineering. Inf. Softw. Technol. **183**, 107751 (2025)
5. Basili, V.R., Caldiera, G., Rombach, H.D.: The goal question metric approach. encyclopedia of software engineering-2 volume set, pp. 528–532. Wiley (1994)
6. Cruzes, D.S., Dybå, T.: Recommended steps for thematic synthesis in software engineering. In: Proceedings of the ESEM 2011, pp. 275–284. IEEE (2011)
7. De Vito, G., Di Martino, S., Ferrucci, F., Gravino, C., Palomba, F.: LLM-based automation of cosmic functional size measurement from use cases. IEEE Trans. Softw. Eng. (2025)

8. Hou, X., et al.: Large language models for software engineering: a systematic literature review. ACM TOSEM **33**(8), 1–79 (2024)
9. Jiang, J., Wang, F., Shen, J., Kim, S., Kim, S.: A survey on large language models for code generation. ACM TOSEM **35**(2), 1–72 (2026)
10. Khalil, M., Bravo, A., Vieira, D., Carvalho, M.M.: Mapping the ai landscape in project management context: a systematic literature review. Systems **13**(10), 913 (2025)
11. Kitchenham, B., Brereton, P.: A systematic review of systematic review process research in software engineering. Inf. Softw. Technol. **55**(12), 2049–2075 (2013)
12. Kitchenham, B., Charters, S.: Guidelines for performing systematic literature reviews in software engineering (2007)
13. Page, M.J., McKenzie, J.E., et al.: The PRISMA 2020 statement: an updated guideline for reporting systematic reviews. BMJ **372**, n71 (2021)
14. Paradis, E., Grey, K.: How much does ai impact development speed? An enterprise-based randomized controlled trial. In: Proceedings of ICSE-SEIP 2025, pp. 618–629. IEEE (2025)
15. Pearce, H., Ahmad, B., Tan, B., Dolan-Gavitt, B., Karri, R.: Asleep at the keyboard? Assessing the security of github copilot's code contributions. Commun. ACM **68**(2), 96–105 (2025)
16. Petersen, K., Vakkalanka, S., Kuzniarz, L.: Guidelines for conducting systematic mapping studies in software engineering: an update. Inf. Softw. Technol. **64**, 1–18 (2015)
17. Project Management Institute: A Guide to the Project Management Body of Knowledge (PMBOK Guide), 6th edn. Project Management Institute, Newtown Square, PA, USA (2017)
18. Project Management Institute (PMI): First Movers' Advantage: The Immediate Benefits of Adopting Generative AI for Project Management (2025). http://bit.ly/48j2tPd. Accessed 25 Mar 2026
19. Valdivia, J., Mauricio, D., Guzmán-Jiménez, R.: Generative artificial intelligence for software development using ISO/IEC 29110 basic profile: gaps and opportunities. IEEE Access (2026)
20. Vaswani, A., Shazeer, N., Parmar, N.: Attention is all you need. In: Advances in Neural Information Processing Systems, vol. 30 (2017)
21. Wohlin, C., Runeson, P., et al.: Experimentation in Software Engineering. Springer, Cham (2012)
22. Wohlin, C.: Guidelines for snowballing in systematic literature studies and a replication in software engineering. In: Proceedings of the EASE 2014, pp. 1–10. ACM, London, UK (2014)

Towards LLM Accelerated Rapid Reviews for Software Tool Discovery - Case for Log Anomaly Detection

Jesse Nyyssölä[1(✉)], Hamza Bin Mazhar[1], Alexander Bakhtin[2], Matteo Esposito[2], Nana Reinikainen[1], Yuqing Wang[1], Ying Song[1], Davide Taibi[2,3], and Mika Mäntylä[1]

[1] University of Helsinki, Fabianinkatu 33, Helsinki, Finland
{jesse.nyyssola,hamza.mazhar,nana.reinikainen,yuqing.wang, ying.song,mika.mantyla}@helsinki.fi

[2] University of Oulu, Pentti Kaiteran katu 1, Oulu, Finland
{alexander.bakhtin,matteo.esposito}@oulu.fi

[3] University of Southern Denmark, Spinderigade 24, Vejle, Denmark
taibi@imada.sdu.dk

Abstract. In software engineering research, the primary outcome is frequently a tool. However, for practitioners and academics alike, it is hard to tell which tools are maintained and do they work out of the box. In this paper, we propose a pipeline to identify relevant studies with LLM screening, extract the tools presented in them, and run them with LLM-based coding agent. To evaluate the feasibility of our approach we focus on software log anomaly detection tools. We begin the study by designing a broad search string that yields 3233 hits from Scopus. We request two LLMs to provide an inclusion probability for each title-abstract pair according to the inclusion and exclusion criteria. From the 3233 exported abstracts, this screening reduced the number of included papers to 569, out of which we could download 470. These papers included 206 unique links and after manual evaluation we determined 83 to be tools. Finally, we ran the LLM-based coding agent on these 83 links, and got 24 successfully running tools. As replicating our approach would require roughly only 4 h of human effort, of which 3 h were manual PDF downloading, and 12 h of LLM running time, this demonstrates promising efficiency when utilizing LLMs in rapid reviews. Because practitioner-built tools often lack academic papers, in the future we aim to expand our analysis to tool-hosting platforms such as GitHub and PyPI. In the future, we plan to formalize our workflow as LLM Agent Skills to make our approach easier to adopt.

Keywords: Rapid review · Large Language Models · Software logs · Anomaly detection · Tool discovery

C. Berger and V. Klös (Eds.): SEAA 2026, LNCS 16864, pp. 295–311, 2027.
https://doi.org/10.1007/978-3-032-36587-3_20

1 Introduction

In software engineering research, the primary outcome is frequently a tool [15]. However, utilizing these tools requires practitioners and academics to search, locate and execute the tools, which is a challenging task given the vast volume of academic literature. This paper introduces an LLM accelerated rapid review methodology to systematically identify and retrieve functional tools from academic publications.

To understand the feasibility of such a methodology, we test our approach on the area of software log anomaly detection. To be crystal clear, we could have selected any software engineering area where tools are prominent. We chose software log anomaly detection because we possess strong expertise in this topic, while also seeking to ensure that our view of the tools in the area is comprehensive. On a more general level, we further motivate our topic selection as follows. Software logs contain information about the execution of the system which is used for monitoring, debugging, and maintenance. However, logs can contain millions of lines that has motivated hundreds of academic studies and tool proposals. Yet, practitioners have emphasized their preference for tools that can be installed in an hour, are easy to use, and can detect anomalies in five seconds [24]. Finding such tools manually can be difficult, which calls for an approach that assesses the tools in a timely manner.

Rapid reviews in software engineering have been endorsed for narrow scoped problem and they are ideal for technology transfer [2]. It has been shown that practitioners are able to apply the outcomes of such reviews [33]. Thus, using rapid reviews to identify tools for log-analysis seems like a perfect fit.

Recently, the use of LLMs has been investigated in systematic reviews in software engineering [9,12,13,31,36] and in other fields [21]. The consensus is that they make many correct decisions, for example in title-abstract screening [12,21], although reliability issues remain and their performance has been found similar to that of master's students as early as 2024 [13]. Yet, the time reduction provided by LLM-based automated paper screening makes it a promising technique for accelerating rapid reviews.

Currently, it is not only humans who may use software engineering tools but also agentic AI. This further motivates our focus on tool discovery. For example, Esposito et al. [8] propose a MAPE-K and agentic AI framework that relies heavily on the continuous ingestion and evaluation of execution logs, making robust, highly scalable tooling a foundational requirement for such agentic architectures. Thus, to realize this vision, we conduct this rapid review of log anomaly detection tools to address the data processing challenges required for successfully automating microservice anomaly detection.

Based on our research objectives, we formulate the following research questions:

- RQ1: To what extent can LLMs be used in the rapid review process for software tool discovery?
- RQ2: How many tools can we identify and successfully run with our process?

The first research question focuses on the process that we are trying to refine, that is, LLM accelerated rapid reviews. By addressing possible strengths or challenges, we provide a substantial academic contribution to future research using similar approaches. The second research question concerns more the output of the pipeline. The set of tools identified by the study is a contribution on its own.

To disambiguate, when we use the term "tool" we refer to software repositories that implement a solution for software log anomaly detection, including replication packages of academic studies. We intentionally do not differentiate between named tools and unnamed replication packages, as the latter may contain functionally equivalent approaches that simply lack a name. In a similar way, when we refer to a repository as successfully running our focus is that it can be installed and executed to produce an output, rather than on its functional correctness or practitioner-readiness (e.g., documentation, containerization).

2 Methodology

To conduct the study, we designed a pipeline from creating the search string all the way to running the tools with an LLM. This section outlines the methodology and reasoning for our choices. To get an overview of our approach including the results found see Fig. 1 and for the LLM selection in the different steps see Table 1. Further details are available in the replication package [28].

Table 1. LLM Pipeline Configuration

Stage	Models Used	Rationale
LLM Screening	Gemini-2.5-Flash, OpenAI/GPT 4.1-Mini	Past work shows an excellent balance of accuracy, speed, and token cost [12]
LLM Repository Runner	Agent Claude Code (Opus 4.6)	Currently the top-performing coding model for execution tasks [38]

2.1 Search String Generation

In our search, we aim to use a very broad search string that yields a lot of hits in order to ensure we do not miss any studies in key word search phase. Consequently, we formulate the following search string that only focuses on software log anomaly detection.

("log anomaly" OR "log-based anomaly" OR "anomaly detection in log*" OR "log analysis") AND ("software" OR "system")

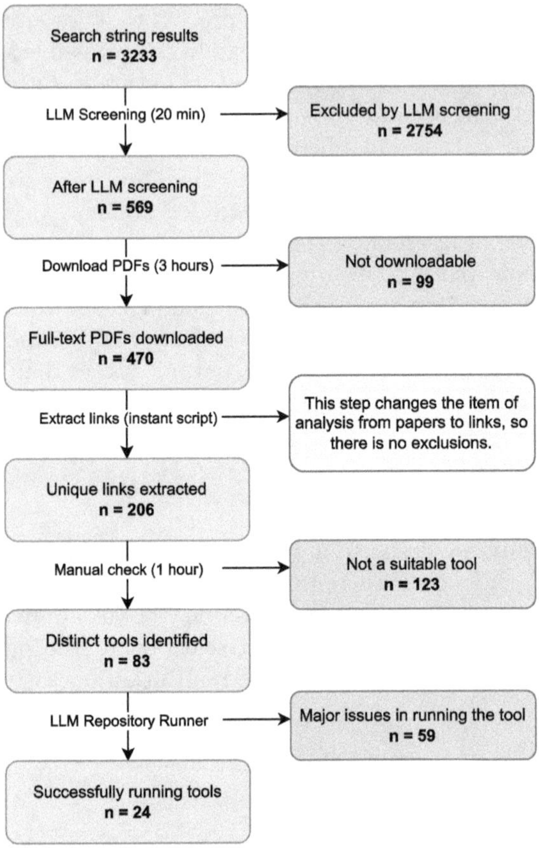

Fig. 1. PRISMA-style flow diagram

The search string resulted in 3233 papers as fetched on January 14th 2026 from Scopus, which is one of the largest academic databases containing titles and abstracts from every major publisher like, IEEE, ACM, Springer, Wiley, etc.

2.2 LLM Abstract Screening

To facilitate abstract screening with LLMs, we use the AISysRev tool [14]. It is designed to take a Scopus export as a CSV and perform screening with the given inclusion and exclusion criteria. As an output, the tool gives an estimated probability for inclusion as assessed by the chosen model(s). We used two models *gemini-2.5-flash* and *openai/gpt-4.1-mini*. As compact models, they are expected to perform with an excellent balance of accuracy, speed, and token cost. Furthermore, gpt-4.1-mini was the top performing model in large-scale study of title-abstract screening [12].

We formulate the following inclusion and exclusion criteria.

- IC1 Studies on "Software log analysis"
- IC2 Within scope "Anomaly detection on software logs"
- EC1 Exclude papers if the target is other than "Anomalies in reliability and testing"

The criteria assess the title and the abstract on three key factors: Topic, scope, and target. These criteria only focus on the content of the expected paper rather than the metadata that is handled by Scopus export. We did not want to exclude secondary studies or datasets, because there is a possibility that they present updated scripts or dependencies. Following the initial LLM screening, we manually validate a stratified sample of 386 abstracts, selected equally from both the included and excluded pools. This sample size, determined using Cochran's formula [5], provides a 95% confidence level for evaluating the accuracy of the LLM screening. Two authors evaluate each abstract, with a third author resolving any disagreements.

2.3 Tool Link Extraction from Full Papers

After title-abstract screening we proceeded to downloading the full papers. Downloading was the most labor intensive part of the whole pipeline as scraping the web page for the download link is generally forbidden in the terms of service of the providers. Our initial test with OpenAlex[1] and Unpaywall[2] APIs could only access roughly 5% of the papers from our sample pool. This forced us to manually download all papers.

We assumed that any important tools mentioned in the papers would accompany a link to the tool home page or repository. We recognize that this may not always be the case; however, for this emerging work, it is a practical design limitation we imposed. For extracting the links from the PDFs, we chose not to leverage LLMs as simple pattern matching for links is very efficient and accurate with regular expressions. Specifically, we created regexes to capture links from GitHub, GitLab, Bitbucket, SourceForge, Zenodo, Figshare, PyPI, and HuggingFace.

2.4 LLM Repository Runner

Figure 2 shows the pipeline for the LLM repository runner. The first step of the pipeline is to clone the project, assuming it is a Git link. In case it is other link, such as Zenodo or Huggingface, the LLM agent can inherently handle the necessary downloads. In the second step, the agent scans the repository for relevant files for installation such as requirements.txt, pyproject.toml and other setup files. In case there are no installation instructions, the agent runs a *grep* command to find import statements. Based on the findings, the agent formulates an action plan that addresses four factors.

[1] https://openalex.org/.
[2] https://unpaywall.org/.

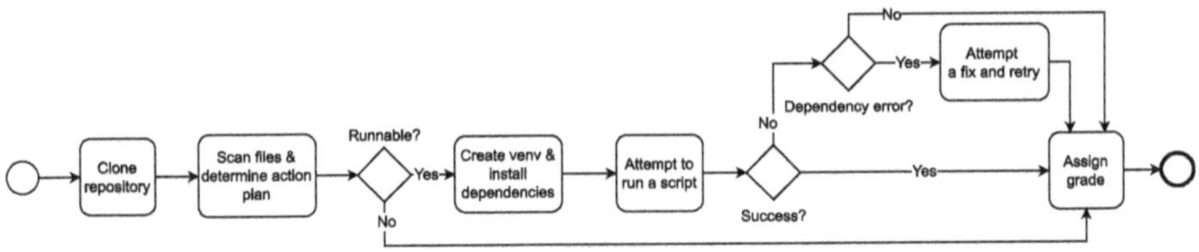

Fig. 2. LLM repository runner pipeline

(1) Is it Runnable? To determine if the tool is runnable, the LLM agent has access to all the files in the repository. We do not define explicit rules for determining if the repository is runnable, it depends on the discretion of the LLM. This filter is intended to address obvious but perhaps unexpected issues, such as no script to run in the first place. In these cases, the repository is simply determined not runnable and the agent ends the process.

(2) Data Feasibility. The data on which to run the script can be bundled with the repository, the README might have a link to download it, it could be a common dataset without a link, it can be an unknown dataset without a link, or the data is not mentioned at all. The agent is instructed to handle the three first options, but the last two are left to the discretion of the agent.

(3) Python Version. Python is by far the most popular language used in software log anomaly detection. As such, the prompt focuses on Python related instructions, but at the same time it does not explicitly forbid trying to run non-Python tools. To determine the correct Python version, the LLM agent utilizes primarily setup or requirement files if they are available. In case the correct Python version is not mentioned, the agent attempts to deduce a suitable version based on the dependencies.

(4) Requirements. Similar to the Python version, the LLM agent uses available files and information to determine how to install the dependencies.

Once the action plan is created and the repository determined to be runnable, the pipeline proceeds to creation of a Python virtual environment and installing dependencies. This is done according to the action plan. Once installed, the LLM agent attempts to run an included script. In case it fails due to a dependency issue, the prompt allows a single attempt to fix it as shown in the "Attempt a fix and retry" box of Fig. 2. Retrying in this means only attempting to run the script, not the whole pipeline. After that, or due to any other error, the agent is instructed to stop trying to fix the repository.

After trying to run the repository script, the LLM agent is instructed to produce a result file of the outcome. It includes status of the run (success vs. failure), a grading for the installation, and a short assessment. We use the following assessment criteria:

- 3 = The tool itself and instructed dependencies worked out of the box, no issues

- 2 = Minor issues like dependencies not explicitly given or there was a small issue with them
- 1 = Significant issues (e.g., install succeeded but run failed)
- 0 = Could not run at all (not runnable, fatal errors, or missing data with no fallback)

We utilize *Claude Code agent* with *Opus 4.6* model due to its performance on coding and data analysis related benchmarks [38]. It reads a pre-written prompt file that instructs all the steps outlined above. To run the setup, we created a dedicated Linux virtual machine with 32 GB of RAM and using 6 cores from Intel Core i7-13700K running on a local computer. This setup introduces limitations on what we can successfully run, specifically on GPU operations as it lacks CUDA support. However, we argue that the environment is justified given that it reflects a common use case. Furthermore, there are security considerations when installing unknown repositories and giving the LLM free rein in the system. These factors favor the use of an isolated environment.

3 Results

In the results section we outline the key findings of each step in our proposed pipeline. Figure 1 shows how the number of included items reduces drastically on each step. Additionally, it contains a rough estimate of how long each step takes to run or perform when assuming that all the data and tools are ready making it essentially reflect the time-cost of re-running our pipeline.

3.1 LLM Title-Abstract Screening Outcomes

Figure 3 shows the average probability of the two models when the papers are sorted by the average probability. This illustrates well the "elbow" [34] where the probability starts rapidly declining. This is a good indicator of a cut-off threshold for inclusion. We selected the start of the elbow at 0.90 probability as the threshold for inclusion which resulted in 569 included papers out of 3233.

Human evaluation validates the LLM screening and our "elbow" cutoff point selection. The Cohen's Kappa was 0.839 between the human consensus and the LLM prediction. This signifies almost perfect agreement on Landis & Koch scale [18]. When considering the human consensus as the ground-truth, the LLM screening reached precision of 0.933, recall of 0.909 and F1-score of 0.921.

For our purpose in conducting a rapid review for tool discovery, these are excellent results that clearly meet our expectations as the results are in the top 5% when compared against SESR-eval results [12]. We think that one reason for such strong results is the data and the criteria, which together form a highly separable set of papers. Many papers are clear includes, even more are clear excludes, and relatively few fall into the ambiguous middle ground. This is evident in Fig. 3, where only about 400 papers are in the middle with probabilities between 0.25 and 0.9.

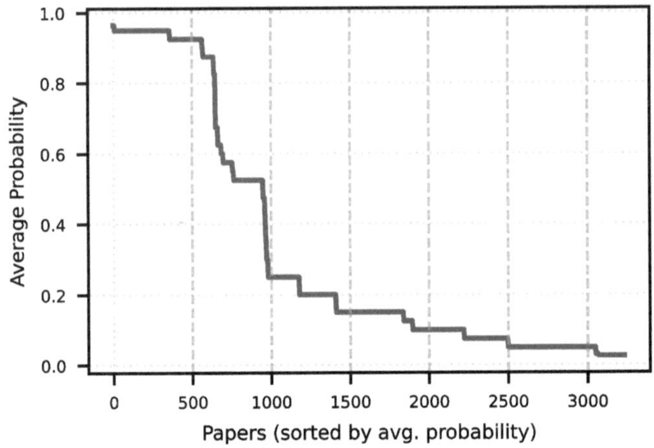

Fig. 3. Average inclusion probability of the papers

3.2 Extracted Tools from Full Papers

From the 569 papers that passed the LLM screening we could download 470. They included 315 links that matched our regexes. There were 206 unique links and 109 duplicates. The most common links in the studies were the repositories for Loghub [42] (33 hits), Loglizer [10] (12 hits), and Logdeep[3] (10 hits).

We estimated 206 links to be a feasible number for manual assessment to determine if the link contains a suitable tool for our study. What we mean by suitability is that, the link actually leads to a tool for software log anomaly detection. In other words, in this step we exclude all non-relevant tools as well as supplementary links such as datasets without tools. Additionally, we excluded forks. The final number of unique links to suitable repositories was 83.

3.3 LLM Repository Runner Execution

Finally, we ran the LLM repository runner as described in Sect. 2.4. This section starts by introducing performance of the installation process, i.e., how successful it is. In addition, we provide an overview on the execution time distribution across the repositories.

Install Performance. The number of repositories of each grade is summarized in Table 2. As shown in the table, the grades 0, 1 and 2 are almost evenly split with most issues caused by dependencies. Unless there are other problems, the extent of the dependency issues appeared to explain the grade to a large degree.

[3] https://github.com/d0nglee/logdeep The Logdeep repository does not have an associated paper; rather, it is a repository for running some popular approaches.

Table 2. Repository install grade distribution and common issues per grade

Grade	# of repos	Common issues
Grade 3	1	No issues
Grade 2	23	Minor dependency issue
Grade 1	22	Missing dependencies, bugs, API incompatibilities
Grade 0	22	Repository not available, unresolvable dependencies
Timed out	15	CPU-bound training, download or processing pipelines
Total	**83**	

The grade 3 repository was LogLead [26]. There were 23 repositories that reached grade 2: aecid-alert-aggregation [17], anomaly-detection-log-datasets [16], BGL_AnoDet [29], BigLog [35], CAT [39], deep-loglizer [3], DeepLog [7], DistilLog [27], FedLAD [20], KnowLog [23], LL-mod-unsupervised [30], LogDeep, LogDLR [41], LogEval [6], LoFI [11], LogGeneratorForAnomalyDetection [37], Loglizer [10], LogRAG [40], Lograph [4], MoLFI [25], NeuralLog [19], OnlineADPipeline [22], and TransSentLog [32]. Note that while the link extraction does not discriminate between primary and secondary studies, this list with its citations was manually collected to try to credit the original authors.

Table 2 shows that 15 repositories exhausted the 20-minutes execution budget. Most timeouts were attributed to CPU-bound training that progressed too slowly to finish within the budget. Additional timeouts occurred due to prolonged dependency resolutions, heavy dataset downloads, or preprocessing pipelines. In few repositories, the agent could not resolve issues related to external datasets.

All repositories in grade 0 did not execute at all. Most of the repositories were not available, they had either been deleted, were private, or were completely empty. Some had hard unresolvable dependencies like requiring CUDA or external API calls with no alternatives. Some had compatibility issues for libraries and Python versions, while a very few had unresolvable dataset availability issues like missing or proprietary datasets, or broken links. In the 83 repositories, there was only one non-Python project. It depended on Java and got grade 0 because the LLM agent could not install Java.

All repositories in grade 1 showed issues that led to partial or failed executions despite heavy agent intervention. Nearly half of the repositories in this grade lacked any dependency specifications, while the other half had outdated or incomplete specifications. A majority of the repositories also contained code bugs, API incompatibilities, or broken imports. In several cases there were hard coded CUDA calls with no CPU fallbacks. There were also issues with datasets and preprocessing scripts.

All repositories in grade 2 required minor agent intervention to become runnable. A vast majority of repositories in this grade had incomplete or incorrect dependency specifications, with some repositories completely missing the specifications. For the missing dependencies, the agent had to infer these from import statements within the code. Some repositories required external data or downloading pre-trained model weights adding to the setup overhead. A couple of repositories in this grade had hardcoded CUDA device references which had to be changed to CPU to allow execution. Despite these issues, all repositories produced meaningful output after low-effort troubleshooting from the agent.

LogLead was the only repository that installed and ran out of the box. One reason that explains LogLead's performance is that it has been maintained after publication to support log analysis research and students who use it in a course.

Execution Times. Running the script for all repositories took approximately 12 h. Figure 4 shows the distribution of execution times as color-coded by the grade of the repository. As expected, we can observe that the majority grade 0 repositories fail in two minutes. This is due to the LLM agent determining early, as instructed in the prompt, that the repository is unrunnable, which ends the process immediately. If running the repository succeeds in five minutes, most of them have grade 2. Conversely, if it succeeds while taking more than five minutes, the majority switch to grade 1. This is logical, as the LLM agent tries to solve issues within the repository, which both takes time and reduces the grading.

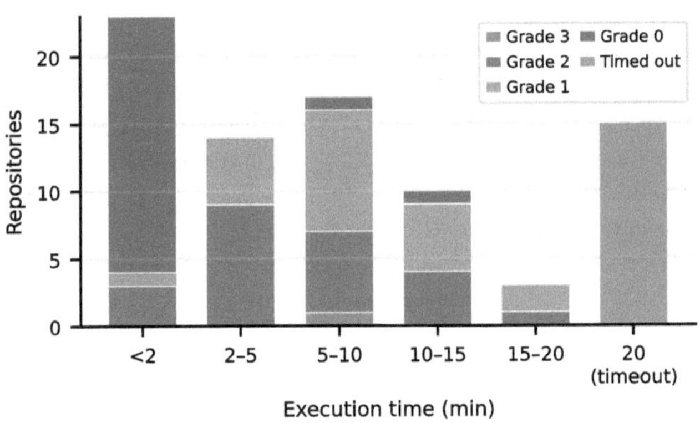

Fig. 4. Distribution of the execution times of the repositories

4 Discussion

The LLM worked surprisingly well in various parts of our pipeline. The result of the abstract screening with LLMs was excellent. Trying to get unknown repositories to run by humans is very time-intensive and exhausting, to the point that studies do not do it to this degree. As such, utilizing the LLM can be seen as improving the quality of the review process as a whole. To address **RQ1**, we argue that the use of LLMs improved both the quality and efficiency of the rapid review process for software tool discovery. For **RQ2**, we presented a list of 24 repositories that received an installation grade of 2 or 3 by the LLM. Although any qualitative assessment of the tools was outside the scope of this paper, the running tools offer a good starting point for anyone who wants to further assess them or integrate them into agentic frameworks such as MAPE-K [8].

One of the main contributions of the LLM-accelerated rapid review pipeline that we propose is the amount of human effort that is automated. A traditional rapid review of a similar scope would take from days to weeks, but our approach took only around four hours of human effort and 12 h of running LLMs. Furthermore, majority of the human effort consists of manually downloading PDFs of the papers. While many major publishers provide Text and Data Mining (TDM) API keys for non-commercial research, integrating these into the pipeline would require managing multiple publisher-specific authentication workflows, which would reduce the portability and reproducibility of our approach. Manual downloading is labour-intensive, but it keeps the pipeline self-contained and the results consistent. For scaling this approach to larger reviews, TDM agreements would become justified. Regarding the LLM run time, it is important to note that it took 12 h to run the 83 repositories sequentially, but outside of rate limits, there is nothing stopping from running several LLM agents in parallel. The 20-minute timeout was chosen both to reflect a realistic practitioner installation scenario [24] and to prevent the agent from entering unproductive loops wasting tokens. For further insight for this study, we ran the 15 repositories that timed out again without a time limit and four of them ran well (grade 2), which is a similar ratio as in those that did not time out.

One of our primary metrics for evaluating a tool is whether it executes successfully. This approach may exclude good methods that have poor replication packages. However, given that replicability is a hallmark of science, ensuring the tool runs remains the responsibility of the original authors, not ours. To characterize what predicts successful execution, we collected GitHub metadata for the 49 CPU-compatible repositories and tested associations with grade outcome. Due to the number of repositories, there were no statistically significant results, but some of them were practically meaningful. For example, repositories that included a dedicated *requirements* file ran successfully at a higher rate (61%) than those without one (38%). Some factors (README length, number of stars, and number of forks), showed a weak positive trend toward successful execution. Repository age and days since last commit did not predict success.

5 Threats to Validity

One notable threat to **Internal validity** is that it is not always clear whether a failure by the LLM runner is caused by the repository or the agent/prompt. Hence, we risk conflating two different things: How good is the repository and how good is the LLM-agent. Another threat is that we conducted the manual assessment of the links only by a single author which is inconsistent with the paper screening validation, but we reason that it is a much more straightforward process with no controversy.

The most obvious threat for **External validity** is that the pipeline was only tested on log anomaly detection tools, and generalization to other SE tool areas is unconfirmed. Another limiting factor is the CPU-only environment where we ran the experiments, and as such we know for certain that the results do not generalize for GPU environments. For better generalizability, using LLM-agents from other providers would also be beneficial. A third threat to external validity, is the potential for evidence loss, i.e., the tools we should have identified. Each instance where a relevant tool is discovered outside our initial search should prompt a critical examination of the reasons, context, and process failures that led to its omission. Another limiting factor is that our pipeline was designed around Python repositories with local dependencies. This does not account for tools which may require Docker containers or cloud infrastructure. However, this is less problematic because research prototypes are often distributed as self contained repositories not utilizing cloud infrastructure, while industrial sources that utilize such infrastructure often do not make their implementation public.

For **Construct validity**, the main threat is that we assume the tool to be "usable" if the LLM-agent manages to run it. In reality, the usability for humans and LLM-agents differ significantly. For example, for a human adjusting vast configuration files would be very laborious while an LLM could manage it in an instant. Conversely, graphical user interfaces are designed to be intuitive for humans, but an LLM-agent might not be able to run such tools at all.

There exist threats to **Conclusion validity** with regards to how the results of this study should be interpreted. They should not be read as saying that only 24 out of 569 log anomaly detection papers provide a good replication package. There are studies in the set that fall outside the scope of tool-oriented research. Additionally, many deep learning based approaches are hardware or time intensive by design. Rather, the 24 tools in 569 papers showcase that in the context of trying to search an easy and fast tool, there are not that many options. However, in this study, we can not guarantee that the running tools produced the correct, expected output. Hence, in terms of output quality of the tools, this study does not intend to place one tool above another.

6 Future Work

As the work in this study is highly novel, we will outline future work as an explicit outcome that relates to the limitations of this study which are summarized in Table 3. The limitations themselves are motivated by the threats to validity presented in the previous section.

Limitation #1: Many significant log analysis tools, such as Angle Grinder[4] and Logfile Navigator[5], are not covered in academic literature and thus fell outside the scope of our rapid review search. **Future work:** Extend our approach beyond academic literature to include public hosting platforms (e.g., GitHub) and grey literature. Combining different sources can help produce a more comprehensive picture than running them individually, and the expected overlap between sources serves as a natural cross-validation of the findings.

[4] https://github.com/rcoh/angle-grinder.
[5] https://lnav.org.

Table 3. Summary of future work by limitation

#	Limitation	Future Work
1	Tools absent from academic literature (e.g., Angle Grinder) not found	Include additional sources, such as GitHub
2	Generalizability: Only evaluated on log anomaly detection tools	Expand to metrics (e.g., CPU, memory) and tracing tools
3	Single OS, limited GPU support, and a 20-minute execution timeout	Aim for more robust environments, develop dynamic timeout
4	Issue location: Repository or LLM agent?	Study LLM runner performance on dataset with groundtruth (e.g., artifact badges)

Limitation #2: At this stage we have tested our approach only on tools for software log anomaly detection. Whether our work generalizes to all software tools requires further study. **Future work:** We aim to expand the method to other software monitoring tool areas, such as those that analyze metrics (e.g., CPU and memory usage) and those that analyze execution traces from modern microservice systems. Furthermore, we aim to increase the generalizability of the repository runner by formalizing the workflow as Agent Skills.

Limitation #3: Limited running environment with one operating system, limited GPU support, and the 20-minute execution timeout. **Future work:** We will explore options to run the repositories in a more robust environment without compromising on information security. Furthermore, the timeout window could be made dynamic if we can identify when the extra time is really necessary (running the tool) as opposed to the LLM agent getting stuck. However, given that practitioners value both ease of use and timely installation [24], the constraints in this study reflect a realistic practitioner scenario, too.

Limitation #4: While we outlined the several reasons for the LLM runner to fail, it is not always clear if the fundamental issue is in the repository or the agent/prompt. **Future work:** Gather a dataset of studies that have artifact review badges. These can serve as a ground truth so that we can expect the artifact to be runnable. If the LLM still fails, we have a good reason to believe the pipeline is not performing adequately.

7 Conclusion

This paper presents an LLM accelerated pipeline for conducting rapid reviews for software tool discovery. We tested our approach on software log anomaly detection tools but we could have chosen any other software engineering area where tools are a typical outcome. We started with a key-word search finding 3233 papers. With the help of LLM abstract screening, regex based link extraction, and finally manual evaluation, we got a list of 83 software tools for log anomaly detection. With the prompt we designed, LLM-based coding agent could eventually run 24 of those with little to no issues.

In the future, we plan to apply our approach to investigate other software monitoring tools. This will provide more evidence of our approach and help make the pipeline more robust. Furthermore, we will extend our approach beyond academic literature for a more comprehensive set of tools. We also plan to formalize our approach as Agent Skills which is an emerging standard for packaging reusable capabilities for LLM agents, as specified in a standard originally developed by Anthropic [1].

Acknowledgments. This work has been funded by the Research Council of Finland (grants n. 359861 and 349488 MuFAno), and by the Finnish Software Engineering Doctoral Research Network, funded by the Ministry of Education and Culture, Finland.

Data Availability. Data is available via our replication package [28].

Disclosure of Interests. The authors have no competing interests to declare that are relevant to the content of this article.

References

1. Anthropic, Agent Skills Contributors: Agent skills: A standardized way to give AI agents new capabilities and expertise (2025). https://agentskills.io
2. Cartaxo, B., Pinto, G., Soares, S.: Rapid reviews in software engineering. In: Felderer, M., Travassos, G. (eds.) Contemporary Empirical Methods in Software Engineering, pp. 357–384. Springer, Cham (2020). https://doi.org/10.1007/978-3-030-32489-6_13
3. Chen, Z., Liu, J., Gu, W., Su, Y., Lyu, M.R.: Experience report: deep learning-based system log analysis for anomaly detection (2022). https://arxiv.org/abs/2107.05908
4. Chu, G., et al.: Anomaly detection on interleaved log data with semantic association mining on log-entity graph. IEEE Trans. Software Eng. **51**(2), 581–594 (2025). https://doi.org/10.1109/TSE.2025.3527856
5. Cochran, W.G.: Sampling Techniques, 3rd edn. Wiley, New York (1977)
6. Cui, T., et al.: LogEval: a comprehensive benchmark suite for LLMs in log analysis. Empir. Softw. Engg. **30**(6) (2025). https://doi.org/10.1007/s10664-025-10701-6
7. Du, M., Li, F., Zheng, G., Srikumar, V.: DeepLog: anomaly detection and diagnosis from system logs through deep learning. In: Proceedings of the 2017 ACM SIGSAC Conference on Computer and Communications Security, CCS 2017, pp. 1285–1298. Association for Computing Machinery, New York (2017). https://doi.org/10.1145/3133956.3134015
8. Esposito, M., et al.: Autonomic microservice management via agentic AI and MAPE-K integration. In: Zdun, U. (ed.) Software Architecture. ECSA 2025 Tracks and Workshops, pp. 105–118. Springer Nature Switzerland, Cham (2026). https://doi.org/10.1007/978-3-032-04403-7_11
9. Felizardo, K.R., Lima, M.S., Deizepe, A., Conte, T.U., Steinmacher, I.: ChatGPT application in systematic literature reviews in software engineering: an evaluation of its accuracy to support the selection activity. In: Proceedings of the

18th ACM/IEEE International Symposium on Empirical Software Engineering and Measurement, ESEM 2024, pp. 25–36. Association for Computing Machinery, New York (2024). https://doi.org/10.1145/3674805.3686666
10. He, S., Zhu, J., He, P., Lyu, M.R.: Experience report: system log analysis for anomaly detection. In: 2016 IEEE 27th International Symposium on Software Reliability Engineering (ISSRE), pp. 207–218 (2016). https://doi.org/10.1109/ISSRE.2016.21
11. Huang, J., et al.: Demystifying and extracting fault-indicating information from logs for failure diagnosis. In: 2024 IEEE 35th International Symposium on Software Reliability Engineering (ISSRE), pp. 511–522 (2024). https://doi.org/10.1109/ISSRE62328.2024.00055
12. Huotala, A., Kuutila, M., Mäntylä, M.: SESR-eval: dataset for evaluating LLMs in the title-abstract screening of systematic reviews. In: 2025 ACM/IEEE International Symposium on Empirical Software Engineering and Measurement (ESEM), pp. 01–12 (2025). https://doi.org/10.1109/ESEM64174.2025.00053
13. Huotala, A., Kuutila, M., Ralph, P., Mäntylä, M.: The promise and challenges of using LLMs to accelerate the screening process of systematic reviews. In: Proceedings of the 28th International Conference on Evaluation and Assessment in Software Engineering, EASE 2024, pp. 262–271. Association for Computing Machinery, New York (2024). https://doi.org/10.1145/3661167.3661172
14. Huotala, A., Kuutila, M., Turtio, O.P., Sipilä, S., Mäntylä, M.: AISysRev – LLM-based tool for title-abstract screening. In: 34th ACM Joint European Software Engineering Conference and Symposium on the Foundations of Software Engineering (FSE Companion 2026), 05–09 July 2026, Montreal, QC, Canada, pp. 1–5 (2026). https://arxiv.org/abs/2510.06708
15. Kotti, Z., Gousios, G., Spinellis, D.: Impact of software engineering research in practice: a patent and author survey analysis. IEEE Trans. Software Eng. **49**(4), 2020–2038 (2023). https://doi.org/10.1109/TSE.2022.3208210
16. Landauer, M., Skopik, F., Wurzenberger, M.: A critical review of common log data sets used for evaluation of sequence based anomaly detection techniques. Proc. ACM Softw. Eng. **1**(FSE) (2024). https://doi.org/10.1145/3660768
17. Landauer, M., Wurzenberger, M., Skopik, F., Hotwagner, W., Höld, G.: AMiner: a modular log data analysis pipeline for anomaly-based intrusion detection. Digit. Threats **4**(1) (2023). https://doi.org/10.1145/3567675
18. Landis, J.R., Koch, G.G.: The measurement of observer agreement for categorical data. Biometrics **33**(1), 159–174 (1977). http://www.jstor.org/stable/2529310
19. Le, V.H., Zhang, H.: Log-based anomaly detection without log parsing. In: Proceedings of the 36th IEEE/ACM International Conference on Automated Software Engineering, ASE 2021, pp. 492–504. IEEE Press (2022). https://doi.org/10.1109/ASE51524.2021.9678773
20. Liao, Y., Keung, J., Mao, Z., Zhang, J., Li, J.: FedLAD: a modular and adaptive testbed for federated log anomaly detection. In: 2025 IEEE International Conference on Autonomic Computing and Self-Organizing Systems Companion (ACSOS-C), pp. 227–232. IEEE Computer Society, Los Alamitos (2025). https://doi.org/10.1109/ACSOS-C66519.2025.00066
21. Lieberum, J.L., et al.: Large language models for conducting systematic reviews: on the rise, but not yet ready for use-a scoping review. J. Clin. Epidemiol. **181** (2025). https://doi.org/10.1016/j.jclinepi.2025.111746
22. Lupton, S., Yu, L., Washizaki, H., Yoshioka, N., Fukazawa, Y.: Assessment of real-world incident detection through a component-based online log anomaly detection

pipeline framework. In: 2023 10th International Conference on Dependable Systems and Their Applications (DSA), pp. 477–478. (2023). https://doi.org/10.1109/DSA59317.2023.00066
23. Ma, L., et al.: KnowLog: knowledge enhanced pre-trained language model for log understanding. In: Proceedings of the IEEE/ACM 46th International Conference on Software Engineering, ICSE 2024. Association for Computing Machinery, New York (2024). https://doi.org/10.1145/3597503.3623304
24. Ma, X., et al.: Practitioners' expectations on log anomaly detection. IEEE Trans. Software Eng. **51**(9), 2455–2471 (2025). https://doi.org/10.1109/TSE.2025.3586700
25. Messaoudi, S., Panichella, A., Bianculli, D., Briand, L., Sasnauskas, R.: A search-based approach for accurate identification of log message formats. In: Proceedings of the 26th Conference on Program Comprehension. p. 167–177. ICPC '18, Association for Computing Machinery, New York (2018). https://doi.org/10.1145/3196321.3196340
26. Mäntylä, M.V., Wang, Y., Nyyssölä, J.: LogLead - fast and integrated log loader, enhancer, and anomaly detector. In: 2024 IEEE International Conference on Software Analysis, Evolution and Reengineering (SANER), pp. 395–399 (2024). https://doi.org/10.1109/SANER60148.2024.00046
27. Nguyen, H.T., Nguyen, L.V., Le, V.H., Zhang, H., Le, M.T.: Efficient log-based anomaly detection with knowledge distillation. In: 2024 IEEE International Conference on Web Services (ICWS), pp. 578–589 (2024). https://doi.org/10.1109/ICWS62655.2024.00078
28. Nyyssölä, J., et al.: Replication package for "towards LLM accelerated rapid reviews for software tool discovery - case for log anomaly detection" (2026). https://doi.org/10.5281/zenodo.19878559
29. Nyyssölä, J., Mäntylä, M.: Event-level anomaly detection on software logs: role of algorithm, threshold, and window size. In: 2024 IEEE 24th International Conference on Software Quality, Reliability and Security (QRS), pp. 649–656 (2024). https://doi.org/10.1109/QRS62785.2024.00070
30. Nyyssölä, J., Mäntylä, M.: Speed and performance of parserless and unsupervised anomaly detection methods on software logs. In: 2024 IEEE 24th International Conference on Software Quality, Reliability and Security (QRS), pp. 657–666 (2024). https://doi.org/10.1109/QRS62785.2024.00071
31. Petersen, K., Gerken, J.M.: On the road to interactive LLM-based systematic mapping studies. Inf. Softw. Technol. **178**, 107611 (2025). https://doi.org/10.1016/j.infsof.2024.107611
32. Pham, T.A., Lee, J.H.: TransSentLog: interpretable anomaly detection using transformer and sentiment analysis on individual log event. IEEE Access 1 (2023). https://doi.org/10.1109/ACCESS.2023.3311146
33. Pizard, S., Lezama, J., García, R., Vallespir, D., Kitchenham, B.: Using rapid reviews to support software engineering practice: a systematic review and a replication study. Empir. Softw. Engg **30**(1), (2024). https://doi.org/10.1007/s10664-024-10545-6
34. Syakur, M.A., Khotimah, B.K., Rochman, E.M.S., Satoto, B.D.: Integration k-means clustering method and elbow method for identification of the best customer profile cluster. In: IOP Conference Series: Materials Science and Engineering, vol. 336, no. 1, p. 012017 (2018). https://doi.org/10.1088/1757-899X/336/1/012017
35. Tao, S., et al.: Biglog: unsupervised large-scale pre-training for a unified log representation. In: IEEE/ACM 31st International Symposium on Quality of Service (IWQoS), pp, 1–11 (2023). https://doi.org/10.1109/IWQoS57198.2023.10188759

36. Thode, L., Iftikhar, U., Mendez, D.: Exploring the use of LLMs for the selection phase in systematic literature studies. Inf. Software Technol. 107757 (2025). https://doi.org/10.1016/j.infsof.2025.107757
37. Uchida, H., Tominaga, K., Itai, H., Li, Y., Nakatoh, Y.: Multi-parameter log anomaly detection with an unsupervised learning approach. In: 2024 International Symposium on Parallel Computing and Distributed Systems (PCDS), pp. 1–5 (2024). https://doi.org/10.1109/PCDS61776.2024.10743635
38. White, C., et al.: LiveBench: a challenging, contamination-free LLM benchmark. In: The Thirteenth International Conference on Learning Representations (2025)
39. Zhang, S., Liu, Y., Zhang, X., Cheng, W., Chen, H., Xiong, H.: CAT: beyond efficient transformer for content-aware anomaly detection in event sequences. In: Proceedings of the 28th ACM SIGKDD Conference on Knowledge Discovery and Data Mining, KDD 2022, pp. 4541–4550. Association for Computing Machinery, New York (2022). https://doi.org/10.1145/3534678.3539155
40. Zhang, W., et al.: Leveraging RAG-enhanced large language model for semi-supervised log anomaly detection. In: 2024 IEEE 35th International Symposium on Software Reliability Engineering (ISSRE), pp. 168–179 (2024). https://doi.org/10.1109/ISSRE62328.2024.00026
41. Zhou, J., et al.: LogDLR: unsupervised cross-system log anomaly detection through domain-invariant latent representation. IEEE Trans. Dependable Secure Comput. **22**(4), 4456–4471 (2025). https://doi.org/10.1109/TDSC.2025.3548050
42. Zhu, J., He, S., He, P., Liu, J., Lyu, M.R.: LogHub: a large collection of system log datasets for AI-driven log analytics. In: 2023 IEEE 34th International Symposium on Software Reliability Engineering (ISSRE), pp. 355–366 (2023). https://doi.org/10.1109/ISSRE59848.2023.00071

Interpersonal Violence and Abuse in Smart Homes: A Systematic Mapping Study

Fazeleh Dehghani Ashkezari[1,2(✉)], Martin Höst[1,2], Kayode S. Adewole[1,2], Klara Svalin[3], and Andreas Jacobsson[1,2]

[1] Department of Computer Science and Media Technology, Malmö University, Malmö, Sweden
{fazeleh.dehghaniashkezari,martin.host,kayode.adewole, andreas.jacobsson}@mau.se

[2] Sustainable Digitalization Research Center, Malmö University, Malmö, Sweden

[3] Department of Criminology, Malmö University, Malmö, Sweden
klara.svalin@mau.se

Abstract. Smart homes are increasingly common in everyday life, offering convenience, automation, energy efficiency, and enhanced security through software services and devices such as smart locks, cameras, and voice assistants. However, their connected and shared nature introduces risks within close relationships, where they can be exploited to facilitate interpersonal violence and abuse. At the same time, they can also be leveraged for mitigation, detection, and victim support. In this study, we conduct a systematic mapping review of 27 studies to identify and categorize how smart home systems can both facilitate and address interpersonal violence and abuse. The findings show that research in this field is imbalanced, with most studies focusing on abuse facilitation, particularly through surveillance, remote control, and access misuse, while fewer studies propose mechanisms for abuse detection and victim support. This suggests a need for more holistic, smart home system-integrated approaches that explicitly address interpersonal risks in smart home design and development, and integrate these concerns into core software engineering activities, including requirements engineering, system design, and validation.

Keywords: Internet of Things · Smart Homes · Interpersonal violence · Technology-facilitated abuse · Requirements Engineering

1 Introduction

Smart connected homes are increasingly integrated into everyday life. They include internet-connected devices and platforms, such as smart locks, cameras, voice assistants, and home automation systems. As an example of the broader Internet of Things (IoT), these systems rely on networked communication and cloud services, integrating sensors, actuators, and intelligent systems to deliver services that enhance comfort and convenience while also promoting safety and

C. Berger and V. Klös (Eds.): SEAA 2026, LNCS 16864, pp. 312–328, 2027.
https://doi.org/10.1007/978-3-032-36587-3_21

improving energy efficiency [9]. However, their connectivity also creates security and privacy risks. Previous research has, among many things, identified vulnerabilities in smart home applications and systems, including weaknesses in authentication and access control [2].

Existing research on smart home security tends to focus primarily on external cybersecurity threats. However, risks can also emerge from within the home environment. Because smart home systems are often shared and remotely accessible, a person with legitimate access may misuse them. In interpersonal contexts, such as between persons living together, misuse can involve monitoring, restricting, threatening, or otherwise controlling others, including intimate partners, family members, or cohabitants [28]. These behaviors align with broader patterns of interpersonal violence and abuse, particularly forms of coercive control.

The World Health Organization (WHO) defines violence as "the intentional use of physical force or power, threatened or actual, against another person or group, that results in or has a high likelihood of resulting in injury, death, psychological harm, maldevelopment, or deprivation" [33]. Within this framework, interpersonal violence refers to violence between individuals and may be physical, sexual, or psychological in nature [20]. Smart home systems may become part of such harmful dynamics by enabling new forms of control and surveillance through technology. At the same time, these systems may also have supportive and protective potential. For instance, they can support forensic investigation and digital evidence reconstruction [13], facilitate the identification of suspicious activities [3,34], and contribute to safety planning and abuse detection [18].

This raises questions for organizations developing smart home systems about how these systems can be abused by perpetrators of interpersonal violence, and how such risks can be addressed through security, privacy, and ethical considerations during system development. One key phase is requirements engineering, where system features, misuse scenarios, and stakeholder needs are evaluated and discussed. During this stage, it becomes possible to identify abuse-enabling system characteristics and consider how systems may detect, mitigate, or respond to interpersonal violence through abuse-aware design decisions.

In prior research [10], we observed that the smart home security field largely focuses on technical concerns, while relational and social harms remain underexplored. Building on this, we conducted a systematic mapping study to examine how smart homes intersect with interpersonal violence and abuse, including the identification of abuse-enabling system characteristics and software engineering implications for abuse-aware smart home development. Specifically, we have studied two main research questions: (RQ1-a) what types of abuse are facilitated by smart home and IoT systems in the context of interpersonal violence, and (RQ1-b) what system characteristics contribute to these kinds of abuse, and (RQ2) what mechanisms in smart home systems can support prevention, detection, and response to interpersonal violence and abuse. The answers to these questions can serve as a basis for development of checklists and guidelines for developers of smart home systems, supporting requirements engineering, threat modeling, and abuse-aware design.

2 Related Work

2.1 Smart Home Security

Research on smart home security has largely focused on technical vulnerabilities in devices, networks, and cloud infrastructures [8,10]. While this has led to progress, it has also meant less attention to how smart homes function as multi-user, social environments [35]. Although some studies have addressed this gap by highlighting user challenges with configuration, access control, and system transparency [12]. Because smart homes are often shared and remotely accessible living spaces, their complexity increases, and technologies intended for the home environment can be misused within interpersonal relationships. Features like remote access, shared accounts, and automation may enable surveillance, control, or harassment without actual technical compromise [12,35]. A study by Ashkezari et al. [10] confirms that smart home research remains fragmented and system-centric, with limited focus on social and contextual factors, especially regarding interpersonal abuse. This limitation aligns with broader software engineering findings that point to that system development often overlooks real-world socio-technical complexity [5]. Overall, smart homes challenge traditional threat models focused on external attackers, and highlight the need to consider insider misuse and more human-centered, context-aware security approaches. Consequently, more research is needed to map the potential for interpersonal violence and abuse in smart homes.

2.2 Interpersonal Violence

Interpersonal violence is an umbrella term for various forms of violence (physical, sexual, or psychological), that occur in close relationships (within families, intimate relationships, in other relationships with people one knows) or is perpetrated by strangers [20].

Interpersonal violence is recognized as a global public health problem, with severe individual and societal consequences [16]. At the individual level, violence causes for instance short-, as well as long-term health consequences, and at the societal level, violence leads to monetary consequences [20]. Violence is a complex problem, and its causes are often described as an interplay between risk factors at different levels including individual (e.g. substance abuse), relational (e.g. violence permissive attitudes in peer-relationships), community-level (e.g. problems with social isolation), and societal (e.g. supportive norms of gender inequality) [16]. Although violence is a complex problem, it is preventable.

In recent years the use of technology in relation to violence, commonly referred to as technology-facilitated violence, has been highlighted [21], referring to "a range of malicious behaviors facilitated in part or in whole through information and communication technologies, or digital media, to commit both online and face-to-face harms" [26]. Such behaviors include stalking, psychological abuse, sexual violence, online harassment. With the increasing adoption of smart home systems, these systems are becoming a tool for facilitating violence in the context of interpersonal relationship. In the context of smart homes, violence often involves continuous surveillance and monitoring, manipulation of connected devices, and attempts to control the victim's living environment [18]. At the same time, these systems may also support detection, mitigation, and victim assistance through features such as monitoring, evidence collection, and alert mechanisms.

2.3 IoT Safety and Security Reviews

Different review papers have been published which are related to this research. For instance, the study in [15] and [11] examine the growing concern of violence against women and explore how IoT technologies can enhance personal safety through the development of Women's Safety Devices (WSDs). The authors review a wide range of IoT- and embedded system-based WSDs such as wearable devices like smart gloves, smart shoes, smart ring, smart cloth, smart jacket, and smart band that can support women during violence.

The study in [6] provides a systematic review of how consumer IoT devices can facilitate cybercrime. It argues that everyday devices, such as smart locks, cameras, and wearables, can create new opportunities for crime harvest. The authors identify key attack methods such as eavesdropping, malware, spoofing, and denial-of-service that attackers have used to perpetrate cybercrime. The review shows that IoT devices can facilitate a wide range of cybercrimes, including burglary via occupancy detection, smart lock exploitation, stalking, identity theft, blackmail, and even physical harm. These harms stem from vulnerabilities in the device design such as poor security consideration, lack of encryption, and weak authentication.

Farooq et al. [11] highlight key limitations in WSDs including their reliance on manual activation, inaccurate predictions due to sensor variability, battery constraints, and dependence on Internet connectivity. In addition, many devices rely heavily on smartphones or pre-registered contacts, which may not always be available [15]. False alarms due to sensor inaccuracies, battery dependency, lack of portability, and privacy concerns are also significant challenges for WSDs adoption.

While the review papers examine IoT for safety and security, they largely focus on external threats and women safety. They do not critically analyze how smart home systems themselves may enable interpersonal violence or abuse, nor do they sufficiently explore system-level mechanisms within smart home systems for prevention, detection, and response to interpersonal violence and abuse.

3 Methodology

This study follows a systematic mapping study (SMS) methodology as outlined by [25] and is guided by the PRISMA framework [24]. The SMS methodology provides a structured and reproducible approach for identifying, categorizing, and analyzing existing literature, enabling a broad overview of the research landscape. The PRISMA framework supports transparency and rigor in the study selection and reporting process by structuring the identification, screening, eligibility, and inclusion phases of the review. The goal of this review is to map and categorize existing research on the intersection between smart home systems and interpersonal violence and abuse, examine how the literature addresses abuse facilitation and intervention mechanisms, and identify research gaps that can inform future smart home design and development.

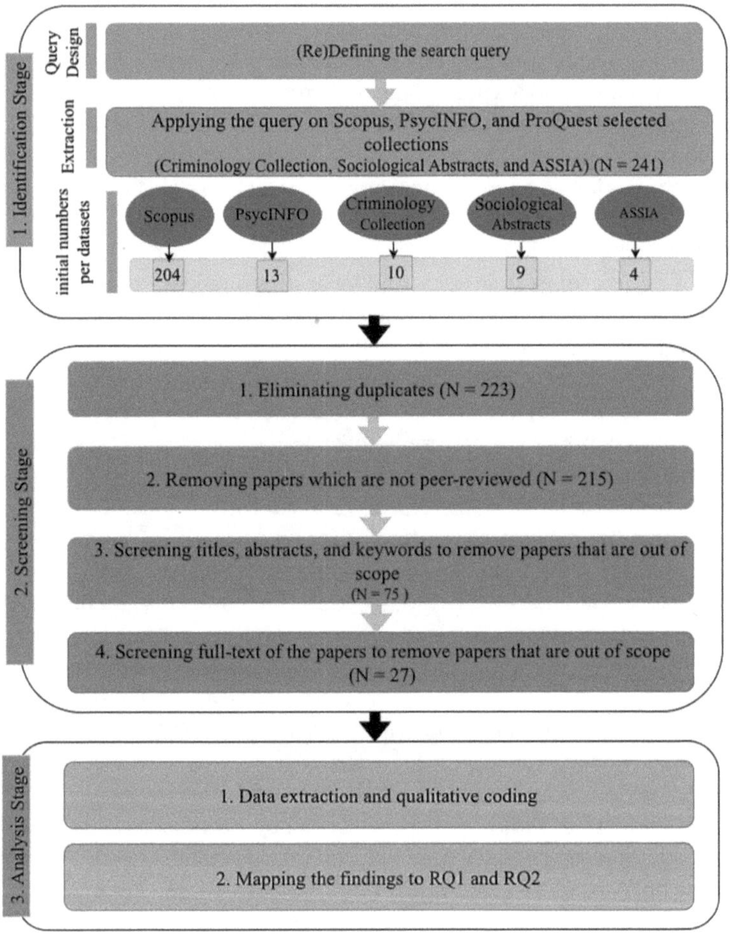

Fig. 1. Research methodology stages.

3.1 Identification Stage

As illustrated in Fig. 1, a systematic search was conducted across multiple academic databases, including Scopus, PsycINFO, and ProQuest database, specifically the Criminology Collection, Sociological Abstracts, and ASSIA, to capture a broad range of research (conducted on 18 February 2026). The search query was iteratively refined through pilot searches to balance recall and precision and separately applied to these databases. The query combines four concept clusters: (1) violence and abuse terms, (2) relational contexts, (3) technology-related terms, and (4) smart home and IoT devices. The full search query is provided in the box below. The search resulted in a total of 241 records across all databases.

Search query used for literature retrieval

```
TITLE-ABS-KEY(
(
    "violen*" OR "abuse" OR "harass*" OR "victim*" OR "stalk*" OR "assault*" OR "aggress*" OR
    "coerci*" OR "threat" OR "intrusion" OR "controlling behavior" OR "controlling behaviour"
)AND(
    "intimate partner" OR "domestic" OR "dating" OR "adolescent dating" OR
    "obsessive relation*" OR "spous*" OR "close relation*" OR "interpersonal"
)AND(
    "technology-facilitated" OR "technology facilitated" OR "technology-assisted" OR
    "technology assisted" OR "technology" OR "tech" OR "technological" OR "digital" OR
    "cyber" OR "electronic" OR "surveillance"
)AND(
    "smart home" OR "connected home" OR "home automation" OR "home assistant" OR "iot" OR
    "smart speaker" OR "smart camera" OR "smart lock" OR "virtual assistant" OR
    "voice assistant" OR "smart environment" OR "smart building" OR "smart microphone" OR
    "alexa" OR "google home" OR "siri" ) )
```

3.2 Screening Stage

The screening process was conducted in multiple steps following the PRISMA guidelines, as illustrated in Fig. 1.

After merging the retrieved records, the duplicates were removed in Screening step 1, resulting in 223 unique papers. In the Screening step 2, non-peer-reviewed publications were also eliminated from the screening process, leaving 215 papers.

In Screening step 3, titles, abstracts, and keywords were reviewed to assess relevance to the research questions. In this step, papers were excluded if they were clearly out of scope. Specifically, studies were removed if they

- did not involve smart home or IoT systems,
- did not relate to interpersonal or domestic contexts, or
- did not provide insights that could directly or indirectly contribute to answering the research questions. This includes studies that do not address either (RQ1) how smart home systems may facilitate or contribute to interpersonal violence and abuse, or (RQ2) how such systems may support prevention, detection, or response mechanisms.

Screening step 3 was conducted in two phases to ensure the quality of the screening process. In the first phase, screening was conducted by a subset of the authors independently for a set of 50 randomly selected articles. The agreement was assessed with the Kappa statistic

$$\kappa = \frac{p_o - p_e}{1 - p_e},$$

where p_0 denotes the observed overall agreement and p_e is the agreement expected by chance. That is, κ, with a maximum value of 1, denotes the proportion of times that the raters agree, corrected for chance agreement, compared to the maximum proportion of times that the raters could agree, also corrected for chance agreement [27].

The first phase was iterated and discussed until sufficient agreement was obtained between the co-authors, and after that the second phase of the screening step was initiated. The motivation for this is that agreement is a sign of quality and indicative of consistent application and shared understanding of the exclusion criteria among co-authors. The first phase of Screening step 3 was iterated twice. In the first iteration, all 5 co-authors reviewed the 50 articles independently. When comparing the results, rather large disagreements were seen. After comparisons and discussions it was found that the PRISMA methodology for exclusion was interpreted in different ways and another iteration was started with the same 50 articles. After the second iteration, where the co-authors reviewed the same 50 articles, the agreement was higher. After these iterations, a κ-value of 0.58 was obtained, which can be interpreted as "moderate" agreement [17]. After analysis it was found that disagreements mainly were due to different classifications of border-line papers, where some authors decided for exclusion but other authors thought that the papers probably would end up being excluded but they decided not to exclude them, just to be certain that they are not missed in case they actually include relevant information. Based on that information and discussion, we proceeded to the second phase of the screening. Following this, the second phase of the screening process was initiated, in which one co-author independently screened all remaining articles.

In Screening step 4, full-text versions of the remaining papers were assessed in detail. Using the same criteria and approach as in the previous stage, papers that were still found to be out of scope were excluded. This resulted in 27 papers eligible for inclusion in the final review.

3.3 Analysis Stage

The final set of included studies was analyzed using a qualitative synthesis approach to address the research questions. The analysis aimed to identify how smart home systems may enable interpersonal violence and abuse (RQ1), and how such systems may support prevention, detection, and response mechanisms (RQ2). For each study, key information was extracted, including study context, methodology, and reported abuse scenarios. Each study was also classified based on the role of IoT within interpersonal abuse (e.g., abuse facilitation, detection, mitigation, or support for victims/survivors), enabling a structured comparison across studies.

First, a qualitative coding process was applied to identify key abuse types described in the studies. Initial categories were informed by the research question and prior literature, including surveillance, remote control, access control misuse, and psychological coercion. Each study was reviewed and assigned one or more abuse types based on its reported findings. In this phase, system characteristics contributing to these abuse types were also identified and captured as much as possible based on the eligible papers included in the study.

Second, the extracted data were mapped to the research questions. Studies focusing on how smart home systems enable or facilitate interpersonal abuse contributed to RQ1. For RQ2, we coded studies based on whether they explicitly proposed mitigation, detection, or support mechanisms. Mitigation mechanisms refer to proactive measures aimed at preventing or reducing abuse, detection mechanisms refer to system capabilities that identify abusive behavior, and support mechanisms refer to system-enabled responses after abuse occurs, such as alerts, assistance, or evidence collection. Only mechanisms explicitly described as system features, design strategies, or technical solutions were included, while studies that discussed challenges or practices without proposing concrete mechanisms were not classified under these categories.

Through this mapping, findings were aggregated across studies to highlight common patterns, compare approaches, and identify gaps in the literature, particularly the imbalance between studies focusing on introducing types of abuse and those proposing effective interventions.

3.4 Threats to Validity

Potential threats to validity were considered in this study, following the commonly accepted categories of construct, internal, external validity, and reliability [32].

Construct validity may be affected by selection bias due to the choice of databases and the design of the search query, which could lead to the omission of relevant studies, particularly those from other databases and gray literature. To reduce this risk, we selected multidisciplinary databases and iteratively refined the search query to improve its coverage. Additionally, we involved researchers from different fields to strengthen conceptual understanding.

Internal validity is affected by factors such as variations in terminology across disciplines, which may limit the completeness of retrieved studies; to address this, the search query was developed using multiple concept clusters and was iteratively refined through pilot searches.

External validity is inherently limited, as the findings are based on the identified articles and thus difficult to generalize beyond the studied context. However, transparency in the research process, including clearly defined exclusion and inclusion criteria, supports future replication. Given the limited studies included, the observed imbalance in research attention across the identified themes should be interpreted as a trend in the current literature rather than a definitive conclusion about the field.

Finally, reliability may be influenced by subjectivity during the study selection process, particularly in the screening stages. To reduce this risk, a calibration step was conducted in which all authors reviewed a shared sample of papers and discussed the inclusion and exclusion criteria to reach a common understanding before applying them to the full dataset.

4 Results

A total of 27 studies were included in the final analysis following the selection process described in Sect. 3. An overview of these studies, including their research methods, key abuse types discussed in the paper, and the roles of smart homes in the context of interpersonal violence and abuse, along with reported mitigation, detection and support mechanisms, is available in this supplementary repository [4].

As shown in the annual distribution (Fig. 2a), although the search query covered publications from the year 2000 onward, all included studies were published after 2019. This highlights the recent emergence of research at the intersection of smart home systems and interpersonal violence and abuse, likely driven by the rapid adoption of IoT systems and increasing awareness of technology-facilitated interpersonal abuse. The included studies span a range of research approaches, including conceptual studies, empirical studies, technical studies, and literature reviews, as illustrated in Fig. 2b. Conceptual studies focus on theoretical reasoning and framework development, representing a substantial portion of the literature and indicating that the field is still developing theoretical and analytical foundations. Empirical studies, involving data-driven approaches such as interviews, surveys, and mixed-methods research, form the second largest portion. In contrast, technical papers, including system design, implementation, and experimental evaluation of smart home systems, represent the smallest portion, suggesting that relatively limited effort has been devoted to implementing and evaluating concrete technical solutions in this domain.

4.1 Types of Abuse and Enabling System Characteristics in Smart Homes

The analysis of the included studies reveals four primary types of abuse facilitated by smart home and IoT systems. The identified abuse categories may overlap, and some studies report abuse scenarios that involve multiple categories. The categories are therefore used to organize recurring themes in the literature rather than as strictly separate forms of abuse. Figure 3 illustrates the distribution of these abuse types across the reviewed studies. These findings indicate that abuse is not limited to isolated technical features, but rather arises from the interaction between data collection capabilities, device control functionalities, and relational power dynamics.

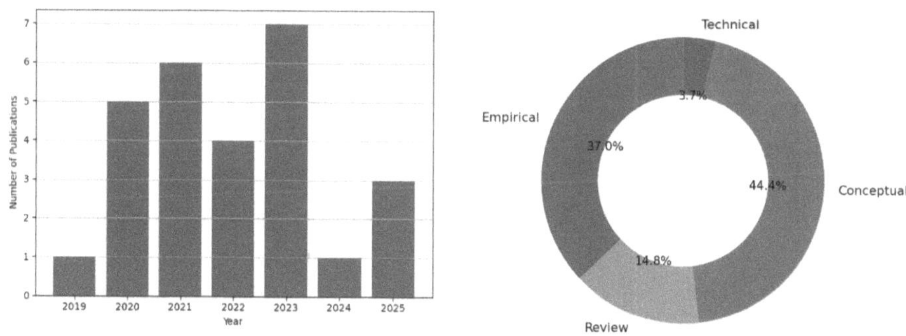

(a) Annual Distribution of Selected Studies

(b) Distribution of Research Strategies

Fig. 2. Overview of study distribution and research strategies.

Surveillance and Monitoring. represent a primary kind of abuse appearing in almost all reviewed studies. These capabilities allow perpetrators to observe victims' activities, movements, and behaviors through interconnected devices such as cameras, sensors, and smart speakers. As shown in Fig. 3, this category includes sub-categories such as location tracking, data logging, and behavioral monitoring. Studies consistently highlight how these features are exploited for abuse. As mentioned by [28,31], IoT devices can be used for covert audio and video monitoring, as well as continuous observation through connected platforms. Such monitoring is often non-transparent, allowing perpetrators to access or manipulate device logs without victims' awareness [1].

These types of abuse are further linked to underlying system characteristics of smart homes. Connected devices support tracking and profiling users' routines and behaviors [22], while continuous sensing and data recording functionalities make such monitoring persistent and difficult to detect [14].

Remote Control and Device Manipulation. are key types of abuse, appearing in the majority of the studies included in our review (see Fig. 3). These types of abuse refer to enabling perpetrators to remotely interact with smart home devices and alter the physical environment. Common actions include controlling lighting, temperature, and appliances, often to disrupt or intimidate victims [19,30].

These types of abuse are enabled by system characteristics such as remote access through mobile applications and the integration and automation of multiple devices, allowing users to manage devices without physical presence [1]. As a result, perpetrators can exert continuous and indirect control over victims' daily life, reinforcing patterns of coercive behavior [31].

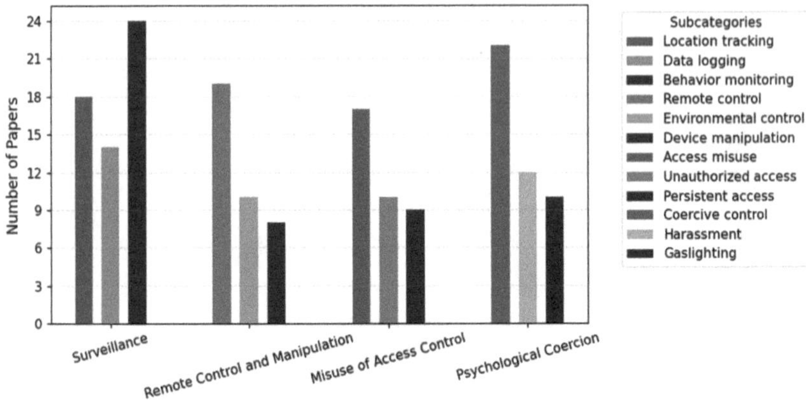

Fig. 3. Types of abuse across interpersonal violence and abuse in smart home studies.

Access Control and Permission Abuse. represent a critical kind of abuse, focusing on controlling who can access and manage smart home systems rather than directly manipulating devices. This includes actions such as unauthorized access, account takeover, and persistent access to shared systems (Fig. 3).

Studies show that perpetrators exploit account structures and permission settings to maintain control. For example, [28,30] describe how abusers retain access to shared devices or accounts after separation from an intimate partner. In addition, [22] highlights how access to personal data and information can be exploited in abusive contexts. Furthermore, [7] show that smart home systems often assign different levels of control to users (e.g., primary and secondary accounts), which can allow one user to exercise greater control over devices and data.

These practices are supported by system characteristics such as shared accounts, limited access differentiation, and low transparency of account activities, which can make it difficult for victims to detect ongoing access or misuse [7,28].

Psychological Coercion and Controlling Behaviors. represent a type of abuse, often emerging through the combined use of surveillance, remote control, and access manipulation. As shown in Fig. 3, and based on studies included in this review, this category includes coercive control, harassment and gaslighting, highlighting that psychological abuse is not a secondary outcome, but a central type of technology-facilitated interpersonal abuse.

Research shows that smart homes can create a sense of constant monitoring and presence [19,31]. Unpredictable device behaviors may be used to intimidate and harass victims, contributing to fear, loss of autonomy, and psychological distress [30]. In some cases, this includes gaslighting, where victims question whether device actions are intentional.

These effects are reinforced by characteristics of smart home systems such as continuous connectivity, automation, and limited transparency, which obscure the source of actions and make abuse difficult to detect. As a result, perpetrators can exert psychological control that may affect victims' perception and sense of safety at home. This is further influenced by the lack of consideration for power imbalance in smart home systems design, allowing these features to be exploited within abusive relationships.

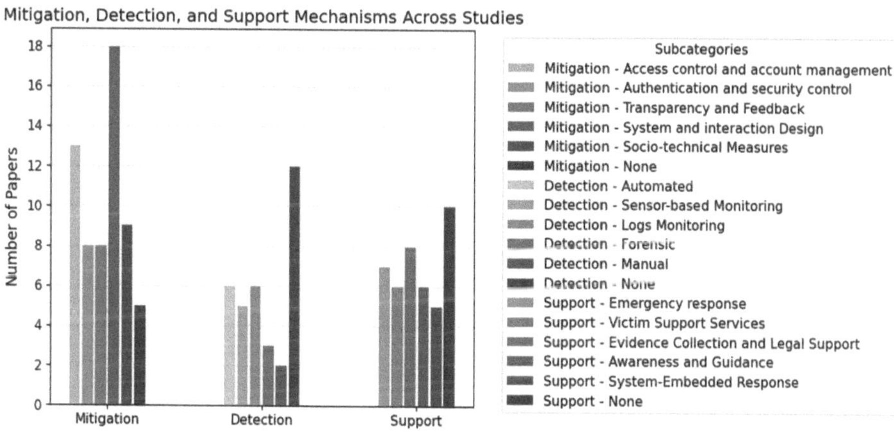

Fig. 4. Mitigation, Detection, and Support Mechanisms discussed across included Studies.

4.2 Prevention, Detection, and Response Mechanisms

Compared to the strong focus on presenting types of abuse, fewer studies propose mechanisms to detect or respond to interpersonal violence and abuse in smart homes. In this review, mechanisms were classified into three categories: mitigation, detection, and support, which correspond to prevention, detection, and response mechanisms as used in the reviewed studies. Mitigation mechanisms focus on preventing or reducing the risk of abuse, detection mechanisms focus on identifying abusive behavior, and support mechanisms focus on assisting victims during or after abusive incidents. This classification focuses on mechanisms, such as system features, design strategies, and technical solutions, extracted from the studies. A mechanism was included if it was explicitly described as enabling prevention, identifying abuse, or supporting victims after an incident. A single study may contribute multiple mechanisms across different categories or subcategories (e.g., a system may include both access control features for mitigation and logging mechanisms for detection). Therefore, the analysis emphasizes the distribution and types of mechanisms across the literature, rather than assigning each paper to a single category.

The following subsections describe each category and its associated mechanisms in detail.

Mitigation Mechanisms. refer to system features, design strategies, and socio-technical approaches that aim to prevent or reduce the risk of interpersonal violence and abuse in smart homes. The identified mitigation mechanisms in the selected studies, span multiple dimensions, as depicted in Fig. 4.

Studies show that mitigation mechanisms focus on reducing power imbalances and preventing misuse through design and system-level features. For example, [18] emphasize abuse-aware design approaches, including multi-user account design, transparency, and improved security controls derived from survivor-informed workshops. Similarly, [1] propose a comprehensive framework that includes multi-user authentication, context-aware access control, and safety-oriented system design.

Detection Mechanisms. refer to system features and technical approaches that aim to identify or reveal instances of interpersonal abuse as they occur or shortly after in smart homes. Unlike mitigation mechanisms, which aim to prevent abuse, detection mechanisms focus on detecting and making abusive behaviors visible. The reviewed studies reveal a diverse set of detection mechanisms, as illustrated in Fig. 4.

Detection mechanisms range from system-level monitoring to automated sensing and analysis, as well as manual identification of abuse through user observation or changes in behavior. For example, [7] highlight the role of system-generated indicators such as access logs, sensor signals, and notifications to reveal hidden monitoring and unauthorized access. In contrast, [23] propose an automated approach using smart microphones and deep learning to detect audio patterns such as screaming, which can then trigger support mechanisms like alerts to notify trusted contacts. These examples show that current detection approaches vary from passive awareness mechanisms to active and automated detection systems. However, detection mechanisms for interpersonal abuse remain limited and are not widely integrated into smart home systems.

Response and Support Mechanisms. focus on assisting victims during or after incidents of interpersonal abuse, enabling help-seeking, recovery, and intervention through system features and support services. What differentiates these mechanisms from mitigation and detection is that, while those mechanisms focus on prevention and identification, response and support emphasize on assisting victims and enabling intervention. The identified mechanisms span multiple approaches, as shown in Fig. 4.

The reviewed studies indicate that response and support mechanisms extend beyond system-level features to include both technical and socio-technical interventions. [29] highlight that smart homes can serve dual roles, not only facilitating abuse but also supporting victims through safety applications, emergency alert systems, and communication tools that enable connection with support networks and recovery processes. Smart homes may also contribute to detection by capturing evidence of abuse through for example monitoring systems or smart devices that are able to record incidents. Additionally, [31] emphasize the need for enhanced training for practitioners, access to specialized expertise, and centralized support resources to better assist victims and address emerging forms of abuse in smart homes.

None of the reviewed studies explicitly address jurisdiction-related integration with local IPV support infrastructures. Associated support mechanisms are generally described as generic support services or trusted contacts, without considering variations in local support infrastructures.

5 Discussion and Conclusion

In this study, we present a structured overview of how smart home systems intersect with interpersonal violence and abuse, highlighting both the risks they introduce and their potential to mitigate, detect and response to such abuse.

The findings suggest that smart homes can enable abuse in multiple ways, shaped by core system features such as connectivity, remote access, shared control, and limited transparency. These kinds of abuse are enabled by core system characteristics such as continuous data collection, remote accessibility, shared account structures, and limited transparency. Notably, abuse emerges not from isolated features but from the interaction between technical capabilities and relational power dynamics, emphasizing the socio-technical nature of smart homes.

Moreover, the review revealed a clear imbalance in the literature. While mitigation mechanisms are relatively well explored, detection and response mechanisms remain limited and fragmented. Detection approaches range from passive mechanisms (e.g., logs and notifications) to automated methods (e.g., sensor-based or AI-driven detection methods). Similarly, response and support mechanisms are often dependent on external services, such as emergency contacts or support organizations, rather than being embedded into smart home systems. The imbalance suggests that the field is still evolving, particularly with respect to detection and support mechanisms. In addition, the fragmentation indicates a lack of cohesive, end-to-end solutions that address prevention, detection, and intervention in a unified manner. This suggests that future research is likely to provide more integrated detection and support solutions. At the same time, it highlights a gap in current smart home systems, which often lack built-in mechanisms for detecting abuse and supporting affected users.

Our findings suggest that risks of interpersonal violence and abuse should be considered as primary design concerns in smart home systems, rather than being treated as secondary issues. Our study can inform system design by contributing to a safety-by-design and abuse-aware design perspective, where potential misuse within close relationships is systematically anticipated and addressed throughout the development life-cycle. In particular, requirements engineering can incorporate abuse scenarios and misuse cases, system design can enforce multi-user access control and transparency mechanisms, and evaluation processes can assess systems not only for security and usability but also for their impact on user safety in shared environments like smart homes. Such approaches extend traditional threat models beyond external attackers to include misuse by insiders with legitimate access, while also considering relational dynamics. Given that the field is still evolving, organizations developing smart home systems should be prepared to revise and adapt their systems as new knowledge becomes available.

Future work should explore how detection and support mechanisms can be designed in ways that are trustworthy, transparent, and sensitive to the needs of different users in shared home environments. This includes understanding how such mechanisms may affect user autonomy, perceptions of safety, and trust in smart home systems. Future reviews could also examine relevant gray literature, including reports from advocacy organizations and public agencies, to determine whether additional mitigation and support approaches are documented outside the peer-reviewed research literature. There is also a need for more empirical and implementation-oriented studies that validate proposed approaches in real-world contexts. From a software engineering standpoint, future research should explore how interpersonal risk analysis can be systematically incorporated into requirements engineering processes, for example by defining abuse scenarios, misuse cases, and stakeholder roles. In addition, there is a need to develop abuse-aware design guidelines that translate these considerations into actionable design decisions, as well as evaluation frameworks that capture both technical and socio-technical dimensions of smart home systems.

Disclosure of Interests. The authors have no competing interests to declare that are relevant to the content of this article.

References

1. Alshehri, A., Salem, M.B., Ding, L.: Are smart home devices abandoning IPV victims? In: 19th International Conference on Trust, Security and Privacy in Computing and Communications (TrustCom), pp. 1368–1375. IEEE (2020). https://doi.org/10.1109/TrustCom50675.2020.00184
2. Ansari, A.M., Nazir, M., Mustafa, K.: Smart homes app vulnerabilities, threats, and solutions: a systematic literature review. J. Netw. Syst. Manag. **32**(2) (2024). https://doi.org/10.1007/s10922-024-09803-1
3. Anthi, E., Williams, L., Słowińska, M., Theodorakopoulos, G., Burnap, P.: A supervised intrusion detection system for smart home IoT devices. IEEE Internet Things J. **6**(5), 9042–9053 (2019). https://doi.org/10.1109/JIOT.2019.2926365
4. Ashkezari, F.D., Höst, M., Jacobsson, A., Adewole, K.S., Svalin, K.: Interpersonal violence and abuse in smart homes: supplementary material (2026). https://zenodo.org/records/19705682, zenodo repository. Accessed 11 June 2026
5. Baxter, G., Sommerville, I.: Socio-technical systems: from design methods to systems engineering. Interact. Comput. **23**(1), 4–17 (2011). https://doi.org/10.1016/j.intcom.2010.07.003
6. Blythe, J.M., Johnson, S.D.: A systematic review of crime facilitated by the consumer Internet of Things: Jm blythe, sd johnson. Secur. J. **34**(1), 97–125 (2021). https://doi.org/10.1057/s41284-019-00211-8

7. Brown, A., Harkin, D., Tanczer, L.M.: Safeguarding the "internet of things" for victim-survivors of domestic and family violence: anticipating exploitative use and encouraging safety-by-design. Violence Against Women **31**(5), 1039–1062 (2025). https://doi.org/10.1177/10778012231222248
8. Bugeja, J., Jacobsson, A., Davidsson, P.: On privacy and security challenges in smart connected homes. In: European Intelligence and Security Informatics Conference (EISIC), pp. 172–175. IEEE (2016). https://doi.org/10.1109/EISIC.2016.044
9. Bugeja, J., Jacobsson, A., Davidsson, P.: Smart connected homes. In: Internet of Things A to Z: Technologies and Applications, pp. 359–384. Wiley (2018). https://doi.org/10.1002/9781119456735.ch13
10. Dehghani Ashkezari, F., Jacobsson, A., Adewole, K.S., Svalin, K., Höst, M.: Research communities in smart homes security: a systematic mapping study. IoT **7**(1), 19 (2026). https://doi.org/10.3390/iot7010019
11. Farooq, M.S., Masooma, A., Omer, U., Tehseen, R., Gilani, S., Atal, Z.: The role of IoT in woman's safety: a systematic literature review. IEEE Access **11**, 69807–69825 (2023). https://doi.org/10.1109/ACCESS.2023.3252903
12. Geeng, C., Roesner, F.: Who's in control? Interactions in multi-user smart homes. In: Proceedings of the CHI Conference on Human Factors in Computing Systems, pp. 1–13 (2019). https://doi.org/10.1145/3290605.3300498
13. Kaushik, K., Bhardwaj, A., Dahiya, S.: Smart home IoT forensics: current status, challenges, and future directions. In: International Conference on Advancement in Computation & Computer Technologies (InCACCT), pp. 716–721. IEEE (2023). https://doi.org/10.1109/InCACCT57535.2023.10141730
14. Köhler, E., Spiekermann, D.: Smart home as a silent witness-a survey. In: Proceedings of the European Interdisciplinary Cybersecurity Conference, pp. 12–16 (2022). https://doi.org/10.1145/3528580.3528583
15. Kommineni, K.K., Basha, S.J., Sandeep, M., Vadana, P.S., Sai, T.S.R., Kumar, D.S.: A review on IoT-based defensive devices for women security. In: 9th International Conference on Advanced Computing and Communication Systems (ICACCS), vol. 1, pp. 99–104. IEEE (2023). https://doi.org/10.1109/ICACCS57279.2023.10113015
16. Krug, E.G., Mercy, J.A., Dahlberg, L.L., Zwi, A.B.: The world report on violence and health. The Lancet **360**(9339), 1083–1088 (2002)
17. Landis, J.R., Koch, G.G.: The measurement of observer agreement for categorical data. Biometrics (1) (1977). https://doi.org/10.2307/2529310
18. Leitão, R.: Anticipating smart home security and privacy threats with survivors of intimate partner abuse. In: Proceedings of the Designing Interactive Systems Conference, pp. 527–539 (2019). https://doi.org/10.1145/3322276.3322366
19. McKay, D., Miller, C.: Standing in the way of control: a call to action to prevent abuse through better design of smart technologies. In: Proceedings of the CHI Conference on Human Factors in Computing Systems, pp. 1–14 (2021). https://doi.org/10.1145/3411764.3445114
20. Mercy, J.A., et al.: Interpersonal violence: global impact and paths to prevention. Inj. Prev. Environ. Health 71–96 (2017). https://doi.org/10.1596/978-1-4648-0522-6_ch5 World Bank
21. Mitchell, M., et al.: Technology-facilitated violence: a conceptual review. Criminol. Crim. Justice **25**(2), 649–669 (2025). https://doi.org/10.1177/17488958221140549
22. Moses, L.B., Breckenridge, J., Gibson, J., Lyons, G.: Technology-facilitated domestic and family violence: protecting the privacy and safety of victim-survivors. Law Technol. Humans **4**(1), 1–17 (2022). https://doi.org/10.5204/lthj.2160

23. Muraleedharan, A., Garcia-Constantino, M.: Domestic violence detection using smart microphones. In: Bravo, J., Ochoa, S., Favela, J. (eds.) Proceedings of the International Conference on Ubiquitous Computing and Ambient Intelligence (UCAmI 2022). UCAmI 2022. LNNS, vol. 594, pp. 357–368. Springer, Cham (2022). https://doi.org/10.1007/978-3-031-21333-5_36
24. Page, M.J., McKenzie, J.E., Bossuyt, P.M., et al.: The prisma 2020 statement: an updated guideline for reporting systematic reviews. BMJ **372**, n71 (2021). https://doi.org/10.1136/bmj.n71
25. Petersen, K., Feldt, R., Mujtaba, S., Mattsson, M.: Systematic mapping studies in software engineering. In: Proceedings of the 12th International Conference on Evaluation and Assessment in Software Engineering (EASE) (2008). https://doi.org/10.14236/ewic/EASE2008.8
26. Quilty, E., Flynn, A.: Technology-facilitated violence in the indo-pacific: a scoping review. Trauma Violence Abuse 15248380251323217 (2025). https://doi.org/10.1177/15248380251323
27. Siegel, S., Castellan Jr., N.J.: Nonparametric Statistics for the Behavioural Sciences. McGraw-Hill, USA (1988)
28. Slupska, J., Tanczer, L.M.: Threat modeling intimate partner violence: tech abuse as a cybersecurity challenge in the internet of things (2021). https://doi.org/10.1108/978-1-83982-848-520211049
29. Sovacool, B., Furszyfer-Del Rio, D.D., Martiskainen, M.: Can prosuming become perilous? Exploring systems of control and domestic abuse in the smart homes of the future. Front. Energy Res. **9**, 765817 (2021). https://doi.org/10.3389/fenrg.2021.765817
30. Stephenson, S., Almansoori, M., Emami-Naeini, P., Chatterjee, R.: It's the equivalent of feeling like you're in jail: lessons from firsthand and secondhand accounts of IoT-Enabled intimate partner abuse. In: 32nd USENIX Security Symposium, pp. 105–122 (2023)
31. Tanczer, L.M., López-Neira, I., Parkin, S.: 'I feel like we're really behind the game': perspectives of the United Kingdom's intimate partner violence support sector on the rise of technology-facilitated abuse. J. Gender-based Violence **5**(3), 431–450 (2021). https://doi.org/10.1332/239868021X16290304343529
32. Wohlin, C., Runeson, P., Höst, M., Ohlsson, M.C., Regnell, B., Wesslén, A.: Experimentation in Software Engineering, 2nd edn. Springer, Cham (2024). https://doi.org/10.1007/978-3-662-69306-3
33. World Health Organization: World Report on Violence and Health. World Health Organization, Geneva, Switzerland (2002). https://iris.who.int/handle/10665/42495
34. Yamauchi, M., Ohsita, Y., Murata, M., Ueda, K., Kato, Y.: Anomaly detection in smart home operation from user behaviors and home conditions. IEEE Trans. Consum. Electron. **66**(2), 183–192 (2020). https://doi.org/10.1109/TCE.2020.2981636
35. Yuan, B., Wan, J., Wu, Y.H., Zou, D.Q., Jin, H.: On the security of smart home systems: a survey. J. Comput. Sci. Technol. **38**(2), 228–247 (2023). https://doi.org/10.1007/s11390-023-2488-3

Assistance to Autonomy: A Systematic Literature Review of Agentic AI Across the Software Development Life Cycle

Spyridon Alvanakis Apostolou[1(✉)], Jan Bosch[1,2], and Helena Holmström Olsson[3]

[1] Department of Computer Science and Engineering, Chalmers University of Technology, Göteborg, Sweden
{spyalv,jan.bosch}@chalmers.se

[2] Department of Mathematics and Computer Science, Eindhoven University of Technology, Eindhoven, The Netherlands

[3] Department of Computer Science and Media Technology, Malmö University, Malmö, Sweden
helena.holmstrom.olsson@mau.se

Abstract. Agentic AI in software product development is increasingly adopted by organizations, yet the field lacks a consolidated synthesis of where adoption is mature, which architectural patterns dominate, and what limitations and coping mechanisms exist in industrial deployments. This systematic literature review addresses these gaps by establishing a body of knowledge as a starting point. Following Kitchenham guidelines, we queried four major research databases, obtaining over 1600 candidate publications. To handle this volume, we developed and validated a domain-agnostic multi-agent screening pipeline that extends prior LLM-assisted review tools by combining automatic metadata curation, inter-agent iterative dialogue, and conflict-resolution defaults that minimize false negatives. From the 92 manually verified primary studies, our thematic synthesis reveals that output verifiability is the primary enabler of agentic adoption: later software development life cycle phases, whose outputs are objectively evaluable through executable feedback, demonstrate the highest maturity and industrial presence, while earlier phases remain almost exclusively academic proofs-of-concept. We identify the Planner-Executor-Reviewer role specialization as the dominant architectural pattern, with the Reviewer agent implementing verifiability through executable feedback loops. Across all challenge categories, industrial mitigation strategies converge on confining agent actions to verifiable, bounded spaces. This study contributes a comprehensive characterization of the current literature on agentic systems in software product development, and a methodological contribution in the form of an AI-assisted tool to automate the screening phase in high-volume SLR domains.

C. Berger and V. Klös (Eds.): SEAA 2026, LNCS 16864, pp. 329–345, 2027.
https://doi.org/10.1007/978-3-032-36587-3_22

Keywords: Agentic AI · Autonomous Systems · LLM agents · Software Development Life Cycle · Software Product Development · Software Engineering · Systematic Literature Review

1 Introduction

The landscape of Artificial Intelligence has evolved rapidly with the advent of Large Language Models (LLMs). The era of generative AI (GenAI) was defined by "passive" interactions, where models generate text in response to explicit human prompts. According to Wang et al. [31], from 2023 the field has been progressing towards agentic AI, which, unlike standard reactive LLMs, is characterized by systems that demonstrate capabilities such as planning, reasoning, use of external tools, self-refinement, and execution of multi-step workflows while requiring minimal human intervention. With this task-oriented behavior, agentic AI pushes the boundaries of traditional LLMs across a wide variety of domains [1,27].

This shift is particularly significant for Software Engineering (SWE). GenAI systems have been integrated into the Software Development Life Cycle (SDLC) as supportive assistants for tasks such as code completion, automated testing, and code generation. The emergence of agentic capabilities reframes the role of GenAI in SWE from assistance to autonomy [11]. Research is increasing rapidly, yet industrial adoption remains in its early stages: inherent LLM limitations, trust concerns, the lack of consolidated architectural patterns, and the rapid obsolescence of underlying models [25] stand as significant barriers to the integration of agentic systems into SDLC phases. As the volume of publications increases rapidly, a systematic synthesis of the current state-of-the-art is necessary. Consequently, this study conducts a Systematic Literature Review (SLR) to analyze and categorize the current state of agentic AI adoption and applications in the SDLC. This is further detailed in the following research questions (RQs):

1. In which phases of the SDLC is agentic AI currently demonstrating the highest maturity and industrial adoption?
2. What architectural patterns (e.g., multi-agent systems, tool use) are predominant in agentic AI implementations?
3. What are the reported challenges in using agentic AI in industrial environments, and how have these limitations been addressed?

The body of literature related to this domain is large and growing rapidly, making traditional manual filtering of publications extremely time-consuming. To address this, we developed and employed a multi-agent system using role-specific LLM agents (Assistant and Evaluator) to automate the screening process and efficiently identify the set of relevant publications.

The contribution of our study is two-fold: first, and most importantly, the results of the systematic literature review, which characterize the current state of agentic AI across the SDLC, while revealing output verifiability as the cross-cutting principle that connects phase maturity, dominant architectural patterns, and industrial mitigation strategies. Second, the multi-agent screening pipeline that extends prior LLM-assisted review tools with automatic metadata curation, inter-agent argumentative dialogue, and inclusion-biased conflict resolution, validated to achieve a low false-negative rate. The remainder of this paper is organized as follows: Sect. 2 analyzes the background of the concept and the related work, Sect. 3 describes the methodology, Sects. 4 and 5 present the research findings, answers to the research questions, and threats to validity, Sect. 6 presents the conclusions and future work, and Sect. 7 provides data and code availability.

2 Background

2.1 The Agentic Turn in SDLC

GenAI was integrated into SDLC phases as an assistant tool through reactive code completion and generation. Tools such as GitHub Copilot, Amazon CodeWhisperer [33], and Meta's CodeCompose [20] demonstrated measurable gains in developer productivity and code generation [5,23]. Nevertheless, the assistants are bounded, responding to explicit prompts without taking autonomous actions beyond immediate output implementations.

As a part of progress, LLM agents extended this baseline by introducing tool integration and a sense-plan-act structure, enabling task-specific automation. However, individual agents remain narrow in scope and operate independently across tasks, lacking features that enhance autonomy [27]. Agentic AI goes further, with capabilities such as task decomposition, persistent memory, and orchestrated autonomy, these systems pursue complex, multi-step goals with minimal human intervention [1,27,28]. Practically, this distinction means agentic systems can span entire SDLC phases rather than individual developer actions.

2.2 Related Work

Research activity in this field has grown substantially since 2023, when the first agentic frameworks for end-to-end development and role-specialized multi agent pipelines began to emerge [31]. Several recent secondary studies approach the topic from complementary angles. He et al. [10] examined 71 primary studies on LLM-based multi-agent systems across the SDLC. Their review is paired with case studies that surface capability limits, and it concludes with a two-phase research agenda focused on individual agent enhancement and, subsequently, agent synergy. A broader synthesis is offered by Liu et al. [18], who survey 106 papers through a dual lens: an SWE perspective spanning individual tasks and end-to-end workflows, and an agent-centric view that analyzes planning, memory, perception, action, and collaboration. Wang et al. [32] take a different direction. Working through 115 papers under a perception-memory-action framework, they flag open issues such as under-explored modalities, hallucination mitigation, and inefficiencies in multi-agent coordination. Otoum and Elkhalili [21] narrow the lens to method categories, namely autonomous coding, multi-agent systems, iterative refinement, and human-agent collaboration, classifying 61 studies along these axes while tracing their temporal evolution and pointing to an early-phase autonomy gap.

Looking beyond software-specific reviews, Bandi et al. [4] cover broader ground. Their analysis of 143 studies across multiple domains contributes concept-level disambiguation of agentic AI paradigms, a comparison of major LLM frameworks, and five architectural models accompanied by evaluation-metric taxonomies. Hosseini and Seilani [11] shift the discussion toward organizational strategy, proposing an adoption framework that addresses business needs, tool selection, and risk management. The practitioner viewpoint is captured by Akbar et al. [3]: drawing on interviews with 21 experts, they argue that agentic AI redefines traditional SDLC phase boundaries through continuous feedback loops and real-time optimization.

We systematically examine peer-reviewed publications on agentic AI across the SDLC, contrasting academic proof-of-concept (PoC) studies with industrially adopted implementations to resolve SDLC-phase maturity (RQ1), architectural patterns in relation to agent autonomy (RQ2), and reported challenges paired with their mitigation strategies in industrial context (RQ3). Critically, rather than organizing findings around agent capabilities or method categories in isolation, our synthesis surfaces output verifiability as the cross-cutting principle that connects phase distribution, architectural design, and industrial mitigation strategies. Beyond the SLR results, the study makes a methodological contribution of a domain-agnostic multi-agent screening pipeline that extends existing LLM-assisted review tools with automatic metadata curation, inter-agent argumentative dialogue, and inclusion-biased conflict resolution, applicable to high-volume SLRs beyond this domain.

3 Methods

3.1 Research Design

As the basis for this SLR, we followed the Kitchenham and Charters guidelines [16]. We consulted an initial list of databases that included: Google Scholar, Scopus, IEEE Xplore, ACM Digital Library, and ScienceDirect. That initial list was further refined to address reproducibility and search functionality issues. Google Scholar was excluded because of the time and location dependence of its results, in addition to an insufficient character limit [8]. ScienceDirect was excluded due to its very restrictive term and boolean limit in advanced search [8]. The refined list, using the terminology defined in [8], consisted of the following libraries:

- IEEE Digital Library http://ieeexplore.ieee.org
- ACM Digital Library http://dl.acm.org
- SpringerLink https://link.springer.com/
- Scopus https://www.scopus.com

3.2 Query

In order to translate the study goal with the research questions to a query structure, we utilized the CIMO (Context, Intervention, Mechanism, Outcome) logic [6]. The key data points extracted included:

- Context: The specific problem domain or application area.
- Intervention: The techniques and methods used at the context.
- Mechanism: The underlying methods and tools employed.
- Outcome: The results achieved, including performance improvements.

The implemented query is the following:

```
("software lifecycle" OR "software development" OR "software product")
AND
("agentic" OR "autonomous agent*" OR "goal-driven agent*" OR "LLM agent*"
     OR ("multi-agent" AND"LLM"))
AND
("tool use" OR "self-reflection" OR "task decomposition" OR "
    orchestration" OR "proactive" OR "goal-driven" OR "task oriented" OR
    "self-adapted")
AND
("automation" OR "accelerat*" OR "efficiency")
```

3.3 Time Frame, Inclusion and Exclusion Criteria

Since the study focuses on agentic AI in SDLC, we limited our review to publications from 2023 onwards, aligning with the timeline identified by Wang et al. [31] who identifies the first agentic frameworks to develop, and thus initiate the transition from standard LLMs to agentic AI as a distinct phase beginning with the advanced reasoning capabilities of models released in early 2023. To avoid collecting unnecessary publications, we employed the timeframe criteria as a filter at the advanced search phase along with the query implementation to each database. Additionally, in order to ensure adherence to the review scope, the inclusion and exclusion criteria shown in Table 1 were curated to be applied to the initial search results. These criteria were designed using the guidance in Kitchenham and Charters [16] and Gough et al. [7].

Along with the time frame filter, we implemented the filter of language during the raw data collection phase when filtered data resulted from the query into the diverse databases.

3.4 Data Analysis Method

Agentic AI is a rapidly evolving domain in which the literature grows continuously, making manual review at scale impractical. This motivated the development of an agile LLM-based tool to reduce reviewer workload. Existing tools such as Rayyan [22] and Abstrackr [30] rely on active learning to prioritize relevant studies. More recently, LatteReview [26] employs role-playing LLM agents

Table 1. Inclusion Criteria

ID	Criteria
1	Publication date within the defined time frame
2	A primary study, not a secondary or a tertiary study
3	Published in a peer-reviewed journal, conference proceeding, or book chapter not in grey literature reports, blog posts, or non-academic publications
4	Published in English
5	Not a duplicate or a version of another included study
6	Discusses LLM agents with particulars matching the agentic characteristic
7	Focuses in software product development
8	Study provides a Proof of Concept (not a vision study)

with hierarchical screening and reasoning transparency. However, LatteReview requires users to manually script agent personas and scoring rules, and expects a complete dataset as input.

To further automate the process and reduce both prompt subjectivity and false negatives, we developed a model- and domain-agnostic six-step pipeline. It requires minimal reviewer input, raw publication metadata (title, DOI, abstract, etc.) and a single detailed prompt containing the research purpose, research questions, and selection criteria. The pipeline includes self-curation of missing abstracts, inter-agent classification discussions, and produces binary relevant/irrelevant labels with full transparency of decisions, reasoning, and agent dialogue.

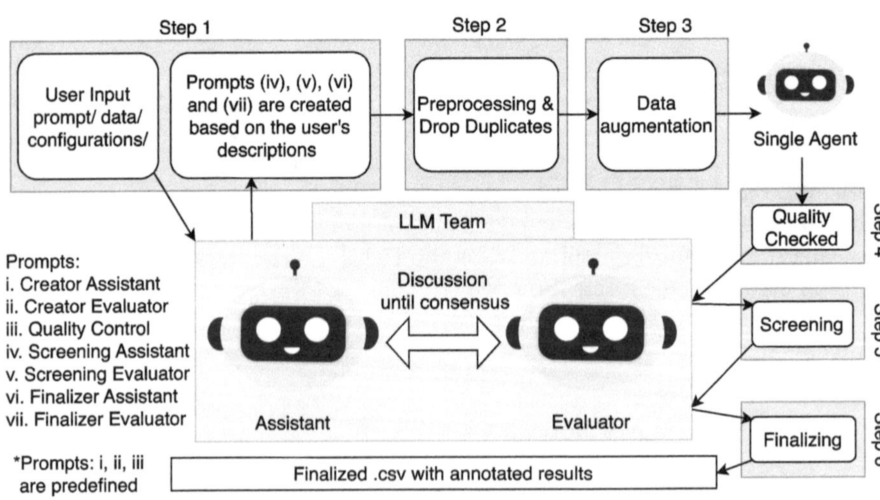

Fig. 1. Analytical workflow of the multi-agent collaboration and consensus mechanism.

In the first step of the workflow, we have two role-playing agents (Assistant and Evaluator) based on the user-provided prompt, respectively they generate and evaluate task-specific prompts for the subsequent phases, only after the reviewer approves the final prompt of each task the process proceeds to the next step. In the second step, raw exports from multiple databases (CSV, RIS, or BIB format) are normalized into a unified CSV with duplicates records removed. In the third step, a self-curation process retrieves missing abstracts via web scraping and API-driven augmentation.

From step four onward, records are filtered against the inclusion criteria. In the Quality Control step, a single agent excludes non-research items (e.g., conference preambles, generic book chapters). A human verification of excluded records lacking abstracts is recommended at this stage to prevent accidental omission of legitimate studies.

In the Screening step, the Assistant and Evaluator agents independently classify each publication against the inclusion/exclusion criteria and high-level domain relevance. It is important to note here that, for every double-agent step, we employed different models in order to minimize classification errors when independent reasoning paths reach the same conclusion. In case of conflict, a structured inter-agent dialogue with iterative argumentation (up to three rounds or until agreement) is triggered to finalize the classification label, unresolved conflicts default to inclusion to minimize false negatives. The purpose of this dialogue is to leverage one agent's reasoning to challenge the other's classification, serving as an additional de-hallucination mechanism. The final Relevance Selection step applies the same multi-agent process, now focused on alignment with the research questions and scope. The complete workflow is illustrated in Fig. 1.

The two-phase (screening and relevance) design serves three purposes: (1) modularity, allowing costlier models to be selectively applied to the smaller candidate set in the final phase only, (2) reduced agent cognitive load, as each phase operates under a constrained set of criteria, and (3) independent evaluability of each stage.

Following the automated pipeline, the candidate relevant publications underwent manual evaluation following a structured two-pass protocol. In the first pass, each selected as relevant study's abstract was first read and applied Criteria 6, 7, and 8 from Table 1 to confirm or reject the automated label. In the second pass, studies confirmed as relevant were read in full to extract responses to at least one of the research questions. Data extraction was guided by a predefined coding sheet capturing: (i) targeted SDLC phase, (ii) evaluation context (academic benchmark vs. industrial deployment), (iii) architectural pattern, and (iv) reported limitations and mitigations.

4 Results

4.1 Query and Data Analysis Implementation

The search was executed across the databases and search systems described in Sect. 3.1, using the query as described in Sect. 3.2. Table 2 summarizes the results acquired from each phase of the process.

We initially provided the prompt-creation agents with a definition and a detailed description of the agentic AI concept, together with all the research questions and the exclusion criteria (except the language and time-range filters, which had already been applied at the database query stage). Based on these inputs, four prompts were automatically generated for the screening and relevance phases. We employed bigger models for the prompt-generation phase (Assistant (A): gpt-5.4, Evaluator (E): gpt-5.2) to ensure high-quality prompt generation, and smaller yet capable models for the subsequent phases to manage cost (A-scr: gpt-5-mini, E-scr: gpt-5-nano, A-rel: gpt-5-mini, E-rel: deepseek-v3).

Table 2. Search Process Results

Source	Raw	Proces.	QC	SC	Relev.	Manual Eval.
ACM	659	605	139	44	16	9
IEEE	289	284	247	106	55	41
Scopus	485	326	315	88	43	32
Springer	276	116	95	27	13	10
Total	**1609**	**1331**	**796**	**265**	**127**	**92**

As illustrated in Table 2, a significant number of records corresponded to generic conference introductions rather than actual research publications and were consequently excluded. After completing the quality-control step, the final number of valid publications was 796. A manual inspection of the generated annotations from this step revealed that only 3 out of the 1331 retrieved records were still missing abstracts while still representing legitimate research publications.

We applied the final two steps of the process. It is worth noting that the screening phase is the most time-consuming step, as a large number of quality checked publication's abstracts must be evaluated by two independent agents. Out of 796 valid publications, 265 passed the screening phase, the remaining 531 were excluded for failing to meet the inclusion criteria beyond those already enforced (date range, publication type, and language, Criteria 1, 3, and 4 in Table 1). The final relevance-selection step identified 127 candidate studies. Following the manual evaluation procedure described in Sect. 3.4, which involved reading the abstracts of all 127 papers, we identified 101 as conceptually relevant, from which we read the full text. Finally, 92 were confirmed as the final relevant set, since 9 papers lacked a PoC and were excluded. Consequently, we identified 26 as false positives produced by the automated pipeline, since only the abstracts were provided to the agents. In addition to this manual verification, a random sample drawn from the quality-control and screening exclusion sets was evaluated to further validate the selection process and ensure that false-negative classifications were minimized.

False Negatives Evaluation. To evaluate the pipeline's reliability, we sampled 100 publications that were excluded by the agent-based stages: 50 excluded during the screening phase and 50 excluded during the final relevance selection phase. Following the central limit theorem rule of thumb, a minimum of 30 samples per stage was considered sufficient to approximate normality in the sampling distribution, and this is why we consider the samples of 50 sufficient. Manual evaluation of each sample was performed to identify any false negatives.

The single false negative identified across the full sample of 100 came from the relevance-selection phase (1/50), while no misclassifications were observed in the screening step (0/50). Extrapolating the observed rate across the full excluded population (669 papers), suggests approximately 7 missed relevant publications in total, and since the sole missed publication originated from the relevance-selection phase, which operates on a smaller candidate set, the true number is likely even lower.

4.2 Thematic Synthesis

Combining the information from the final set of 92 publications, we structured the answers to our initial research questions.

RQ1. In which phases of the SDLC is agentic AI currently demonstrating the highest maturity and industrial adoption?

The phase distribution of the final publications set is summarized in Table 3. From 92 studies only 13 were developed and evaluated in an industrial context, while the rest 79 represent academic PoC studies evaluated on benchmarks or controlled experimental settings. For both types of studies we can observe from Table 3 that the phases of the SDLC that demonstrate higher representation are **Testing & QA**, **Maintenance**, **Deployment**, and **Coding & Implementation** indicating that agentic AI maturity is concentrated in post-development phases.

The dominance of post-development phases reflects an important characteristic. They include tasks from which the performance can be verified through objective, executable feedback (e.g., test results, compiler outputs, fault localization traces, and log signals). These concrete results provide the agents a specific state to improve during self-refinement loops, which can be implemented without human evaluation.

On the industrial side, the concentration in Testing & QA reflects the state, that testing is a time consuming and labour intensive phase of the SDLC, and its outcomes are verifiable. Publications in this concept target high-cost bottlenecks with clear success criteria, from GUI testing of production desktop and web applications to automotive software release gatekeeping [15] and structural testing of agentic systems themselves [17]. Moreover, Deployment & Operations tasks follow the same logic, as AIOps agents monitor structured operational signals (e.g., metrics, logs, and CI/CD states), which outputs can be evaluated against concrete production thresholds for service performance anomaly detection [13,15].

The underrepresentation of Coding & Implementation and Maintenance with industrial implementation does not necessarily translate as lack of research effort in these areas. Academic studies classified under these phases demonstrate that the majority rely on test execution as primary verification mechanism. Studies targeting code generation, automated debugging, and program repair (corresponding examples of systems: EvoMAC, SoapFL, and RGD), validate their contributions through unit tests or benchmarks such as HumanEval or Defects4J [12,14,24]. Notably, Maintenance, Coding & Implementation from the literature are not fully distinguished by the Testing & QA phase, since the correctness of the agents outputs is eventually evaluated by a form of testing. This suggests that Testing & QA represents an entry point for industrial agentic adoption, while the integration of agentic systems in Maintenance or Coding & Implementation require agents to operate on large industrial codebases with legacy systems, undocumented constraints, and evolving requirements that controlled benchmarks do not capture.

Table 3. Distribution of Primary Studies by SDLC Phase and Evaluation Context

SDLC Phase	Industrial	Academic	Total
Maintenance	1	19	20
Testing & QA	5	13	18
Cross-cutting (multiple phases)	4	11	15
Deployment & Operations	2	12	14
Coding & Implementation	0	12	12
Requirements Analysis	0	7	7
Project Management	1	2	3
Design & Architecture	1	2	3
Total	**13**	**79**	**92**

Finally, Requirements Analysis, Design & Architecture, and Project Management represent the least explored phases, almost exclusively in academic settings. While limited in volume, the industrial context studies in Design & Architecture and Project Management demonstrate that meaningful agentic integration is feasible even in early SDLC stages, ranging from formal architectural verification [29] to agile sprint planning automation [2].

RQ2. What architectural patterns (e.g., multi-agent systems, tool use) are predominant in agentic AI implementations?

The predominant architecture across the selected studies is multi-agent role specialization. In this concept complex SWE tasks are decomposed in sequential or graph-based pipelines of agents, each assigned with a specific and bounded responsibility. The most common structure is Planner → Executor → Reviewer, with an Orchestrator agent managing the flow of the sub-processes. Notably, this structure pattern appeared in all the SDLC phases publications. Moreover, the rationale is to reduce the cognitive load of the agents by narrowing their scope in order to produce more predictable and accurate outcomes, while additionally structured typed inter-agent communication methods (e.g., via JSON or LangGraph state graphs) in many occasions replaced free text handoffs with formally typed state transitions. A key example of an industrial case study, illustrates why this structure succeeds in practice. A two-agent Planner-Actor configuration is used for software release gatekeeping [15], where the Planner applies Chain-of-Thought reasoning with self-consistency to generate a release strategy, and the Actor executes from a predefined atomic action vocabulary with self-reflection for error correction. Restricting the Actor to a fixed action set was key to industrial adoption, as it bounds operational risk without sacrificing the reasoning flexibility of the Planner, achieving a separation between what to do and how to do it safely.

Beyond agent role decomposition, memory and retrieval architectures form the second structural axis of the surveyed systems. Memory and information retrieval with Retrieval-Augmented Generation (RAG) is implemented as a baseline mechanism for injecting domain-relevant context. Interestingly, we mostly find variations in industrial studies. For an agentic RAG system (validated in production settings at Apple) [9], the authors developed a hybrid vector-graph knowledge system to preserve structural relationships between test artifacts and requirements, addressing this way the loss of relational context in flat retrieval. Similarly, the Codebase-Aware Generative Agents system [19] uses a Zero-Shot Dependency Mapping Knowledge Graph as a shared memory layer across agents. By combining deterministic static code parsing with constrained LLM extraction, this approach enables reasoning over structural code relationships, addressing architectural blindness.

RQ3. What are the reported challenges in using agentic AI in industrial environments, and how have these limitations been addressed?

This research question focuses on industrial studies, in which agentic systems are developed and evaluated under real-world company-specific contexts. Before we dive into it, it is important to note that there is a difference on perspective between academic and industrial based studies, nevertheless the limitations are similar. Academic implementations mostly focus on performance and feasibility under controlled experimental conditions, while industrial case studies attempt to address reliability issues to ensure consistency. Overall, the most common limitations we found in studies are the following: non-deterministic behavior, information overload, hallucinations, and scalability.

Non-determinism and Hallucinations: Non-determinism and hallucinations in LLM outputs are universally acknowledged. In most studies (from both categories) the predominant coping mechanism is iterative self-correction loops, in which systems identify their own mistakes based on results from the evaluation method (e.g., testing, compiler output, logs, metrics). An extra feature to narrow the scope of agents is role assignments with detailed instructions or chain of thought to provide information about steps, rather than letting the agents finding them on their own. Industrial studies, while adopting these coping mechanisms, implement additional constraint layers. More specifically, systems developed for domain-specific information implement a terminology knowledge base with semantic meanings to enhance the understanding of the agents, additionally in the same study, the complexity of the two-agent system were mostly assigned to one agent for transparency and interpretation reasons, while the second agent had a pre-defined action space [15]. The latter is widely employed in industrial studies with variations (tool calling or API communication) or structured outputs of agents in order to reduce hallucinations from unstructured text. Notably, in a different perspective industrial study instead of trying to force the AI to be perfectly predictable, built a rigorous, automated safety net around the AI to catch it if it makes a mistake [17], representing a shift that agents are not only tools but also subjects of verification.

Scalability: Agentic AI systems in industrial contexts mostly operate on large codebases, distributed microservices, and continuous streams of logs. More specifically, scalability concerns in industrial contexts span computational cost, execution time, and context size. Multi-agent iterative loops and tree-search strategies (e.g., Monte Carlo exploration) introduce costs that grow non-linearly with task complexity. While in most studies task-decomposition is enough narrow the scope of the agent, cases that manage real time monitoring needs extra steps. For example, systems employed for continuous and massive-scale operations utilize a combination of decentralized execution with task delegation in containerized Kubernetes environments, and dynamic stream processing via engines that compute metrics over sliding time windows of data [13]. Other common solutions, target stage-specific pass/fail tests to reject intermediate errors directly rather than propagate them to later pipeline steps.

Context Management and Information Overload: In industrial environments, the information stream is heterogeneous and continuous, as context is imported from source code, execution logs, documentation, and architectural artifacts. This limitation is not independent of the aforementioned ones, since in many occasions large information that exceeds the context window increases the likelihood of hallucinations or incomplete answers, while additionally requires more computational time increasing the latency and the demand of sources to avoid bottlenecks. As described in RQ2, a common mitigation strategy in both industrial and non-industrial studies is the use of RAG to address this challenge. However, specifically in industrial contexts, a flat vector retrieval alone is unable to preserve structural relationships between artifacts. The CA-SAF system [19] addresses this with a Zero-Shot Dependency Mapping Knowledge Graph, replacing flat retrieval with graph-based reasoning over structural code relationships. Similarly, another testing system uses a hybrid vector-graph representation that preserves business-logic relationships between test artifacts and requirements [9]. These approaches represent architectures where retrieval is structurally grounded rather than semantically approximate.

4.3 Synthesis and Discussion

Examining the three RQs jointly reveals a unifying principle: *output verifiability* operates as the primary enabler of agentic adoption, and its influence is traceable across phase distribution, architectural design, and industrial mitigation strategy.

RQ1 shows that the phases with the highest maturity and industrial presence (Testing & QA, Deployment & Operations, and Maintenance) are those whose outputs are objectively evaluable via executable feedback. Requirements Analysis and Design & Architecture, remain almost exclusively in academic PoC territory. This asymmetry suggests that the current ceiling of industrial agentic adoption is defined by the availability of ground-truth feedback at the task level.

RQ2 highlights this at the architectural level. The dominant Planner-Executor-Reviewer pattern is not only a coordination structure, the Reviewer agent is the verifiability mechanism, providing the feedback that grounds iterative refinement. The industrial preference for hybrid vector-graph retrieval over flat RAG adds a structural layer for verifiability to the information-access layer. Finally, RQ3 shows that industrial mitigations across all challenge categories converge on confining agent actions to bounded, verifiable spaces (predefined actions, structured outputs, stage-wise pass/fail tests).

These observations imply that extending agentic integration into early SDLC phases is, first and foremost, a problem of designing phase appropriate feedback mechanisms rather than of improving model capability.

5 Threats to Validity

Threats to Internal Validity: The search strategy was systematically defined and implemented across multiple major databases, although relevant studies may have been omitted due to query keyword limitations or database coverage. The automated pipeline was designed to minimize false negatives, to validate this we sampled excluded publications from two distinct phases of the six-step process and projected the estimated false-negative rate (≈1%) to the larger excluded set, estimating ≈7 misclassified studies. Furthermore, relevance decisions depend on predefined prompts and specific LLM models, meaning prompt inaccuracies or future model changes may introduce systematic variability in classification outcomes that cannot be fully controlled.

Threats to External Validity: This review focuses on peer-reviewed publications from 2023 onwards. Grey literature was deliberately excluded, as peer-reviewed studies provide methodological transparency and independent validation, however this entails an information loss since industrial agentic AI practices frequently emerge in grey literature prior to formal publication. Additionally, many industrial studies rely on proprietary data and organization-specific workflows, limiting the transferability of reported architectures and mitigation strategies across contexts.

Threats to Temporal Validity: Given the rapid evolution of agentic AI, the findings reflect the literature available at the time of data collection. However, the identification of open challenges and research gaps provides a forward-looking perspective that partially mitigates this limitation.

6 Conclusions and Future Work

This systematic literature review synthesizes the current state of agentic AI in software product development based on 92 primary studies identified through a structured search across four major scientific databases. The screening process was accelerated by a multi-agent pipeline that extends existing LLM-assisted review approaches with automatic metadata curation, inter-agent dialogue, and inclusion-biased conflict resolution, validated to achieve a low false negative rate.

The thematic synthesis across the three research questions reveals a unifying principle: output verifiability is the primary enabler of agentic AI adoption. RQ1 shows that the phases with the highest industrial presence (Testing & QA, Deployment & Operations, and Maintenance) are those whose outputs are objectively evaluable through executable feedback (test results, compiler outputs, operational metrics). Earlier lifecycle phases remain almost exclusively as purely academic PoCs, constrained by the absence of ground-truth feedback signals. RQ2 identifies the Planner-Executor-Reviewer role specialization as the dominant architecture, where the Reviewer implements verifiability within iterative refinement loops. RQ3 shows that across reported challenge categories (non-determinism, hallucinations, scalability, and context overload), industrial mitigation strategies consistently converge on confining agent actions to verifiable, bounded spaces.

Future Work: The most consequential open direction is extending agentic integration into other SDLC phases, which requires establishing phase-appropriate verifiability mechanisms to enable the iterative feedback loops that currently drive adoption in post-development stages. A second direction concerns the long-term assessment of production-scale agentic systems, evaluating their maintainability, adaptability, and reliability under evolving codebases and shifting requirements, conditions that controlled benchmarks do not capture. Finally, establishing empirical comparison protocols between multi-agent architectures across SDLC phases would allow practitioners to make principled decisions about agent autonomy and orchestration design.

7 Data and Code Availability

To facilitate the reproducibility of our methodology, we have made the complete replication developed tool available in an online repository.[1]. This repository contains the source code of the developed multi-agent pipeline, the specific prompts utilized for the Assistant and Evaluator agents, and the raw datasets resulting from the query implementation across the four queried databases.

Acknowledgments. This study was funded by Software Center.

Disclosure of Interests. The authors have no competing interests to declare that are relevant to the content of this article.

References

1. Acharya, D.B., Kuppan, K., Divya, B.: Agentic AI: autonomous intelligence for complex goals—a comprehensive survey. IEEE Access **13**, 18912–18936 (2025). https://ieeexplore.ieee.org/abstract/document/10849561
2. Adapa, C., Anjana, A., Rahim, R., Victor, A.: A multi-agent AI framework for agile workflow automation, issue resolution, and developer performance evaluation. In: 2025 IEEE International Conference for Women in Innovation, Technology & Entrepreneurship (ICWITE), pp. 1–6. IEEE (2025)
3. Akbar, M.A., Khan, A.A., Hamza, M., et al.: Agentic AI in software engineering: practitioner perspectives across the software development life cycle (2025). https://papers.ssrn.com/abstract=5520159
4. Bandi, A., Kongari, B., Naguru, R., et al.: The rise of agentic AI: a review of definitions, frameworks, architectures, applications, evaluation metrics, and challenges. Future Internet **17**(9) (2025). https://www.mdpi.com/1999-5903/17/9/404
5. Becker, J., Rush, N., Barnes, E., Rein, D.: Measuring the Impact of Early-2025 AI on Experienced Open-Source Developer Productivity (2025). http://arxiv.org/abs/2507.09089
6. Denyer, D., Tranfield, D., van Aken, J.E.: Developing design propositions through research synthesis. Organ. Stud. **29**(3), 393–413 (2008). https://doi.org/10.1177/0170840607088020
7. Gough, D., Thomas, J., Oliver, S.: An Introduction to Systematic Reviews. SAGE (2017)
8. Gusenbauer, M., Haddaway, N.R.: Which academic search systems are suitable for systematic reviews or meta-analyses? Res. Synth. Methods **11**(2), 181–217 (2020). https://doi.org/10.1002/jrsm.1378

[1] https://doi.org/10.5281/zenodo.20670298.

9. Hariharan, M., Arvapalli, S., Barma, S., Sheela, E.: Agentic RAG for Software Testing with Hybrid Vector-Graph and Multi-Agent Orchestration (2025). http://arxiv.org/abs/2510.10824
10. He, J., Treude, C., Lo, D.: LLM-Based Multi-Agent Systems for Software Engineering: Literature Review, Vision and the Road Ahead (2025). http://arxiv.org/abs/2404.04834
11. Hosseini, S., Seilani, H.: The role of agentic AI in shaping a smart future: a systematic review. Array **26**, 100399 (2025). https://www.sciencedirect.com/science/article/pii/S2590005625000268
12. Hu, Y., Cai, Y., Du, Y., et al.: Self-Evolving Multi-Agent Collaboration Networks for Software Development (2024). http://arxiv.org/abs/2410.16946
13. Ji, X., Zhang, L., Zhang, W., et al.: LEMAD: LLM-empowered multi-agent system for anomaly detection in power grid services. Electronics **14**(15), 3008 (2025). https://www.mdpi.com/2079-9292/14/15/3008
14. Jin, H., Sun, Z., Chen, H.: RGD: Multi-LLM Based Agent Debugger via Refinement and Generation Guidance (2024). http://arxiv.org/abs/2410.01242
15. Khoee, A.G., Yu, Y., Feldt, R., et al.: GoNoGo: An Efficient LLM-based Multi-Agent System for Streamlining Automotive Software Release Decision-Making (2024). http://arxiv.org/abs/2408.09785
16. Kitchenham, B., Charters, S.: Guidelines for performing systematic literature reviews in software engineering. Keele (2007)
17. Kohl, J., Kruse, O., Mostafa, Y., et al.: Automated structural testing of LLM-based agents: methods, framework, and case studies (2026). http://arxiv.org/abs/2601.18827
18. Liu, J., Wang, K., Chen, Y., et al.: Large Language Model-Based Agents for Software Engineering: A Survey (2025). http://arxiv.org/abs/2409.02977
19. Mavani, V.K.: Codebase aware generative agents for the SDLC: automating documentation, dependency analysis and test generation. In: 2026 IEEE 5th International Conference on AI in Cybersecurity (ICAIC), pp. 1–4 (2026). https://ieeexplore.ieee.org/document/11395666
20. Murali, V., Maddila, C., Ahmad, I., et al.: AI-assisted code authoring at scale: fine-tuning, deploying, and mixed methods evaluation. Proc. ACM Softw. Eng. **1**(FSE), 48:1066–48:1085 (2024). https://doi.org/10.1145/3643774
21. Otoum, N., Elkhalili, N.: Methods and techniques of agentic software engineering: a systematic literature review. IEEE Access **14**, 7443–7465 (2026). https://ieeexplore.ieee.org/abstract/document/11343819
22. Ouzzani, M., Hammady, H., Fedorowicz, Z., Elmagarmid, A.: Rayyan—a web and mobile app for systematic reviews. Syst. Rev. **5**(1), 210 (2016). https://doi.org/10.1186/s13643-016-0384-4
23. Peng, S., Kalliamvakou, E., Cihon, P., Demirer, M.: The Impact of AI on Developer Productivity: Evidence from GitHub Copilot (2023). http://arxiv.org/abs/2302.06590
24. Qin, Y., Wang, S., Lou, Y., et al.: SoapFL: a standard operating procedure for llm-based method-level fault localization. IEEE Trans. Softw. Eng. **51**(4), 1173–1187 (2025). https://ieeexplore.ieee.org/document/10891926
25. Raheem, T., Hossain, G.: Agentic AI systems: opportunities, challenges, and trustworthiness. In: 2025 IEEE International Conference on Electro Information Technology (eIT), pp. 618–624 (2025). https://ieeexplore.ieee.org/abstract/document/11103638

26. Rouzrokh, P., Khosravi, B., Rouzrokh, P., Shariatnia, M.: LatteReview: A Multi-Agent Framework for Systematic Review Automation Using Large Language Models (2025). http://arxiv.org/abs/2501.05468
27. Sapkota, R., Roumeliotis, K.I., Karkee, M.: AI Agents vs. Agentic AI: a conceptual taxonomy, applications and challenges. Inf. Fusion **126**, 103599 (2026). http://arxiv.org/abs/2505.10468
28. Schneider, J.: Generative to Agentic AI: Survey, Conceptualization, and Challenges (2025). http://arxiv.org/abs/2504.18875
29. Tahat, A., Amundson, I., Hardin, D., Cofer, D.: Agree-dog copilot: a neuro-symbolic approach to enhanced model-based systems engineering. In: International Conference on Bridging the Gap between AI and Reality, pp. 117–137. Springer, Heidelberg (2025). https://doi.org/10.1007/978-3-032-07132-3_8
30. Wallace, B.C., Small, K., Brodley, C.E., et al.: Deploying an interactive machine learning system in an evidence-based practice center: abstrackr. In: Proceedings of the 2nd ACM SIGHIT International Health Informatics Symposium, IHI '12, pp. 819–824. Association for Computing Machinery, New York (2012). https://doi.org/10.1145/2110363.2110464
31. Wang, L., Ma, C., Feng, X., et al.: A survey on large language model based autonomous agents. Front. Comp. Sci. **18**(6), 186345 (2024). https://doi.org/10.1007/s11704-024-40231-1
32. Wang, Y., Zhong, W., Huang, Y., et al.: Agents in Software Engineering: Survey, Landscape, and Vision (2024). http://arxiv.org/abs/2409.09030
33. Yetiştiren, B., Özsoy, I., Ayerdem, M., Tüzün, E.: Evaluating the Code Quality of AI-Assisted Code Generation Tools: An Empirical Study on GitHub Copilot, Amazon CodeWhisperer, and ChatGPT (2023). http://arxiv.org/abs/2304.10778

Large Language Models for Fuzz Testing in Microservices: A Systematic Literature Review

Ying Song[1], Ke Ping[1], Yuqing Wang[1], and Xiaozhou Li[2](✉)

[1] University of Helsinki, Helsinki, Finland
{ying.song,ke.ping,yuqing.wang}@helsinki.fi
[2] Free University of Bozen-Bolzano, Bolzano, Italy
xiaozhou.li@unibz.it

Abstract. Microservice systems (MSS) increasingly rely on heterogeneous APIs whose combinatorial input space and stateful dependencies challenge traditional fuzz testing. Meanwhile, Large Language Models (LLMs) have recently been introduced to enhance fuzzing with semantic reasoning over specifications, inputs, and runtime feedback. This paper presents a systematic literature review (SLR) of LLM-assisted fuzz testing for microservices to synthesise how LLMs are applied, evaluated, and what challenges remain. Following established SLR guidelines, we analyze 20 primary studies published between 2024 and 2026. Results show LLMs are mainly used as semantic input generators in black-box fuzzing, with a growing shift towards agent-based and retrieval-augmented architectures, improving valid input generation and modestly increasing coverage and vulnerability detection. However, evaluation remains heterogeneous, with limited benchmark standardization, scarce cost reporting, and a bias toward single-service experiments, highlighting a gap with real-world multi-service systems. This review provides a taxonomy of LLM roles and integrations, a consolidated view of evaluation practices, and a mapping of open challenges to research directions, supporting the design and deployment of LLM-driven fuzzing in microservices.

Keywords: Large Language Models · Fuzz Testing · Microservices · REST API Testing · Systematic Literature Review

1 Introduction

Microservice architectures are widely adopted in modern software systems. They decompose applications into loosely coupled services that interact through APIs [3]. While this improves scalability and maintainability, it also introduces significant testing challenges. In particular, the large parameter spaces of APIs, inter-parameter dependencies, and multi-step workflows across services make systematic testing in microservice systems (MSS) challenging [11,15].

C. Berger and V. Klös (Eds.): SEAA 2026, LNCS 16864, pp. 346–362, 2027.
https://doi.org/10.1007/978-3-032-36587-3_23

Fuzz testing has been widely used to address this problem, as it can automatically generate and execute diverse inputs to explore large numbers of test scenarios and detect failures such as crashes and server errors [19]. However, existing API fuzzers still have limitations. They often generate invalid inputs, struggle to satisfy complex constraints, and fail to reach deeper program states [5,10]. They also lack the ability to use API documentation, interpret error responses, or handle dependencies between inputs and business logic [5,10]. These limitations become more serious in MSS, where interactions span multiple services, depend on context, and are often not clearly specified [13,14].

Recent advances in large language models (LLMs) provide new capabilities for understanding and generating information from diverse sources, such as API specifications, source code, logs, error messages, and request–response traces [2]. These capabilities have been increasingly applied to fuzz testing, where LLMs are used to generate inputs, guide mutations, analyze responses, and coordinate testing workflows [14]. Although early results are promising, existing work is scattered across different domains, techniques, and evaluation settings, and has not been systematically analyzed. Despite the growing body of work, there is no consolidated understanding of how LLMs are applied to fuzz testing in MSS, or how effective these approaches are in practice. Existing secondary studies either focus on LLM-based fuzzing in other domains or on MSS testing without LLMs, leaving a clear gap at their intersection.

To address this gap, this paper presents a systematic literature review (SLR) of LLM-based fuzz testing in MSS. Following established guidelines for evidence-based software engineering [9], we employ a protocol-driven methodology that includes structured search, dual-reviewer screening, quality assessment, and data synthesis. The SLR aims to systematically synthesise existing studies on the integration of LLMs into fuzzing for MSS, analyze how these approaches are evaluated and their reported effectiveness, and identify key limitations and research gaps.

The contribution of this study is threefold: (1) provides a structured taxonomy of LLM roles, fuzzing paradigms, and integration patterns in MSS testing; (2) consolidates evaluation practices across the literature, highlighting common metrics, baselines, and experimental limitations; and (3) identifies key research gaps, e.g., the lack of realistic multi-service benchmarks and cost-aware evaluation, and maps them to concrete future directions.

The remainder of the paper is organized as follows. Section 2 positions our work against existing surveys. Section 3 presents the methodology. Section 4 reports the results. Section 5 discusses implications and open challenges. Section 6 outlines threats to validity. Section 7 concludes the paper.

2 Related Work

Our work relates to two lines of secondary literature: SLRs on LLM-based fuzzing and SLRs on microservice testing. We discuss each and then identify the gap addressed by our review.

SLRs on LLM-Based Fuzzing. Recent SLRs focus on LLM-based fuzzing tend to organise the literature by application domain rather than by fuzzing technique. For example, Huang et al. [7] provide the most comprehensive review to date, surveying LLM-fuzzer integrations across binary, compiler, protocol, and DL-library targets, and characterising the roles LLMs play as seed generators, mutators, and harness synthesisers. Xu et al. [18] review LLMs for cybersecurity tasks including web fuzzing, intrusion detection, and penetration testing. He et al. [6] focus on LLM-driven fuzzing of smart contracts, where the LLM guides exploration toward vulnerable code regions. Kaniewski et al. [8] review LLM-based software vulnerability detection more broadly, with fuzzing as one of several detection strategies.

SLRs on Microservice Testing. While MSS testing has been widely studied in SLRs, fuzzing and LLM-based techniques are not covered in these studies. For instance, Ghani et al. [4] and Waseem et al. [16] catalogue testing techniques, levels, and challenges in the microservice literature up to 2020, identifying integration and end-to-end testing as the dominant concerns and flagging the lack of standardised tooling. Ponce et al. [12] update this picture with a more recent SLR of 74 primary studies organised along the SWEBOK testing taxonomy, reporting system testing as the most investigated level and highlighting the growing role of AI-assisted approaches without analysing them in depth.

Positioning. The two lines of secondary literature above do not cover the intersection of LLM-based fuzzing and MSS. LLM-based fuzzing reviews focus on other software domains, while MSS testing reviews do not focus on fuzzing or LLMs. Our SLR addresses this intersection: fuzz testing as a technique, LLMs as the AI component, and MSS as the system under test.

3 Methodology

We follow the guidelines for systematic reviews in software engineering proposed by Kitchenham et al. [9] and complement them with Wohlin's snowballing procedure [17]. The goal is to identify, evaluate, and synthesise existing research on the use of Large Language Models (LLMs) for fuzz testing in microservice-based systems. The process of this study is depicted in Fig. 1.

Consistent with established SLR practice, the review process comprises five stages: (1) Research question definition, (2) Search strategy and source selection, (3) Inclusion and exclusion screening, (4) Quality assessment, and (5) Data extraction & synthesis.

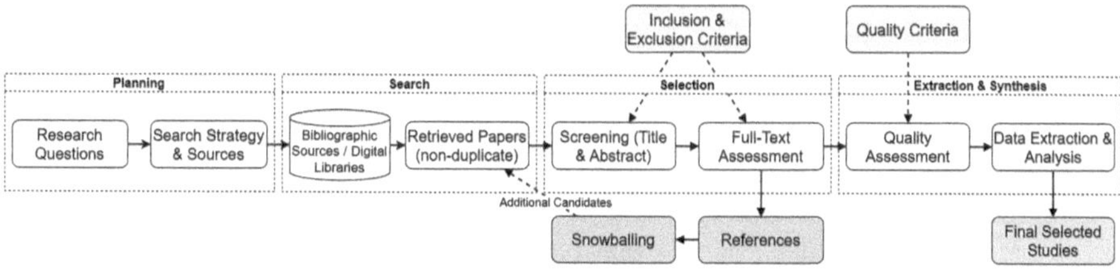

Fig. 1. Systematic literature review (SLR) search and selection process.

3.1 Research Question Definition

The research questions were defined to systematically characterise how LLMs are applied in fuzz testing for microservices and to assess the maturity of the field. In line with the guidance by Kitchenham et al., RQs are explicitly formulated to guide the search process, data extraction, and synthesis. The primary research questions are:

- **RQ1.** How are Large Language Models applied to support fuzzing in microservice systems?
- **RQ2.** How are LLM-based approaches for microservice fuzzing evaluated, and what effectiveness do they achieve?
- **RQ3.** What are the open challenges and future research directions?

These RQs are motivated by the need to characterise the design space and assess the maturity of the field. Specifically, RQ1 classifies LLM roles and their integration with fuzzing paradigms such as black-box, gray-box, and white-box fuzzing. RQ2 examines evaluation practices, including target systems, metrics, baselines, and reported effectiveness. RQ3 identifies open challenges and maps them to future research directions. Together, these RQs support a three-part synthesis: (1) a descriptive mapping of techniques and design choices (RQ1), (2) an assessment of evaluation practices and reported effectiveness (RQ2), and (3) an analysis of open challenges and future research directions (RQ3). The structure is consistent with established SLR practices, where the RQs explicitly drive data extraction and analysis and align with the workflow shown in Fig. 1.

3.2 Search Strategy and Sources

A comprehensive search strategy was designed to maximize the coverage of relevant studies while maintaining precision. Following best practices, the search combines automated database querying with a carefully constructed Boolean query. The final search string is structured along three dimensions:

1. **LLM-related terms**:
```
("large language model*" OR LLM* OR "generative AI" OR "gen AI"
OR "foundation model*" OR GPT* OR ChatGPT* OR Claude* OR
Gemini* OR Llama* OR Copilot* OR Codex* OR DeepSeek* OR Grok*
OR agent*)
```

2. **Testing/fuzzing terms:**
```
("automated API testing" OR "REST API security testing" OR
"REST API test*" OR "OpenAPI testing" OR "Swagger testing" OR
fuzzing OR "fuzz testing" OR "fuzzer" OR "input generation" OR
"test case generation" OR "automated testing")
```
3. **System context terms:**
```
(microservice* OR "micro-service*" OR "micro service*" OR
"service-oriented architecture" OR SOA OR "distributed system*"
OR "web service*" OR API OR "RESTful" OR GraphQL)
```

The search was conducted across major digital libraries commonly used in software engineering SLRs, including IEEE Xplore, ACM Digital Library, Scopus, Web of Science. These sources are consistent with Kitchenham et al.'s recommendation to search multiple repositories to reduce bias [9]. Furthermore, we also complemented the results with preprint articles from arXiv due to the fast-moving domain. In addition to automated database searches, we also employed backward and forward snowballing to improve coverage of relevant studies [17]. All studies identified through snowballing were subjected to the same inclusion/exclusion criteria and screening procedures.

3.3 Inclusion and Exclusion Screening

Explicit inclusion and exclusion criteria were defined to ensure consistency and reduce selection bias, as recommended in the SLR guidelines (Table 1).

Table 1. Inclusion and exclusion criteria.

Inc./Exc.	Criteria
Inclusion	explicitly applies, proposes, or evaluates LLMs/generative AI/agentic AI for automated testing or fuzzing-related practices of API-based, service-oriented, distributed, or microservice systems
Exclusion	Irrelevant topic (no LLM *or* no fuzzing/testing *or* no MSS context)
	Non-English source
	Inaccessible full text
	Studies that test LLMs/agentic-AI *themselves*
	Published before 2023 (emergence of modern LLMs)
	Other secondary studies

The inclusion and exclusion criteria were defined to ensure a precise alignment with the research scope while maintaining methodological rigor. In particular, the inclusion criterion directly addresses the RQs, while the exclusion criteria were designed to systematically remove sources that could introduce bias or irrelevance. This design follows established SLR practices that emphasize clearly defined, reproducible selection criteria to improve validity and consistency.

The screening process was conducted in two phases: (1) Title and abstract screening and (2) Full-text review. To improve reliability, each article was reviewed by two researchers with disagreements resolved by a third researcher.

3.4 Quality Assessment

To evaluate the rigor and reliability of the included studies, a structured quality assessment was performed. The assessment is based on established criteria derived from the DARE framework used in previous SLRs [9]. The quality of each study was evaluated along four dimensions, including (1) clarity and appropriateness, (2) search strategy completeness, (3) validity assessment, and (4) reporting adequacy, with each criterion scored using a three-point scale. We set the selection threshold to be 6 out of 12. The assessment process was conducted by two reviewers with the quality score set by the average of two.

3.5 Data Extraction and Synthesis

A structured data extraction form was defined to systematically collect relevant information from each study. The extracted data aligns directly with the research questions and includes: Bibliographic information (title, venue, year), LLM characteristics (model type, usage), LLM role (e.g., input generator, mutation operator, oracle) Fuzzing type (black-box, grey-box, white-box), Target system (e.g., microservices, REST APIs), Evaluation setup (datasets, benchmarks, metrics), Availability of replication packages. Data extraction was performed by one researcher and validated by a second reviewer to ensure accuracy and consistency, following standard SLR practice [9]. For synthesis, we adopted a qualitative and descriptive approach, complemented by quantitative summaries where applicable, enabling both evidence aggregation and research gap identification.

4 Results

We first describe the corpus (Sect. 4.1), then present the answers to RQ1 (Sect. 4.2), RQ2 (Sect. 4.3), and RQ3 (Sect. 4.4). Throughout, primary studies are cited with the labels [SP1] - [SP20] cross-referenced in Appendix.

4.1 Corpus Overview

The 20 included studies span 2024 (2 papers), 2025 (13 papers) and 2026 (5 papers), reflecting that LLM-assisted fuzzing of microservices is an emergent topic. Figure 2 presents the distribution of the selected studies, showing both the yearly publication trend and the proportion of document types in the corpus. Venues include top-tier software engineering conferences (e.g., ICSE, FSE), specialized journals (e.g., IEEE TIFS, IEEE TSC), domain-specific venues and arXiv pre-prints, capturing the fast-evolving nature of the field. In terms of system focus, the corpus is dominated by REST-based APIs with limited representation of GraphQL, CGI/IoT services, and hybrid architectures, suggesting a narrow empirical base. Notably, only a small number of studies report industrial-scale cases, e.g., ByteDance and Volkswagen, while the majority rely on benchmark or single-service setups, highlighting a gap between current research and real-world multi-service environment practices. The full list of selected primary studies is shown in the Appendix.

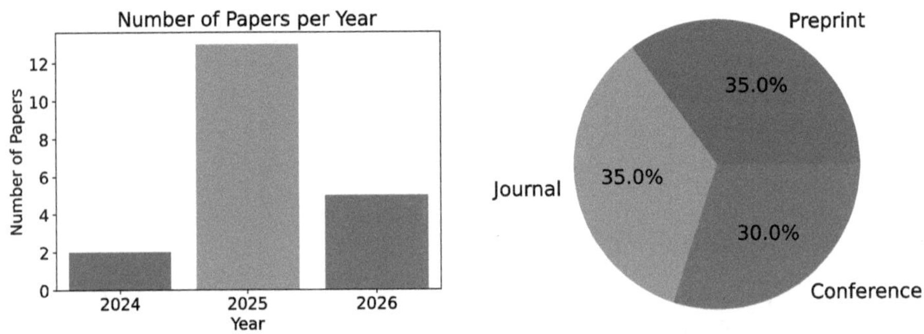

(a) Number of papers per year (b) Distribution of document types

Fig. 2. Overview of the selected studies: (a) yearly publication trend and (b) distribution of document types.

4.2 RQ1: How are LLMs Applied to Support Fuzzing in MSS?

We analyze RQ1 along four dimensions: *which LLMs*, *which roles* they play in the pipeline, *which fuzzing visibility* they assume, and *how* they are integrated.

LLMs in Use. As shown in Table 2, GPT-family models are the most common choice, but open-source and smaller models are also used, including Llama, Mistral, Qwen, DeepSeek, CodeBERT, and fine-tuned or quantised Llama variants. This diversity suggests that the field has not converged on a single canonical model; instead, reproducibility, cost, and local deployment increasingly influence model selection.

LLM Role in the Fuzzing Pipeline. As shown in Table 3, LLMs are predominantly used as input generators, especially in black-box settings (16 studies), compared to a much smaller number in grey-box (1 study) and white-box settings (1 study). In contrast, the use of LLMs as mutation operators is limited, with only a few studies exploring this role in grey-box (1 study) and white-box (1 study) settings. Similarly, LLM-based oracles appear in both black-box (6 studies) and grey-box settings (2 studies), but remain relatively underexplored

Table 2. Models used in each primary study.

Category	Studies	Examples
GPT family	[SP1], [SP2], [SP3], [SP4], [SP6], [SP11], [SP12], [SP13], [SP14], [SP15], [SP16], [SP17], [SP19]	GPT-3.5/3.5-turbo; GPT-4 family (4, 4o, 4o-mini, 4.1-mini); GPT-5 Mini; GPT-5.2-Codex; o1/o1-mini; Azure OpenAI
Other proprietary	[SP2], [SP4], [SP15]	Claude (3.5/3.7 Sonnet; Opus 4.6); Gemini (1.5, 2.0, 2.5)
Open-source models	[SP2], [SP6], [SP8], [SP19], [SP20]	Llama 3 / 3.1 (8B, 70B); DeepSeek V3.1 & R1; Mistral-Instruct 7B; Phi-3 Mini Instruct; WizardLM v1.2 13B
Fine-tuned/Quantised	[SP7], [SP18]	CodeBERT; LlamaREST-IPD/EX
Other/unspecified	[SP5], [SP9], [SP10]	StarCoder/StarCoderChat; Doubao-pro-128k; Not specified

overall. Agent-based approaches employ LLMs as orchestrators in five studies in black-box settings, with little presence in other settings. Overall, the results show a clear concentration of LLM usage in input generation for black-box fuzzing, while their adoption in other roles are explored much less, and grey-box and white-box settings remain relatively underrepresented.

Table 3. LLM roles × fuzzing visibility (one paper may appear in multiple cells).

LLM role	Black-box	Grey-box	White-box
Specification Generator	[SP11], [SP16], [SP17]	–	–
Input Generator	[SP1], [SP2], [SP4], [SP5], [SP6], [SP8], [SP10], [SP11], [SP12], [SP13], [SP15], [SP16], [SP17], [SP18], [SP19], [SP20]	[SP9]	[SP14]
Mutation Operator	[SP10], [SP17], [SP20]	[SP7]	[SP14]
Oracle / Analyzer	[SP1], [SP2], [SP4], [SP10], [SP18], [SP19]	[SP7], [SP9]	[SP14]
Orchestrator	[SP2], [SP6], [SP8], [SP16], [SP19]	–	–

Integration Approach. Table 4 summarizes how LLMs are integrated into fuzzing pipelines across different dimensions. Prompt-based integration is the most common pattern, with iterative approaches using feedback being more prevalent than one-shot generation. Several recent studies adopt multi-agent architectures. For knowledge augmentation, program analysis (4 studies) and system data such as logs or traffic (3 studies) are more commonly used than retrieval-based approaches (2 studies). In contrast, learning-based integration is less common overall, with only limited use of reinforcement learning or model adaptation techniques.

4.3 RQ2: How are LLM-Based Microservice Fuzzers Evaluated?

RQ2 covers target systems, metrics, baselines, and reported effectiveness, consolidating the per-study evaluation profile.

Table 4. Integration approaches (grouped by dimension).

Integration approach	Studies
Prompting strategy	
One-shot generation	[SP5], [SP10], [SP15]
Execution feedback loop	[SP4], [SP11], [SP16], [SP17], [SP20]
Architecture	
Multi-agent	[SP1], [SP6], [SP8], [SP16], [SP19]
Knowledge augmentation	
Retrieval-augmented generation (RAG)	[SP2], [SP8]
Program analysis	[SP7], [SP9], [SP14], [SP20]
Traffic/log/specification mining	[SP9], [SP15], [SP17]
Learning	
Reinforcement learning (incl. multi-agent)	[SP2], [SP12], [SP13], [SP18]
Fine-tuning/quantization	[SP7], [SP18]

Target Systems. Table 5 groups the evaluation targets into three categories: open benchmark services, deliberately vulnerable APIs, and industrial or real-world systems. However, most studies focus on evaluating individual REST services rather than cooperating microservice clusters, leaving cross-service workflows underexplored.

Metrics. Table 6 shows that evaluation metrics cluster into four families: coverage, effectiveness, input quality, and cost. Coverage and effectiveness metrics are the only families reported in a comparable form across most studies therefore provide the common ground for cross-study comparison. Input quality metrics are concentrated in studies that focus on parameter or sequence generation, while cost-related metrics are reported by fewer than half of the studies. Overall, the breadth illustrates that the community has not yet converged on a benchmark suite, and the diversity of metrics remains a key obstacle to analysis.

Table 5. Target systems used in the primary studies.

Category	Studies	Target systems
Open benchmark services	[SP11], [SP12], [SP13], [SP16], [SP18], [SP19], [SP20]	FDIC, OhSome, Spotify, LanguageTool, RestCountries, Genome-Nexus, GitLab, PetStore
Deliberately vulnerable APIs	[SP8], [SP11]	VAmPI, CrAPI, OWASP Juice Shop
Industrial/real-deployment systems	[SP5], [SP6], [SP7], [SP9], [SP11], [SP15]	ByteDance microservices; Volkswagen Group IT REST APIs; in-vehicle SPAPI; Light-OAuth2 microservice cluster; 20 Android backends; Azure/AWS/GCP cloud APIs

Table 6. Evaluation metrics reported in the primary studies.

Family	Studies	Metrics
Coverage-based	[SP1], [SP2], [SP3], [SP5], [SP11], [SP12], [SP13], [SP14], [SP15], [SP16], [SP18]	Line, branch, and method coverage; API/operation coverage; schema coverage; basic-block coverage; log-template coverage
Effectiveness	[SP2], [SP3], [SP6], [SP7], [SP9], [SP10], [SP11], [SP12], [SP13], [SP16], [SP17], [SP18]	Number of confirmed bugs or vulnerabilities; unique 5xx server errors; 500-error counts as proxy oracle; CVEs assigned; pass rate and fault detection; root-cause categorisation
Input quality	[SP5], [SP8], [SP10], [SP11], [SP15], [SP17], [SP18]	Valid-input/pass rate; valid-sequence increase; value-generation precision; inter parameter dependency (IPD) detection accuracy; false-positive parameter rate; syntactic correctness of generated tests
Cost/engineering	[SP1], [SP4], [SP6], [SP8], [SP9], [SP14], [SP15], [SP16], [SP17]	Token usage; processing time; GPU/CPU speedup; energy consumption; deployment effort; generation and execution time

Baselines. Table 7 shows that traditional fuzzers are the dominant baseline. A small group of studies compares only against other LLMs which weakens the strength of their effectiveness claims. Three studies compare against *human-written* test suites or expert ground truth, an important sanity check that is otherwise rare. In addition, replication packages are released by 11 out of 20 studies (55%), which facilitates reproducibility and enables further empirical validation.

4.4 RQ3: Open Challenges and Future Research Directions

As shown in Table 8, the open challenges of LLM-based microservice fuzzing reflect a shift from feasibility-oriented prototypes to deployable testing systems. Methodologically, current approaches still struggle with guarded branches, hallucinated or invalid tests, and complex inter-parameter or OpenAPI dependencies, suggesting that prompt-based generation alone is insufficient. Evaluation remains limited by the absence of unified microservice benchmarks and by the frequent reliance on weak oracles such as 5xx responses, which cannot fully capture functional or security failures. From an engineering perspective, token cost, latency, compute overhead, non-determinism, and IP/compliance concerns directly hinder CI/CD integration. At the theoretical level, existing systems provide limited guarantees that LLM-generated tests satisfy API grammars, protocol constraints, or distributed authorisation logic.

Table 7. Baselines and replication artefacts in the primary studies.

Baseline category	Studies	Details
Traditional fuzzers	Most studies	RESTler (9); EvoMaster (8); Morest (5); ARAT-RL (4); foREST, RESTTESTGEN, RESTCT (1)
LLM-only comparisons	[SP4], [SP8], [SP19]	Compared only against other LLMs, limiting the strength of effectiveness claims
Human-written/expert ground truth	[SP5], [SP6], [SP15]	Compared against human-written test suites or expert ground truth, providing an important but rare sanity check
Replication packages	11/20 (55%)	Generally good release rate supporting reproducibility; studies [SP19] and [SP20] do not provide artefacts

Overall, the result suggests that future research should move beyond simply adding LLMs to fuzzing pipelines. Progress will depend on three directions: microservice-aware designs that combine LLMs with static or symbolic analysis, dependency graphs, runtime feedback, and cross-API reasoning; cost-aware deployment strategies based on smaller, quantised, or domain-specific models with deterministic decoding; and correctness-aware generation methods such as grammar-guided decoding, verified post-conditions, and stronger functional or security oracles. In this sense, the next stage of LLM-assisted microservice fuzzing should focus not only on generating more realistic inputs, but also on making the resulting systems scalable, reproducible, and suitable for industrial deployment.

5 Discussion

The synthesis in Sect. 4 reveals several key observations about the current state of LLM-assisted fuzz testing in MSS and its implications for research and practice.

Architectural Convergence. The field is converging on black-box, feedback-driven, and agentic fuzzing pipelines that combine LLM-based input generation, response/log analysis, and lightweight orchestration. This shared template helps cumulative progress, but pure black-box pipelines may soon face diminishing returns without richer external signals such as source code, dependency graphs, runtime traces, or service-level observability.

Table 8. Open challenges and corresponding future-work directions.

Dimension	Open challenges	Future directions
Methodology	Limited coverage on guarded branches; hallucinated or invalid tests; weak handling of inter-parameter dependencies and incomplete specifications ([SP1], [SP5], [SP8], [SP10], [SP11], [SP12], [SP14], [SP16], [SP17], [SP18], [SP19], [SP20])	Hybrid LLM + static/symbolic analysis; self-reflective feedback loops with LLM-as-judge oracles; IPD-aware fine-tuning and specification mining ([SP1], [SP2], [SP11], [SP14], [SP15], [SP16], [SP17], [SP18], [SP19], [SP20])
Evaluation	Lack of unified microservice benchmarks; reliance on weak 5xx-only oracles ([SP8], [SP15], [SP16], [SP17])	Standardised authorisation and log-coverage benchmarks; functional and response-difference oracles ([SP8], [SP15], [SP16], [SP17])
Engineering	High compute, token, and latency cost; limited CI/CD integration; non-determinism and IP/compliance concerns ([SP1], [SP2], [SP5], [SP8], [SP9], [SP14], [SP15], [SP17], [SP18], [SP19])	Smaller, quantised, or domain-specific LLMs; on-prem deployment; deterministic decoding; CI/CD-friendly tooling ([SP1], [SP2], [SP5], [SP9], [SP15], [SP18], [SP20])
Theory	Lack of formal correctness guarantees; difficulty modelling distributed authorisation logic ([SP5], [SP7], [SP8], [SP10])	Constrained, grammar guided generation; verified post-conditions; cross-API dependency reasoning ([SP2], [SP7], [SP8], [SP10])

Microservice Realism Gap. Most evaluations still target isolated REST services rather than cooperating microservice clusters. Cross-service workflows, distributed authorisation, asynchronous queues, service-mesh policies, and sidecar interactions are rarely tested. Therefore, reported gains in validity, coverage, or bug discovery may not fully reflect performance in production microservice environments.

Cost and Deployability. Token cost, latency, energy consumption, non-determinism, and compliance concerns remain major barriers to CI/CD adoption. This makes smaller, quantised, fine-tuned, or domain-specific models increasingly attractive, especially when they can run on-premise. Model downsizing is thus a deployment requirement, not merely an optimisation.

Implications. Practitioners should combine LLM fuzzing with program analysis or dependency information when available, and prefer locally deployable models when cost or compliance is critical. Researchers should prioritise microservice-cluster benchmarks, cost-aware evaluation, and correctness-aware generation using grammars, specifications, or verified post-conditions.

6 Threats to Validity

Here, we discuss threats to validity following the categorization proposed by Ampatzoglou et al. that fits software engineering secondary studies, covering study selection, data and research validity [1].

Study-Selection Validity. The completeness of the selected corpus may be affected by the search strategy and source coverage. Although we queried major digital libraries, e.g., IEEE Xplore, ACM DL, Scopus, WoS, and complemented them with snowballing, relevant studies may have still been missed. We include pre-prints from ArXiv to capture the fast-evolving nature of this research area, their non-peer-reviewed status may introduce variability in study quality and maturity. The inclusion and exclusion criteria were designed to align closely with the research scope, though borderline cases required subjective judgment. To mitigate this, a dual-reviewer screening process with conflict resolution was applied, but residual selection bias may remain.

Data Validity. Threats arise from potential inaccuracies or inconsistencies in data extraction and classification. Hence, categorical fields (LLM role, fuzzing type, integration approach) were extracted using a controlled vocabulary. Nonetheless, some studies report hybrid or implicit configurations, which require the interpretation of the reviewers. Furthermore, heterogeneity in reporting, e.g., metrics, model details, or experimental setups, limits direct comparability across studies and may introduce bias in synthesis. To reduce errors, data extraction was performed by one researcher and cross-checked by another, although minor inconsistencies may persist.

Research Validity. The synthesis and interpretation of results are subject to researcher bias, particularly in taxonomy design and qualitative aggregation. The synthesis was performed primarily by a single reviewer with cross-checking despite the fact that three reviewers were involved in extraction. Although the protocol-driven methodology aligned with the SLR guidelines, the categorization of LLM roles, integration patterns, and evaluation practices reflects informed but subjective decisions. Furthermore, the lack of standardized benchmarks and metrics across primary studies constrains the strength of generalizable conclusions. To mitigate these threats, we focused on consistent patterns across multiple studies and avoided overgeneralization of isolated results. The corpus skews towards REST-based systems with minimal representation of GraphQL, RPC, and other API paradigms, which constrains the applicability of conclusions to broader microservice ecosystems. Industrial evidence is concentrated in a small number of large-scale case studies, which may not generalize to organizations with different scales, technology stacks, or regulatory contexts. To mitigate these threats, we focus on recurring patterns across multiple studies and avoid overgeneralizing isolated results.

7 Conclusion

We presented a systematic literature review of LLM-assisted fuzz testing for microservice systems, synthesizing 20 primary studies published between 2024 and 2026. The results show a clear convergence where LLMs are mainly used as semantic input generators in black-box fuzzing, with increasing adoption of closed-loop, multi-agent and RAG-augmented architectures that incorporate oracle and orchestration roles. Meanwhile, LLMs improve valid input generation and modestly enhance coverage and vulnerability detection, but evaluation remains inconsistent, with limited cost reporting and a bias toward single-service experiments over realistic microservice systems. Notably, the key challenges persist across literature including the cost–effectiveness trade-off, lack of standardized benchmarks, weak oracles, and no formal guarantees. The field is converging on three directions: (1) smaller or fine-tuned models for efficiency, (2) hybrid LLM–program analysis approaches, and (3) standardized, cost-aware multi-service benchmarks. Overall, although LLMs significantly enhance fuzzing, integration into scalable, reproducible, and industry-ready pipelines requires more realistic microservice-level evaluation frameworks.

Acknowledgements. This work is supported by FAST, the Finnish Software Engineering Doctoral Research Network, funded by the Ministry of Education and Culture, Finland. This work is also supported by the Research Council of Finland (grant id: 359861, the MuFAno project). This work is also funded by the EuroHPC Joint Undertaking and its members including top-up funding by the Ministry of Education and Culture.

Disclosure of Interests. The authors have no competing interests to declare that are relevant to the content of this article.

Appendix The Selected Papers (SP_s)

[SP1] Nooyens, R., Bardakci, T., Beyazıt, M., & Demeyer, S. (2025, September). Test amplification for rest apis via single and multi-agent llm systems. In

IFIP International Conference on Testing Software and Systems (pp. 161–177). Cham: Springer Nature Switzerland.

[SP2] Liu, S., Marefat, S., Tsai, O., Chen, Y., Deng, Z., Wang, J., & Tayebi, M. A. (2025). PrediQL: Automated Testing of GraphQL APIs with LLMs. arXiv preprint arXiv:2510.10407.

[SP3] Shi, C., Yu, J., Zhao, Z., Chen, J., & Zhang, F. (2025). CGIFuzz: Enabling Gray-Box Fuzzing for Web CGI of IoT Devices. IEEE Transactions on Information Forensics and Security.

[SP4] Altin, M., Mutlu, B., Kilinc, D., & Cakir, A. (2025). Automated Testing for Service-Oriented Architecture: Leveraging Large Language Models for Enhanced Service Composition. IEEE Access.

[SP5] Poth, A., Rrjolli, O., & Arcuri, A. (2025). Technology adoption performance evaluation applied to testing industrial REST APIs. Automated Software Engineering, 32(1), 5.

[SP6] Wang, S., Yu, Y., Feldt, R., & Parthasarathy, D. (2025). Automating a complete software test process using llms: An automotive case study. arXiv preprint arXiv:2502.04008.

[SP7] Yijun, L., Shuhao, L., Zufeng, W., Zhizhong, W., Jianwen, H., & Lei, Z. (2025, December). SemFuzz: A Semantic-Guided Fuzzing Framework for Detecting Unauthorized API Access in Mobile Applications. In 2025 22nd International Computer Conference on Wavelet Active Media Technology and Information Processing (ICCWAMTIP) (pp. 1–5). IEEE.

[SP8] Pasca, E. M., Delinschi, D., Erdei, R., & Matei, O. (2025). LLM-Driven, Self-Improving Framework for Security Test Automation: Leveraging Karate DSL for Augmented API Resilience. IEEE Access.

[SP9] Wang, J., Chen, S., Liu, Y., Deng, Y., Zhang, L., Fu, Y., & Liu, B. (2025, June). TestGPT-Server: Automatically Testing Microservices with Large Language Models at ByteDance. In Proceedings of the 33rd ACM International Conference on the Foundations of Software Engineering (pp. 192–203).

[SP10] Chen, J., Chen, Y., Pan, Z., Chen, Y., Li, Y., Li, Y., ... & Shen, Y. (2024). Dyner: Optimized test case generation for representational state transfer (rest) ful application programming interface (api) fuzzers guided by dynamic error responses. Electronics, 13(17), 3476.

[SP11] Zheng, T., Shao, J., Dai, J., Jiang, S., Chen, X., & Shen, C. (2024). Restless: Enhancing state-of-the-art rest api fuzzing with llms in cloud service computing. IEEE Transactions on Services Computing, 17(6), 4225–4238.

[SP12] Stennett, T., Kim, M., Sinha, S., & Orso, A. (2025, April). Autoresttest: A tool for automated rest api testing using llms and marl. In 2025 IEEE/ACM 47th International Conference on Software Engineering: Companion Proceedings (ICSE-Companion) (pp. 21–24). IEEE.

[SP13] Kim, M., Stennett, T., Sinha, S., & Orso, A. (2025, April). A Multi-Agent Approach for REST API Testing with Semantic Graphs and LLM-Driven Inputs. In Proceedings of the IEEE/ACM 47th International Conference on Software Engineering (pp. 1409–1421).

[SP14] Li J., Shen J., Su Y., & Lyu M. R. (2026). MioHint: LLM-assisted Mutation for Whitebox API Testing. arXiv preprint arXiv:2504.05738 .
[SP15] Reinikainen, N., Mäntylä, M., & Wang, Y. (2026). Assessing REST API Test Generation Strategies with Log Coverage. arXiv preprint arXiv:2604.07073.
[SP16] Kogler, L., Ehrhart, M., Dornauer, B., & Enoiu, E. P. (2025). RESTifAI: LLM-Based Workflow for Reusable REST API Testing. arXiv preprint arXiv:2512.08706.
[SP17] Decrop, A., Devroey, X., Papadakis, M., Schobbens, P. Y., & Perrouin, G. (2024). You Can REST Now: Automated REST API Documentation and Testing via LLM-Assisted Request Mutations. arXiv preprint arXiv:2402.05102.
[SP18] Kim, M., Sinha, S., & Orso, A. (2025). Llamaresttest: Effective rest api testing with small language models. Proceedings of the ACM on Software Engineering, 2(FSE), 465–488.
[SP19] Han, X., & Zhu, H. (2025). MASTEST: A LLM-Based Multi-Agent System For RESTful API Tests. arXiv preprint arXiv:2511.18038.
[SP20] Liu, C. H., Chen, S. L., & Li, K. Y. (2026). REST API Fuzzing Using API Dependencies and Large Language Models. Engineering Proceedings, 120(1), 42.

References

1. Ampatzoglou, A., Bibi, S., Avgeriou, P., Verbeek, M., Chatzigeorgiou, A.: Identifying, categorizing and mitigating threats to validity in software engineering secondary studies. Inf. Softw. Technol. **106**, 201–230 (2019)
2. Deng, Y., Xia, C.S., Peng, H., Yang, C., Zhang, L.: Large language models are zero-shot fuzzers: fuzzing deep-learning libraries via large language models. In: Proceedings of the 32nd ACM SIGSOFT International Symposium on Software Testing and Analysis, pp. 423–435 (2023)
3. Dragoni, N., et al.: Microservices: yesterday, today, and tomorrow. In: Present and Ulterior Software Engineering, pp. 195–216 (2017)
4. Ghani, I., Wan-Kadir, W.M.N., Mustafa, A., Imran Babir, M.: Microservice testing approaches: a systematic literature review. Int. J. Integrat. Eng. **11**(8), 65–80 (2019). https://doi.org/10.30880/ijie.2019.11.08.008
5. Golmohammadi, A., Zhang, M., Arcuri, A.: Testing restful APIs: a survey. ACM Trans. Softw. Eng. Methodol. **33**(1), 1–41 (2023)
6. He, Z., et al.: Large language models for blockchain security: a systematic literature review. arXiv preprint arXiv:2403.14280 (2024)
7. Huang, L., Zhao, P., Ma, L., Chen, H.: On the challenges of fuzzing techniques via large language models. In: 2025 IEEE International Conference on Software Services Engineering (SSE), pp. 162–171 (2025). https://doi.org/10.1109/SSE67621.2025.00028
8. Kaniewski, S., Schmidt, F., Enzweiler, M., Menth, M., Heer, T.: A systematic literature review on detecting software vulnerabilities with large language models. arXiv preprint arXiv:2507.22659 (2025)

9. Kitchenham, B., Brereton, O.P., Budgen, D., Turner, M., Bailey, J., Linkman, S.: Systematic literature reviews in software engineering-a systematic literature review. Inf. Softw. Technol. **51**(1), 7–15 (2009)
10. Manes, V.J.M., et al.: The art, science, and engineering of fuzzing: a survey. IEEE Trans. Softw. Eng. **47**(11), 2312–2331 (2019)
11. Miao, T., Shaafi, A.I., Song, E.: Systematic mapping study of test generation for microservices: approaches, challenges, and impact on system quality. Electronics **14**(7), 1397 (2025)
12. Ponce, F., Verdecchia, R., Miranda, B., Soldani, J.: Microservices testing: a systematic literature review. Inf. Softw. Technol. **188**, 107870 (2025). https://doi.org/10.1016/j.infsof.2025.107870
13. Reinikainen, N., Mäntylä, M., Wang, Y.: Assessing REST API test generation strategies with log coverage. arXiv:2604.07073 (2026)
14. Wang, J., et al.: TestGPT-server: automatically testing microservices with large language models at ByteDance. In: Proceedings of ACM SIGSOFT Symposium on the Foundations of Software Engineering (FSE) (2025). https://doi.org/10.1145/3696630.3728545
15. Wang, Y., Kadiyala, H., Rubin, J.: Promises and challenges of microservices: an exploratory study. Empir. Softw. Eng. **26**(4), 63 (2021)
16. Waseem, M., Liang, P., Márquez, G., Salle, A.D.: Testing microservices architecture-based applications: a systematic mapping study. In: 2020 27th Asia-Pacific Software Engineering Conference (APSEC), pp. 119–128 (2020). https://doi.org/10.1109/APSEC51365.2020.00020
17. Wohlin, C.: Guidelines for snowballing in systematic literature studies and a replication in software engineering. In: Proceedings of the 18th International Conference on Evaluation and Assessment in Software Engineering, pp. 1–10 (2014)
18. Xu, H., et al.: Large language models for cyber security: a systematic literature review. ACM Trans. Softw. Eng. Methodol. (2025). https://doi.org/10.1145/3769676
19. Zhang, M., Arcuri, A.: Open problems in fuzzing restful APIs: a comparison of tools. ACM Trans. Softw. Eng. Methodol. **32**(6), 1–45 (2023)

Software Process and Product Improvement

Commit-Aware Learning-Based Test Case Prioritization for Continuous Integration

Lorenzo Abbondante and Gerardo Canfora(✉)

Department of Engineering, University of Sannio, Benevento, Italy
canfora@unisannio.it

Abstract. Regression testing in Continuous Integration (CI) pipelines is increasingly costly due to the growing size and execution frequency of test suites. Test Case Prioritization (TCP) mitigates this problem by reordering tests to expose faults earlier. However, most existing techniques rely primarily on historical execution data and coverage metrics, neglecting the rich structural information contained in code changes. We propose a commit-aware, learning-based TCP method that combines structural properties of version-control diffs, test coverage relations, and historical execution behavior into a unified predictive model. Preliminary findings show that including commit structural semantics enhances regression fault detection and enables robust, generalizable learning-based TCP in CI environments.

Keywords: Test Case Prioritization · Continuous Integration

1 Introduction

In modern Agile and DevOps environments, software systems evolve continuously through rapid and incremental development cycles. Continuous Integration (CI) and Continuous Deployment (CD) pipelines automate the process of building, testing, and deploying new code as soon as it is committed to the shared repository. Although these practices significantly improve responsiveness and shorten delivery times, they also increase the frequency with which large regression test suites must be executed. Test Case Prioritization (TCP) addresses this challenge by reordering test execution so that test cases with the highest probability of revealing faults are executed earlier.

Over the past two decades, many researchers have investigated TCP strategies. However, most methods rely heavily on historical execution data, overlooking the contextual information contained in the code changes that trigger each CI cycle. Indeed, although version-control repositories encode rich signals about code evolution, very few TCP techniques leverage the information conveyed by commits, including the number of altered files, the added or removed lines, and the churn level, although this information has long been recognized as a strong predictor of fault-proneness.

C. Berger and V. Klös (Eds.): SEAA 2026, LNCS 16864, pp. 365–372, 2027.
https://doi.org/10.1007/978-3-032-36587-3_24

We address this gap by introducing a *commit-aware, machine-learning-based TCP method* that integrates version control diffs, test coverage information, and historical outcomes into a unified predictive model. By learning the relationships between code evolution and test failures, the proposed approach bridges the traditional "black-box" (based on execution history) and "white-box" (based on coverage measures) paradigms into a strategy suitable for CI environments.

2 Related Work

TCP has been extensively studied in the context of regression testing and CI, with the goal of accelerating fault detection by reordering the execution of the tests. We focus on learning-based TCP methods that treat prioritization as a predictive ranking problem, learning from historical execution data, coverage, and code metrics [12].

Early industrial approaches applied supervised classifiers to predict failing tests based on execution history and change-aware features [5,7,11], while later work employed ensemble models and automated hyperparameter tuning to improve robustness [9]. While some authors focus on model training, others define tools to collect the features evaluated in their approach [17].

More recent research explores reinforcement learning and learning-to-rank formulations, enabling adaptive prioritization under CI feedback loops [2–4,13]. Deep learning approaches further model long-term execution patterns and sequential dependencies using neural and recurrent architectures [10,14–16].

Most learning-based approaches rely predominantly on execution history and coverage signals, while structural commit semantics remain weakly exploited, particularly in cross-project generalization settings. The method proposed in this paper directly addresses this limitation by embedding commit-level diff semantics into a unified learning framework and evaluating it under cross-project validation.

3 The Method

Our commit-aware, learning-based TCP method aims at predicting, for each test suite and each commit, the probability of observing at least one failure and to prioritize tests accordingly.

Given a commit c_t, we build a feature vector for each test suite that encodes: (i) historical execution behavior, (ii) structural coverage relations between tests and production code, and (iii) commit-level change relevance signals. A supervised machine-learning model estimates the probability that a given test suite will fail under c_t, and test suites are ranked in descending order of predicted failure probability.

Each test suite under a given commit is represented by a compact set of features. All features are computed using only information available prior to executing the current test run, ensuring leakage-free learning. The complete formal definition of features and the process to compute them is provided in the replication package [1].

Commit-Aware (Diff-Based) Features. Commit-aware features capture the structural properties of code changes introduced by the current commit. From the version-control diff, we extract basic change metrics such as: the number of modified files, added lines, and removed lines.

These metrics are originally defined at file or class level. To obtain test-level representations, we associate each test suite with the production classes it covers, using a heuristic mapping [1], and propagate diff information from modified classes to their corresponding test suites. If a test suite covers multiple modified components, diff metrics are aggregated.

The resulting features capture the relevance of each test suite with respect to the current change, capturing both the size of the change and its proximity to the code exercised by the test.

Historical Features. These features summarize the past behavior of test suites. We consider: (i) the previous pass rate, representing the most recent execution outcome, and (ii) a weighted historical pass rate, computed over multiple past versions.

The weighted pass rate combines temporal recency with commit similarity, assigning higher importance to recent executions and to past commits with similar change intensity. This feature estimates the expected reliability of a test suite under the current commit.

Coverage Features. Coverage features describe the structural relationship between test suites and production code. We compute: (i) the suite coverage ratio, indicating how much of the system is exercised by the test suite, and (ii) a combined coverage–diff signal, capturing the extent to which a test suite covers recently modified components.

This combination allows the model to identify test suites that are both structurally broad and directly exposed to the latest code changes.

4 Experimental Setup

This section describes the experimental methodology adopted to evaluate the proposed commit-aware TCP approach. We report research questions, dataset and data processing strategies, evaluation metrics, design and analyses. Our automated data collection pipeline, detailed implementation artifacts and scripts are provided in the publicly available replication package [1].

4.1 Research Questions

We address the following research questions:

- **RQ1:** Can commit-aware features improve test failure prediction?
- **RQ2:** Does improved failure prediction translate into more effective test case prioritization?

To answer **RQ1**, we evaluate failure prediction performance using Precision–Recall AUC (PR-AUC) and F1-score. These metrics are appropriate for highly imbalanced classification problems, as they emphasize performance on the minority (failing) class.

To answer **RQ2**, we evaluate test case prioritization effectiveness using: (i) Average Percentage of Faults Detected (APFD), that measures the average rate of fault detection per percentage of test suite execution [6]; (ii) Speedup, measuring the reduction in First-Time-To-Failure relative to chronological execution.

4.2 Dataset

We evaluate the proposed approach on five projects from the Defects4J benchmark [8], namely *Math*, *Lang*, *Jsoup*, *Time*, *JacksonDatabind.* Defects4J provides real-world Java faults, reproducible regression testing scenarios, and versioned project histories. Each project consists of multiple faulty program versions, associated test suites, and execution outcomes.

We apply SMOTE oversampling and random undersampling or parameter tuning to address dataset imbalance and an exponentially weighted moving average mechanism for data imputation of missing values.

4.3 Machine Learning Models

We evaluate two representative supervised learning models with complementary characteristics: gradient-boosted decision trees (XGBoost) and a feedforward neural network (MLP). XGBoost is well suited for imbalanced tabular data and provides interpretable feature importance, while MLPs can capture non-linear interactions among heterogeneous features. Both models are trained to estimate the probability that a test suite will fail under a given commit.

4.4 Design

We use a leave-one-out cross-project strategy: five different clusters each with four training projects and a test project. In the evaluation of the results, we consider only four out of the five folds. The fold where the *Time* project represents the test set is kept out of the evaluation as this project, due to its structure, is an outlier with all datapoints in the positive class.

First, we train the models including all the selected features, and evaluate the classification performance and the prioritization scores. Then, to quantify the contribution of diff-based information, we perform an ablation study in which we retrain the models after removing all commit-aware features.

The goal of the ablation study is to evaluate whether the inclusion of commit-aware features produces statistically significant improvements in both classification and prioritization performance. We test the following hypotheses:

- H_{01} (classification): the removal of diff-based features does not change classification performance;

- H_{02} (prioritization): removing diff-based features does not change the effectiveness of TCP.

We use the Wilcoxon signed-rank test for statistical significance and Cliff's delta for effect size, and report Q1, median (Q2), and Q3 descriptive statistics.

5 Results and Discussion

This section presents the experimental results, addressing the research questions.

5.1 RQ1: Commit-Aware Feature Effectiveness on Test Failure Prediction

The ablation study highlights the critical role of the diff features in the classification performance of both the XGBoost and the MLP models. When these features are removed, performances degrade across all four projects, as shown in Table 1. Specifically, F1 and PR-AUC values drop from high-performance levels to near-zero values, indicating that the models lose their discriminative power without these specific inputs.

The analysis of the bootstrap quartiles reveals large differences in performance stability between the two experimental configurations. With diff-based features, the models exhibit a robust statistical profile, characterized by high median values and narrow interquartile ranges across the validation folds. This indicates that the predictive performance is not only elevated but also highly consistent, with minimal variance in the model's output. In contrast, the removal of these features outlines a collapse of the distribution. In the ablation scenario, the entire quartile spread shifts toward zero, and the upper bounds fail to reach meaningful classification thresholds. The absence of overlap between the distributions of the two scenarios confirms that the diff-based signals are not merely additive enhancements but are the foundation required for the models to achieve any discriminative capability.

Statistical analysis in Table 2 confirms this impact. The Cliff's delta for both models and all classification metrics is 1.000, meaning a large effect size and demonstrating that the with-features configuration consistently outperforms the baseline across all folds. Furthermore, the Wilcoxon signed-rank test exhibits a p-value of 0.0625 for all metrics. Although the p-value does not cross the conventional 0.05 significance threshold, it corresponds to the smallest attainable p-value for a sample size of $n = 4$ under this test, indicating the strongest evidence that could be obtained with the current experimental design.

5.2 RQ2: Improved Prediction Effectiveness on Fault Detection

The analysis of the prioritization quartiles reveals a distinct behavioral shift compared to the total collapse observed in the classification task, as shown in Table 3. The APFD Gain demonstrates a surprising resilience in the absence of

Table 1. Classification report for both models on each fold. For each metric we report the Q1, Q2 and Q3 values. The number of bootstrap replications is 5000 per fold.

Metric	XGBoost		MLP	
	Yes diff f.	No diff f.	Yes diff f.	No diff f.
Lang				
F1	(0.922, 0.939, 0.956)	(0.000, 0.022, 0.039)	(0.845, 0.870, 0.891)	(0.126, 0.151, 0.180)
PR-AUC	(0.857, 0.891, 0.923)	(0.024, 0.028, 0.033)	(0.898, 0.923, 0.951)	(0.057, 0.074, 0.094)
JacksonDatabind				
F1	(0.909, 0.941, 0.962)	(0.018, 0.034, 0.051)	(0.815, 0.857, 0.900)	(0.000, 0.000, 0.000)
PR-AUC	(0.964, 0.980, 0.996)	(0.014, 0.018, 0.023)	(1.000, 1.000, 1.000)	(0.052, 0.072, 0.095)
Jsoup				
F1	(0.863, 0.879, 0.895)	(0.000, 0.000, 0.000)	(0.291, 0.325, 0.359)	(0.046, 0.061, 0.076)
PR-AUC	(0.908, 0.928, 0.946)	(0.069, 0.076, 0.083)	(0.329, 0.364, 0.400)	(0.050, 0.055, 0.060)
Math				
F1	(0.882, 0.895, 0.908)	(0.011, 0.015, 0.019)	(0.743, 0.760, 0.778)	(0.015, 0.019, 0.023)
PR-AUC	(0.791, 0.817, 0.841)	(0.009, 0.010, 0.011)	(0.452, 0.477, 0.504)	(0.007, 0.009, 0.010)

diff-based features. This indicates that the models retain a good ability to order test suites effectively by leveraging residual signals, such as historical pass rates or coverage data. However, this resilience does not translate to the Speedup metric. Here, the removal of diff-based features causes a drastic degradation. This dichotomy suggests that, while the models can achieve a generally good sorting quality without diff features, they lose the ability to identify the first failure immediately.

This dichotomy is statistically confirmed by Table 2: the Cliff's δ for APFD gain indicates only a moderate effect size compared to the maximum separation seen in classification, whereas the Speedup metric reveals a large Mean δ Confidence Interval, confirming that, while general ordering is robust, the ability to rapidly detect failures is strictly dependent on diff-based features.

Table 2. Cliff's δ and Wilcoxon p-value and mean δ CI (low-high interval) for XGBoost and MLP metrics on each fold prediction. Number of bootstrap samples: $n = 5000$; alternative hypothesis for Wilcoxon signed-rank test: `alternative='greater'`; number of pairs: $p = 4$. Mean δ represents the per-fold difference between the two mean metric values from the with and without features scenario.

Metric	XGBoost			MLP		
	Cliff δ	p-value	Mean δ CI	Cliff δ	p-value	Mean δ CI
F1	1.000	0.0625	0.877–0.912	1.000	0.0625	0.383–0.821
PR-AUC	1.000	0.0625	0.820–0.928	1.000	0.0625	0.388–0.889
APFD gain	0.500	0.0625	0.053–0.169	0.375	0.0625	0.140–0.509
Speedup	0.750	0.0625	258.750–1622.643	0.500	0.0625	0.232–116.418

Table 3. Prioritization metrics for both models on each fold. For each metric we report the Q1, Q2 and Q3 values. The number of bootstrap replications is 5000 per fold.

Metric	XGBoost		MLP	
	Yes diff f.	No diff f.	Yes diff f.	No diff f.
Lang				
APFD Gain	(0.506, 0.553, 0.599)	(0.453, 0.503, 0.552)	(0.501, 0.547, 0.594)	(0.477, 0.522, 0.571)
Speedup	(809, 983, 1173)	(62, 79, 99)	(801, 975, 1168)	(127, 161, 202)
JacksonDatabind				
APFD Gain	(0.664, 0.711, 0.753)	(0.607, 0.654, 0.697)	(0.659, 0.709, 0.751)	(0.596, 0.644, 0.685)
Speedup	(504, 663, 745)	(20, 25, 31)	(568, 648, 728)	(14, 16, 18)
Jsoup				
APFD Gain	(0.541, 0.566, 0.589)	(0.326, 0.360, 0.392)	(0.440, 0.466, 0.492)	(-0.112, -0.073, -0.033)
Speedup	(36, 43, 51)	(6, 7, 8)	(15, 19, 23)	(6, 9, 14)
Math				
APFD Gain	(0.459, 0.482, 0.505)	(0.334, 0.363, 0.392)	(0.460, 0.485, 0.510)	(0.395, 0.422, 0.450)
Speedup	(1864, 2149, 2455)	(88, 103, 121)	(3273, 4168, 5218)	(78, 101, 126)

6 Conclusion

We introduced a commit-aware, learning-based approach for Test Case Prioritization in Continuous Integration environments. By integrating structural information extracted from version-control diffs with historical execution data and coverage metrics, our method explicitly accounts for the characteristics of the current code change when prioritizing test execution.

Empirical evaluation on five Defects4J projects shows that commit-level signals play a central role in enabling accurate failure prediction.

Future work will extend the evaluation to industrial datasets, explore richer semantic representations of commits, and investigate online and incremental learning strategies to improve adaptability to long-running CI pipelines.

References

1. Abbondante, L., Canfora, G.: Replication package for commit-aware learning-based test case prioritization for continuous integration. Zenodo (2026). https://doi.org/10.5281/zenodo.19355771
2. Alrakban, N.A., Alrashoud, M., Abdullah-Al-Wadud, M.: Optimizing test case prioritization with meta deep reinforcement learning in continuous integration. IEEE Access **13**, 172435–172455 (2025). https://doi.org/10.1109/ACCESS.2025.3617387
3. Bagherzadeh, M., Kahani, N., Briand, L.C.: Reinforcement learning for test case prioritization. IEEE Trans. Softw. Eng. **48**(8), 2836–2856 (2022). https://doi.org/10.1109/TSE.2021.3070549
4. Bertolino, A., Guerriero, A., Miranda, B., Pietrantuono, R., Russo, S.: Learning-to-rank vs ranking-to-learn: strategies for regression testing in continuous integration.

In: ICSE '20: 42nd International Conference on Software Engineering, pp. 1–12. ACM (2020). https://doi.org/10.1145/3377811.3380369
5. Busjaeger, B., Xie, T.: Learning for test prioritization: an industrial case study. In: Proceedings of the 24th ACM SIGSOFT International Symposium on Foundations of Software Engineering, pp. 975–980. ACM (2016). https://doi.org/10.1145/2950290.2983954
6. Elbaum, S.G., Malishevsky, A.G., Rothermel, G.: Test case prioritization: a family of empirical studies. IEEE Trans. Softw. Eng. **28**(2), 159–182 (2002). https://doi.org/10.1109/32.988497
7. Hajri, I., Goknil, A., Pastore, F., Briand, L.C.: Automating system test case classification and prioritization for use case-driven testing in product lines. Empir. Softw. Eng. **25**(5), 3711–3769 (2020). https://doi.org/10.1007/S10664-020-09853-4
8. Just, R., Jalali, D., Ernst, M.D.: Defects4j: a database of existing faults to enable controlled testing studies for java programs. In: International Symposium on Software Testing and Analysis, ISSTA, pp. 437–440. ACM (2014). https://doi.org/10.1145/2610384.2628055
9. Khan, M.A., et al.: An end-to-end test case prioritization framework using optimized machine learning models. In: IEEE International Conference on Software Testing, Verification and Validation, pp. 1–8. IEEE (2024). https://doi.org/10.1109/ICSTW60967.2024.00014
10. Mahdieh, M., Mirian-Hosseinabadi, S., Etemadi, K., Nosrati, A., Jalali, S.: Incorporating fault-proneness estimations into coverage-based test case prioritization methods. Inf. Softw. Technol. **121**, 106269 (2020). https://doi.org/10.1016/J.INFSOF.2020.106269
11. Marijan, D.: Comparative study of machine learning test case prioritization for continuous integration testing. Softw. Qual. J. **31**(4), 1415–1438 (2023). https://doi.org/10.1007/S11219-023-09646-0
12. Pan, R., Bagherzadeh, M., Ghaleb, T.A., Briand, L.C.: Test case selection and prioritization using machine learning: a systematic literature review. Empir. Softw. Eng. **27**(2), 29 (2022). https://doi.org/10.1007/S10664-021-10066-6
13. da Roza, E.A., do Prado Lima, J.A., Vergilio, S.R.: On the use of contextual information for machine learning based test case prioritization in continuous integration development. Inf. Softw. Technol. **171**, 107444 (2024). https://doi.org/10.1016/J.INFSOF.2024.107444
14. Sharif, A., Marijan, D., Liaaen, M.: Deeporder: deep learning for test case prioritization in continuous integration testing. In: IEEE International Conference on Software Maintenance and Evolution, pp. 525–534. IEEE (2021). https://doi.org/10.1109/ICSME52107.2021.00053
15. Vescan, A., Gaceanu, R.D., Szederjesi-Dragomir, A.: Neural network-based test case prioritization in continuous integration. In: 38th IEEE/ACM International Conference on Automated Software Engineering, pp. 68–77. IEEE (2023). https://doi.org/10.1109/ASEW60602.2023.00014
16. Vescan, A., Tiutin, C.: Test case prioritization based on neural networks classification: a replication study and hyper-parameter optimization using Taguchi methods. IEEE Access **13**, 118082–118095 (2025). https://doi.org/10.1109/ACCESS.2025.3586144
17. Yaraghi, A.S., Bagherzadeh, M., Kahani, N., Briand, L.C.: Scalable and accurate test case prioritization in continuous integration contexts. IEEE Trans. Softw. Eng. **49**(4), 1615–1639 (2023). https://doi.org/10.1109/TSE.2022.3184842

Quality Metrics for LLM-Generated Asset Administration Shells: A Perturbation-Based Evaluation Approach

Janek Groß(✉), Elena Zentgraf, and Jens Heidrich

University of Applied Sciences Mainz, Mainz, Rhineland-Palatinate, Germany
janek.gross@hs-mainz.de

Abstract. The rapid digital transformation of manufacturing, often referred to as Industry 4.0, relies on seamless interoperability between physical and software assets. A central enabler is the Asset Administration Shell (AAS), a standardized digital representation of such assets. Recent advances in large language models (LLMs) enable the generation of AAS submodels from unstructured sources such as product datasheets but raise challenges for quality assurance. In particular, unexpected errors, the lack of ground-truth references, and the absence of standardized quality metrics hinder reliable adoption. In this work, we evaluate quality metrics for AI-generated AAS using a perturbation-based evaluation framework. By systematically degrading AAS generation along multiple dimensions, we assess how well different metrics reflect quality changes. Based on a dataset of 200 products from multiple manufacturers, we generate 6,400 AAS instances using GPT-4o-mini, Qwen3, and DeepSeek-R1. Our results show that metrics based on exact matching of property names and similarity-based soft matching of property values, in particular value-based recall and name based F1 score, provide the most reliable indicators of quality degradation. Furthermore, we quantify the impact of different perturbation types and analyze differences across model families and product segments. These findings support the selection of suitable metrics, the tuning of LLM-based pipelines, and the integration of AI-generated AAS into industrial applications.

Keywords: Quality Metrics · Evaluation · Asset Administration Shell · Large Language Models · Information Extraction · Digital Twins · Industry 4.0

1 Introduction

Asset Administration Shells (AAS) [5,6] provide standardized digital representations of hardware and software assets (see Fig. 1). They define common semantics for properties and services and enable interoperable digital twins in Industry 4.0. The AAS is also increasingly discussed as a basis for Digital Product Passport implementations, an EU-driven effort for sharing product lifecycle information.

C. Berger and V. Klös (Eds.): SEAA 2026, LNCS 16864, pp. 373–389, 2027.
https://doi.org/10.1007/978-3-032-36587-3_25

As such, a large number of AAS must be created and maintained to cover the variety of assets used in modern manufacturing and across supply chains.

An AAS consists of one or more submodels that organize information about an asset, such as technical characteristics, documentation, or lifecycle data. In this work, we focus on technical data submodels. Within a submodel, properties describe specific characteristics (e.g., rated voltage or operating temperature). Usually, each property is linked to a *ConceptDescription* specifying its semantic meaning, data type, unit, and other metadata. AAS can be serialized in XML, JSON, or RDF/Turtle formats and are commonly distributed as AASX archives containing the AAS and supplementary files.

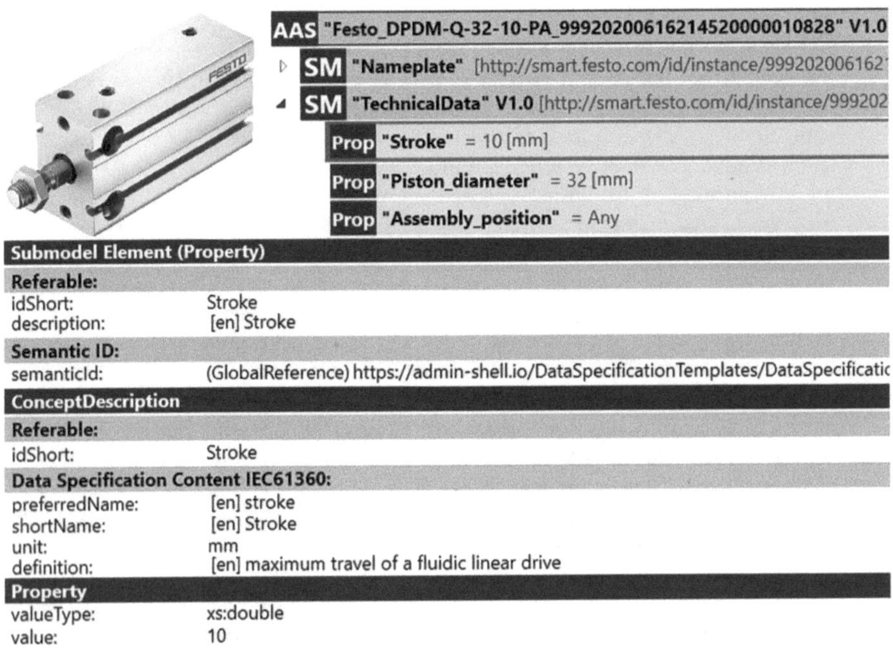

Fig. 1. Example AAS [7] with three technical properties and property metadata.

Typically, manufacturers generate AAS from internal product data. However, if company-foreign or legacy products need to be modeled, manual extraction of properties from datasheets or technical documentation is required. This process is time-consuming, error-prone, and requires domain expertise.

Information extraction (IE) is the task to derive structured, machine-readable information from unstructured sources such as tables or natural-language text [2, 4]. In the context of AAS creation, IE enables systematic extraction of product properties from technical documents. Traditionally, IE systems required extensive domain-specific annotation and complex pipelines. Recent advances in large language models (LLMs), particularly instruction tuning and function calling, have significantly lowered this barrier. LLMs now enable the construction of IE pipelines without supervised training, leading to emerging LLM-based AAS generation tools [10,19,22]. While these tools are promising, they remain unreliable and often produce unexpected results, raising critical questions about output validity and quality.

To enable trustworthy use of LLM-based tools for AAS generation, suitable quality metrics are necessary. Such metrics serve both the evaluation and optimization of generation tools including choice of model, prompting strategies and other hyperparameters. Defining suitable quality metrics, however, is non-trivial. AAS content is often non-unique: the same product can be described using different classification systems (e.g., ECLASS, ETIM, or company-specific schemes). Moreover, variations in naming, alternative units, or permissible structure complicate the application of standard IE metrics such as precision, recall, and F1 score. Furthermore, in many current LLM-based AAS generation approaches, multiple IE steps—such as entity recognition, normalization, and template mapping—are performed within a single prompt-response cycle, making step-by-step evaluation difficult when intermediate outputs are not exposed. While multi-stage LLM-based pipelines with explicit intermediate outputs are conceivable, the tools considered in this study expose only the final generated AAS and are therefore evaluated end-to-end. Together with the scarcity of labeled datasets, this underscores the need for tailored evaluation approaches.

In this work, we propose an empirical methodology for the evaluation of AAS quality metrics based on controlled perturbations of the generation process. By systematically degrading AAS instances, we analyze how well different metrics reflect changes in quality. Our research addresses the following questions: (1) Which metrics best reflect AAS quality degradation under controlled perturbations? (2) How do perturbation types and model characteristics affect AAS generation quality? (3) How does AAS quality vary across manufacturers and product segments? RQ1 establishes how to meaningfully compare AAS quality metrics. Once the best metrics in their category have been identified, they can be used as measurement instruments to investigate the impact of perturbations and product-specific factors on generated AAS quality in RQ2 and RQ3.

Our contributions are (i) a set of AAS-specific quality metrics, including full-reference and no-reference variants, (ii) a perturbation-based evaluation methodology for systematically assessing metric performance, and (iii) an empirical analysis of AAS quality across perturbation types, model families, manufacturers, and product segments. These contributions support the selection and benchmarking of AAS generation tools, enable automated quality assurance, and facilitate the integration of AI-assistants into industrial processes.

The remainder of this paper is structured as follows. Section 2 examines relevant background and related work. In Sect. 3, the study design, including the evaluated metrics, the perturbation-based evaluation approach, and the experimental setup is described. Section 4 presents empirical results. Section 5 discusses the implications of the findings. Section 6 outlines threats to validity. Lastly, Sect. 7 concludes the paper and highlights directions for future work.

2 Background and Related Work

This section reviews relevant work on the evaluation of information extraction and LLM-based systems.

Traditional software quality models such as ISO/IEC 25010 [8,20] provide valuable frameworks for assessing software products based on characteristics such as functionality, reliability, and maintainability. However, these models primarily target conventional software and do not readily extend to structured artifacts such as AAS submodels. In contrast, our work focuses on the empirical evaluation of concrete quality metrics tailored to such AI-generated artifacts, rather than proposing an encompassing quality model.

The evaluation of generative models like LLMs poses a challenge due to the complexity of the output domain. It is common practice to evaluate LLMs on benchmark tasks with a unique, short answer to provide a general indication of model performance, but these benchmarks may not reflect performance in other, domain-specific tasks. For example, translation and summarization are commonly evaluated using metrics such as BLEU [15] and ROUGE [12], which rely on n-gram overlap between generated and reference texts. However, these metrics are not well suited for structured outputs, where fields are short and multiple semantically equivalent representations may exist.

Information extraction (IE) research is closely related to the AAS generation use case. IE systems typically combine tasks such as named entity recognition (NER) [11], relation extraction (RE) [23], and slot filling [21], and are evaluated on labeled datasets using precision, recall, and F1 score. For AAS generation, however, labeled data for individual extraction steps is not available, and these IE steps (i.e. recognition of technical properties, value and unit normalization, mapping to AAS template) are often performed within a single LLM interaction. As a result, for approaches that do not expose intermediate results, evaluation must be performed end-to-end and requires adaptations of classical metrics, such as soft matching for property names and values. These adaptations increasingly rely on AI-based methods like embedding-based similarity, to account for permissible variations and the absence of a unique correct output (e.g., color: gray vs. colour: grey).

Similar challenges arise in the evaluation of other multi-step LLM-based systems, such as retrieval-augmented generation (RAG) where output quality is difficult to assess directly. Recent work has therefore explored alternative evaluation strategies that closely align with our setting. These include indirect metrics based on downstream task performance and LLM-based judgments. These works also evaluate their methods through correlation with human judgments and test systems with intentionally varied retrieval quality.

For example, Sander and Dietz [18] assess RAG systems based on their ability to support follow-up questions, providing an indirect measure of output quality. Es et al. [3] propose RAGAS, an automated framework that uses LLM prompting and embeddings to evaluate relevance and faithfulness. Building on that, Saad-Falcon et al. [17] apply prediction-powered inference [1] to align automated evaluations with human judgments. To evaluate their approach, they simulate systems with controlled retrieval performance, which inspired the perturbation-based evaluation approach used in this work.

Overall, existing work highlights both the limitations of traditional evaluation methods for structured outputs and the need for more flexible, task-specific evaluation strategies. Building on insights from IE and RAG evaluation, our work introduces a framework for systematically benchmarking AAS quality metrics, even in the absence of high-quality labeled reference data.

3 Study Design

This study systematically evaluates quality metrics for AI-generated Asset Administration Shells (AAS) using a perturbation-based framework. We deliberately degrade AAS generation along multiple dimensions to analyze how sensitively and consistently different metrics reflect quality changes.

The overall evaluation pipeline is illustrated in Fig. 2. Starting from product datasheets and corresponding AAS, we construct structured prompts that combine the unstructured datasheet content with a predefined property dictionary derived from the reference AAS. This dictionary specifies the expected properties, including their names, value types, and units, and serves as a schema to guide the extraction process.

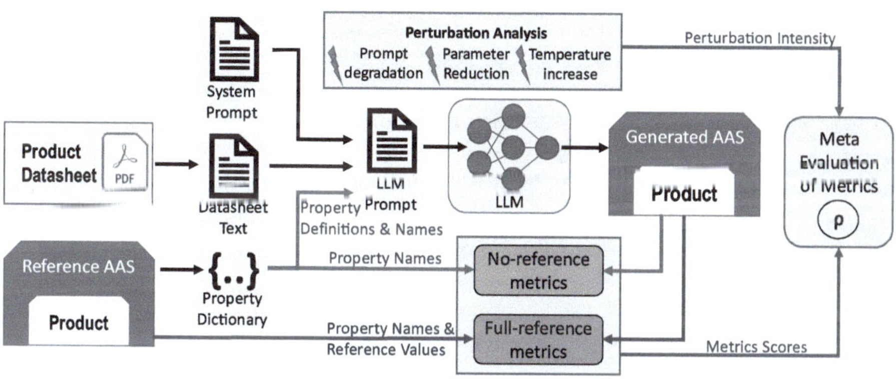

Fig. 2. Overview of the perturbation-based evaluation pipeline. Values for properties given by a *Property Dictionary* are extracted from a *Product datasheet* and converted into AAS format. Controlled perturbations are applied to the generation process, and the resulting AAS instances are evaluated using quality metrics. To compare different quality metrics, their scores are then correlated with perturbation intensity to assess their sensitivity to known quality degradations.

Based on these prompts, AAS instances are generated using LLM-based information extraction. The model is instructed to extract values for the specified properties and return the results in a structured format, which is then transformed into a technical data submodel of the AAS.

To simulate varying quality levels, controlled perturbations are introduced at different stages of the generation process, including prompt degradation, temperature variation, and the use of different model sizes. These perturbation classes were selected because prompt design, model selection, and inference parameter configuration are influencing LLM output quality and represent common practical decisions in real-world deployments. Consequently, they provide realistic and controllable sources of variation in the completeness and correctness of the extracted properties.

The resulting AAS instances are evaluated using both full-reference and no-reference metrics. Full-reference metrics compare generated properties and values against the reference AAS, while no-reference metrics assess intrinsic plausibility, such as alignment with the expected property schema and the presence of missing values.

Finally, a meta-evaluation step analyzes the relationship between perturbation intensity and metric scores. By correlating metric values with controlled degradations, we assess how sensitively and consistently each metric reflects changes in AAS quality.

The following subsections describe the evaluated metrics, perturbation mechanisms, dataset, and experimental setup.

3.1 AAS Quality Metrics

We define a set of AAS-specific quality metrics for evaluating AI-generated AAS. The metrics are intended to support researchers and practitioners in assessing and comparing the quality of generated AAS as well as improving AAS generation tools. Consequently, the metrics focus on technical properties and values within AAS submodels, either by measuring their correspondence to a reference artifact or by assessing their intrinsic plausibility. Broader aspects such as schema compliance, adherence to AAS templates, or practical usability are not considered, as they can be addressed by deterministic validation tools or require different evaluation goals.

We distinguish between two complementary types of metrics: **full-reference metrics** and **no-reference metrics**. Full-reference metrics compare a generated AAS against a reference and assess similarity in structure, properties, and values. While interpretable and reliable, such references are often unavailable in practice. No-reference metrics instead assess plausibility based on intrinsic characteristics, such as alignment with expected property names or missing values, making them suitable for large-scale quality assurance. Both types are therefore complementary.

To match generated properties to reference properties, we use a two-step procedure. First, similarity scores are computed for all property pairs using either normalized Levenshtein distance or cosine similarity of embeddings. Second, an optimal one-to-one assignment between generated and reference properties is computed from the resulting similarity matrix, ensuring that each generated property is matched at most once and maximizing overall similarity. A similarity threshold is applied to classify matches, optimized via grid search to maximize correlation with perturbation intensity.

For full-reference metrics, matched property values are additionally compared. Numeric values must fall within a tolerance threshold, while string values are evaluated using similarity thresholds.

Table 1. Overview of the evaluated metrics dimensions: reference type, matching type, and IE metric.

Dimension	Characteristics	Description
Reference Type	**Name** (no reference values required) **Value** (requires reference values)	Whether metric compares property names (against prompt) or property values (against reference AAS).
Matching Type	**Exact** (string equality) **Embedding-based** (cosine similarity) **String-based** (normalized-Levenshtein-distance-based similarity)	How property names are matched. For similarity-based matching, pairs match if similarity exceeds a threshold τ. Numeric values match if their relative difference is below 1%.
IE Metric	**Precision** **Recall** **F1 Score**	Standard information extraction metrics computed after the matching.

Overall, we evaluate 18 metrics covering all combinations of three dimensions: (i) reference type (names vs. values), (ii) matching type (exact, embedding-based, string-based), and (iii) information extraction metric (precision, recall, F1). Table 1 summarizes these dimensions. These metrics provide a simple yet effective basis for evaluating structured outputs, enabling both controlled benchmarking and scalable quality checks.

3.2 Perturbation-Based Evaluation Approach

To evaluate metric effectiveness, we introduce controlled perturbations during AAS generation to simulate varying quality levels. Metric sensitivity is then assessed by measuring the rank correlation (Spearman's ρ) between perturbation intensity and metric scores. We consider three perturbation types:

LLM Temperature Variation. The temperature parameter controls output randomness. Lower values produce deterministic outputs, while higher values increase diversity but typically degrade performance in logic tasks [16]. We exploit this effect to vary output quality.

Model Size Reduction. Model size is reduced using smaller or distilled variants. While the functionality is largely preserved, performance degradation can be observed [9], enabling controlled quality variation.

Prompt Degradation. The input prompt plays a central role in guiding the LLM and is therefore a potential leverage point for introducing controlled perturbations [14]. To analyze metric sensitivity, we apply a set of complementary perturbations at varying intensity levels (0.0–1.0). These perturbations introduce both syntactic and semantic distortions while preserving the overall task intent. The following perturbation types are used:

- `Semantic Drift`: Up to 10% of tokens are replaced with contextually plausible synonyms (WordNet [13]), introducing subtle shifts in meaning.
- `Grammar Degradation`: A portion of grammatical elements such as determiners, adpositions, auxiliary verbs, and punctuation are removed based on part-of-speech tagging, reducing syntactic clarity.
- `Information Ambiguity`: Hedge phrases (e.g., "maybe," "or something") are inserted at random positions (up to 10% of tokens), increasing ambiguity.
- `Contextual Irrelevance`: Grammatically correct but semantically unrelated sentences are inserted after up to 10% of sentences, introducing distracting context.
- `Lexical Noise`: Up to 10% of characters are modified (substitution, deletion, insertion, transposition) to simulate typographical errors.

All perturbations are scaled according to the specified intensity and applied jointly, resulting in a gradual transition from clean to heavily degraded prompts.

An example of prompt perturbation at maximum intensity (1.0) is shown in Table 2. The perturbed version is obtained by sequentially applying all perturbation types, resulting in a heavily distorted but still partially interpretable prompt. Despite severe degradation, LLMs often recover the task intent, highlighting both their robustness and the challenge of evaluating quality.

Table 2. Original prompt and the maximally perturbed prompt (intensity 1.0). Perturbations are applied incrementally from mild to severe levels for metric evaluation.

Original Prompt	Perturbed Prompt (Intensity = 1.0)
You act as a text API to extract technical properties from a given datasheet. The datasheet will be surrounded by triple backticks ("').	You cat textula matter API to estrat you know technical a liottle bti ropejrtes given datasheet datasheet surrounded tyripebackticks

3.3 Dataset and Preprocessing

The evaluation is based on 200 products from four manufacturers (A–D), with 50 products each. Products were selected to maximize product diversity, while excluding incomplete or unusable data. Most products belong to the ECLASS segments "27: Electrical engineering" and "51: Fluid Power." Table 3 summarizes dataset statistics.

AASX files were preprocessed to ensure compatibility with the basyx-python-sdk. This included normalizing deprecated URIs, correcting file references, merging duplicate properties, standardizing decimal formats, and sanitizing idShort identifiers. Products were excluded if they used AAS version less than 3, lacked technical data submodels, or had unreadable datasheets. Additionally, only products with at least 10 purely technical properties not related to company or product identification were included.

To account for company-specific structures, a custom property dictionary was derived for each AAS, specifying property names, definitions, value types, and units. Table 4 summarizes the configurations.

The code to run the experiments and links to the product data is publicly available[1].

Table 3. Data statistics. Number of technical properties per product and product coverage shown by the number of ECLASS categories (including broad product segments and increasingly detailed product groups, classes, and subclasses).

Company	Product count	Average property count (Std. Dev.)	Segment count	Group count	Class count	Subclass count
A	50	35.4 (12.3)	1	1	1	5
B	50	36.8 (4.8)	2	5	6	18
C	50	86.4 (33.9)	1	5	6	8
D	50	23.9 (9.7)	3	10	21	30
Overall	200	45.6 (30.6)	4	17	33	60

3.4 Models and Experimental Procedure

We evaluate both proprietary and open-source LLMs. Proprietary experiments use GPT-4o-mini via the OpenAI API, while open-source evaluations use Qwen3 (0.6B–32B) and DeepSeek R1 (1.7B–70B) via a self-hosted Ollama deployment. All experiments were conducted on GPU-enabled nodes of an HPC cluster.

The pipeline constructs prompts from datasheets and property dictionaries, instructing the model to extract property records. A JSON schema was used to structure the LLM output as a list of records with *name*, *value*, *unit* and text *reference* for each record, ensuring machine-readable results.

Generated AAS are evaluated using the defined metrics, and perturbations are applied to analyze metric sensitivity under controlled conditions.

[1] https://github.com/janek-gross/perturbation_based_evaluation.

Table 4. Fields used in the creation of custom property dictionaries for different manufacturers.

Company	Property Name	Definition	Value Type	Unit	Selection Constraints	ECLASS Release
A	id_short	description	string	None	> 15 properties	11.0
B	display_name	concept_description.description	value_type	unit*	ECLASS ids not ending in 90–99 > 32 properties	12.0
C	preferred_name*	definition*	value_type	unit*	-	12.0
D	preferred_name*	definition*	value_type	unit*	> 9properties	14.0

4 Results

We first report data statistics to provide an overview of the generation results. In total, we generated 6,400 technical data submodels across 32 experimental conditions, covering different perturbation levels, model variants, and companies. Overall, 231,276 properties were extracted from 200 product datasheets.

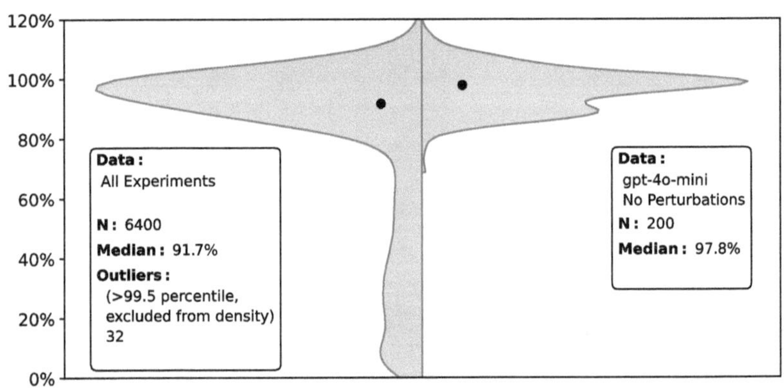

Fig. 3. Distribution of the ratio of extracted to prompted properties. Values larger than 100% indicate LLM-hallucinations or duplicate extractions. Values smaller than 100% indicate incomplete extractions.

On average, 83.5% of the prompted properties were extracted (correct or false) per submodel. In a baseline scenario without perturbations, GPT-4o-mini extracted values for 96.8% of prompted properties. Figure 3 shows the distribution of the ratio of extracted to prompted properties. The left density includes all perturbations, while the right density represents an unperturbed baseline scenario.

4.1 Metric Performance

We evaluate metric performance by analyzing the correlation between metric scores and perturbation intensity. Metric performance is assessed using Spearman's rank correlation between metric values and the intensity of controlled perturbations (temperature, model size, and prompt degradation), addressing RQ1 and RQ2.

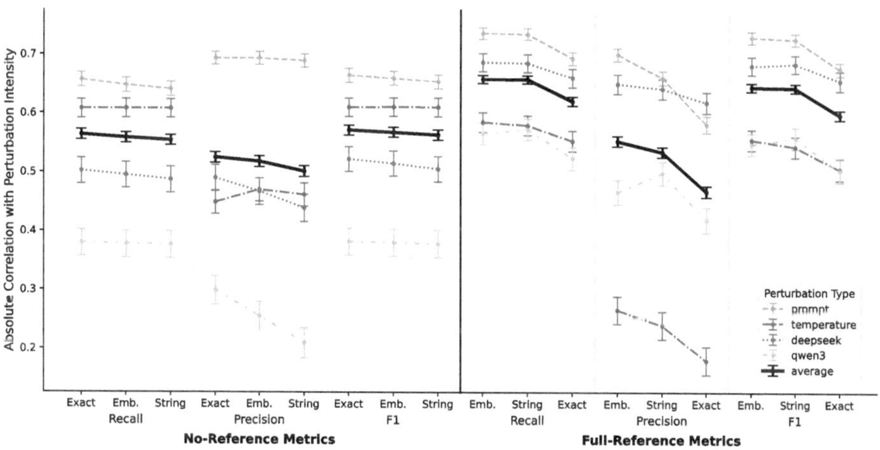

Fig. 4. Metric sensitivity measured as Spearman's rank correlation with perturbation intensity. Error bars indicate the standard error of the correlation.

The results are shown in Fig. 4, which reports the absolute value of the Spearman correlation between metric scores and perturbation intensity for all combinations of reference type, matching strategy and information extraction metric (see Table 1). Higher values indicate greater sensitivity of a metric to quality degradation.

Several consistent trends emerge. In the no-reference setting, embedding-based matching performed better than string-based matching. However, neither provided a clear advantage over simple exact matching. For illustration purposes in Fig. 4, we therefore apply a consistent matching threshold of $\tau = 0.88$ to both string- and embedding-based no-reference metrics even though these metrics would otherwise default to exact matching with an optimal matching threshold very close or equal to $\tau = 1.0$. **No-reference F1** scores exhibited the strongest monotonic relationships with perturbation intensity.

We utilize these observations and fix name-matching to exact matching in the full-reference setting to isolate the effect of value matching. In this scenario, soft matching based on embeddings resulted in the highest correlations. Among all candidates, **full-reference recall**, where cosine similarity was applied to values of exactly matching property names, achieved the highest average correlation ($\rho = 0.65$) at a value matching threshold of $\tau = 0.88$. In both settings, precision-based metrics showed limited sensitivity to quality variations.

4.2 Impact of Perturbations

We next analyze the impact of perturbation types and model configurations on AAS generation quality, addressing RQ2. Figure 5 illustrates the effects of different perturbations on the most sensitive metric full-reference recall, with perturbation intensity normalized between 0 and 1. Baseline performance for each model is indicated by markers on the left.

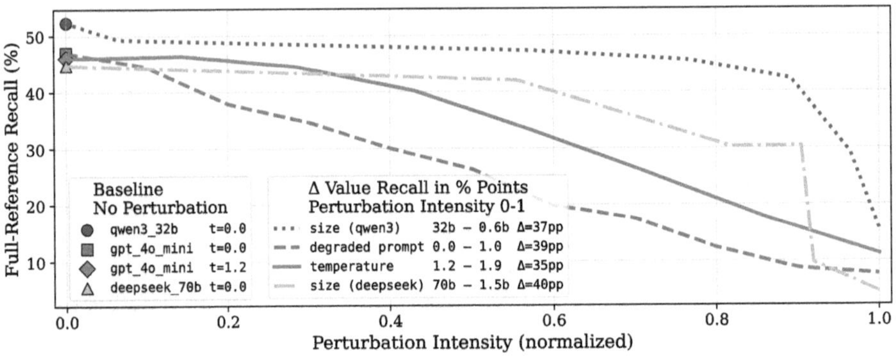

Fig. 5. Effect of perturbation types on value recall.

Across all perturbations, performance decreases by 35–40 percentage points, confirming that all perturbation types substantially degrade AAS quality. The effect of model size is distinctly non-linear: performance declines gradually for large models but drops sharply below approximately 8 billion parameters, suggesting a non-linear, potentially logarithmic relationship between model size and quality. This behavior further justifies the use of Spearman's rank correlation, which captures monotonic but non-linear relationships.

In contrast, both temperature increases and prompt degradation show a more linear degradation trend across the tested ranges. Interestingly, in the baseline scenario, the open-source model Qwen3:32b achieves the best performance, indicating that architecture and training method can outweigh high parameter count alone.

4.3 Manufacturer and Product Segment Analysis

Finally, we analyze how AAS quality varies across manufacturers and product segments (RQ3). Figure 6 compares both dimensions using strip plots overlaid with boxplots. The left plot shows differences between manufacturers, while the right plot highlights variation across product segments.

ANOVA indicates statistically significant differences between manufacturers for both no-reference and full-reference metrics ($p < 0.001$), with effect sizes of $\eta^2 \approx 0.13$–0.17, suggesting that company affiliation explains a moderate portion

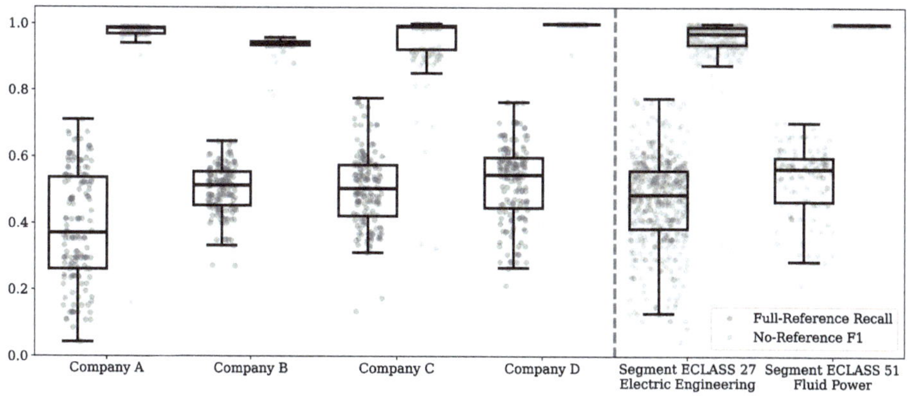

Fig. 6. AAS quality across manufacturers and product segments.

of the observed variance. This indicates that product-specific characteristics have a stronger influence on AAS quality than manufacturer-specific factors.

At the segment level, Fluid Power products tend to achieve higher scores than Electrical Engineering products, although substantial variability remains within each segment. For no-reference metrics, a ceiling effect is observed, with many samples receiving near-perfect scores, reflecting that only indirect quality signals are captured in the absence of reference values.

5 Discussion

The results provide several insights into the evaluation of AI-generated AAS and the behavior of different quality metrics. A key finding is that for matching property names, simple, interpretable metrics based on exact matching outperform more complex similarity-based approaches. This indicates that exact matching more reliably captures quality degradation—such as missing or incorrectly named properties—whereas embedding-based approaches, although intended to capture semantic similarity, introduce noise in settings where precise and standardized terminology is required. However, for the comparison of property values, exact matching turns out too restrictive. Here, a soft matching based on similarity which permits spelling variations and semantically equivalent phrasing leads to the most sensitive metrics.

From a practical perspective, these findings are directly relevant for Industry 4.0 applications. In industrial pipelines, quality assessment must be transparent, reproducible, and easy to integrate. The identified metrics meet these requirements and can be used for benchmarking AAS generation tools, monitoring extraction quality, and supporting acceptance decisions prior to system integration. In particular, no-reference metrics remain attractive for scalable quality assurance in scenarios where reference AAS are unavailable. However, the evaluated no-reference metrics were considerably less sensitive to perturbations than full-reference approaches, indicating substantial room for improvement.

At the same time, the results highlight limitations of metric-based evaluation. Optimizing a system with respect to a single metric can lead to metric overfitting, where models exploit metric-specific weaknesses rather than improving actual output quality. This is particularly relevant for no-reference metrics, which capture quality only indirectly and may exhibit ceiling effects, as observed in our experiments. In practice, robust evaluation therefore requires a combination of complementary metrics and, where necessary, human-in-the-loop validation.

The perturbation-based methodology itself provides additional insights. While the results indicate that current LLM-based AAS extraction quality remains limited, suitable quality metrics are a prerequisite for improving these systems. By systematically degrading inputs and analyzing metric responses, the proposed approach enables controlled and reproducible assessment of metric sensitivity without requiring labeled ground-truth data. This approach is not limited to AAS generation and can be applied to other structured information extraction tasks and LLM-based systems with end-to-end evaluation requirements.

Finally, differences across model families, manufacturers, and product segments indicate that AAS generation quality depends on both model characteristics and data properties. While larger models tend to perform more robustly, the results also show that architecture and training can outweigh parameter count. Variation between product segments further suggests that domain-specific factors, such as terminology consistency and the number and complexity of properties, significantly influence extraction performance. These findings highlight the importance of context-aware evaluation and caution against relying on single benchmark scenarios.

6 Threats to Validity

Our evaluation is subject to several threats to validity.

Construct Validity. A central threat concerns the operationalization of AAS quality. In this work, quality is primarily measured through the correctness and completeness of extracted property names and values in technical data submodels. Although these measurements are important, they do not cover all aspects of AAS quality, such as appropriateness in a specific industrial context, compliance with domain-specific modeling conventions, or usefulness for downstream applications. In particular, proposed no-reference metrics measure plausibility only indirectly and fail to detect semantic errors.

Internal Validity. Our perturbation-based methodology assumes that increasing perturbation intensity corresponds to decreasing AAS quality. Although this assumption is well motivated for the considered perturbation types, such as prompt degradation, temperature increase, and model size reduction, the relationship may not always be strictly monotonic for all models and products.

Furthermore, the optimization of similarity thresholds based on correlation with perturbation intensity may bias the evaluation in favor of metrics that align particularly well with our perturbation design.

Conclusion Validity. The conclusions drawn from the statistical analyses may be affected by variability in product characteristics, model behavior, and perturbation effects. While the dataset and number of generated AAS are substantial, some subgroup analyses, for example by manufacturer or product segment, are based on smaller effective sample sizes. Furthermore, Spearman's rank correlation only measures monotonic relationships, but overlooks non-monotonic effects.

External Validity. The generalizability of our findings is limited by the scope of the dataset and the evaluated models. Our experiments are based on 200 products from four manufacturers and focus on technical data submodels, with strong representation from specific ECLASS segments. The results may therefore not directly transfer to other industrial domains, other types of AAS submodels, or different product documentation styles. In addition, only a selected set of proprietary and open-source LLMs was evaluated, so the findings may not fully generalize to other model families or future model generations.

7 Conclusion and Future Work

In this work, we presented a systematic empirical framework for evaluating the quality of AI-generated Asset Administration Shells (AAS). By combining full-reference and no-reference metrics with a perturbation-based evaluation methodology, we enabled a controlled and reproducible analysis of how different metrics reflect variations in AAS quality. Our results show that metrics based on exact matching of names and similarity-based matching of values provide the most reliable indicators of quality degradation across different perturbation types. These findings support the use of soft-matching techniques for benchmarking AAS generation tools in case of non-unique spelling and phrasing of property values.

Beyond the specific results, the proposed perturbation-based methodology provides a general approach for evaluating metrics in scenarios where labeled ground truth is scarce or unavailable. It enables systematic comparison of metrics under controlled conditions and can be transferred to other structured information extraction tasks and LLM-based systems.

In future work, we plan to extend this approach in several directions. First, we aim to incorporate expert assessments to better align automated metrics with human judgment and to calibrate metrics in realistic evaluation settings. Second, we will investigate more advanced evaluation methods, including semantics-aware and LLM-based metrics, to address the limitations observed for the no-reference metrics evaluated in this study, and analyze their sensitivity under controlled perturbations. Third, we plan to extend the study to additional AAS submodels and broader industrial domains to assess the generalizability of our findings. Finally, we aim to integrate the proposed metrics into adaptive evaluation pipelines that support continuous quality monitoring and improvement of AI-assisted AAS generation systems.

Acknowledgments. This work was supported by the research training group "Dependable AI Assistants for the Management of Dynamic Production Systems and Supply Chains (VAMoS)" at Mainz University of Applied Sciences and the Rheinland-Palatinate Technical University of Kaiserslautern-Landau, funded by the Ministry of Science and Health of Rhineland-Palatinate. The authors gratefully acknowledge this support.

Disclosure of Interests. The authors have no competing interests to declare that are relevant to the content of this article.

References

1. Angelopoulos, A.N., Bates, S., Fannjiang, C., Jordan, M.I., Zrnic, T.: Prediction-powered inference. Science **382**(6671), 669–674 (2023). https://doi.org/10.1126/science.adi6000
2. Deng, S., Ma, Y., Zhang, N., Cao, Y., Hooi, B.: Information extraction in low-resource scenarios: Survey and perspective. In: 2024 IEEE International Conference on Knowledge Graph (ICKG), pp. 33–49 (2024). https://doi.org/10.1109/ickg63256.2024.00013
3. Es, S., James, J., Espinosa Anke, L.E., Schockaert, S.: RAGAs: automated evaluation of retrieval augmented generation. In: Proceedings of the 18th Conference of the European Chapter of the Association for Computational Linguistics: System Demonstrations, pp. 150–158. Association for Computational Linguistics (2024). https://doi.org/10.18653/v1/2024.eacl-demo.16
4. Han, R., Peng, T., Yang, C., Wang, B., Liu, L., Wan, X.: An empirical study on information extraction using large language models. arXiv preprint arXiv:2305.14450 (2023). https://doi.org/10.48550/arXiv.2305.14450
5. Industrial Digital Twin Association: Specification of the asset administration shell part 1: Metamodel. Technical report IDTA 01001, IDTA (2023)
6. Industrial Digital Twin Association: Specification of the asset administration shell part 3a: Data specification – iec 61360. Technical report IDTA 01003-a-3-0, IDTA (2023)
7. Industrial Digital Twin Association: Aasx samples (nd). https://github.com/admin-shell/io. Accessed. 08 June 2026
8. International Organization for Standardization: Iso/iec 25010:2011 systems and software engineering - systems and software quality requirements and evaluation (square) - system and software quality models. Technical report, ISO (2011)
9. Kaplan, J., et al.: Scaling laws for neural language models. arXiv preprint arXiv:2001.08361 (2020). https://doi.org/10.48550/arXiv.2001.08361
10. Kaya, F., Şanlı, E., Albayrak, Ö., Ünal, P., Kirci, P.: Asset administration shell tool comparison: a case study with real digital twins used in petrochemical industry. Sensors **25**(7) (2025). https://doi.org/10.3390/s25071978
11. Li, J., Sun, A., Han, J., Li, C.: A survey on deep learning for named entity recognition. IEEE Trans. Knowl. Data Eng. **34**(1), 50–70 (2022). https://doi.org/10.1109/TKDE.2020.2981314

12. Lin, C.Y.: ROUGE: a package for automatic evaluation of summaries. In: Text Summarization Branches Out, pp. 74–81. Association for Computational Linguistics, Barcelona (2004). https://aclanthology.org/W04-1013/
13. Miller, G.A.: WordNet: a lexical database for English. Commun. ACM **38**(11), 39–41 (1995). https://doi.org/10.1145/219717.219748
14. Moradi, M., Samwald, M.: Evaluating the robustness of neural language models to input perturbations. In: Proceedings of the 2021 Conference on Empirical Methods in Natural Language Processing, pp. 1558–1570. Association for Computational Linguistics (2021). https://doi.org/10.18653/v1/2021.emnlp-main.117
15. Papineni, K., Roukos, S., Ward, T., Zhu, W.J.: BLEU: a method for automatic evaluation of machine translation. In: Proceedings of the 40th Annual Meeting of the Association for Computational Linguistics, pp. 311–318. Association for Computational Linguistics, Philadelphia (2002). https://doi.org/10.3115/1073083.1073135, https://aclanthology.org/P02-1040/
16. Renze, M.: The effect of sampling temperature on problem solving in large language models. In: Findings of the Association for Computational Linguistics: EMNLP 2024, pp. 7346–7356. Association for Computational Linguistics (2024). https://doi.org/10.18653/v1/2024.findings-emnlp.432
17. Saad-Falcon, J., Khattab, O., Potts, C., Zaharia, M.: ARES: an automated evaluation framework for retrieval-augmented generation systems. In: Proceedings of the 2024 Conference of the North American Chapter of the Association for Computational Linguistics: Human Language Technologies (Volume 1: Long Papers), pp. 338–354. Association for Computational Linguistics (2024). https://doi.org/10.18653/v1/2024.naacl-long.20, https://aclanthology.org/2024.naacl-long.20/
18. Sander, D.P., Dietz, L.: EXAM: how to evaluate retrieve-and-generate systems for users who do not (yet) know what they want. In: DESIRES. pp. 136–146 (2021). https://ceur-ws.org/Vol-2950/paper-16.pdf
19. Vogel, J.A., et al.: Extraction of technical data using LLMs: experience report and evaluation based on asset administration shells. In: Automation 2025: Human-centric Automation, pp. 153–168. VDI (2025)
20. Wagner, S., et al.: Operationalised product quality models and assessment: the quamoco approach. Inf. Softw. Technol. **62**, 101–123 (2015). https://doi.org/10.1016/j.infsof.2015.02.009
21. Witte, C., Cimiano, P.: Intra-template entity compatibility based slot-filling for clinical trial information extraction. In: Proceedings of the 21st Workshop on Biomedical Language Processing, pp. 178–192. Association for Computational Linguistics, Dublin (2022). https://doi.org/10.18653/v1/2022.bionlp-1.18
22. Xia, Y., Xiao, Z., Jazdi, N., Weyrich, M.: Generation of asset administration shell with large language model agents: toward semantic interoperability in digital twins in the context of industry 4.0. IEEE Access **12**, 84863–84877 (2024). https://doi.org/10.1109/ACCESS.2024.3415470
23. Zhao, X., et al.: A comprehensive survey on relation extraction: recent advances and new frontiers. ACM Comput. Surv. **56**(11) (2024). https://doi.org/10.1145/3674501

Adopting InnerSource in a Public Sector Organization: A Case Study

Muhammad Usman[1(✉)], Johan Linåker[2], Deepika Badampudi[1], and Hannes Salin[3]

[1] Department of Software Engineering, Blekinge Institute of Technology, Karlskrona, Sweden
{muhammad.usman,deepika.badampudi}@bth.se
[2] RISE Research Institutes of Sweden, Lund, Sweden
johan.linaker@ri.se
[3] Swedish Transport Administration, Borlänge, Sweden
hannes.salin@trafikverket.se

Abstract. InnerSource (IS) is increasingly viewed as a way to improve large-scale software development. However, evidence on its adoption in public sector organizations remains limited. This paper reports a study of IS adoption in a Swedish Public Sector Organization. Drawing on nine semi-structured interviews and an internal workshop with 13 participants, we examine motivations, challenges, and improvement strategies for IS adoption. The results show that the main motivations are improving reuse, strengthening cross-team collaboration, and enabling faster and more cost-efficient development. Key challenges relate to a lack of an open culture and mindset, management of reusable assets (e.g., ownership, documentation, and code visibility), and ways of working (e.g., siloed practices and limited time for contributions). The study also identified improvements to address challenges, including fostering an enabling culture and mindset for IS and knowledge sharing, strengthening management support, and establishing internal platforms and governance for reusable assets.

Keywords: InnerSource · Software Reuse · Open Source

1 Introduction

Public sector organizations (PSOs) are increasingly developing and maintaining software-intensive systems to support their operations and service delivery. A census of Swedish government agencies illustrates this growth, with some agencies employing more than 100 developers [2]. In large organizations where software is developed and maintained across different units, challenges in coordination and reuse can arise. The census identified software reuse as a potential area for improvement [2]. Furthermore, as software development scales across organizations with multiple units and teams, it is crucial to coordinate and synchronize development efforts to improve reuse and avoid duplicate effort.

C. Berger and V. Klös (Eds.): SEAA 2026, LNCS 16864, pp. 390–398, 2027.
https://doi.org/10.1007/978-3-032-36587-3_26

Innersource (IS) refers to the adoption of open source software development practices within organizational boundaries and has emerged as a promising solution to address the challenges of large-scale software development [4,6]. One of the key motivations is to decrease duplication of effort and improve internal reuse by making common reusable assets discoverable and easier to contribute to across organizational silos [1,4,5,13]. Previous studies also suggest that IS adoption is motivated by human and social factors, such as forming stronger internal communities, encouraging contributions, and improving employees' job satisfaction [13,16]. While these benefits are well recognized, IS adoption and scaling do not come without challenges, such as resistance to change [4], a lack of management support [1], insufficient time to contribute to IS projects, and concerns about ownership of IS projects [4,8,13]. Challenges such as these often require the establishment of structured governance, practices, and an overall cultural shift within the organization [5,13,15].

Although the adoption and scaling of IS have been extensively studied in private-sector organizations, there is limited empirical evidence on IS adoption in PSOs. PSOs often have limited IT and engineering capabilities, due to a tradition of outsourcing and IT procurement [2,9]. However, some PSOs have large internal IT divisions consisting of several sub-units and teams responsible for a large portfolio of software applications. The hierarchical structure of PSOs' IT divisions increases the likelihood of duplicate functionality, fragmented ownership of similar assets, and limited systematic reuse. Adopting IS is a potential solution to address some of these issues. However, there is not much research on IS adoption in PSOs (with some notable exceptions [10]). This study aims to address this gap by presenting a study of IS adoption in a PSO with a large IT division responsible for managing a large portfolio of applications.

Our study, through an exploratory case study at the Swedish Transport Administration (STA), represents an early effort to further explore this potential. We ask the following research questions (RQs):1) *What is the motivation for adopting IS in PSOs?*, 2) *What are the challenges in adopting IS in PSOs?*, and 3) *How can the identified challenges be addressed?* The findings provide empirical evidence on the motivations, challenges, and improvement strategies associated with IS adoption, offering a foundation for understanding how IS can be introduced and supported in PSOs.

2 Research Methodology

We conducted an exploratory case study [12] to answer the RQs.

2.1 Case Organization and Unit of Analysis

The case organization is the Swedish Transport Administration (STA), a Swedish PSO responsible for planning, construction, operation, and maintenance of Sweden's roads and railway infrastructure. STA operates in a large-scale, heavily regulated environment where digitalization and software systems play a central role, and has an annual budget of approximately 97 billion SEK (approximately 10.24 billion USD) [14].

Our study focuses in particular on the Information and Communication Technology (ICT) division at STA, which includes around 1,700 employees and contractors, with roughly 350–400 software developers and architects. Software development work is organized within a hybrid governance model combining the PM3 framework [11] with agile practices such as Scrum and Kanban.

An estimated 80–90 software engineering teams are located across four departments within the ICT division, either developing their own systems, customizing third-party systems, or maintaining commercial off-the-shelf (COTS) systems. In total, roughly 4–500 applications are developed.

Within the context of the ICT division case at STA, the unit of analysis for our study is the development practices (e.g., development, maintenance, sharing, integration) related to common reusable assets. During the study period, no established IS practices were in place, although a smaller set of code repositories was available in the local TRV Hub. In addition, no official strategies or documents on open or inner sourcing were officially communicated within ICT at the beginning of the study.

2.2 Data Collection and Analysis

We used two data sources: 1) Data collected from nine semi-structured interviews for this study, and 2) Notes from an internal workshop at the case organization.

The relevant interviewees, representing a mix of roles and teams, were identified by the main contact person (fourth author) at STA (see Table 1. The interviews (half-hour long) were conducted remotely (via Microsoft Teams) and recorded with the permission of the interviewees. The fourth author did not participate in any interview. In addition to the questions about demographic information (e.g., role, experience, team), the interviews included questions about our three RQs. The interviewees were first asked about the motivation and need for adopting IS in the organization. Next, we asked them about the potential challenges of adopting IS practices and their suggestions for addressing them.

After the interviews, an internal workshop was held within the ICT division to discuss IS adoption. The workshop was attended by 13 participants (including the two interviewees) from the ICT division. The discussion points were recorded in a document, which we have used in this study as an additional data source.

The Microsoft Team's auto-generated transcripts of the interviews were used for data analysis. The text segments were grouped and included under the broader topics that correspond to the aspects covered in the interview guide (i.e., motivation for IS, challenges, and improvement suggestions). The second and third authors then performed a thematic analysis [3] to identify the themes under each of these topics. The identified themes were discussed and refined in a meeting (approximately one hour long in-person meeting) between the first three authors. Later, the analysis results were further discussed in a joint meeting (approximately 1.5 h, onsite) among all four authors at one of the STA offices.

Table 1. Interviewees

Role (STA experience)	Description
1) Team lead (3 years)	He is also a solution architect. He works with 15 people from different delivery sections in the transport and traffic control systems area.
2) Manager (7 years)	His two teams (15 people) work on the railroad and traffic systems.
3) Team lead (2 years)	His team (eight members) works on railroad and traffic systems.
4) Developer (1 year)	His team (six members) is responsible for managing the developer platforms.
5) Developer (8 years)	His team (two members) is responsible for the observability platform.
6) Architect (4 years)	He works with 8–10 teams that are responsible for case management, web, and e-commerce applications.
7) Manager (6 years)	He manages two teams that are responsible for software solutions in technical documentation for the railroads in Sweden.
8) Developer (10 years)	His team (four members) is responsible for a system that manages how different contractors are doing infrastructure (e.g., roads). maintenance
9) Developer (6 years)	His team (ten members) is responsible for developing applications for internal users, mainly the business and management side.

The workshop document was also coded to identify the IS's motivating factors, challenges, and areas for improvement.

3 Results

This section presents the results of the RQs.

3.1 RQ1: Motivation for IS

Improving reuse is a leading motivator for adopting IS. Four interviewees highlighted it as the main reason behind IS adoption. It was also highlighted as a main factor in the workshop. An interviewee, while explaining the motivation for adopting the IS stated: "*I think it's a good path to go. If it's reusable, then other people can use it and like extend it to their needs.... You don't have to reinvent the wheel again.* ". Improving cross-team collaboration was also highlighted as a motivation for adopting IS, both in the interviews (two interviewees) and the workshop. In the workshop, IS is highlighted as a mechanism that could promote collaboration and help break down silos. An interviewee explained it as: "*it's necessary that we cooperate more and to help each other with and use things from the code to do that. [IS] can be a way to make this happen, so we should cooperate more between the teams.*". The interview (two interviewees) and workshop participants also highlighted faster and more cost-effective development as a motivating factor for adopting IS. This relates to reuse, i.e., IS helps improve reuse, which in turn helps teams developing with reuse to reduce their development costs and improve delivery time.

The workshop participants also identified additional motivating factors. IS could accelerate innovation within the organization by establishing mechanisms for improved cross-team collaboration, open and transparent processes, and knowledge-sharing opportunities. The workshop participants also highlighted that, since IS encourages code sharing, it would improve code quality by enabling code to be reviewed, reused, and contributed to by more people. Lastly, the workshop participants also reflected that adopting IS would help STA become an attractive and modern workplace where developers are encouraged and supported to work on interesting ideas and new technologies beyond their regular work, thereby helping them upskill their competence. Table 2 presents the list of motivating factors identified through interviews and the workshop.

Table 2. Motivators, challenges, and improvements for InnerSource (IS) adoption.

No.	Factor	Interviews	Workshop
Motivators for IS adoption			
1	To improve reuse across the entire organization	✓	✓
2	To improve cross-team collaboration	✓	✓
3	To achieve faster and cost-efficient development	✓	✓
4	To lower maintenance effort	✓	-
5	To accelerate innovation	-	✓
6	To improve quality through more eyes	-	✓
7	To be an attractive and modern workplace	-	✓
Challenges in IS adoption			
1	Lack of open mindset and culture	✓	✓
2	Ownership of reusable assets	✓	✓
3	Working in silos	✓	✓
4	Code sharing and visibility	✓	✓
5	Documentation of reusable assets	✓	✓
6	Lack of time for reuse and collaboration	✓	-
7	Prioritizing own work	✓	-
8	Explaining InnerSource value	✓	-
9	Security clearance for code sharing	✓	-

(*continued*)

3.2 RQ2: IS Adoption Challenges

Several common IS adoption challenges were identified in the interviews and the workshop (see Table 2 for details). First, the lack of an open mindset and culture

Table 2. (*continued*)

No.	Factor	Interviews	Workshop
Improvements to support IS adoption			
1	Enabling culture and mindset for open collaboration	✓	✓
2	Knowledge sharing across teams and units	✓	✓
3	Internal platform for sharing reusable assets	✓	✓
4	Documentation of reusable assets	✓	✓
5	Upper management support and guidance	✓	-
6	Dedicated time for IS collaborations	✓	-
7	Meritocracy before hierarchy	-	✓
8	Clear responsibility and ownership	-	✓
9	Prioritize small changes and quick feedback	-	✓
10	Promote reuse and sharing of existing assets	-	✓
11	Clear processes and guidelines for contributions	-	✓

for supporting cross-team and unit collaboration is identified as a challenge in the interviews (four interviewees) and the workshop. An interviewee highlighted it as: "*It doesn't have anything to do with the governmental work or anything. It's just culture and mentality. And then some organizations do have a more the culture where that's more appreciated, which makes it easier.*" The ownership of reusable assets was also discussed as a potential challenge in the interviews (four interviewees) and workshop - i.e., who will take the responsibility for the ownership and maintenance of the reusable asset. An interviewee explained it as: "*If you take the initiative to start something and that you will be the only one who maintains the code. That's I think it could be something that scares you off to start something like this.*". Another challenge that acts as a barrier to IS adoption is that teams and units work in their silos, which limits the possibilities to identify and implement opportunities for co-developing common assets. Furthermore, the interview (four interviewees) and workshop participants also highlighted barriers in sharing and accessing code (e.g., due to security concerns) and other artifacts as a challenge in adopting IS in the organization. Finally, another common challenge in the interviews and the workshop relates to the documentation of reusable assets. For assets intended for reuse by multiple teams, the requirements for proper documentation are more stringent; otherwise, reusers may not be able to understand or reuse them.

3.3 RQ3: Improvements

Both interview and workshop participants shared several improvements to support IS adoption in the organization (see Table 2 for a complete list). First, the interview (three interviewees) and workshop participants suggested addressing the question of culture and mindset within the organization. They would like to see initiatives that foster a culture and mindset where collaboration across teams and units comes naturally. This, perhaps, also relates to Improvement 5 in Table 2, which is about upper management support and guidance. An interviewee explained it as: "*it's a mindset shift maybe that's need to take place that we should collaborate more because I think at the moment we are mostly Looking inside each team and we solve everything inside the teams*". Another interviewee reflected on it as: "*The system developers need to talk to each other, not the managers or others. So it's a culture question, I think.*" Another related improvement suggestion is about creating opportunities for sharing knowledge across teams. The workshop participants suggested measures such as establishing chat channels, organizing hackathons, and teams organizing demos of their applications for others. Establishing an internal platform where the information about the IS projects and reusable assets (e.g., links to code repos, relevant owners, and related wikis and communication channels) is available for everyone in the organization was also shared as an improvement by interview (three interviewees) and workshop participants. This internal platform should allow efficient search and classification features so that it is easy to find relevant assets. The interview and workshop participants also suggested to improve the documentation of reusable assets (e.g., by AI-generated documentation).

The workshop participants also suggested some additional improvements. They suggested to promote meritocracy in the IS process so that the contributions and ideas are evaluated on the basis of their quality, not by the designation of the proposer. Potential contributors do not contribute to avoid becoming maintainers and owners of common assets. To address that, the workshop participants suggested clarifying the rules regarding ownership and appointing owners. The workshop participants also suggested that promoting reuse (over reinventing the wheel) should be an organizational focus area. Lastly, they also suggested formulating contributions guidelines so that contributors know what is expected from them when they send their commits and pull requests to a common asset.

4 Discussion and Conclusion

The findings highlight reuse as a main incentive, which, in many ways, can also be considered an enabler of other incentives, such as faster, more cost-efficient development. Higher degrees of collaboration and more eyes on the code may help accelerate innovation and quality, and decrease maintenance efforts, again leading to potentially faster and more cost-efficient development. In this sense, increased reuse or collaboration is not the end goal. The rationale for adopting IS should ideally be viewed holistically, considering cost, innovation, competency, culture, and employer branding as the main goals. These values can resonate with management and secure their support for introducing IS into the organization. In general, the incentives (improving reuse, fostering cross-team collaboration, and achieving faster and more efficient development and maintenance) align well with software-intensive organizations [13,16].

For challenges, a similar alignment between industry and the case organization is reiterated, e.g., regarding asset ownership, culture and mindset, siloed work practices, and incentivizing the adoption and implementation of IS [5,7,13,15]. To some degree, security clearance stands out, as some interviewees reported that their specific products were considered too sensitive or classified, even for internal disclosure. In STA's case, this can be seen in light of their responsibility for the physical infrastructure used for transport and mobility, as well as their role in national security. In terms of improvements, our observations reiterate industry best practices, e.g., establishing internal forges, better documentation, management support, dedicated time and mandate for collaboration, and advocacy and training for reuse [1,5,7,13,15].

The similarities, both in terms of perceived benefits, challenges, and improvement opportunities, indicate the potential to transfer practice from industry to a public-sector context. However, it should be noted that this should not serve as a potential generalization for PSOs at large. The STA has strong development capacity, with a complex team and product structure, which, anecdotally, can also translate to industrial contexts. PSOs, however, often have a tradition of outsourcing and procuring developer capacity, or solutions, with IT departments generally being small or limited to a product owner level [2,9]. As we are limited by a single case, future research should investigate the potential for IS across PSOs more broadly with different types of characteristics.

An aspect missing from our research and warranting special attention in future work is how the concept of IS can be extended to an inter-PSO (or intra-governmental) practice. PSOs within the same government may overlap and have similar needs to varying degrees, and internal sharing and reuse can be a means of transferring the same incentives for IS adoption from a single PSO to a cross-government level. The interviewees highlighted design systems for internal and external e-platforms as examples of solutions that are commonly redeveloped but where collaboration is now emerging, e.g., at the Swedish Public Employment Service. While the latter case concerns an open-source solution, there will be cases where a solution is not suitable for release as open source, yet can still be shared as a government-internal asset. Aspects such as security and classified access can be expected to prevent some sharing, as well as the generalizability of solutions and components. Still, in areas such as infrastructure and tooling, standardization and overlap may potentially be higher, as also indicated by the internal teams surveyed through the interviewees at STA.

The limitations of the study include a relatively small sample of interviewees in a large organization. To some extent, it was addressed by incorporating the workshop discussion into the analysis. The results were discussed jointly by all authors to avoid misinterpretation. In the future, we plan to expand the study by organizing workshops and focus groups at STA, to, for example, complement and prioritize challenges and improvements, and identify future focus areas.

References

1. Badampudi, D., Usman, M., Chen, X.: Large scale reuse of microservices using CI/CD and innersource practices-a case study. Empir. Softw. Eng. **30**(2), 1–46 (2025)

2. Borg, M., Olsson, T., Franke, U., Assar, S.: Digitalization of Swedish government agencies: a perspective through the lens of a software development census. In: Proceedings of the 40th International Conference on Software Engineering: Software Engineering in Society, pp. 37–46 (2018)
3. Braun, V., Clarke, V.: Using thematic analysis in psychology. Qual. Res. Psychol. **3**(2), 77–101 (2006)
4. Capraro, M., Riehle, D.: Inner source definition, benefits, and challenges. ACM Comput. Surv. (CSUR) **49**(4), 1–36 (2016)
5. Chen, X., Usman, M., Badampudi, D.: Using innersource for improving internal reuse: an industrial case study. In: Proceedings of the 27th International Conference on Evaluation and Assessment in software engineering, pp. 348–357 (2023)
6. Cooper, D., Stol, K.J.: Adopting Innersource. O'Reilly Media, Incorporated (2018)
7. Edison, H., Carroll, N., Morgan, L., Conboy, K.: Inner source software development: current thinking and an agenda for future research. J. Syst. Softw. **163**, 110520 (2020)
8. InnerSource Commons: State of innersource 2024 (2024). https://innersourcecommons.org/documents/surveys/State.of.InnerSource.2024.pdf
9. Marco-Simó, J.M., Pastor-Collado, J.A.: It outsourcing in the public sector: a descriptive framework from a literature review. J. Glob. Inf. Technol. Manag. **23**(1), 25–52 (2020)
10. Martin, G., Lippold, A.: Forge. mil: a case study for utilizing open source methodologies inside of government. In: Ifip International Conference On Open Source Systems, pp. 334–337. Springer, Cham (2011)
11. Nordström, M.: Pm3 Evolutionen: En Innovationsberättelse Från Systemförvaltning Till It-governance, Linköping University Electronic Press (2014)
12. Runeson, P., Host, M., Rainer, A., Regnell, B.: Case Study Research in Software Engineering: Guidelines and Examples. Wiley, Hoboken (2012)
13. Stol, K.J., Avgeriou, P., Babar, M.A., Lucas, Y., Fitzgerald, B.: Key factors for adopting inner source. ACM Trans. Softw. Eng. Methodol. (TOSEM) **23**(2), 1–35 (2014)
14. Swedish Transport Administration: Trafikverkets årsredovisning 2025. Technical report diva2:2040315, Swedish Transport Administration (2025). https://trafikverket.diva-portal.org/smash/record.jsf?pid=diva2:2040315
15. Usman, M., Badampudi, D., Smith, C., Nayak, H.: An ecosystem for the large-scale reuse of microservices in a cloud-native context. IEEE Softw. **39**(5), 68–75 (2022)
16. Wan, Z., et al.: What motivates software practitioners to contribute to inner source? In: Proceedings of the 30th ACM Joint European Software Engineering Conference and Symposium on the Foundations of Software Engineering, pp. 132–144 (2022)

HARP-ML Framework: A Hybrid Assisted Refactoring Pipeline for ML Code Smells

Gargie Tambe(✉) and Y. Raghu Reddy

Software Engineering Research Center (SERC), International Institute of Information Technology, Hyderabad, India
gargie.tambe@research.iiit.ac.in, raghu.reddy@iiit.ac.in

Abstract. The increasing adoption of machine learning (ML) systems has led to ML-specific code smells that degrade maintainability, reproducibility, and scalability. While prior research has focused primarily on detecting such smells, automated refactoring support remains limited. This paper proposes HARP-ML (Hybrid Assisted Refactoring Pipeline for ML code smells), a framework that classifies ML code smells into two categories: Type I smells, which are syntactically localized and resolved through Concrete Syntax Tree (CST) transformations validated by Property-Based Testing (PBT), and Type II smells, which involve control flow and execution context and are addressed using a Small Language Model (SLM) with a focused context window. We evaluate HARP-ML on four ML code smells across two benchmarks: curated experimental kits, where HARP-ML achieves a 97.5% refactoring success rate, and 14 real-world repositories from the NICHE dataset, where it achieves 87.7%. Results confirm that deterministic CST-based transformations are sufficient and verifiable for syntactically localized smells, while SLM-based reasoning is necessary for context-dependent fixes.

Keywords: Machine Learning Systems · Technical Debt · ML Code Smells · Automated Refactoring · Small Language Models · Property-Based Testing · Software Maintainability

1 Introduction

As Machine Learning (ML) systems move into production, the maintainability of their codebases becomes as critical as model performance. However, ML-specific risk factors such as tightly coupled data dependencies and weakened abstraction boundaries frequently manifest as technical debt and code smells [3,7,10]. Because rapid prototyping environments prioritize experimentation over disciplined engineering, ML code typically exhibits lower quality than traditional software [2]. Despite growing awareness, tool support is limited. General-purpose linters produce frequent false positives [4], and while recent work has advanced ML smell *detection* [6], systematic *refactoring* techniques remain underexplored.

C. Berger and V. Klös (Eds.): SEAA 2026, LNCS 16864, pp. 399–407, 2027.
https://doi.org/10.1007/978-3-032-36587-3_27

To bridge this gap, we propose HARP-ML[1] (Hybrid Assisted Refactoring Pipeline for Machine Learning). HARP-ML classifies ML code smells into Type I (syntactically localized, deterministic) and Type II (context-dependent, requiring semantic reasoning). Type I smells are resolved via Concrete Syntax Tree (CST) transformations validated by Property-Based Testing (PBT), while Type II smells are addressed using a Small Language Model (SLM) operating over a focused context window. Evaluated on curated experimental kits [6] and 14 real-world repositories from the NICHE dataset [9], HARP-ML achieved refactoring success rates of 97.5% and 87.7%, respectively. To evaluate this approach, we address the following research questions:

RQ1: How effective is HARP-ML at resolving Type I and Type II ML code smells in controlled environments?
RQ2: How does HARP-ML perform when deployed against real-world ML repositories?

The rest of the paper is structured as follows: Sect. 2 outlines related work. Section 3 details the dual-pathway HARP-ML framework. Section 4 presents the evaluation and threats to validity, followed by conclusions in Sect. 5.

2 Background and Related Work

Prior work has extensively studied the emergence of machine learning-specific code smells and the accumulation of hidden technical debt driven by unstable data dependencies and weakened abstraction boundaries [2,7]. Empirical studies indicate that while ML projects inherit traditional software smells, they also introduce complex semantic issues tied directly to data pipelines and model behavior [2]. To manage these risks, researchers have proposed various static and notebook-aware tools. General-purpose linters apply Abstract Syntax Tree-based rule checking, while specialized tools like MLSmellHound [3] and CodeSmile [6] effectively address project-level engineering smells. However, these tools focus almost exclusively on detection, leaving the complex task of automated resolution through refactoring heavily underexplored.

To bridge this resolution gap, recent work has drawn on learning-based Automated Program Repair (APR) [11], utilizing Large Language Models to recommend semantics-aware refactorings that traditional rule-based techniques cannot achieve [5]. However, a major limitation of generative edits in ML pipelines is the high risk of hallucinated fixes, which necessitate explicit validation to prevent silent behavioral regressions during training or inference. As a more reliable alternative for constrained tasks, Small Language Models (SLMs) offer highly efficient, context-aware reasoning [1], while property-based testing (PBT) provides a principled mechanism for the oracle-free verification of behavioral invariants [8]. Building on these foundations, HARP-ML addresses both structural

[1] The replication package for this study is available at https://github.com/garguy07/HARP-ML-Supplementary.

and semantic challenges by combining rule-based Concrete Syntax Tree transformations, SLM-driven reasoning, and property-driven verification into a unified refactoring pipeline.

3 Proposed Framework

HARP-ML is a hybrid refactoring framework designed to address ML-specific code smells. It focuses strictly on resolution rather than detection: given a code snippet, an identified smell type, and its location within the source file as produced by a static smell detector such as CodeSmile [6], the framework determines and applies the appropriate transformation. As shown in Fig. 1, the framework routes smells through one of two pathways according to the nature of the required fix. This reflects the distinction between transformations that can be guaranteed through rule-based structural analysis and those that require contextual semantic reasoning. HARP-ML introduces no new detector, instead leveraging CodeSmile [6]. Its novelty lies in ML smell classification and a dual-pathway refactoring pipeline.

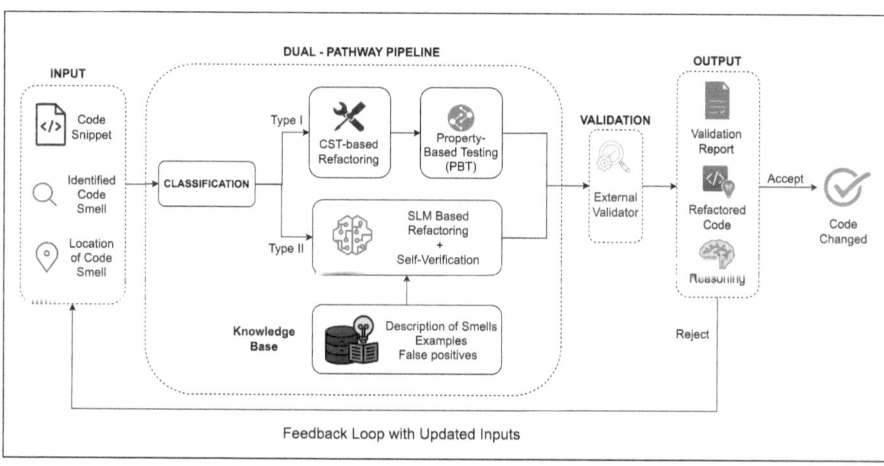

Fig. 1. Overview of the HARP-ML framework.

Classification. To formalize the distinction of transformations needed, two authors independently classified 22 smells from Zhang et al. [10] against a predefined criterion. Smells were classified as Type I if their fix is syntactically complete and verifiable within a single statement without broader context, and Type II if their resolution depends on control flow or execution context (cross-file smells were marked out-of-scope). Disagreements were resolved through discussion. In the current prototype, we implement two representative smells from each category.

Type I smells are structural anti-patterns resolvable within a localized code block. They typically correspond to API misuses with strict, deterministic fixes. For example, the *Pandas Chain Indexing* smell (e.g., `df["A"]["B"]|` may return a copy instead of a view; fixing it by replacing it with the safer `df.loc[:,("A", "B")]` accessor is syntactically complete and can be verified locally. Another example is the *Dataframe Conversion API* smell, where replacing `df.values` with `df.to_numpy()` is a direct, context-free API substitution. The key characteristic is that the fix does not require reasoning about model behavior, data flow, or training logic.

Type II smells arise from complex interactions between API calls or the broader logic of an ML pipeline. For instance, the smell *PyTorch Gradients Not Cleared* arises when `optim-izer.zero_grad()` is absent before `loss.backward()`, causing gradients to accumulate improperly across iterations. Fixing this requires analysing control flow to identify the correct insertion point within the training loop (as shown in Fig. 2). Another example is the *Merge API Parameter Not Explicitly Set* smell, where fixing a `df.merge()` call requires understanding surrounding DataFrame schemas from context to infer appropriate parameters. In such cases, rule-based approaches become infeasible.

```
# Smell: zero_grad() missing, gradients accumulate across iterations
# Fix: zero_grad() inserted at correct position
for epoch in range(num_epochs):
    optimizer.zero_grad()
    out = model(X)
    loss = criterion(out, y)
    loss.backward()
    optimizer.step()
```

Fig. 2. Gradients Not Cleared smell fixed by SLM.

Dual-Pathway Refactoring Pipeline. The refactoring engine consists of two specialized pathways designed to address structurally deterministic and context-dependent ML code smells.

Type I Pathway - Deterministic CST Refactoring: For Type I smells, preserving original code formatting is essential. Because standard ASTs discard details like whitespace and comments, the engine operates on a Concrete Syntax Tree (CST) to retain formatting nodes and ensure seamless integration. Transformations are deterministic and smell-specific; the Chain Indexing fix, for instance, replaces nested `Subscript` nodes with a unified `loc` accessor. Correctness is validated via Property-Based Testing (PBT), which establishes invariant templates to assert behavioural equivalence between the original and refactored code. PBT also acts as a false-positive filter: if a valid test cannot be instantiated, it signals a likely detector misclassification, safely routing the instance to human review instead of silently refactoring.

Type II Pathway - Contextual SLM Refactoring: For Type II smells, static rules are insufficient because resolution depends on control flow and execution context. The system therefore routes these instances to an SLM alongside a structured knowledge base (containing smell descriptions, canonical fixes, and known FP patterns) to ensure suggestions are grounded in smell-specific semantics rather than generic edits. The pathway employs two collaborating instances: a *refactoring model* that proposes the fix, and a *verification model* that independently evaluates it. Instead of isolating the flagged line, the framework extracts a fixed context window capturing the enclosing training loop, relevant variables, and optimizer sequences. Prompting the SLM with this window ensures fixes integrate naturally into the existing code structure rather than acting as decontextualised patches. To minimize hallucinations, the verification model checks whether the smell persists in the refactored output. Failed cases are flagged for human review, while successful fixes are applied in-place with the model's reasoning stated as an inline comment.

Validation and Feedback Loop. The outputs of both pathways which include the refactored code with inline reasoning, flagged false positives, and unresolved instances, are forwarded to the *Validation* step. An external smell detector reanalyses the refactored code to determine whether the targeted smell has been eliminated. This step is applied uniformly across both pathways. The final output of the system falls into one of four states:

1. **Successful Resolution:** The original detected smell is no longer present, and the code structure is improved, with no new issues introduced.
2. **Smell Persistence:** The refactoring transformation failed to resolve the targeted issue.
3. **Regression or New Smells:** The transformation introduced syntax errors, altered semantics, or created new types of technical debt.
4. **False Positive Detection:** Particularly relevant for the SLM pathway, the system may determine that the initial smell flagged by the detector was a false positive, meaning the smell was left by intention, and no refactoring was actually necessary.

Following this automated step, the system presents both the refactored code and the corresponding validation report to the developer. This Human-in-the-Loop (HITL) design is critical for maintaining trust in automated tools for ML pipelines. The developer acts as the final decision-maker, manually verifying the refactored outputs before integration. If the developer accepts the proposed changes, the refactoring is finalized. However, if the developer rejects the refactoring due to semantic inaccuracies, style preferences, or an unaddressed edge case, the *Feedback Loop* (refer to Fig. 1) is triggered. The specific reasons for rejection, combined with the validation report, are fed back into the processing module as a new set of inputs. This allows HARP-ML to adjust its understanding and generate a refined solution.

4 Results

Experimental Setup. The HARP-ML prototype integrates CodeSmile [6] as its external validator. We evaluate four smells exhibiting high detection precision (>0.8): *Chain Indexing* and *Dataframe Conversion API* as Type I, and *Gradients Not Cleared* and *Merge API Parameter* as Type II. Evaluation spans two datasets: self-contained experimental kits from CodeSmile, and a subset of 14 medium-sized, highly-rated real-world repositories from the NICHE dataset [9]. For the Type I pathway, the framework utilizes a deterministic structural transformation engine driven by Property-Based Testing (PBT) for validation. The Type II pathway is powered by a Small Language Model (SLM) configured to ensure highly deterministic code generation and minimize hallucinations, firmly grounding its semantic reasoning via a structured, smell-specific knowledge base. Finally, the developer feedback loop is strictly capped at a maximum of three iterations. Notably, during our evaluation, no single instance required more than two refinement iterations to reach a final state.

We evaluate the framework using two primary metrics summarized in Table 1. The *False Positive Rate* measures the proportion of total flagged instances correctly identified as intentional code requiring no modification. The *Refactoring Rate* evaluates the framework's success on genuine smell instances, defined as the ratio of successfully resolved instances to the total flagged instances excluding verified false positives. All detected false positives were manually verified by the authors.

Table 1. HARP-ML refactoring performance across both datasets.

Dataset	Smell	Pathway	Raw Instances	FPs Detected	Resolved	Failed	RR
Exp. Kits	Chain Indexing	CST + PBT	84	0	84	0	100%
	Dataframe Conversion API	CST + PBT	17	4	12	1	92.3%
	Gradients Not Cleared	SLM	12	2	8	2	80.0%
	Merge API Parameter	SLM	13	0	13	0	100%
NICHE	Chain Indexing	CST + PBT	45	3	40	2	95.2%
	Dataframe Conversion API	CST + PBT	7	1	6	0	100%
	Gradients Not Cleared	SLM	37	12	18	7	72.0%
	Merge API Parameter	SLM	9	1	7	1	87.5%
Experimental Kits Total			**126**	**6 (4.8%)**	**117**	**3**	**97.5%**
NICHE Total			**98**	**17 (17.3%)**	**71**	**10**	**87.7%**

RQ1: Performance in Controlled Environments. Evaluating HARP-ML against the CodeSmile experimental kits yielded an overall refactoring rate of 97.5%. As Table 1 demonstrates, the CST pathway successfully resolved all Chain Indexing instances, while the SLM effectively inferred join parameters for all Merge API instances. Furthermore, the PBT module proved effective as a false-positive filter by safely routing four DCA instances to human review after failing to construct `st.DataFrames()` strategies for non-DataFrame objects.

RQ2: Deployment on Real-World Repositories. To assess robustness against complex codebases, we deployed HARP-ML against the NICHE repositories, achieving an 87.7% refactoring rate. The CST pathway maintained high efficacy (95.2% for Chain Indexing, 100% for DCA). Figure 3 illustrates a successful, real-world structural transformation where the deterministic engine safely replaces an ambiguous `.values` call with the explicit `.to_numpy()` API.

```
def get_salt_existence():
    train_mask = pd.read_csv(settings.LABEL_FILE)
    salt_exists_dict = {}
    # Smell: df.values has inconsistent return behaviour
     for row in train_mask.values:
    # Fix: df.to_numpy() guarantees consistent array conversion
     for row in train_mask.to_numpy():
        salt_exists_dict[row[0]] = 0 if (row[1] is np.nan
            or len(row[1]) < 1) else 1
    return salt_exists_dict
```

Fig. 3. DCA smell refactored by HARP-ML on a real-world NICHE repository.

5 Discussion

The results validate our dual-pathway architecture: deterministic issues require structured rules, while contextual issues need semantic reasoning. The Type I pathway's high reliability underscores the value of CSTs in preserving original formatting without the overhead or unpredictability of generative models. Furthermore, PBT proved essential as a safety mechanism, intercepting false positives (e.g., standard Python lists misclassified as DataFrames) by failing to instantiate valid test strategies and safely routing them to human review. Conversely, the SLM pathway faced higher complexity in real-world code, causing a 28.3% FP rate in NICHE, primarily for the Gradients Not Cleared smell. Often, `optimizer.zero_grad()` was correctly placed but flagged by the detector due to intervening statements; the SLM successfully identified these as intentional and refrained from refactoring. However, failed instances highlight single-file context limitations: because intentional gradient accumulation or target DataFrame schemas were often defined in external modules, the SLM lacked cross-file context and safely abstained rather than risking a hallucinated modification.

Threats to Validity. Our evaluation is subject to certain limitations. First, HARP-ML's performance is inherently bounded by the precision of the external detector (CodeSmile); our results reflect only instances it flags, though our PBT module successfully intercepts some upstream false positives. Second, while evaluating on 14 NICHE repositories addresses the simplicity of the curated experimental kits, this sample represents only a fraction of real-world ML projects, limiting broader generalizability. Finally, our primary success metric relies on re-running CodeSmile to confirm smell absence, creating a construct validity concern by depending on its precision as both the upstream detector and downstream validator. While PBT rigorously guarantees behavioral equivalence for Type I transformations, our Type II verification currently checks structural improvements (e.g., parameter presence or correct API ordering) rather than end-to-end training convergence. Evaluating the downstream behavioral impacts of SLM-generated patches remains a critical area for future work.

6 Conclusion and Future Work

We presented HARP-ML, a hybrid refactoring framework that targets machine learning code smells by separating them into deterministic Type I syntax transformations and contextual Type II semantic patterns. Evaluated across the CodeSmile experimental kits and 14 real-world repositories from the NICHE dataset, HARP-ML achieved a 97.5% refactoring success rate on controlled instances and 87.7% on real-world code. The results validate the core premise of our two-level architecture: deterministic, structurally localized anti-patterns should be resolved via Concrete Syntax Trees (CST) paired with Property-Based Testing (PBT) for guaranteed verification, while Small Language Models (SLMs) operating over focused context windows should be reserved for distinguishing intentional design choices from genuine semantic smells.

Despite these promising results, our evaluation highlighted key limitations that dictate our future research direction. The most prominent constraint is the single-file scope of the current prototype. For example, several SLM failures within the NICHE dataset occurred because crucial training loop objects or target DataFrame schemas were defined in external modules. Without cross-file referencing, the model lacked the required global context to confidently execute modifications and safely abstained. Resolving this context retrieval bottleneck by introducing repository-level dependency tracking is our immediate next step.

Furthermore, verifying functional and behavioral equivalence for Type II refactorings remains an open challenge. While PBT provides rigorous guarantees for Type I syntactic patches, an equivalent strategy for semantic ML adjustments, such as proving that training loss curves are preserved after inserting a missing gradient clearing statement, remains unsolved. Future work will investigate metamorphic testing frameworks to validate training loop semantics. Additionally, we plan to expand HARP-ML's coverage to the remaining smells in established taxonomies, integrate interpretability features for auditable SLM refactorings, and evaluate our tools against the full NICHE dataset to comprehensively assess scalability.

Disclosure of Interests. The authors have no competing interests to declare that are relevant to the content of this article.

References

1. Asvydyte, G., Pandey, S.K., Chand, S.: How well small language models can be adapted for software maintenance and refactoring tasks. In: Scanniello, G., Lenarduzzi, V., Romano, S., Vegas, S., Francese, R. (eds.) Product-Focused Software Process Improvement. PROFES 2025. LNCS, vol. 16361, pp. 506–515. Springer, Cham (2026). https://doi.org/10.1007/978-3-032-12089-2_36
2. Bogner, J., Verdecchia, R., Gerostathopoulos, I.: Characterizing technical debt and antipatterns in ai-based systems: a systematic mapping study. In: 2021 IEEE/ACM International Conference on Technical Debt (TechDebt), pp. 64–73. IEEE (2021). https://doi.org/10.1109/techdebt52882.2021.00016
3. Kannan, J., Barnett, S., Cruz, L., Simmons, A., Agarwal, A.: Mlsmellhound: a context-aware code analysis tool. In: Proceedings of the ACM/IEEE 44th International Conference on Software Engineering: New Ideas and Emerging Results, pp. 66–70. ICSE-NIER '22, Association for Computing Machinery, New York, NY, USA (2022). https://doi.org/10.1145/3510455.3512773
4. van Oort, B., Cruz, L., Aniche, M., van Deursen, A.: The prevalence of code smells in machine learning projects. In: 2021 IEEE/ACM 1st Workshop on AI Engineering - Software Engineering for AI (WAIN), pp. 1–8 (2021). https://doi.org/10.1109/WAIN52551.2021.00011
5. Pucho, A., Ferreira, A., Cirilo, E., Cafeo, B.: Refactoring python code with llm-based multi-agent systems: an empirical study in ml software projects. In: Anais do XXXIX Simpósio Brasileiro de Engenharia de Software, pp. 678–684. SBC, Porto Alegre, RS, Brasil (2025). https://doi.org/10.5753/sbes.2025.11033
6. Recupito, G., Giordano, G., Ferrucci, F., Di Nucci, D., Palomba, F.: When code smells meet ml: on the lifecycle of ml-specific code smells in ml-enabled systems. Empir. Softw. Eng. **30**(5) (2025). https://doi.org/10.1007/s10664-025-10676-4
7. Sculley, D., et al.: Hidden technical debt in machine learning systems. In: Proceedings of the 29th International Conference on Neural Information Processing Systems - Volume 2, pp. 2503–2511. NIPS'15, MIT Press, Cambridge, MA, USA (2015)
8. Wauters, C., De Roover, C.: Property-based testing within ml projects: an empirical study. In: 2024 IEEE International Conference on Software Maintenance and Evolution (ICSME), pp. 648–653 (2024). https://doi.org/10.1109/ICSME58944.2024.00067
9. Widyasari, R., et al.: NICHE: a curated dataset of engineered machine learning projects in python. In: 2023 IEEE/ACM 20th International Conference on Mining Software Repositories (MSR), pp. 62–66. IEEE Computer Society, Los Alamitos, CA, USA (2023). https://doi.org/10.1109/MSR59073.2023.00022
10. Zhang, H., Cruz, L., van Deursen, A.: Code smells for machine learning applications. In: Proceedings of the 1st International Conference on AI Engineering: Software Engineering for AI, pp. 217–228. CAIN '22, Association for Computing Machinery, New York, NY, USA (2022). https://doi.org/10.1145/3522664.3528620
11. Zhang, Q., Fang, C., Ma, Y., Sun, W., Chen, Z.: A survey of learning-based automated program repair. ACM Trans. Softw. Eng. Methodol. **33**(2) (2023). https://doi.org/10.1145/3631974

GAppium+: A Tool for Gamified Testing With Appium Inspector

Lorenzo Laudadio(✉), Alessandro Costantino, Riccardo Coppola, and Marco Torchiano

Department of Control and Computer Engineering, Polytechnic University of Turin, Turin, Italy
{lorenzo.laudadio,riccardo.coppola,marco.torchiano}@polito.it, alessandro.costantino@studenti.polito.it

Abstract. Exploratory testing of mobile applications is a critical yet cognitively demanding activity, often perceived as tedious and repetitive. Gamification has emerged as a promising technique to address this challenge, by embedding game-design mechanics into non-ludic contexts to foster engagement and performance. In this paper, we present GAppium+, a gamified extension of Appium Inspector, a widely adopted tool for exploratory testing of mobile applications. GAppium+ enriches the testing experience through a set of mechanics – badges, leaderboards, levels, coverage tracking, and profile customization – grounded in established gamification theory. We report on a preliminary in-vivo evaluation conducted with PhD/scholarship students, who interacted with GAppium+ under controlled conditions. Post-session questionnaire results indicate a generally positive reception: participants rated gamification favorably overall (avg. 3.73/5), with badges scoring highest in terms of motivational impact (avg. 4.10/5), and broad agreement that gamification is a viable and beneficial approach for exploratory testing.

Keywords: Software Testing · End-To-End Testing · Gamification

1 Introduction

Software testing is an essential step in the software development process. Modern web and mobile applications – due to the richness of their user interfaces – require extensive End-to-End (E2E) testing, which focuses on the system features and behaviors, typically carried through the Graphical User Interface (GUI) of the Application Under Test (AUT). E2E testing is often exploratory, i.e., it leverages human expertise and creativity to freely traverse the GUI in an unstructured way.

However, traditional testing approaches are frequently perceived as tedious, monotonous, and lacking immediate motivation for practitioners [9]. A technique that is frequently used to increase engagement in testing activities is Gamification, defined as *the application of game-design mechanics in non-ludic context*

C. Berger and V. Klös (Eds.): SEAA 2026, LNCS 16864, pp. 408–416, 2027.
https://doi.org/10.1007/978-3-032-36587-3_28

[4]. Theoretical advancements in Gamification have defined sets of instruments and mechanics – such as scoreboards, achievements, competition mechanisms – that have gained increasing traction in the field of software engineering and testing [6], and have been proved beneficial in increasing practitioners' motivation and performance [3].

In this paper, we detail GAppium+, an extension of an original tool prototype to enact gamification mechanics within Appium Inspector, a popular exploratory testing tool for mobile applications [7][1]. We frame and motivate the implemented mechanics and provide a preliminary evaluation of the tool, to answer the following research questions: ***(RQ1)*** *What is the attitude of testers toward the adoption of gamification in Exploratory Testing activities?;* ***(RQ2)*** *Which gamification features are perceived as most useful, influential, and motivating by software testers in the context of Exploratory Testing?;* ***(RQ3)*** *What is the perceived usability of the proposed tool as assessed by software testers?*

The remainder of the paper is structured as follows: Sect. 2 reports details about related work in the field of gamified E2E testing; Sect. 3 describes the tool, focusing on the implemented gamification mechanics; Sect. 4 describes the preliminary evaluation that was performed for the tool; Sect. 5 concludes the paper and provides future research directions.

2 Background and Related Work

Gamification has emerged as a widespread practice in Software Engineering, with increasing attention on its application to software testing. Several gamified tools have been developed and validated to be applied to software testing practices. Gamekins employs game mechanics aligned with commits in software repositories, allowing developers to earn points for completing challenges and compete with colleagues on leaderboards. The system has demonstrated effectiveness in motivating developers to write more test cases in a CI/CD pipeline [8].

IntelliGame, a gamification plugin for IntelliJ IDEA, specifically targets IDE-based testing activities, and its capabilities in motivation and productivity was demonstrated in a study involving nearly 200 participants in an educational setting [10]. A gamified version of Scout, a tool for exploratory mobile testing, had positive influences in how testers created test cases for web applications, with increased testing coverage and efficiency in bug finding [3].

As recent Multivocal Literature Reviews report, the applications of Gamification mechanics to mobile testing activities are still fewer than in the web application testing domain [6]. Our work aims to contribute to this under-explored area, by proposing a gamification-based approach tailored to mobile testing activities.

2.1 The Octalysis Framework

The design of the gamification mechanics of Gappium+ is based on the Octalysis Framework, developed by Yu-kai Chou [2]. The Octalysis framework defines

[1] The GAppium+ source can be found at: https://doi.org/10.5281/zenodo.19821744.

eight principal human motivators, named *core drives* (CDs). Octalysis can be leveraged as both a design framework to develop gamified platforms and an evaluation tool to assess the presence of gamified elements in an existing activity or tool.

The CDs are further categorized along two axes: Left Brain vs Right Brain (extrinsic vs intrinsic motivation) and White Hat vs Black Hat (positive vs negative motivation).

The eight CDs of gamified activities are *CD1 - Epic Meaning and Calling* (users feel part of something bigger than themselves), *CD2 - Development and Accomplishment* (motivation through progress, goals, and overcoming challenges), *CD3 - Empowerment of Creativity and Feedback* (engagement through creativity and experimentation), *CD4 - Ownership and Possession* (attachment formed by owning or customising something), *CD5 - Social Influence and Relatedness* (motivation driven by social interaction, competition, and belonging), *CD6 - Scarcity and Impatience* desire triggered by limited or hard-to-get rewards, *CD7 - Unpredictability and Curiosity* (engagement through surprise and uncertainty), *CD8 - Loss and Avoidance* (motivation based on fear of losing progress or missing opportunities).

2.2 Appium, Appium Inspector, GAppium

As the result of our previous research efforts, we developed a prototype tool, Gappium, based on the Appium framework and on the Appium Inspector tool. **Appium** is open-source, platform-independent test automation framework used to test native, mobile, and hybrid applications [1]. Testers can write automated test scripts (using languages like Java, Python, JavaScript) that interact with the UI elements. **Appium Inspector** is a debugging and inspection tool provided within the Appium framework. It allows testers to visually inspect the mobile application's UI at runtime. It also allows to record and replicate interactions against the GUI of the Application Under Test (AUT). **GAppium** is a tool that extends the existing functionalities of Appium Inspector by adding a Gamification tab. In its first version, GAppium implements the following basic gamification features: setting of a *Username*; awarding *Points* when interacting with specific widgets for the first time or when discovering a new "page" (defined as a set of widgets); earning *Badges* on certain events; a *Leaderboard*, which only displays a few preset users along with their scores; a *Progress bar* indicating the percentage of widgets already interacted with; a *Counter* for the number of "pages" discovered in the current session.

The main limitations of the prototype version of the tool is that only CD2 (*Development and Accomplishment*) and CD4 (*Ownership and Possessions*) of the Octalysis framework are covered.

3 Tool Description

The main purpose of the Gappium+ tool is to integrate new gamification features alongside existing ones, in order to create a gamified exploratory testing tool that can trigger an even greater number of CDs.

GAppium+ implements the following features:

Quality of life: Recalibrated widget management system that only considers those that are relevant for determining the gamification-related metrics (i.e. *clickable* ones).

Glowing choice: Orange boxes can be displayed on the screen to highlight widgets the user has never interacted with. This supports the GUI testing process and triggers the CD7 gamification technique *"Glowing choice"*, which draws curiosity by visually guiding users toward possible next actions.

Level and score: A level system based on points has been introduced. Points are awarded upon discovery of new items and/or specific tasks, triggering CD2. Animations provide immediate feedback, enhancing engagement and encouraging interaction, triggering CD3.

User profile: A section allowing users to customize their username and icon has been introduced to trigger the CD4 *"Build-from-scratch"* technique, whereby users develop a sense of ownership over what they create, fostering greater involvement with the platform.

Badges: New badges have been added based on level, pages, coverage, leaderboard rankings, and special objectives, alongside a dedicated section displaying all available badges. Locked badges reveal extra information, upon reaching level 10. This triggers the CD3 technique *"Milestone Unlock"* and the CD6 technique *"Evolved UI"*, progressively exposing features as the user advances.

Leaderboard: The leaderboard is populated with preset users and displays level, badge count, and ranked position for each, with sorting available by any of these parameters. This triggers the CD2 *"Urgent Optimism"* technique, which positions users within reach of immediate improvement, avoiding discouragement when goals appear unattainable.

Impatience and Fear of Missing Out: Alerts motivate users toward specific levels or goals, such as notifying them that only one unvisited widget remains on the current "page". This triggers CD6 and, notably, the CD8 technique *"FOMO Punch"*, which prompts action by surfacing what users risk missing if they do not engage.

Bonus Rewards: Variable or random extra rewards, typically points, are granted upon reaching specific levels or goals. This triggers CD7 techniques such as *"Variable/Random, Sudden, and Rolling Rewards"*. Since these rewards are most frequent in the early stages of use, the CD1 technique *"Beginner's Luck"* is also triggered.

Score Booster: A randomly-activated score multiplier doubles or triples points earned for up to two minutes. This triggers the CD3 technique *"Boosters"*, which empowers users for a limited time, and, through its countdown timer, the CD8 technique *"Evanescent Opportunities"*, whereby the visible timer instills urgency by emphasizing the scarcity of remaining time.

Figure 1 shows an overview of the gamification tab in Gappium+. Figure 2 shows a comparison between the Octalysis self-evaluation of the first version of GAppium and the GAppium+ version[2].

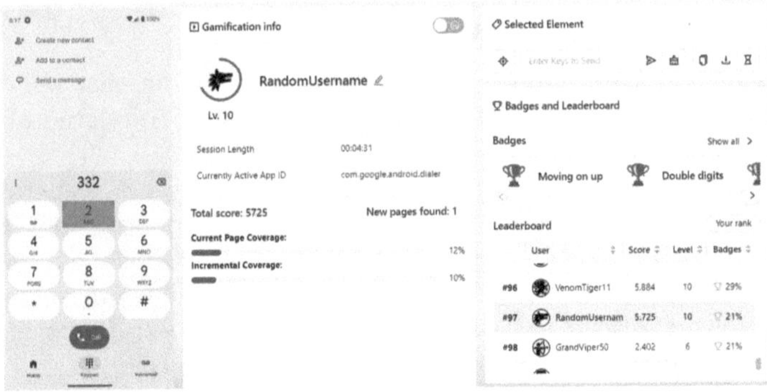

Fig. 1. Overview of the gamification section in GAppium+.

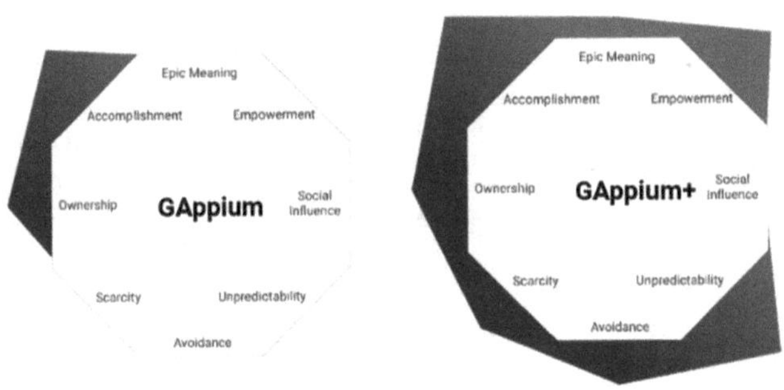

Fig. 2. Octalysis self-evaluation of the two GAppium versions.

4 Preliminary Evaluation

We ran an interactive in-vivo evaluation of the Gappium+ tool with ten PhD/scholarship student volunteers working in our laboratory at Politecnico di Torino. The participants were selected based on their availability during the experimental phase, and they had mixed academic backgrounds and different levels of expertise with mobile development and software testing (shown in Fig. 3, where ME = Management Engineering, DE = Cinema and Digital Media Engineering, CE = Computer Engineering, B = Biology).

[2] This graphical representation has been made with the online Octalysis Tool, available at https://yukaichou.com/octalysis-tool/.

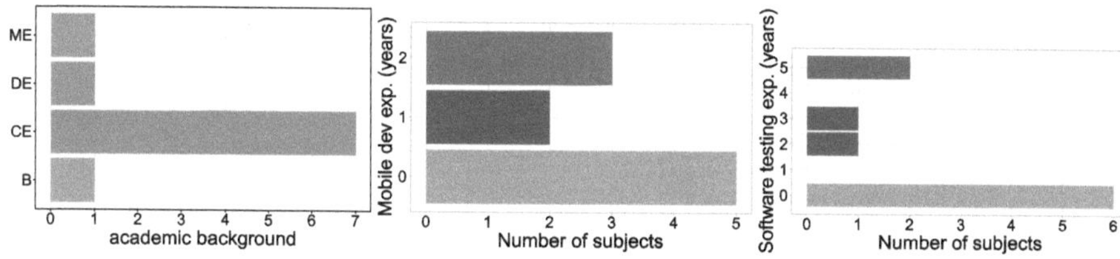

Fig. 3. Academic background, Mobile development and Software testing experience of the participants.

The evaluation consisted of an in-vivo experience where the subjects interacted with the GAppium+ tool under controlled conditions, simulating a real-world scenario. The subjects were asked to perform exploratory testing on *OmniNotes*[3], an open-source notes application, with no particular constraints. They received brief training on GAppium+, but they were not informed about the presence of gamification mechanics, allowing them to discover them independently. After a 15-minute testing session, participants completed a Likert scale questionnaire (1 = Completely Disagree, 5 = Strongly Agree) covering usability (SUS), general gamification satisfaction [5] and individual gamification features. Table 1 lists the questions, with their IDs[4].

Figures 4, 5 and 6 show the distribution of the answers respectively for the usability-related questions, the gamification-related questions and the specific gamification features questions.

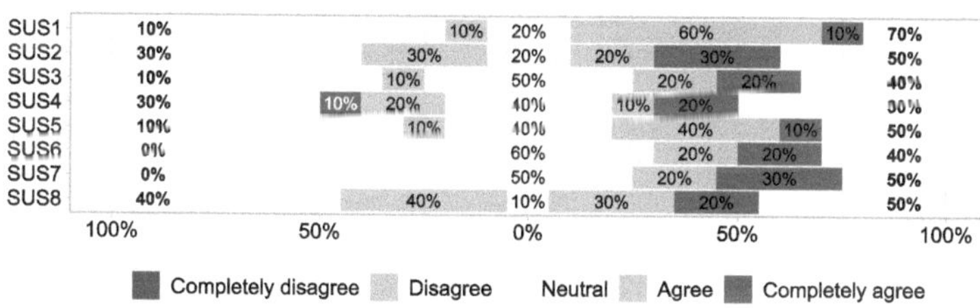

Fig. 4. Distribution of the Likert answers on SUS questions.

General attitudes toward gamification (G1–G4) were rated positively (avg. 3.95/5), with perceived appropriateness (G3: 4.30) and future adoption intent (G2: 4.30) scoring highest, therefore allowing us to answer positively to RQ1. Regarding RQ2, coverage emerged as the strongest feature overall (avg. 4.55/5), with participants finding it both useful (GC1: 4.70) and influential on their behavior (GC2: 4.70). Badges also scored well (avg. 4.12/5), consistently across

[3] https://github.com/federicoiosue/Omni-Notes.

[4] The complete list of questions and answers can also be found at: https://doi.org/10.5281/zenodo.19825435.

Table 1. List of questions in the questionnaire

ID	Text
SUS questions	
SUS1	I may use this type of application for my testing activities in future.
SUS2	The application was more complex than necessary.
SUS3	The application was easy to use.
SUS4	I would need external technical support to use the application.
SUS5	The various features of the application were well integrated.
SUS6	There was too much inconsistency in the application.
SUS7	I believe that most people could quickly learn to use the application.
SUS8	I needed to acquire a significant amount of info. before using the application.
Specific experience-related questions	
S1	I found the explanations provided by the instructors to be sufficiently clear.
S2	It was clear to me which paths to explore in order to test the application.
Gamification-related questions	
G1	The gamification elements were clear and understandable.
G2	If I were to conduct ET in the future, I would be in favor of using gamification.
G3	I believe that using gamification for ET is a good idea.
G4	I believe that gamification aspects could improve my productivity.
GAMEX questions	
GMX1	I had fun using the application.
GMX2	While using the application, I lost track of time.
GMX3	I found the application to be frustrating to use.
GMX4	I felt autonomous in using the application.
GMX5	I felt confident in using the application.
Specific gamification features *(B = badges, L = leaderboards, C = customization, P = progress indicator, V = levels)*	
GF1	I believe that the F feature is useful.
GF2	I believe that the F feature has influenced my usage of the application.
GF3	I appreciated the F feature.
GF4	The F feature motivated me in ET.

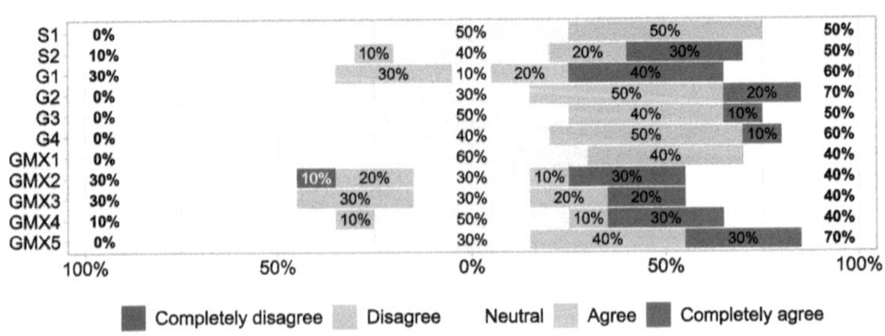

Fig. 5. Distribution of the Likert answers on gamification questions.

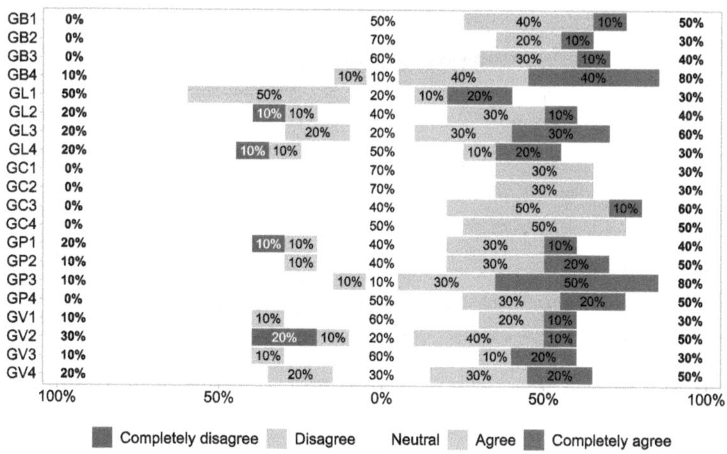

Fig. 6. Distribution of the Likert answers on gamification features questions.

all four items. Leaderboards remained the weakest gamification feature (avg. 3.23/5). Notably, Customization dropped to the lowest score among all groups (avg. 2.77/5), driven by low perceived influence (GP2: 2.10) and motivational impact (GP4: 2.30), suggesting that avatar and username personalization has limited relevance in a testing context. Finally, concerning RQ3, usability was deemed appropriate (SUS1–SUS8: 3.66/5)[5]. The frustration item (GMX3: 2.30) is the only notably negative signal within the gamification-related aspects.

5 Conclusion

In this paper, we presented GAppium+, a gamified extension of Appium Inspector designed to increase engagement and motivation in exploratory mobile application testing. The tool enriches the testing experience through a set of mechanics – badges, leaderboards, levels, coverage tracking, and profile customization – grounded in established gamification theory. A preliminary in-vivo evaluation conducted with PhD students showed overall positive reception, particularly toward coverage tracking and badges, which scored highest among all gamification features. Leaderboards and customization were less effective, the former likely due to the limited cohort size undermining competitive dynamics, the latter suggesting that aesthetic personalization carries limited motivational weight in a testing context. These results, while encouraging, should be interpreted with caution given the small sample size and the homogeneity of the participant pool. Future work will focus on refining the interface to address usability concerns and the frustration observed during the the evaluation, extending the evaluation to a larger and more diverse population, possibly evaluating the long-term effects

[5] Being SUS2, SUS4, SUS6, and SUS8 negatively worded, they were inverted (6 - score) prior to averaging.

of gamification exposure as well, exploring the relationship among gamification and testing effectiveness, and investigating whether the observed engagement translates into measurable improvements in testing coverage and defect detection. Longitudinal studies will also be needed to assess whether the motivational effect of gamification mechanics is sustained over time.

References

1. How does appium work? https://appium.io/docs/en/latest/intro/appium/
2. Chou, Y.K.: Actionable gamification: Beyond points, badges, and leaderboards, Packt Publishing Ltd. (2019)
3. Coppola, R., Fulcini, T., Ardito, L., Torchiano, M., Alègroth, E.: On effectiveness and efficiency of gamified exploratory gui testing. IEEE Trans. Softw. Eng. **50**(2), 322–337 (2023)
4. Deterding, S., Khaled, R., Nacke, L.E., Dixon, D.: Gamification: Toward a definition. In: CHI 2011 Gamification Workshop Proceedings, vol. 12, pp. 1–79. Vancouver (2011)
5. Eppmann, R., Bekk, M., Klein, K.: Gameful experience in gamification: Construction and validation of a gameful experience scale [gamex]. J. Interact. Mark. **43**, 98–115 (2018) https://doi.org/10.1016/j.intmar.2018.03.002, https://www.sciencedirect.com/science/article/pii/S1094996818300124
6. Fulcini, T., Coppola, R., Ardito, L., Torchiano, M.: A review on tools, mechanics, benefits, and challenges of gamified software testing. ACM Comput. Surv. **55**(14s), 1–37 (2023)
7. Laudadio, L., Coppola, R., Torchiano, M., Fulcini, T.: Gappium: A framework to enact gamification mechanics in appium inspector. In: 2025 IEEE/ACM Workshop on Gamification in Software Development, Verification, and Validation (Gamify), pp. 9–12. IEEE (2025)
8. Straubinger, P., Fraser, G.: Gamekins: Gamifying software testing in jenkins. In: Proceedings of the ACM/IEEE 44th International Conference on Software Engineering: Companion Proceedings, pp. 85–89. (2022)
9. Straubinger, P., Fraser, G.: A Survey on What Developers Think About Testing. In: 2023 IEEE 34th International Symposium on Software Reliability Engineering (ISSRE), pp. 80–90 (2023). https://doi.org/10.1109/ISSRE59848.2023.00075, https://ieeexplore.ieee.org/abstract/document/10301252, iSSN: 2332-6549
10. Straubinger, P., Fulcini, T., Garaccione, G., Ardito, L., Fraser, G.: Gamifying testing in intellij: A replicability study. Proc. ACM Softw. Eng. **2**(ISSTA), 2407–2429 (2025)

Bridging Stakeholder Needs and Requirements via Multi-perspective Goal Modeling: A Case Study of Administrative Digital Transformation in Japan

Momoe Kobayashi[1(✉)], Takako Nakatani[2], and Takashi Kobayashi[1]

[1] School of Computing, Institute of Science Tokyo, Yokohama, Japan
m.kobayashi@sa.comp.isct.ac.jp, tkobaya@comp.isct.ac.jp
[2] Graduate School, The Open University of Japan, Chiba, Japan
tinakatani@ouj.ac.jp

Abstract. Software development aims to deliver products that fulfill stakeholder goals. However, conflicting interests and uneven influence within an organization often produce fragmented or incomplete requirements. A structured and multiperspective analysis of stakeholder goals is therefore necessary to understand these divergences and to form a holistic view of the organizational landscape. This paper proposes a method that integrates the strengths of KAOS and iStar while maintaining compliance with IEEE 29148. By enabling the analysis of individual stakeholder perspectives alongside primary system goals aligned with organizational strategies, the method supports the derivation of valid requirements specifications. We illustrate the initial feasibility of this approach through a case study on Administrative Digital Transformation initiatives in Japan.

Keywords: Stakeholder-centric Goal Model · IEEE 29148 · KAOS · iStar · Requirements Engineering

1 Introduction

ISO/IEC/IEEE 29148:2018 [7] emphasizes that the requirements must be validated against real-world needs. However, insufficient distinction between needs and requirements remains a challenge, introducing significant ambiguity during technical derivation [12]. To mitigate these risks, needs must be systematically transformed into requirements, with strict traceability ensuring that every system element is linked to an originating need [12]. This process is complicated because stakeholders possess diverse and often conflicting needs shaped by their interests [16]. In large-scale organizations, differing levels of influence and intertwined concerns further increase the complexity of analyzing these needs [11].

While IEEE 29148 standard defines the structure and content for Business, Stakeholder, and Software Requirements Specifications, it focuses primarily on

C. Berger and V. Klös (Eds.): SEAA 2026, LNCS 16864, pp. 417–426, 2027.
https://doi.org/10.1007/978-3-032-36587-3_29

the *what* of requirements rather than the *how* [7]. As a result, the standard lacks a rigorous process and offers limited systematic support for transforming abstract needs into a coherent, traceable set of requirements. To bridge this gap, existing research has proposed supplementing the textual descriptions of IEEE 29148 with graphical representations, such as the Multiview Modeling Framework [18]. Although these approaches improve understanding, they often fail to systematically capture goal conflicts among stakeholders or the logical derivation from needs to concrete requirements.

Goal-Oriented Requirements Engineering (GORE) fills this gap in IEEE 29148 by modeling the WHY, WHAT, and WHO of requirements [9]. By refining stakeholder intentions into measurable specifications [21], frameworks like iStar [2] facilitate conflict resolution through socio-technical analysis, offering a comprehensive approach to systematic requirements engineering.

Based on these challenges, this study addresses the following RQs:

- ▹ RQ1: What extent can a goal model represent the systematic relationships between stakeholder needs and requirements?
- ▹ RQ2: How effectively does the goal model capture the differing and potentially conflicting needs of stakeholders?

To answer RQs, we propose a stakeholder-centric goal-modeling method that systematically represents needs and requirements. Rooted in goal-oriented analysis [15], this approach detects obstacles while evaluating complex stakeholder dependencies. A case study of Administrative DX (Digital Transformation) initiatives in Japan showed that the resulting model yielded new insights.

The remainder of this paper is organized as follows. Section 2 covers preliminaries (IEEE 29148, KAOS, iStar). Section 3 describes the proposed method. Section 4 presents a case study on Administrative DX. We conclude with findings and future work.

2 Preliminary Research

This section establishes the theoretical foundation for our study by reviewing international standards for requirements engineering and the primary goal-oriented modeling frameworks. We first discuss the general landscape of goal-oriented analysis before detailing the specific methodologies that serve as candidates for our proposed approach.

2.1 IEEE 29148

IEEE 29148 [7] standardizes the progression from business needs to system requirements, ensuring quality through defined attributes and lifecycle management. It mandates a traceable hierarchy in which Business (BRS) and Stakeholder (StRS) requirements are refined into Software Requirements (SRS). Complementing this structure, the Concept of Operations (ConOps) and the Operational Concept (OpsCon) define the high-level mission and detailed operational context, ensuring alignment with business intent. Consequently, IEEE 29148 serves as a critical benchmark for both industry and research in requirements engineering practices.

However, while this standard establishes the structure, it does not provide a robust framework for the process of transforming needs into requirements. In this research, it is essential to distinguish stakeholder needs from system requirements, linking organizational expectations to technical obligations via traceable transformation. Lacking a systematic approach, a persistent gap often arises between final specifications and initial stakeholder intent.

2.2 Landscape of Goal-Oriented Requirements Engineering Methodologies

Guided by Horkoff and Yu's taxonomy [6], which categorizes methods by engineering objectives, we identify four Goal-Oriented Requirements Engineering (GORE) methodologies. These are selected for their ability to perform forward and backward satisfaction analysis, thereby bridging the gap between stakeholder needs and system requirements by evaluating how design alternatives impact primary goals.

KAOS: KAOS generates consistent requirements documents by mapping goal and object models to predefined templates, ensuring traceability from strategic goals to technical specifications [14,17,20]. However, its stakeholder analysis capabilities are limited. Approaches like SysML/KAOS [13,19] focus on verifying subsystem compliance rather than distinguishing individual stakeholder origins, making it difficult to trace and resolve conflicting needs during refinement.

Attributed Goal-Oriented Requirements Analysis (AGORA) extended basic KAOS by incorporating attribute values into goal graphs [10].

iStar: The iStar framework models the social context of requirements (the why, who, and how) by mapping dependencies among actors [2,8]. This perspective helps analysts identify organizational vulnerabilities and opportunities arising from inter-actor dependence. iStar comprises two main components: the Strategic Dependency model and the Strategic Rationale model.

Tropos was developed from the iStar framework, introducing an agent-oriented software methodology grounded in the concepts of agents and goals [5].

2.3 Synthesis and Research Gap

Existing methodologies lack a unified process that strictly adheres to IEEE 29148 while preserving distinct stakeholder perspectives. As Horkoff and Yu [6] note, effective analysis requires forward and backward reasoning to evaluate how candidate solutions impact each stakeholder original needs. However, current frameworks present a trade-off: KAOS offers rigorous refinement but lacks social nuance, while iStar captures social dependencies but lacks formal operationalization. To address this, we propose an integrated method that combines KAOS formal refinement with iStar social analysis. This approach ensures the completeness of stakeholder requirements (StRS) and strict adherence to the IEEE 29148 hierarchical refinement process.

Table 1. Comparison Summary of Goal Models

	KAOS	iStar2.0	Proposed Model
Primary Strength	Mission-critical systems	Business ecosystem understanding	Systems with diverse user bases
Decomposition	Strict AND/OR refinement	Internal rationale analysis	Strict AND/OR refinement
Responsibility	Goal-to-agent responsibility assignment	Organizational dependency networks	Organizational dependency networks

3 Approach

3.1 Method

While IEEE 29148 [7] defines three major processes including system requirements definition, our scope is to derive organizational and stakeholder-level goals prior to full system specification. Therefore, this study strictly focuses on the first two processes: "Business or Mission Analysis" and "Stakeholder Needs and Requirements Definition." These processes generate the Operational Concept (OpsCon), which details essential stakeholder challenges and serves as a critical artifact for requirements analysis. However, capturing diverse stakeholder perspectives within this framework remains challenging. To address this, we propose a method that integrates KAOS and iStar. The KAOS component decomposes high-level goals to assess agent responsibilities and domain assumptions [17,20], while the iStar component maps dependencies and influence relations among intentional elements [2,8]. This synthesis provides a holistic view of stakeholder objectives, facilitating the systematic derivation of requirements.

3.2 Modeling of Stakeholder-Centric Goals

The proposed goal model is constructed using goals and AND/OR decompositions. Through these refinements, we employ the NeedBy link to analyze the tasks and resources required to achieve goals and to identify dependency relationships, following iStar2.0. This represents diverse stakeholder goals in complex social settings. Furthermore, we incorporate traceability links from top-level goals to end-level subgoals and apply conflict links, adapted from KAOS, to evaluate high-level design alternatives. Together, these mechanisms enable the model to represent divergent stakeholder goals while supporting the evaluation of alternative designs. Table 1 summarizes the comparison of goal models. The goal structure of the proposed model is detailed in Sect. 4.

3.3 Operationalizing IEEE 29148 Processes

IEEE 29148 [7] defines a hierarchy in which organizational objectives are refined into system elements. Our method operationalizes this by using goal-oriented reasoning to decompose strategic objectives into system-level goals, producing a baseline of requirements for design. This process follows five structured steps.

Step 1: Identifying stakeholder concerns
The process begins by eliciting stakeholder concerns as softgoals, supporting IEEE 29148 Business or Mission Analysis. By articulating the fundamental rationale for system development, this step clarifies how the system supports stakeholder interests, establishing a foundation for solution selection.

Step 2: Defining behavioural goals
Define behavioural goals as measurable system states, grounded in explicit environmental assumptions. This transforms stakeholder concerns (from Step 1) into structured Stakeholder Needs, where any behaviour satisfying these states constitutes valid goal fulfillment.

Step 3: Specifying tasks and resources
Introduce tasks as functional services that operationalize behavioural goals, requiring physical or informational resources. This combination allows for the systematic evaluation of solution alternatives in terms of feasibility and strategic alignment. In cases of divergent needs, this evaluation identifies areas of consensus to derive commonly accepted stakeholder requirements.

Step 4: Delineating stakeholder scopes
Define individual stakeholder scopes that encompass As-Is problems, constraints, and opportunities. By restricting each scope to elements under stakeholder responsibility, this step ensures clear duty separation and supports requirement prioritization based on relevance.

Step 5: Validating traccability
Validate traceability by refining softgoals into verifiable behavioural goals and deriving tasks. This structured representation fulfills IEEE 29148 traceability constraints by ensuring every requirement links directly to its stakeholder origin, creating a coherent, auditable baseline for the Software Requirements Specification (SRS).

These steps are applied iteratively to maintain strategic alignment and reveal stakeholder dependencies. This process operationalizes IEEE 29148 by providing a visual, logical representation of needs and requirements. The resulting model serves as a baseline for validation of traceability, and stakeholder approval constitutes explicit agreement on the requirements.

This framework aligns with GORE core dimensions: Step 1 clarifies the **WHY** by uncovering system goals through domain reasoning; Steps 2–3 address the **WHAT** by specifying capabilities and constraints; and Steps 45 articulate the **WHO** by assigning responsibilities and validating traceability. Thus, they produce a coherent, consensus-oriented baseline for IEEE 29148 compliance.

4 Case Study

We applied our proposed method to the Administrative DX initiative at Adachi-ward municipal office in Tokyo to address the RQs. Our evaluation focuses on the residence certificate update procedure using the self-service counter system. This system, promoted by the Digital Agency of Japan [1,3,4], aims to enhance resident convenience and reduce staff workload by eliminating handwritten applications through digital technology.

4.1 Application Process

In this paper, we interpret the policy objectives published on the Digital Agency website as stakeholder requirements. Building on this mandate, we apply our proposed method to refine these high-level objectives into implementable requirements. The website describes as follows.

As-Is, Problems: *Stalled administrative reform burdens residents with redundant data entry and long waits, while staff face repetitive explanations, extensive verification, and complex tasks dependent on experience.*

To-Be, Deliverables: *While the Digital Agency streamlines online applications via the "No-Visit Service Counter," municipal offices must adopt "One-Stop" and "Once-Only" models to support non-digital users.*

Outcomes, Digital Transformation: *Using ID cards and data for seamless services, the Digital Agency reduces burdens on residents and staff, aiming to create a digitally inclusive society focused on well-being.*

4.2 Application Results

We defined stakeholders as Residents and Local government, and constructed stakeholder-centric goal models following the steps outlined in Sect. 3.3. Due to space limitations, this article presents only the resident-centric goal model. We omitted goal post-conditions; however, each post-condition specifies the state that must hold after the goal is achieved, as indicated within its square.

Figure 1 illustrates resident-centric goals. **First**, we identified the problems that must be addressed, and interpreted their resolution as residents' softgoals, represented as clouds. Significant conflicts emerged among several softgoals, particularly those related to online applications. **Second**, we refined these softgoals into explicit behavioural goals, represented as squares and expressed using passive verbs. Each goal depends on specific environmental assumptions, such as the availability of digital devices (`#5,#13,#16`), support staff (`#22`), or online

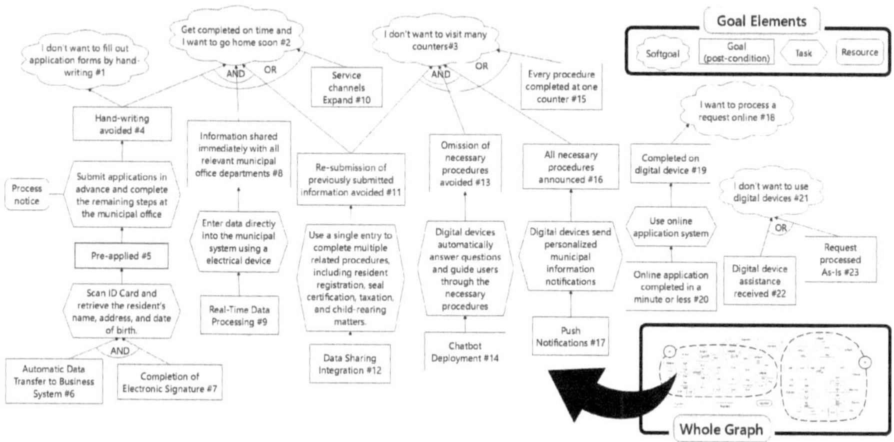

Fig. 1. Resident-centric Goal Model.

systems (#19). **Third**, we decomposed the goals into tasks using AND/OR decompositions. These tasks are represented as hexagons and expressed using active verbs, which sequentially derive subgoals. We also used NeedBy links to identify required resources, represented as rounded rectangles. This repeatable process revealed multiple solution paths, specifically identifying the goals that contribute to the Administrative DX, from which the most appropriate options can be selected (One-Stop service (+): #11--#14,#16,#17, Once-Only service (+): #4--#9,#11,#12, In-Person service (-): #22,#23). **Fourth**, we delineated the scope of residents along the refinement branches using explicit traceability links. **Fifth**, we verified that goals were correctly derived from softgoals and decomposed into tasks and subgoals

4.3 Evaluation

We evaluate the proposed method using the application example. First, our proposed goal model framed problem-oriented statements, logically linking them to derived solution-oriented statements. This structure captures the systematic decomposition of high-level stakeholder needs into functional requirements. For example, the resident-centric model refines overarching softgoals into specific subgoals such as "Chatbot," "Push Notifications," and "Support Staff" to directly accommodate individual preferences and circumstances.

This reasoning is underpinned by GORE [14]. We proposed a goal model integrating KAOS and iStar, that links stakeholder needs (WHY) to the functional goals (WHAT), thereby creating a structured path for deriving requirements and making explicit the owners (WHO). By aligning this construction process with IEEE 29148 specifically supporting Business/Mission Analysis and Stakeholder Needs/Requirements Definition, the model ensures secure traceability between high-level objectives and implementation requirements. Consequently, these findings allow us to answer RQ1 positively.

Second, our model defines the scope of each stakeholder and initial softgoals, capturing a wide variety of diverse and conflicting needs. For example, resident-centric goals reveal differing views on technology. By applying KAOS logical decomposition to these top-level goals, we discovered potential conflicts both within and across stakeholder scopes, such as the direct conflict between maintaining "As-Is" operations and adopting "To-Be" digital services. Identifying these conflicts at the goal level provides explicit design alternatives for systematic trade-off analysis. Consequently, these findings suggest the initial feasibility of the model, supporting a positive answer to RQ2.

4.4 Discussion

The case study demonstrates that modeling stakeholder desires as softgoals and refining them into verifiable goals via KAOS provides a robust basis for requirements. By incorporating tasks, resources, and delegation, our approach defines concrete operational means and reveals dependencies often overlooked in single-perspective analyses. This method effectively operationalizes IEEE 29148 Business/Mission Analysis by bridging high-level needs and technical requirements, addressing the standard's lack of specific transformation mechanisms. Thus, this method is particularly useful for analyzing systems designed for diverse user groups, such as public-interest systems. However, ensuring full compliance with the standard's recursive processes across all hierarchical layers remains a primary challenge due to the complexity of step-by-step refinement.

The prescriptive nature of goals [14,20] enables multiple satisfaction paths, essential for managing diverse stakeholder interests in Administrative DX [16]. By surfacing divergences early and distinguishing problem-oriented concerns from solution-oriented specifications, our method facilitates the transformation of natural language needs into unambiguous requirements. However, as the underlying transformation mechanism requires further clarification, future work will focus on formalizing the mapping between stakeholder concerns and system specifications. This will ensure complete satisfaction of high-level needs and refine iterative alignment with IEEE 29148.

5 Conclusion

This paper presents a stakeholder-centric goal-modeling method that bridges the gap between needs and requirements by integrating KAOS and iStar. This synthesis enables a multidimensional analysis of dependencies and obstacles, offering a holistic view of how individual requirements influence overall goal satisfaction. A case study on Japanese Administrative DX demonstrated the initial feasibility of the method in systematically representing diverse and often conflicting softgoals. The results confirm that our approach maintains strict alignment with

IEEE 29148 processes while addressing the complexity of large-scale digital initiatives.

The results confirm that the model effectively maps needs to requirements (RQ1) and captures conflicting stakeholder interests (RQ2). Although the current representation provides insights into these divergences, future refinement will improve IEEE 29148 alignment, thereby enhancing the robustness of conflict analysis.

Future work will extend this method to AI-driven development, addressing the need for stakeholder alignment in systems whose capabilities evolve over time, an area of growing importance. We also plan to develop tools for directly generating software requirements from goal models, thereby strengthening end-to-end traceability from high-level visions to technical specifications.

Acknowledgments. This study was partially funded by JSPS KAKENHI (#22H03567, #26K02888, #26K02889).

References

1. Adachi Ward, Tokyo Metropolitan Government: Adachi ward official website: No-write service now available! (2025). https://www.city.adachi.tokyo.jp/sesaku/madoguchidx.html, Accessed 4 Apr 2026) (in Japanese)
2. Dalpiaz, F., Franch, X., Horkoff, J.: istar 2.0 language guide. arXiv preprint arXiv:1605.07767 (2016)
3. Digital Agency Japan: Initiatives for digital transformation of local government service counters (2025). https://digital-gov.note.jp/n/n54f3241091f4, Accessed 4 Apr 2026 (in Japanese)
4. Digital Agency Japan: Local government service counter DX paperless one-stop service counter (2025). https://www.digital.go.jp/policies/cs-dx, Accessed 4 Apr 2026 (in Japanese)
5. Giorgini, P., et al.: Goal-oriented requirements analysis and reasoning in the tropos methodology. Eng. Appl. Artif. Intell. **18**(2), 159–171 (2005)
6. Horkoff, J., Yu, E.: Analyzing goal models: different approaches and how to choose among them. In: Proceedings of ACM Symposium on Applied Computing (SAC), pp. 675–682 (2011)
7. ISO/IEC/IEEE: International Standard - Systems and software engineering – Life cycle processes – Requirements engineering. ISO/IEC/IEEE 29148:2018(E)
8. istarwiki.org: i* Wiki Home, iStar Guides (2011). http://istarwiki.org/tiki-index.php, Accessed 4 Apr 2026
9. Kadakolmath, L., Ramu, U.D.: iStar goal model to Z formal model translation and model checking of CBTC moving block interlocking system. Formal Aspects Comput. **36**(1), 1–45 (2024). https://doi.org/10.1145/3633065
10. Kaiya, H., Horai, H., Saeki, M.: AGORA: attributed goal-oriented requirements analysis method. In: Proceedings of IEEE Joint International Conference on Requirements Engineering (RE), pp. 13–22 (2002). https://doi.org/10.1109/ICRE.2002.1048501
11. Khan, F.M., et al.: A comparative systematic analysis of stakeholder's identification methods in requirements elicitation. IEEE Access **10**, 30982–31011 (2022)

12. Kubin, A., Wagenmann, S., Reichert, F., Mandel, C., Albers, A.: Stakeholder needs in systems engineering: A proposal for a formal definition. In: Proceedings of IEEE International Systems Conference (SysCon), pp. 1–8 (2023)
13. Laleau, R., Semmak, F., Matoussi, A., et al.: A first attempt to combine sysml requirements diagrams and b. Innovations Syst. Softw. Eng. **6**, 47–54 (2010)
14. van Lamsweerd, A.: Requirements Engineering. John Wiley & Sons (2009)
15. Letier, E., van Lamsweerde, A.: Obstacle analysis in requirements engineering: Retrospective and emerging challenges. IEEE Trans. Softw. Eng. **51**(3), 795–801 (2025). https://doi.org/10.1109/TSE.2025.3534318
16. Li, R., Verhagen, W.J., Curran, R.: Stakeholder-oriented systematic design methodology for prognostic and health management system: Stakeholder expectation definition. Adv. Eng. Inform. **43**, 101041 (2020)
17. Respect, -I.A.K., Tutorial - Objectiver: (2007). tutorial V1.0
18. Selvyanti, D.: The requirements engineering framework based on iso 29148: 2011 and multi-view modeling framework. In: Proceedings of International Conference on Information Technology Systems and Innovation (ICITSI), pp. 128–133 (2017)
19. Tueno Fotso, S.J., Frappier, M., Laleau, R., Mammar, A., Leuschel, M.: Formalisation of SysML/KAOS goal assignments with B system component ecompositions. In: Integrated Formal Methods (IFM 2018), pp. 377–397 (2018)
20. Van Lamsweerde, A.: Goal-oriented requirements engineering: A guided tour. In: Proceedings Fifth IEEE International Symposium on Requirements Engineering (ISRE), pp. 249–262 (2001)
21. Yamamoto, K., Saeki, M.: Attributed goal-oriented analysis method for selecting alternatives of software requirements. IEICE Trans. Inf. Syst. **E91-D**(4), 921–932 (2008). https://doi.org/10.1093/ietisy/e91-d.4.921

Security in a Workflow: Exploring Role-Based Agentic Architectures for Vulnerability Handling

Srijita Basu(✉) and Miroslaw Staron

Chalmers University of Technology and University of Gothenburg,
Göteborg 417 56, Sweden
{srijita.basu,miroslaw.staron}@gu.se

Abstract. Secure software engineering in practice is a multi-stage workflow involving vulnerability analysis, remediation, and fix verification. However, current LLM-based software security approaches often focus on isolated tasks such as detection or patch generation, with limited attention to agentic architectures reflecting industrial workflow. This creates a gap between existing LLM-based vulnerability-handling methods and real-world practices. In this paper, we study a role-based agentic workflow for vulnerability analysis and mitigation consisting of Planner, Analyzer, Fixer, and Verifier roles. To explore the effect of static-analysis tool, the analyzer agent was integrated with the CodeQL in one of the workflows. The models used include *nemotron-cascade-2:30b, qwen3-coder-next, and gpt-oss:120b*. Our evaluation uses 25 real-world C/C++ vulnerabilities. The study reports 44% vulnerability detection accuracy comparable to GPT 5.5 and 19% fix accuracy. We also list implications from this study in context of software security practitioners.

Keywords: analyzer · fixer · planner · security · verifier · vulnerability

1 Introduction

Secure software engineering has become an essential part of modern software development, as security vulnerabilities directly affect quality, reliability, and trust. In industrial practice, vulnerability handling is typically not a single-step task but a structured workflow involving vulnerability analysis, remediation, and fix verification. With the benefits of large language models (LLMs), LLM-assisted cybersecurity capability is advancing rapidly, e.g., XBOW topped the HackerOne US leaderboard[1], Google Big Sleep finds real-world vulnerabilities showing that LLMs are moving from synthetic evaluation towards operational bug discovery[2], DARPA AI Cyber Challenge (AIxCC) at DEF CON 33 (security conference) exhibited high efficiency in vulnerability detection and patching[3].

[1] https://xbow.com/blog/top-1-how-xbow-did-it.
[2] https://therecord.media/google-big-sleep-ai-tool-found-bug.
[3] https://aicyberchallenge.com/.

C. Berger and V. Klös (Eds.): SEAA 2026, LNCS 16864, pp. 427–444, 2027.
https://doi.org/10.1007/978-3-032-36587-3_30

However, current research remains fragmented. Existing studies often focus on isolated tasks such as vulnerability detection [1], repair benchmarking [2], or patch generation [3], while comparatively limited attention has been paid to workflow-oriented agentic architectures [4] that reflect how security activities are organized in real software engineering processes. Prior work in LLM-based software engineering suggests that agent collaboration quality depends on factors such as role alignment, interaction patterns, and consistency between generated code and accompanying reasoning [5,6]. However, these insights have largely been studied in general software engineering settings, with much less attention to security aspects. This motivates examining whether similar structured agentic designs are useful in secure software engineering.

In addition, there is still limited work exploring tool-augmented agentic workflows and Model Context Protocol (MCP)-style skill integration for low-level systems languages such as C and C++, which remain widely used in safety-critical systems. Compared with high-level languages such as Python or Java, vulnerabilities in C/C++ often depend on low-level memory semantics, pointer manipulation, buffer management, and execution behavior, making both diagnosis and remediation more challenging for LLMs [7]. This creates a gap between current LLM-based vulnerability handling methods and the needs of practical secure software engineering, particularly in settings where contextual reasoning, explainability, transparent outcomes, and reliable tool support are essential.

In this paper, we investigate a role-based agentic workflow for vulnerability analysis and mitigation as an initial security-focused software process improvement mechanism for secure software engineering. In this context, process improvement means making security activities more structured, repeatable, transparent, and reviewable by decomposing vulnerability handling into explicit stages such as investigation planning, vulnerability analysis, patch generation, and fix verification. We instantiate the workflow in CrewAI and compare two variants: i) Planner, Analyzer, Fixer & Verifier and ii) Planner, Analyzer with MCP CodeQL integration, Fixer & Verifier. We conducted a focused exploratory study of whether workflow-oriented role separation and the addition of static-analysis capability at the analysis stage can improve the quality of vulnerability detections, generated patches, and verification outcomes. The evaluation is performed on 25 curated real-world C/C++ Common Vulnerabilities and Exposures (CVEs) spanning five Common Weakness Enumeration (CWE) categories (CWE-787, CWE-476, CWE-190, CWE-125, CWE-191). The selection was based on frequently encountered CWEs as elaborated later, and for each CWE, the most recent CVE instances were selected for which we could extract enough information required for formulating the ground-truth comprising of the vulnerability details from Natioanl Vulnerability Database (NVD) and patched version of the code provided in the repository under study. This was necessary for later evaluation.

This study is motivated by two research questions: 1) *RQ1*: How effective is the proposed role-based agentic workflow as an initial exploratory mechanism for studying process-oriented vulnerability analysis, patch generation, and fix verification? 2) *RQ2*: How does integrating MCP tool based skills into the Analyzer stage affect the quality of downstream workflow outcomes, including detections, generated patches, and verification results?

We position this work as a methodology-oriented exploratory study rather than a large-scale benchmark. The smaller curated dataset was chosen deliberately to support detailed stage-wise analysis of the proposed workflow, including how planner guidance, role separation, and CodeQL-supported diagnosis affect vulnerability analysis, patch generation, and verification. The main contributions of this paper are as follows: *1) Propose and evaluate an end-to-end role-based agentic architecture for vulnerability detection, patch generation, and fix verification, 2) Design a static Planner module for guiding vulnerability investigation in industry-relevant C projects. The results largely vary with and without the planner guidance, & 3) Provide an initial curated reference set of 25 real-world C/C++ vulnerability instances together with ground-truth vulnerability metadata, developer-provided fixes, and LLM-generated outputs. Also the CrewAI framework code with agent flows, prompt designs, etc., is provided as an open research material for reproducibility.* Beyond empirical comparison, we discuss the implications of such workflows for secure software engineering, including the continuous need for human-in-the-loop oversight in security-critical settings.

2 Related Work

Recent work has shown growing interest in LLM-based multi-agent systems for software engineering more broadly. He et al. [8] provide a systematic review of 71 primary studies and argue that multi-agent systems can improve autonomy, robustness, and scalability across software engineering tasks, including code generation, quality assurance, maintenance, and end-to-end development workflows. Their review is important in positioning agentic systems as a broader software engineering trend.

A first line of security-oriented work studies multi-agent support for *secure code generation*. AutoSafeCoder [9] combines a Coding Agent, a Static Analyzer Agent, and a Fuzzing Agent in an iterative loop to improve the security of LLM-generated Python code, reporting a 13% reduction in vulnerable outputs relative to a baseline model. This work is valuable in showing that role separation and tool-supported feedback can improve security outcomes, but its focus is on secure code generation (only Python). In a related but single-pipeline repair setting, LLM4CVE [3] proposes an iterative LLM-based vulnerability repair process for real-world CVEs, using repeated feedback, prompt engineering, and Low-Rank Adaptation (LoRA)-enhanced generation to synthesize candidate patches and compare them against trusted fixes using metrics such as CodeBLEU, human quality judgment, and end-to-end compilation. While this work demonstrates the promise of iterative LLM-based repair, it does not explicitly decompose vulnerability handling into distinct roles such as planning, diagnosis, fixing, and verification.

A second line of work focuses on *vulnerability detection.* VulAgent [1] addresses project-level vulnerability detection through a multi-agent hypothesis-validation pipeline. It uses specialized agents to surface candidate vulnerable code, aggregates findings, constructs explicit vulnerability hypotheses, and validates them against program context, improving average accuracy by 7% and reducing false positives by about 36% on PrimeVul and SVEN. This is highly relevant in showing the importance of context-sensitive reasoning and staged analysis for vulnerability detection. However, its scope is detection-centric, it does not extend into patch generation, independent fix verification, or a workflow designed around secure software engineering stages.

A third line of work has emphasized *evaluation settings and workflow realism.* CVE-Bench [2] argues that existing vulnerability-repair benchmarks are limited because they often reduce the task to simple code input-output pairs. It therefore proposes a more realistic evaluation setup with interactive environments, tool use, and multiple levels of CVE information, including black-box and white-box settings. On 509 CVEs across four languages and 120 repositories, the evaluated agent repairs only about 21% of cases at best, and performs substantially worse under black-box information settings. In a more workflow-complete direction, MAVM [10] proposes a multi-agent framework for end-to-end *recurring* vulnerability management, integrating a vulnerability knowledge base with detection, confirmation, repair, and validation, and outperforming baselines by 31.9%-45.2% in repair accuracy on recurring vulnerability cases. MAVM is especially relevant because it moves closer to real security workflows, but it targets recurring vulnerability management and patch porting with repository-level historical knowledge rather than file-level vulnerability analysis and mitigation in low-level C code.

In summary, existing work has explored secure code generation, vulnerability detection, iterative repair, realistic benchmarking, and recurring vulnerability management. Several of these studies already demonstrate the value of multi-agent decomposition and tool support. However, there remains limited work on *role-based, workflow-oriented architectures for secure software engineering* that explicitly separate investigation planning, vulnerability diagnosis, patch generation, and fix verification in a way that mirrors industrial security review practice. In addition, prior work has given limited attention to MCP-style tool integration in the analysis stage for low-level C vulnerabilities under a controlled exploratory setup. Our work takes an initial step toward this gap by studying two role-based workflows on CrewAI framework curated on real-world C CVEs, with emphasis on the quality of detections, generated patches, and verification outcomes rather than benchmark-scale throughput.

3 Methodology: Workflow Design and Evaluation Setup

We selected some vulnerability instances (CVEs) from the NVD, recorded the associated details, and the vulnerable and patched code files. Later we provided the vulnerable code to our CrewAI based architecture and asked for vulnerability detection and patch generation. Finally, we compared the output with the developer-provided patched version. The details of the workflow design, experimental setup, and analysis procedure are provided in the following sub-sections. In total, the experimental setup yielded 150 workflow executions (25 CVEs $\times$ 3 models $\times$ 2 workflow variants).

3.1 Data Collection: CWE, Repository and CVE Selection

We constructed a curated vulnerability set tailored to the needs of this study rather than directly adopting an existing benchmark dataset (CrossVul, BigVul, SVEN, DiverseVul [11], etc.). This gave us tighter control over code scope, vulnerable-to-patched version alignment, vulnerability difficulty, and the presence of clearly documented ground-truth.

We restricted the study to the C programming language in order to keep the evaluation setting controlled and focused on a low-level system language where vulnerability reasoning is often more challenging. Compared to higher-level languages such as Python or Java, C vulnerabilities depend more frequently on memory operations, pointer behavior, bounds handling, and other low-level semantics, making it a suitable setting for studying tool-augmented agentic workflows.

We selected five CWE categories that occur frequently in C-related vulnerability reports: **CWE-476 (Null Pointer Dereference), CWE-125 (Out-of-bounds Read), CWE-191 (Integer Underflow), CWE-190 (Integer Overflow or Wraparound), and CWE-787 (Out-of-bounds Write).** Selection was guided by the prevalence of these weakness classes in public NVD records[4] and MITRE 2025 CWE Top 25 list[5] and by their relevance to common low-level security issues in C programs. We then identified repositories that were widely used and had a significant number of reported vulnerabilities. Table 1 summarizes the repositories considered, together with their associated CVEs counts as per NVD, GitHub popularity indicators, and the number of CVEs considered from each repository for our study.

Within these repositories, we searched for CVEs belonging to the selected CWE categories and applied the following inclusion criteria:

1. We prioritized *recent vulnerability* instances in order to keep the study aligned with contemporary coding practices and vulnerability reporting.
2. We retained only those CVEs for which both the *vulnerable code* version and the corresponding *patched version* could be reliably recovered.

[4] https://nvd.nist.gov/general/visualizations/vulnerability-visualizations/cwe-over-time.

[5] https://cwe.mitre.org/top25/archive/2025/2025_cwe_top25.html.

Table 1. Repositories considered for CVE selection.

Repository	NVD CVEs	GitHub stars	CVEs Selected for study
freerdp/freerdp	167	13.1k	5
nanomq/nanomq	33	2.5k	4
AcademySoftwareFoundation/ openexr	84	1.8k	8
wolfSSL/wolfssl	107	2.8k	8

3. We selected cases with sufficiently *clear public documentation of the vulnerability*, including its nature, likely root cause, exploitation path, and security impact, so that workflow outputs could be meaningfully compared against available ground truth.
4. To avoid restricting the evaluation to small or narrowly scoped examples, we selected CVEs whose affected files exhibited substantial *variation in size*, ranging from approximately 700 to 20,000 lines of code. We also ensured *diversity in vulnerability localization*, including both cases where the weakness was concentrated in a single line or operation and cases where it extended across multiple lines of code. This allowed the study to examine workflow behavior under different levels of contextual and structural complexity.
5. Finally, we limited the number of instances to five CVEs per CWE category, yielding a total of 25 CVEs, because the goal of this study is not large-scale statistical benchmarking but an initial exploratory assessment of the quality of workflow outputs across representative vulnerability cases.

The complete list of 25 CVEs, together with their metadata (including CVE ID, CWE ID, vulnerable file name, vulnerable line numbers, severity, security impact, and exploitation path when available), as well as the corresponding vulnerable and patched code files, is provided in the replication repository[6]. This study is intentionally conducted at the vulnerable file level rather than the full repository level. At the next level we would extend this to a repository level to understand how does the presence of the entire repository information and structure affect the end results (keeping all other settings intact).

3.2 Model Selection

We prioritized open-source LLMs in this study. This choice was motivated not only by reproducibility and deployability considerations, but also by prior discussions with cybersecurity practitioners in industrial settings, which indicated reservations about sending potentially sensitive source code to proprietary hosted models. Locally deployable or openly controllable models were viewed as more compatible with internal security and compliance expectations. We initially began with a pool of 25 candidate models, selected from publicly discussed

[6] https://github.com/SriAbir/SecurityAgentWorkflow.

coding and reasoning capable LLMs[7]. Next, we used Inspect Evals' built-in CyberMetric task (`cybermetric_80`)[8] as a preliminary feasibility filter to identify models with sufficient cybersecurity-oriented knowledge for downstream use in the workflow. Based on this step, we retained the top 8 models as presented in Table 2. From this set, we selected three final LLMs, `nemotron-cascade-2:30b`, `qwen3-coder-next`, and `gpt-oss:120b` while ensuring that all selected models supported MCP-based tool integration. This enabled consistent comparison across workflow variants. To keep it simple, during each execution we used the same model to instantiate all the three roles (Vulnerability Analyzer, Fixer and verifier).

Table 2. Preliminary model screening

Model	Accuracy	Stderr	Skill Integration
gpt-oss:120b	0.988	0.012	Yes
qwen3-coder-next:latest	0.950	0.025	Yes
nemotron-cascade-2:30b	0.975	0.018	Yes
llama3:70B	0.950	0.025	No
gemma4:31b	0.988	0.012	No
deepseek-r1:32b	0.988	0.012	No
glm-4.7-flash:bf16	0.950	0.025	No
qwen3.6:35b	0.975	0.018	Yes

3.3 Role-Based Workflow

We implement the proposed workflow in CrewAI[9] as a base layer because its explicit role-based orchestration model and easy skill/tool integration settings aligns well with our security workflow design and additional MCP skill customization. In this design, CrewAI is used to coordinate role assignment, task sequencing, and context passing across workflow stages. Our contribution is not a modification of CrewAI itself, but the design and exploratory study of a security-oriented workflow instantiated on top of it. The workflow as depicted in Fig. 1 is organized around four roles, *Planner, Vulnerability Analyzer, Fixer, and Verifier*, each with a narrowly scoped responsibility and a restricted output format. The workflow has two variants, the first one (Workflow 1) without skill integration (Planner, Analyzer, Fixer, Verifier) is described as follows.

- The Planner serves as the investigation-guidance stage. In the present study, this role is implemented as a rule-based static planner rather than

[7] https://ollama.com/search?q=llama.
[8] https://github.com/CyberMetric.
[9] https://docs.crewai.com/.

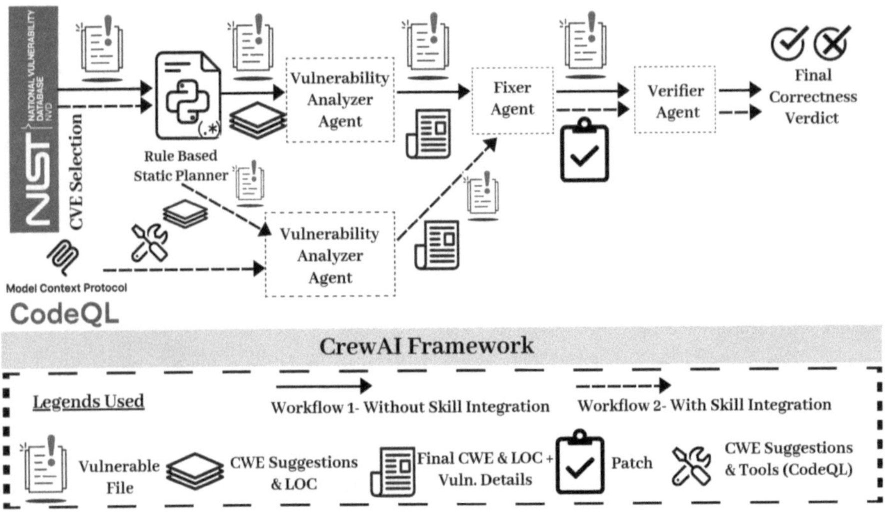

Fig. 1. Role based Workflow for Secure Software Development.

an LLM agent. The planner (.py file) scans the input C code for predefined vulnerability-relevant patterns (Fig. 2) and highlights likely investigation regions together with corresponding analysis focus. It uses regular-expression-based matching to identify patterns associated with common C weakness classes, including classic buffer overflow operations, out-of-bounds memory access risks, potential null pointer de-references, and integer-overflow/underflow related allocation issues. It returns detected issue regions and a set of prioritized vulnerability themes, which are then used only as guidance for the downstream Analyzer.

- The Vulnerability Analyzer is an LLM based agent that performs the main technical diagnosis of the vulnerable code. It receives the source code together with the planning context and is instructed to determine the primary vulnerability, assign the CWE, identify the vulnerable lines of code, explain the root cause, trace the source-to-sink or input-to-dangerous-operation flow, and characterize the security impact. To preserve role separation, the Analyzer is explicitly constrained to use the Planner output only as guidance and not to restate the plan or propose a patch. This makes the Analyzer the principal decision-making stage of the workflow.
- The Fixer (LLM-based) is responsible for remediation. Given the vulnerable source code and prior analysis context, it produces a minimal secure patch targeted at the vulnerability diagnosed by the Analyzer. Its output is restricted to the patched code together with a concise explanation of the unsafe behavior removed, the security control or validation added, and why the patch addresses the root cause. The Fixer is deliberately prevented from redoing the entire diagnosis, which allows the study to separate vulnerability understanding from patch construction.

– The Verifier agent acts as an independent post-remediation assessment stage. Given the original source code and prior task context, it evaluates whether the proposed patch actually resolves the vulnerability identified by the Analyzer. The Verifier is instructed to assess whether the same vulnerability was addressed, whether the root cause rather than only the symptom was removed, whether the unsafe source-to-sink path was disrupted, whether attacker-controlled input can still reach the dangerous operation, and whether residual risk or correctness regressions remain. It returns a structured verification verdict together with patch-level concerns.

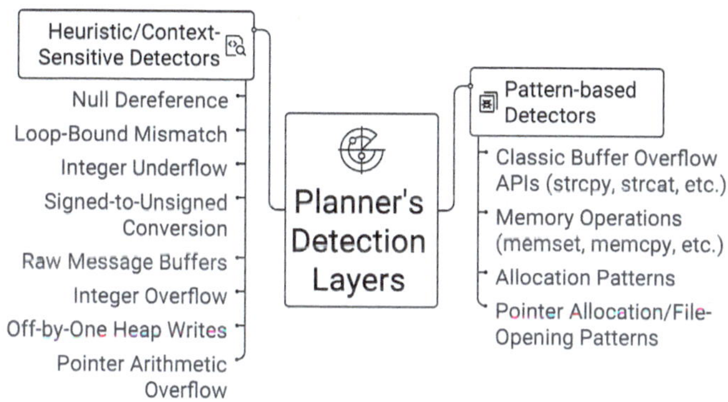

Fig. 2. Planner Detection Logic.

In the second variant i.e., Workflow 2, (Planner, Analyzer with MCP CodeQL integration, Fixer, Verifier), MCP CodeQL[10] integration equips the Analyzer with an additional static-analysis skill during the diagnosis stage. CodeQL is particularly appropriate in our setting because it provides built-in support for C and C++, including dedicated C/C++ library, standard query packs, and security and quality query suites for static analysis [15]. We relied on CodeQL's built-in C/C++ security analysis capabilities exposed through the MCP integration and did not develop custom CodeQL queries for this study. The Analyzer records the CodeQL MCP tools it uses and the contribution of each tool to the diagnosis, but remains responsible for validating or rejecting that evidence against the actual code.

We present the role descriptions and workflow logic at a conceptual level in this paper. The full role prompts, task specifications, and implementation details are provided in the accompanying replication repository[11].

[10] https://mcpmarket.com/server/codeql.
[11] https://github.com/SriAbir/SecurityAgentWorkflow.

3.4 Execution Environment and Run Settings

The experiments were executed on two servers, 1) Server 1 with Windows was equipped with an AMD Ryzen 9 9950X CPU, 128 GB RAM, and an NVIDIA RTX 5090 GPU, 2) Server 2 ran on Linux and used an NVIDIA GB10 platform with 128 GB RAM and 128 GB unified memory along with GB 10 NVIDIA GPU. The workflow implementation was developed in Python 3.10.12 using CrewAI v1.14.2.

To keep the experimental conditions consistent, the same role prompts were used across all selected models within each workflow variant. Likewise, the same static Planner was used in both workflow variants, so that the only architectural difference between them was the Analyzer's access to MCP CodeQL in Workflow 2. This allowed the comparison to focus on the effect of tool-augmented analysis rather than changes in workflow structure. Each CVE instance was executed twice for each model and workflow variant. Across these repeated runs, we did not observe major differences in the outcomes. In particular, cases that failed to give the correct solution in the first run did not become succeed in the second run, and cases that succeeded remained stable. For this reason, we do not report per-run details separately and instead discuss the consolidated outcomes. The temperature was set to 0.5 for all model runs. No manual editing was performed on intermediate agent outputs during workflow execution. Outputs generated by the Planner, Analyzer, Fixer, and Verifier were passed between stages according to the predefined task structure.

3.5 Data Analysis and Evaluation

Ground Truth Definition. For each selected CVE, ground truth was derived from the publicly available vulnerability description, primarily by following the advisory URL referenced on the corresponding NVD page, together with the associated repository artifacts. For the *Vulnerability Analyzer*, the reference information consisted of: i) the associated CWE type, ii) the vulnerability location (i.e., the lines containing the vulnerable logic), iii) the root-cause description, iv) the exploitation path when available, and v) the security impact. For the *Fixer*, the primary ground truth was the developer-provided patched code, evaluated semantically rather than by exact textual matching. For the *Verifier*, ground truth was defined by whether the generated patch correctly removed the vulnerability identified in the reference case, broke the unsafe path or condition that enabled it, and avoided introducing obvious residual risk or regression.

Rubric-Based Manual Assessment. The outputs produced by the workflow were evaluated through a *manual, rubric-based assessment* against the reference ground truth defined above. Two authors independently did the assessment, and inter-rater agreement of $\kappa = 0.83$ (almost perfect agreement) was measured using Cohen's kappa [12]. All disagreements were then resolved through discussion, and the agreed labels were used in the final analysis. This approach was adopted because the study focuses on the semantic quality of security reasoning and

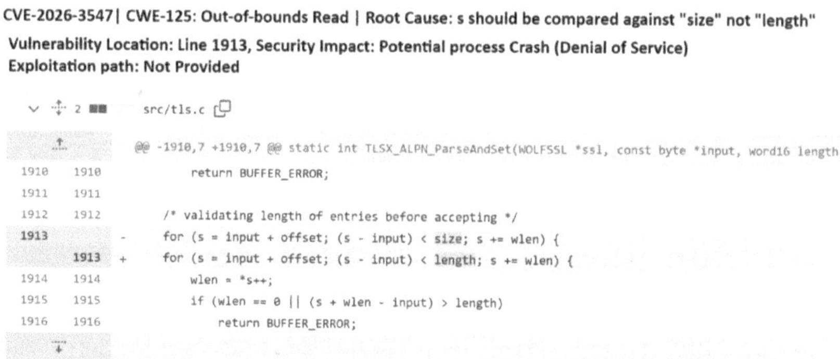

(a) Ground-truth for vulnerability & patch for CVE-2026-3547.

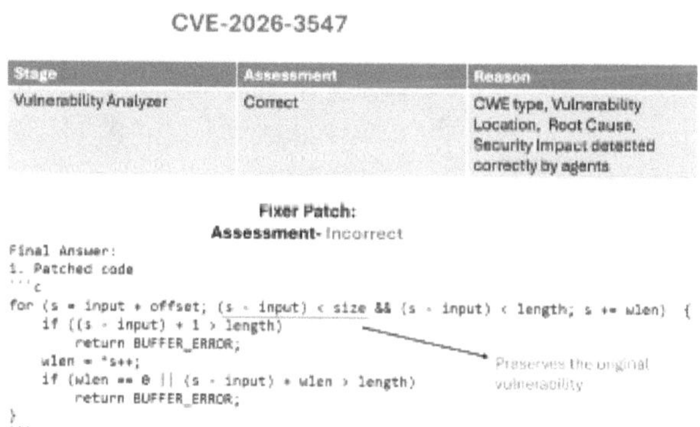

(b) Assessment of an agent-generated patch. Although the agent correctly identified the vulnerability, its fix retained `size` in the loop condition, thereby preserving the original boundary-checking flaw.

Fig. 3. Example: Ground Truth and Assessment for CVE-2026-3547.

patching outcomes rather than on exact textual similarity. In particular, multiple secure outputs may differ syntactically while still addressing the same underlying vulnerability. Accordingly, each workflow stage was assessed using predefined criteria and mapped to a small set of qualitative labels.

For the *Vulnerability Analyzer*, we assessed the correctness of, i) CWE assignment, ii) vulnerable line(s) or code region, iii) quality of the root-cause explanation, iv) reported exploitation or input-to-dangerous-operation flow, and v) security impact. Based on these criteria, Analyzer outputs were labeled as *Correct*, *Partially Correct*, or *Incorrect*. For the *Fixer*, we assessed: i) whether the generated patch addressed the vulnerability diagnosed in the reference case, ii) whether the patch was semantically comparable to the trusted developer fix, and iii) whether it introduced obvious unsafe behavior, regressions, or overly broad modifications. Based on these criteria, Fixer outputs were labeled as *Comparable*, *Partially Correct*, *Incorrect*, and *Better*. For the *Verifier*, we assessed: i) whether the reported verdict (*fixed*, *partially fixed*, or *not fixed*) was consistent with the reference case, ii) whether the reasoning correctly judged root-cause removal, and iv) whether residual risk or possible regressions were meaningfully identified. Based on these criteria, Verifier outputs were labeled as *Accurate*, and *Inaccurate*.

Table 3 presents the rubrics for labeling the workflow outputs. Additionally, Fig. 3 presents an example of ground truth and assessment.

4 Results and Implications

We report overall Analyzer, Fixer, and Verifier accuracy as the percentage of cases in which each role produced the correct outcome relative to the ground truth. While significant observations are highlighted here, the detailed results are present in the shared repository.

Vulnerability Analyzer: Figure 4 shows a clear dependence of analyzer performance on both the model and the availability of CodeQL-MCP support, with notable variation across CWEs.

Without CodeQL-MCP, *nemotron-cascade-2:30b* is the strongest overall analyzer. It achieves the highest proportion of fully correct vulnerability detections for *CWE-125, CWE-190, and CWE-787. qwen3-coder-next* performs moderately well on *CWE-476 and CWE-787*, but is weaker on *CWE-191*, where its outputs are mostly only partially correct. *gpt-oss:120b* is the weakest analyzer in the no-CodeQL setting.

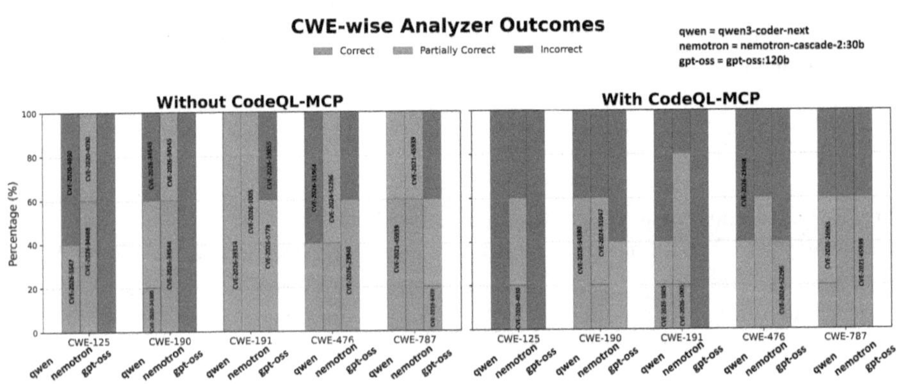

Fig. 4. Results: Vulnerability Analyzer.

With CodeQL-MCP, the impact is mixed rather than uniformly positive. *qwen3-coder-next* improves on *CWE-190* and shows some gains on *CWE-191*, but remains weak on *CWE-125 and CWE-476. nemotron-cascade-2:30b* remains the most balanced model overall, with strong results on *CWE-190 and CWE-787*, and a reasonable mix of correct and partially correct outcomes on *CWE-191 and*

Table 3. Rubric used for manual assessment of workflow outputs.

Stage	Assessment	Decision rule
Analyzer	Correct	When all the 5 assessment criteria matches with ground truth
	Partially Correct	The vulnerable line(s) of code are identified correctly but one or more of the other criteria do not match ground truth OR CWE-ID and root cause identified correctly but one or more of the other criteria do not match ground truth
	Incorrect	Both the CWE-ID and vulnerable line(s) of code are identified incorrectly
Fixer	Comparable	The patch is semantically similar to ground truth
	Partially Correct	The patch contains semantically similar logic to the ground truth but introduces additional buggy logic, inappropriate for the code
	Incorrect	The patch is totally different from ground truth and does not resolves the vulnerability at all
	Better	The patch contains additional security controls over the ground truth which is suitable for improving the code security
Verifier	Accurate	The verifier gives the verdict which is similar to our evaluation after comparison with ground truth
	Inaccurate	The verifier gives the verdict which is different from our evaluation after comparison with ground truth

CWE-476. In contrast, gpt-oss:120b continues to struggle even with CodeQL-MCP, with a small improvement for *CWE-787*.

Across CWE categories, *CWE-787 and CWE-476* appears to be the easiest class overall, producing the largest share of correct localizations across models and settings. While *CWE-191* is the hardest, with very few fully correct results. *CWE-125* also remains challenging, especially for *qwen3-coder-next and gpt-oss:120b* in the CodeQL-assisted setting. Overall, the results suggest that *CodeQL-MCP* helps selectively rather than universally, and that *nemotron-cascade-2:30b* gives the best accuracy across weakness types under our controlled experimental settings.

The analyzer results suggest that most failures arose from two main sources: (i) the Planner failed to surface the required vulnerability pattern, accounting for **16%** of cases, and (ii) even when the Planner provided the correct signal, the Analyzer often struggled to prioritize the most relevant vulnerability cue. A small number of failures were also linked to misleading CodeQL outputs that diverted the analysis. Exact vulnerable-region detection reached **52%** accuracy in without CodeQL-MCP workflow and **56%** in with CodeQL-MCP workflow. In a few instances, limited code context may also have contributed to failure, suggesting that full-repository access could further improve analyzer performance.

Fixer: The fixer results (Fig. 5) indicate that repair remains substantially more difficult than detection.

Among the three models, *nemotron-cascade-2:30b* shows the most balanced fixer behavior, producing some comparable or partially correct repairs across multiple CWEs. The strongest outcomes appear for *CWE-476*, where some fixes are actually better than the ground truth, and for *CWE-787*, where *nemotron-cascade-2:30b* achieves the highest proportion of comparable repairs. In contrast, *CWE-191* remains the most difficult category.

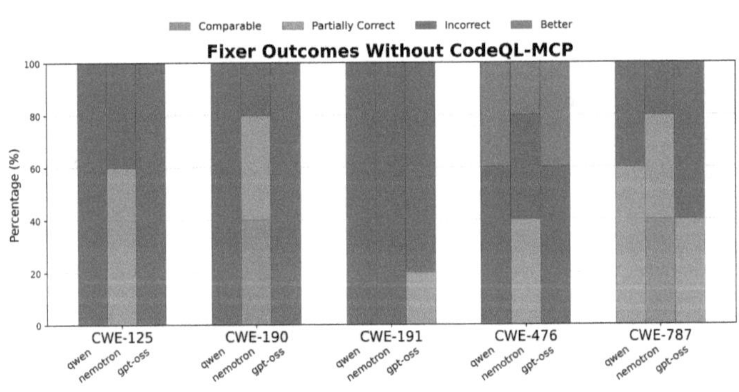

Fig. 5. Results: Fixer.

Since fixer accuracy did not vary much between the with-CodeQL and without-CodeQL settings (expected, since CodeQL was integrated with the analyzer rather than the fixer) we presented the without-CodeQL results in Fig. 5.

In case of the Fixer agent, **24%** of the generated patch contained additional logic in addition to what was actually required to mitigate the vulnerability. Additionally, under such cases, we observed instances where the additional logic was of no harm (though not required) as well as certain instances where these unnecessary updates resulted in to buggy logic.

Verifier: Verifier accuracy was highest for *nemotron-cascade-2:30b* (**69%**), followed by *qwen3-coder-next* (**44%**) and *gpt-oss:120b* (**38%**).

Baseline, Ablation Studies & Summary: Table 4 summarizes the overall detection and fix accuracy across the evaluated workflows (all of them with *nemotron-cascade-2:30b*) and the baseline setting. We measure accuracy as the percentage of cases that match the ground truth, with separate scores for vulnerability detection and fix generation. Within our evaluated models and settings, Workflow 1 with *nemotron-cascade-2:30b* performs best (comparable to GPT 5.5 in detection accuracy), the Planner is critical for detection quality, and CodeQL support has a larger effect on analysis than on fixing.

Answer- RQ1 & RQ2: The role-based agentic workflow without CodeQL using *nemotron-cascade-2:30b*, achieved **44%** detection accuracy which was comparable to GPT 5.5, while fix accuracy was lower at **19%** and verifier reached **69%** accuracy. Removing the Planner reduced correct detections by **45%**, underscoring the importance of explicit planning and role separation. Workflow 2 with CodeQL yielded **31%** detection accuracy and **13%** fix accuracy. These findings indicate that tool integration alone is insufficient; its benefit depends on whether the Analyzer can correctly interpret and prioritize the additional hints.

Table 4. Final accuracy summary across workflows with Baseline Comparison

Workflow / Setting	Detection Accuracy (%)	Fix Accuracy (%)
Workflow 1 (without CodeQL)	44	19
Workflow 2 (with CodeQL)	31	13
Workflow 1 (without CodeQL) (without Planner)	25	13
Workflow 2 (with CodeQL) (without Planner)	19	6
Baseline (*OpenAI GPT-5.5.*)	44	44

5 Discussion

Our discussion is mainly based on practitioner insights with whom we had a detailed session where we presented these results. We wanted to understand how our approach would be beneficial to them and in what ways they would like to apply or integrate our framework in their secure software engineering process. The highlights of the discussions are as follows:

- It was interesting to see how the planners could directly influence the Analyzer's approach. It could be better to have a human intervention at this step (right after planner) who could prioritize the planner hints before we send the same to the Analyzer
- Though the Fixer gave some partially correct patch, it could still be beneficial for the practitioners. E.g., if 3 out of 5 statements added by the Fixer are correct, a human-in-the-loop process could be followed to filter out the correct remediation steps and ignore the others.
- It is a challenge to cope up with the everyday releases of newer and more powerful models. It is hard to understand which could be better over the other. Therefore, through our work we try to shift the focus on the underlying role-based workflow rather than the models. Though an initial screening for filtering out some candidate models is essential but the main aim s to refine and finetune the architecture and integration techniques.
- Finally, though the current CodeQL skill integration did not heavily improve the performance of the system, there still remains ample scope to modify the way the MCP skill results are being used or explore other skills in the workflow.

6 Threats to Validity

Following the validity perspectives discussed by Wohlin [13] and Staron [14], we summarize the main threats as follows.

Construct Validity. The study evaluates workflow quality through a manual, rubric-based assessment of analyzer, fixer, and verifier outputs. Although this is suitable for judging semantic adequacy in a small exploratory study, some subjectivity remains in assigning qualitative labels such as *Correct*, *Partially Correct*, or *Comparable*. To reduce this threat, we defined explicit evaluation criteria and grounded the assessment in publicly available CVE descriptions, associated CWE labels, vulnerable code regions, and trusted patched versions.

Internal Validity. The workflow behavior may be influenced by model stochasticity and tool interaction effects. To reduce this threat, we used the same prompts across models within each workflow, kept the same static Planner in both workflow variants, and repeated each CVE execution twice. Since repeated runs did not materially alter the outcome categories, results are reported at the consolidated case level.

External Validity. The study uses a curated set of 25 real-world C-language CVEs across five CWE categories. While this supports controlled exploratory evaluation, it limits generalizability to other vulnerability classes, programming languages, and repository-scale workflows. The findings should therefore be interpreted as early evidence rather than broad statistical claims.

Conclusion Validity. The study relies on a limited set of three LLMs and one tool-augmented variant using MCP CodeQL integration. Although the workflow design, role prompts, and artifacts are provided in the replication repository, broader replication across additional models and tool configurations is needed to assess stability fully.

7 Conclusion and Future Work

This paper explored a role-based agentic workflow for vulnerability analysis and mitigation in C/C++. The results suggest that explicit role separation with a strongly designed planner can support improved vulnerability detection. Also, CodeQL-based tool support showed mixed effects denoting that tool-integration needs to be done in a way that can be prioritized and interpreted by the agents as per requirement. At the same time, the uneven quality of generated patches reinforces the continued need for human-in-the-loop review in security-critical settings.

These findings position workflow-oriented agentic architectures as a promising direction for security-focused software process improvement, while motivating future studies on larger datasets and broader tool and model settings. Future studies is specifically aimed towards designing different workflow alternatives (with multiple analyzers, judges, refinement loops, etc.). Also a repository level analysis in future could help improve the detection and mitigation process (more code context and transparent inter-file relations).

Acknowledgments. This paper has been partially financed by Software Center, www. software-center.se, a collaboration between Chalmers, the University of Gothenburg, and 17 companies. The paper has also been partially funded by the SFO Transport/AoA Transport at the University of Gothenburg and Chalmers University of Technology.

References

1. Wang, Z., Li, G., Li, J., Zhu, H. and Jin, Z.: VulAgent: Hypothesis-Validation based Multi-Agent Vulnerability Detection. arXiv preprint arXiv:2509.11523 (2025)
2. Wang, P., Liu, X., Xiao, C.: Cve-bench: Benchmarking llm-based software engineering agent's ability to repair real-world cve vulnerabilities. In Proceedings of the 2025 Conference of the Nations of the Americas Chapter of the Association for Computational Linguistics: Human Language Technologies (Volume 1: Long Papers), pp. 4207–4224 (2025)
3. Fakih, M., et al.: Llm4cve: Enabling iterative automated vulnerability repair with large language models. In: 2025 28th Euromicro Conference on Digital System Design (DSD), pp. 592–599. IEEE (2025)
4. Singh, A., Ehtesham, A., Kumar, S., Khoei, T.T.: Enhancing AI systems with agentic workflows patterns in large language model. In: 2024 IEEE World AI IoT Congress (AIIoT), pp. 527–532. IEEE (2024)
5. Basu, S., et al.: Understanding Conversational Patterns in Multi-agent Programming: A Case Study on Fibonacci Game Development. arXiv preprint arXiv:2605.24138 (2026)

6. Sun, S., Staron, M.: Literate Programming with LLMs?-A Study on Rosetta Code and CodeNet. IEEE Trans. Softw. Eng. **52**(2), 468–487 (2026). https://doi.org/10.1109/TSE.2025.3629828
7. Ahmed, M.B.U., Harzevili, N.S., Shin, J., Pham, H.V., Wang, S.: SecVulEval: Benchmarking LLMs for real-world C/C++ vulnerability detection. arXiv preprint arXiv:2505.19828 (2025)
8. He, J., Treude, C., Lo, D.: Llm-based multi-agent systems for software engineering: Literature review, vision, and the road ahead. ACM Trans. Softw. Eng. Methodol. **34**(5), 1–30 (2025)
9. Nunez, A., Islam, N.T., Jha, S.K., Najafirad, P.: Autosafecoder: A multi-agent framework for securing llm code generation through static analysis and fuzz testing. arXiv preprint arXiv:2409.10737 (2024)
10. Zheng, Z., Zhou, J., Hu, X., Gao, Y., Pan, S.: Multi-Agent End-to-End Vulnerability Management for Mitigating Recurring Vulnerabilities. arXiv preprint arXiv:2601.17762 (2026)
11. Ding, Y., et al.: Vulnerability Detection with Code Language Models: How Far are We?. In 2025 IEEE/ACM 47th International Conference on Software Engineering (ICSE), pp. 1729–1741. IEEE (2025)
12. Cohen, J.: A coefficient of agreement for nominal scales. Educ. Psychol. Measur. **20**(1), 37–46 (1960)
13. Wohlin, C., Runeson, P., Höst, M., Ohlsson, M.C., Regnell, B., Wesslén, A.: Experimentation in software engineering, vol. 236, Springer, Cham (2012)
14. Staron, M.:Action research in software engineering, p. 50. Springer, Cham (2020)
15. Youn, D., Lee, S., Ryu, S.: Declarative static analysis for multilingual programs using CodeQL. Softw. Pract. Exp. **53**(7), 1472–1495 (2023)

Software Analytics: Mining Software Open Datasets and Repositories

Empirical Study on Engineering Decisions in Multi-agent Reinforcement Learning Systems

Deepansha Chowdhary[1(✉)] and Uwe Zdun[2]

[1] UniVie Doctoral School Computer Science (DoCS), University of Vienna, Vienna, Austria
deepansha.chowdhary@univie.ac.at
[2] Faculty of Computer Science, Research Group Software Architecture, University of Vienna, Vienna, Austria
uwe.zdun@univie.ac.at

Abstract. Multi-agent reinforcement learning (MARL) is increasingly used in real-world coordination tasks, yet little is known about how MARL systems are engineered in practice. We present an empirical repository-mining study of 187 open-source GitHub repositories comprising 12,205 files (9,957 Python, 2,090 YAML, and 158 JSON). Using automated static analysis and manual repository screening, we examine engineering decisions in algorithm adoption and hyperparameter configuration, environment integration, and multi-agent implementation patterns. Our results show that open-source MARL development is concentrated around a small set of algorithm families, especially PPO, DQN and QMIX, and that algorithm use co-occurs with recurring library and environment combinations. Hyperparameter practice is largely limited to a small set of recurring defaults, while specialized variants tend to involve larger hyperparameter sets than their base algorithms. Repositories most often realize multi-agent behavior through simple structural patterns, such as instantiating multiple agents or defining multiple agent classes, whereas specialized multi-agent abstractions occur less frequently. These findings provide an empirical baseline for current MARL engineering decisions and highlight opportunities to improve standardization in hyperparameter specification, environment integration, and multi-agent abstractions.

Keywords: Reinforcement Learning · Multi-Agent Systems · Repository Mining · Empirical Software Engineering · RLOps

1 Introduction

Multi-agent reinforcement learning (MARL) [4] is increasingly used to address coordination problems in domains such as production automation, autonomous

C. Berger and V. Klös (Eds.): SEAA 2026, LNCS 16864, pp. 447–464, 2027.
https://doi.org/10.1007/978-3-032-36587-3_31

driving [24], smart grids [21], and robotics [17]. Alongside this growth, an ecosystem of frameworks, libraries, and tools has emerged to support MARL development, including RLlib [14], Stable-Baselines3 [19], and BenchMARL [3]. These frameworks provide templates, defaults, and environment integrations, but they do not by themselves show how practitioners combine algorithms, libraries, environments, and multi-agent patterns across projects.

This creates an important empirical gap. Although prior work has studied MARL algorithms, benchmarks, and theoretical properties [7,10,20,25], much less is known about engineering decisions in open-source MARL systems. In particular, we lack cross-project evidence on which algorithms are adopted in practice, how they are configured, which environments and libraries they are combined with, and how multi-agent functionality is realized in code. These questions matter for reproducibility because many MARL engineering decisions, including hyperparameters, environment wrappers, and implementation structure, are only partially documented in papers and tutorials [8,15,16].

To address this gap, we conduct an empirical repository-mining study of open-source MARL projects on GitHub. We examine how existing methods are engineered in practice, focusing on algorithm adoption, hyperparameter configuration, environment integration, and multi-agent design patterns across real-world repositories. Our study addresses the following research questions:

- **RQ1:** Which algorithms are most prevalent in MARL implementations, and how frequently are multi-agent variants adopted compared to single-agent baselines?
- **RQ2:** How consistent are hyperparameter configurations across MARL implementations, and which parameters show consensus versus high variability?
- **RQ3:** Which recurring combinations of algorithms, libraries, environments, and multi-agent patterns appear across MARL repositories?

2 Background and Related Work

Prior empirical work has shown that implementation details in reinforcement learning can be as consequential as algorithmic innovations. In single-agent deep RL, Engstrom et al. [6] showed that code-level choices such as normalization, gradient clipping, and initialization can substantially affect performance, while Andrychowicz et al. [1] identified the impact of specific design and hyperparameter choices through large-scale empirical analysis. Similar observations have been reported in MARL. Papoudakis et al. [18] found that independent learners can remain competitive in some settings, Yu et al. [27] showed that implementation details such as value normalization and epoch tuning are critical to MAPPO performance, and Christianos et al. [5] demonstrated that the effectiveness of parameter sharing depends strongly on the environment. Framework and benchmark papers have defined much of the current MARL implementation landscape. RLlib [14], PettingZoo [26], MARLlib [11], BenchMARL [3], and JaxMARL [22] provide abstractions for multi-agent training, policy mapping, parameter sharing, and environment standardization, while platforms such as SMAC [23] shape how MARL systems are built and evaluated. However, these works primarily describe framework capabilities, benchmark ecosystems, and recommended abstractions rather than how practitioners actually combine algorithms, libraries, environments, and multi-agent patterns across open-source implementations.

Complementary software engineering and tooling studies have examined practical challenges in RL system development. Henderson et al. [9] and Liaw et al. [15] highlighted reproducibility challenges and the importance of hyperparameter optimization infrastructure, Ntentos et al. [16] studied architectural design patterns in RL systems, and Fu et al. [8] revisited common practices in cooperative MARL. These studies provide important insights into RL engineering, but they do not characterize engineering decisions across a broad dataset of open-source MARL repositories. Our work addresses this gap by examining how MARL systems are engineered in practice, including algorithm adoption, configuration, environment and library use, and multi-agent structure.

3 Research Methodology

We analyzed 187 public GitHub repositories implementing MARL, comprising 12,205 files (9,957 Python, 2,090 YAML, and 158 JSON). Repositories were identified through GitHub Search API queries using broad MARL-related text and topic terms, while excluding algorithm and framework-specific search terms to reduce retrieval bias. The discovery queries included terms such as *marl*, variants of *multi-agent reinforcement learning*, and related GitHub topic labels. The full query list is included in the replication package.

Candidates were filtered in two stages. First, automated filters excluded forks, archived repositories, and non-Python repositories; we restricted the dataset to Python repositories because our detector pipeline relies on Python-specific static analysis, including AST parsing. We further removed repositories whose topics indicated coursework or tutorial content (e.g., tutorial, course, homework, thesis, demo), repositories whose name, description, or topics did not indicate both a multi-agent and a reinforcement-learning context, and repositories with fewer than 2 contributors or fewer than 10 commits to exclude toy and single-developer projects [12]. We retained repositories with activity after 1 October 2023. Prior work has used 12-month [2] and 24-month [13] thresholds to identify inactive projects. We chose this cutoff to balance inclusion of maintained but infrequently updated repositories with a focus on recent MARL practice. The dataset snapshot used in this study was collected in April 2026. Second, we manually screened the remaining repositories to retain only those that implement or apply MARL. We inspected each repository's README, directory structure, source files, and configuration files, retaining repositories that contained executable code or configurations for training, evaluating, or applying RL with multiple agents. We excluded repositories that only mentioned MARL in documentation, collected paper lists, provided environments without agents,

Table 1. Indicators used by the multi-agent detector.

Indicator	Detection intuition
Instantiation of multiple agents	Code explicitly creates or configures more than one agent through constructor parameters or assignments.
Multiple agent classes	A module defines two or more classes whose names contain *Agent*, suggesting distinct agent roles or behaviors.
Multi-agent modules/imports	Imports from modules or classes whose names indicate multi-agent functionality (e.g., *MultiAgentEnv*), suggesting use of specialized multi-agent utilities.
Parallel environment detected	Assignments to names such as *VecEnv* or variables containing *parallel*, indicating vectorized or parallelized environment execution.
Multiple buffers	Imports of two or more classes whose names end in *buffer*, suggesting separate replay or storage buffers.
Multiple policies	Imports of more than one symbol containing *Policy*, suggesting management of multiple policy networks.
Multi-agent environment references	Assignments to *env_name* or *env_id* whose string values contain *multi*, suggesting a multi-agent environment variant.

implemented general RL frameworks without a concrete MARL application, corresponded to core RL/MARL frameworks or libraries (e.g., Stable-Baselines3, RLlib, CleanRL, PettingZoo), or matched search terms without implementing MARL. Manual screening was conducted by the first author; ambiguous cases were revisited after the initial pass and assessed against the same inclusion and exclusion criteria. This yielded 232 candidate repositories, of which 187 remained after screening. Metadata for all included and excluded repositories is available in the replication package.

The detailed algorithm-level analysis as seen in Sect. 4 was data-driven rather than based on a predefined selection of algorithms. We first applied the algorithm detector to the full repository dataset and then focused the analysis on the most prevalent detected algorithm families. The main analysis therefore covers PPO, DQN, Q-Learning, MAPPO and QMIX, which were the five most frequently observed families in the dataset. Less frequent algorithms and variants are retained in the repository-level variant summaries, but are not analyzed with the same level of detail to avoid overinterpreting patterns supported by only a smaller number of repositories.

To study engineering decisions directly from source code and configuration files, we implemented five static detectors for algorithm usage, environment setup, hyperparameter definitions, library usage, and multi-agent patterns. Using parsed Python files and YAML configurations, the detectors identify algorithms, environment setup patterns, hyperparameters, and RL libraries. Multi-agent pattern detection specifically relies on the seven indicators listed in Table 1.

4 Results

This section presents results on algorithm adoption and configuration, environment setup and integration, and multi-agent design patterns. We focus on usage patterns, frequency distributions, and cross-repository variation. The data are available in the replication package (Sect. 8).

Table 2. Environment prevalence across the 126 repositories in which at least one environment was detected (repositories may use multiple environments; % = share of those 126 repositories)

Category	Environment	Repos	%	Category	Environment	Repos	%
General-purpose	Gymnasium	65	51.6	Game-based	Atari	12	9.5
	PettingZoo	58	46.0		GridWorld	19	15.1
	SMAC/SMACv2	38	30.2		OpenSpiel	20	15.9
	MPE	40	31.7		GFootball	10	7.9
	Overcooked	10	7.9	Cont. control	MuJoCo	16	12.7
Cooperative MARL	RWARE	9	7.1		MaMuJoCo	9	7.1
	VMAS	6	4.8	Domain-specific	SUMO	10	7.9
	MeltingPot	5	4.0		MiniGrid	4	3.2
	LBF	7	5.6				
	Hanabi	3	2.4				

4.1 Environment Setup and Integration

Repository-level environment definitions can be grouped by primary backend or environment family. Table 2 summarizes their distribution across the 126 repositories in which at least one environment was detected. Gymnasium is the most common backend, appearing in 51.6% of these repositories (65/126; 95% Wilson CI [42.9, 60.1]). Among MARL-specific environments, PettingZoo appears in 46.0% of repositories (58/126; 95% CI [37.6, 54.7]), while SMAC/SMACv2 and MPE appear in 30.2% (38/126; 95% CI [22.8, 38.7]) and 31.7% (40/126; 95% CI [24.3, 40.3]) of repositories, respectively. Full 95% Wilson confidence intervals for repository-level prevalence proportions are provided in the replication package.

Figure 1 and Table 3(a) show how the five most prevalent algorithms (*PPO*, *DQN*, *Q-Learning*, *MAPPO*, and *QMIX*) are implemented across libraries in our dataset. **PyTorch** is the most widely used library across all five algorithm families, appearing in 65.4%–81.7% of repositories per algorithm, with the lowest share observed for MAPPO (65.4%). Beyond PyTorch, **Ray/RLlib** shows non-trivial adoption for PPO (24.5%) and MAPPO (15.4%) implementations. **Stable-Baselines3** appears primarily alongside PPO and DQN and is absent from QMIX implementations entirely. In contrast, **TensorFlow** appears less consistently and is concentrated in specific algorithms, with the highest share for DQN (15%) and QMIX (13.6%). **JAX** shows comparable adoption to TensorFlow in QMIX (13.6% each). Gymnasium and PettingZoo are included in the table as environment libraries commonly used with MARL algorithm implementations, rather than as training frameworks.

As shown in Fig. 1, we examined temporal shifts in library adoption by grouping repositories into contiguous 2-year creation-year bins and computing, for each bin, the share of repositories in which a library was detected in at least one file. We use three bins: 2020–2021 ($n = 18$), 2022–2023 ($n = 45$), and 2024–2025 ($n = 73$), and omit 2018–2019 due to a small cohort ($n = 5$). Under this definition, adoption of PyTorch rises from 83.3% in 2020–2021 to 90.7% in 2024–2025, whereas TensorFlow declines from 27.8% to 8%. Because bin sizes are modest and proportions are not mutually exclusive, we report per-bin n and 95% Wilson confidence intervals to communicate uncertainty in these estimates.

Table 3. Repository-level summaries of algorithm, library, environment, and variant usage. In (a), percentages are computed over repositories where the column algorithm was detected (n in parentheses). Counts in (c) are non-exclusive, since repositories may implement multiple variants within a family.

(a) Algorithm-library distribution across repositories

Library	PPO *(n=110)*	DQN *(n=60)*	Q-Learning *(n=43)*	MAPPO *(n=52)*	QMIX *(n=44)*
PyTorch	83 (75.5%)	49 (81.7%)	32 (74.4%)	34 (65.4%)	34 (77.3%)
Gymnasium	46 (41.8%)	27 (45.0%)	12 (27.9%)	20 (38.5%)	10 (22.7%)
Ray/RLlib	27 (24.5%)	9 (15.0%)	2 (4.7%)	8 (15.4%)	4 (9.1%)
PettingZoo	18 (16.4%)	3 (5.0%)	0 (0.0%)	5 (9.6%)	0 (0.0%)
SB3	19 (17.3%)	7 (11.7%)	1 (2.3%)	1 (1.9%)	0 (0.0%)
TensorFlow	4 (3.6%)	9 (15.0%)	5 (11.6%)	1 (1.9%)	6 (13.6%)
JAX	11 (10.0%)	3 (5.0%)	5 (11.6%)	6 (11.5%)	6 (13.6%)

(b) Algorithm-environment co-occurrence

Algorithm	Gymnasium	PettingZoo	MPE	SMAC	OpenSpiel	GridWorld
PPO	41	34	31	26	15	12
DQN	24	25	15	14	9	9
Q-Learning	18	15	21	22	12	8
MAPPO	26	21	26	22	10	6
QMIX	21	19	25	26	11	4

(c) Repository-level prevalence of variants within selected algorithm families

Family	Variant	Repos	Family	Variant	Repos
DDPG	DDPG	33	PPO	PPO	110
DDPG	MADDPG	32	PPO	MAPPO	52
DQN	DQN	60	PPO	IPPO	31
DQN	DDQN	13	PPO	HAPPO	10
DQN	Double DQN	12	PPO	VDPPO	2
DQN	Rainbow	10	QMIX	QMIX	44
DQN	Dueling DQN	8	QMIX	VDN	34
DQN	DRQN	6	QMIX	WQMIX	5
DQN	QRDQN	6	SAC	SAC	36

4.2 Algorithm Selection and Configuration

This subsection examines which algorithm families practitioners adopt, how variants are distributed within those families, and where hyperparameter choices converge or diverge. The five most prevalent algorithms in our dataset are PPO (110 repositories), DQN (60), MAPPO (52), QMIX (44), and Q-Learning (43). Percentages in this subsection are computed over configuration files within the corresponding algorithm family.

High Consensus: QMIX shows the strongest hyperparameter consistency among the five algorithm families. As shown in Table 7, *double_q* = True is the only key exceeding 85% prevalence (85.9%). *target_update_interval* = 200 (80.8%), *buffer_size* = 5,000 (80.8%), and *mixing_embed_dim* = 32 (81.8%) also show strong, though slightly lower, consensus.

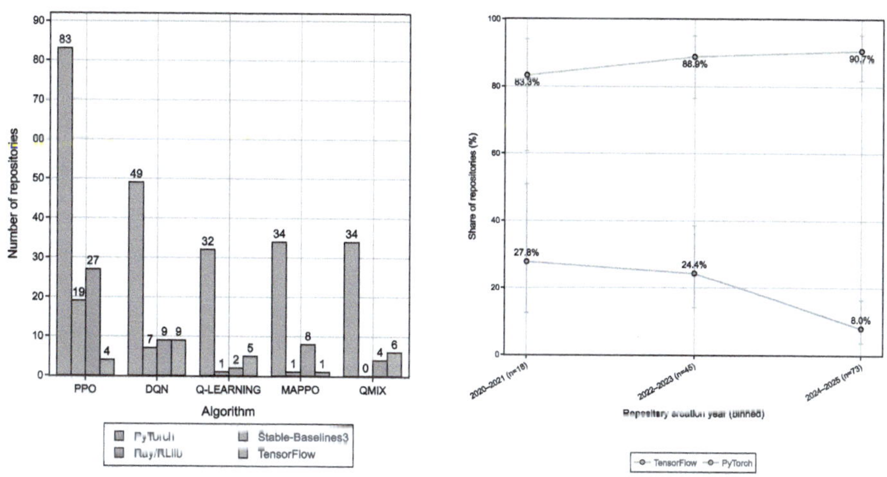

Fig. 1. RL library adoption patterns: algorithm-library usage (left) and PyTorch vs. TensorFlow adoption by repository creation year (right).

Table 4. Common PPO hyperparameter values across 395 YAML files.

Hyperparameter	Most frequent	2nd most frequent	3rd most frequent
gae_lambda	0.95 (274, 69.4%)	0.9 (3, 0.8%)	0.8 (1, 0.3%)
discount_factor	0.99 (228, 57.7%)	0.98 (21, 5.3%)	0.95 (16, 4.1%)
learning_rate	0.0007 (150, 38%)	0.0005 (45, 11.4%)	0.0004 (41, 10.4%)
activation	relu (184, 46.6%)	leaky_relu (47, 11.9%)	tanh (11, 2.8%)
vf_coef	1.0 (137, 34.7%)	0.25 (59, 14.9%)	0.5 (52, 13.2%)
ent_coef	0.01 (220, 55.7%)	0.0 (28, 7.1%)	0.000002 (1, 0.3%)

Table 5. Common MAPPO hyperparameter values across 2184 YAML files.

Hyperparameter	Most frequent	2nd most frequent	3rd most frequent
learning_rate	0.0007 (531, 38.9%)	0.001 (194, 14.2%)	0.0004 (102, 7.5%)
discount_factor	0.99 (1010, 73.9%)	0.95 (129, 9.4%)	0.98 (105, 7.7%)
representation	Basic_RNN (540, 39.5%)	Basic_MLP (357, 26.1%)	Basic_Identical (143, 10.5%)
activation	relu (912, 66.8%)	leaky_relu (240, 17.6%)	tanh (11, 0.8%)
running_steps	10000000 (376, 27.5%)	1000000 (248, 18.2%)	2000000 (138, 10.1%)
buffer_size	5000 (297, 21.7%)	128 (169, 12.4%)	100000 (147, 10.8%)
use_grad_clip	False (668, 48.9%)	True (463, 33.9%)	–
grad_clip_norm	0.5 (821, 60.1%)	10 (296, 21.7%)	100.0 (12, 0.9%)
use_actions_mask	False (560, 41%)	True (444, 32.5%)	–

Table 6. Common DQN and Q-Learning hyperparameter values across 92 and 175 YAML files.

	DQN		Q-Learning	
Hyperparameter	Most frequent	2nd most frequent	Most frequent	2nd most frequent
buffer_size	200000 (50, 28.6%)	100000 (32, 18.3%)	5000 (47, 51.1%)	100000 (8, 8.7%)
target_update_interval	500 (50, 28.6%)	100 (47, 26.9%)	200 (47, 51.1%)	100 (9, 9.8%)
learning_rate	0.001 (90, 51.4%)	0.0001 (53, 30.3%)	0.0007 (34, 37.0%)	0.001 (13, 14.1%)
discount_factor	0.99 (148, 84.6%)	0.9 (2, 1.1%)	0.99 (53, 57.6%)	0.9 (8, 8.7%)

Moderate Consensus: PPO and MAPPO show partial convergence around a small set of recurring hyperparameters. In PPO, the clearest recurring values are *gae_lambda* = 0.95 (69.4%) and *ent_coef* = 0.01 (55.7%) (Table 4). MAPPO (Table 5) shows a similar pattern, with recurring use of *discount_factor* and *activation*, while still varying in architectural choices such as representation (*Basic_RNN*: 39.5%, *Basic_MLP*: 26.1%). Taken together, these results suggest partial standardization around a limited set of defaults rather than broad agreement across all hyperparameters.

Low Consensus: DQN and Q-Learning exhibit the lowest degree of standardization. As shown in Table 6, both families vary substantially in *buffer_size*, *target_update_interval*, and *learning_rate*. Although *discount_factor* is the most stable hyperparameter in Q-Learning, its most common value, 0.99, still appears in only 57.6% of files, indicating limited value-level convergence.

Tables 8 and 9 summarize hyperparameter variability across algorithm families using the coefficient of variation (CV) for continuous parameters and normalized Shannon entropy for discrete ones. Among continuous parameters, *discount_factor* is the only consistently stable hyperparameter across all five families, with CV values below 0.06; *gae_lambda* is similarly stable in PPO and MAPPO, with CV values below 0.08. In contrast, *learning_rate*, *buffer_size*, *batch_size*, and *running_steps* show substantial variability, indicating limited convergence beyond a small set of shared defaults. Among discrete parameters, *policy*, *use_actions_mask*, and *agent* remain highly variable in several families.

Table 7. Top 3 values for common hyperparameter keys for QMIX.

Hyperparameter	Most frequent	2nd most frequent	3rd most frequent
buffer_size	5000 (160, 80.8%)	100000 (13, 6.6%)	2000 (4, 2.0%)
target_update_interval	200 (160, 80.8%)	100 (11, 5.6%)	10 (1, 0.5%)
double_q	True (170, 85.9%)	–	–
mixing_embed_dim	32 (162, 81.8%)	128 (13, 6.6%)	64 (8, 4.0%)
hypernet_embed	64 (105, 53.0%)	32 (60, 30.3%)	128 (12, 6.1%)
running_steps	10000000 (31, 30.7%)	1000000 (18, 17.8%)	2000000 (12, 11.9%)

Table 8. Hyperparameter variability across algorithm families (CV for continuous parameters; $n \geq 15$).

Hyperparameter	DQN	MAPPO	PPO	Q-Learning	QMIX
High consensus (CV < 0.1)					
discount_factor	0.010	0.014	0.055	0.031	0.007
gae_lambda	–	0.075	0.011	–	–
High variability (CV > 0.4)					
learning_rate	5.261	5.501	0.534	1.172	0.479
buffer_size	1.007	4.673	2.182	2.758	3.062
batch_size	0.682	1.320	3.483	1.608	1.765
running_steps	2.003	2.056	1.087	1.057	0.950

use_grad_clip is fully standardized in DQN, PPO, and Q-Learning, but shows near-maximum disagreement in MAPPO (0.976), indicating that gradient clipping practice is not standardized across MAPPO implementations. *double_q* reaches full consensus across all families where it appears. *use_rnn* shows moderate variability in most families but crosses into high variability in Q-Learning (0.811). *representation* shows moderate variability throughout, suggesting only partial convergence on architectural choices.

Figure 2 shows substantial variation in the median number of hyperparameter keys per configuration file, ranging from 3 to 42 across algorithms with at least 15 configuration files. The highest medians occur in *WQMIX* (42), *PDQN* (33), and *Double DQN* (31), whereas simpler baselines such as *FACMAC* (3), *DDPG* (6), and *SAC* (6) remain in the single digits. More specialized variants also tend to require larger hyperparameter sets than their base algorithms: *DQN* has a median of 9 keys, compared with 25–31 across its distributional variants; *PPO* increases from 10 to 12 in *IPPO* and 11 in *MAPPO*; and *QMIX* (15) and *VDN* (9) exceed Q-Learning (7). Overall, this suggests that configuration burden tends to increase with algorithm specialization.

4.3 Multi-agent Practices

We report repository-level prevalence of multi-agent implementation indicators across the five algorithm families and their variants (Fig. 3). Each heatmap cell shows the number of repositories in which an algorithm or variant exhibits a given indicator. Across base algorithms, *Instantiation of multiple agents* and *Multi-agent modules or classes found* show the highest prevalence. For example, *Instantiation of multiple agents* appears in 84.5% of PPO repositories (93/110; 95% Wilson CI [76.6, 90.1]). Other indicators occur less frequently, including *Multiple agent classes found* (25–45 repositories), *Multiple buffers found* (10–17), *Multiple policies found* (8–19), and *Parallel environment detected* (6–15). Variants follow the same relative ordering as their base algorithms but at lower absolute counts: among PPO variants, IPPO shows the highest counts (29 repositories for *Instantiation of multiple agents*), while HAPPO and VDPPO appear far less frequently. In the DQN family, Double DQN leads (15 repositories), and among Q-Learning variants, IQL (27) exceeds Double Q-Learning (21). WQMIX appears in substantially fewer repositories than QMIX (5 versus 43 for *Instantiation of multiple agents*). *Multiple buffers found* consistently shows the lowest prevalence across all families. Full 95% Wilson confidence intervals are provided in the replication package.

5 Validation

We validated five detectors: Multi-agent categorization, algorithm, library, environment, and hyperparameter detectors. Validation samples were generated from the detector outputs using scripts included in the replication package. For instance-level precision, we sampled detected occurrences for the algorithm, library, environment, and MARL-indicator detectors; for hyperparameters, we sampled detected configuration files. To reduce sampling bias towards large repositories, instance/file-level samples were stratified by repository. For recall, we sampled repositories or files from the dataset and manually checked whether the corresponding construct was present but missed by the detector. Each sampled item was manually inspected against the surrounding source-code or configuration context. A true positive required that the detected evidence correspond to the intended construct, rather than appearing only in comments, documentation, unrelated variable names, generic configuration files, or non-training artifacts. Validation was conducted by the first author, with ambiguous cases revisited after the initial pass. We report precision with 95% Wilson confidence intervals and, where feasible, recall at the repository or file level. Results are summarized in Tables 10 and 11; complete validation samples and scripts are provided in the replication package.

Environment Detector. Of 100 reported instances, 75 were true positives (precision = 0.750, 95% CI [0.657, 0.825]). Among 67 repositories manually confirmed to contain an environment setup, 57 were detected (recall = 0.851, 95% CI [0.747, 0.917]). The false negatives mainly concerned non-standard, domain-specific instantiation patterns or repositories with minimal executable code.

Table 9. Discrete hyperparameter variability across algorithm families (normalized Shannon entropy; 0 = full consensus, 1 = maximum disagreement; $n \geq 15$).

Hyperparameter	DQN	MAPPO	PPO	Q-Learning	QMIX
High variability (entropy > 0.8)					
policy	0.881	0.885	0.998	0.000	0.993
use_actions_mask	0.000	0.990	0.995	0.439	0.622
agent	0.878	0.876	0.666	0.258	0.486
use_grad_clip	0.000	0.976	0.000	0.000	0.107
use_rnn	–	0.662	0.684	0.811	0.582
Moderate variability (0.1 < entropy ≤ 0.8)					
representation	0.616	0.615	0.652	0.555	0.378
activation	0.145	0.387	0.607	0.000	0.000
use_parameter_sharing	–	0.358	0.689	0.000	0.253
Complete consensus (entropy = 0)					
double_q	0.000	0.000	–	0.000	0.000

Table 10. Environment detector validation

Level	Value	What was checked
Instance-level (detector-reported occurrences)		
Sampled instances	100	(repo, file, occurrence) outputs flagged by detector
TP/FP	75/25	True env instantiation/wrapping vs. non-env matches
Precision	0.750	95% CI: [0.657, 0.825]
Repository-level (coverage of env setup)		
Human-positive repositories	67	Repos manually confirmed to contain env setup code
TP/FN	57/10	Repo detected vs. repo missed
Repo level recall	0.851	95% CI: [0.747, 0.917]

Note: Precision = $TP/(TP + FP)$ over sampled instances; repo-level recall = $TP/(TP + FN)$ over repositories manually confirmed to contain env setup code.

Algorithm and Library Detectors. Manual checks confirm an algorithm detector precision of 0.890 (89/100; 95% CI [0.814, 0.937]) and repository-level recall of 0.953 (61/64; 95% CI [0.871, 0.984]). Its false positives arose from clues based solely on names or from closely related variants assigned canonical names. The library detector achieved instance-level precision of 1.000 (100/100; 95% CI [0.963, 1.000]) and repository-level recall of 1.000 (69/69; 95% CI [0.947, 1.000]).

MARL Detector. The classifier achieves repository level precision of 0.895 and recall of 0.785; MARL indicators yield instance-level precision of 0.760 (76/100; 95% CI [0.668, 0.833]) and repository-level recall of 0.896 (69/77; 95% CI [0.808, 0.946]) (full CIs in Table 11). False positives stem from non-MARL agentic tools;

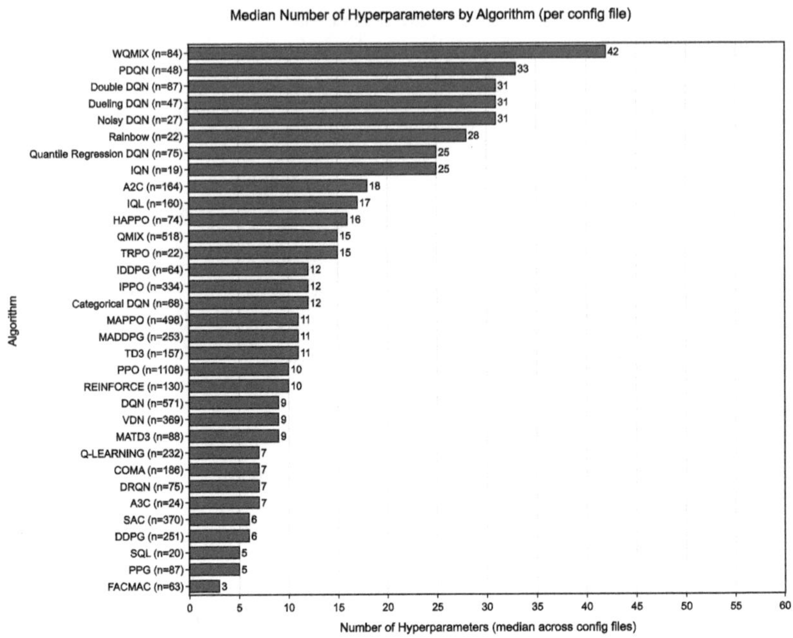

Fig. 2. Median number of hyperparameters by algorithm (algorithms with $n \geq 15$ configuration files).

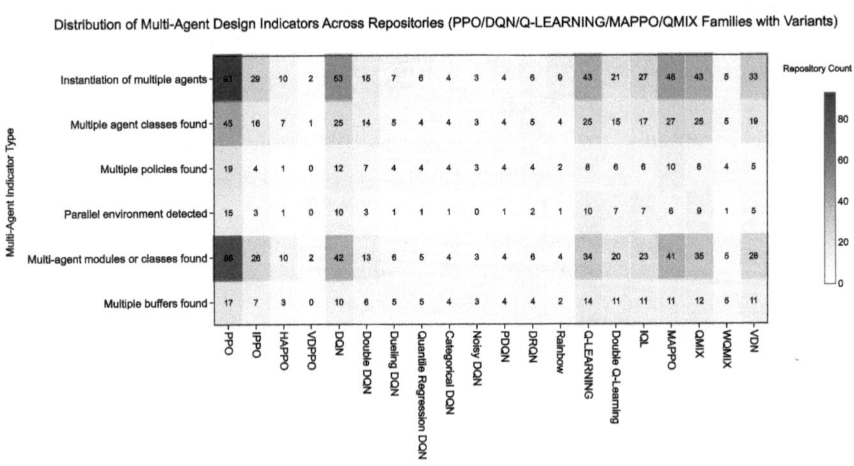

Fig. 3. Distribution of multi-agent indicators across RL algorithms.

false negatives from multi-agent structures implemented via indirect wrappers rather than standard APIs.

Hyperparameter Detector. Across 100 configuration files, precision was 0.890 (89/100; 95% CI [0.814, 0.937]) and file-level recall was 0.986 (71/72; 95% CI

[0.925, 0.998]). The false positives included generic CI YAML files and non-training configuration files.

6 Discussion

This section interprets our findings in relation to the research questions from Sect. 1 and discusses implications for practitioners and researchers.

6.1 RQ1: Algorithm Prevalence and Variant Adoption

RQ1 examined which algorithm families are most prevalent in open-source MARL repositories and how variant adoption appears within these families. The five most prevalent algorithms in our dataset are PPO (110 repositories), DQN (60), MAPPO (52), QMIX (44), and Q-Learning (43). Variant-level counts in Table 3 show that the relationship between base algorithms and their variants differs across families: PPO remains prevalent but coexists with substantial MAPPO and IPPO usage, DQN variants are more fragmented, DDPG and MADDPG show nearly equal repository prevalence, and the QMIX family includes both QMIX and VDN as strongly represented methods. These patterns indicate that variant adoption is family-specific: some families remain centered on a widely reused baseline, whereas others are organized around several specialized variants that are themselves reused across repositories. More specialized variants also tend to involve larger hyperparameter sets than their base algorithms (Fig. 2). DQN has a median of 9 hyperparameter keys, whereas distributional DQN-style variants reach 25–31; PPO increases from 10 to 12 in IPPO and 11 in MAPPO; and QMIX (15) and VDN (9) exceed Q-Learning (7).

For Practitioners. Widely reused families such as PPO and QMIX provide practical starting points, but adapting single-agent baselines to multi-agent settings through configuration changes alone may not capture important architectural differences, and practitioners should verify that such adaptations match their requirements.

For Researchers. The lower adoption of multi-agent-specific algorithms relative to single agent counterparts highlights an important question for future work: whether implementation complexity and configuration burden hinder reuse. Investigating what drives variant adoption remains an important direction, particularly in families where no single variant has achieved broad community reuse.

Table 11. Validation results for detection systems

Detector	Level	n	TP	FP	Precision [95% CI]
Algorithm	Instance	100	89	11	0.890 [0.814, 0.937]
Library	Instance	100	100	0	1.000 [0.963, 1.000]
Hyperparameter	File	100	89	11	0.890 [0.814, 0.937]
MARL indicators	Instance	100	76	24	0.760 [0.668, 0.833]
Detector	Level	n	TP	FN	Recall [95% CI]
Algorithm	Repository	64	61	3	0.953 [0.871, 0.984]
Library	Repository	69	69	0	1.000 [0.947, 1.000]
Hyperparameter	File	72	71	1	0.986 [0.925, 0.998]
MARL indicators	Repository	77	69	8	0.896 [0.808, 0.946]
Detector	Level	n	TP/FP	TN/FN	Precision/Recall [95% CI]
MARL classifier	Repository	80	51/6	9/14	0.895 [0.789, 0.951]/0.785 [0.670, 0.867]

Note: Wilson CIs throughout. Precision validated at instance/file level; recall measured against human-labeled positive sets at repo/file level.

6.2 RQ2: Consistency and Variability of Hyperparameters

RQ2 examined the extent to which MARL repositories converge on common hyperparameter conventions. Across the five most prevalent algorithm families, only a narrow shared core of hyperparameter choices appears consistently reused across repositories: *discount_factor* = 0.99 is stable throughout, and *gae_lambda* shows similarly strong convergence where applicable. Beyond this small core, however, hyperparameter practice is fragmented and strongly family-dependent. QMIX exhibits the strongest standardization, with *double_q* = True as the only key exceeding 85% prevalence (85.9%) and several others clustered just below, whereas PPO and MAPPO show only partial convergence around a limited set of recurring defaults. In contrast, DQN and Q-Learning display the weakest standardization, with substantial variation in training-scale and optimization parameters such as *buffer_size*, *batch_size*, and *learning_rate*. Tables 8 and 9 reinforce this pattern: a small number of parameters behave like widely reused defaults, while most hyperparameter choices remain highly variable across repositories. These patterns suggest that open-source MARL development relies on only a limited set of hyperparameter conventions, with much of the remaining tuning logic encoded in family-specific or project-specific choices rather than broadly shared practice.

For Practitioners. Parameters with high consensus (e.g., discount_factor = 0.99, gae_lambda = 0.95) may serve as reasonable starting points, while high-variability parameters such as buffer sizes, learning rates, and running steps likely require domain-specific tuning. More advanced algorithms also tend to involve larger hyperparameter sets, increasing development and debugging effort.

For Researchers. The limited standardization of hyperparameters beyond a few recurring defaults highlights the need for systematic studies of sensitivity and transferability across MARL settings. Evidence-based configuration guidance could help separate reusable defaults from task or algorithm-specific parameters and reduce trial and error in open-source MARL development.

6.3 RQ3: Recurring Combinations of Engineering Decisions

RQ3 examined which engineering decisions in MARL repositories recur together across algorithms, libraries, environments, and multi-agent patterns. PyTorch is the most widely used library across all five algorithm families, while other libraries appear in more family-specific combinations. Algorithm-environment pairings similarly show consistency rather than independent choices: PPO co-occurs frequently with Gymnasium, PettingZoo, SMAC, and MPE; DQN and Q-Learning are often paired with Gymnasium, PettingZoo, and SMAC-based environments; and QMIX co-occurs most strongly with SMAC. At the structural level, the most prevalent multi-agent indicators across families are *Instantiation of multiple agents* and *Multi-agent modules or classes found*, while more specialized patterns such as *Multiple policies found* and *Multiple buffers found* occur less frequently. These results suggest that engineering choices tend to appear in recurring combinations rather than as isolated decisions. Some pairings are concentrated around established benchmark ecosystems, such as QMIX with SMAC. The higher prevalence of simple structural patterns indicates that repositories in our dataset more often realize multi-agent behavior through straightforward implementation structures than through complex coordination-specific ones.

For Practitioners. When adopting an algorithm, practitioners may benefit from examining which libraries, environments, and structural patterns commonly accompany it in existing repositories (Table 3, Fig. 3). These recurring combinations can serve as practical reference points, though not as universally appropriate solutions.

For Researchers. The recurring combinations of engineering decisions in our dataset suggest that studies of individual factors, such as algorithms or hyperparameters, should account for implementation context, including library, environment, and system structure. The limited use of specialized multi-agent architectures also raises the question of whether their added complexity yields practical benefits.

7 Threats to Validity

Internal Validity. The dataset was compiled using GitHub search queries and broad MARL-related filtering criteria; repositories using unconventional names, descriptions, or topic labels may have been missed. We mitigated this by using diverse search terms, applying consistent inclusion and exclusion criteria, manually screening candidate repositories, and documenting repository metadata in the replication package. The resulting dataset should therefore be interpreted as a broad but not exhaustive sample of observable open-source MARL repositories.

External Validity. This study focuses on open-source MARL repositories on GitHub, so the findings primarily reflect engineering practices visible in public repositories. Proprietary or industrial MARL systems may follow different development processes, quality standards, and deployment constraints. The analyzed repositories also vary in maturity, maintenance activity, and intended purpose. A detailed stratification by repository quality or production readiness is outside the scope of this study; hence, our analysis focuses on broad engineering decisions observable in public MARL repositories at the time of data collection.

Construct Validity. Our static detectors may not fully capture design intent. This is most relevant for multi-agent indicators, where terms such as *Agent*, *Policy*, *Buffer*, or *multi* may reflect naming conventions or partial implementations rather than deliberate architectural choices. However, these indicators characterize structural patterns within repositories already identified as MARL implementations during manual screening; they are not used to classify repositories. We mitigated this risk through stratified manual validation and report precision, recall, and confidence intervals throughout. Since the environment and MARL-indicator detectors have lower precision than the remaining detectors, findings on environment usage and multi-agent structures should be interpreted as approximate prevalence estimates rather than exact measurements.

Validity of Conclusions. This study provides a descriptive empirical baseline rather than causal evidence on which practices lead to better performance. Some analyses are reported at the repository level while others, particularly hyperparameter summaries, are reported at the file level; repositories with more configuration files contribute proportionally more to file-level counts. We make the unit of analysis explicit in each table and interpret file-level results as configuration patterns in the analyzed dataset rather than as independent developer decisions. Future work could complement these findings with controlled experiments evaluating the impact of specific configuration choices on MARL performance.

8 Conclusion

Our study provides an empirical characterization of engineering decisions across 187 open-source MARL repositories. Open-source MARL development is concentrated around a small number of algorithm families, especially *PPO*, *DQN*, *QMIX*, and their variants. Hyperparameter standardization remains limited beyond a few recurring defaults, with substantial variation across repositories and a higher configuration burden in more specialized variants. Multi-agent behavior is more often realized through simple structural patterns such as agent instantiation and multiple agent classes than through specialized coordination abstractions, algorithms, libraries, or environments, and algorithms, libraries, environments, and multi-agent patterns co-occur in recurring combinations rather than appearing independently. These results provide an empirical baseline of current MARL practice and highlight opportunities for stronger standardization, improved tooling, and controlled studies of the impact of configuration on performance.

Acknowledgments. This work was supported by: FFG (Austrian Research Promotion Agency) project MODIS (no. FO999895431); project BEAM (no. FO999933314).

Disclosure of Interests. The authors have no competing interests to declare that are relevant to the content of this article.

Data Availability. The replication package is available at: https://doi.org/10.5281/zenodo.19656029.

References

1. Andrychowicz, M., et al.: What matters in on-policy reinforcement learning? A large-scale empirical study (2020). https://arxiv.org/abs/2006.05990
2. Avelino, G., Constantinou, E., Valente, M.T., Serebrenik, A.: On the abandonment and survival of open source projects: an empirical investigation. In: 2019 ACM/IEEE International Symposium on Empirical Software Engineering and Measurement (ESEM), pp. 1–12. IEEE (2019)
3. Bettini, M., Prorok, A., Moens, V.: Benchmarl: benchmarking multi-agent reinforcement learning. J. Mach. Learn. Res. **25**(217), 1–10 (2024)
4. Busoniu, L., Babuska, R., De Schutter, B.: A comprehensive survey of multiagent reinforcement learning. IEEE Trans. Syst. Man, Cybern. Part C (Appl. Rev.) **38**(2), 156–172 (2008)
5. Christianos, F., Schäfer, L., Albrecht, S.V.: Shared experience actor-critic for multi-agent reinforcement learning (2021). https://arxiv.org/abs/2006.07169
6. Engstrom, L., Ilyas, A., Santurkar, S., Tsipras, D., Janoos, F., Rudolph, L., Madry, A.: Implementation matters in deep RL: a case study on PPO and TRPO. In: International Conference on Learning Representations (2019)
7. Foerster, J.N.: Counterfactual multi-agent policy gradients. In: AAAI (2018)
8. Fu, W., Yu, C., Xu, Z., Yang, J., Wu, Y.: Revisiting some common practices in cooperative multi-agent reinforcement learning (2022). https://arxiv.org/abs/2206.07505
9. Henderson, P., Islam, R., Bachman, P., Pineau, J., Precup, D., Meger, D.: Deep reinforcement learning that matters. In: Proceedings of the AAAI Conference on Artificial Intelligence, vol. 32 (2018)
10. Hernandez-Leal, P., Kartal, B., Taylor, M.E.: A survey and critique of multiagent deep reinforcement learning. Auton. Agent. Multi-Agent Syst. **33**(6), 750–797 (2019)
11. Hu, S., et al.: Marllib: a scalable and efficient multi-agent reinforcement learning library. J. Mach. Learn. Res. **24**(315), 1–23 (2023)
12. Kalliamvakou, E., Gousios, G., Blincoe, K., Singer, L., German, D.M., Damian, D.: The promises and perils of mining github. In: Proceedings of the 11th Working Conference on Mining Software Repositories, pp. 92–101 (2014)

13. Khondhu, J., Capiluppi, A., Stol, K.J.: Is it all lost? A study of inactive open source projects. In: IFIP International Conference on Open Source Systems, pp. 61–79. Springer, Cham (2013)
14. Liang, E., et al.: Rllib: abstractions for distributed reinforcement learning. In: International Conference on Machine Learning, pp. 3053–3062. PMLR (2018)
15. Liaw, R., Liang, E., Nishihara, R., Moritz, P., Gonzalez, J.E., Stoica, I.: Tune: a research platform for distributed model selection and training. arXiv preprint arXiv:1807.05118 (2018)
16. Ntentos, E., Warnett, S.J., Zdun, U.: Supporting architectural decision making on training strategies in reinforcement learning architectures. In: 2024 IEEE 21st International Conference on Software Architecture (ICSA), pp. 90–100. IEEE (2024)
17. Orr, J., Dutta, A.: Multi-agent deep reinforcement learning for multi-robot applications: a survey. Sensors **23**(7), 3625 (2023)
18. Papoudakis, G., Christianos, F., Schäfer, L., Albrecht, S.V.: Benchmarking multi-agent deep reinforcement learning algorithms in cooperative tasks (2021). https://arxiv.org/abs/2006.07869
19. Raffin, A., Hill, A., Gleave, A., Kanervisto, A., Ernestus, M., Dormann, N.: Stable-baselines3: reliable reinforcement learning implementations. J. Mach. Learn. Res. **22**(268), 1–8 (2021)
20. Rashid, T., et al.: Qmix: monotonic value function factorisation for deep multi-agent reinforcement learning. In: ICML, vol. 80, p. 4295–4304 (2018)
21. Roesch, M., Linder, C., Zimmermann, R., Rudolf, A., Hohmann, A., Reinhart, G.: Smart grid for industry using multi-agent reinforcement learning. Appl. Sci. **10**(19), 6900 (2020)
22. Rutherford, A., et al.: Jaxmarl: multi-agent RL environments and algorithms in JAX. Adv. Neural. Inf. Process. Syst. **37**, 50925–50951 (2024)
23. Samvelyan, M., et al.: The starcraft multi-agent challenge. CoRR **abs/1902.04043** (2019)
24. Shalev-Shwartz, S., Shammah, S., Shashua, A.: Safe, multi-agent, reinforcement learning for autonomous driving. arXiv preprint arXiv:1610.03295 (2016)
25. Sunehag, P., et al.: Value-decomposition networks for cooperative multi-agent learning. arXiv preprintarXiv:1706.05296 (2017)
26. Terry, J.K., Black, B.J.: Pettingzoo: gym for multi-agent reinforcement learning. In: NeurIPS Datasets and Benchmarks Track (2021)
27. Yu, C., et al.: The surprising effectiveness of PPO in cooperative, multi-agent games (2022). https://arxiv.org/abs/2103.01955

Selecting GitHub Repositories for Electroencephalography-Based Code Quality Assessment

Sophie Chaveli(✉), Steve Counsell, Stephen Swift, and Mahir Arzoky

Department of Computer Science, University of London, Brunel, UK
{sophie.chaveli,steve.counsell,stephen.swift,mahir.arzoky}@brunel.ac.uk

Abstract. Selecting Java code for *in vitro* experiments where human participants are asked to assess its quality is a non-trivial task. As a priority, we would want to ensure that as *diverse* a set of Java language constructs, idioms and features were included in the selected code. This paper proposes a systematic methodology for selecting a representative and reproducible subset of small, human-readable GitHub repositories for researchers conducting human-centred software engineering studies. Java projects were randomly sampled from GitHub and their suitability was justified through the use of machine learning and statistical analysis techniques. Subset selection was performed using heuristic search methods - specifically Hill Climbing and Simulated Annealing to maximise diversity with respect to a set of carefully targeted and selected code-based metrics. The resulting dataset was constructed as the union of unique repositories across multiple candidate subsets, each of which was independently validated to outperform random selection. While the approach is particularly suited to studies using electroencephalography (EEG), it could apply equally to a broad range of experimental settings where human participants are required to look at and assess code.

Keywords: GitHub · Dataset Creation · Software Metrics · Electroencephalography · Machine Learning · Heuristic Search

1 Introduction

Common approaches for assessing software code quality in the past have relied on generating a wide variety of software metrics from a large codebase using an automated tool and then inspecting the generated data for outliers or unusual patterns in the generated data [1,2]. Peer review has also been used as a visual approach for identifying problems in code using a manual inspection approach. The motivation for using each is clear - fixing defects late in the development process can be up to thirty times more costly than addressing them in early testing phases [3]. On the other hand, assessing code for its quality in an *in vitro* experimental setting using human participants also brings its own challenges. Most

C. Berger and V. Klös (Eds.): SEAA 2026, LNCS 16864, pp. 465–481, 2027.
https://doi.org/10.1007/978-3-032-36587-3_32

importantly, how do we choose code that is of a manageable size for the experimental subjects in a time-restricted experimental setting and yet still contain a diverse set of language features? Code with relatively large numbers of comments, code that has excessive loop constructs, assignment statements or code that makes sole use of polymorphic methods, for example, may skew the assessment by the experimental subjects; a combination of code features is less likely to cause that effect. Moreover, large-scale repositories and benchmark datasets [4,5] are usually optimised solely for use in machine learning or static analysis applications limiting their suitability for studies where humans are required to assess code for its quality. These challenges are made worse in the context of cognitive measurement techniques such as *electroencephalography* (EEG), a non-invasive method which records electrical brain activity *via* electrodes placed on the scalp. For such studies, the wider the variation in stimuli (i.e., code features) the better, since different language constructs will probably evoke different sets of cognitive responses in each of the experimental subjects, thereby giving a far richer data set and providing more wide-reaching study conclusions.

The aim in this paper is to describe the construction of a dataset to support investigations into the relationship between developers' cognitive responses captured through EEG devices and perceived code quality. We propose a repeatable methodology for constructing subsets of GitHub repositories tailored to human-centred and EEG-based code evaluation. We first sample Java projects from GitHub and apply filtering criteria based on structural properties to ensure that selected repositories are of sufficient size and readability for experimental use. Machine learning techniques are then used to distinguish smaller systems from larger repositories. Finally, we formulate subset selection as a combinatorial optimisation problem and apply heuristic search methods, specifically Hill Climbing and Simulated Annealing to select a diverse set of repositories. This selection is based on software and GitHub metrics and maximises Euclidean distance, ensuring maximal diversity within experimental constraints. While motivated in this instance by EEG based code quality assessment, the methodology could be applied to any empirical study requiring carefully selected real-world software systems where humans have to review/assess code.

The work in this paper thus makes the following two key contributions. Firstly, it offers a description of the dataset construction problem in human-centred software engineering, highlighting the need for smaller, interpretable code suitable for human analysis and EEG-based studies. Secondly, it provides a reproducible GitHub Java repository filtering pipeline and generalisable methodology for constructing representative, small-scale and cognitively accessible code datasets for human-centred empirical software engineering research. The remainder of this paper is organised as follows. In Sect. 2, we review relevant background and related work. Section 3 describes the methodology; in Sect. 4, we present and discuss results before outlining threats to validity (Sect. 5). Finally, Sect. 6 draws conclusions and suggests directions for future work.

2 Background

Although previous work has explored human interaction with source code in relation to comprehension and perceived quality, the community has given scant attention to rigorous dataset selection (and the features it contains). Controlled experiments using artificially constructed or simplified code snippets [6,7] provide strong experimental control, but lack validity since they do not reflect the complexity of real-world software systems. Often, only *toy* examples are used, because they are small - but of course they lack industrial-strength complexity. In contrast, studies based on open-source repositories [8] offer realism but are typically limited to manually selected projects and do not provide a reproducible approach for constructing representative datasets from large-scale sources such as GitHub. Consequently, there is a methodological "gap" in the construction of datasets which are both a) representative of real software systems and b) suitable for controlled experimental or EEG-based evaluation.

Many EEG studies in software engineering are relatively short, typically lasting between thirty minutes and one hour, with short breaks incorporated throughout the experiment. For example, Peitek et al., [9] found that a sixty-minute experiment with a 'voluntary break after twenty minutes and forty minutes' was effective for maintaining participant engagement. The dataset used was taken from the authors' GitHub replication repository and comprised 32 code snippets totalling 754 Lines Of Code (LOC) as reported by GitHub. This corresponds to a mean of 23.6 LOC per snippet, with a standard deviation of 7.1. Similarly, Calcagno et al., [10] designed an experiment consisting of three tasks, with a total duration of approximately 28 min. However, very little detail about the code dataset used was discussed. Yeh et al., [11] used 12 code snippets described as: 'as small as possible' with an average of 1.9 LOC per snippet [6]. These studies suggest that experimental sessions involving neurophysiological measurements should remain brief to avoid fatigue and maintain participant attention, which in turn motivates the use of smaller software systems according to the approach described in this paper.

Code review studies such as those by Kemerer & Paulk [12] suggest that reviews should typically examine between 140 and 280 lines of code per hour and should not exceed approximately two hours in total. Additionally, industry guidelines from organisations such as Google and the Linux Kernel Project [13, 14] recommend keeping code changes small. On the other hand, some studies suggest a broader upper bound for practical review sizes, especially for Java systems. Kudrjavets et al., [15] reported that an acceptable size for a code review was approximately 800 LOC. Additionally, Nanz & Furia [16] observed that Java programs (the language used in this study) are, on average, 2.22.9 times longer than programs written in functional or scripting languages. This further justifies the use of a somewhat larger Total Lines of Code (TLOC) threshold. In terms of the uniqueness of our research, we know of no work in the EEG world where a dataset has been produced using the combined techniques of data mining and software metrics.

3 Methodology

3.1 Selection of GitHub Sample

A random sampling approach was adopted to obtain a representative set of projects, implemented using the GitHub REST API. The design of the data collection process was informed by practical constraints, including API rate limits of 5k requests per hour for authenticated requests. Java was selected as the focus of this study due to its widespread adoption and the availability of mature analysis tools; this also enabled consistent and automated extraction of software metrics, since most tools are applicable to just one language. Restricting the dataset to a single language also reduced variability and supported more reliable comparison across projects. As of 2025, the GitHub API reported that GitHub hosted over 17 million public Java repositories. Even at the authenticated limit, retrieving metadata for all Java repositories would require approximately 3,400 h (approx. 141 days) of continuous requests, excluding repositories created during that period. As a result, exhaustive analysis was not a viable option. The challenge is both the scale of available repositories and ensuring that the sampled dataset is representative of the diversity of projects on GitHub. In the context of human-subject EEG experiments, this is particularly important since biased or homogeneous code samples may influence participant responses and reduce the validity and impact of observed effects. Naïve sampling strategies, such as selecting only recent or highly active repositories risked introducing temporal and activity-based biases.

To address these sampling issues, several random 30-day windows were selected between the launch of GitHub in 2008 and the most recently completed year at the time of data collection (2024). Within these windows, Java repositories were retrieved through the GitHub API. Because results are paginated (up to 100 per page), a random page and repository were selected iteratively to maintain temporal randomness while remaining within rate limits. To capture a diverse range of repository sizes, measured in TLOC, a random sample of 1,000 Java repositories was selected from the population providing an estimated $\pm 3\%$ margin of error at a 95% confidence level if sampling for a feature such as TLOC. The sample size was chosen to balance representativeness with feasibility, ensuring adequate coverage of the TLOC distribution while remaining suitable for detailed analysis. Ten repositories with no code were removed, along with one repository excluded for inappropriate content. This gave a final dataset of 989 repositories. Following repository selection, their GitHub metadata and current codebase (as of 25 August 2025) were downloaded. Each repository was then assigned a unique identification number based on its alphabetical position. The following GitHub metadata metrics were included:

- `stargazers_count`: The number of users who have starred the repository, indicating its popularity within the developer community.
- `forks_count`: The number of times the repository has been forked, reflecting reuse or independent development by other users.

- open_issues_count: The number of unresolved issues associated with the repository, suggesting ongoing maintenance needs or potential problems.
- subscribers_count: The number of users subscribed to repository updates, indicating continued interest in its development.

3.2 Software Metrics Extracted

The selected software metrics were collected to support two objectives. Firstly, they characterised repository size and structural complexity, providing context for interpreting human assessments of readability in subsequent experiments. Secondly, they were intended to capture a wide set of structural code properties (e.g., size, complexity and distributional characteristics) allowing analysis of which software attributes most influenced code quality. *Understand* (v7.1, available at scitools.com) was the static analysis tool used to generate the metrics across all repositories and was executed on the full sample containing 25,280,071 TLOC. The resulting metrics were collated and categorised according to a scope (i.e., Method, Class or File), grouped using typical statistical summaries (see Table 1). Certain metrics, such as MaxCyclomatic representing the maximum McCabe Cyclomatic Complexity [17] observed within a given scope, were preferred over cumulative measures (e.g., total Cyclomatic Complexity), since they are less sensitive to project size and provide more interpretable indicators of structural complexity across repositories of varying scale.

3.3 Machine Learning Classification Pipeline

This study adopts a threshold of 1,000 TLOC as a pragmatic compromise between ensuring sufficient implementation detail and maintaining readability within a limited review period. Although heuristic, and somewhat larger than thresholds used in prior studies, this value captures a point at which repositories exhibit meaningful structural characteristics without becoming impractical to read. To support this choice, machine learningbased classification is used to compare repositories above and below the threshold, demonstrating that it provides a meaningful boundary.

Four distinct datasets were constructed from available repositories, each corresponding to a different preprocessing configuration. The number of datasets was determined pragmatically to provide a manageable yet sufficiently diverse set of variations, enabling systematic comparison across preprocessing strategies. The data was split into smaller subsets to improve computational efficiency and enable effective model training and evaluation. Feature complexity was addressed through the selective removal of certain variables, both to reduce computational burden and to assess the relative importance and effectiveness of individual features within the modelling process. Finally, particular attention was given to the prevention of *data leakage*, defined as the inclusion of features that directly encode or trivially approximate the target variable (e.g., repository metrics such as number of files that are strongly correlated with TLOC). Such features can

Table 1. Extracted software metrics per scope.

Metric	Scope
Internal metrics (avg/min/max/std)	
CountLine	F, C, M
CountLineBlank	F, C, M
CountLineCode	F, C, M
CountLineCodeDecl	F, C, M
CountLineCodeExe	F, C, M
CountLineComment	F, C, M
RatioCommentToCode	F, C, M
MaxCyclomatic	F, C
MaxNesting	F, C, M
MaxInheritanceTree	C
Repository-level maxima (max)	
MaxCyclomatic_max	R
MaxInheritanceTree_max	R
MaxNesting_max	R
Repository totals (count)	
numberOfFiles	R
numberOfPackages	R
numberOfClasses	R
numberOfMethods	R
Lines of code (total / avg)	
TLOCFile/averageFileLength	F
TLOCClass/averageClassLength	C
TLOCMethod/averageMethodLength	M
F = File, C = Class, M = Method, R = Repository	

inflate performance estimates by implicitly encoding the target through proxy relationships. To mitigate this risk, all features were systematically reviewed for direct or indirect association with the classifier. This process combined an initial manual inspection by the authors with an independent assessment by a large language model (ChatGPT v.04-mini). To mitigate hallucinations, the human research team systematically verified all outputs. Any disagreement, regardless of whether it originated from a human reviewer or the large language model, triggered a panel review.

Features were classified using a traffic-light scheme as follows: red indicated a direct or near-deterministic relationship with TLOC, orange a potential proxy relationship and green representing no meaningful association. Based on this traffic light system, the resulting four datasets differ in their treatment of TLOC-related features and the application of normalisation. Minmax normalisation, which scales values between 0 and 1 by subtracting the minimum value of a feature and dividing by its range, was chosen to ensure that all metrics were comparable. This was primarily applied to compositional metrics describing the distribution of line types within files (e.g., `CountLineCodeExe_File_avg`, `CountLineComment_File_avg`). By contrast, metrics representing the total number of lines in a file (e.g., `CountLine_File_avg`, `CountLine_File_max`) were not normalised, since they reflect absolute scale rather than relative composition. The following datasets were created by following this procedure:

- **Dataset A:** Features with an obvious relationship to TLOC (those categorised as red in the traffic light system) were removed or min–max normalised (those categorised as orange in the traffic light system).
- **Dataset B:** All features were retained, with selected metrics min–max normalised.
- **Dataset C:** Features with an obvious relationship to TLOC were removed and all remaining metrics were min–max normalised.
- **Dataset D:** All features were retained and all metrics were min–max normalised.

A machine learning pipeline was implemented using *scikit-learn* [18] (v1.7.2). *Scikit-learn* has been used extensively in this area to analyse software systems [7,19]. The dataset comprised 311 repositories below 1,000 TLOC (as measured by *Understand*) and 678 above this threshold. Machine learning models were trained to predict a binary class label indicating whether a repository exceeded 1,000 TLOC. Performance was assessed using 10-fold cross-validation, repeated 100 times per model, with mean results recorded. Hyperparameters were tuned via *scikit-learn*'s GridSearch. The selected methods cover the principal categories of machine learning, excluding neural networks due to the complexity of their optimisation. The following machine learning methods were therefore investigated:

- Random Forest (RF): Constructs a collection of decision trees, aggregating their outputs to produce a final classification.
- Logistic Regression (LR): Models the probability of class membership via a logistic function.
- Naïve Bayes (NB): Applies Bayes' theorem, assuming feature independence, to estimate the posterior probability of each class.
- Support Vector Machine (SVM): Identifies the optimal separating hyperplane that maximises the margin between classes.
- K-Nearest Neighbour (KNN): Assigns a class label based on the majority vote of the k nearest neighbours in the feature space.

Following the selection of Dataset C based on the machine learning experiments (Sect. 4.1), results showed that projects could be reliably distinguished using the 1,000 TLOC threshold. This motivated further investigation into which metrics were driving this separation and whether non-informative features could be removed to improve the efficiency of subsequent analyses. A MannWhitney U test was therefore applied to identify metrics that significantly differed between projects above and below 1,000 TLOC. P-values were adjusted using both the False Discovery Rate and Bonferroni corrections to control for multiple comparisons. All metrics were found to be statistically significant ($p \leq 0.05$) except for `Count_LineBlank_Method_min`, `forks_count`, `stargazers_count`, and `MaxNesting_Method_avg`. Based on these results, three derived datasets were constructed:

- **Dataset E1**: Contained only metrics that were found to be statistically significantly different.
- **Dataset E2**: Contained only metrics that were not statistically significantly different.
- **Dataset E3**: Contained all metrics, regardless of statistical significance.

3.4 Heuristic Search

From each of the three datasets (**E1**, **E2**, and **E3**), five repositories were selected using two heuristic search algorithms to maximise the likelihood of obtaining a sufficient number of unique repositories. We note that the number five was chosen arbitrarily and may be adjusted in future iterations of the experiment. These selections were combined and the unique repositories formed the final dataset (**Dataset F**) used in the experiment. Selecting a subset with maximally diverse features exemplifies the 'Maximum Diversity Problem', which has been proven to be NP-hard [20]. As a result, an exhaustive search over all possible subsets was infeasible, since there are 23,474,070,697 distinct five-element subsets of the 311 elements. Consequently, the final subset was obtained using two heuristic optimisation algorithms: Random Restart Hill Climber (RRHC) and Simulated Annealing (SA). The two algorithms were selected as they are widely adopted, standard methods in the literature [21,22] and are known to produce consistent and reliable outputs. Additionally, this paper is intended as a proof of concept and therefore focuses on commonly used methods that are representative of standard practice, rather than necessarily the most optimal alternatives. The RRHC is an optimisation algorithm based on hill climbing, which iteratively moves to neighbouring solutions that improve a given fitness function. RRHC performs multiple short Hill Climbing runs from different random starting points, allowing broader exploration of the search space and reducing the likelihood of becoming trapped in local optima - see Algorithm 1.

SA further addresses this limitation by probabilistically accepting worse solutions, enabling escape from local optima and improving the chance of locating the global optimum. The probability of accepting inferior solutions is controlled by a temperature parameter, which gradually decreases according to a cooling rate. Early in the search, high temperatures promote exploration, while lower temperatures at a later stage favour fitness improvements - see Algorithm 2.

The fitness function, which the heuristic algorithms sought to maximise, was

Algorithm 1. Random Restart Hill Climbing

Require: Number of restarts R, maximum iterations per restart $Iter$
Ensure: Approximate optimal solution S_{best}

```
Initialise S_best as null
Initialise f_best = -∞ {Assuming a maximisation problem}
for r = 1 to R do
    Initialise S as a randomly generated solution
    for i = 0 to Iter - 1 do
        Compute the fitness F = fitness(S)
        Generate a neighbouring solution S' of S by swapping an element of S with
        a randomly chosen element not in S.
        Compute the fitness F' = fitness(S')
        if F' > F then
            Accept the new solution: S = S'
            Compute fitness F = fitness(S)
        end if
    end for
    if F > F_best then
        Update best solution: S_best = S
        Update best fitness: F_best = F
    end if
end for
return S_best
```

designed to select the most dissimilar repositories, exposing participants to a broad range of codebases. This enables clearer identification of positively and negatively evaluated characteristics and patterns in developers' assessments of code attributes. To calculate the fitness function:

Let $V = 1, 2, \ldots, n$, let $I \subset V$ such that $|I| = k$ (a fixed constant), and then let $S = [I]$, i.e. S is the list version of subset A. As well, note that the choice of ordering does not affect the value of the fitness function, as all pairwise combinations are considered regardless of order. Each repository S_i is represented by a feature vector $\mathbf{x}_{S_i} \in \mathbb{R}^m$, where m is the number of features and $x_{S_i,\ell}$ denotes the value of the ℓ-th feature of repository S_i.

The distance between two repositories S_i and S_j is given by the Euclidean distance (here, ψ is used to represent distance, departing from its usual notation) between their respective feature vectors:

$$\psi_{S_i, S_j} = \sqrt{\sum_{\ell=1}^{m} \left(x_{S_i,\ell} - x_{S_j,\ell}\right)^2} \tag{1}$$

These distances collectively define a symmetric, non-negative distance matrix $\Psi \in \mathbb{R}^{n \times n}$, with entries $\psi_{ij} \in \mathbb{R}$ satisfying:

$$\psi_{ij} \geq 0, \quad \psi_{ij} = \psi_{ji}, \quad \psi_{ii} = 0 \tag{2}$$

Algorithm 2. Simulated Annealing Procedure

Require: Initial temperature T_0, number of iterations *Iter*, cooling rate α
Ensure: Approximate optimal solution S

Initialise S as a randomly generated solution
for $i = 0$ to $Iter - 1$ **do**
  Compute fitness $F = \text{fitness}(S)$
  Generate a neighbouring solution S' by applying a small change to S
  Compute fitness $F' = \text{fitness}(S')$
  if f' is worse than f **then**
    Compute acceptance probability $P = \text{PR}(f', f, T_i)$
    Generate a random number $u \sim \text{Uniform}(0, 1)$
    if $p < u$ **then**
      Reject the new solution and retain S
    else
      Accept the new solution: $S = S'$
      Compute fitness $F = \text{fitness}(S)$
    end if
  else
    Accept the new solution: $S = S'$
  end if
  Update temperature: $T_{i+1} = \lambda T_i$
end for
return S

The fitness function $f(S)$ is defined as the sum of pairwise distances between all repositories in the selected subset S:

$$f(S) = \sum_{i=1}^{k-1} \sum_{j=i+1}^{k} \psi_{S_i, S_j} \tag{3}$$

For SA, the `Starting Temperature` (T_0) is dependent on the dataset being investigated. An appropriate initial temperature is estimated using a sacrificing sub-algorithm. The probability of accepting a worse solution comes from the Boltzmann constant thanks to the physical system the algorithm is based on which can be simplified down to:

$$P = e^{-\Delta f / T_i} \tag{4}$$

where P is the probability of accepting a worse solution, Δf is change in fitness and T_i is the current temperature. Setting the chance that the SA algorithm should accept a worse solution at e^{-1} at the very beginning of the run, the formula can be written as:

$$e^{-1} = e^{-\Delta f / T_0} \tag{5}$$

Rearranging, $T_0 = \Delta f$. Therefore, 10% of the total runs are allocated to determining a suitable initial temperature [23]. A random starting subset is generated, and its fitness evaluated. A small change is made and the new fitness recalculated. If the new fitness is worse, the decrease is added to a cumulative sum

Table 2. Summary fitness statistics from random restarts and calculated algebraic average results.

Dataset	Average	Median	Std Dev	Maximum	Algebraic Average
E1	13.9	13.2	5.2	35.5	13.9
E2	1.7	1.6	0.8	5.9	1.7
E3	14.1	13.4	5.3	36.6	14.1

to estimate the average fitness loss. The initial acceptance probability for worse solutions is set to $e^{-1} \approx 0.37$ and gradually reduced according to the cooling rate in subsequent runs.

Cooling Rate (λ) is calculated using the following formula [23]:

$$\lambda = \sqrt[\text{Iter}]{\frac{T_{\text{Iter}}}{T_0}} \tag{6}$$

where *Iter* = iterations, $T_{\text{Iter}} = 0.001$.

Both the Hill Climbing and Simulated Annealing algorithms were configured to operate under an equivalent computational budget (number of iterations) to ensure a fair comparison. Each algorithm was evaluated over 100 independent runs, with 100,000 iterations per run, giving a total of 10,000,000 iterations per method. For the RRHC approach, each run was divided into 10 independent restarts of 10,000 iterations each, whereas the SA algorithm employed a single continuous search per run using the full 100,000-iteration budget.

4 Results

4.1 Classification Results

For the machine learning classification, all datasets achieved high classification accuracy across the chosen models. RF consistently produced the highest average accuracy (98.4%), while KNN performed the weakest (89.5%). Datasets A and C achieved accuracies of 97.0% and 97.1%, respectively, both with an F-measure of 0.966. Datasets B and D achieved the highest overall performance, with accuracies of 99.7% and F-measures of 0.997. Despite slightly lower accuracy compared to Datasets B and D, Dataset C was selected for the heuristic search algorithms. This decision was made because it achieved strong performance while excluding features directly related to TLOC, thereby reducing potential data leakage and improving the robustness of the model.

4.2 Heuristic Search Results

To establish a baseline for comparison and assess the heuristic search algorithms' effectiveness, one million separate random subsets of five items each were drawn from the dataset, with the fitness of each subset calculated. Results can be found in Table 2.

Additionally, a theoretical average of the entire dataset can be calculated as follows: We define the fitness function (as discussed in Eq. 3) as

$$f(S) = \sum_{i=1}^{k-1} \sum_{j=i+1}^{k} \psi(S_i, S_j) \tag{7}$$

For the purposes of this proof, we will work with an alternative fitness function defined as:

$$\hat{f}(S) = \sum_{i=1}^{k} \sum_{j=1}^{k} \psi(S_i, S_j) = \sum_{i=1}^{k} \sum_{j=1}^{k} \psi_{ij} \tag{8}$$

Given that $\psi(i,i) = 0$, it is clear (without loss of generality) that

$$\hat{f}(S) = 2f(S) \tag{9}$$

We wish to compute the average fitness of all possible instances of S. To do this, we first consider how many times any two arbitrary items will appear in the same subset S. We can calculate this by rephrasing the problem as follows: consider a bag with n balls, where two are marked T and U, respectively. We then draw k balls. The probability that T and U are drawn is

$$\Pr(T \text{ and } U \text{ drawn}) = \frac{2}{n} \times \frac{1}{n-1} \times \binom{k}{2} = \frac{k(k-1)}{n(n-1)} \tag{10}$$

Hence, the number of times T and U will appear together if we consider all combinations of S is

$$\binom{n}{k} \times \frac{k(k-1)}{n(n-1)} = \frac{n!}{k!(n-k)!} \times \frac{k(k-1)}{n(n-1)} \tag{11}$$

Simplifying, we get

$$\frac{(n-2)!}{(k-2)!((n-2)-(k-2))!} = \binom{n-2}{k-2} \tag{12}$$

We can now rephrase the average of $\hat{f}(S)$ over all instances of S as the sum of all possible $\psi(i,j)$ multiplied by the number of times i and j appear together, divided by the total number of possible S:

$$\text{Average } \hat{f}(S) = \sum_{i=1}^{n} \sum_{j=1}^{n} \frac{k(k-1)}{n(n-1)} \psi(i,j) = \frac{k(k-1)}{n(n-1)} \times \text{Sum}(\Psi) \tag{13}$$

where $\text{Sum}(\Psi) = \sum_{i=1}^{n} \sum_{j=1}^{n} \psi_{ij}$ denotes the sum of all entries in Ψ. Finally, the average of $f(S)$ is

$$\frac{1}{2} \text{ Average } \hat{f}(S) \tag{14}$$

For the currently selected sample, the theoretical average was calculated for each dataset and the results can be seen in Table 2. As shown, the theoretical

Table 3. HC vs SA Data

Dataset	HC	SA	Fitness
E1	36, 573, 699, 923, 963	36, 573, 699, 923, 963	39.2
E2	N/A	446, 484, 544, 592, 923	8.4
E3	36, 573, 699, 923, 963	36, 573, 878, 923, 963	39.9

Table 4. Final dataset for experiments.

ID	TLOC	GitHub ID	Description
36	300	`/ALRubinger/jboss-as-deployment`	Deployment Contracts for JBoss Application Server
446	48	`/joaomlneto/travis-ci-tutorial-java`	Using travis-ci in a Java project
484	271	`/kitplummer/PosRepToKml`	Position Report to KML
544	51	`/lydonchandra/rydex`	Basic project scaffold with test suite
573	997	`/mayooresan/Android-TamilUtil`	Convert Unicode string to Bamini, Anjal, TAB, TAM and TSCII
592	118	`/mihasya/sample-java-nio-server`	Small async server in Java
699	117	`/qht1003077897/hellocharts-line`	Modified implementation of an Android charting library
923	27	`/winks/projectfoo`	Calculates the difference between the square of the sum and the sum of the squares of numbers from 1 to 100
963	15	`/YuhannciaMaryS/Java_substring`	Starter template for a Java Substring method

averages were found to be the same as the average of the million sample subsets also found in Table 2 which allows researchers to gain an understanding of their datasets without having to generate and test large numbers of samples. The outputs of the heuristic search algorithms are presented in Table 3 and consistently outperformed the random selections and calculated averages shown in Table 2. Consistency between repeats was assessed using the Jaccard index [24]; all results obtained using SA produced a value of 1. The RRHC algorithm produced consistent results for datasets **E1** and **E3**, whereas dataset **E2** yielded an average Jaccard index of 0.58. 16 unique combinations were identified; however, all combinations resulted in the same fitness value. Due to the large number of combinations, they have been marked as N/A in Table 3 for space and clarity. These fitness values were lower than those achieved by SA and, consequently, have not been included in the final results.

4.3 Final Dataset

The final dataset **Dataset F** was constructed by aggregating all unique values as shown in Table 4. It comprises 1,944 TLOC, which participants can scan without requiring full comprehension or modification. The median TLOC is 117, with a mean of 216 and standard deviation of 292.7. Typically, software engineering datasets are very large in size, however the inclusion of only nine repositories in this specific dataset is particularly beneficial for the intended purpose. The compact size enables feasible human review, while the nine repository total allows for an average allocation of approximately seven minutes per repository in subsequent experiments (subject to adjustment depending on repository size). The selected repositories, shown in Table 4, span diverse topics that include server deployment, novice coding projects and encoding conversions. High fitness values ensure that repository features are widely distributed, making the chosen repositories highly dissimilar. In the experiments we plan to use this dataset for, participants will rank these repositories according to perceived quality. The high dissimilarity of the repositories will make it easier to determine which metrics participants consider important and these rankings will be analysed together with recorded EEG data.

5 Threats to Validity

Any study with and empirical component needs to consider threats to its validity. With respect to *internal* validity, only the *Understand* metrics tool was employed in this study. Nevertheless, it is a well-established and reliable software analysis tool, widely adopted within the software engineering research community [25,26]. To mitigate selection bias, the sole criterion applied to the sample was that it comprised Java-based projects; otherwise, the sample was entirely random. Heuristic searches employed a sufficient number of iterations as determined from the convergence graphs.

Regarding *external* validity, the study analysed only Java code. However, Java is one of the most widely used programming languages and is currently the fourth most hosted language on GitHub. It is also the most popular Object-Oriented language on GitHub, as of 2025. Additionally, the proposed experiment is focused on programming capability not on language. The dataset was sufficiently large to provide a reasonable representation of the broader population, though the focus on smaller repositories may affect the generalisability of the findings. Furthermore, only public GitHub repositories were considered, which may not be representative of private or enterprise software systems.

To address *construct* validity and to ensure that the final results were suitable for use in the subsequent project, each selected repository was manually reviewed in order to assess its overall quality and relevance. The effectiveness of EEG outcomes will be assessed in future work. Finally, in terms of *conclusion* validity, particular care was taken to account for the probabilistic limitations associated with heuristic search methods. To mitigate these issues, all runs were repeated and their consistency evaluated using the Jaccard index across an appropriate number of iterations. For the machine learning techniques, each was repeated a sufficient number of times with each run using ten fold cross validation and all runs finally averaged with standard deviation taken into account. For the statistical tests, significance was confirmed using both the FDR and Bonferroni corrections.

6 Conclusions and Future Work

This paper has presented a novel approach for selecting a dataset of appropriately sized codebases for experimental studies. A random sample of Java projects was obtained from GitHub and the use of smaller repositories was justified through the application of several machine learning classification techniques and statistical tests; this demonstrated a significant distinction between repositories containing more than 1,000 TLOC and those containing fewer. Subsequently, two heuristic search algorithms were applied to identify a subset of repositories that best satisfied the experimental requirements outlined in this paper. The repositories chosen were found to be the most dissimilar from a metrics standpoint from each other which will help determine importance when ranked by participants in our planned EEG experiments.

For future work, each repository could be analysed for additional metrics such as code smells or commit frequency. Finally, other programming languages such as Python could be investigated using a similar methodology with notice paid to the chosen metrics dependent on the language type. Building on the dataset presented in this paper, we plan to conduct an experimental study in which software engineers from both academia and industry will review code snippets while wearing an EEG cap. Participants' assessments of code quality will be analysed alongside their physiological data, with the aim of investigating whether EEG signals, combined with machine learning techniques, can be used to support and enhance debugging and code review processes.

References

1. Basili, V.R., Briand, L.C., Melo, W.L.: A validation of object-oriented design metrics as quality indicators. IEEE Trans. Softw. Eng. **22**(10), 751–761 (1996). https://doi.org/10.1109/32.544352
2. Fenton, N.E., Pfleeger, S.L.: Software Metrics: A Practical and Rigorous Approach, 2nd. edn. International Thomson (1996). ISBN 978-1-85032-275-7
3. Tassey, G.: The economic impacts of inadequate infrastructure for software testing final report prepared for. Technical report, National Institute of Standards and Technology (2002)
4. Ray, B., et al.: A large scale study of programming languages and code quality in github. In: Proceedings of the 22nd ACM SIGSOFT International Symposium on Foundations of Software Engineering, pp. 155–165. ACM (2014). https://doi.org/10.1145/2635868.2635922. ISBN 9781450330565

5. Sharma, T., Kessentini, M.: QScored: a large dataset of code smells and quality metrics. In: Proceedings of the 2021 IEEE/ACM 18th International Conference on Mining Software Repositories, MSR 2021, pp. 590–594. Institute of Electrical and Electronics Engineers Inc., (2021). https://doi.org/10.1109/MSR52588.2021.00080. ISBN 9781728187105
6. Gopstein, D., et al.: Understanding misunderstandings in source code. In: Proceedings of the ACM SIGSOFT Symposium on the Foundations of Software Engineering, vol. Part F130154, pp. 129–139. Association for Computing Machinery (2017). https://doi.org/10.1145/3106237.3106264. ISBN 9781450351058
7. Goncales, L.J., et al.: An empirical evaluation of machine learning techniques to classify code comprehension based on EEG data. Expert Syst. Appl. **203** (2022). https://doi.org/10.1016/j.eswa.2022.117354. ISSN 09574174
8. Scalabrino, S., et al.: Automatically assessing code understandability. IEEE Trans. Softw. Eng. **47**, 595–613 (2021). https://doi.org/10.1109/TSE.2019.2901468. ISSN 19393520
9. Peitek, N., et al.: Correlates of programmer efficacy and their link to experience: a combined EEG and eye-tracking study. In: ESEC/FSE 2022 - Proceedings of the 30th ACM Joint Meeting European Software Engineering Conference and Symposium on the Foundations of Software Engineering, pp. 120–131. Association for Computing Machinery, Inc. (2022). https://doi.org/10.1145/3540250.3549084. ISBN 9781450394130
10. Calcagno, A., et al.: EEG monitoring during software development. In: IEEE 20th Mediterranean Electrotechnical Conference (MELECON), pp. 325–329. IEEE (2020). https://doi.org/10.1109/MELECON48756.2020.9140717. https://ieeexplore.ieee.org/document/9140717/. ISBN 978-1-7281-5200-4
11. Yeh, M.K.-C., et al.: Detecting and comparing brain activity in short program comprehension using EEG. In: IEEE Frontiers in Education Conference (FIE), pp. 1–5. IEEE (2017). https://doi.org/10.1109/FIE.2017.8190486. http://ieeexplore.ieee.org/document/8190486/. ISBN 978-1-5090-5920-1
12. Kemerer, C.F., Paulk, M.C.: The impact of design and code reviews on software quality: an empirical study based on PSP data. IEEE Trans. Softw. Eng. **35**, 534–550 (2009). https://doi.org/10.1109/TSE.2009.27. ISSN 00985589
13. Google. Small CLs. https://google.github.io/eng-practices/review/developer/small-cls.html. Accessed 03 Aug 2026
14. The kernel development community. Everything you ever wanted to know about Linux -stable releases. https://www.kernel.org/doc/html/v4.15/process/stable-kernel-rules.html. Accessed 03 Aug 2026
15. Kudrjavets, G., Rastogi, A.: Does code review speed matter for practitioners? Empirical Softw. Eng. **29** (2024). https://doi.org/10.1007/s10664-023-10401-z. ISSN 15737616
16. Nanz, S., Furia, C.A.: A comparative study of programming languages in Rosetta code (2015)
17. McCabe, T.J.: A complexity measure. IEEE Trans. Softw. Eng. **SE-2**, 308–320 (1976). https://doi.org/10.1109/TSE.1976.233837. ISSN 0098-5589
18. Buitinck, L., et al.: API design for machine learning software: experiences from the scikit-learn project. In: ECML PKDD Workshop: Languages for Data Mining and Machine Learning, pp. 108–122 (2013)
19. Chouchen, M., et al.: Predicting code review completion time in modern code review (2021). http://arxiv.org/abs/2109.15141

20. Martí, R., et al.: Heuristics and metaheuristics for the maximum diversity problem. J. Heuristics **19**, 591–615 (2013). https://doi.org/10.1007/s10732-011-9172-4. ISSN 1381-1231. 10.1007/s10732-011-9172-4
21. Mann, A., Swift, S., Arzoky, M.: Applying graph partitioning-based seeding strategies to software modularisation. In: Smith, S., Correia, J., Cintrano, C. (eds.) Applications of Evolutionary Computation, pp. 240–258. Springer, Cham (2024). https://doi.org/10.1007/978-3-031-56852-7_16. ISBN 978-3-031-56852-7
22. Dalavi, A.M., Gomes, A., Husain, A.J.: Bibliometric analysis of nature inspired optimization techniques. Comput. Ind. Eng. **169** (2022). https://doi.org/10.1016/j.cie.2022.108161. ISSN 03608352
23. Swift, S., et al.: Consensus clustering and functional interpretation of gene-expression data. Genome Biol. **5**, R94 (2004). https://doi.org/10.1186/gb-2004-5-11-r94. https://genomebiology.biomedcentral.com/articles/10.1186/gb-2004-5-11-r94. ISSN 1474-760X
24. Leskovec, J., Rajaraman, A., Ullman, J.D.: Mining of Massive Datasets, p. 82, 3rd edn. Cambridge University Press (2020). ISBN 9781108476348
25. Capiluppi, A., et al.: Detecting Java software similarities by using different clustering techniques. Inf. Softw. Technol. **122**, 106279 (2020). https://doi.org/10.1016/j.infsof.2020.106279. ISSN 09505849
26. Sultana, K.Z., Anu, V., Chong, T.-Y.: Using software metrics for predicting vulnerable classes and methods in Java projects: a machine learning approach. J. Softw. Evol. Process **33** (2021). https://doi.org/10.1002/smr.2303. ISSN 2047-7473

Cryptography Bill of Materials Generation and Consumption: A Mining Study from GitHub

Sabato Nocera(✉) and Giuseppe Scanniello

Department of Computer Science, University of Salerno, Fisciano, Italy
{snocera,gscanniello}@unisa.it

Abstract. A *Cryptography Bill of Materials* (*CBOM*) is a machine-readable inventory of cryptographic components—*e.g.,* algorithms, keys, and certificates—that enables practitioners to assess risks ranging from classical cryptographic failures to post-quantum threats. However, despite growing regulatory and security pressure to operationalize cryptographic governance, there is little empirical evidence on the available open-source CBOM tools. To address this gap, we conducted a mining study of GitHub repositories that host CBOM tools: *generation tools* that extract cryptographic components from software artifacts to produce CBOMs, and *consumption tools* that analyze generated CBOMs to derive actionable insights. Our results reveal a generation–consumption disparity: 46 repositories host generation tools, while only seven host consumption tools. Community engagement appears limited: 93.48% of generation tools and 100% of consumption tools have no dependent repositories. Qualitative analysis indicates that generation tools can produce CBOMs using static, dynamic, or hybrid techniques over diverse artifacts (*e.g.,* source code, container images, and network-exposed services), whereas consumption tools can derive actionable visualizations and reports from CBOMs.

Keywords: Cryptography Asset Management · Cryptography Bill of Materials · Cryptographic Agility · SBOM · Software Bill of Materials

1 Introduction

Software products rely on cryptography to ensure fundamental security properties such as confidentiality, integrity, authentication, and non-repudiation [8]. However, the use of weak cryptographic algorithms undermines this foundation and exposes software products to significant risks [24]. These risks are further exacerbated by advances in quantum computing, which represent a new frontier in computational power and information processing [16]. For instance, problems such as integer factorization—on which much of public-key cryptography relies—are considered infeasible for classical computers when large integers are involved, yet could be solved by quantum computers running Shor's algorithm [16]. In

C. Berger and V. Klös (Eds.): SEAA 2026, LNCS 16864, pp. 482–499, 2027.
https://doi.org/10.1007/978-3-032-36587-3_33

this scenario, managing cryptographic components—*e.g.*, cryptographic keys, certificates, tokens, and algorithms—across source code and third-party components becomes essential for responding to incidents involving cryptographic failures [24]. To address this need, Cryptography Bills of Materials (CBOMs) have been introduced [25]. A CBOM is a structured, machine-readable document providing a comprehensive inventory of cryptographic components and their dependencies (see Fig. 1 for an example). The analysis of CBOMs enables practitioners to detect potential cryptographic weaknesses and support remediation. For instance, CBOMs can reveal the use of weak cryptographic algorithms, thereby supporting mitigation strategies such as quantum readiness assessments and post-quantum migration planning for quantum-vulnerable algorithms [25].

CBOMs are a specialized type of Software Bills of Materials (SBOMs) [20]. The latter have been enforced by international stakeholders—including the European Union [7] and the United States [17]—to describe generic software components and manage software supply chains. CBOM extends this concept to cryptographic components, addressing also specific requirements in terms of cryptography asset management and post-quantum cryptography readiness [30]. CBOM tools can be characterized as generation and consumption tools. Generation tools analyze software artifacts to detect and extract component information and produce CBOMs, while consumption tools analyze those CBOMs to derive actionable insights (*e.g.*, insights on replacing a weak cryptographic algorithm).

Despite the urgency reflected in international mandates, CBOM remains an emerging and underexplored technology. In fact, there is a critical lack of empirical evidence regarding the availability of the tools required to operationalize CBOM. Without a clear understanding of the open-source landscape, practitioners are left without a reliable toolbox to operationalize CBOMs. To address this gap, we conducted a mining study of GitHub repositories to characterize the current landscape of open-source tools for CBOM generation and consumption.

We identified 162 candidate repositories and verified 64 as hosting CBOM tools: 46 generation tools, seven consumption tools, and 11 tools supporting both generation and consumption, thus indicating an imbalance toward generation. Community engagement appears limited, as 93.48% (43 out of 46) of generation tools, 100% of consumption tools, and 100% of tools supporting both generation and consumption lack dependent repositories—*i.e.*, other GitHub repositories that make use of such CBOM generation/consumption tools. Our qualitative analysis revealed that generation tools can produce CBOMs through static, dynamic, or hybrid techniques over diverse artifact types, while consumption tools can transform CBOMs into actionable outputs to support security and risk management. Overall, these results provide a foundational baseline for researchers and a guide for practitioners working toward CBOM operationalization.

2 Background and Related Work

In this section, we present background notions and review related literature.

```
{"bomFormat":"CycloneDX","specVersion":"1.7","version":1,
 "serialNumber":"urn:uuid:3e671687-395b-41f5-a30f-a58921a69b79",

 "metadata":{"component":{"type":"application","name":"Acme Application",
 "version":"1.0","bom-ref":"acme-application"}},

 "components":[
  {"type":"cryptographic-asset","bom-ref":"aes128gcm",
   "name":"AES-128-GCM-128-12",
   "cryptoProperties":{"assetType":"algorithm",
    "algorithmProperties":{
      "primitive":"ae","algorithmFamily":"AES","mode":"gcm",
      "executionEnvironment":"software-plain-ram",
      "implementationPlatform":"x86_64","certificationLevel":["none"],
      "cryptoFunctions":["keygen","encrypt","decrypt","tag"],
      "classicalSecurityLevel":128,"nistQuantumSecurityLevel":1},
    "oid":"2.16.840.1.101.3.4.1.6"}},

  {"type":"library","bom-ref":"crypto-library",
   "name":"Crypto library","version":"1.0.0"},

  {"type":"library","bom-ref":"some-library",
   "name":"Some library","version":"1.0.0"}
 ],

 "dependencies":[
  {"ref":"acme-application","dependsOn":["crypto-library"]},
  {"ref":"crypto-library","provides":["aes128gcm"],"dependsOn":["some-library"]},
  {"ref":"some-library"},{"ref":"aes128gcm"}
 ]}
```

Fig. 1. Example of a CBOM in JSON format and CycloneDX standard [9].

2.1 Background on SBOMs and CBOMs

A software supply chain comprises software products built from layered, reusable components, such as libraries and packages [32]. An SBOM provides a structured, machine-readable representation (*e.g.*, XML or JSON) of all components within a software product, covering both open-source and proprietary elements along with key details such as versions, vendors, licenses, disclosed security vulnerabilities, and dependency relationships [18,20]. To enable automated processing, several standards define uniform, machine-readable schemas for SBOMs, allowing their integration with tools such as security scanners. Among these, the most widely adopted standards are CycloneDX and SPDX [20,27,34].

SBOMs can be extended to represent a wide range of inventories [26], which has led to the introduction of CBOM for specifying cryptographic components [25]. Managing cryptography is indeed challenging due to limited visibility into which components depend on which cryptographic assets, hindering risk assessment and mitigation [25]. CBOM addresses these challenges by enabling the monitoring and mitigation of cryptographic risks.

Figure 1 shows an example of a CBOM sourced from an open-source repository publicly available on GitHub [9]. This repository contains examples of Bills of Materials (BOMs), including CBOMs and traditional SBOMs, that conform to the CycloneDX standard.

- This CBOM is structured according to the CycloneDX 1.7 specification, as indicated by the fields `bomFormat` and `specVersion`. The former declares that the document follows the *CycloneDX* standard, while the latter specifies compliance with version *1.7* of that standard. The `version` field is set to *1*, indicating the initial revision of the CBOM. The `serialNumber` field assigns a globally unique identifier to the CBOM instance, enabling unambiguous referencing, including by other SBOMs.
- The `metadata` section describes the primary software `component` that the CBOM concerns. In this case, this component is of `type` *application* and has `name` *Acme Application* with `version` *1.0*. The attribute `bom-ref` assigns a unique internal identifier, *acme-application*, which is later used in the dependency graph to express relationships to other components.
- The `components` array enumerates all the components comprising the software supply chain of the application. The first component is a *cryptographic-asset* identified by the reference *aes128gcm* and named *AES-128-GCM-128-12*. It represents the AES–128 algorithm operating in Galois/Counter Mode (GCM) with a 128-bit key and the standard 96-bit (12-byte) IV length. The `cryptoProperties` field specifies that this asset is an *algorithm* and provides the corresponding metadata. The field `primitive` is *ae*, indicating authenticated encryption, and the `algorithmFamily` is *AES* with mode *gcm*. The `executionEnvironment` is *software-plain-ram*, meaning that the algorithm runs as a software implementation in standard system memory, while `implementationPlatform` is *x86_64*. The `certificationLevel` is set to *none*, indicating that no formal cryptographic certification applies. The list of `cryptoFunctions` shows that the implementation supports key generation, encryption, decryption, and authentication tag computation. The `classicalSecurityLevel` is 128 bits, and the `nistQuantumSecurityLevel` is 1, reflecting the expected reduction in symmetric-key strength under quantum adversaries. Finally, the `oid` encodes the standard object identifier associated with AES–128–GCM. The second and third components are libraries, identified by the references *crypto-library* and *some-library* and named *Crypto library* and *Some library*, respectively. Both are listed at version *1.0.0*. Although no additional metadata is provided for these components, their specific roles become clear in the dependency section.
- The `dependencies` section encodes the directed dependency graph that specifies how the previously defined components relate to one another. Each entry associates a component, identified by its (bom-)`ref`, with the components it either depends on or provides. The first dependency entry shows that the root application, *acme-application*, depends on *crypto-library* via the `dependsOn` field, indicating that the application relies on this cryptographic library. The second entry shows that *crypto-library* depends on another software component, *some-library*, and additionally `provides` the cryptographic asset *aes128gcm*, meaning that it contains an implementation of the AES–128–GCM algorithm. The final two entries, referring to *some-library* and *aes128gcm*, list these components without additional relationship fields. Their

presence indicates that they are nodes in the dependency graph but do not themselves depend on any other component.

2.2 Related Work on CBOMs

Risks of cryptographic failures, including post-quantum threats, have motivated approaches for managing cryptographic components based on CBOM. For example, von Nethen *et al.* [31] presented a framework where CBOMs document cryptographic components. Burkhart and Tellenbach [5] proposed a roadmap combining the creation of cryptographic inventories and risk assessment with the use of CBOMs. Jena [14] likewise positions CBOM as a pillar in quantum security readiness. While these works [5,14,31] underscore the relevance of cryptographic inventories and CBOMs, they lack details on how to generate them.

Yamamuro *et al.* [35] systematize the challenges of automated cryptography discovery and inventory tools. Unlike CBOM generation tools, which focus on source and binary code, other tools may use broader sources and track how cryptography is applied in practice. Kundu and Kompella [15] developed a research prototype that monitors quantum-related risks in cryptographic components. Using observability and dependency graphs, this prototype generates cryptography supply chains and CBOMs, then assesses the risk of each component for post-quantum readiness. Bögli *et al.* [3] developed a framework for orchestrating various CBOM generation tools and analyzing their outputs. Their results also revealed discrepancies among generated CBOMs, underscoring the need for systematic evaluation. Hirsch and Raab [11] argued that current CBOM generation tools fail to clarify which cryptographic mechanisms are security-critical or how architectural decisions constrain changes and affect security attributes and risk. To address these gaps, they proposed an approach connecting CBOMs to threat modeling, security attributes, and architectural decisions, making cryptographic decisions explicit and traceable. Zhang [36] also argued gaps in current CBOM generation tools and envisioned enhancing CBOMs with code-level information, linking cryptographic uses to call graphs, dataflow slices, and protocol roles.

While prior work has motivated the adoption of CBOM [5,14,31], argued the limitations of existing generators [3,11,35,36], and proposed novel approaches [3,11,15], there remains a lack of empirical evidence on the availability of open-source CBOM generation and consumption tools. CBOM can be adopted only when practitioners can both (i) generate CBOMs from software artifacts, and (ii) consume the generated CBOMs to derive actionable insights (*e.g.*, remediation guidance). Shortcomings on either side—such as lack or immaturity of CBOM generation or consumption tools—can hinder CBOM adoption. Motivated by this limitation, we conducted a mining study of GitHub repositories hosting tools for CBOM generation and consumption, providing practitioners with guidance for selecting CBOM tools and offering researchers an empirical foundation to identify future directions, including gaps in generation and consumption approaches.

3 Methodology

Our methodology follows a repository mining research design, aligned with the ACM SIGSOFT Empirical Standards and, in particular, the criteria established for "repository mining" [6]. Below, we describe the adopted methodology.

3.1 Goal and Research Questions

Our goal is to analyze repositories related to CBOM, publicly available on GitHub, for the purpose of characterizing the current landscape of open-source tools for CBOM generation and consumption. GitHub was selected given its central role in being the leading platform for collaborative software development and hosting of open-source software [23,28]. The study adopts the perspectives of both practitioners and researchers. Practitioners would benefit from guidance on CBOM adoption, particularly in identifying tools for both generating and consuming CBOMs. Researchers would have an empirical basis to assess CBOM tool maturity, including identifying gaps and spotting emerging trends. Based on this goal, we devised the following two Research Questions (RQs):

RQ1. *Are tools for CBOM generation and consumption hosted on GitHub?*

This RQ aims to investigate whether tools for CBOM generation and/or consumption are publicly available on GitHub and, if so, which repositories host them and how prevalent they are. Answering this RQ would help practitioners identify candidate CBOM tools to integrate into their software projects and assess their readiness (*e.g.*, very recent tools may indicate limited maturity). For researchers, the findings would provide an empirical foundation to evaluate CBOM generation and consumption tooling and offer initial evidence to assess the extent to which CBOMs are being adopted in practice.

RQ2. *What are the characteristics of CBOM generation and consumption tools hosted on GitHub?*

This RQ aims to examine both how CBOMs are generated and which capabilities are available for their consumption (*e.g.*, storage or visualization). Answering this RQ would enable practitioners to make more informed decisions when selecting CBOM tools that best fit their needs. For researchers, the findings would serve as a foundation for CBOM tool comparison and benchmarking, as well as reveal missing or inaccurate functionalities that warrant further research.

3.2 Data Collection

The data collection was performed on April 22, 2026, and leveraged the GitHub REST API [10] to retrieve repositories to be included in our study. We employed 16 distinct search queries designed to capture formal terminology (*e.g.*, `cryptography bill of materials`), hyphenated variations (*e.g.*, `cryptography-bill-of-materials`), and acronyms (*e.g.*, `CBOM`). We report the comma-separated list of queries below.

```
cryptography bill of materials, cryptography-bill-of-materials, cryptography
bills of materials, cryptography-bills-of-materials, cryptographic
bill of materials, cryptographic-bill-of-materials, cryptographic
bills of materials, cryptographic-bills-of-materials, crypto bill
of materials, crypto-bill-of-materials, crypto bills of materials,
crypto-bills-of-materials, CBOM, CBOMs, crypto-bom, crypto-boms.
```

Once the repositories were identified, we issued individual queries to collect full metadata (*e.g.*, repository description, creation dates, stars, forks, and subscribers) and the contents of their `README.md` files. To minimize false positives from the API search indexing, each repository's content was further verified for the presence of the original query term. Lastly, we parsed the GitHub Dependency Graph [2] to count the number of repositories that depend on those identified through the GitHub REST API search. A repository listed as a dependent (*i.e.*, a dependent repository) declares the corresponding CBOM tool as a dependency, thereby enabling its use within that repository.

3.3 Data Analysis

Below, we describe the data analysis performed to address each RQ.

RQ1: Are tools for CBOM generation and consumption hosted on GitHub? We verified that each identified repository corresponded to a CBOM generation and/or consumption tool. As no automated method exists to classify repositories in this respect, we applied the following procedure to each repository:

1. We examined the repository description and the `README.md` file in the root directory to assess evidence that the given repository could support CBOM generation and/or CBOM consumption—*e.g.*, explicit references to generating CBOMs or supporting consumption use cases such as CBOM visualization. Based on this evidence, we labeled the repository as a "CBOM generation tool," a "CBOM consumption tool," or both when it supported both generation and consumption use cases.
2. When the repository description and the `README.md` file did not provide sufficient evidence to deem the given repository as a CBOM generation and/or consumption tool, we extended the inspection to the repository contents. We inspected files across directories and subdirectories, focusing on source code and code comments related to CBOM generation and consumption. In case we found evidence that the repository could support CBOM generation and/or CBOM consumption, we labeled the repository as a "CBOM generation tool," a "CBOM consumption tool," or both when it supported both generation and consumption use cases.
3. We discarded the given repository in case we found no evidence that it could support either CBOM generation or CBOM consumption.

After labeling each repository as a "CBOM generation tool," "CBOM consumption tool," or both, we counted the number of repositories in each category to estimate how many such tools were publicly available on GitHub at the time of the study. Then, for each labeled repository, we plotted repository creation timelines separately for generation and consumption tools to illustrate when these tools first emerged on GitHub. For instance, very recent tools may indicate limited maturity. Finally, by distinguishing between generation and consumption tools, we computed descriptive statistics (*i.e.,* quartiles and the proportion of zero values) for stars, forks, subscribers, and dependents. These metrics can serve as proxies for community engagement on GitHub (*e.g.,* [1,4,13,20]). For instance, repositories without dependents indicate no downstream use as a declared dependency on GitHub, suggesting limited engagement by the community.

RQ2: What are the characteristics of CBOM generation and consumption tools hosted on GitHub? For each repository labeled as a "CBOM generation tool," "CBOM consumption tool," or both, we performed a qualitative content analysis [12] of the repository description and the `README.md` file. The analysis used predefined categories, namely *CBOM generation* and *CBOM consumption*, which served as guiding codes and aligned with our goal of characterizing the current landscape of open-source tools for CBOM generation and consumption. For each repository, we reviewed the description and `README.md` file and extracted all excerpts that described the tool's functionality (*e.g.,* supported inputs and output formats). In particular, we extracted relevant excerpts describing how the tool generates CBOMs (*e.g.,* through static analysis) and/or how it supports their consumption (*e.g.,* storage). We then synthesized the extracted excerpts to derive the qualitative characterization for CBOM generation and CBOM consumption reported in our results. This characterization is independent of the repositories' labeling (*i.e.,* "CBOM generation tool," "CBOM consumption tool," or both), as its purpose is to describe the characteristics related to CBOM generation and CBOM consumption in their own right.

4 Results

In this section, we report the results per RQ. All data is available online [21].

4.1 RQ1: Are Tools for CBOM Generation and Consumption Hosted on GitHub?

A total of 162 repositories were retrieved via the GitHub REST API; after verification, 64 were confirmed as CBOM tools. Of these, 46 were classified as generation tools, seven as consumption tools, and 11 as supporting both, indicating that generation tools are more prevalent than consumption tools on GitHub.

Figure 2 shows the cumulative number of CBOM tools over time. Generation tools first appeared in December 2019, with activity resuming in December 2022 and accelerating from late 2024 into early 2025; the most recent generation tool

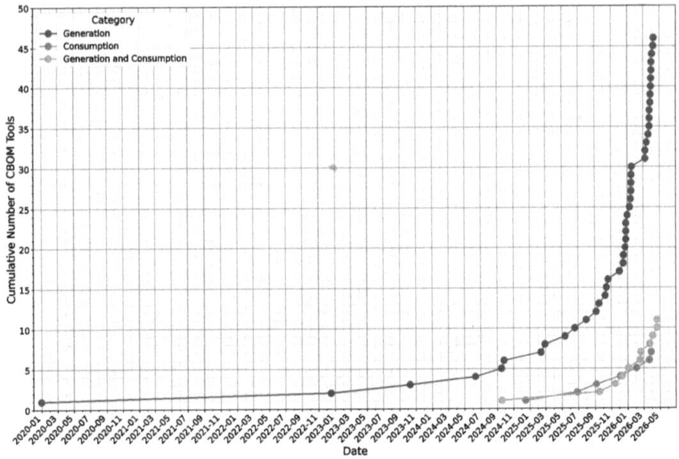

Fig. 2. Number of CBOM generation and consumption tools created over time.

Table 1. Descriptive statistics for stars, forks, subscribers, and dependent repositories.

Tool	Metric	Statistic					
		Minimum	Q1	Median	Q3	Maximum	% 0
Generation	Stars	0	0	1	3	951	47.83%
	Forks	0	0	0	1	241	67.39%
	Subscribers	0	0	0	0.75	12	73.91%
	Dependents	0	0	0	0	186	93.48%
Consumption	Stars	0	0	0	0.5	166	71.43%
	Forks	0	0	0	1	9	71.43%
	Subscribers	0	0	0	1	4	57.14%
	Dependents	0	0	0	0	0	100%
Generation & Consumption	Stars	0	0	0	0	92	81.82%
	Forks	0	0	0	0	38	90.91%
	Subscribers	0	0	0	0	8	81.82%
	Dependents	0	0	0	0	0	100%

dates to April 2026. Consumption tools appeared later, first in December 2024, then resumed in June 2025 and grow steadily through March 2026. Tools supporting both CBOM generation and consumption first appeared in September 2024, resumed in September 2025, and increase notably from late 2025 to early 2026; the latest such tool was created in April 2026.

Table 1 shows that engagement is generally low across CBOM tools, and that the distributions are highly skewed: a few repositories account for most of the engagement, while the majority receive little or none. For CBOM generation tools, the maximum values are 951 stars, 241 forks, 12 subscribers, and 186

Table 2. Summary of the characteristics of CBOM generation and consumption.

Aspect	CBOM Generation	CBOM Consumption
Primary goal	Automatically identify cryptographic components and generate machine-readable CBOMs.	Transform, interpret, analyze, and manage CBOMs to support operational use.
Covered elements	Algorithms, protocols, certificates, keys, tokens, secrets, and their relationships.	Cryptographic components of CBOMs and their associated properties and relationships.
Inputs	Source code, libraries, container images, and network-exposed services.	CBOM files, typically represented in structured formats such as JSON.
Main techniques	Primarily static analysis; also dependency analysis, dynamic runtime tracing, infrastructure-level inspection, and hybrid and compositional approaches (*e.g.*, combination of multiple scanners).	Parsing, file conversion, visualization, rule-based analysis, policy checks, data querying and management (*e.g.*, filtering, search, upload, storage, and retrieval), and comparison of multiple CBOMs.
Outputs	CBOMs (*e.g.*, in CycloneDX and JSON), in some cases enriched with contextual relationships and security-relevant metadata.	Usable and actionable representations (*e.g.*, dashboards, spreadsheets), and reports and summaries (*e.g.*, also in HTML).
Security support	May generate CBOMs with weak algorithm detection, post-quantum readiness assessments, migration recommendations, and compliance support (*e.g.*, NIST guidance).	May assess CBOMs against security requirements, detect weak, deprecated, or quantum-vulnerable components, and provide severity/scores and remediation guidance.

dependents, yet typical engagement remains near zero. The minimum and the first quartile (Q1) are zero for all metrics, and the median is non-zero only for stars, where it is one; forks, subscribers, and dependents remain zero at the median. Even at the third quartile (Q3), values are small at three stars, one fork, and 0.75 subscribers, while dependents are still zero. The prevalence of zero values further highlights the limited engagement of most CBOM generation tools: 47.83% have no stars, 67.39% have no forks, 73.91% have no subscribers, and 93.48% have no dependent repositories. CBOM consumption tools exhibit a similar pattern. Some repositories reach moderate engagement, with maximum values of 166 stars, nine forks, and four subscribers, but dependents are zero throughout. The minimum, the Q1, and the median are zero across all metrics, while the Q3 remains low at 0.5 stars, one fork, and one subscriber. Accordingly, 71.43% of CBOM consumption tools have no stars, 71.43% have no forks, 57.14% have no subscribers, and 100% have no dependent repositories. CBOM tools that support both generation and consumption also show low engagement. Aside from a few repositories with maximum values of 92 stars, 38 forks, and eight subscribers, all descriptive statistics from the minimum through Q3 are zero, and dependents remain zero even at the maximum. Accordingly, 81.82% of generation-and-consumption tools have no stars, 90.91% have no forks, 81.82% have no subscribers, and 100% have no dependent repositories.

4.2 RQ2: What are the Characteristics of CBOM Generation and Consumption Tools Hosted on GitHub?

In the remainder of this section, we present the characteristics identified through the qualitative analysis for both CBOM generation and CBOM consumption. These characteristics are summarized in Table 2 and described below.

CBOM Generation. CBOM generation tools rely on automated scanners that identify cryptographic components and produce machine-readable CBOMs. These components involve a broad spectrum, including algorithms (*e.g.,* AES, RSA), protocols (*e.g.,* TLS), certificates, keys, tokens, and secrets. CBOM generation tools can also capture relationships among these elements—for instance, protocols that use specific algorithms (*e.g.,* TLS 1.3 using ECDH/secp256r1), libraries that implement cryptographic primitives, and applications that import those libraries. This modeling enables a contextual view of how cryptography is implemented and used across a system.

In terms of analysis techniques, CBOM generation targets a wide range of artifacts, including source code (notably Java, Python, and JavaScript), container images, and network-exposed services. CBOMs are typically generated in the CycloneDX standard as JSON files, reflecting a growing convergence toward standardized representations. For certain ecosystems—such as Java—the precision and completeness of the generated CBOMs can depend heavily on the scanner's ability to resolve symbols across dependencies. Most CBOM generation tools primarily employ static code analysis, while others extend coverage through dependency analysis (*e.g.,* augmenting SBOM generation with cryptographic scanning), dynamic techniques based on runtime tracing, infrastructure-level inspection of containers and network services, and hybrid approaches that integrate multiple data sources.

CBOM generation tools can be integrated into DevOps workflows via command-line interfaces, plugins, and Continuous Integration/Continuous Delivery (CI/CD) pipelines, enabling continuous and automated CBOM generation. For example, Sonar Cryptography Plugin is integrated into SonarQube and can detect cryptographic assets during code analysis to generate CBOMs as part of the CI/CD pipeline. Other static analysis tools, such as CodeQL and Semgrep, have also been leveraged to support CBOM generation.

Several CBOM generation tools go beyond simple inventory creation by enriching CBOMs with security-relevant information, such as the detection of weak cryptographic algorithms, post-quantum cryptography readiness assessments, migration recommendations, and compliance support aligned with standards such as NIST IR 8547 or NIST FIPS 203/204/205. Some CBOM generation tools acknowledge their current limitations—such as incomplete language support and partial coverage of cryptographic assets—and, in doing so, encourage the open-source community to extend, refine, and integrate these tools.

Finally, CBOM generation can be compositional: tools can orchestrate other tools within their workflows. For instance, CBOMkit (developed by IBM Research and now maintained by the Post-Quantum Cryptography Alliance) combines multiple scanners—leveraging the Sonar Cryptography Plugin for source code analysis alongside an additional tool for inspecting container images and directories—to produce comprehensive CBOMs.

CBOM Consumption. CBOM consumption tools can transform CBOMs into more usable and actionable representations, for instance, by converting formats such as JSON into spreadsheets or dashboards. Several CBOM consumption tools also provide reporting and export capabilities, including the generation of HTML reports and summarized views tailored to different stakeholders, such as auditors and security engineers. More recent solutions introduce artificial intelligence–assisted summaries and natural-language querying of CBOM data; however, these features are primarily intended to support interpretation rather than automate decision-making.

Another prominent characteristic concerns CBOM visualization. CBOM consumption tools in this space offer interfaces ranging from basic viewers to fully interactive dashboards, enabling graphical exploration of cryptographic components and their relationships. These visualizations can be complemented by filtering, search, and navigation functionalities that facilitate exploratory analysis and comprehension of complex cryptographic inventories.

CBOM consumption tools can also support compliance and risk analysis by ingesting CBOMs and evaluating them against security requirements. This includes rule-based or policy-driven checks targeting aspects such as algorithm strength, certificate validity, and post-quantum cryptography readiness. In this context, tools may classify cryptographic assets according to established standards (*e.g.*, NIST categories) and identify weak or deprecated algorithms. The outcomes of these analyses can be expressed through scoring mechanisms, severity levels, and detailed reports, sometimes accompanied by remediation guidance.

Finally, CBOM consumption tools can address data management and integration concerns. They can expose APIs and rely on backend storage systems (*e.g.*, databases) to support the upload, storage, querying, and retrieval of CBOMs. This enables integration into broader workflows and facilitates continuous monitoring scenarios. Additional capabilities include the comparison of multiple CBOMs—such as semantic diffing and benchmarking across different generators—allowing tracking and analyzing changes in the cryptographic posture over time.

5 Discussion

In this section, we discuss the results and outline implications for practitioners and researchers, concluding with possible threats to validity.

5.1 Overall Discussion and Implications

A first notable aspect concerns the numerical distribution of tools: CBOM generation is more represented than CBOM consumption. This imbalance suggests that the community has focused on generating CBOMs, while less effort has been devoted to operationalizing their use. The temporal analysis reinforces this interpretation. CBOM generation tools emerged earlier and have shown a more pronounced growth trajectory than CBOM consumption tools. This pattern may, however, not be unexpected. CBOMs must be created before they can be consumed, making an initial emphasis on generation reasonable. Moreover, the act of generating CBOMs can itself provide valuable insights, even in the absence of downstream consumption. The existence of dual-purpose tools that support both CBOM generation and consumption points to an emerging shift toward integrated CBOM solutions. However, this integration is still relatively recent, as outlined by the temporal analysis. **Practitioners** could progressively adopt CBOM practices, for example, starting with generation tools and subsequently incorporating consumption capabilities.

Both CBOM generation and consumption tools exhibit low overall engagement within GitHub. This mirrors an early trend also observed in SBOM adoption [19,29,34]. While a few tools attain higher engagement, the distributions of stars, forks, subscribers, and dependent repositories are highly skewed: most repositories receive little to no attention and show no evidence of downstream usage by dependent repositories. This pattern reinforces the view that CBOM remains experimental or exploratory, with limited integration into widely adopted software engineering practices. **Researchers** could be interested in investigating the limited engagement in CBOM tools, including aspects related to usability, developer experience, and adoption barriers within real-world workflows. Empirical studies involving practitioners would be especially valuable to better understand these challenges and inform CBOM tool design.

CBOM generation supports the automated discovery of cryptographic assets—*e.g.,* algorithms, protocols, certificates, keys, tokens, and secrets—across heterogeneous software artifacts such as source code, container images, and network-exposed services. Beyond producing a flat inventory, generation tools can capture relationships among assets and dependencies, yielding a contextual view of how cryptography is implemented and used within a system. This is essential for understanding complex cryptographic configurations and their propagation across components. To extract this information, tools rely on a range of techniques, including static code and dependency analysis, dynamic methods based on runtime tracing, infrastructure-level inspection, and hybrid approaches that combine multiple data sources. Many generation tools are also delivered as command-line utilities, plugins, and CI/CD integrations, which lowers the barrier to adoption. This is particularly relevant for **practitioners**: CBOM generation can be added to existing development pipelines (*e.g.,* as a CI/CD step) with minimal setup and without substantial changes to their workflows.

We also observed some limitations affecting CBOM generation, including incomplete support for different programming languages, partial coverage of cryptographic assets, and challenges related to the precision and completeness of the generated CBOMs. These findings are consistent with prior work that argued the limitations of existing CBOM generation tools [3,11,35,36] and open several promising directions for future investigation. For example, **researchers** could be interested in improving the completeness and accuracy of current CBOM generation techniques (*e.g.*, by improving dependency resolution capabilities or combining multiple generation techniques).

On the consumption side, several tools focus on the visualization, reporting, and transformation of CBOM data. The integration of data management, compliance, and risk analysis capabilities further positions CBOMs as a foundation for security assessment, enabling the identification of issues, the assignment of severity levels, and the recommendation of remediation strategies for cryptographic weaknesses and post-quantum readiness. For this reason, once CBOM generation is established, **practitioners** should integrate consumption tools to assess their cryptographic posture and operationalize CBOM-driven governance.

The emphasis on the visualization, reporting, and transformation of CBOM data reflects an effort to bridge the gap between machine-readable CBOMs and human-interpretable insights that can inform security decisions. Similar challenges have been observed for SBOM [19,22,34]. This also underscores an important direction for **researchers** concerning bridging the gap between insights generated from CBOM consumption and action. Current CBOM consumption tools focus on reporting and assessment; extending them toward automated or semi-automated remediation and policy enforcement mechanisms would enhance their practical impact and enable more effective operationalization of CBOMs.

5.2 Threats to Validity

Below, we discuss potential threats to the validity of our results following the classification by Wohlin *et al.* [33]. Threats to internal validity are not discussed, as this study does not investigate causal relationships.

Construct Validity. A potential threat to construct validity relates to the data collection process and the possibility of incomplete coverage of relevant repositories due to search limitations. To mitigate the risk of omitting relevant repositories, we defined a comprehensive set of search queries, comprising 16 distinct formulations. These queries included both commonly used terminology (*e.g.*, `CBOM`) and semantically related expressions describing the same concept (*e.g.*, `crypto bill of materials`). We acknowledge that GitHub repositories for CBOM generation or consumption may exist without explicitly mentioning our search queries and may therefore not be retrieved through the GitHub REST API search. To reduce false positives introduced by limitations in API search indexing, we checked each identified repository for the presence of the original query terms. Lastly, we acknowledge a threat to construct validity related to the operationalization of the metrics used to capture community engagement, *i.e.*, stars, forks, subscribers, and dependents. Although these metrics are provided by GitHub and can serve as useful proxies for community engagement, they may not fully capture the phenomenon under investigation. For instance, the number of dependents may be affected by accuracy concerns due to limitations in the GitHub Dependency Graph [2], and zero dependents does not necessarily imply a lack of use, as some tools may be intended for standalone use (*e.g.*, command-line interface tools) rather than as dependencies (*e.g.*, libraries).

Conclusion Validity. A possible threat to conclusion validity concerns potential subjectivity in labeling repositories as CBOM generation and/or consumption tools and in the qualitative analysis, since a single author conducted the assessment. To mitigate this risk, ambiguous and unclear cases were discussed with the other author, and final decisions were made jointly.

External Validity. We acknowledge that findings derived from a limited number of repositories—such as the CBOM tools identified in this study—may have restricted generalizability beyond the specific contexts in which they were observed. For example, they may reflect isolated perspectives, early-stage development efforts, or context-specific practices rather than broadly established trends. As such, these findings should be interpreted with caution and in light of the exploratory nature of this research. Our results may also not generalize beyond GitHub (*e.g.*, industrial software or alternative open-source platforms such as GitLab or Bitbucket). Finally, we acknowledge that the lack of repository selection criteria, such as excluding personal or inactive projects, might limit the representativeness of our context with respect to real-world practice.

6 Conclusion

We conducted a mining study of GitHub repositories to characterize the landscape of open-source Cryptography Bill of Materials (CBOM) generation and consumption tools. Our findings show that the CBOM tooling landscape is expanding but still immature. The ecosystem is currently unbalanced, with a stronger emphasis on generation compared to consumption. While this reflects a natural progression—as CBOMs must first be produced before they can be used—it also highlights a gap in the operationalization of CBOMs. The emergence of tools supporting both generation and consumption suggests a shift toward more integrated solutions, although this trend is still recent. Furthermore, the overall limited engagement of CBOM tools indicates that the technology remains at an exploratory stage, with minimal integration into widely adopted software engineering practices. Overall, our results suggest that CBOM technology is at an early yet promising stage of evolution. Increasing regulatory pressure on software supply chains and cryptographic governance is likely to drive further adoption. In this context, practitioners can begin by adopting CBOM generation and progressively incorporating consumption tools to support analysis and decision-making. For researchers, several opportunities remain open, including improving the completeness and accuracy of CBOM generation, exploring hybrid and compositional approaches, investigating usability and adoption barriers, and advancing the integration of CBOMs (*e.g.*, consumption) with automated security remediation mechanisms.

Acknowledgments. This work has been financially supported in part by the project "TeleRiab4Fra: TeleRiabilitazione ad alta tecnologia per il trattamento del paziente FRAgile" (grant n. PNC0000007, CUP: B53C22006950001).

Data Availibility Statement. We have made all data and scripts publicly available online [21].

Disclosure of Interests. The authors have no competing interests to declare that are relevant to the content of this article.

References

1. Alfadel, M., Costa, D.E., Shihab, E., Mkhallalati, M.: On the use of dependabot security pull requests. In: 2021 IEEE/ACM 18th International Conference on Mining Software Repositories (MSR), pp. 254–265. IEEE (2021)
2. Bifolco, D., Romano, S., Nocera, S., Francese, R., Scanniello, G., Di Penta, M.: An empirical study on the accuracy of github's dependency graph and the nature of its inaccuracy. Inf. Softw. Technol. **187**, 107854 (2025). https://doi.org/10.1016/j.infsof.2025.107854
3. Bögli, R., Spieler, J., Kehrer, T.: BF-CBOM: uncovering cryptographic assets through comparative CBOM analysis at scale. In: 34th IEEE/ACM International Conference on Program Comprehension (2026)
4. Borges, H., Hora, A., Valente, M.T.: Understanding the factors that impact the popularity of github repositories. In: 2016 IEEE International Conference on Software Maintenance and Evolution (ICSME), pp. 334–344. IEEE (2016)
5. Burkhart, M., Tellenbach, B.: Quantum readiness: recommendations for enterprises. In: Quantum Technologies: Trends and Implications for Cyber Defense, pp. 155–162. Springer, Cham (2025)
6. Chatterjee, P., Sharma, T., Ralph, P.: Empirical standards for repository mining. In: 19th International Conference on Mining Software Repositories (2022)
7. ENISA: Guidelines for Securing the Internet of Things (2020). http://www.enisa.europa.eu/publications/guidelines-for-securing-the-internet-of-things
8. ENISA: Cryptography (2026). https://www.enisa.europa.eu/topics/digital-identity-and-data-protection/cryptography
9. GitHub: Example of CBOM (2025). https://github.com/CycloneDX/bom-examples/blob/master/CBOM/Example-With-Dependencies/bom.json
10. GitHub, Inc.: Github rest API (2026). https://docs.github.com/en/rest
11. Hirsch, E., Raab, K.: Architecture-derived cboms for cryptographic migration: a security-aware architecture tradeoff method. arXiv preprint arXiv:2603.22112 (2026), accepted at the Magics Workshop, co-located with Eurocrypt 2026
12. Hsieh, H.F., Shannon, S.E.: Three approaches to qualitative content analysis. Qual. Health Res. **15**(9), 1277–1288 (2005)
13. Hu, X., Chen, Z., Situ, L., Pan, X., Shi, J.: Identification of important software based on software dependency graph. Scientometrics **130**(7), 3961–3985 (2025)

14. Jena, J.: The quantum security deadline: Building crypto-agility against'harvest now, decrypt later'threats. Eur. J. Comput. Sci. Inf. Technol. **13**(52), 35–52 (2025)
15. Kundu, A., Kompella, R.: Quantum-resistant security: PQC readiness and research challenges. In: 2025 62nd ACM/IEEE Design Automation Conference (DAC), pp. 1–4. IEEE (2025)
16. Nielsen, M.A., Chuang, I.L.: Quantum Computation and Quantum Information. Cambridge University Press (2010)
17. NIST: Executive Order 14028 (2021). https://www.nist.gov/itl/executive-order-14028-improving-nations-cybersecurity
18. Nocera, S., Di Penta, M., Francese, R., Romano, S., Scanniello, G.: If it's not sbom, then what? How Italian practitioners manage the software supply chain. In: 2024 IEEE International Conference on Software Maintenance and Evolution (ICSME), pp. 730–740 (2024). https://doi.org/10.1109/ICSME58944.2024.00077
19. Nocera, S., Penta, M.D., Ahmed, F., Romano, S., Scanniello, G.: What we know about aiboms: results from a multivocal literature review on artificial intelligence bill of materials. ACM Trans. Softw. Eng. Methodol. (2026). https://doi.org/10.1145/3786773
20. Nocera, S., Romano, S., Di Penta, M., Francese, R., Scanniello, G.: On the adoption of software bill of materials in open-source software projects. J. Syst. Softw. **230**, 112540 (2025). https://doi.org/10.1016/j.jss.2025.112540
21. Nocera, S., Scanniello, G.: Cryptography Bill of Materials Generation and Consumption: A Mining Study from GitHub - Artifact (2026). https://doi.org/10.6084/m9.figshare.32124022
22. Oberhauser, R.: VR-SBOM: visualization of software bill of materials and software supply chains in virtual reality. In: International Symposium on Business Modeling and Software Design, pp. 52–70. Springer, Cham (2025)
23. Onsori Delicheh, H., Cardoen, G., Decan, A., Mens, T.: Automation and reuse practices in github actions workflows: a practitioner's perspective. ACM Trans. Softw. Eng. Methodol. (2026)
24. OWASP: A04:2025 Cryptographic Failures (2025). https://owasp.org/Top10/2025/A04_2025-Cryptographic_Failures/
25. OWASP: Authoritative Guide to CBOM (2025). https://cyclonedx.org/guides/OWASP_CycloneDX-Authoritative-Guide-to-CBOM-en.pdf
26. OWASP: Authoritative Guide to SBOM (2025). https://cyclonedx.org/guides/OWASP_CycloneDX-Authoritative-Guide-to-SBOM-en.pdf
27. Soeiro, L., Robert, T., Zacchiroli, S.: Wild sboms: a large-scale dataset of software bills of materials from public code. In: 2025 IEEE/ACM 22nd International Conference on Mining Software Repositories (MSR), pp. 164–168. IEEE (2025)
28. StackOverflow: Developer Survey (2022). http://survey.stackoverflow.co/2022
29. Stalnaker, T., Wintersgill, N., Chaparro, O., Di Penta, M., German, D.M., Poshyvanyk, D.: Boms away! inside the minds of stakeholders: a comprehensive study of bills of materials for software systems. In: Proceedings of the 46th IEEE/ACM International Conference on Software Engineering, pp. 1–13 (2024)
30. The White House: Memorandum on Promoting United States Leadership in Quantum Computing While Mitigating Risks to Vulnerable Cryptographic Systems (2022). https://www.presidency.ucsb.edu/documents/memorandum-promoting-united-states-leadership-quantum-computing-while-mitigating-risks
31. Von Nethen, N., Wiesmaier, A., Alnahawi, N., Henrich, J.: PMMP-PQC migration management process. In: Proceedings of the 2024 European Interdisciplinary Cybersecurity Conference, pp. 144–154 (2024)

32. Williams, L., et al.: Research directions in software supply chain security. ACM Trans. Softw. Eng. Methodol. **34**(5), 1–38 (2025)
33. Wohlin, C., Runeson, P., Höst, M., Ohlsson, M.C., Regnell, B., Wesslén, A.: Experimentation in Software Engineering, vol. 236. Springer, Cham (2012)
34. Xia, B., Bi, T., Xing, Z., Lu, Q., Zhu, L.: An empirical study on software bill of materials: where we stand and the road ahead. In: 2023 IEEE/ACM 45th International Conference on Software Engineering (ICSE), pp. 2630–2642. IEEE (2023)
35. Yamamuro, H., Uemura, S., Fukushima, K.: SoK: challenges for implementing automated cryptography discovery and inventory tool. In: Proceedings of the 12th International Conference on Information Systems Security and Privacy - Volume 2: ICISSP, pp. 157–168. INSTICC (2026)
36. Zhang, L.: Toward quantum-safe software engineering: a vision for post-quantum cryptography migration (2026). arXiv:2602.05759 arXiv preprint accepted at the Poster Track of ICSE 2026

Mining Architectural Quality Under Agentic AI Adoption: A Causal Study of Java Repositories

Oliver Aleksander Larsen(✉) and Mahyar T. Moghaddam

SDU Software Engineering, University of Southern Denmark, Odense, Denmark
{olar,mtmo}@mmmi.sdu.dk

Abstract. AI coding tools are now used by a majority of developers, and agentic use of these tools has popularized the practice colloquially called "vibe coding". Yet causal evidence on their effect on software architecture is scarce. Prior causal work has measured code-level outcomes (complexity, static analysis warnings); whether such degradation propagates to architecture-level outcomes remains unknown. We mine 151 open-source Java repositories, 74 with detectable agentic AI adoption (identified via configuration files and `Co-Authored-By` commit trailers) and 77 propensity-matched controls, across a 13-month per-repository window yielding 1,811 monthly Arcan snapshots. We estimate the causal effect of adoption on architectural smell density (ASD) with a staggered difference-in-differences design and the Borusyak imputation estimator, applying a causal design recently used for code-level metrics to the architecture level. Total smell counts are essentially unchanged (+1.1%, $p = 0.82$) while lines of code grow +12.8% ($p = 0.003$); the resulting 6.7% ASD decline ($p = 0.004$) is therefore a denominator effect rather than an architectural improvement. Per-type estimates and robustness checks (wild cluster bootstrap, Lee bounds, stale-observation sensitivity) corroborate the pattern; pre-trends are flat (Wald $p = 0.90$), consistent with parallel trends. Density-normalized outcomes can mislead when treatment affects system size: raw counts and explicit decomposition are required for causal mining studies of AI tool adoption. The complete replication package, including the curated 151-repository monthly panel, is publicly available.

Keywords: architectural smells · architectural erosion · AI-assisted development · vibe coding · mining software repositories · difference-in-differences

1 Introduction

AI coding tools have moved from inline autocomplete to fully agentic operation: given a natural-language intent, tools such as Cursor, GitHub Copilot, Claude Code, and Aider generate, edit, and refactor code across multiple files [4,5,

C. Berger and V. Klös (Eds.): SEAA 2026, LNCS 16864, pp. 500–516, 2027.
https://doi.org/10.1007/978-3-032-36587-3_34

16]. The resulting paradigm, popularized as "vibe coding" by Karpathy [25], leaves observable artifacts in repositories: tool-specific configuration files, which encode project-specific directives consistent with agentic engagement [22], and `Co-Authored-By` commit trailers; neither signal arises from inline autocomplete. These artifacts make agentic adoption visible to repository mining at scale, even as practitioner surveys report concerns about long-term maintainability [14,39].

These concerns have empirical support at the code level. He et al. [20] studied 806 Cursor-adopting repositories using a staggered difference-in-differences (DiD) design and found that AI adoption increases static analysis warnings by 30% and code complexity by 41%. Yet code-level complexity and architectural quality are distinct: a method with high cyclomatic complexity does not necessarily create a cyclic dependency; a duplicated code block does not produce a hub-like component. Esposito et al. [13] showed that 33.8% of static analysis warnings never co-occur with any architectural smell, confirming that code-level and architectural degradation are only partially overlapping concerns. Whether code-level degradation propagates to architecture-level degradation remains unanswered.

The gap matters. Architectural smells are recurring structural anti-patterns in a system's dependency graph [15] and are indicators of architectural erosion [19,21] that affects maintainability and evolvability [23,33]. Qualitative work suggests the risk is real [3], yet no study has measured architectural impact with a causal mining design.

The code-level evidence above predicts that agentic AI adoption should increase architectural smell density (ASD), particularly structural anti-patterns plausibly arising from file-scoped generation. RQ1–RQ3 test that prediction at the architectural level; RQ4 decomposes any observed ASD effect into numerator and denominator channels.

RQ1: Does the adoption of agentic AI coding tools affect architectural smell density (ASD) in open-source Java repositories?

RQ2: Which categories of architectural smells show the largest treatment effect?

RQ3: How does the effect on ASD evolve over time after agentic AI tool adoption?

RQ4: Is the observed ASD effect driven by changes in architectural smell counts (numerator), code volume (denominator), or both?

We mine 151 open-source Java repositories, 74 with observable agentic AI adoption (detected via configuration files and `Co-Authored-By` trailers) and 77 propensity-matched controls [31,36], yielding 1,811 monthly Arcan snapshots [6,32] over 13 months per repository. The causal effect on ASD is estimated with a staggered difference-in-differences design and the Borusyak imputation estimator [9], applied here at the architectural level (one abstraction higher than He et al. [20]).

ASD declines by 6.7% ($p = 0.004$), the opposite-direction finding to that prediction. Decomposition reveals the mechanism: total smell counts are essentially unchanged (+1.1%, $p = 0.82$) while code volume grows substantially (+12.8%,

$p = 0.003$); the decline is therefore a composition effect driven by the denominator. Pre-trends are flat (Wald $p = 0.90$), consistent with parallel trends.

This paper contributes: (1) a causal mining pipeline (151 repositories, 1,811 monthly snapshots, Borusyak DiD on architectural metrics) reusable for other AI-tool quality outcomes; (2) a methodological warning that density-normalized outcomes mislead when treatment affects system size, requiring explicit numerator/denominator decomposition; (3) the first causal evidence on architecture-level effects of agentic AI adoption, consistent with divergence between code- and architecture-level effects [13,20]; and (4) a complete open-source replication package with the curated 151-repo monthly panel.

2 Background and Related Work

2.1 AI Coding Tools and the Detection Problem in Repository Mining

AI tools are now used by 63.2% of professional developers [35]. The major tools (GitHub Copilot, Cursor, Claude Code) have each evolved beyond inline autocomplete to offer agentic capabilities: given a natural-language intent, the tool autonomously generates, edits, and refactors code across multiple files [4,5,16]. Practitioner accounts describe developers accepting AI-generated code with minimal structural review [14,25,39].

The key distinction for repository mining is between *usage modes*, not between tools. In autocomplete mode, the developer accepts inline suggestions; no project-level configuration is needed and no attribution metadata is produced. In agentic mode, developers create tool-specific configuration files (which encode project-specific directives [22]) and produce `Co-Authored-By` commit trailers; neither artifact arises from autocomplete-only usage. Any detection strategy based on repository artifacts (including ours and He et al.'s [20]) therefore observes only agentic usage (Sect. 3.2). This is also the mode posing the greatest architectural risk: agentic tools operate at file and function scope, while architecture is an emergent property of inter-module relationships [8].

2.2 Architectural Erosion and Architectural Smells

Perry and Wolf [29] formalized software architecture as the set of design decisions governing a system's structural organization. *Architectural erosion* is the gradual divergence between intended and implemented architecture [19,21]. *Architectural smells* operationalize erosion as detectable structural anti-patterns in dependency graphs [15]. We measure four types, each violating a known design principle [27,28]:

- **Cyclic Dependency (CD):** circular dependency chains among packages, violating the Acyclic Dependencies Principle.
- **Unstable Dependency (UD):** a package depending on a less-stable package, violating the Stable Dependencies Principle.

- **Hub-Like Dependency (HL):** a component with both high fan-in and high fan-out, undermining modularity.
- **God Component (GC):** an oversized package concentrating too many responsibilities, violating modularity.

We detect these smells with Arcan [6], with reported precision in the 70–100% range across Java projects [6,32]. Architectural smell density (ASD = total smells / KLOC) is used as a proxy for the rate of erosion; erosion proper requires comparison against an intended architecture [19], which is unavailable for open-source projects at scale. ASD requires decomposition when treatment affects code volume (Sect. 4.5).

2.3 Empirical Studies of AI-Assisted Development

He et al. [20] conducted the closest predecessor study: a staggered DiD analysis of 806 Cursor-adopting repositories, reporting +30% static-analysis warnings and +41% complexity alongside higher development velocity. We follow their mining design one abstraction level higher: from SonarQube's intra-method metrics to Arcan's inter-package metrics. Esposito et al. [13] confirmed the gap between these two levels: 33.8% of static analysis warnings are architecturally benign, unassociated with any smell, indicating that code-level findings cannot be assumed to translate to architecture-level effects.

Beyond causal studies, Cotroneo et al. [11] found AI-generated code more prone to vulnerabilities, while Yetiştiren et al. [41] report mixed quality results across major AI tools; both are cross-sectional and measure code-level properties exclusively. Amasanti and Jahić [3] survey practitioners about architectural-quality concerns under AI assistance, finding mixed signals; Waseem et al. [39] document related qualitative concerns. Jiang and Nam [22] characterized Cursor configuration files across 401 repositories, finding project-specific directives consistent with agentic engagement. A companion study by Agarwal et al. [1] extends He et al.'s analysis by distinguishing IDE-based AI assistants from autonomous coding agents, finding larger quality effects for agentic usage. These studies establish a code-level signal but do not address the architectural channel; the present work fills that gap.

2.4 Architectural Smell Evolution

Longitudinal studies of smell evolution provide the baseline against which AI-induced changes must be assessed. Sas et al. [33] found that smells persist, compound, and resist removal: erosion is the natural trajectory of organic development. Gnoyke et al. [17] confirmed these patterns across 485 releases of 14 open-source systems. Our DiD design controls for this natural trajectory by measuring the *differential* change in treated repositories relative to controls. Related work links smells to reduced maintainability [23], validates Arcan against LLM-based detection [38], and identifies conformance checking as underexplored [34].

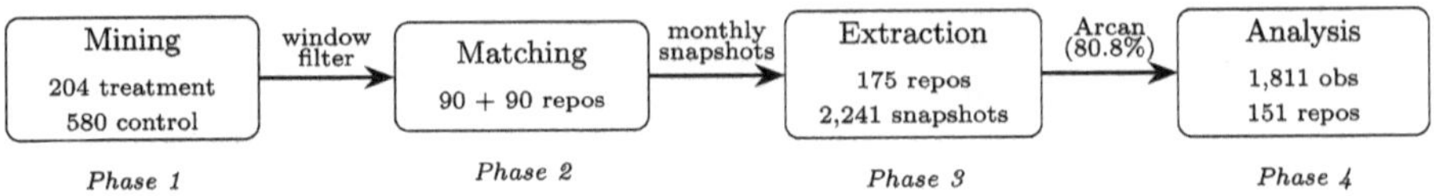

Fig. 1. Study pipeline with sample sizes at each stage.

Summary. No prior work applies a causal mining design to measure the architectural impact of AI-assisted development. The closest causal precedent (He et al.) operates on code-level metrics; the closest architectural-level work (Amasanti and Jahić) is qualitative.

3 Mining Design and Statistical Model

3.1 Study Design

We employ a staggered difference-in-differences (DiD) design to estimate the causal effect of observable agentic AI adoption on architectural quality. Figure 1 summarizes the four phases (mining, matching, extraction, analysis) whose sample sizes we trace below. Treatment is the first detectable adoption of an agentic AI coding tool (Sect. 3.2); controls are matched non-adopters observed over the same calendar periods. Each repository contributes a 13-month window (six pre-adoption, adoption month, six post-adoption). The unit of analysis is the repository-month; the primary outcome is log(ASD + 1) with ASD = total_smells/KLOC (thousand lines of code); effects are reported as $100 \times (\exp(\hat{\beta}) - 1)\%$ (approximate under $\log(x+1)$; see Sect. 4.5 for the strict-log specification on positive observations). Identification relies on repository and time fixed effects under parallel trends. Repository sampling follows the methodological caveats of Kalliamvakou et al. [24] (forks and inactive repositories filtered).

3.2 Treatment Detection and Sample Construction

Treatment Identification. AI tool adoption is identified through two categories of repository artifacts. First, tool-specific configuration files per tool: Cursor (`.cursorrules`, `.cursor/rules/`), Copilot (`.github/copilot-instructions.md`), Claude Code (`CLAUDE.md` or `claude.md`), Aider (`.aider.conf.yml`, `.aider.model.settings.yml`), and Codex (`AGENTS.md`). Second, `Co-Authored-By` commit trailers matching known AI tool patterns.

Detection Patterns. Each configuration marker is matched as a literal pathspec via `git log --all --diff-filter=A`; all markers are file pathspecs except `.cursor/rules/`, which is a directory pathspec (any addition under it counts). Commit-message signals are matched via `git log --all -E --grep` against four POSIX-ERE patterns: three case-insensitive `Co-Authored-By:` trailers naming `Claude`, `aider`, or `Copilot`, plus the literal subject-line tag `(aider)` that the Aider CLI appends to commits it authors. The adoption date is the earliest event across both signal types. Ambiguous markers (`CLAUDE.md`/`claude.md`, `AGENTS.md`) are content-validated, while high-reliability markers (`.cursorrules`, `copilot-instructions.md`, `.aider.*`) are accepted directly. Full patterns and code are in the replication package.

Both categories indicate configured, agentic usage rather than inline autocomplete, which produces no detectable artifacts (Sect. 2.1). The construct measured is observable agentic AI adoption, distinct from the broader behavioral pattern of accepting AI output without review. Undetected autocomplete in controls induces attenuation bias, making estimates conservative.

Sensitivity to Autocomplete Contamination. If a fraction c of controls use undetected AI tools, attenuation bias yields $\hat{\beta}_{\text{true}} \approx \hat{\beta}_{\text{obs}}/(1-c)$ [2]; the corrected effect at the empirical $c = 8.9\%$ is -7.4%, amplifying rather than altering the neutrality conclusion.

Tool composition (matched/post-Arcan retained): Claude Code 52/44 (one of which also uses Aider), Copilot 21/14, Cursor 16/15, Codex 1/1. Single-event sensitivity is in Sect. 4.7; tool-stratified analysis in Sect. 4.6. We validate the proxy empirically via temporal alignment: LOC growth emerges at adoption dates (Sect. 4.5).

Inclusion Criteria. Treatment candidates satisfy: (1) Java as primary language; (2) GitHub repository size $\geq$2,000 KB at mining time as a code-volume proxy (LOC and package counts are post-hoc Arcan outputs); (3) $\geq$2 commits per month on average; (4) $\geq$6 months pre-adoption history; and (5) $\geq$3 months post-adoption history. These criteria yield 90 treatment repositories from 204 candidates (Fig. 1).

Control Matching. The control pool comprises 580 Java repositories without detectable AI markers. We perform 1:1 nearest-neighbor matching [31,36] on Euclidean distance over six standardized covariates (four log-transformed to address skew: stars, forks, commits, size), with a propensity-score caliper of $0.2 \times \text{SD}(\text{logit}(\hat{p}))$ [7,30]. Matching yields 90 pairs (the 90+90 in Fig. 1). Post-matching, four of six covariates satisfy $|\text{SMD}| < 0.1$ (standardized mean difference; below 0.1 is well balanced); repository size ($\text{SMD} = 0.18$) and commit count ($\text{SMD} = -0.12$) exceed it, addressed via covariate adjustment in Sect. 4.7.

3.3 Architectural Smell Extraction

Monthly Snapshots and Arcan Analysis. For each repository-month we extract the last commit before the first of the month (`git rev-list --first-parent --before`) and materialize it as a temporary working copy. Of the 180 matched repositories (90 treatment, 90 control), 5 controls are dropped before analysis for having no resolvable commit in their study window (insufficient git history), leaving 175 repositories (90 treatment, 85 control) that yield 2,241 monthly snapshots. Each snapshot is analyzed with Arcan 2 CLI [6] (trial edition, pinned Docker image) detecting the four smell types from Sect. 2.2; analysis succeeded for 1,811 of 2,241 snapshots (80.8%, failures from JVM memory limits or incompatible structures). A further 24 repositories with zero successful snapshots (16 treatment, 8 control) are excluded, yielding the final panel of 1,811 observations across 151 repositories (74 treatment, 77 control). Total attrition is thus 29 of 180 matched repositories (16.1%; Sect. 6).

Metrics. Primary outcome: ASD = total_smells/KLOC, aggregated across class and package granularity (a container-only sensitivity is in Sect. 4.7). Cyclic dependencies dominate (mean CD = 333 vs. <10 for other types), so we complement aggregate ASD with per-type analysis (RQ2), balanced-ASD, and total-count decomposition. Secondary metrics: efferent coupling (Ce), instability ($I = Ce/(Ca + Ce)$), and distance from the main sequence. All outcomes log-transformed as $\log(x + 1)$. The primary specification uses fixed effects only; the secondary specification, two-way fixed effects with the Sun and Abraham [37] interaction-weighted correction (TWFE-SA), additionally adjusts for monthly contributors.

3.4 Statistical Model

Because repositories adopt at different calendar months (staggered adoption), standard two-way fixed effects estimation can produce biased estimates under heterogeneous treatment effects [12,18]. We therefore employ estimators designed for staggered settings, and adopt Borusyak imputation as primary because, unlike standard TWFE, it never uses already-treated repositories as controls and so stays unbiased under heterogeneous treatment effects.

Primary Estimator: Borusyak Imputation. Following Borusyak et al. [9]:

$$\log(\text{ASD}_{it} + 1) = \alpha_i + \gamma_t + \beta \cdot D_{it} + \varepsilon_{it} \tag{1}$$

where i indexes repositories, t months, α_i and γ_t are repository and time fixed effects, and $D_{it} = 1$ once repository i has adopted. The imputation procedure fits on untreated observations (controls plus pre-adoption periods of treated), predicts counterfactual $\hat{Y}_{it}(0)$ for treated post-adoption observations, and estimates the average treatment effect on the treated (ATT) as $\widehat{\text{ATT}} = \overline{Y_{it} - \hat{Y}_{it}(0)}$. Standard errors are clustered at the repository level.

Architectural metrics exhibit high inertia (intraclass correlation ICC = 0.979); fixed effects absorb between-repository variance, isolating within-repo treatment effects. GC nulls should be interpreted as potentially underpowered (77.5% zero-inflation).

Secondary Estimator and Event Study. The Sun and Abraham [37] interaction-weighted estimator provides an independent concordance check. Event-study coefficients are estimated for $h \in \{-6, \ldots, +6\}$ with $h = -1$ as reference; a Wald test on $h = -6$ through $h = -2$ jointly zero is the parallel-trends falsification check. Post-adoption coefficients trace the trajectory (RQ3).

Table 1. Main diff-in-diff estimates: effect of AI tool adoption on architectural smell density (log ASD).

	Borusyak	TWFE-SA
ATT ($\hat{\beta}$)	−0.0698***	−0.0681***
	(0.0239)	(0.0238)
Effect (%)	−6.7%	−6.6%

$^{*}p < 0.1$; $^{**}p < 0.05$; $^{***}p < 0.01$
Both: 1,811 obs., 151 repos, repo and time FE, SEs clustered by repo.

Denominator Decomposition (RQ4). Since ASD is a ratio (smells/KLOC), a treatment effect can reflect changes in the numerator, the denominator, or both. We run separate DiD models on log(total_smells+1) and log(KLOC+1) to identify the mechanism.

Robustness Checks. Pre-registered: a placebo test at a fake adoption date and an alternative matching specification (subsumed by Mahalanobis with regression adjustment). Added post-results: wild cluster bootstrap [10,40] (few-cluster robustness); Lee [26] bounds (worst-case attrition); smells per package; stale observations; Bacon decomposition (staggered-DiD weighting); size stratification; container-only. Post-hoc: tool-type stratification; dose-response.

4 Results

4.1 Sample and Descriptive Statistics

The final panel comprises 1,811 observations across 151 repositories (74 treatment, 77 control), after excluding 29 of 180 matched repositories (16.1%; Section 6). Groups are comparable in size (mean KLOC: 44.9 vs. 45.2), maturity (73.8 vs. 80.1 months), and stars (918 vs. 920). ASD is right-skewed (median = 3.0, max = 58.8), motivating the log transformation. Treatment repos exhibit higher mean ASD (6.1 vs. 5.1); with ICC = 0.979, repository fixed effects absorb this variation.

4.2 RQ1: Effect of AI Adoption on Architectural Smell Density

Table 1 reports the main DiD estimates. The Borusyak imputation estimator yields $\hat{\beta} = -0.070$ (SE = 0.024, 95% CI [−0.117, −0.023], $p = 0.004$), corresponding to 6.7% lower ASD in repositories with observable agentic AI adoption. Sun and Abraham confirms concordance (−6.6%, $p = 0.005$). Against the theoretical expectation of architectural degradation (Sect. 1), the negative point estimate is the opposite-direction finding; the mechanism behind the headline number is the focus of Sect. 4.5.

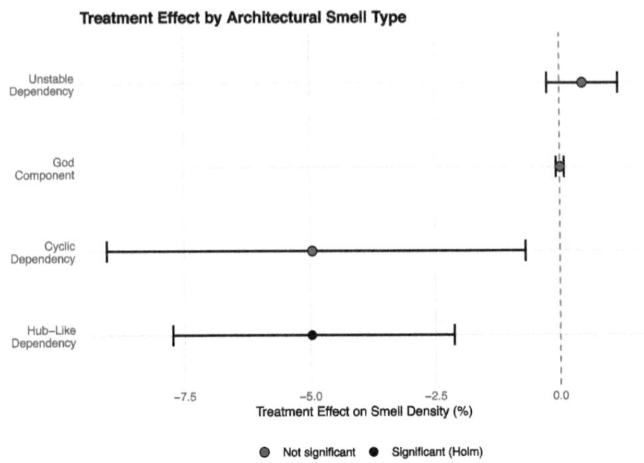

Fig. 2. Per-type treatment effects (Borusyak imputation) with 95% CIs. Filled markers: significant after Holm correction.

4.3 RQ2: Disaggregated Effects by Smell Type

Figure 2 presents per-type treatment effects (Borusyak imputation). Because we test four smell types, we report Holm-adjusted p-values, which raise the bar so multiple tests do not yield a false positive. Hub-like dependency density decreases by 5.0% ($p = 0.001$; Holm-adjusted $p = 0.003$), the only type surviving multiplicity correction. Cyclic dependency shows a comparable estimate (−5.0%, $p = 0.023$) but is non-significant after Holm adjustment ($p = 0.070$). UD and GC show no significant density change ($p = 0.205$, $p = 0.877$). The GC null likely reflects low power: 77.5% of repo-months record zero god components.

Raw UD counts show a suggestive increase of 5.8% (raw $p = 0.032$; Holm-adjusted across four raw-count tests, $p = 0.128$). The density null masks this marginal signal, discussed in Section 5.1. Density and count tests answer distinct mechanistic questions, with family-wise error controlled within each family.

4.4 RQ3: Dynamic Treatment Effects

Figure 3 presents the event study. Pre-period coefficients ($h = -6$ to $h = -2$) cluster near zero, and the Wald test cannot reject joint nullity ($\chi^2 = 1.64$, df = 5, $p = 0.896$), consistent with the parallel trends assumption (here a high p-value is reassuring: no divergence before adoption).

Post-adoption, the effect appears immediately at $h = 1$ (−5.5%) and grows to −9.5% by $h = 6$, consistent with cumulative code growth diluting smell density (Sect. 4.5). The effect is still expanding at $h = 6$, so longer post-adoption windows are needed to see whether smell counts eventually grow in step with LOC and the density gap closes.

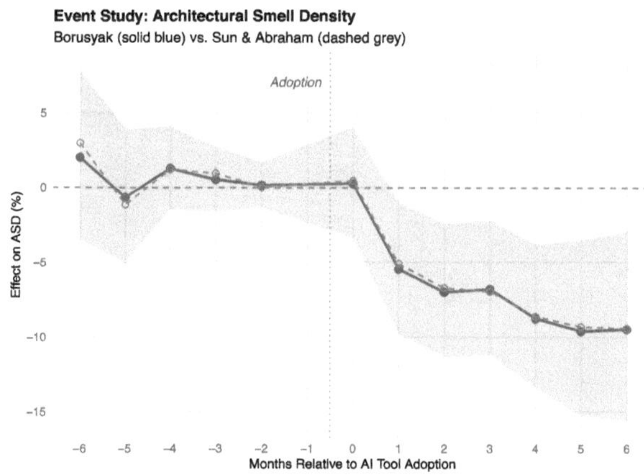

Fig. 3. Event study: ASD effect by relative month. Pre-period coefficients near zero (Wald $p = 0.896$); post-adoption effect grows to $\sim -9.5\%$ at $h = 6$. Sun & Abraham overlay (grey dashed) confirms concordance.

4.5 RQ4: Decomposing the ASD Effect

The 6.7% ASD reduction could reflect fewer smells (numerator) or faster code growth (denominator). Separate DiD models (Fig. 4) reveal the mechanism. Raw smell counts are unchanged (+1.1%, $p = 0.82$) while code volume grows significantly faster in adopters than controls (+12.8%, $p = 0.003$). The ASD decrease is a composition effect: the marginal code carries lower smell density than the pre-existing codebase. A strict-log specification on positive observations (which preserves the ratio identity that $\log(x+1)$ approximates) yields $\hat{\beta} = -0.139$ (−13.0%, $p < 0.001$), implying an even larger denominator share than under $\log(x+1)$.

Per-type raw counts confirm the pattern: CD, HL, and GC show no significant absolute changes (all $p > 0.25$). UD shows a suggestive increase (+5.8%, raw $p = 0.032$; Holm-adjusted $p = 0.128$), the strongest per-type signal though non-significant after multiplicity correction. Coupling metrics (Ce, I, D) are similarly stable (all $p > 0.05$). Package count also grows (+9.7%, $p = 0.032$), yet smell counts remain unchanged despite expanding modular structure. The methodological implication for empirical mining is discussed in Section 5.2.

4.6 Exploratory: Treatment Heterogeneity by Tool

Tool-stratified Borusyak estimates are consistently negative (Codex, $n_T = 1$, omitted): Claude Code ($n_T = 44$, −5.1%, $p = 0.039$), Copilot ($n_T = 14$, −4.0%, $p = 0.005$), and Cursor ($n_T = 15$, −13.5%, $p < 0.001$). Magnitudes differ (Cursor strongest), but with a non-significant dose-response interaction ($p = 0.716$) and post-hoc stratification, the larger Cursor effect is a hypothesis for replication, not a finding.

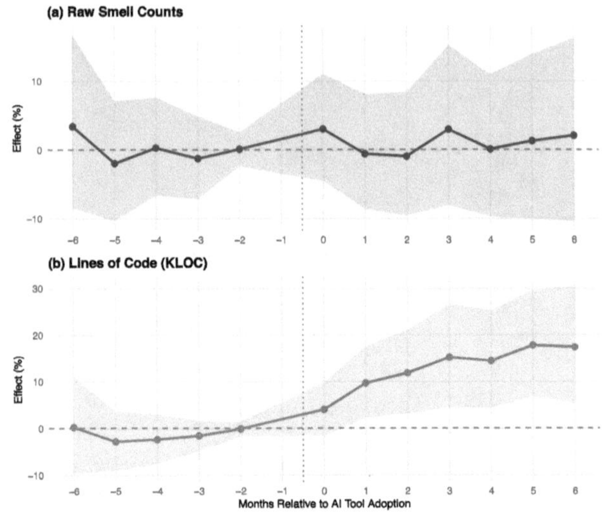

Fig. 4. Decomposition: separate DiD on raw smell counts (top) and LOC (bottom). Smells unchanged (+1.1%, $p = 0.82$); LOC grows significantly (+12.8%, $p = 0.003$).

4.7 Robustness Checks

Table 2 reports supplementary analyses. Covariate adjustment yields −6.6% ($p = 0.004$). The Bacon decomposition reports 89.1% of the TWFE weight from clean comparisons (80.2% treated-vs-never-treated, 8.9% treated-vs-not-yet-treated) and 10.8% from the potentially-biased later-vs-already-treated comparison, which the Borusyak primary estimator avoids by construction; a placebo at a fake adoption date ($t - 3$) is null ($p = 0.427$). The wild cluster bootstrap [10,40] (small-sample-safe significance) yields −6.0% ($p = 0.010$); Lee [26] bounds (worst-case attrition) span [−9.9%, −2.3%] (both negative, though the upper-bound CI includes zero, $p = 0.239$). Size-stratified estimates are consistent (−6.3%/−7.2%); balanced ASD (−4.6%, $p < 0.001$) and a multi-event restriction excluding repositories with a single detection event (≥ 2 events, −6.8%, $p = 0.020$) retain significance, indicating the result is not driven by one-off configuration commits. Container-level (package) smells alone (an outcome restriction; −3.0%, $p = 0.074$) are directionally consistent but attenuated. Only aggressive stale filtering ($N = 94$, $p = 0.223$) attenuates to non-significance; the effect is directionally consistent (−3% to −8%, or −13% under strict-log) across all other specifications.

5 Discussion

5.1 Code Growth Without Proportional Architectural Degradation

Architectural smells are topological: cyclic dependencies require mutual package imports; hub-like dependencies require excessive fan-in and fan-out. Neither

Table 2. Supplementary analyses: denominator decomposition, inference robustness, attrition bounds, and sample sensitivity.

Analysis	ATT ($\hat{\beta}$)	SE	95% CI	p-value	Effect (%)
Denominator decomposition					
Raw smell count	0.0108	0.0486	[−0.0845, 0.1061]	0.8246	1.1%
LOC growth (log KLOC)	0.1201***	0.0401	[0.0415, 0.1986]	0.0027	12.8%
Smells per package	−0.0318*	0.0171	[−0.0653, 0.0018]	0.0636	−3.1%
Inference robustness					
Wild cluster bootstrap	−0.0615***	0.0249	[−0.1098, −0.0129]	0.0097	−6.0%
Attrition bounds (Lee 2009)					
Upper bound (pessimistic)	−0.0229	0.0195	[−0.0611, 0.0152]	0.2387	−2.3%
Lower bound (optimistic)	−0.1046***	0.0192	[−0.1422, −0.0671]	0.0000	−9.9%
Sample sensitivity					
Excl. stale (≥3 zero-mo, N=94)	−0.0413	0.0339	[−0.1078, 0.0252]	0.2234	−4.0%
Excl. stale (≥6 zero-mo, N=128)	−0.0556**	0.0251	[−0.1048, −0.0063]	0.0269	−5.4%
Packages ≥ 30 (N=109)	−0.0590***	0.0216	[−0.1013, −0.0167]	0.0063	−5.7%
Balanced ASD (equal type weight)	−0.0469***	0.0139	[−0.0742, −0.0196]	0.0007	−4.6%
Excl. outliers (KLOC ≥ 1)	−0.0791***	0.0188	[−0.1159, −0.0423]	0.0000	−7.6%

$^{*}p < 0.1$; $^{**}p < 0.05$; $^{***}p < 0.01$. Primary ASD estimate: $\hat{\beta}$=-0.070, p=0.004.

increases despite growth in code volume (+12.8%) and package count (+9.7%, $p = 0.032$), suggesting new modules integrate without creating structural violations. UD's suggestive count increase (+5.8%, raw $p = 0.032$; Holm-adjusted $p = 0.128$) would, if confirmed by replication, be consistent with AI tools preferentially adding imports to less-stable packages [28]. It does not survive multiplicity correction.

The limited warning-smell overlap (33.8% non-co-occurring [13]) offers a candidate, untested reconciliation with He et al. [20]: AI tools may write more complex code within modules while respecting between-module boundaries.

5.2 A Methodological Lesson for Density-Normalized Mining Outcomes

Without decomposition, the −6.7% result would invite the misleading headline "AI tools improve architecture." The correct interpretation is that adopters grow code volume faster than matched controls without a proportional increase in architectural violations. This generalizes: any density-normalized metric (defects/KLOC, vulnerabilities/KLOC, churn/KLOC) where treatment plausibly affects KLOC requires explicit decomposition. He et al.'s [20] raw-count SonarQube metrics show warning growth (+30%) exceeding LOC growth (+28.6%), indicating per-line degradation at the code level. Smells are topological yet ASD normalizes by KLOC (volumetric): the smells-per-package alternative normalization (a denominator change: −3.1%, $p = 0.064$) shows a smaller, marginal effect consistent with the denominator explanation.

5.3 Implications

For Practitioners. These findings do not support escalating architectural safeguards in response to agentic AI adoption in the short term, but they warrant three monitoring practices: (1) track raw smell counts alongside ASD, since density alone will look improving even when counts are stagnant; (2) treat 6-month windows as preliminary and re-examine at 12+ months given the trajectory at $h = 6$ shows no inflection; and (3) monitor coupling metrics (Ce, I) alongside smell counts as a complementary signal.

For Researchers. Density-normalized outcomes require numerator/denominator decomposition under any treatment plausibly affecting system size. The highest-value extensions are greenfield projects (where AI influences architecture from inception), longer observation windows, and dependency-graph topology diffs to identify AI-introduced edges.

6 Threats to Validity

Internal Validity. *Differential attrition* is the most serious concern. From the matched 90+90, 16/90 treatment (17.8%) and 13/90 control (14.4%) were lost (5 controls dropped pre-Arcan for insufficient git history; 24 repositories, 16 treatment and 8 control, lost during Arcan analysis to JVM memory limits, concentrated among the largest projects). Lee bounds bracket the effect at $[-9.9\%, -2.3\%]$: both bounds are negative, but the upper bound's 95% CI includes zero ($p = 0.239$). Under worst-case attrition, the effect cannot be distinguished from null. *Parallel trends* are supported by the event study Wald test ($p = 0.896$), though this cannot exclude smooth pre-treatment effects absorbed by repository fixed effects. *Estimator sensitivity:* Borusyak and TWFE-SA agree closely ($-6.7\%/-6.6\%$). The Bacon decomposition (Sect. 4.7) confirms 89.1% of weight comes from clean comparisons, the bias Borusyak avoids by construction. *Stale observations:* 19.3% of consecutive month-pairs share identical commits; aggressive filtering ($N = 94$) attenuates the effect to non-significance, though moderate filtering ($N = 128$, $p = 0.027$) retains it. *Interference:* we assume no spillover between units (SUTVA): shared libraries or fork relationships could violate this assumption, though any spillover would attenuate estimates toward zero. *Co-adoption and selection:* the treatment may capture a modernization bundle. Repository fixed effects and matching mitigate time-invariant confounders, but unobserved time-varying changes could confound the estimate.

External Validity. We focus on mature Java OSS systems to isolate architectural effects where structure is already established; findings apply to short-term effects under agentic AI usage. The effect may differ in greenfield projects where AI influences architecture from inception, or under strict governance constraining AI-generated changes. Generalization is further limited by language (Java, an Arcan constraint). Survivorship is a further threat: repositories abandoned before sampling are invisible, potentially biasing toward neutrality.

Construct Validity. *AI adoption proxy:* our treatment captures observable agentic AI usage through configuration artifacts and commit metadata. Treated repositories are a purposive subset, restricting external validity. While this excludes autocomplete-only usage (false negatives) and may include one-off experiments (false positives), prior work shows such artifacts encode project-specific directives [22]. We validate this proxy empirically (Sect. 3.2): temporal alignment and cross-signal consistency support its reliability. Excluding single-event repos retains significance (-6.8%, $p = 0.020$). *Control contamination:* 8/90 matched controls (8.9%) showed AI markers during their study windows. The corrected effect is -7.4% (Sect. 3.2), and the qualitative pattern (significant ASD decline, unchanged raw counts, large LOC growth) is unchanged. *Arcan and architecture operationalization:* Arcan precision is reported in the 70–100% range [6, 32]. The trial edition was used. Arcan detects smells at class and package level: our primary ASD aggregates both, with 57% of cyclic dependencies at class level. A container-only sensitivity (-3.0%, $p = 0.074$) is directionally consistent but non-significant. We operationalize architecture through dependency-graph structure, which does not capture design intent, conformance, or semantic violations. *ASD normalization:* the ratio metric conflates numerator and denominator changes. This is addressed via explicit decomposition (Sect. 4.5) and alternative normalization (smells per package, $p = 0.064$). *Reproducibility:* mitigated by detection-pattern disclosure (Sect. 3.2), pinned tool versions, fixed random seeds, and a complete replication package.

7 Conclusion

This study presented the first causal mining study of agentic AI adoption's effect on software architecture, analyzing 1,811 monthly snapshots across 151 Java repositories with a staggered difference-in-differences design. The apparent 6.7% ASD reduction is a composition effect: repositories with observable agentic AI adoption exhibit increased code volume without proportionally more architectural smells. We find no evidence that the observed agentic AI tools degrade software architecture in established projects over a six-month window, though under worst case attrition the confidence interval includes zero.

Future work should extend the observation window and study greenfield projects. Dependency-graph topology diffs are needed to confirm the mechanism. The denominator-decomposition lesson generalizes to any density-normalized mining outcome under size-affecting treatment, and we encourage empirical AI-tool studies to adopt this practice by default.

Data Availibility Statement. The replication package (pipeline scripts, processed monthly panel, configurations, fixed seeds, Docker setup) is archived on Zenodo (https://doi.org/10.5281/zenodo.20510047) and mirrored at https://github.com/Oliver1703dk/seaa2026-replication-package; all tables and figures reproduce via `make analyze`.

References

1. Agarwal, S., He, H., Vasilescu, B.: AI IDEs or autonomous agents? Measuring the impact of coding agents on software development (2026), accepted at MSR 2026
2. Aigner, D.J.: Regression with a binary independent variable subject to errors of observation. J. Econometrics **1**(1), 49–59 (1973). https://doi.org/10.1016/0304-4076(73)90005-5
3. Amasanti, G., Jahić, J.: The impact of AI-generated solutions on software architecture and productivity: results from a survey study. In: Software Architecture: ECSA 2025 Tracks and Workshops. LNCS, vol. 15982, pp. 89–104. Springer, Cham (2025). https://doi.org/10.1007/978-3-032-04403-7_10
4. Anthropic: Claude Code: An agentic coding tool. Software tool (2025)
5. Anysphere: Cursor: The AI code editor. Software tool (2024)
6. Arcelli Fontana, F., Pigazzini, I., Roveda, R., Tamburri, D.A., Zanoni, M., Di Nitto, E.: Arcan: a tool for architectural smells detection. In: Proceedings of the IEEE International Conference on Software Architecture Workshops (ICSAW), pp. 282–285 (2017). https://doi.org/10.1109/ICSAW.2017.16
7. Austin, P.C.: Optimal caliper widths for propensity-score matching when estimating differences in means and differences in proportions in observational studies. Pharm. Stat. **10**(2), 150–161 (2011). https://doi.org/10.1002/pst.433
8. Bass, L., Clements, P., Kazman, R.: Software Architecture in Practice. 4th edn. Addison-Wesley (2021)
9. Borusyak, K., Jaravel, X., Spiess, J.: Revisiting event-study designs: robust and efficient estimation. Rev. Econ. Stud. **91**(6), 3253–3285 (2024). https://doi.org/10.1093/restud/rdae007
10. Cameron, A.C., Gelbach, J.B., Miller, D.L.: Bootstrap-based improvements for inference with clustered errors. Rev. Econ. Stat. **90**(3), 414–427 (2008). https://doi.org/10.1162/rest.90.3.414
11. Cotroneo, D., Improta, C., Liguori, P.: Human-written vs. AI-generated code: a large-scale study of defects, vulnerabilities, and complexity. In: Proceedings of ISSRE, pp. 252–263 (2025). https://doi.org/10.1109/ISSRE66568.2025.00035
12. de Chaisemartin, C., d'Haultfœuille, X.: Two-way fixed effects estimators with heterogeneous treatment effects. Am. Econ. Rev. **110**(9), 2964–2996 (2020). https://doi.org/10.1257/aer.20181169
13. Esposito, M., Robredo, M., Arcelli Fontana, F., Lenarduzzi, V.: On the correlation between architectural smells and static analysis warnings. Softw. Qual. J. **33**(4), 33 (2025). https://doi.org/10.1007/s11219-025-09730-7
14. Fawzy, A., Tahir, A., Blincoe, K.: Vibe coding in practice: motivations, challenges, and a future outlook—a grey literature review. In: Proceedings of ICSE-SEIP (2026). arXiv:2510.00328, to appear
15. Garcia, J., Popescu, D., Edwards, G., Medvidovic, N.: Toward a catalogue of architectural bad smells. In: Proceedings of the International Conference on the Quality of Software Architectures (QoSA), pp. 146–162 (2009). https://doi.org/10.1007/978-3-642-02351-4_10
16. GitHub: GitHub Copilot: Your AI pair programmer. Software tool (2025)
17. Gnoyke, P., Schulze, S., Krüger, J.: Evolution patterns of software-architecture smells: an empirical study of intra- and inter-version smells. J. Syst. Softw. **217**, 112170 (2024). https://doi.org/10.1016/j.jss.2024.112170
18. Goodman-Bacon, A.: Difference-in-differences with variation in treatment timing. J. Econometrics **225**(2), 254–277 (2021). https://doi.org/10.1016/j.jeconom.2021.03.014

19. van Gurp, J., Bosch, J.: Design erosion: problems and causes. J. Syst. Softw. **61**(2), 105–119 (2002)
20. He, H., Miller, C., Agarwal, S., Kästner, C., Vasilescu, B.: Speed at the cost of quality: how Cursor AI increases short-term velocity and long-term complexity in open-source projects (2025), accepted at MSR 2026
21. Hochstein, L., Lindvall, M.: Combating architectural degeneration: a survey. Inf. Softw. Technol. **47**(10), 643–656 (2005)
22. Jiang, S., Nam, D.: Beyond the prompt: an empirical study of Cursor Rules. In: Proceedings of the 23rd International Conference on Mining Software Repositories (MSR) (2026). arXiv:2512.18925, to appear
23. Jolak, R., Karlsson, S., Dobslaw, F.: An empirical investigation of the impact of architectural smells on software maintainability. J. Syst. Softw. **225**, 112382 (2025). https://doi.org/10.1016/j.jss.2025.112382
24. Kalliamvakou, E., Gousios, G., Blincoe, K., Singer, L., German, D.M., Damian, D.: An in-depth study of the promises and perils of mining GitHub. Empir. Softw. Eng. **21**(5), 2035–2071 (2016). https://doi.org/10.1007/s10664-015-9393-5
25. Karpathy, A.: Vibe coding. X (formerly Twitter) (2025). https://x.com/karpathy/status/1886192184808149383
26. Lee, D.S.: Training, wages, and sample selection: estimating sharp bounds on treatment effects. Rev. Econ. Stud. **76**(3), 1071–1102 (2009). https://doi.org/10.1111/j.1467-937X.2009.00536.x
27. Lippert, M., Roock, S.: Refactoring in Large Software Projects: Performing Complex Restructurings Successfully. Wiley, Hoboken (2006)
28. Martin, R.C.: Agile Software Development: Principles, Patterns, and Practices. Prentice Hall (2003)
29. Perry, D.E., Wolf, A.L.: Foundations for the study of software architecture. ACM SIGSOFT Softw. Eng. Notes **17**(4), 40–52 (1992)
30. Rosenbaum, P.R., Rubin, D.B.: Constructing a control group using multivariate matched sampling methods that incorporate the propensity score. Am. Stat. **39**(1), 33–38 (1985). https://doi.org/10.1080/00031305.1985.10479383
31. Rubin, D.B.: Bias reduction using Mahalanobis-metric matching. Biometrics **36**(2), 293–298 (1980). https://doi.org/10.2307/2529981
32. Sas, D., Avgeriou, P.: An architectural technical debt index based on machine learning and architectural smells. IEEE Trans. Softw. Eng. **49**(8), 4169–4195 (2023). https://doi.org/10.1109/TSE.2023.3286179
33. Sas, D., Avgeriou, P., Uyumaz, U.: On the evolution and impact of architectural smells–an industrial case study. Empir. Softw. Eng. **27**, 86 (2022)
34. Schmid, L., et al.: Software architecture meets LLMs: a systematic literature review (2025)
35. Stack Overflow: Stack overflow developer survey 2024. Online survey (2024)
36. Stuart, E.A.: Matching methods for causal inference: a review and a look forward. Stat. Sci. **25**(1), 1–21 (2010). https://doi.org/10.1214/09-STS313
37. Sun, L., Abraham, S.: Estimating dynamic treatment effects in event studies with heterogeneous treatment effects. J. Econometrics **225**(2), 175–199 (2021). https://doi.org/10.1016/j.jeconom.2020.09.006
38. Tessa, C., Bochicchio, M., Arcelli Fontana, F.: Exploring architectural smells detection through LLMs. In: Proceedings of the 19th European Conference on Software Architecture (ECSA). LNCS, vol. 15929, pp. 90–98. Springer, Cham (2025). https://doi.org/10.1007/978-3-032-02138-0_6
39. Waseem, M., et al.: Vibe coding in practice: flow, technical debt, and guidelines for sustainable use (2025)

40. Webb, M.D.: Reworking wild bootstrap-based inference for clustered errors. Can. J. Econ. **56**(3), 839–858 (2023). https://doi.org/10.1111/caje.12661
41. Yetiştiren, B., Özsoy, I., Ayerdem, M., Tüzün, E.: Evaluating the code quality of AI-assisted code generation tools: an empirical study on GitHub Copilot, Amazon CodeWhisperer, and ChatGPT (2023)

Author Index

C. Berger and V. Klös (Eds.): SEAA 2026, LNCS 16864, pp. 517–518, 2027.
https://doi.org/10.1007/978-3-032-36587-3

FSC
www.fsc.org
MIX
Papier | Fördert
gute Waldnutzung
FSC® C083411

Kolibri 360 GmbH
Ferdinand-Jühlke-Straße 7
99095 Erfurt, Deutschland
produktsicherheit@kolibri360.de